RAND MCNALLY
COLLEGE
PUBLISHING
COMPANY / CHICAGO

Developing Second-Language Skills:

THEORY TO PRACTICE

SECOND EDITION

KENNETH CHASTAIN

University of Virginia

W9-CKS-263

76   77   78   10   9   8   7   6   5   4   3   2

Copyright © 1976 by Rand McNally College Publishing Company

Copyright © 1971 by The Center for Curriculum Development, Inc.

All Rights Reserved

Printed in U.S.A.

Library of Congress Catalog Card Number 75-16806

To Jan, Brian, and Michael, and to the memory of Kevin

Fray Luis de León was teaching at the University of Salamanca when he was arrested and taken to prison. The story is told that upon being released, he began his first lecture with the following words, "As we were saying. . . ." The second edition of any work should be much more than a repetition of what the author was saying in the first. The selection of approach and content is perhaps more of a problem in the second edition than in the first. On the one hand, abandonment of the total content of the first edition would certainly arouse suspicions as to its validity. On the other hand, failure to incorporate new insights and to consider new directions in the field would be tantamount to admitting a lack of awareness of the new growth in an ever-changing field. Too, in my own case the omission of new material would constitute a repudiation of the necessity of staying abreast of current developments in order to achieve the goal of "educational engineer," which I espoused in the first edition.

The title of the second edition has been changed to *Developing Second-Language Skills: Theory to Practice* because the term *second language* is broader than *modern language* and creates a more positive image than *foreign language*. However, the basic philosophy of this second edition is in harmony with that of the first. To be prepared to grow in their chosen profession, teachers must have a basic understanding of and familiarity with both the "science" and the "art" of teaching; and comprehension of the "science" must precede the development of the "art." Just as in Chomsky's theory of linguistics, the acquisition of some degree of competence is a prerequisite to productive and growing performance in the classroom. Both prospective and practicing teachers must be concerned with their ability to grow. Each of us should be evolving into what we can be. In no fundamental sense can a "bag of tricks" substitute for an expandable "blueprint."

Too, the second edition continues the systematic and conscious polarization of various dichotomies currently being discussed in professional journals. Although the first edition concentrated on cognitive factors in second-language learning, this edition treats the affective domain as well. The examination of extreme positions has been selected purposefully as a means of clarifying differences and of promoting more complete comprehension of each position. As does any teacher, I have my own particular preferences, which should become clear to the reader, but there is no conscious attempt to brainwash any reader just as there is no intent to deny modifications and/or blends of any of the extremes discussed in this edition. My goal in preparing this edition was the development of intelligent practitioners of the science and art of teaching, not the subtle philosophical entrapment of the unwary into any given "camp."

Nor have I, in any sense, rejected my original contention that teaching style is personal. No teacher should feel obligated to conform to any general theory or movement. Her style should be her own, and it should grow out of knowledge of theory, familiarity with current practice and methodology, insight into student individuality, her own personality, and the results she obtains in the classroom. However, ineptitude cannot be justified by the untenable rationalization that the classroom situation is due to personal style. That is obviously true, but it is also obviously true that good teaching and bad teaching do exist. Whatever the teacher's style, it must produce good results to qualify as good teaching. Most teachers prefer to sample, select, and discard as they grow personally and professionally. Having a variety of teaching skills will give them much greater flexibility and will allow them to provide much more adequately for individual differences among students. At the same time, no teacher can justifiably ignore what is happening in society, education, psychology, linguistics, psycholinguistics, and second-language teaching. Change for the sake of change is unwise, but refusal to remain receptive to productive innovations is synonymous with stagnation.

No major organizational changes have been made in the format of this edition. The first part still deals primarily with theory, and the second part attempts to put the theory into practice. The discussion of the teaching process itself is still based on three components: (1) defining objectives, (2) developing teaching procedures to accomplish these objectives, and (3) evaluating the results. This model is applicable to audio-lingual classes and to cognitive classes; it is equally applicable to the traditional classroom organization and to the more recent "individualized" classes.

The content and arrangement of the treatment of theory have been altered considerably. The chapters on first-language learning and research now precede the chapters dealing with audio-lingual and cognitive approaches to teaching. The research chapter now treats both cognitive and affective-social factors in learning. Results of studies comparing audio-lingual and cognitive methods or components of these methods are included in the chapters treating each approach. In line with the more recent trends to emphasize the individual in the instructional process in second-language teaching, two new chapters have been added: "The Student" and "Diversifying Instruction." Another new chapter, "Why a Second Language?," has been placed first in the book, reflecting my opinion that our profession must concern itself with answering this question.

Changes made in the discussion of practice involve emphasis more than actual reorganization. Additional classroom exercises have been included to supplement the more general descriptions of the first edition. The goal has been to provide a clue to the direction and types of activities that might be used in the classroom without giving so many as to stifle the potential creativity of the teacher. No book can provide all the types of exercises that teachers will require, *if* they are to satisfy the needs of all their students. Therefore, they should begin immediately to originate new ideas for student activities. A new chapter on meeting student needs has been added. It seems irrefutable that meeting the needs of modern-day students must be a prime consideration in the classroom, second-language or otherwise. Another new chapter, "Teaching Culture," has been included, reflecting the increased emphasis on cultural goals in second-language teaching.

The revision of the chapter format to include a chapter outline at the beginning of each chapter and a list of words to be defined, discussion questions, and activities at the end of each chapter has several objectives. First, hopefully the chapter outline will focus the students' attention on the general goals of the chapter. The definitions will help the students to learn the terms needed to comprehend the basic concepts of each chapter. The discussion questions at the end of the chapter should help the students to review the content of the chapter and to organize the information. (I agree wholeheart-edly with Ausubel that true comprehension can only come about through meaningful learning. Each reader should summarize the basic concepts presented in each chapter in his own words before proceeding to new material.) The activities should also help him to begin the direct application of the ideas contained in the chapter to practical contexts. In addition, many of the discussion questions and suggested activities should help the students to go beyond the confines of this text. I urge both instructors and students to consider other questions and activities that would serve to broaden the understanding and the application of any of the concepts presented in this book.

One of the most interesting and exciting rewards of having written the first edition has been the gratifying privilege of meeting so many teachers and students who have used the book. I have most truly appreciated their many kind comments, and I have enjoyed becoming acquainted with all of those who have taken the time to introduce themselves and to chat for a few moments. I am indeed grateful to have the opportunity to prepare a second edition. My desire is that the second edition will be an asset to teachers and prospective teachers alike in considering and questioning the various components of the teaching process as they formulate their individual teaching philosophies. My hope is that the second edition will bring me into contact with as many new friends as the first.

In closing, I readily acknowledge my indebtedness and gratitude to Charles H. Heinle and Rand McNally College Publishing Company for encouraging, promoting, and publishing this second edition; to Carlyle Carter for her careful work in editing my original manuscript; to Terry Gamba and Gilbert Jarvis for providing examples in German and French respectively for the chapter on evaluation; to Gary Dielman (German), Gilbert Jarvis (French), and Kathryn Orth (German) for assisting with various examples in the language skills chapters; to Virginia Kruse for her dedication to teaching and her inspiration to her methods students; to Gil Jarvis for the insights that have stimulated much of my thinking and influenced many of my ideas; to Ben Christensen, Pierre Cintas, Ernie Frechette, Alan Garfinkel, Roberta Lavine, Ted Mueller, Phil Smith, Dave Wolfe, and the authors of reviews for the various journals for their many helpful suggestions; to my methods students for their stimulating questions, observations, and discussions; to Jan for preparing the manuscript; and to Jan, Brian, and Michael for their continued love and patience.

Kenneth Chastain
University of Virginia
Charlottesville, Virginia

CONTENTS

Part One: Theory

In each era certain problems receive more attention and recognition than others. Similarly, proposed solutions vary according to the prevailing attitudes favored during that particular period. These tidelike movements of action and reaction, however, are not representative of the entire pool of ideas available to the "educational engineers," who make use of all available resources, combining them into the most propitious mixture given their own individuality and that of their students. Only in the classroom at the scene of the action and in concert with all the individuals involved can the most appropriate and productive decisions be made. These decisions are not spontaneous and extemporaneous, because they are based on knowledge and experience. Neither can they be prepackaged and shipped to the anxious teacher like some convenience food in the supermarket, because the truly germane proposals must be geared to the exigencies of the situation and the participating students within the realistic limits of the teacher's own capabilities.

During the fifties and sixties, methodology was the guiding light that was to lead second-language teachers along paths to increased student achievement and fluency. When the expected bilingual products failed to materialize, many of the leaders in second-language education turned away from methodology and began to seek new solutions to old problems. Currently, the emphasis is on curricular organization of classroom instruction as a means of diminishing the undesirable attrition rate in second-language classes, of increasing enrollment in second-language classes, and of responding to the needs of individual students.

As was true at the time when the first edition was prepared, teachers and/or prospective teachers are faced with several important dichotomies in the field of second-language teaching. Do they favor a mechanistic or a mentalistic approach to teaching? Do they believe in inductive or deductive explanations of new material? Do they plan to utilize conditioning drills or reasoning exercises? Should they be "educational broadcasters" or "facilitators of learning"? Do they intend to promote extrinsic or intrinsic motivation? Do they hope to establish a teacher-centered class or a student-centered class?

All the questions in the preceding paragraph condense to a single issue, the external versus internal control of learning. Is the learning process to be controlled and shaped externally by the teacher and other agents of the educational system, or are the learners to be granted an important role in their education? Is the student to be viewed as a piece of clay to be molded or as an active participant in the learning process? This is not to imply that the teacher must choose one or the other. All teachers have the option to position themselves at any point on the continuum between the two extremes, and they do not have to remain in the same position indefinitely. They may change from year to year, from class to class, from student to student, from one type of learning situation to another, and from one type of learning task to another, as circumstances warrant. Too, it must be recognized that seating arrangements and curricular organization are no guarantee that a particular stress is indeed being put into practice. An individualized class may be characterized as teacher-centered and externally controlled just as the traditional classroom setup may emphasize student-centered, internally focused learning activities.

The question of position on the continuum is not so important as whether or not the stance taken by the teacher is the most facilitative one for maximum student achievement given student background, cognitive style, personality, self-concept, interests, goals, and needs; available school facilities; and teacher personality and capabilities. In order to make intelligent choices, the teacher needs to be familiar with contemporary, and past, currents in society, education, linguistics, psychology, sociology, anthropology, etc. as well as methodological and curricular trends. It is doubtful that any teacher ever acquires all the information needed in all possible situations, but it is this responsibility for continuing to learn, to evaluate, to reconsider, and to create that constitutes one of the most exciting aspects of a teaching career.

Since no single text can incorporate all topics, a decision must be made as to those areas that are most important in the formation of a knowledgeable base from which to develop an intelligent personal teaching style. The present text is seen as a springboard to further reading plus additional examination, discussion, expansion, extrapolation, and practice of the contained concepts. The reader is urged to grow beyond what has been presented here.

This book has been prepared keeping in mind the aforementioned teachers' needs to make intelligent choices. The purpose of part I is to examine theoretical and research support for each extreme of the external-internal continuum. Chapter 1 summarizes support for second-language study. Chapter 2 provides a historical perspective to the current situation. Chapter 3 surveys differing viewpoints of first-language learning. Chapter 4 presents results of research studies in both the cognitive and affective domains. Chapter 5 outlines the audio-lingual method, giving its principal theoretical bases, its basic classroom practice, and the major research studies supporting it. Chapter 6 does the same for the cognitive approach. Chapter 7 stresses student individuality. Chapter 8 deals with the diversification of instruction to provide for student individuality. The Conclusion summarizes Part I.

WHY A SECOND LANGUAGE?

INTRODUCTION

There are many valid reasons for studying a second language. Second-language teachers should be "ready, willing, and able" to expound on any and/or all of them to fellow teachers, guidance personnel, administrators, interested public, and students whenever the opportunity arises. In fact, they will hopefully be prepared to create the appropriate situations. All reasons may not be valid for all groups, and the teacher should be cognizant of the varying needs. Too, the advantages cited may be presented in different terms to the different groups involved. Individually and collectively, second-language teachers should be able to outline clearly and forcefully why they believe in second-language study and to explain how any given classroom activity contributes to the accomplishment of these goals. The focus of this chapter is on this "why" of second-language teaching.

One day a mother mouse was taking her children for a walk. As the unsuspecting family rounded the corner of a building, they suddenly found themselves confronting the twitching whiskers of a hungry cat delighted to find such a tantalizing and unprotected delicacy within striking distance. Surveying the dangerous situation instantly, the quick-witted and learned mother raised herself to her greatest height, drew in a huge breath of air, and barked, "Wuff! Wuff!" at the top of her voice. As the startled cat disappeared down the street, she turned to her darlings and said knowingly, "See how it pays to know a second language."

Nothing could change the complexion of second-language teaching more than a clientele committed to the study and learning of second languages. In this respect, second-language teachers in many other countries are more fortunate than those in the United States. While we in this country discuss ways and means of justifying the inclusion of second languages in our curriculum, the *UNESCO-FIPLV Survey of Foreign Language Teaching and Learning Today* (1975) reveals two principle concerns in other parts of the world: (1) at what age to begin the second language, and (2) at what age to begin the third language. It would be wonderful if the public and students could be imbued with a sense of need for language study. It would be marvelous if the profession could demonstrate to them the relevance of language learning as easily as the mother mouse did to her offspring.

The need to formulate a list of rationales acceptable to our various clientele is one of the highest priorities, if not the highest, in second-language education in the United States. In order to affirm the value of second-language study we must believe in ourselves and what we are trying to do. Otherwise, no one will take our discipline seriously, and our worst nightmares will become an unfortunate reality. Jarvis (1974) refers to this possibilility as a "self-fulfilling" prophesy in which "we feel worthless and thereby become useless." Belief in ourselves and what we are attempting to accomplish must become a reality. Only then will we be capable of establishing a supporting base of operations among the public, the administrators, and, last but not least, the students. The good will and encouragement of each of these groups must be cultivated carefully and constantly if second-language study is to flourish. Public good will must be earned and maintained. We must become conscious of and sensitive to our public image, and we must adopt positive public relations practices.

This pressing need for appropriate and acceptable justifications for second-language study is characterized by two basic implications. First, the reasons for language study may be, and likely will be, different for the varied and varying clientele; and second, we must be prepared to deliver the skills, or the knowledge, or the abilities, or the sensitivity, or the values that we profess.

BREAKING THE BARRIER

The urge to know and to grow intellectually, to push one's knowledge into new areas, is so strong and so universal that one of the most severe punishments known to man is stimulus deprivation. Almost before children are entirely aware of their beds, they are eager to explore their rooms. The individual's learning is a process of liberation, of freeing oneself from the confines of present circumstances in order to gain a greater comprehension of the world.

As we grow out of the confines of our immediate environment, we find other limitations—our cultural and linguistic heritage. The outer boundaries of the growing awareness of each individual is determined to a large extent by language experience, including first- as well as second-language experience. The same statement can be made of the third language and even beyond, but the liberating hurdle is the second. An acquaintanceship in breadth with the contemporary, interdependent world can be expanded considerably by one's linguistic and cultural abilities to benefit from the accumulated knowledge in languages and cultures other than one's own.

One acceptable manner in which to break through these cultural cocoons is the experience of becoming familiar with and gaining insights from another language and another culture through the study of a second language. The liberating value of stepping outside one's own language and one's own culture explains why language study has traditionally been a cornerstone in a liberal education. Language study is the only satisfactory way of gaining these cultural and linguistic insights. Substitutes may be more palatable, but they are likely to be less rewarding.

Of course, the individual, and society in general for that matter, is under no obligation to pursue an education in breadth. Chastain (1974, p. 374) says:

> The concept of education in breadth can be abandoned, but such action in no wise eliminates the need. It only ignores that basic need and eventually leads to a sad state of unrealized shallowness and myopia, a condition usually not correctable by the victim himself, because he is unlikely to be aware of his vacuity. The condition is not painful, of course, and it may even be characterized by a state of light-hearted euphoric bliss, i.e., ignorance is bliss.

The lack of concern among some segments of the public and of the student body merely serves to place an even greater responsibility upon the members of the profession to make the students and public aware of these needs and to meet them.

The image problem facing second-language education is serious, as the following table well illustrates:

Table 1.1: Percent Growth (Second-Language Study) Between Surveys (Major Languages)

1960–65	1965–68	1968–70	1970–72
59.9	9.2	−1.8	−11.5

Source: Brod (1973, p. 59)

Surveys indicate, however, that second-language study is supported by a much higher percentage of students, even among those who are fulfilling a language requirement, than commonly held opinion would lead us to believe. (See chapter 2, "Perspectives," for additional information.) Too, we should not lose sight of the fact that other traditional academic subjects, such as English, mathematics, and science, are suffering from some of the same problems of image and enrollment as second languages.

BENEFITS OF BREAKING THE CULTURAL AND LINGUISTIC BARRIERS

One of the basic components of growth and expansion of awareness is comparison. As one becomes acquainted with other people, he learns more about himself by comparison. Knowing other people makes it possible for individuals to develop a greater understanding of themselves, just as exploring the variations in another culture presents the necessary contrasts needed to enable individuals to see more fully into the complexities of their own society. The same fundamental principle applies to language study as well. Studying a second language provides a comprehension of the connotations of words and the building blocks of expression that is unimagined prior to the study of a second language. Can there be any doubt that a more complete knowledge of oneself, of one's culture, and of one's language is a valid and worthwhile goal of any educational program?

One word of caution at this point. None of the desirable outcomes of second-language study presented in the preceding paragraph are automatically attained in a second-language classroom. The teacher must present opportunities for the students to learn about the lives, the social patterns, and the values of people in other countries, and to become acquainted with the phonological, semantic, and syntactical system of the language they are studying. The profession must not only sell the product, but the teachers must see to it that the goods are delivered.

Internal Benefits

Internal benefits refer to the changes that occur within the individual during second-language study. These benefits are primary. Other related benefits are secondary and depend upon the internal pluses for their validity and practical importance. This is not to say that the student, or even society, will stress the internal benefits. They may well stress the external, practical possibilities to a much greater extent. As second-language teachers we may even have to emphasize the external in order to accomplish the internal.

This section deals with internal benefits only. The discussion treats the following internal benefits of second-language study: insight into life, tolerance, knowledge of the complexities of language, flexibility, discipline, and the acquisition of new learning skills. One internal benefit that students can acquire through second-language study is an insight into life and life styles that enables them to appreciate more fully their own situation both personally and culturally. This insight helps them to begin to answer the questions "Who am I?" and "How do I fit in?" As they gain a more complete understanding of themselves and their environment, they are more capable of directing their own activities and of relating to surrounding circumstances.

As students become more familiar with other cultural and societal patterns, they can develop tolerance for different life styles. The word *can* is used because individual reaction depends upon the manner in which this information is presented and studied. Certainly, in the modern world and in modern pluralistic societies, the goal of tolerance is an important one, and the second-language teacher should be conscious of the need to strive for positive reactions toward others and other cultural systems without alienating the students or without attempting to denigrate their own cultural values. The acquisition of this ability to operate comfortably in the presence of dissimilar attitudes and values will spare the individuals a great deal of psychological discomfort.

Having a greater insight into the complexities and the potentials of language is a definite plus to the individual who seeks to comprehend the world and to cope with it. Language, it must be remembered, controls not only one's speech, but one's thoughts and one's view of the world as well. For example, different cultural viewpoints are reflected in such an everyday occurrence as a mother's words of caution to a misbehaving child. In the English-, Italian-, and Greek-speaking worlds, the mother says, "Be good." The French-speaking mother says, "Be wise." The German-speaking mother says, "Get in line." In Scandinavia the mothers say, "Be kind." The Hopi Indian mother says, "That is not the Hopi way." (Goldschmidt).

It has been theorized that second-language study can enhance the individual's ability to cope with new situations. Forced by the nature of the discipline to deal with previously unencountered cultural ideas and linguistic structures, the learner acquires the flexibility needed in a fast changing world. Alter (1970) maintains that society has entered a stage of accelerated change and that the study of second languages can help the student adapt to a world in transition. She argues that second-language learning is the only subject in the curriculum that can serve this purpose since other subjects, such as mathematics, are not entirely new and strange to the student. Jarvis (1974) echoes these thoughts, saying that second-language study can prepare the student for the trauma of "future shock" in that "the ability to cope with the unfamiliar can be a powerful outcome of foreign language study." He chides second-language educators, however, stating that "too often *we have made our students victims of the unfamiliar, rather than beneficiaries.*"

Flexibility in this case relates principally to psychological factors. However, an intellectual flexibility, which enhances the individual's cognitive powers, is also a possible outcome of second-language study. Educational psychologists have been able to promote the development of certain aspects of creativity, especially in the area of divergent thinking, by means of selected learning activities (Treffinger & Gowan, 1971). Landry (1974) reported that scores of FLES students obtained from tests of divergent thinking, especially flexibility and originality, were higher than those of students who had not studied a second language. Potential investigators of the effects of second-language study would be well advised to attempt to replicate these findings with students at the junior high and high school levels.

Although the word *discipline* may be less than popular in some quarters at the present time, discipline is necessary for the successful completion of innumerable tasks. Language is one of those subjects in the curriculum that does require consistent effort and energy to progress successfully. The ability to persevere is a definite asset in school as well as out, and a certain persistence and "stick-to-itiveness" can be one of the positive outcomes of second-language study. Second-language study is one of the most beneficial content areas in this respect, because students are forced to learn the material rather than to rely on a base of information that they may already have. Too, it is a subject area that must be mastered in small segments as the students proceed through the course.

Few would argue with the statement that the study of a second language is different in many respects from the study of other subjects in the curriculum. As a result, the student needs to adopt different and varying approaches to learning when studying a second language. Since it is now rather widely and readily recognized that there is a variety of learning skills, the study of a second language can be an asset in the acquisition of new learning skills. One study conducted several years ago found that students who had studied a second language in high school had a higher grade-point average in their studies at the university than those students who had no second-language experience. These findings persisted even when the students from the same percentile ranges on intelligence were compared (Skelton, 1957).

External Benefits

External benefits encompass what can be done with the knowledge, skills, insights, and sensitivities gained from second-language study. They may be beneficial in a practical, social way as people come into contact with persons from other nations, cultures, and/or subcultures, in travel and other leisure activities, and/or as a primary or secondary skill in one's chosen profession.

After having experienced a second culture and its language, the individual has the potential for relating more fully and effectively with others. These possibilities apply in the case of other cultures and to other subcultures within one's own general culture. In this respect, one should not lose sight of the fact that to a certain extent culture has various levels and various components just as language does. Each individual speaks an ideolect of a dialect within his language group. In this sense each of us operates according to his own unique culture pattern as well as within a subculture group and in a general overall cultural, societal group. The recognition and comprehension of the diversity involved will enable the individual to participate in more meaningful, more satisfactory, and more productive relationships with others. These relationships give personal satisfaction to the individual who enjoys making friends with members of other cultures. A political benefit derived from the understanding of cultural diversity is the informed citizenship that results and that can form a base for promoting a smoother operating and more cooperative community and national spirit.

The nation needs individuals capable of communicating to citizens of other countries in their own tongue. Such a capability is highly desirable in the State Department and foreign service, in commerce and business, and in relationships involving individual citizens having no other reason to communicate than to get acquainted and to share ideas. Nor can a country in the modern world ignore the effects of world opinion. Abandoning the study of second languages while most of the students in other countries are pursuing the study of one or more second languages for an extended period of time damages our image abroad.

Second-language skills are needed for maximum enjoyment and benefit during travel to foreign countries. Most second-language teachers would agree that one of the most educational experiences a person can have is to spend some time in a foreign country. However, the benefits that one derives from such an experience depend upon knowledge of the language and the culture. Exposure in and of itself in no way insures educational rewards as a result of being in the country. What is there must be recognized and experienced.

Dennis Gabor in his book *Inventing the Future* says modern society faces three grave dangers: (1) atomic annihilation, (2) overpopulation, and (3) too much leisure time. Science can find answers to the first two problems. The third presents more serious complications. At this time in the history of civilization, humanity is incapable of busying itself constructively during long periods of leisure. Second-language study can be a very enjoyable and beneficial leisure-time activity. In the first place, learning a second language can be fun in itself. Secondly, people can use their leisure time to keep up with the language, travel, see foreign films, eat in ethnic restaurants, make new acquaintances, listen to short wave, and read books, magazines, and newspapers in the second language.

Some students will use their second language as a primary skill in their careers, such as teaching, translating, and interpreting. In the teaching field there are positions available, but it must be admitted that currently there is a surplus of teachers. Both translating and interpreting are special skills that require a much greater familiarity with the second language than can be obtained in the typical undergraduate curriculum. At this point, encouraging large numbers of students to specialize in second-language study with the expectation of a career in teaching, translating, or interpreting is unrealistic. On the other hand, interested and capable students certainly should not be discouraged from majoring in a second language. Positions are and will continue to be available. However, the students should be made aware of the tight job market at the present time.

A more realistic and viable approach is to point out to the students the various possibilities for employing second-language skills as an extra asset that they can offer a prospective employer in fields such as social work, medicine, law, political science, and publishing.

When one considers the use of a second-language as an auxiliary skill, one's mind almost immediately turns to American firms that conduct business abroad, or foreign firms that conduct business in the United States. The international nature of business continues to grow at a phenomenal pace. Over 3,200 U.S. companies have branches or representatives overseas, and over 1,500 foreign firms have business connections in the U.S. The *Modern Language Journal* in March of 1974 quoted an article in the *Wall Street Journal* which reported that corporate requests for second-language training had risen ten times in two years, the Thunderbird Graduate School of International Management expected an increased enrollment of 50 percent over 1972, and the Berlitz courses in second-language instruction for corporate executives were flourishing (Durette, 1974). One business executive is quoted as follows: "I have tried to establish Latin American business ties since 1959. I finally decided to learn Spanish around 1965, and after I became proficient in 1967, my business with Spanish-speaking countries soared from nothing to over 20 million dollars yearly" (Honig & Brod, 1974, p. 9).

The bleeding balance of payments, which plagues the economy of the United States, and the extent of American investment abroad and foreign investment in this country underscore the absolute necessity of elevating the nation's second-language skills. American investments abroad now total more than 86 billion dollars, which is an increase of over 600 percent in the last twenty years, and foreign investment has reached a mark of over 14 billion, which is more than three times the former amount (Honig & Brod, 1974).

In addition to foreign business in the United States, there are many needs for second-language skills in the United States itself. There are many speakers of languages other than English living in this country. Doctors, lawyers, public officials, media personnel, educators, service employees, and people engaged in business in areas with large concentrations of non-English speaking populations can make use of second-language skills to their advantage and to the advantage of the people involved. Also, the number of foreign visitors to the U.S. is increasing enormously. The U.S. has not yet begun to develop the vast potential of the international tourist trade. Even though the numbers of foreign visitors to the U. S. is gradually catching up to those going abroad "only *2 percent* of America's hotels and motels have bilingual or multilingual staff in key guest-contact positions" (Honig & Brod, 1974, p. 5). The potential in this one area alone lies practically untapped.

Is the world really shrinking? Here are some figures indicating the extent of interchange and interdependence among nations. In 1972, 7,700,000 Americans went abroad. That number was a 1,083 percent increase over 1950. The same year 3,800,000 foreigners came to the U. S., an increase of 1,219 percent. Trade between free-world nations was $371.1 billion, a rise of 565 percent since 1952. In 1971 Americans had $86 billion invested in other countries, an increase of 629 percent, and foreign investment in the U. S. had reached $13.7 billion, a rise of 303 percent. In 1972 Americans made or received 35,000,000 phone calls, an increase of 3,789 percent over 1950 (*U.S. News and World Report*, 1973).

One future consequence of the economic and political international interdependence among nations may be to relieve the second-language teachers in this country from having to defend the place of their subject in the curriculum. As the general public becomes aware of the economic possibilities of and the political and economic need for second languages as auxiliary skills in fields as diverse as social work and government service, the obvious, being obvious, will not need to be justified. Future prospects along with current needs should encourage those of us in the profession to do what we can to strengthen second-language learning at the present time.

HANDLING THE PERSISTENT CRITIC

What does the proponent of second-language learning do when, after presenting all the valid and relevant reasons for second-language study she can muster, the reaction she gets is just as negative as it was in the beginning? First, she can suggest that her unenlightened challenger consider what the world would be like if no one had ever learned a second language. (This would be a good exercise in creativity as well as an enlightening exercise for students!) She might also ask the critic to contemplate what the world would be like at the present time if no one in the modern world could communicate in a second language.

In reply to the obdurate who claims, "Everything of any importance is available in English," or complains, "I've forgotten all the French and German I ever learned, and I've done all right," the ultimate comeback is that of William Riley Parker (1971, p. 19) who put this type in his place saying, "Blind men get along, too, but the difference is that one can admire their triumph over handicap."

The complaint against the language requirement has been long and loud. Such a typical reaction is entirely comprehensible to this author who was forced into his first exposure to second-language learning during his sophomore year in college by an identical requirement. However, the resultant satisfaction arising from such an experience is by no means isolated. Here is how James Michener (1974, pp. 193–94) describes his fateful introduction to Spanish:

> If Swarthmore College in 1925 had employed even a half way decent guidance counselor, I would have spent my life as an assistant professor of education in some Midwestern university. Because when I reported to college, it must have been apparent to everyone that I was destined for some kind of academic career. Nevertheless, I was allowed to take Spanish, which leads to nothing, instead of French or German, which as everyone knows are important languages studied by serious students who wish to gain a Ph.D.
>
> I cannot tell you how often I was penalized for having taken a frivolous language like Spanish instead of a decent, self-respecting tongue like French. In fact, it led to the sacrifice of my academic career.
>
> Still, I continued to putter around with Spanish, eventually finding a deep affinity for it. In the end, I was able to write a book about Spain which will probably live longer than anything else I've done. In other words, I blindly backed into a minor masterpiece. . . . It was Spanish that opened up for me a whole new universe of concepts and ideas.[1]

Getting anyone who has not benefited from a profitable second-language experience to comprehend the limitations of his ethnocentric background and the liberating influence of attaining familiarity with a second language and a second culture constitutes a severe challenge to even the most persuasive. Perhaps Mark Twain through Huck and Jim can accomplish the task for us. Huck has been discussing French princes who come to the United States:

> "Den he cain't git no situation. What he gwyne to do?"
> "Well, I don't know. Some of them gets on the police, and some of them learns people how to talk French."

---

[1]Michener (1974, pp. 193–94). Reprinted by permission of the William Morris Agency, Inc., as Agent for James A. Michener.

"Why, Huck, doan' de French people talk de same way we does?"

"*No*, Jim; you couldn't understand a word they said—not a single word."

"Well, now, I be ding-busted! How do dat come?"

"*I* don't know; but it's so. I got some of their jabber out of a book. S'pose a man was to come to you and say Polly-voo-franzy. What would you think?"

"I wouldn't think nuffn; I'd take en bust him over de head.". . .

"Shucks, it ain't calling you anything. I's only saying, do you know how to talk French?"

"Well, den, why couldn't he say it?"

"Why, he *is* a-saying it. That's a Frenchman's *way* of saying it."

"Well, it's a blame ridicklous way, en I doan' want to hear no mo' 'bout it. Dey ain' no sense in it."

"Looky here, Jim; does a cat talk like we do?"

"No, a cat dón't."

"Well, does a cow?"

"No, a cow don't, nuther."

"Does a cat talk like a cow, or a cow talk like a cat?"

"No, dey don't."

"It's natural and right for 'em to talk different from each other, ain't it?"

"Course."

"And ain't it natural and right for a cat and a cow to talk different from *us*?"

"Why, mos' sholy it is."

"Well, then, why ain't it natural and right for a *Frenchman* to talk different from us? You answer me that."

"Is a cat a man, Huck?"

"No."

"Well, den, dey ain't no sense in a cat talkin' like a man. Is a cow a man?—er is a cow a cat?"

"No, she ain't either of them."

"Well, den, she ain't got no business to talk like either one er the yuther of 'em. Is a Frenchman a man?"

"Yes."

"*Well*, den! Dad blame it, why doan' he *talk* like a man? You answer me *dat*!"

I see it warn't no use wasting words. . . . So I quit.

CONCLUSION

Let's not quit. The validity of second-language learning has not diminished in the slightest. Our task is to make the public aware of the benefits to be gained from broadening their experience and amplifying their potential through second-language study.

REVIEW AND APPLICATION

DISCUSSION AND ACTIVITIES

1. Why did you decide to study a second language? Why did your friends?
2. Why did you decide to major, or minor, in a second language?
3. Which of the reasons for second-language study presented in this chapter do you support? What reasons would you add?
4. Discuss how you might justify the study of second languages to parents, administrators, counselors, students.
5. How can second-language study be made more relevant?
6. Role play an interview between a principal attempting to refute all justifications for second-language learning and a second-language teacher attempting to convince him that he can justify the subject to the public and to the students.
7. Examine the ramifications of how the world would be different if no one had ever learned to speak a second language and if no one did at the present time.
8. Outline ways and means of informing the public and the students of our goals in second-language teaching.
9. Present any ideas you have or any practices you are familiar with for establishing and maintaining good public relations between the modern-language department and the public.
10. What would you tell your students on the first day of class to inform them, and perhaps to convince them, of the reasons for second-language study?

SELECTED REFERENCES

Alter, M. P. (1970) *A Modern Case for German.* Philadelphia: American Association of Teachers of German. Pp. 18–19.

Bomse, M. D. (1973) Meeting the Needs and Interests of Students and the Community. *ADFL Bulletin,* 5: 40–41.

Brod, R. I. (1973) Foreign Language Enrollments in U.S. Colleges—Fall 1972. *ADFL Bulletin,* 5:59.

Brod, R. I. (1974) Careers and the Foreign Language Department. *ADFL Bulletin,* 6: 16–22.

Chastain, K. (1974) The Relevance of Requirements. *Intellect,* 103: 373–74.

Cormier, R. J. (1974) Foreign Languages and the Liberal Arts. *ADFL Bulletin,* 6: 23–25.

Durette, R. (1974) Notes and News. *Modern Language Journal,* 58: 124–25.

Edgerton, M. F. (1971) A Philosophy for the Teacher of Foreign Languages. *Modern Language Journal,* 55: 5–15.

Fuller, C. S. (1974) Language-Oriented Careers in the Federal Government. *ADFL Bulletin,* 6: 45–51.

Gold, P. J. (1973) Why Spanish? *Canadian Modern Language Review,* 29: 32–35.

Goldschmidt, W. A Word in Your Ear. A program in the series *Ways of Mankind* presented and distributed by the National Association of Educational Broadcasters.

Grittner, F. M. (1972) Behavioral Objectives, Skinnerian Rats, and Trojan Horses. *Foreign Language Annals,* 6: 52–60.

Hanzeli, V. E. (1971) Foreign Language Teachers and the "New" Student: A Review Article. *Modern Language Journal,* 55: 15–21.

Harrison, A. T. (1973) What Can I Do With It?—Vocational Counseling for Language Students. *ADFL Bulletin,* 5: 37–39.

Harvey, W. (1974) Helping Guidance Counselors See the Value of Foreign Languages. *ADFL Bulletin,* 5: 5–6.

Honig, L. J., and Brod, R. I. (1974) Foreign Languages and Careers. *Modern Language Journal,* 58: 157–85.

Jarvis, G. (1974) What *Really* Comes From Studying a Foreign Language. Keynote Address, ACTFL Convention.

Kimpton, J. R. (1975) What Is French For? *French Review,* 48: 735–40.

Kirylak, L. (1973) Foreign Language Career Preparation. *ADFL Bulletin,* 5: 42–47.

Landry, R. G. (1974) A Comparison of Second Language Learners and Monolinguals on Divergent Thinking Tasks at the Elementary School Level. *Modern Language Journal,* 58: 10–15.

Liddy, C. R., et al. (1973) The Case for French in the Secondary School Program. *Canadian Modern Language Review,* 29: 14–18.

Lippman, J. N. (1974) Rationale for Language Study. In G. Jarvis (Ed.), *The Challenge of Communication.* Skokie, Ill.: National Textbook. Pp. 37–69.

Michener, J. (1974) On Wasting Time. *Reader's Digest,* 105: 193–96.

Parker, W. R. (1961) *The National Interest and Foreign Languages.* (3rd ed.) Washington, D.C.: Department of State.

Parker, W. R. (1971) Why a Foreign Language Requirement? *The Case for Foreign-Language Study.* New York: MLA/ACTFL Materials Center. P. 19.

Reinert, H. (1970) Student Attitudes Toward Foreign Language—No Sale! *Modern Language Journal,* 54: 107–12.

Reinert, H. (1972) Truth in Packaging . . . for Foreign Languages. *Modern Language Journal,* 56: 205–9.

Roeming, R. F. (1971) Bilingualism and National Interest. *Modern Language Journal,* 55: 73–81.

Ryder, F. G. (1973) A Matter of Image. *ADFL Bulletin,* 5: 5–11.

Sandrock, J. P. (1972) Languages and the Humanities: Our Roots and Responsibility. *ADFL Bulletin,* 4: 15–17.

Savaiano, E. (1974) The FL Requirement, a Liberal Education, and You. *ADFL Bulletin,* 5: 11–14.

Schaefer, W. D. (1973) Foreign Languages and the National Interest. *Foreign Language Annals,* 6: 460–64.

Shuman, R. B. (1971) Let's Get Foreign Language Teachers Out of Our Public High Schools. *Modern Language Journal,* 55: 21–26.

Skelton, R. B. (1957) High School Foreign Language Study and Freshman Performance. *School and Society,* 85: 203–5.

Steiner, F. (1974) Career Education and Its Implications at the National Level. *Modern Language Journal,* 58: 186–91.

Treffinger, D. J., and Gowan, J. C. (1971) An Updated Representative List of Methods and Educational Programs for Stimulating Creativity. *Methods and Educational Programs for Stimulating Creativity,* 5: 127–39.

Troyanovich, J. M. (1972) Foreign Languages and the Dodo Bird: A Lesson from Darwin. *Foreign Language Annals,* 5: 341–44.

Turner, P. R. (1974) Why Johnny Doesn't Want to Learn a Foreign Language. *Modern Language Journal,* 58: 191–96.

U.S. News and World Report (1973) It's a Shrinking World. *Accent on* ACTFL (September): 18–19. (Reprinted from *U.S. News and World Report,* June 11, 1973.)

Valdes, M. E. (1974) Toward a New Relevance in Language Teaching. *Canadian Modern Language Review,* 31: 50–54.

Yalden, J. (1973) A Case for Studying Spanish. *Canadian Modern Language Review,* 29: 36–42.

PERSEPCTIVES

The Beginnings

Breaking Away from the Past: Revolution to Civil War

Boom Period: Civil War to World War I

Isolationism and Involvement: World War I to 1952

International Commitment to Internal Dissent: 1952 to the Late Sixties

Protest to Participation: Late Sixties to the Present
    Characteristics of the Period
    Trends in the Schools
    Problems in Education
    Trends in Second-Language Teaching
    Effects of Abolishing the Language Requirement
    Trends in Psychology, Linguistics, and Sociology

The Future

INTRODUCTION

The study of the past may not unlock the closed doors of the future, but an acquaintance with what has preceded certainly provides a key to the understanding of the way things are and why they are as they are. Whether or not such knowledge actually improves future prospects is debatable, but certainly individuals who are aware of change and the forces behind it are more capable of anticipating and adjusting to the continuous innovations in their life and work. The teacher, especially, needs to be attuned to the tenor of the times and be able to adjust to the curriculum revisions brought about by shifting political, economic, and social conditions. Teaching does not occur in a vacuum. Any subject occupies a position in the curriculum in order to meet a need of all or part of the school population. Second-language teaching is no exception. As conditions change, the course objectives are altered.

    The purpose of this chapter is to put into perspective the changing climates that have affected second-language teaching in order that teachers may better comprehend the forces that influence their profession. The historical facts included are presented only as a necessary basis for the clarification of the various cause-and-effect relationships and interrelationships that have rather effectively determined the course taken by second-language teaching. In each historical period, the discussion proceeds from a general overview of the period to its educational system and type of second-language teaching. In the later periods, an examination of related influences from the fields of psychology, linguistics, and sociology is included.

THE BEGINNINGS

The work-filled life of the early settlers was centered in their religious faith. In the somber and authoritarian atmosphere, discipline was stressed, and social, religious, and moral conformity was demanded. Control in local affairs was exercised by the ruling theocracy. Political and economic matters were controlled by England. As far as possible, within the limits of the new environment, the institutions established were extensions of those in Europe at that time. There was no time to develop new institutions; nor was the desirability or need for such changes felt. The people spent their energies establishing themselves in a new and often hostile environment. Faithful to their religion, dedicated to the task of making new homes, and kept in line by strict rules and regulations, the colonists were left little reason or opportunity for reflection or innovation.

The educational system was a reflection of the existing conditions and beliefs. Life was an expression of religious faith, and the schools were a part of that life. The schools were established to insure that each person, in keeping with the obligation set forth during the Reformation, know how to read the Bible. In the words of the "Old Deluder Satan Act" of 1647 they were to counteract and to nullify the ". . . one chief project of that old deluder Satan—to keep men from a knowledge of the Scriptures. . . ." The curriculum and the materials read were religious in nature, and the primary qualifications for a teacher were religious orthodoxy and good moral character.

As important as it was to learn to read and write, little emphasis was placed on higher learning. Most children had too much to do to spend much time in school. The few who attended secondary school went to a Latin grammar school. The goal of these schools was also a religious one. The purpose of studying Latin and Greek was to gain a better understanding of the Scriptures. Those students who wished could continue their religious training at Harvard before taking their place among the ministers, lawyers, or teachers of the colonies.

Little can be said about modern languages during this period because little importance was attached to them. The Renaissance tradition of studying the classics and the need to study Latin and Greek in order to comprehend more clearly the Bible's teachings completely dominated the early educational scene. The few who learned a modern language did so either by studying with a private tutor or by studying abroad.

BREAKING AWAY FROM THE PAST: REVOLUTION TO CIVIL WAR

Having completed the initial physical phase of the colonization, the inhabitants of the original colonies began to have some extra time to devote to improvements in their political and economic system. In Europe the winds of change were blowing, and, young and enthusiastic, the new country was listening to its whispers. What they were hearing was coming mostly from the French writers of the eighteenth century. The ideas of the French intellectuals with regard to government, mixed with the colonists' independent pioneer spirit and a growing consciousness of self, culminated in the Revolutionary War. After the war came the problems associated with establishing a new government and a new nation. The westward expansion continued unabated throughout the period. A cultural nationalism developed, and the United States became quite sensitive to foreign opinion. Toward the latter part of this era the country was preoccupied with another problem, the question of slavery and later the Civil War.

The dominant note in education during this period was one of change. Prior to the Revolutionary War, the Latin grammar school had met the needs of the times. Afterwards, the trend was away from the traditional ways of doing things. The ideas of the Age of Enlightenment affected all aspects of society, including education. Expanding trade and commerce also influenced the educational needs of society. The focus of the country was beginning to widen, and the curriculum reflected this expansion. The emphasis on religion gave way to increased secular interests, with the exception of the period immediately following the Great Awakening, and church control of the schools gave way to political control. Demands arose for instruction in the social graces and for practical preparation for careers in trade and commerce. The apprentice system was basic prior to this period, but now the need was to include training for a trade as an important part of the curriculum. In other words, the pragmatic character of America was beginning to assert itself. As early as 1731, bookkeeping and modern languages were taught in New York as a part of the program leading toward a career in foreign trade. Franklin's academy was established in 1751, and the offerings began to include a greater variety of subjects. The first high school, the English Classical School, was founded in

1828. By the time of the Civil War, the Latin grammar school had been largely replaced by the academies and the high schools.

The teaching of modern languages in the schools actually began in the middle decades of the eighteenth century. The times had changed. The dominant role of religion in society had diminished. The classic tradition of the schools was cracking under the pressure to assume some of the responsibility for practical career training. Merchants and businessmen needed young men trained in bookkeeping and modern languages to participate in the increasingly important field of international commerce. Others felt that the curriculum was too narrow and that it should be expanded to include other subjects. Although not embraced wholeheartedly, modern languages were accepted into the curriculum during this period. In spite of the efforts of men like Franklin and Jefferson, who recommended that modern languages be included in the curriculum, many still considered modern languages a frill subject. In their opinion, such subjects lacked the necessary difficulty to be one of the fundamental courses in the curriculum. Tradition was behind the classics. Many years elapsed in the process of establishing modern languages as a bona fide course in its own right.

BOOM PERIOD: CIVIL WAR TO WORLD WAR I

At the end of the Civil War the people of the United States were free to turn their energies toward developing the nation. The period between the Civil War and World War I was one of unprecedented expansion internally and internationally. Business prospered. Industry grew. The economy flourished. Immigrants flowed into the country. People flocked to the cities. There was constant activity and change. The period was one of almost uncontrollable growth and development as the country was converted into an industrial giant among nations. During this era the United States grew up and assumed a position as a world power in international affairs.

This was also a period of tremendous growth and change for the schools. Not only were there more and more people, but also a larger percentage of the children enrolled in school. The number of pupils doubled in every decade from 1800 to World War I. As society became more and more urbanized, the schools were called on to assume responsibilities for such things as sewing, cooking, woodworking, metal crafts, etc., which had formerly been learned at home. As the steady trend toward tax-supported public schools continued, the academy, which had been basically a private system, declined; and the high school gradually assumed the characteristics of today's modern comprehensive high school.

Although modern languages had gained a foothold in the curriculum in the eighteenth century, there was no sudden shift in interest toward modern language study. Enrollments rose slightly as the academies and the high schools replaced the Latin grammar school. Latin remained strong, even in the curriculum of the academies and high schools. Enrollment in Latin, for example, rose to a high of 50.6 percent of the total high school enrollment in 1900. Afterwards, as the high school population of school-age children and the character and purpose of the secondary schools began to change, enrollments in Latin began to decline (Kant, 1970, p. 403).

During the boom period following the Civil War, the number of students studying modern foreign languages rose along with the increasing school population. By 1890, 16.3 percent of the high-school population was studying French and German. German was by far the most popular language. In 1915, 24.4 percent of the high-school students were taking German. Spanish made little headway until just before World War I (Kant, 1970, p. 403).

In this period of change and expansion, one would expect similar innovations in the teaching of modern languages. Such was not the case. Enrollments rose, but the model for teaching was based on the past, not on any new techniques. The growth was present, but not the changes. Modern languages were still a stepchild in the curriculum, and the difficult task was still to convince the public and the educators that they belonged there. In order to prove that modern languages could provide the necessary mental discipline required in the school program, modern-language teachers copied the traditional classroom methods of the classics. The result was that modern languages were gradually accepted, but at first they conformed to the objective of supplying the needed intellectual discipline. This goal was approved by the teachers who founded the Modern Language Association of America (MLA) in 1883.

The present-day modern-language teacher should not be too quick to condemn the teachers of this period for their apparent capitulation to classical methodology. Opinion was such that other types of teaching probably would not have been accepted. Too, one must keep in mind that from the beginnings of the country to World War I, the dominant approach to learning in general was based on faculty psychology. This theory stemmed from the belief that the brain was much like a muscle that needed to be exercised, the tougher the exercise the better. Learning was like the medicine of the day, bitter and tough to swallow. Therefore, modern-language classes based on traditional teaching methods involving huge amounts of memorization and translation were justified in terms of tradition, both from the classics and from psychology.

Toward the end of this period, however, forces were set in motion that were to have considerable influence on teaching methods. World War I itself, of course, caused profound changes in the society. The first experimental psychology laboratory was opened in Germany in 1879. Soon after, psychological laboratories were established in the United States. Psychology came to be viewed as a science, and resultant theories from these early years have had a great deal of influence on the educational system and on language teaching ever since. Another influence on language teaching was the introduction of the "direct method."[1]

ISOLATIONISM AND INVOLVEMENT: WORLD WAR I TO 1952

The American people were quite disillusioned after World War I. President Wilson's dream of a war to end all wars burst. The League of Nations failed. There was a withdrawal, an urge to disengage from international affairs. The desire was to avoid all foreign contacts and involvements. This period was followed by the "Gay Twenties," the gilded days of fun and frolic. The country was driven by a compulsion to "live it up." It was almost as if a national reaction to the previous period of disenchantment had emerged. The country basked in its prosperity, and the future promised even better things to come. Suddenly the stock market crashed, signaling the beginning of the long depression years, which did not actually end until the beginning of World War II. Then came the war itself, which required a total commitment of the country's energies and resources. The aftermath, too, required tremendous effort and aid to rebuild countries destroyed by the war. America did not withdraw this time but became increasingly occupied with international problems.

The nation's schools continued to grow at a rapid rate. With the passage of the child-labor laws and compulsory school attendance laws in the early part of the century, now most school-age children were enrolled in school. Of course, this rapid growth was aided by the vast economic support available in this country. The direction taken in this period in education was toward greater flexibility. The number of courses offered was gradually increased. Also, the number of responsibilities that education assumed was expanded. Summer recreation programs were begun. Swimming pools were built. Education for the physically and mentally handicapped was established. In short, the educational objective was to develop the total capability of all children. The American goal of providing an educational system responsive to the needs of all students, not just the academically talented, was drawing closer to a reality.

The effects of the war and the postwar isolationist sentiment upon the

---

[1]Using the direct method, the teacher endeavors to teach oral skills directly in the second language without reference to the mother tongue.

teaching of modern languages were almost disastrous. The enrollment in German dropped from 24.4 percent in 1915 to .6 percent in 1922 (Kant, 1970, p. 403). Although French and Spanish, especially the latter, reaped temporary benefits from the negative sentiment toward German, enrollment in these two languages soon began a decline, which continued until well after the end of World War II. In 1948, only 13.7 percent of the high-school population was enrolled in modern languages. (That was down from a high of 35.9 percent in 1915). Latin also suffered, dropping from 37.3 percent in 1915 to 7.8 percent in 1948 (Kant, 1970, p. 403).

The study of modern languages was affected not only by distrust and dislike for all things foreign and by the country's depressed economic condition, but also by the consequences of the "progressive" education movement of the thirties. According to this philosophy, an outgrowth of the functionalist psychology and pragmatic philosophy of James and Dewey, the curriculum was to be geared toward "life adjustment" education.[2] As late as 1945, the "Harvard Report" recommended modern-language study only for the college bound. Increasing numbers of colleges eliminated language entrance and degree requirements.

From World War I to 1952, modern languages, which had little background to assist them in maintaining their position in the schools, were again in trouble. Even the centuries-old Renaissance tradition of the classics was not sufficient to spare Latin from undergoing a decline. There appeared to be little concern for language teaching in the United States. After World War I and throughout the depression years, the country was too busy with its own internal problems to be very much interested in other languages and other cultures.

In spite of the fact that declining enrollments indicated that drastic changes in modern-language teaching were needed, little was done. Immediately after World War I, an attempt was made, in reaction to the criticism of returning soldiers who had not been able to communicate in a foreign language, to teach the oral skills via the "direct method." However, that attempt was soon abandoned. The complaint was that the method was too time consuming. The grammar-translation approach of the classics continued.[3] In 1929, a study sponsored by the Modern Language Association of America under the direction of Algernon Coleman recommended a reading approach. Its findings had indicated that most students do not go beyond two years of study in a foreign language. Therefore, the committee concluded that the only practical objective was reading. The conclusions of this study were widely

---

[2]According to functionalist psychology and pragmatic philosophy, only those types of teaching-learning activities that the students could use in life situations were to be included in the curriculum.

[3]Grammar-translation teaching emphasizes the study of grammar and translation of sentences as a means of learning a second language.

accepted, even though many teachers were not happy with them. As a result, special, graded reading materials based on word counts were prepared. As time passed, many teachers reverted to grammar-translation methods as a way of teaching reading. Many had never abandoned the security of their traditional techniques. Some teachers espoused a more eclectic approach that involved the oral use of the language as well as the written.[4] No approach, apparently, was successful in attracting large groups of students.

Although the future was dark, and many in the field of modern-language education were disparaging, the light was rising that was to lead the way and to brighten the prospects of modern languages after 1952. In the twenties, and even before, a few cultural anthropologists and linguists had initiated work among the Indians. Since these tribes had no written language, the historical linguistic approach did not suffice. The result was a new approach to the study of languages, descriptive linguistics. One of the leaders in this new field was Leonard Bloomfield.

In addition to being a linguist, Bloomfield was extremely interested in, and highly critical of, methods of teaching modern languages. He felt that grammar-translation practices were not the way to teach a foreign language. According to him, oral language was primary and should be given primary stress in the classroom. Too, language learning should involve a process of overlearning necessary structural forms rather than a superficial exposure to written grammatical exercises. Later, it was the Bloomfieldian linguists, members of the American Council of Learned Societies, who were instrumental in establishing intensive language courses at various colleges and universities. At the outbreak of World War II, the government turned to these innovators for leadership in the development of intensive language courses to teach much-needed language skills to Armed Forces personnel.

The theories of the linguists, as put into practice in the Army Specialized Training Program (ASTP), did indeed produce graduates who were able to function in the language. When the public learned of this success, they were surprised and pleased, surprised that an American could learn a foreign language so quickly, and pleased that it was possible. The next reaction was to ask why this had not been done before. Shortly thereafter, searching and uncomfortable questions were directed at the schools. However, the school structure was not such that the ASTP program could be transferred directly into the typical program. Not until after 1952 were adaptations developed that would fit the school situation.

Interesting and related events were also taking place in psychology. During the late nineteenth and early part of the twentieth century, psychology

---

[4]The eclectic approach is a middle-of-the-road selection of workable techniques and activities from various methods.

was able to establish itself as a science and to separate itself from philosophy and physiology. Wundt was the first to apply scientific methods to introspection. His followers became known as the structuralists. Their objective was to study the states of the mind. In 1900 the functionalists separated from the structuralists. Functionalists were interested in behavior as well as mental processes, and they placed special stress on the changing mental processes in adjusting to the environment. The next school to appear was that of the behaviorists. They rejected all forms of introspection. In their striving for complete scientific objectivity, i.e., for recording only those phenomena observable by others, some went to the point of denying the existence of conscious thought because thought cannot be observed. The recording of overt behavior was to be the only basis for objective descriptions of psychological studies. The behavioristic theories of this early period later grew into stimulus-response (S-R) theories of learning.

In part, behavioristic, mechanistic theories of learning were an outgrowth of comparative psychological studies in which the similarity of animal and human learning was compared. Thorndike, for example, believed that learning in animals and simple learning in humans were the same, a process of establishing a connection between a stimulus and its response through trial-and-error. Many present S-R learning theories are based on extrapolations to human learning from experiments in the animal laboratory. In part, they were a reaction to the stress on mental discipline that had dominated the view of learning for so long. In part they occurred as a reaction to introspection as a scientific method in psychology.

The first of the cognitive theories of learning was introduced in Germany around 1912 by Wertheimer. His theories stressed the totality of the situation as opposed to the parts and pieces of the mechanistic theories proposed earlier. Later, Kohler described examples of insightful behavior displayed by apes in problem-solving situations and concluded that S-R theories were not sufficient to explain the apes' actions (Mouly, 1973).

Behaviorism caught on quite quickly in this country and rapidly assumed a dominant position in psychological circles. Becoming widespread in the twenties, behavioristic explanations of learning were those most commonly accepted during this whole period from World War I to 1952. The preeminence of mechanistic learning theories was to continue until the emerging popularity of cognitive psychology in the fifties and sixties. Thus, it is not surprising to learn that Bloomfield and Bloomfieldian linguists accepted behavioristic interpretations of learning. These beliefs regarding learning coupled with Bloomfield's distaste for the mental discipline approach to language teaching and his analysis of oral stimuli and responses while studying conversations between the Indians explain many of the basic tenets of the Army Specialized Training Programs. This close connection between descriptive linguistics and stimulus-response learning theories and teaching techniques has continued to the present.

INTERNATIONAL COMMITMENT TO INTERNAL DISSENT: 1952 TO THE LATE SIXTIES

From the end of World War II to the late sixties the United States had an almost uninterrupted period of growth and prosperity. Along with prosperity, however, the country experienced various internal and international problems. As one of the leaders of the free world, the United States was involved in a continual series of confrontations in the hot and cold Cold War.

Additional problems on the homefront, such as integration, the "war on poverty," inflation, pollution, and a dissatisfied youth, led to an ever increasing number of crises. So, although the period was characterized by material plenty, for a vast majority of the people the economic growth was accompanied by persistent turmoil. Although enjoying the highest standard of living in the history of mankind, the American people, and the people of the world for that matter, had to live in a world of constant frustration and insecurity. This was an age of material comfort but psychological discomfort, an age of crisis.

America's commitment to educate its youth continued to grow and expand. School enrollments increased at enormous rates, especially as the postwar baby population reached school age. In 1900, 6.4 percent of the seventeen-year olds in the country were high-school graduates. The figure in 1956 was 62.3 percent and rising. At the college level, the rate was equally rapid. In 1870, 9,371 received the A.B. degree, 1,478 the M.A. degree, and 1 the Ph.D. degree. In 1963, 450,592 obtained the bachelor's degree, 91,418 the master's degree, and 12,822 the doctorate, (Atkinson & Maleska, 1965, p. 157). The continuing emphasis was on keeping greater numbers of students in school for more years.

As well as growing to include larger numbers of students, education also expanded its offerings and its scope. From headstart and kindergarten to the Job Corps to postgraduate fellowships, the trend was toward broadening the educational programs available. Night school, summer school, college extension classes, etc. offered an almost unlimited variety of educational opportunities for adults, part-time students, young people with handicaps, etc., to further their education.

The curriculum was to include expanded academic, vocational, and general education programs. The course offerings at some universities became so vast and so varied that it would require hundreds of years to take all the courses. Curricular revisions as well as new technological advances in media were utilized to improve instruction. New approaches to teaching, such as team teaching, nongraded classes, individualized instruction, programmed learning, flexible scheduling, etc. were developed to improve learning within the various curricula.

Innovations in the educational system seemed to have reflected the unprecedented pace of life in general. Yet, education underwent attacks from both internal and external sources. The criticism was that the changes involved mostly facilities, administrative procedures, and equipment and that the approach to teaching young people had changed little. Some critics viewed current practice more in terms of "miseducation" than of education.

Modern-language teaching, which had appeared on the brink of being ousted from the curriculum in the thirties and forties, enjoyed a period of prosperity and rising enrollments during the fifties and sixties. America's continued commitments abroad and the interdependency among the peoples of the modern world fostered a climate in which international understanding and cooperation were of prime importance. The study of modern languages was considered basic to developing and promoting good will and friendship among the nations of the world.

Even though the climate was right for expanding modern-language study, a great deal of effort and energy had been necessary to reverse the previous downward trend and to institute a rebirth in modern-language study. From the end of the war until 1952 there was much frustration but little activity. However, in 1952, William Riley Parker was appointed head of the newly organized foreign-language section of the MLA. The leadership supplied by this office, coupled with that of other leaders in the field, eventually initiated the movement necessary to energize the profession. In 1954, the first edition of Parker's *The National Interest and Foreign Languages* was published. In this report the position taken was that the availability of Americans who could speak a foreign language in times of emergency such as the one that occurred in World War II and in the constant relationships with governments of other countries was a matter of "national interest." Thus, national defense was added to the list of reasons given for studying modern languages.

The National Interest and Foreign Languages was one of the most important and most influential books in the history of modern-language teaching. It provided the needed impetus, the awaited catalyst, to renew interest in the study of modern languages and to revitalize the profession. Activity in the field of modern languages in this country began to increase. The results of these efforts were seen in the National Defense Education Act of 1958, which recognized foreign languages as being critical to the country's security and provided funds for stimulating the study of languages.

The infusion of government funds into the field brought renewed vigor to an almost lifeless profession. Millions of dollars were made available to retrain teachers and to purchase language laboratories and other electronic equipment. Projects for preparing new materials, such as the MLA project in which a group of experts developed the audio-lingual Spanish text, *Modern Spanish,* and the Glastonbury project, which culminated in the publication of the A-LM series, were funded. In addition to the sudden availability of government funds, other events were taking place that added to the sudden successes enjoyed by modern-language education. The launching of Sputnik by the Russians in 1957 startled the world and prompted a doubtful attitude toward the qualities of the American educational system. In 1959, Conant in his book *The American High School Today* urged that greater emphasis be placed on the academic aspects of the curriculum. Also, rapidly increasing contacts between peoples in international trade, travel, and educational and cultural exchanges focused attention on the need for language learning in the modern, interdependent world.

Change comes slowly in most cases, but this was a revolution. Teachers everywhere were going to meetings, to workshops, and to institutes to learn about the audio-lingual approach to teaching modern languages. The professional journals were filled with articles explaining the new techniques and procedures. The whole profession was overflowing with previously unknown energy, excitement, and enthusiasm. Within a few short years, the audio-lingual approach became the dominant methodology.

Enrollments rose with the enthusiasm. At last it was "in" to study modern languages! In the public secondary schools, the percentage of the high school population studying modern languages increased from 16.4 percent in 1958 to 21.7 percent in 1960, to 24.2 percent in 1962, and to 26.4 percent in 1965 (Kant, 1970, p. 403). At the university level, 31.7 percent more students were studying modern languages in 1963 than in 1960, and 24.8 percent more in 1965 than 1963 (Kant, 1969, p. 259). The number of graduate students studying modern languages increased 77.8 percent between 1960 and 1963, and 15.1 percent from 1963 to 1965 (Kant, 1969, p. 259).

By the early sixties, the study of modern languages seemed to have found a place in the sun. Pleased language teachers basked in the warmth of public favor and dedicated themselves to producing the bilinguals needed by the nation. However, such bliss was not long to continue. Results did not meet initial expectations. A trickle of criticism of the audio-lingual approach began to appear, a trickle that grew to considerable proportions and was reflected in revisions of first-edition audio-lingual texts.

The audio-lingual approach was, in effect, the adaptation of the ASTP language programs to the school situation. The basic tenets continued to be those espoused by the Bloomfieldian linguists in establishing their first intensive language courses. Although primarily linguists, much of their influence was on the methods and classroom techniques employed in the "new" methodology. The basic viewpoint, as far as learning theory was concerned, was that of the stimulus-response school of psychology. At a time when other subjects such as math and chemistry were emphasizing comprehension of principles and conceptual understanding, modern-language teaching was emphasizing rote learning and drill procedures.

While descriptive linguists were in the midst of the audio-lingual revolution and while their influence was at its peak, other movements were beginning that were to challenge their views of learning and of language. First, cognitive psychologists began increasingly to question the stimulus-response learning theories upon which its teaching techniques were based. The growing acceptance of learning theories based on mathematical models, neurophysiological models, and information-processing models caused psychologists to reconsider earlier behavioristic models. Second, new ideas about language, stimulated by Chomsky's *Syntactic Structures* published in 1957, gave rise to the generative-transformational school of linguistics. The innovative viewpoints of the transformationalists resulted in restructured thinking as to what language is. In both instances the explanations provided were more complex than those previously given and accepted.

Compounding the problems caused by the disunity within the profession and related fields during the latter part of the sixties was the changing mood of the nation itself. Some leaders began to talk in terms of disengaging from the entangling array of international commitments in which the country had become involved. The concern of the people shifted to social problems, and student interest reflected this changing concern. Enrollments in the behavioral and social sciences skyrocketed as young people sought courses they felt were relevant to their interests in social change. Along with this movement toward social sciences in the curriculum arose a mounting criticism of, and attack on, the practice of having required courses. In many schools and colleges, the language requirement, which had been restored in the fifties and sixties, was once again being discarded.

Whatever the causes, the evidence was quite clear that the drive begun in the early fifties and continued into the sixties had lost much of its force by the late sixties. Modern-language teachers were no longer confident in their methodology or sure of their objectives. Enrollments were declining. In fact, the percent of change in foreign-language enrollment between 1965 and 1968 was a plus 5.7 percent, but the total school enrollment rose 7.0 percent (Kant, 1970, p. 411). Of course, part of this figure can be explained by the fact that the numbers of Latin students continued to decline, but the percentage of students studying a modern language increased only 1.3 percent between 1965 and 1968 (Kant, 1970, p. 403). This was a much lower increase than at any time since the early fifties. In the universities and colleges, the increase was also less, 14.4 percent from 1965 to 1968 (Kant, 1969, p. 259). At the graduate level, the increase for the same three-year period was 3.2 percent (Kant, 1969, p. 248).

PROTEST TO PARTICIPATION: LATE SIXTIES TO THE PRESENT

Characteristics of the Period

President Johnson's unexpected decision not to seek a second term as president was a direct result of the strong public reaction being generated against the continuation of the war in Viet Nam. The first isolated mutterings of discontent against the war had grown into an angry roar of protest as government support among the people eroded. At the same time, the seething coals of dissatisfaction in the face of a seemingly unresponsive bureaucracy burst into open flame as protests, demonstrations, sit-ins, and marches became common place. Demands replaced discussion as segments of the population became disenchanted with traditional governmental processes as a means of promoting change. As the conscience of the minority became the conscience of the majority, the American government took steps to disengage from the unwanted and unsupported war.

This time of protest was characterized by the following trends or movements:

1. Many people strongly desired to end the seemingly interminable conflict in Viet Nam. Frustrated by efforts to deal with the government, protest leaders turned to practices successfully followed by earlier southern integration leaders to accomplish their goal.
2. The protest movement became widespread and popular due to the desire of many people, especially many of the nation's youth, who wanted to have a voice in their future.
3. Reflecting this attitude, many institutions and organizations have made efforts to incorporate more people, especially youth, into the decision-making process.
4. Concurrently, a negative reaction toward and a rejection of such tactics, capped by the tragedy at Kent State, as a means of accomplishing desired goals occurred.
5. Concomitant to the protest movement has been a tendency by some members of society to reject traditional morals and values. As a result some have adopted new life styles.
6. One effect of the rejection of bigness, bureaucracy, technology, and impersonalization has been a strong and almost universal emphasis on

minorities and individuals. The ideal of the "melting pot" has given way to the goal of a pluralistic society. The process of socialization has taken a back seat to individual differences.

7. Growing awareness of the hazards of technologically produced pollution and the capability of modern society to destroy itself have led to disillusionment and disenchantment with modern science and with education for not producing solutions to society's problems.

Trends in the Schools

Fischer (1971, p. 561) states, "Schooling will sooner or later reflect significant changes in the culture." The present educational system is no exception. Such readily apparent trends and practices in contemporary education as the following are direct outgrowths of the major movements in contemporary society in general: (1) pluralism;[5] (2) individualization; (3) rejection of earlier values; (4) consideration of the "total" student; (5) student desire to participate in governing the school; (6) student lack of interest in school curriculum; (7) emphasis on "how" to learn, not "what" to learn; (8) taxpayer and parent reactions against high taxes and low results; and (9) competency-based education.

First, there is a great deal of disagreement and turmoil in schools just as in society as a whole. This situation can be traced in some respects to the desire to accommodate a pluralistic culture in American society. In Fischer's (1971, p. 561) words, "In the final analysis, in an open, pluralistic culture, schools must learn to function in the midst of controversy and conflict." In addition, the patterns that different groups would like to follow in establishing their ideal educational program depend to a large extent upon their philosophy. Based on their philosophies, educators can be termed *romantics, structuralists,* or *social reformers.* The romantics would choose individual freedom in learning as their number one priority. They object to the 1984 trend of social engineering; they question acceptance of authority, conformity instead of individuality, the use of competition and grades to coerce student effort, and the imposition of program content that may have no personal meaning for the student. The structuralists would change the organization and control of the schools. They urge integration, compensatory education, assistance for the poverty stricken, community schools, and the voucher plan.[6] The social reformers would use education to transform society. They see the schools as the means toward the improvement of society in general (Shields, 1973).

The stress on the individual has been reflected in the schools. Many

---

[5]*Pluralism* stresses diversity rather than conformity. One person described a conformist culture as being a "melting pot," while a pluralistic culture is more like a "salad bowl."

[6]Under the *voucher plan,* parents are given vouchers to pay for their children's education, which they may use at an approved educational institution of their choice.

schools have attempted to develop programs and classes geared toward individual needs rather than group needs. Individualization of instruction in general and specific programs, such as Individually Guided Education (Klausmeier et al., University of Wisconsin) and Individually Prescribed Instruction (Glaser et al., University of Pittsburgh), are a direct outgrowth of this influence from society as a whole. Within the schools there is much greater emphasis on the freedom to be oneself than was true in the past. One now hears a great deal about student rights and the need to respect the democratic rights of students.

The rejection of many attitudes and values formerly accepted by students has resulted in marked changes in student behavior. As the trend toward turning away from the adult cultural patterns crept down into the secondary schools and into the elementary schools, the changes in dress codes were reflective of inner changes as well. For example, a strong reaction against requirements of any kind is a basic part of the typical student attitude. In some areas alternative schools and/or free schools have been established. Many students rejected the Puritan work ethic as well. Discipline has deteriorated in many schools, and many students take their studies less seriously. The average score on the SAT examinations has dropped each year for ten consecutive years. In 1974 approximately half of the entering freshmen at the University of California at Berkeley were required to take remedial English. Growing numbers of students were graduating from high school with a reading ability below fourth-grade level.

A trend correlated closely to pluralism, individuality, and changing values has been the increased attention being given to the "total" student, not just his cognitive ability. Researchers and educators are attempting to consider and explore the components of the affective domain and the effects each component may have on personality, social adjustment, and academic achievement. All student factors appear to be interrelated, and it is becoming more and more apparent that the school and the teacher need to consider the entire student if maximum success is to be achieved.

Students are voicing more and more the desire to participate in the governing of the school. They are given more freedom and more opportunities to express their opinions than in the past. No longer are students willing to accept as a matter of fact and in an unquestioning fashion what they were told in school.

In spite of their increased participation in the decision-making processes of the schools, many students still seem uninterested in the offerings of the school. Many experts attribute this lack of interest to the outmoded school programs and feel that interest would be increased if the curriculum was more related to the students' world. Some people are saying that in order to become a part of the students' lives the educational program must expand beyond the walls of the school building. They emphasize that school and learning should not be considered as being synonomous, and they urge the "deschooling" of society.[7]

The contemporary world is changing fast. Will what a student learns now be of any real value in twenty years? If not, the course content is not nearly so important as the skills that the student is acquiring. In short, learning how to learn in a rapidly changing society is infinitely more beneficial than specific knowledge the student may be gaining. In order to implement this goal, educators are calling for instructional programs in which students are active participants in what and how they learn.

A negative reaction has been growing among parents and taxpayers in response to what has been occurring in the schools and to the requests for increased financial aid to the schools. Taxpayers are resisting higher taxes more and more and demanding accountability from the educational system. Schooling is costing more, but student achievement and discipline have apparently dropped. Those who have vested interests in the schools, i.e., those who pay the bills and those whose children attend the schools, want to know why. In response to this reaction some states are adopting programs of competency-based education. Under this program, measurable behavioral descriptions are written that specify exactly what responsibilities and duties everyone on the administrative staff and faculty have. The objective is to create a tightly knit system that can be held accountable for the students who complete its instructional program. By preparing written behavioral objectives, the educational system can specify what the teachers should be doing and what the students should be able to do.

Many educators reject competency-based education as being a technological, industrial model that has no place in the educational system. They feel that the goals of education far exceed the narrow limits of behavioral objectives. In their opinion, the education of a student simply is too vast and too complex to be stated in behavioral terms, and schools that already have many characteristics of the mass-production factory system should not adopt additional industrial practices. The question of how to insure quality education with regard to high-level cognitive abilities, attitudes, and values seems to have no readily available solutions at the present time.

Problems in Education

The schools have been caught in the middle of opposing pressures pulling and pushing them in different directions. Some critics accuse them of being authoritarian, inhumane, irrelevant, and unresponsive to student needs. Such

---

[7]Those in favor of "deschooling" feel that too much emphasis has been placed on learning in the schools. They point out that in fact most learning takes place outside the classroom and urge that curricula be developed in which students are given credit for this outside learning.

titles as *Crisis in the Classroom, Children Under Pressure, Death at an Early Age, How Children Fail,* and *Murder in the Classroom* leave little doubt as to the authors' opinions about the educational system. Other writers hold contrary views. Dobay (1973), for example, contends that a crisis indeed exists in the nation's classrooms, but that the problem is directly attributable to the erosion of discipline and academic standards that has been allowed to occur. Too, the move toward a conceptualization of society as being pluralistic has multiplied the demands upon the curriculum in the schools that have not been encountered in the past.

To compound their difficulties, educators are being forced under present conditions to seek solutions to the problems of education in a situation in which they have lost much public confidence and financial support. In addition, enrollments that had continued to rise almost continuously now are beginning to drop. The "baby boom" of World War II has passed through the schools, and the birth rate is declining in the nation. The *Statistical Abstract of the United States 1974* states that the number of children under five years old declined as follows: 1960—20.3 (million); 1965—19.8; 1970—17.2; and 1973—16.7.

In the past, the schools have faced perplexing problems, but none that seem to demand more radical solutions than those confronting educators at present. Innovative curricula are necessitated by a profound break with educational criteria of the past. Up to this point in the history of education, the major stress has been on increasing the number of years in school and on increasing the numbers of students and the numbers of programs. Now the concern is shifting to qualitative aspects of the curriculum, which are much more difficult to comprehend and to make primary objectives of the educational system. According to Fischer (1971, p. 562), "The entire range of current discussion centering on individualization, learning styles, teaching styles, differentiated staffing, performance criteria, integrated schooling, the education of the gifted, the new curricula, and a host of other topics shows the influence of qualitative ideals at work."

Mouly (1973, p. vi) summarizes the many currents in contemporary education as follows:

> The public school has been undergoing major changes ranging from a shift from the self-contained classroom to team teaching to greater emphasis on relevance, on the one hand, and behavioral objectives, behavior modification techniques, and accountability, on the other hand. Integration, for instance, has accelerated the need for a greater understanding of minority classes, not only those in the ghettos. Meanwhile, recent emphasis on humanism, e.g., the Third Force, has led to greater interest in the child as a unique individual, with a sense of purpose and a capacity for growth and self-determination—and, as a corollary, to a greater awareness that education is valuable to the extent that it is

personally meaningful. In the process, it has altered the role of the teacher and otherwise forced a major reconstruction of the pedagogical as well as philosophical outlook.

Trends in Second-Language Teaching

The developments in modern-language teaching have paralleled closely those trends occurring in society and education in general. The shift has been toward the individualization of instruction as the focus has been placed on self-pacing of learning and on emphasizing student responsibility for learning.

The acceptance of a pluralistic society has stimulated the establishment of bilingual education programs in areas containing speakers of a language other than English. The state of Texas, for example, now requires the establishment of such programs. Also, there has been increased interest in the Francophile world and the incorporation of French Africa and French-speaking Canada into the study of French. At McGill University, efforts are continuing to discover ways and means to improve bilingual education in Canada.

A reflection of the acceptance of a pluralistic society has been the increased emphasis on culture in the second-language class. Some leaders in the field have recommended that culture be made the primary objective in language learning. The language skills per se would be the goal only to the extent that they were necessary to acquire cultural knowledge and information.

In response to other changing student attitudes, language education has moved in several directions to stimulate interest and to counter the cries for relevance. For example:

1. Many second-language teachers have individualized their classes. Learning activity packages, which can be completed at the students' own pace, are often used. Students are permitted to go as rapidly or as slowly as they need to complete the material in each package.
2. In view of the admitted fact that many students enrolled in second-language classes cannot communicate efficiently in the language they are studying, many teachers emphasize communicative skills as the most acceptable goal in language teaching. Students must be shown that they can learn to use a second language and that they can take tangible skills away from the language class.
3. Culture has been given greater emphasis in the language class. Teachers feel that if students can relate to the speakers of the second language, they will be more interested in the language.
4. Many teachers have begun to stress the practical aspects of having a language skill. Hopeful teachers have tried stressing the career opportunities for speakers of a second language as a means of convincing the student of the practical advantages of second-language study.

5. Language teachers have sought to divorce themselves from the elite image surrounding their subject. Leaders in the field have begun to call for language courses suitable for all students in the schools, not just the academic elite.
6. Ideas from values education and group dynamics are being introduced into second-language teaching in order to incorporate content more directly applicable to the student's life and interest.
7. Summer language camps, foreign visitors and correspondence, magazines and newspapers, films, radio broadcasts, and travel abroad are seen as a means of establishing a closer contact between the student's culture and that of the language being studied.
8. Exploratory programs are being initiated in the middle schools and junior high schools to interest the students in studying language later in their schooling.
9. Mini-courses are being developed as a means of maintaining and enhancing student interest in language study and of meeting a greater variety of student interests and schedules.

Effects of Abolishing the Language Requirement

As the student rejection of requirements grew, modern-language teachers again found themselves in a period of less favorable circumstances for modern-language teaching. The first focal point of attack was the language requirement. This movement was initiated at the university level, but when the language requirements were dropped at the university level, many students at lower levels, who had enrolled in language courses primarily in preparation for attending college, found other courses more to their liking. In fact, the favorable trend of increasing enrollments that had continued during the latter fifties and early sixties suddenly reversed in 1968 and began to decline. The *Digest of Educational Statistics 1973* states that between 1968 and 1970 the total enrollment in foreign languge dropped from 30.6 percent of the total school population to 28.3 percent. Enrollment in modern languages declined from 27.7 percent to 26.4 percent. Spanish was the only language to escape the general trend, but not by much, as enrollment increased from 13.4 percent to 13.6 percent. The number of students in French and German dropped from 10.4 percent to 9.2 percent and from 3.3 percent to 3.1 percent respectively. Karsen (1974, p. 15) reported that between 1966 and 1970, 45 percent of the nation's colleges and universities "modified, reduced, or eliminated entrance or graduation requirements." From 1968 to 1970 enrollments in higher education rose 12.9 percent while the number of students registered in modern foreign languages declined slightly (.5 percent). In the period 1970–1972, university enrollment increased 8.6 percent while the study of modern foreign languages declined by 9.7 percent. French dropped by 18.4 percent, German by 12.6 percent, Spanish by 6.3 percent, and Latin by 11.6 percent. At the same time, enrollments grew in some of the less commonly taught languages (Brod, 1973). Subjective estimates indicate that this trend away from second-language study has accelerated until recently, when local situations seem to indicate that the low point may have been reached. At some schools enrollments are not only holding their own but rising, thereby implying that quality programs can attract students to second-language study.

Trends in Psychology, Linguistics, and Sociology

The disciplines of psychology, linguistics, and sociology, from which second-language learning theories draw much valuable information, have not undergone the radical transformation that second-language teaching has in the last few years. With respect to language learning, much of the effort in these areas has been devoted to research attempting to substantiate the internal theories of language and learning, which at this time have been widely accepted as being the most powerful models proposed to date.

In general, current learning theories are basically similar to those previously proposed by the cognitive psychologists and the linguistic theories of Chomsky. The most widely accepted theories of learning are those that acknowledge the crucial role the student plays in the learning process. The writings of Piaget, Bruner, Ausubel, and the phenomenologists have had an important impact on the comprehension of the individual's cognitive development and of the individual's contribution to his own learning. The major part of the activity in linguistics has revolved around attempts to prove or disprove various aspects of Chomsky's theories. The two principal innovations are the suggestion by Fillmore that language study should concentrate on case relationships in the sentence rather than on the subject and the verb and the contention by supporters of generative-semantic theory that the key to meaning in language resides in the semantic component of language rather than the syntactical (Greene, 1972).

The stress on the total student in the classroom has given rise to the need for additional information from the fields of psychology and sociology. The affective domain is now considered to be as influential as the cognitive in determining student achievement and success in the classroom. In addition, it is increasingly apparent that the student does not learn in an isolated environment, and it is undeniably obvious that the school, in preparing the student to participate productively in a democratic society, must concern itself with the socialization of the student. Past and present social influences on the learner are important factors in determining student success or failure in any given classroom, and future success and happiness will be dependent upon the degree to which the student adapts to the surrounding social structure.

Overall, recent trends in psychology, linguistics, and sociology support the importance of internal processes and of the role of the individual in learning. This statement should not be construed as a denial of external, extrinsic factors. Assigning the central role in learning to the internal, mental processes in no way denies the importance of conditioning, i.e., external reinforcement in learning activities in some skills and for some students. Motivation to learn can be extrinsic as well as intrinsic. From the teacher's point of view, the latest descriptions of the various factors influencing her teaching and the student's learning make her job that much more complicated and require that her knowledge and expertise extend into more areas. In short, she must now consider the students' attitudes, feelings, and social adjustment as well as their cognitive capacities and the subject matter being taught. What an interesting and exciting challenge and what possibilities exist for implementing qualitative educational goals!

THE FUTURE

What direction will second-language teaching take in the future? Predictions are always hazardous and often foolhardy, and anticipating future trends is perhaps more difficult now than at the writing of the first edition of this text. Much depends on the future economic conditions of the nation. The economic situation depends in turn upon the availability of large quantities of low-cost energy. If the energy crisis can be solved, current trends in second-language teaching will probably continue. If the economy worsens, society's interests will turn inward, and language learning will be less important than at present. The scarcity of positions for graduates of higher education has already fostered a more serious student attitude and intensified pressure for high grade-point averages. This trend may spread to the high schools as well. Although the tendency in recent years to encourage everyone to seek a college education seems to have reached its peak, for those who do plan to attend college, however, the desire to do well in "academic" subjects may provide an incentive to enroll in second-language classes. Too, both society and education are now in an extreme position with regard to individuality and permissiveness. If the pendulum swings toward greater emphasis on socialization and more rigid requirements and stricter discipline, the schools of tomorrow may resemble those of yesterday more than what present trends would indicate.

Based on present conditions and trends, one would expect the following developments:

1. Instruction will become more student centered. Chosen teaching-learning objectives and activities will be based on student attitudes and feelings as

well as on cognitive abilities. Prime consideration will be on both the learner as a person and the person as a learner.

2. The teacher will attempt to relate the course content to student experience, interests, and goals.

3. As the teaching procedures are developed, the teacher will attempt to match instruction with cognitive style, personality, attitudes, and social characteristics of the students. Meanwhile, the choice of methods will be based on what works in a given situation with a given objective.

4. A second language is an asset in many different fields of work and study. Already some schools are offering courses geared toward the acquisition of specific expressions and specialized vocabulary. If the trend toward a pluralistic society continues, more courses of this type will be offered.

5. Values and group dynamics activities will provide a bridge to relating to the students and to stimulating their interest in second-language learning.

6. Teachers will seek to introduce the students to the culture of the second language. However, before they can do this well, they will need much assistance from textbook authors and publishers of classroom materials.

7. Teachers will stress communicative competence as the goal of language classes.

8. Second-language teachers will continue to seek ways to stimulate interest in their subject. One way will be to concentrate on public awareness of the need for the contributions gained from the study of second languages. A definite asset in support of the profession's efforts to sell their product is the increasingly interdependency among nations. Hopefully, in the profession's efforts to maintain interest and enrollments it will not sacrifice quality programs in favor of "warm bodies."

9. The public will be in favor of more stability and fewer innovations than in the past. There will still be a desire for improvement, but the public cannot be stimulated continuously by the expectation of new trends without becoming skeptical of the similarity between the new promises and those of previous proposals, which were eagerly adopted only to be abandoned when a new cure-all for educational ills appeared on the scene.

10. The public will insist that both subject matter and socialization be emphasized in school. Teachers will be obliged to insist upon achievement and to demonstrate that it has been accomplished. To do so, teachers will need to insist upon cooperation and effort in the classroom. Permitting students not to learn or to be undisciplined and uncooperative is a disservice to them and to society. Teachers must accept the fact that their responsibility extends beyond the mere scope of the subject they are teaching.

CONCLUSION

Throughout most of the history of the United States, second-language teaching has had to justify continually its presence in the curriculum. Although the late fifties and early sixties were a welcome relief from this overall trend, current indications are that second-language education will not be so popular in the near future. Nor will any other academic subject. The teaching profession must work to prove its worth to young people whose primary needs revolve around two basic problems in modern society: acquiring self and social identity. Developing curricula that meet the individual needs of students requires much time and effort, but the results and rewards are worth the investment. The necessity of having to be concerned about offering worthwhile courses that attract students and that achieve desired goals can be considered nothing less than an impetus toward constant professional growth and quality curricula. Already the signs are encouraging. The profession is searching for ways and means of improving methods and curricula. New and interesting textual materials are being published. The vision of what constitutes good language teaching has expanded and is expanding considerably. In spite of the current situation, language teachers are doing the best job of teaching they ever have. The future offers tremendous potential, and the prospects look quite exciting.

REVIEW AND APPLICATION

DEFINITIONS
1. behavioristic psychology, p. 24
2. communicative skills, p. 34
3. competency-based education, p. 32
4. descriptive linguistics, p. 23
5. direct method, p. 21
6. eclectic approach, p. 23
7. faculty psychology, p. 20
8. grammer-translation, p. 22
9. individualized instruction, p. 26
10. pluralism, pluralistic society, p. 30
11. self-pacing, p. 34
12. socialization vs. individualization, pp. 30, 37
13. stimulus-response theories, p. 24
14. "total" student, p. 31

DISCUSSION
1. Summarize briefly the principal characteristics of the society of each period. How did society's objectives change in each, and what effect did these changes have on the schools? Compare and contrast the different periods.

2. Describe the changing character of the school curriculum and of the school student body from the beginnings until the present day.
3. What philosophy of education do you favor for the schools? Which group has been most influential in recent years?
4. Can more be done to take advantage of student input into the decision-making process in the schools? Should more be done? Give examples. How do your views agree with or differ from those of current high school students, high school teachers, and high school principals?
5. Outline some of the changes that will take place in the typical classroom if the affective domain is considered to be equally as important as the cognitive. That is, how will the classroom differ from that in which you were a student? To what degree is this change desirable, undesirable, or basic?
6. Discuss the apparent lack of student interest in the current curriculum. What is the cause of this lack of interest? Have students always been this way? What do you think would turn them on? What might be done in a second-language class?
7. How do you think students can be prepared for the future? What types of knowledge and/or skills do they need?
8. Discuss the idea of putting educational objectives into behavioral terms. Does this trend reflect efficiency or external, mechanical control of desired learning outcomes?
9. In your opinion, why have enrollments in second-language classes dropped? What can be done to increase the numbers of students taking second languages? Why is the percentage of high school students taking a second language so small? Compare the figures with those of other countries. How can this difference be explained?
10. React to the list of expected future developments presented in this chapter. With which do you agree and with which do you disagree? What others would you add?

ACTIVITIES
1. Visit some high school classes to try to get a feel for what the high school students like and dislike about school.
2. Compare the students' responses with what a teacher, counselor, and an administrator would say about student likes and dislikes.
3. Visit a traditional, lock-step classroom, an individualized class, and a class organized according to Individually Guided Education (IGE) or Individually Prescribed Instruction (IPI). Discuss the various characteristics of each and your reaction to each.
4. Survey local schools in general and local second-language classes to determine what is being done to combat student lack of interest and to make the curriculum more pertinent to the student.

5. Interview a high school principal to see what new programs have been instituted in the school during the last five years and to determine how change is accomplished. If they have a student-centered curriculum, how has it been implemented, and what is the student response? What have been the teacher and student responses to innovations? What does the principal see as present and future trends?

SELECTED REFERENCES

Alden, D. W. (1970) The Threat to the College Language Requirement. *ADFL Bulletin,* 1:11–19.

Alden, D. W. (1974) The Status of French. *French Review,* 48:7–16.

Allen, E. D. (1971) The Foreign Language Teacher as a Learner in the Seventies. *Modern Language Journal,* 55:203–7.

Allen, J. E. (1972) Crisis in Confidence: The Public and its Schools. *Education Digest,* 35:5–8.

Banathy, B. H. (1968) Current Trends in College Curriculum: A Systems Approach. In E. M. Birkmaier (Ed.), *The Britannica Review of Foreign Language Education,* vol. 1. Chicago: Encyclopaedia Britannica. Pp. 105–40.

Bereiter, C. (1972) Moral Alternatives to Education. *Interchange,* 3:25–41.

Birkmaier, E. M. (1971) The Meaning of Creativity in Foreign Language Teaching. *Modern Language Journal,* 55:345–53.

Bolinger, D. (1971) Let's Change Our Base of Operations. *Modern Language Journal,* 55:148–56.

Bono, J. D. (1970) Languages, Humanities and the Teaching of Values. *Modern Language Journal,* 54:335–47.

Brod, R. (1973) Foreign Language Enrollments in U. S. Colleges—Fall 1972. *ADFL Bulletin,* 5:56–57.

Chamberlin, L. J. (1973) Process-Centered Education for a Changing Tomorrow. *Intellect,* 102:101–3.

Childers, J. W. (1964) *Foreign Language Teaching.* New York: Center for Applied Research in Education.

Dobay, C. M. (1973) A Look at What Lies Behind the Crisis in Our Schools. *Education Digest,* 39:44.

Dusel, J. P. (1970) Implications of Elimination of the Foreign Language Requirement, *ADFL Bulletin,* 1:19–21.

Fantini, M. D. (1973) Education by Choice. *NASSP Bulletin,* 57:10–19.

Fischer, L. (1971) Social Foundations. In D. W. Allen and E. Seifman (Eds.), *The Teacher's Handbook.* Glenview, Ill.: Scott Foresman. Pp. 561–62.

Freeman, S. A. (1971) Modern Language Teaching: Problems and Opportunities for the Seventies. *Modern Language Journal,* 55:141–48.

Garfinkel, A. (1974) The Public Image of Foreign Language Instruction, 1972–1973. *Modern Language Journal,* 58:108–12.

Greene, J. (1972) *Psycholinguistics.* Middlesex, England: Penguin Books. P. 84.

Grittner, F. M. (1969) *Teaching Foreign Languages.* New York: Harper & Row. Pp. 1–38.

Gross, N. (1973) Critical Questions for Contemporary Education. *Intellect,* 102:24–26.

Hansen, K. H. (1963) *Public Education in American Society.* Englewood Cliffs, N.J.: Prentice-Hall. Pp. 1–23.

Hilgard, E. R., and Atkinson, R. C. (1967) *Introduction to Psychology.* (4th ed.) New York: Harcourt, Brace & World. Pp. 13–23.

Holschuh, A., and Lafayette, R. C. (1974) Hedgehog versus Hare: Changes in Foreign Language Teaching. *The Review,* 17:1–11.

Honig, L. J., and Love, F. W. D. (1973) *Options and Perspectives.* New York: Modern Language Association of America.

Hoye, A. G. (1969) Let's Do Our Thing—Flexibility. *Modern Language Journal*, 53:481–84.

Jarvis, G. A. (1972) Teacher Education Goals: They're Tearing Up the Street Where I Was Born. *Foreign Language Annals*, 6:198–205.

JeKenta, A. W., and Fearing, P. (1968) Current Trends in Curriculum: Elementary and Secondary Schools. In E. M. Birkmaier (Ed.), *The Britannica Review of Foreign Language Education,* vol. 1. Chicago: Encyclopaedia Britannica. Pp. 141–78.

Kant, J. G. (1969) Foreign Language Registrations in Institutions of Higher Education, Fall 1968. *Foreign Language Annals,* 3:247–304.

Kant, J. G. (1970) Foreign Language Offerings and Enrollments in Public Secondary Schools, Fall 1968. *Foreign Language Annals,* 3:400–58.

Karsen, S. (1974) Alternatives in College Foreign Language Programs. *Language Association Bulletin,* 26:15.

Kelly, L. G. (1969) *25 Centuries of Language Teaching.* Rowley, Mass.: Newbury House.

Krohn, R. (1970) The Role of Linguistics in TEFL Methodology. *Language Learning,* 20:103–8.

Lafayette, R. C. (1972) Diversification: The Key to Student-Centered Programs. *Modern Language Journal,* 56:349–54.

Lawson, J. H. (1971) Is Language Teaching Foreign or Dead? *Modern Language Journal,* 55:353–57.

Leamon, M. P. (1974) Some Modest Suggestions. *Modern Language Journal,* 58:225–29.

McCuaig, M. G. (1973) Concerns and Trends. *Canadian Modern Language Review,* 30:12–18.

McGreary, E. (1965) Schools for Fearlessness and Freedom. *Phi Delta Kappan,* 46:257.

Manning, W. (1972) The Credibility Gap That Is Neutralizing the Public Schools. *American School Board Journal,* 159:31–32.

Mouly, G. L. (1973) *Psychology for Effective Teaching.* (3rd ed.) New York: Holt, Rinehart and Winston. Pp. vi, 29–30.

Northeast Conference Reports (1971) *Leadership for Continuing Development.* J. W. Dodge, ed. New York: MLA/ACTFL Materials Center.

Oliva, P. (1969) The Teaching of Foreign Languages. Englewood Cliffs, N.J.: Prentice-Hall. Pp. 2–10.

Ornstein, J., and Gage, W. W. (1964) *The ABC's of Languages and Linguistics.* Philadelphia: Chilton. Pp. 56–67.

Papalia, A., and Zampogna, J. (1974) The Changing Curriculum. In G. A. Jarvis (Ed.), *The Challenge of Communication.* Skokie, Ill.: National Textbook. Pp. 299–328.

Parker, W. R. (1961) *The National Interest and Foreign Languages.* (3rd ed.) Washington, D.C.: Department of State. Pp. 84–96.

Pearl, A. (1972) *The Atrocity of Education.* St. Louis: New Critics Press.

Potter, E. J. (1971) Revitalization of Foreign Language Programs in Higher Education. *Foreign Language Annals,* 5:206–10.

Rivers, W. M. (1972) From Pyramid to the Commune: The Evolution of the Foreign Language Department. *ADFL Bulletin,* 3:13–17.

Ruch, F. L. (1948) *Psychology and Life.* (3rd ed.) Chicago: Scott Foresman. Pp. 35–40.

Schaefer, W. D. (1972) The Plight and Future of FL Learning in America. *ADFL Bulletin,* 3:5–8.

Seelye, H. N. (1971) A Hard Look at Hard Times: A Reaction to Superintendent Lawson's "Is Language Teaching Foreign or Dead?" *Modern Language Journal,* 55:358–61.

Seigneuret, J. C. (1971) Teaching French in the 70's. *French Review,* 45:104–13.

Shields, J. J., Jr. (1973) The New Critics in Education. *Intellect,* 102:16–20.

Smith, V. H. (1973) Alternative Public Schools: What Are They? *NASSP Bulletin,* 57:4–9.

Strasheim, L. A. (1970) The Anvil or the Hammer. *Foreign Language Annals*, 4:48–56.

Strasheim, L. A. (1971) "Creativity" Lies Trippingly on the Tongue. *Modern Language Journal*, 55:339–45.

U.S. Government Printing Office (1973) *Digest of Educational Statistics*. Washington, D.C.: U.S. Government Printing Office. Pp. 41–42.

U.S. Government Printing Office (1974) *Statistical Abstract of the United States 1974*. Washington, D.C.: U.S. Government Printing Office. P. 114.

Walker, D. F. (1974) Educational Policy Is Flapping in the Wind. *Education Digest*, 39:2–5.

Willbern, G. (1968) Foreign Language Enrollments in Public Secondary Schools, 1965. *Foreign Language Annals*, 1:239–53.

FIRST-LANGUAGE LEARNING

The External, Mechanistic View
  The Development of Speech
    Earliest Sounds
    Babbling
    Lalling
    Echolalia
    True Speech
  Implications of the External, Mechanistic View for Second-Language
    Learning

Internal, Mentalistic Views
  A Neurophysiological Interpretation
    Implications of the Neurophysiological Interpretation for
      Second-Language Learning
  The Nativistic and Cognitive Models
    The Development of Language
    An Internal, Mentalistic Model of First-Language Acquisition
    How Children Learn Language
    Implications of the Nativistic and Cognitive Models for
      Second-Language Learning

Error Analysis
  Interlanguage Errors
  Intralanguage Errors
  Implications of Error Analysis for Second-Language Learning

INTRODUCTION

It has been common in second-language teaching in recent years to justify classroom procedures on the basis of first-language learning. As logical as this practice may seem on first consideration, such comparisons are somewhat tenuous due to the fact that the circumstances surrounding children below school age and children school age or older are dissimilar. Young children do not know how to read or write at the time they are learning their mother tongue; second-language learners do. Young children are surrounded by the language; second-language learners in the normal classroom situation are not. Young children are highly motivated to learn the language in order to communicate with their family and friends; second-language learners may not have such a strong incentive. Young children do not already know another language system; second-language learners do. Young children do not have a rather complete knowledge of the world around them; second-language learners often do. Young children have a long exposure time in which to acquire the language skills; second-language learners do not. Young children have not reached a high level of mental, social, and emotional maturity; second-language learners either have, or at least are more advanced.

Qualifying the premise that second-language learning is based on the first language should not, however, discourage further investigation in the area of first-language learning. Additional insights may be gained that will be of interest and of value to second-language teachers. The purpose of this chapter is to discuss first-language learning from both the external, mechanistic point of view and from internal, mentalistic points of view and to extrapolate certain implications from each for the second-language teacher.

THE EXTERNAL, MECHANISTIC VIEW

The Development of Speech

Van Riper (1950, p. 3) makes the following comment concerning speech: ". . . Mothers, as well as fathers, miss almost completely the most fascinating part of the child's entire development—the growth of his speech. More complicated than walking, more human than eating, the mastery of talking is probably going to be for all time his greatest accomplishment." Naturally, such an important process has been of great interest through the years. Although there is some disagreement as to which sounds are produced during certain stages of development, there are certainly broad areas of agreement among the writers on the subject. It is generally agreed that the acquisition of the mother tongue is a long process fraught with difficulties. Speech is not an all-or-nothing ability. The Staats (1962, p. 836) speak of the "continued shaping of speech through successive approximation." Furthermore, the literature continually emphasizes the fact that children must be taught the language, and that parents must teach this most complex of human skills. At the same time, however, parents are cautioned not to be over-attentive to their children's speech. Young children progress best where the "happy mean" is applied. In short, although the process is long and difficult, given sufficient models to imitate and sufficient opportunity to practice, the child learns best by himself without having his attention focused on language as such or on his pronunciation. To him, language is a tool to use in order to communicate and to satisfy his needs, not to take apart and examine for errors or inconsistencies. Also commonly accepted among the various researchers is the fact that especially in the beginning, ". . . speech is a total physiological, psychological, and organismical development" (Richardson, 1959, p. 276).

There are various stages seemingly identifiable in theory, at least, in the acquisition of one's native language. It must be immediately pointed out that these different stages exist on a continuum much like the speech process itself and that there is no distinct break between them. The researchers also continually stress the importance of individual differences that affect the ages at which babies progress from one stage to another.

M. M. Lewis (1957, p. 14), a recognized authority on infant speech, has based the beginnings of the long speech process on ideas of Charles Darwin. According to Darwin, a baby's cry can be compared to the bleat of a hungry lamb. This cry of hunger is just one among several movements that the lamb makes in its urgent desire to attain nourishment. This cry is not deliberately produced but is part of the newborn's bodily struggle as it reacts to its discomfort. Therefore, in response to the question of when does a child begin to learn to speak, Lewis answers, "The answer is, if not at the moment of birth, then certainly the first day. For as soon as a child cries and someone pays attention to his cry, the first step has been taken; the essentials of language are there: one person makes a sound which another person interprets." Other writers agree with this statement. Most feel that the first vocalizations of the newborn baby, the first cries at birth, are the beginnings of language.

Earliest sounds   The earliest noises that babies make are the discomfort sounds, and these sounds are the natural result of their agitated body state and their struggles for relief. These sounds are shrill, nasalized vowel sounds. These vowel sounds are produced in the front of the mouth with a tense facial expression as a result of the baby's discomfort. At other times the baby is quiet (Lewis, 1957). These early cries are *involuntary* responses to hunger, pain, etc. Toward the end of this early period, the cries begin to have differences in vocal tones, and the mother can begin to identify the reasons for crying (Ainsworth, 1950).

In addition to the discomfort sounds, babies learn to make comfort sounds. These sounds are relaxed, deeper, and without a nasal quality. Like the discomfort sounds, these sounds are produced naturally as a result of the body state of the baby. Unlike the discomfort sounds, they lack urgency and are relaxed and contented. Lewis (1957, p. 18) concludes, "From all this we see that discomfort cries and gurgling noises have their special forms and qualities from the very fact that they are expressive; and how all the world over they must be the same cries and noises."

Next, consonant sounds begin to be heard when the baby is uncomfortable. Since the need to cry in a state of distress is much more powerful than the comfort sounds, consonant sounds are first noticed when a baby is in a state of discomfort. The early consonants in discomfort cries are as follows:

"wa . . . wa . . . wa . . . wa
la . . . la . . . la . . . la
nga . . . nga . . . nga . . . nga
ha . . . ha . . . ha . . . ha" (Lewis, 1957, p. 19).

Lewis (1957) explains the appearance of these sounds as being a result of the fact that distress cries come in bursts. Each pause for breath will cause a constriction of some part of the air passage. For example, if a child who has cried "a . . . a . . . a" from birth closes his lips with each burst, the sound now becomes *wa.* Later the child will add the sounds *ma* and *na* to his repertoire of discomfort sounds.

Babbling The second stage in the development of language is generally referred to as *babbling.* Berry and Eisenson (1942, p. 3) state, "The babbling stage may be considered a training and preparatory period for later articulate utterance." In other words, it is during this stage that the baby really begins to practice the variations of our sound system. Lewis (1957) emphasizes the relation of the babbling stage to the later comfort situations in which the baby, after a feeding and while lying on his back, begins to add consonants to his collection of vowel sounds used when he is comfortable. He has saliva in his mouth and is perhaps making swallowing movements. As a natural result of this situation, the baby begins to make some of the back consonant sounds such as *gu, ga, ka, cha,* and *ru.* The later consonant sounds of a satisfied baby include *ma, pa, ba, ta,* and *da.*

Van Riper has some interesting comments with regard to babbling. He points out that babies do not suck with their lips alone. The tongue is placed against the upper gum ridge behind the teeth and then pulled down. If the baby does this while exhaling, the *t, d, l,* or *n* sounds are produced. In fact Van Riper (1950, p. 17) states, "Sucking and swallowing are the parents of many of our consonants. Other consonants are illegitimate."

Up to this point, all babies everywhere make the same sounds. For example, the Spanish *v* sound, which is difficult for speakers of English, is practiced regularly. One investigator, by recording a baby's vocalizations during the first year, concluded that a baby makes all possible sounds and gradually loses them as he is reinforced by the sounds he hears in his environment (Staats & Staats, 1962).

The following quote from Van Riper (1950, p. 18) will illustrate why the babbling stage is so important:

> Babbling is so vitally important in the learning of talking that adults with defective speech are sometimes taught to do it by the hour. If speech sounds are to be mastered, they must be felt and heard both simultaneously and successively. The child must imitate himself before he can ever imitate others. When the child's vocal play is prevented by illness or almost constant crying, the onset of true communicative speech is almost sure to be delayed. Deaf babies start babbling about the same time normal children do but they soon lose interest, and teaching them to talk correctly is a very difficult task. It is interesting that mirrors hung over the cribs of deaf babies prolong and increase the babbling.

Babbling occurs because the child is happy and contented. Happy, contented children babble more and talk sooner. This fact again emphasizes the important role that parents play in the entire speech process. For example, the fact that children reared in orphanages are generally slow in the speech-development process is probably due to lack of personal attention. Furthermore, babbling, which is a result of being happy, excites the baby, and he babbles even more. There seems to be a kinesthetic excitement created by the action of producing the sounds that induces repetition. The role of babbling and being content is demonstrated by the fact that by the end of the third month, babies are using twice as many consonants and vowels in "vocal play" as in discomfort states (Van Riper, 1950).

In general, the development of vowel sounds begins in the front of the mouth or perhaps with the middle vowel *a* and proceeds toward the back of the mouth. On the other hand, the consonants begin with the velar sounds due to saliva and swallowing movements. Next to develop are the labial and alveolar sounds as a result of sucking movements. The dental and palatal sounds develop last in the child's sound system.[1]

Lalling   The next stage is that of *lalling*. Berry and Eisenson (1942, p. 4) give the following description: "Lalling, which usually begins during the second six months of the child's life, may be defined as the repetition of *heard* sounds or

---

[1]These terms refer to the points of articulation or pronunciation. *Velar* sounds are made at the back of the mouth near the velum. *Labial* sounds are made with the lips, and *alveolar* sounds are produced at the ridge behind the teeth. *Dental* sounds involve the teeth, and *palatal* sounds are articulated at the roof of the mouth.

sound combinations." For the first time then, hearing others becomes important in the speech-development process. However, the repetition of sounds heard is merely for the pleasure of oral activity and not as an environmental response. Beginning with this stage, the child's progress may be affected by defective hearing or an inability to discriminate among the various speech sounds.

Echolalia   The speech-learning process soon develops into constant imitation of sounds in the environment. This stage, called *echolalia* by Berry and Eisenson (1942), is further practice in sound manipulation and preparation for actual talking. It is during this stage, which begins about the age of nine or ten months, that the parents hear the first *dadas* and *mamas*. However, as of yet children have no real comprehension of the significance of what they are saying. Smith (1960) states that by the end of the first year, the most important single factor in speech development is imitation.

Van Riper (1950) emphasizes repeatedly the importance of imitation in the speech-development process. Nonsense noises made by adults and children's responses to them are the beginning of children's social intercourse, and from this social intercourse speech is born. Van Riper feels that the imitation should start with movements and gestures rather than speech. According to Van Riper, the process of imitation continues through intonation patterns and finally words. However, the words should be very short at first and such that children are capable of imitating them. He disagrees with the theory that we should speak to children only in an adult manner. His point is that we should begin on their level because only in this manner will they be encouraged to imitate us. Gradually the syllables stretch into words, the words into phrases, and the phrases into sentences.

True speech   Gradually, these sounds become associated with meanings, and the child progresses into the last stage of speech development, *true speech,* at the age of twelve to eighteen months. Berry and Eisenson (1942, p. 5) define this stage: "By *talking* we mean that the child *intentionally* uses conventionalized sound patterns (words) and that his observable behavior indicates that he anticipates a response appropriate to the situation and the words he is uttering." Babies learn their first words through a successive series of events: imitation, comprehension, gesture, vocal play, and expressive noises. According to Van Riper (1950, pp. 49–51) the earliest words spoken by children are as follows:

mama	(mother)
dada	(father)
bah or ba-ba	(bye-bye or ball or baby)
kaaka	(cake or crackers)

titta	(tick-tock or sister)
puh-puh	(puppy or papa or pipe)
ha	(hat or here)
pitty	(pretty)
dih	(drink)
wah or wa-wa	(water or bow-wow)
pee or peek	(peekaboo)
nanna	(nurse or substitute mother)
nuh-nuh	(no)

Babies all over the world speak pretty much the same first words, but doting and anxious parents give their first words different meanings. For example:

German: dada (there it is!), baba (father), wow-wow (dog), mama (mother)

French: papa (father), mama (mother), non-non (no), wa-wa (dog)

Russian: mama (mother), tata (father), baba (grandmother), da (give).

This ready acceptance of the child's early speech demonstrates two points very clearly: (1) the stages of successive approximation the child goes through in learning to speak, and (2) the importance of parental encouragement.

In discussing the latter stages of a child's progress toward actual communication, Gesell (1940, p. 43) makes the following comment:

Jargon at eighteen months, words at two years, sentences at three years—such in outline is the order of growth. This outline, however, oversimplifies the developmental forces at work. Words at two years are different from words at three years. At two years, words are little more than lingual-laryngeal patterns, rooted in a total action pattern, or they are mere habit formations. Two acquires words. Three uses them. At three, words are more fully disengaged from the gross motor system and become instruments for designating percepts, concepts, ideas, relationships.

At the age of three, then, the child appears capable of true speech. However, he still makes many pronunciation errors. As Long (1957, p. 15) puts it, "The onset of the verbal stage is usually loaded with oral inaccuracies. . . ." The parent must keep in mind two important ideas: (1) that the goal is distinct speaking, not perfect articulation, and (2) that talking must be fun for the child. Mange (1959, p. 4) assures parents who have worries about their child's pronunciation when he says, ". . . most children have very little awareness of their own errors which are present during the speech development period. As autocritical abilities develop, however, awareness and modification in the articulatory pattern follows rapidly until an essentially adult pattern is reached by eight years of age."

The preceding description of first-language acquisition outlines a process in which, from the onset of lalling, children imitate the speech they hear around them. In doing so they often make errors in their imitation. However, children's language gradually approaches the adult model as they are reinforced by the people with whom they come in contact, especially their parents. Those sounds and forms that are not needed or are incorrect are slowly extinguished due to lack of reinforcement. With the exception of Gesell and Mange, who refer to internal mental processes on the part of the learner at advanced stages, the quoted authors conceive of first-language learning as a mechanistic process in which the learners' language is shaped by the reinforcements they receive from their surroundings.

Implications of the External, Mechanistic View for Second-Language Learning

What are some of the implications from the above description of the process of learning our native language that may be applied to second-language learning? To repeat what was said in the first paragraph of this chapter, it should be obvious that the two processes are greatly different due to chronological time in the life of the individual and her situation at the time of learning the language, if for no other reasons. First, it must be kept in mind that the first-language learning process is a series of successive approximations to adult language. This entire process continues in most children for a number of years, in spite of the fact that they need the language in order to operate as others do in their environment, and in spite of being continually surrounded by the language. During these years of learning, the emphasis is on the ability to communicate.

The following is a list of possible extrapolations from first- to second-language learning.

1. Students and parents should be made aware of the length of time necessary to learn a language.
2. Imitation and reinforcement play an important role in first-language learning.
3. Teachers should continually keep in mind the length of the process as well as the fact that students approach language usage rather than suddenly acquire it. It is not an all-or-nothing process.
4. One common error is the insistence on a natural-speed rendition. The model is thus incomprehensible (and only *after* comprehension does learning begin), and it is impossible for the student to repeat it. All parents

slow down for their children; why not teachers? Liamina (1964) says that only by age two can a child repeat as fast as an adult. The teacher must remember, however, to speed up once the appropriate stage of ability is reached in order to aid in the students' successive stages approach to native speech.

5. The same principle is applicable to grammar and pronunciation as well. If the teacher spent more time concentrating on what the student is saying rather than how he is saying it, the process would be more rapid as well as more enjoyable. Ainsworth (1950) in "Speech in the Home" says, "All through the early years, the child must *never* be impressed with the fact that he has failed to respond correctly or to reproduce sounds accurately. The child's best efforts must be accepted as satisfactory." Later he adds, "Another practical suggestion is to refrain from making the correction at the time the error is made. Whenever you correct a child immediately after his mistake, you are throwing him completely off balance by interfering with his main concern, that of communicating with you."

6. Point number 5 leads to another concept, that of class content. Drills are needed, but too often they are accepted as an end rather than a means to an end—speech. The important goal in language is that of communication, even if there are some grammatical errors and the pronunciation is not perfect. Drills should be limited to the relatively minor role consistent with their function and purpose in language acquisition. Drills often lack meaning except to the linguist and the teacher. Students must be taught to convey meaning through speech. The speech itself, as in the native tongue, can be polished during the continuing process of speech expansion.

7. Motivation, the perpetual problem in language classes, should cease to be such an obstacle if the emphasis is switched from mechanics to practicality, from constant correction to continual encouragement. *The students' confidence, usually shaky as they begin language study, must be carefully preserved.*

8. During the complete process, abundant opportunity for practice along with an adequate model should be provided the students. If the teacher provides the model and the opportunity to talk, her role has been filled. The students then may learn a second language if they so desire. The quoted authors point out that, given a model and the opportunity to talk, children will learn their native language. This process should not be interfered with too much or language acquisition is more difficult. The same seems to be true in second-language learning. Many try to teach a language rather than provide a context in which the students may practice and learn a language.

9. Obviously, first-language learners communicate, and communicate quite

satisfactorily, although not perfectly in the beginning stages, from the onset of language to the point at which they reach the adult level of proficiency. Second-language learners, too, can operate at a multitude of functional levels that are suitable to their purposes, but that are not perfect models of native speech.

INTERNAL, MENTALISTIC VIEWS

A Neurophysiological Interpretation

From a neurophysiological point of view, learning a language is made possible by a highly developed central nervous system, by specialized brain mechanisms.[2] Animals have no such mechanisms. They can communicate in an elementary fashion via certain sounds and cries. They can, for example, communicate the idea of danger with cries of alarm, but they do not have the necessary mechanism in their cerebral cortex to speak. Nor is their brain sufficiently developed to master ideational speech.

Although young children's ability to learn language apparently decreases as they grow older, they are born with the potential "speech mechanisms" that make it possible for them to learn and to use language. Given the appropriate surroundings in which they hear a language, they will learn that language. The questions of concern are "How does the child acquire language?" and "What role do the brain mechanisms play in the language-learning process?"

The first step the child takes is to learn the concept. Penfield uses the example of a mother taking the child outside. As she does so she says, "Bye-bye." Gradually, the child acquires the idea of what *bye-bye* means. Once the child has the concept, it is stored in the memory as a "concept unit."

The next step is to learn the sound or sounds that signify the concept. Knowing the concept is not enough if speech is to be acquired. The child must learn the word that designates the learned concept. This "word-sound unit" is then stored at a different location in the brain. Next the child must establish an automatic reflex connection between the "word-sound unit" and its correlated "concept unit."

Up to this point in language learning the child has little advantage over the family dog. The dog, too, can learn the concept of going outside and the word that stands for that concept. Its reactions when someone mentions *bye-bye*

---

[2]This discussion is an abbreviated summary of Penfield's views as outlined in his article, "The Learning of Languages." For a more complete presentation of his ideas, the reader should consult the article itself in *Foreign Language Teaching.* (J. Michel, ed.) listed in the Selected References section of this chapter.

indicate that it knows a treat is in store. But beyond this point the dog cannot go. Only the children can take the next step. Only they have been born with a sufficiently elaborate and complex set of neuronal connections that allow them to speak. In order to communicate, children must activate a "verbal unit." This mechanism activates the muscles that are used to pronounce the words representing the concept.

When children begin to connect words in order to express themselves, an additional process becomes involved. They must select the words that they plan to use. Penfield stresses that the connection between thought and expression is not automatic. Humans make a conscious selection of the words and forms they need to communicate. This selectivity is made possible by the "centrencephalic system," which is "the system of central organizing connections that makes available to conscious thinking the many different neuronal mechanisms within the brain."

This, in a very simplified sense, is the pattern for learning a language. During the acquisition process, there is a time lapse of two to seven months from the time a concept is first heard until it is used meaningfully by the child. As children grow, they add "reading units" and "writing units." At first these units are selected consciously, but with practice they can become automatic. A person writing, for example, does not always have to pay conscious attention to his writing. The connections become so well established that thinking the thought is sufficient to have it appear on the written page.

Implications of the neurophysiological interpretation for second-language learning The preceding description of the neurophysiological processes developed in first-language learning contain the following implications for second-language learning:

1. Mental processes are basic to language learning. The teacher should concentrate on understanding and acquisition of concepts prior to practice.

2. Once the concepts have been learned, the students need practice in activating the "verbal units," the "writing units," and the "reading units" in order to increase their fluency in using the language.

3. Since school-aged children already have hundreds of concepts stored as "concept units," might it not be possible, and preferable, to help them learn vocabulary in the second language by associating new words with the known concepts? This approach would be a variation from the audio-lingual approach, which attempts to establish a "coordinate" set of concepts. It would also differ from the grammar-translation approach, which attempts to form associations between the "word-sound units" of the two languages, i.e., to teach vocabulary without taking advantage of known concepts or to connect words in the native language with words in the second language.

The Nativistic and Cognitive Models

The development of language The ultimate objective of transformational-generative linguistics is to understand what language is and how it operates.[3] In this sense the study of language is closely associated with the field of psychology. As Lenneberg (1964, p. 78) asks, "Might it not be possible that language ability—instead of being the consequence of intelligence—is its cause?" If the goal is to comprehend language more fully, the ideal place to begin is with children's acquisition of their mother tongue. It is this desire to understand language itself better that has fostered increased attention among psycholinguists on first-language learning.

Former studies of language learning stressed word counts and pronunciation. The object was to describe the language as spoken. The emphasis was on phonology, morphology, and semantics. Language learning was viewed as a product of imitation and reinforcement. However, stimulated by Chomsky's theory of language and language learning, newer studies have focused on the acquisition of syntax and the development of competence.[4] McNeill (1966, p. 17) states, "It is possible to describe performance without explaining it, but if we wish to explain performance, we must show how it derives from competence. . . ." In other words, the crucial aspect of comprehending how language and mind interact is to determine the role of language in the process of converting thought to expression and vice versa. However, before performance can be explained, competence must be understood.

As the psycholinguists have studied first-language learning from this new perspective of syntax, a new viewpoint has developed.[5] In the first place, these studies reveal that elementary competence underlying functional language performance is acquired in a relatively short period of time. Speech in a grammatical sense usually occurs around the time the child is one-and-one-half years old. By the time she is three-and-one-half, she already has the elementary syntactical patterns of the language. The accomplishment of this tremendously complex task in a period of two years, compared with the child's cognitive achievements in other areas, is little short of amazing.

The fact that children can handle elementary syntactical patterns at age three-and-one-half does not mean that they have reached the adult language level, however. In fact, the more researchers explore first-language acquisition, the more they are impressed by the length and the complexity of the

---

[3]Except where indicated otherwise, this discussion reflects the ideas, in general, of McNeill in the two sources listed in the Selected References section of this chapter. For a more complete understanding of his ideas the reader should consult both papers.

[4]For a summary of Chomsky's theories, see chapter 6, pages 136–41.

[5]*Syntax* refers to the arrangement of words in a communicative utterance.

process. Contrary to earlier belief that the child has mastered the language syntactical system by the age of five or six, Chomsky (1969) found that the grammar of a child of five is still significantly different from that of an adult and that it is not until she is around ten that her language is essentially that of the adult.

Theoreticians and researchers in the area of first-language learning now seem relatively certain that children's utterances are not a reduced imitation of adult speech. Close examination of the words children use and the way they put them together indicates that certain combinations and forms occur that are not to be found in adult speech. However, the combinations the children use do have a definite pattern, even though it does not correspond to the adult system of combining words. Therefore, the conclusion is that children develop their own simple linguistic competence, i.e., grammar rules, which makes their speech patterns possible.

It has been found that young children usually do not imitate a new pattern prior to incorporating that pattern into their own language system. For example, a child will not repeat, "Daddy is going to work," until he has reached a certain level of linguistic and cognitive maturity. Only after he has begun to use the -ing form of the verb will he repeat the sentence as he hears it. Ervin and Brown found that approximately 10 percent of all child utterances were imitations (McNeill, 1966).

The stand has also been taken that language is not learned by means of repetition and practice. Patterns within the language system are much more influential in language acquisition. This conclusion is based on the fact that children first learn irregular verb forms. The irregular verbs are the most common and are, therefore, the verbs with which children come in contact first and with which they have the most practice. Yet, as soon as they acquire a regular pattern, such as the past tense of regular verbs in English, they extend the pattern to include the irregular verbs that they have practiced repeatedly and that, up to this point, they have handled correctly. For some time thereafter, they continue to say "goed" and "seed," etc. McNeill (1966, p. 71) states, ". . . the amount of practice given to a feature is less relevant to language acquisition than the ability of a child to notice that a feature is part of a pattern."

Language is not learned by analogy. In order to acquire language children must develop hierarchical structures in their language system. Yet, these hierarchical structures are not apparent in overt, adult speech which children receive from their surroundings. The necessary knowledge is hidden within the deep structure of the language.[6] Therefore, it would be impossible for them to analogize that which is not available for analogy. For example, in the

---

[6]*Deep structure* is discussed in chapter 6, p. 140.

sentences: "I like raising flowers," "I like amusing stories," and "I like entertaining guests," there is no surface indication that the sentences are different. However, when the native speaker of English attempts to insert the word *the* in the sentences, the fact that they are not the same is readily apparent (Saporta, 1966).

Lenneberg (1966) argues that language is not learned due to a psychological need. He cites the cases of deaf-mute children who seem to be as happy psychologically as those who have learned to speak. Nor does he feel that language is developed by means of "training procedures and extrinsic response-shaping." Instead, he maintains that language is acquired as a normal corrolary of the typical maturation process. When children are ready, they will learn the language, and neither their parents nor anyone else can speed up this developmental sequence. He gives the example of a father attempting to get a child to say, "Daddy, bye-bye." The child until a certain age will not join the two words into a single phrase, even though she may "babble" much longer utterances. The block apparently does not result from a lack of motor development but of cognitive development. In the average child, language is not conditioned or hastened, but ". . . emerges by an interaction of maturation and self-programmed learning" (Lenneberg, 1966, p. 239).

An internal, mentalistic model of first-language acquisition If children do not learn to speak by imitation, practice, and reinforcement, how do they learn the language? What is the process whereby children learn to connect words in order to express meaning?

As children's cognitive functions mature, they begin to use one-word sentences, i.e., holophrastic sentences. *Wah-wah* may mean "I want a drink," "I had a drink," "Let's go play in the pool," or any number of things connected with water. It has been suggested that children quickly abandon this holophrastic means of communication for two reasons: (1) the mind would shortly be filled with a "cognitive clutter," which would overtax its capabilities, and (2) the communications of such a system are ambiguous and imprecise.

Therefore, for the sake of efficiency and exactness children progress as they mature to the formation of a grammar that allows them to produce the exact expressions they need. At first this grammar is quite simple. The first sentences are made up of two-word expressions, such as the following examples given by McNeill (1965):

allgone	boy
byebye	sock
big	boat
more	milk
pretty	vitamins

> my   plane
> see   hot

The words listed above fall into two classes, an open class and a pivot class. Words in the open class correspond to naming words (i.e., nouns) in the language. Words in the pivot class correspond to function words (i.e., verbs) in the language. By combining pivot words and open words or open words with other open words, the child achieves an elementary, but satisfactory, manner of self-expression. The important factor in this development of grammar is that learning a system enables the child to spin out needed language in its infinite variety from a limited corpus of material.

How children learn language   Gradually, the child's simple grammar acquires the complexity of the adult model. But a description of the process does not explain how it all takes place. The answer of the mentalists is that the child is born with an innate capability for language acquisition. As children mature cognitively and linguistically, this innate predisposition for language learning enables them to compare their language system with the adult system. The deep structure that they produce at first is modified by means of rules of transformation to enable them to produce the surface structure that they hear.[7] It is the children's "innate linguistic endowment" that enables them to formulate "linguistic hypotheses," and it is by means of these hypotheses compared with the language they receive that they manage to conform to adult speech. In McNeill's (1965, p. 32) words, "Languages have deep features, unmarked in overt speech, precisely because children possess the specific linguistic capacities that correspond to them. Otherwise, deep features would be unlearnable."

THE NATIVISTIC EXPLANATION

It is on this point of the learner's innate capability for language acquisition that nativistic theory and cognitive theory disagree. Those who hold to the nativistic theory of first-language learning maintain that the child is born with an indwelling predisposition to learn a language. They refer to this innate component as a language acquisition device (LAD). They base their conclusions on the following observations:

1. Only humans have the physiological and psychological means to participate in sustained speech.
2. Given a typical environment, all children learn language. In fact, suppression of language learning would be almost impossible.
3. The sequence in which grammatical structures are acquired seems to be

---

[7]*Surface structure* is discussed in chapter 6, p. 140.

practically the same for all people, and the beginning of language usage and the minimal achievement in language skills seem to be relatively unaffected by cultural or linguistic variations.

4. Certain characteristics of phonology, semantics, and syntax appear to be universal.

THE COGNITIVE EXPLANATION

On the other hand, those who hold to a cognitive theory of first-language acquisition feel that children are born with the ability to learn. They hold that children's cognitive capacities make it possible for them to acquire many types of knowledge and skills including language and language skills, but they do not feel that children are born with a mental mechanism specifically designed for language learning per se. That is, children have certain mental abilities that make all types of learning, as well as language learning, possible (Butler, 1974).

Based on the latest research findings in first-language acquisition, both nativistic and cognitive theorists conceive of first-language learning as an internal process that is creative and rule-governed. Given the fact that the words and word combinations children first use do not correspond to the adult system, they conclude that children are creating their own language. Given the fact that the child's language follows a definite pattern, they conclude that she is creating language according to some rule-governed system. This apparent existence of a child grammar implies that the mind of the child is an active agent in the language acquisition process. As she learns the language, she uses certain learning strategies to formulate rules appropriate to the level of her cognitive development. These rules then become the basis for her participation in the "creative construction" of language (Dulay & Burt, 1974).

First-language acquisition is a dynamic and self-correcting process. Given the fact that the child's grammar system changes from rather simple beginnings to a rather complex set of rules at the adult level, theorists conclude that the system undergoes an evolutionary process. Given the facts that children hear only surface structure manifestations of language meanings and that their language tends to resist attempts to change it prior to their own incorporation of a pattern, the theorists conclude that children gradually modify their language system, changing it to conform with that of the language they receive. And how is this changing process explained? The mentalistic theorists say that the language users formulate language as hypotheses which they test against the language they receive. As time passes and as their cognitive abilities mature, they gradually acquire the adult system.

Another important aspect of the process of first-language acquisition is that the learner participates in natural communication situations. Dulay and Burt (1973) define a natural communication situation as having two characteristics: (1) the attention of the producer and the receiver is focused on the content of the message, not its form; and (2) the meaning of the communication is established by the existence of clearly understood referents.

Implications of the Nativistic and Cognitive Models for Second-Language Learning   The nativistic and cognitive models of first-language learning imply the following tenets for second-language learning:

1. Competence must be developed first.
2. Language usage is based on the acquisition of rules.
3. Language usage is productive, i.e., the speaker can produce language appropriate to a given situation.
4. First-language learning proceeds from deep structure to surface structure. Second-language learning reverses this process. Might it be possible to provide insights into deep structure for adult learners prior to presenting them with surface structures of the language? McNeill (1965) mentions the possibility of teaching child grammar to adults in order that they first learn the deep structure.
5. Adult learners of a second language need assistance in formulating the appropriate hypotheses about language. The proper choice of explanation and exercises might assist them to internalize the necessary language competence.
6. Typically, the surface structure of the second language is imposed upon the deep structure of the native language. The teacher should expect this native-language influence and not be upset by it.
7. Language learners generate their own set of language rules. They then test the appropriateness of these rules by comparing them with the language they hear used.
8. The learner must be given opportunities to develop language hypotheses and to test them against the language model.
9. Communication does not require a perfected language system.
10. First-language learners focus on meaning rather than on syntax (Butler, 1974). Second-language teachers have tended to stress syntax rather than meaning.
11. The acquisition of irregular structures in first-language learning proceeds from (a) not using a particular structure to (b) occasional use with no errors or overgeneralizations to (c) increased use with errors and overgeneralizations to (d) correct usage (Butler, 1974). Certainly, second-language learners will pass through a period of incorrect usage or at least incomplete control of a pattern prior to total mastery of the structure.
12. Language learning and language usage are creative processes. Therefore, the second-language learner should participate in the "creative construction" use of language.

13. The teacher should concentrate on establishing natural communication situations for practice at the "real" language level. Communicative competence cannot be acquired in a vacuum, i.e., in situations devoid of meaning or meaningful purpose.

ERROR ANALYSIS

Teachers of second languages tend to forget that even first-language learners commit a multitude of errors as they progress over a period of years from initial utterances to adult speech patterns. The external, mechanistic view is that such errors result from an imperfect imitation of the adult sample. Correct speech is shaped over a period of years by reinforcing desired responses. The internal view is that during the acquisition process the learner's self-generated grammar system does not conform to that of the adult language system. Given the time, practice, and cognitive maturity, learners will gradually bring their language into line with that of other adult speakers.

Interlanguage Errors

Second-language teachers are concerned with the cause and elimination of errors in second-language classes. Until recently, most linguists believed that errors were due to interference from the mother tongue. On this basis, they placed a great deal of importance on contrastive analysis. The feeling was that if linguists could analyze carefully and completely the systems of both the first and the second languages, they would be able to predict the errors that would occur during second-language learning. This theory was based on the tenet that language was primarily a set of conditioned verbal habits. Errors in second-language learning would occur at those points at which the two language systems were dissimilar. The solution was a systematic analysis of both languages followed by the prescription of pattern drills to overcome first-language habits.

Recent investigations of the errors made by second-language learners have revealed surprising statistics. Although some errors are the direct result of native-language interference, the percentage is not so large as had been believed. The errors tabulated by Dulay and Burt (1973) indicated that only 3 percent of the errors in their study were due to interference. Hanzeli (1975, p. 8) states that researchers in contrastive analysis ". . . like Corder, Selinker, Burt, and George, have proved conclusively that the traditional contrastive analysis of two grammars cannot predict the frequency and hierarchy of learners' errors."

Intralanguage Errors

If second-language errors cannot be accounted for on the basis of interference from the mother tongue, from what source do the errors originate? The answer the researchers give is that they are not interlanguage errors, but intralanguage errors. An intralanguage error is not the result of conflict with the native language but the result of some problem in the acquisition of the second language itself. Intralanguage errors arise from the lack of congruity between the second-language learner's set of language rules and those of the native speaker. These errors are termed *developmental* or *restructuring* errors because they are the direct result of the learners' attempts to create language based on their hypotheses about the language system they are learning. In a study by Dulay and Burt (1973), 85 percent of the errors among second-language learners were developmental. Another study by Dulay and Burt (1974) reported that child speakers of Chinese and Spanish acquired eleven English structures in the same sequence, thus providing research support for the thesis that strategies for all learners are similar and that the mother tongue is not the major influence in second-language learning.

The data seem to imply that second-language learners approach language learning much as first-language learners do. That is, they formulate a self-created interim language system, practice "creative construction," and then compare the results with the feedback they receive from the language around them. According to Dulay and Burt, both first- and second-language learning involve the same two internal processes: "creative construction" and testing of hypotheses about the language (Ott et al., 1973). Studies by Dulay and Burt (1973) support the belief that all language learners all over the world use similar learning strategies, and that these strategies control the order of acquisition of syntactical structures.

The conclusions drawn in the preceding paragraphs have been derived from studies of child second-language learners, adult second-language learners, and first-language learners. Researchers have found that errors in first- and second-language learning are predictable but that the errors are different. In both cases the errors result from learner-created rules which are then tested and revised by the learner. It was found that learners corrected intralanguage errors sooner than interlanguage errors (Scott & Tucker, 1974).

Implications of Error Analysis for Second-Language Learning

The most recent research in errors of second-language learners support the following assumptions regarding second-language learning:

1. Errors occur both as a result of interference from the mother tongue and as a result of incomplete interim grammars of the learner.
2. Hopefully, future research will furnish more information about learner

strategies. These insights may provide clues as to more efficient teaching-learning procedures.

3. Apparently, both first- and second-language learning is characterized by the creation of language and by the comparison of the learner's interim language system with that of adult or native speech. As has been true throughout this examination of first- and second-language learning, the implication is that we, as second-language teachers, should be much more tolerant of student errors in the initial and intermediate stages of language learning.

CONCLUSION

Thus, the same mechanistic-mentalistic distinction made in the fields of linguistics and psychology also influences interpretations of first-language learning. Dulay and Burt (1973, p. 245) state, "In the last fifteen years of first-language research the emphasis has shifted from a search for environmental factors such as reinforcement and frequency of stimulus-response associations to a search for the innate ability of the human child to organize speech data."

Fodor (1966, p. 112) supports the cognitive stance when he states, "Notice that imitation and reinforcement, the two concepts with which American psychologists have traditionally approached problems about language-learning, are simply useless here." Krech (1969, p. 374) concurs, saying, "Whatever value so-called reinforcement or stimulus-response theories of learning may have for describing acquisition of motor skills by people, maze-learning by rats, and bar-pressing by pigeons—these theories are assessed as completely trivial and utterly irrelevant when it comes to understanding . . . the acquisition of language by the child."

Recent studies in first-language learning have convinced the researchers that language is much more than a collection of conditioned verbal responses. As Miller (1964, p. 99) explains, ". . . syntactic and semantic habits must have a character that linguists call *productive*. It is their productivity that distinguishes our linguistic rules from our other, simpler habits. On the basis of a finite exposure to grammatical and meaningful utterances, we are able to deal with an infinite variety of different and novel utterances." It is believed that the comprehension of the native speaker's "competence" is the key to understanding the "productivity" of language. Undoubtedly, the young child learning her mother tongue can "use what she knows." Typically the second-language learner knows many words and the basic language structures; yet she finds herself unable to "use what she knows." Further studies may provide insights into why this stumbling block exists in second-language learning. *If the psychological and cognitive processes of first-language learning can be* duplicated or reactivated in second-language learning, perhaps modern-language teachers will indeed be able to teach large numbers of students to use a second language.

Until that time arrives, if it ever does, the teacher must rely on her intuitive extrapolations of the implications of first-language learning with reference to second-language teaching. The position taken in this chapter is that at present, modern-language teachers should not, and cannot, duplicate the process of first-language learning, but that they can gain many valid and applicable insights by considering the various viewpoints regarding native-language acquisition.

REVIEW AND APPLICATION

DEFINITIONS

1. child grammar, p. 59
2. cognitive view, p. 59
3. creative construction, p. 59
4. developmental errors, p. 62
5. error analysis, p. 61
6. hypotheses in language learning, p. 59
7. interlanguage vs. intralanguage errors, pp. 61–62
8. LAD, p. 58
9. nativistic view, p. 58
10. neurophysiological, p. 53
11. open and pivot classes, p. 58
12. syntax, p. 55

DISCUSSION

1. Discuss the similarities and differences between first- and second-language learning.
2. Summarize the two basic interpretations of first-language learning. What are the similarities and differences between the two?
3. What are the implications of each interpretation for second-language teaching?
4. What has been learned from the study of language learners' errors?
5. Discuss the implications of interlanguage errors and intralanguage errors.
6. Which of the implications of first-language learning do you feel to be the most important in the second-language class? Which can you, as a second-language teacher, most easily and most productively incorporate into your teaching philosophy? Which, in your opinion, are not applicable?
7. How can the productive aspect of first-language learning be duplicated in second-language learning?

ACTIVITIES

1. Interview a non-native speaker of English and list his errors.
2. Talk to a young child and note her errors.

3. If class interest and class time permit, each class member might read one article on bilingual education, an important area of language teaching that is not being considered in this text, and summarize its contents for the class.

SELECTED REFERENCES

Ainsworth, S. (1950) Speech in the Home. In W. Johnson (Ed.), *Speech Problems of Children.* New York: Grune & Stratton. Pp. 47–66.

Ausubel, D. P. (1964) Adults Versus Children in Second-Language Learning: Psychological Considerations. *Modern Language Journal,* 48:420–24.

Bailey, N., et al. (1974) Is There a "Natural Sequence" in Adult Second Language Learning? *Language Learning,* 24:235–43.

Berry, M. F., and Eisenson, J. (1942) *The Defective in Speech.* New York: F. S. Crofts. Pp. 3–5.

Brown, R. (1973) *A First Language: The Early Stages.* Cambridge, Mass.: Harvard University Press.

Butler, L. C. (1974) Language Acquisition of Young Children: Major Theories and Sequences. *Elementary English,* 51: 1120–23, 1137.

Chomsky, C. S. (1969) *On Language Learning from 5 to 10: The Acquisition of Syntax in Children.* Cambridge, Mass.: M.I.T. Press.

Dulay, H. C., and Burt, M. K. (1973) Should We Teach Children Syntax? *Language Learning,* 23:245–58.

Dulay, H. C., and Burt, M. K. (1974) A New Perspective on the Creative Construction Process in Child Second Language Acquisition. *Language Learning,* 24:253–78.

Dulay, H. C., and Burt, M. K. (1974) Natural Sequences in Child Second Language Acquisition. *Language Learning,* 24:37–53.

Ervin-Tripp, S. M. (1973) *Language Acquisition and Communicative Choice.* Stanford, Calif.: Stanford University Press.

Fodor, J. A. (1966) How to Learn to Talk: Some Simple Ways. In F. Smith and G. A.

Miller (Eds.), *Genesis of Language: A Psycholinguistic Approach.* Cambridge, Mass.: M.I.T. Press. P. 112.

Gesell, A., et al. (1940) *The First Five Years of Life.* New York: Harper. P. 43.

Hanzeli, V. E. (1975) *Learner's Language: Implications of Recent Research for Personalized Instruction.* Paper presented at the Kentucky Foreign Language Conference, April 25.

Hymes, J. L., Jr. (1963) *The Child Under Six.* Englewood Cliffs, N.J.: Prentice-Hall.

Krech, D. (1969) Psychoneurobiochemeducation. *Phi Delta Kappan,* 50:374.

Lenneberg, E. H. (1964) A Biological Perspective of Language. In E. H. Lenneberg (Ed.), *New Directions in the Study of Language.* Cambridge, Mass.: M.I.T. Press. P. 78.

Lenneberg, E. H. (Ed.) (1964) *New Directions in the Study of Language.* Cambridge, Mass.: M.I.T. Press.

Lenneberg, E. H. (1966) The Natural History of Language. In F. Smith and G. A. Miller (Eds.), *Genesis of Language: A Psycholinguistic Approach.* Cambridge, Mass.: M.I.T. Press. P. 239.

Lewis, M. M. (1936) *Infant Speech.* London: Kegan Paul.

Lewis, M. M. (1957) *How Children Learn to Speak.* London: Harrap. Pp. 14, 17–21.

Liamina, G. (1964) Development of the Speech and Environmental Orientation of Two-Year-Olds. *Soviet Education,* 6:15–23.

Long, C. L. (1957) *Will Your Child Learn to Talk Correctly?* Albuquerque, N. Mex.: New Mexico Publishing. P. 15.

McNeill, D. (1965) Some Thoughts on First and Second Language Acquisition. Mimeographed. Harvard University: Center for Cognitive Studies. Pp. 32, 35.

McNeill, D. (1966) Developmental Psycholinguistics. In F. Smith and G. A. Miller (Eds.), *Genesis of Language: A Psycholinguistic Approach.* Cambridge, Mass.: M.I.T. Press. Pp. 17, 71–72.

Mange, C. V. (1959) *An Investigation of the Relationships Between Articulatory Development and Development of Phonetic Discrimination and Word Synthesis Abilities in Young Mentally Retarded Children and Normal Children.* Syracuse, New York: Syracuse University Research Institute. P. 4.

Menýuk, P. (1971) *The Acquisition and Development of Language.* Englewood Cliffs, N.J.: Prentice-Hall.

Miller, G. A. (1964) Language and Psychology. In E. H. Lenneberg (Ed.), *New Directions in the Study of Language.* Cambridge, Mass.: M.I.T. Press. P. 99.

Morley, M. E. (1957) *The Development and Disorders of Speech in Childhood.* Edinburgh, Scotland: E. & S. Livingston.

Mysak, E. D. (1961) Organismic Development of Oral Language. *Journal of Speech and Hearing Disorders,* 26:377–84.

Oller, J. W., Jr. (1972) Contrastive Analysis, Difficulty, and Predictability. *Foreign Language Annals,* 6:95–106.

Ott, C. E., et al. (1973) The Effect of Interactive-Image Elaboration on the Acquisition of Foreign Language Vocabulary. *Language Learning,* 23:197–206.

Penfield, W. (1953) A Consideration of the Neurophysiological Mechanisms of Speech and Some Educational Consequences. *Bulletin of the American Academy of Arts and Sciences,* 5.

Penfield, W. (1967) The Learning of Languages. In J. Michel (Ed.), *Foreign Language Teaching.* New York: Macmillan. Pp. 192–214.

Politzer, R. L. (1974) Developmental Sentence Scoring as a Method of Measuring Second Language Acquisition. *Modern Language Journal,* 58:245–50.

Reber, A. S. (1973) On Psycholinguistic Paradigms. *Journal of Psycholinguistic Research,* 2:289–319.

Richardson, P. C. (1959) Developing Fundamental Speech Patterns. *Volta Review,* 61:276–82.

Saporta, S. (1966) Applied Linguistics and Generative Grammar. In A. Valdman (Ed.), *Trends in Language Teaching.* New York: McGraw-Hill. P. 90.

Scholnick, E. K., and Adams, M. J. (1973) Relationships Between Language and Cognitive Skills, Passive-Voice Comprehension, Backward Repetition, and Matrix Permutation. *Child Development,* 44:741–46.

Scott, M. S., and Tucker, G. R. (1974) Error Analysis and English-Language Strategies of Arab Students. *Language Learning,* 24:69–97.

Smith, D. W. (1960) Factors Affecting Speech Development. *Education,* 80:452–54.

Smith, F., and Miller, G. A. (Eds.) (1966) *Genesis of Language: A Psycholinguistic Approach.* Cambridge, Mass.: M.I.T. Press.

Staats, A. W., and Staats, C. K. (1962) A Comparison of the Development of Speech and Reading Behavior with Implications for Research. *Child Development,* 33:831–46.

Taylor, B. P. (1974) Toward a Theory of Language Acquisition. *Language Learning,* 24:23–35.

Templin, M. C. (1957) *Certain Language Skills in Children.* Minneapolis: University of Minnesota Press.

Van Riper, C. (1950) *Teaching Your Child to Talk.* New York: Harper. Pp. 3, 14, 17–18, 35–45, 49–51.

Wardhaugh, R. (1971) Theories of Language Acquisition in Relation to Beginning Reading Instruction. *Language Learning,* 21:1–26.

Woodsworth, J. A. (1973) On the Role of Meaning in Second-Language Teaching. *Language Learning,* 23:75–88.

RESEARCH

Research on Affective-Social Variables
>   Self-Concept
>   Personality
>   Motivation
>   Social Development
>   Values and Morals

Research on Cognitive Variables
>   Intelligence
>   Cognitive Style

Research on Learning
>   Meaningful Learning
>   Practice
>   Feedback and Reinforcement
>   Acquisition, Retention, and Recall of Information
>   Transfer

Specific Studies
>   Stressing Oral Language Skills
>>   Listening Training
>>   The Effect of the Written Word on Student Pronunciation
>>   Transfer of Learning Across Sense Modalities
>>   Prereading Period
>>   Motivation in Classes Stressing Oral Skills
>   Acquiring and Using Structure

Methodological Comparisons

Aptitude-Treatment Interaction

Future Research

INTRODUCTION

Undoubtedly the prime source of knowledge for the teacher is her own classroom experience based on past procedures, performances, and results. However, she should realize that experience is not the *only* teacher. Research studies in second-language education and related fields are an additional source of valuable information, and the teacher should keep abreast of the latest findings. Empirical results can provide guidelines within which subjective interpretations can operate. Scientific teaching without the artful expression of the teacher's personality is lifeless and mechanical, but subjective teaching unaccompanied by periodic adjustments based on theory and research can be myopic, inefficient, and unproductive. Teaching practices should be continually reviewed in light of the latest research findings, and appropriate modifications should be made. The purpose of this chapter is to examine relevant research in areas related to second-language learning.

Scholars' use of the word *experiment* is often confusing. Many use *experiment* to refer to any undertaking in which "something new or different" is attempted. Others attach research significance to the word. Consequently, a great number of the articles published in journals and reviews are not scientific, comparative studies based on research design and statistical analysis but are subjective evaluations. Obviously, the teacher needs to read both types of articles, but she should be able to separate empirical research from personal preference. The discussion in this chapter deals primarily with empirical research.

RESEARCH ON AFFECTIVE-SOCIAL VARIABLES

Critics charge that schools have concerned themselves with students' cognitive development to the neglect of their psychological, emotional, and social growth. The questions to be answered with regard to affective-social variables contain four dimensions. First, what are the various student feelings, attitudes, values, and social relationships that can be identified? Second, how does each, separately and collectively, affect learning? Third, what can be done to promote the development of satisfactory affective and social characteristics? Fourth, how can the teaching-learning process be fitted to varying student needs?

These questions obviously cannot be discussed completely in this brief review of related research. The issues are complex, and the concerted efforts of the teaching profession for an extended period of time will be required to attack selected problems and to arrive at some answers. Since affective factors and social interaction have not received the amount of attention devoted to the cognitive aspects of education in the past, research in this area is not so extensive, so easily undertaken, nor so readily accepted. Gaining consistent results in the affective area is rather difficult, and determining and controlling the exact variables involved are quite logically complex. Too, justifying one's preference for one instructional system or another or for one program or another on perceived student attitudes does not satisfy the scientific mind in search of empirical support for education practices.

It is now generally accepted that the separation of a student's cognitive capabilities from his emotional, psychological state is impossible. Mahmoudi and Snibbe (1974) conducted a comparative study in which they manipulated the teacher's expectations, actions, and attitudes in order to determine the extent to which student response conforms to the "self-fulfilling prophesy" implied in the teacher's actions. In their study, those students exposed to a high degree of warmth, love, acceptance, respect for the rights of others, and positive expectations of a good semester were characterized by increased achievement, decreased tension, and increased mental health.

Kohn and Rosman (1974) state that the student's social-emotional involvement in the class consists of three main factors: (1) interest and curiosity, (2) acceptance of classroom routine and rules, and (3) task orientation. The student may come to class with a natural desire to learn and to explore unknown material, or that interest may be developed in class. In addition to motivating interest, however, classroom achievement also depends on student willingness to participate within the limits of necessary classroom operational procedures and to work toward the completion of instructional goals. The ideal classroom goal is a situation in which all three factors work together to promote learning.

Self-Concept

Research shows that students who have a good self-concept will achieve more in their studies. Alvord and Glass (1974) found a significant correlation between self-concept and achievement at the three grade levels included in their data. Other studies showed that the relationship between self-concept and achievement was reciprocal. A good self-concept improved achievement, and at the same time better grades enhanced the student's self-concept. Given the insecurity often experienced by second-language learners, one would suspect that a strong self-concept would facilitate second-language learning. In a study related directly to achievement in second-language learning, Prawer (1974, p. 9) concluded that the "self-concept as a foreign-language student and the foreign-language grade are mutually reinforcing variables, since the self-concept is a composite of personal expectation, perceived feedback, and subjective reaction."

A study by Brown and MacDougall (1973) reinforced the following hypotheses:

1. Given an opportunity to examine procedures for improving the self-concept of their students, teachers do modify classroom behavior, and this change in behavior does result in a more positive self-image on the part of their students.
2. Socioeconomic status does seem to affect teacher judgment of students.
3. The teacher's treatment of any given student in class tends to influence the other students' perception of that student.

Personality

Since personality is inseparably related to intelligence and cognitive style, it is to be expected that personality will exert an important influence on the learner's aptitudes, interests, and goals. Farnham-Diggory (1972) discusses the following seven personality characteristics as being critical in the classroom.

1. Persistence, Impulsivity, and Hyperactivity. The range on this factor is from that of the student who is able to stick with his task to that of one who is not able to do so.
2. Tolerance for Delay of Gratification. Rewards are necessary components of purposeful behavior, but some students need to be given immediate rewards while others are more willing to wait.
3. Anxiety and Defensiveness. The continuum on this personality factor extends from the student who is not at all concerned and who consequently fails to attend to her responsibilities in the learning situation to the student who is so burdened by his anxiety that his achievement is diminished. Anxiety that leads to improved performance is most likely not damaging to the personality.
4. Dependency and Growth. On the one hand, the teacher has to contend with the student's dependency needs, and on the other, she has the obligation to promote independence and growth in the students.
5. Assertiveness, Agressiveness, and Hostility. The classroom teacher has the task of toning down the dominant personalities in class without stunting their potential, while at the same time supporting the meek and timid in the growth of their own personalities.
6. Egocentrism and Self-Esteem. The individual's first task is to be confident in herself. The teacher's role is to assist in the development of an adequate and a realistic ego image. Once this prerequisite is attained, learning will be enhanced.
7. Feelings versus Behavior. The complex relationship between feelings and behavior is crucial to the establishment of a productive learning atmosphere

in the classroom, but the underlying cause and effect of relationships influencing behavior is sometimes difficult to ascertain.

In one study students were permitted to choose a class in which they could follow the traditional lecture-objective examination format, an independent study project, or a small-group discussion class. After the selection, the researchers identified the dominant personality factors of each of the three groups. Students choosing the conventional class (86 percent) were characterized by a dislike for uncertainty, a lack of interest in many areas of knowledge and in the higher-level cognitive skills, a concern for what others think of them, a greater dependency need than the other students, a low interest in new and different experiences, a greater need for reassurance, a certain amount of caution and insecurity, a need for order and neatness, a feeling that they are not in control of their lives, and less perseverance than the other students. Those students who chose the independent study group (3 percent) were more intellectually curious, more desirous of breaking away from restraints, more determined and persevering, and more in need of autonomy. Those who enrolled in the small-group discussion sessions (11 percent) were in between the other two groups with three exceptions: they tended toward a greater interest in social interaction, a more serious academic attitude, and a greater desire for fun activities (Baker, Bakshis, & Tolone, 1974).

The way students react to success or failure has received considerable attention in educational research. Researchers have divided the reactions into two personality types: *internal* and *external* locus of control. *Internals* attribute success or failure to their own ability and effort; *externals* consider success or failure to be determined by outside forces over which they have little or no control. Internals blame themselves for failure, while externals fix the blame on external conditions. In this sense, external orientation serves as a type of ego defense device (Davis & Davis, 1972). In the learning situation, internals concentrate more on the information being presented while externals are more affected by social conditions in the classroom (Pines & Julian, 1972). Internals are more resistant to attempts to influence behavior than externals (Borden & Hendrick, 1973). Internals and externals seem to prefer different types of learning. Externals prefer chance situations; internals prefer situations in which their own ability is a factor in determining success or failure. Alegre and Murray (1974) state that verbal conditioning is greatest in externals and least in internals. Krovetz (1974) maintains that the cognitive processes are different for internals and externals: the former stressing internal processes and the latter external conditions.

Motivation

Motivation is perhaps more widely mentioned at professional meetings, in professional journals, and in teacher conversations than any other student characteristic. In spite of its obvious importance and the amount of attention motivation has received, not a great deal is known about the components of motivation nor about how to stimulate or enhance student motivation. Cofer and Appley (1964), in their book *Motivation: Theory and Research,* state that it is clear that a comprehensive, definitive psychology of motivation does not exist.

Noar (1972, p. 3) lists two emotional needs that are crucial to motivation in classroom instruction. First, the student must be accepted, and second, he must achieve. Motivation in the classroom involves each individual's efforts to satisfy these two needs. She expresses these needs saying, "In addition to finding acceptance in life, every human being, especially as he is growing up, must have experiences in which he achieves, accomplishes, is successful."

Achievement motivation in the school consists of three components: cognitive drive, ego-enhancement, and affiliation. Cognitive drive involves the need to know and understand one's surroundings. Ego-enhancement consists of the individual's need for a sense of adequacy and self-esteem. According to Ausubel and Robinson (1969, p. 359): "On the average, ego-enhancement motivation seems clearly the strongest motivation available during the active portion of an individual's academic and vocational career." Affiliation denotes individuals' need for social approval from their group (Ausubel & Robinson, 1969). As learners attempt to cope with their situation, their motivation may vary from inadequate to the point of being apathetic to a maximally efficient level or to so high that their achievement is hindered (Mouly, 1973, p. 338). McClelland and Watson (1973) found that students high in need for social power sought to distinguish themselves publicly and took higher risks to do so.

Not all students are motivated by the certainty of success. The reaction to programmed instruction is a good example of the boredom that can result for some students when the certainty of a correct response is a basic characteristic of the learning materials. Atkinson has theorized that achievement-oriented students perfer a learning task in which there is a moderate ratio between success and failure. On the other hand, students who anticipate a possible failure choose tasks with either a high or a low chance of success (Machr & Sjogren, 1971). Students high in achievement motivation tend to relax after success and to work harder after failure. Students high in need to avoid failure do poorer work after failure and better work as a result of success. Highly motivated students should experience challenge and occasional failure. Students high in need to avoid failure should receive much positive feedback and encouragement. Research does not support the use of either positive or negative feedback in all cases for all types of students (Weiner, 1969). Not all students are motivated by the same system of rewards and punishment. Introverts tend to respond with maximum effort when praised. Extroverts do their best in response to criticism (Lipe & Jung, 1971).

Some students are generally motivated intrinsically; others extrinsically. Schwartz (1972) lists the intrinsic motivators as anxiety, need to achieve, self-concept, and aspirations; and the extrinsic motivators as sociocultural influences and social reinforcers. She adds that intrinsic motivation for learning reaches its peak during the preschool years. Intrinsic models of motivation emphasize plans, cognitive drive, and need to avoid failure as well, while extrinsic theories stress response reinforcement and behavior modification.

Weiner (1969) lists four basic theoretical positions regarding motivation.

1. *Associative theory,* which postulates specific responses connected to certain stimuli.
2. *Drive theory,* which postulates drives triggered by a need to correct some type of imbalance in the organism.
3. *Cognitive theory,* which stresses purposive behavior based on plans, cognitive drive, level of aspiration, need for achievement, and need to avoid failure.
4. *Psychoanalytic theory,* which is a psychological theory of motivation stressing internal processes.

Social Development

The student does not learn in isolation. Her classroom behavior and achievement are influenced by her home life and her social status in the community, the school, and the classroom. Her acceptance of the teacher and the other students and their acceptance of her constitute a major factor in the enthusiasm and willingness with which she participates in the classroom activities. The social climate of the class will play a major role in the success of the class to further the process of socialization of individual members and in academic achievement.

Several factors affect the social relationships within the class itself. Some students hold the teacher in high esteem; some students prefer to learn in group activities with their own peers; and others are inclined toward more independent types of activities (Johnson & Johnson, 1974). In an investigation of cooperative and competitive classroom atmospheres, Wheeler and Ryan (1973) reported more favorable student attitudes in the cooperative class, although the results did not indicate any significant difference between the two groups on achievement. Levenson and LeUnes (1974) found that student reaction toward the instructor is influenced by similarity or dissimilarity of attitudes. Brown and Richard (1972) reported an interdependence between self-concept and social responsibility.

Values and Morals

Student values are as varied as the other components of individuality. Some students do not value an education at all; some students conceive of school as a means toward a better job; and others place a high value on the intellectual aspects of education (Johnson & Johnson, 1974). A wide disparity exists among students as to what is important to them and how they accomplish their goals.

Student actions are determined to a large extent by their moral development. The most recent models postulate an increasingly complex moral system related quite closely to the individual's cognitive growth. Rest (1973) did a study to investigate the hierarchical development of moral judgment as postulated by Kohlberg. The results supported the thesis that each stage of moral development is cognitively different from and more cognitively complex than the preceding stage, that each succeeding stage is more conceptually adequate for the individual, that there are upper limits as to what moral principles the individual can comprehend, and that there are lower limits as to what moral guidelines are acceptable to an individual. This study indicates that the teacher should be cognizant of varying levels of moral judgment in the classroom.

RESEARCH ON COGNITIVE VARIABLES

Cognition refers to the individual's intellectual operations by which knowledge is gained about ideas or perceptions. The term encompasses all the internal processes activated during perceiving, comprehending, practicing, organizing, storing, recalling, transferring, and manipulating information. Obviously, the concept of cognition is directly related to internal theories of learning. External theories focus on stimuli and the resultant responses.

Intelligence

The concept of intelligence remains an area of disagreement among psychologists and ordinary people alike. Just what intelligence is has not been settled to everyone's satisfaction. There are at least four major viewpoints. Biologists see intelligence in the evolutionary sense as "adaptation to the environment." The ordinary person's view is that intelligence is "the ease of learning new structures and skills." Piaget has conceptualized intelligence as the "coordination of mental operations that facilitate adaptation to the environment." Guilford has postulated a multifaceted model of intelligence consisting of the "interaction of different types of *mental processes* and *contents* to produce various *mental products*" (Kagan, 1971, pp. 655–57).

Although there is no general agreement as to the definition of intelligence, psychologists do agree in two areas. (1) Cognitive abilities grow, and (2) cognitive abilities may vary from individual to individual. Cognitive growth has some generally recognized characteristics. First, the child's horizon expands intellectually and temporally from his immediate surroundings to more distant contexts. Second, the child acquires an increasingly expanded capacity to deal with symbols, especially abstract symbols. The best example of this ability is his use of language. Third, the child's memory grows. Fourth the child's mental growth is characterized by a gradual increase in his ability to reason (Mouly, 1973).

Individual differences in intelligence are present at birth and are distinguishable variables thereafter. One study reported measurable individual difference in the "general amount of reactivity and speed of reactivity to stimulation" at birth (Stiles & McCandless, 1969, p. 121). Ausubel and Robinson (1969) cite a table prepared by Merrill that indicates that approximately one half the IQ scores fall between 90 and 110. Only a small number of people score higher than 140 or lower than 60. The fact that intellectual ability varies from individual to indivdual is indicated not only by direct measures such as standardized intelligence tests, but also by studying individual performances on tasks involving mental operations. Klausmeier and Ripple (1971, p. 445) provide the following description: "On all the [intellectual] . . . behaviors, the children of low IQ were less effective than were those of high IQ. More important, the differences in behavior give clues as to why failure was experienced more frequently by the children of low IQ. For example, more children of high than low IQ used a logical approach, noted and corrected mistakes, and verified solutions. More children of low than high IQ made random approaches to the problem, offered incorrect solutions, and did not persist in attempts at solving the problem."

Cognitive Style

Not only is there a wide range of intellectual abilities, there is also a definite variability in the way individuals employ their intelligence as they approach learning situations. The evidence is overwhelmingly in support of individual cognitive styles in learning. Some learners are more analytical than others. The trend as one matures is to become more analytical, but individual differences never completely disappear. The less analytical learner is "more impulsive and more susceptible to immediate perceptual experiences" and more "impatient for answers." The more analytical thinker is "more independent." This description implies a basic connection between cognitive style and personality (Stiles & McCandless, 1969). Thorsland and Novak (1974) report that individual differences in adopting an intuitive or analytical approach to the solution of a problem can be identified. Students high in both have a significant advantage over others, who must compensate in some way to learn the material.

Some learners are field-dependent while others are field-independent. The former are more dependent on their surrounding circumstances, while the latter are more independent in their thinking and in their actions. Walters and Sieben (1974) quote various studies reporting that field-dependent children are less ambitious, less persevering, less theoretical, more dependent, more likely to accept external authority, and less tolerant of ambiguity. The authors add that field-dependent children do better in a class that provides a great deal of guidance and support, while field-independent children seem to learn better in an open, self-directed environment. The suggestion was made that teaching styles be adjusted to learning requirements of the students.

The manner in which information is received varies from student to student. Mouly (1973) refers to Klein's distinction between *sharpeners*, learners who are flexible in the face of new evidence or new situations, and *levelers*, learners who seem unable to change their previous mental set.

In his review of concept formation, Sax (1969) quotes a study which found that bright children learn by using hypotheses in the development of concepts. Children of average intelligence learn by developing stimulus-response associations. Jensen suggests what he terms *Level I* learners, who learn best by mechanistic methods, and *Level II* learners, who learn best by following a mentalistic approach (Weiner, 1972). King, Roberts, and Kropp have hypothesized that students scoring high on an inference test should do best learning deductively while those students with high scores on a word-grouping test would learn better inductively (Weiner, 1972). Lower ability students need instruction that forces them to pay attention to and to differentiate among details. Higher ability students prefer instruction involving the manipulation of symbolic materials and concepts (Salomon, 1972).

Research evidence indicates that individuals have different perceptual styles: they prefer to learn with different kinds of sensory information (Temple, 1974). An extension of this preference is the effect the type of perception has on the processing of the information being acquired. Bernstein (1974) refers to several studies that have investigated visually minded versus nonvisually minded thinkers. The results support the thesis that some individuals think and remember visually while others use language cues. That there is a difference between the two types of thinkers is supported by physiological evidence—the brain waves of visual and nonvisual thinkers are different. Efforts to improve student ability in a nonpreferred mode have been largely unsuccessful. The implication of this research is that some students may learn more efficiently with abstract explanations while others need to visualize the problem.

Some individuals are more capable of handling complex abstract concepts than others. In a study examining the level of mental operations attained by disadvantaged students at the junior high and high school levels, Nordland, Lawson, and Kahle (1974) reported that of the junior high students in their sample 86.4 percent were operating at the concrete operational level or below. In the senior high sample 86.8 percent were at the concrete operational level or below. These results point out the variability of the students' capabilities of handling abstract concepts and mental operations. Both at the junior high and high school levels, large numbers of students remain at a level at which concrete examples and representations of material to be learned are necessary.

Cognitive style is a product of both cognitive and affective factors. After reviewing the relevant research, Gordon (1969) stated that cognitive style is a direct outgrowth of one's life experiences. The cognitive style of students coming from a low socioeconomic class, for example, is more visual, kinesthetic, concrete, short-term in outlook, and less able to delay gratification than that of students from an upper socioeconomic class. Ramirez and Price-Williams (1974) obtained results that indicated that members of groups which emphasize respect for family and authority, group identity, and shared family and friends tended to be more field-dependent. Individuals from groups which stress questioning of convention and individuality tended to be more field independent. They also found that teachers tend to give higher grades to those students having a cognitive style matching that of the teacher. Denny (1974) lists three aspects of cognitive style, all of which involve affective as well as cognitive variables: (1) conceptual style—analytic, relational, and inferential; (2) cognitive tempo—impulsive or reflective; and (3) attentional styles—constriction versus flexibility, i.e., more versus less easily distracted.

Cognitive style refers not only to how the individual processes information but also to the number of ideas generated. Those students who have a high degree of *fluency* in their thoughts, who are *flexible* in considering alternatives, and who can then *elaborate* from the initial idea to more complex constructs are said to be creative. Goor (1974) states that highly creative students respond more, generate more information, work more productively on hypotheses, and are better able to view their own work objectively and to criticize it than noncreative students. Studying the relationship of creativity to course grade in a second-language class, Chastain (1975) found that in many cases there was a significant correlation between student creativity scores and student grades in a second-language course.

RESEARCH ON LEARNING

Meaningful Learning

The concepts of meaningful learning in general and meaningful verbal learning in particular are of rather recent formulation. Meaningful learning is learning that is understood by the student and that he can relate to his previous knowledge. Meaningful learning has been a major target of speculation and research in recent years. Ausubel (1968, p. 504) states, "Providing guidance to the learner in the form of verbal explanation of the underlying principles almost invariably facilitates learning and retention and sometimes transfer as well. Self-discovery methods or the furnishing of completely explicit rules, on the other hand, are relatively less effective." Based on the results of this research, learning by discovery is not held in such high esteem at present as it was earlier. In discovery learning, the student learns, or "discovers," the basic content and principles for himself by studying instances or examples of what he is to learn. In fact, Ausubel (1968, p. 497) asserts," . . . Actual examination of the research literature allegedly supportive of learning by discovery reveals that valid evidence of this nature is virtually nonexistent."

Recent studies have obtained results supporting the desirability of verbal receptive learning over discovery learning. In verbal receptive learning, students listen to prepared explanations of rules and principles to be learned. Chalmers and Rosenbaum (1974) stated that students can learn concepts by observation and that there is less error on a transfer task. The assumption was made that learning by observation results in greater flexibility. In a study with first-, third-, and sixth-grade pupils, the pupils learned rules at all levels of difficulty faster than pupils taught by discovery methods and were superior in all measures of retention and transfer. Francis (1975) adds, however, that discovery learning in the past has been found to facilitate the discovery of new rules and that, in general, motivation has been higher in discovery learning.

The acquisition of new behavior or new knowledge apparently depends a great deal upon how the individual perceives the task or material to be learned. Perception, in turn, is colored and influenced by the individual's past learning. For learning to be most efficient, perception must be meaningful. Witkin (1969, p. 53) quotes Gould's definition of perception as "sensory experience which has gained meaning or significance. When, as the result of learning experience, one understands the relationships of objects which were previously merely raw, undifferentiated sensory experiences, he is said to perceive these objects." Egan and Greeno (1973) determined that (1) more skills were necessary to learn by discovery than by rules; (2) material learned by discovery is integrated into the cognitive network, while material learned by rules results in the addition of new structure; and (3) students who do not have the needed related abilities for discovery learning do better learning with rules. Gagné (1970) says that " . . . The most dependable condition for the insurance of learning is the prior learning of prerequisite capabilities."

Meaningful perception implies cognitive interpretation by the individual. Beyond the level of perception, cognition plays an even greater role. Briggs and Hamilton (1964, p. 596) state: "There is increasing evidence that, for meaningful learning, the roles of overt responding, practice, and reinforcement can be overemphasized, to the neglect not only of subsumption and other cognitive processes. . . ."[1] Anderson (1970, p. 353) describes attention as involving both awareness and encoding of stimuli. He recognizes that "students tend to follow a principle of least effort" and that "when it is possible to short-circuit the instructional task, students will often fail to learn what a lesson is intended to teach them." He suggests that teachers should structure the "characteristics of instructional tasks so as to force students to do all the processing required for learning" (Anderson, p. 363).

Various studies support an emphasis on meaning in learning. The results of Dawson's study (1967) indicated that classical conditioning in humans is inevitably accompanied by an awareness of relationships. Mascolo (1967) found that students in courses in which the material is organized around key concepts do much better than students in courses in which the content is not so organized. After a review of the literature for the last fifty years and a study of his own, Dubois (1967) concluded that most results favor deduction in learning. Ausubel (1969, p. 132) supports the use of "advance organizers" in meaningful learning. He says, "The use of expository organizers to facilitate the learning and retention of meaningful verbal material is based on the premise that logically meaningful material becomes incorporated most readily and stably in cognitive structure insofar as it is subsumable under specifically relevant existing ideas. It follows, therefore, that increasing the availability in cognitive structure of specifically relevant subsumers—by implanting suitable organizers—should enhance the meaningful learning of such material. Research evidence . . . , in fact, confirms this supposition." Studies by Slock (1975) and Young (1975) found that students studying with materials containing advance organizers were superior in achievement and retention to students studying materials without advance organizers.

Some authors feel that the success of induction or deduction in learning depends on individual learning preferences. Frederick and Klausmeier (1970) describe the theories of Messick, who feels that individuals have different cognitive styles or information-processing habits. In an investigation of this topic by Laughlin (1969), the data indicated that the receptive learning is more effective for a "more difficult conceptual task" but that the opposite is true for tasks that are less difficult.

How important is meaningful learning in the acquisition of language? On the basis of his findings, Smith (1969, p. 4784-B) concluded that the S-R model is inadequate and that "language is better typified as the acquisition of 'rules.'" Rutherford (1968) stated that the central task of the second-language teacher is to make the students aware of the deep structures in the language. Studies by Blumenthal (1967), Blumenthal and Boakes (1967), and Johnson

---

[1] *Subsumption* refers to the learners' incorporation of new information into their existing knowledge system.

(1965), all support the hypothesis that the native speaker's language ability is based on an intuitive knowledge of rules.

Practice

External theories of learning emphasize the necessity of overt response to a stimulus. On the other hand, internal theories support the position that learning can take place through the process of covert responses, even in the absence of overt responses. Cognitive theorists are not opposed to practice, but they maintain that understanding should precede practice. Psychological studies concerning the role of repetition, imitation, and practice are relevant to this problem and to the selection of appropriate teaching/learning activities in the classroom.

Rock (1957, p. 193) precipitated a great deal of research on the subject when he concluded that "repetition plays no role in the formation (as distinct from strengthening) of associations, other than that of providing the occasion for new ones to be formed, each in a single trial." Estes (1960) stated that Kimble and associates found that only the first few trials were effective in strengthening stimulus-response bonds. Murdock and Babick (1961) concluded that repetition had no discernible effect on recall. Although unwilling to accept Rock's conclusion, Clark et al. (1960, p. 23), after having obtained similar results, called for further studies and stated: "If, therefore, his results are confirmed, if they are not artifacts of his method, which still has to be proved, then all of the modern-day theories of learning that are based on repetition, or some form of it, will have to be abandoned or very radically modified."

Associated with a great deal of repetition is the phenomenon of verbal satiation. Some research shows that constant repetition tends to weaken or actually cause a total lapse of meaning of the repeated word on the part of the subject. One article reported a dissipation of meaning within three or four seconds. The theoretical explanation of this loss through repetition is that after a period of continually activating the environmental referent associated with the word, an inhibiting factor develops causing a loss of the mediators involved (Lambert & Jakobovits, 1960). Hull's reactive inhibition postulate states: "As a word is repeated, the trace associated with it, and with its meaning, as well as the connection between the two, are repeatedly activated, and should lead to their own inhibition. Repeated activation of the traces and bonds limits their further activation" (Wertheimer & Gillis, 1958, p. 79).

A great deal of research has been done in the area of observational learning and imitation. On the basis of their work, Bandura and Walters concluded that "new behavior units, or chunks of behavior, are learned initially through observing and imitating a model, rather than being shaped through successive approximations involving differential reinforcement" (Klausmeier & Ripple, 1971, p. 50). Although this line of research dealt originally with the learning of social behavior, the basic procedures have been expanded to other areas of learning. In one study, Rosenthal and Zimmerman (1973) found that practice in which the student was required to perform without error was far less effective than observation of a model. In a later study, Zimmerman and Rosenthal (1974) reported that a physical, overt response interfered with vicarious learning. After reviewing the research on imitative behavior, Flanders (1968) concluded that the acquisition of complex, unfamiliar behavior, whether it be verbal or nonverbal, is possible, even by very young children, without any overt response having actually occurred.

One purpose of practice is to refine initial learning to the skill level. In a review of skill learning, Posner and Keele (1973, p. 805) point out that the term *skill* refers to "those processes producing expert, rapid, and accurate perform-ance" and that this definition can be applied to internal mental processes as well as physical actions. Even though they limit their review to a consideration of skilled motor movement, Posner and Keele indicate that an information processing approach is supported by the research being done in the field. The data indicate that central systems of control underlie physical movement. This internal control of movement may be explained on the basis of S-R chains acquired through kinesthetic reinforcement or on the basis of a "central motor program control." Studies support the thesis that movement is guided by an internalized mental model, which the learner tries to achieve. The existence of such an internalized model means that at some stages in the development of a skill, especially in the initial stages during which the model is established, overt, physical practice may be unnecessary. Instead, mental practice involving observation of models and verbal guidance may be more beneficial.

An examination of six reviews surveying sixty-one studies comparing overt and covert responding revealed thirty-three with no significant difference, eighteen favoring overt responding, four favoring covert, and six containing interactions.[2] These reviews lead to the conclusion that in many situations and with many types of learning overt responses are not necessary. In cases involving psychomotor skills, some practice is obviously necessary. Too, covert response is not synonymous with no response. The learner is still actively involved in the teaching-learning process (Levie & Dickie, 1973).

Ausubel (1968, p. 291) asserted that, "Research findings . . . indicate that subjects who respond covertly not only learn and retain verbal material as well as or better than subjects who construct their responses, but also do so more efficiently in terms of learning time." At the same time, however, Ausubel

---

[2]*Interaction* is a research term implying that some students learn better by one method, while other students learn more by another method.

(1968, p. 276) maintained that, "On theoretical grounds there are many reasons for believing that repetition is typically required not only for the retention of adequately clear, stable, and valid meanings (and often for their acquisition as well), but also for the degree of consolidation of antecedent portions of sequentially organized subject matter that is necessary for efficient learning of subsequent portions."

Mouly (1973) also defends practice as an important variable in the learning process. In his opinion, practice (1) assists in overcoming those factors that cause the student to forget, (2) provides opportunities to modify the existing cognitive structure associated with the information being learned, and (3) gives students a chance to determine their comprehension of the material presented. However, he warns that practice does not necessarily produce improvement and that practice will in all likelihood be of little benefit unless the student understands the purpose of the practice. The best type of practice activity is that involving previously learned material being employed in the acquisition of more advanced work.

Feedback and Reinforcement

External theories of learning stress that learning consists basically of conditioning connections between selected stimuli and desired responses. Reinforcement occupies a central and crucial role in this behavioristic learning strategy. In order for this bond between the stimulus and its response to be formed, the response must be reinforced. With external learning strategies, desired behaviors are reinforced or rewarded. Undesired behaviors are ignored or given negative reinforcement. In no case are the learners' actions examined by the learners for areas in need of improvement. Theorists who hold to a model of learning based on internal mental processes, however, talk in terms of feedback rather than reinforcement. With internal learning strategies, learners are presented a description of the desired learning as they attempt to learn; they are given information delineating what they are doing well and what they are doing poorly. This data supplies the necessary knowledge of performance that enables learners to improve performance. The information received by the learner serves as a guide for altering cognitive structure, which in turn modifies subsequent behavior. Students have less need of feedback during meaningful learning due to the fact that their own comprehension enables them to be more aware of appropriate responses (Mouly, 1973).

External theorists have insisted upon the immediate reinforcement of responses. Recent studies have obtained results indicating that delayed feedback may be just as effective. English and Kinzer (1966, p. 147) found that one-hour and two-hour delays in giving correct responses were superior to immediate reinforcement. They conclude, "It has been assumed for many years that immediate knowledge of results is superior to feedback delay. Such an assumption, however, was based upon the findings of research on lower animals or human learning of motor skills and nonsense verbal material." Sassenrath and Younge (1969) reported that there was no difference between immediate reinforcement and delayed feedback on immediate retention, but that delayed feedback was better for retention. In an experiment by More (1969), there were four feedback groups: immediate, two-and-one-half-hour, one-day, and four-day. The two-and-one-half-hour and one-day groups scored significantly higher on retention than the other two. The author feels that the results indicate that immediate reinforcement "may actually inhibit retention learning."

Some writers stress the role of cognition, as opposed to conditioning, in the reinforcement process. Lampron (1967, p. 1709-B) suggests that many so-called S-R bonds are actually the result of "varying degrees of awareness or implicit self-instruction" in arriving at the desired behavior. Crum's research (1969, p. 3479-B) also supports the role of cognition in acquiring desired responses. His results indicate that "initial instructional set or elicitation procedure" is an important factor in increasing the probability of any given response. Reinforcement alone was less effective. The importance of reinforcement is apparently greater in the case of rote learning than of meaningful learning (Ausubel, 1968).

In a review of the literature related to knowledge of results, Levie and Dickie (1973) reported that the importance of feedback varies depending upon the learner's situation. Feedback is of little value when the students are correct, of slight value when they are in doubt, and of great value if the students' answers are incorrect. Telling the learner what their mistakes are is superior to telling them that they have made a mistake.

Feedback may be of two types: *intrinsic,* which refers to the effect of knowing correctly the material being learned; and *extrinsic,* which has to do with some reward or punishment unrelated to the specific content itself (Glaser & Cooley, 1973). The use of positive reinforcers is a basic component of behavior modification techniques to mold student behavior by external means. The proper use of appropriate reinforcers has long been postulated as a significant factor in student motivation. Studies have been reported in which the use of rewards, such as social approval, has led to gains in achievement. However, the results indicate that different types of reinforcement may be needed with students from different socioeconomic levels. Another study focusing on the effects of delayed and immediate feedback found that delayed feedback produced higher achievement, but that immediate reinforcement was a positive factor in stimulating task perseverance (Della-Piana & Endo, 1973). Although most of the current literature favors the use of rewards rather than punishments, Walker and Buckley (1972) surveyed the literature and could find no convincing preference for either. They determined that punishment and negative feedback can serve to increase effort and motivation.

Acquisition, Retention, and Recall of Information

Clouse (1969) found that the type of cue given had more effect on acquisition and retention than the number of cues. Guthrie (1967) stated that instruction containing rules improved the speed of learning and the retention of material. One writer has suggested that the acquired knowledge is stored in the memory in deep-structure language units (Rohrman, 1968). Two other writers have hypothesized that information is not stored as words at all, but as nonverbal, cognitive representations (Rosenfield, 1968; Johnson, 1968). Once the material has been learned, individual differences in retention are apparently slight (Shuell & Keppel, 1970).

Several factors are influential in the acquisition and retention of knowledge: subsumption, intent to learn, type of material, organization of material, and appropriateness of material. Ausubel and Fitzgerald (1961), in support of Ausubel's theory of subsumption of acquired knowledge into the learner's existing cognitive structure, reported that students who were familiar with Christianity learned more and retained more information after having studied Buddhism. Klausmeier and Ripple (1971, p. 610) quote the results of several studies related to retention and recall. Intent to learn has been found to be an important variable in the acquisition and retention of material. Another factor is the type of material being learned. Ideas are retained much longer and more completely than facts, while facts are retained longer and more completely than nonsense syllables (p. 599). The organization of the material facilitates initial learning and promotes retention (p. 591). Another crucial variable seems to be the appropriateness of the material for each student's level of achievement. Content that is beyond the student's capability is inadequately learned and therefore imperfectly retained (pp. 611–12).

Underwood has divided memory into various types of attributes. The first category includes those attributes independent of the learning task:
1. Temporal attribute, remembering the time something happened.
2. Spatial attribute, remembering where something was located.
3. Frequency attribute, remembering the number of times something occurs.
4. Modality attribute, remembering something through auditory or visual recollection of experience.

The second category consists of those attributes dependent upon the task:
1. Acoustic attribute, remembering something on the basis of its sound.
2. Visual attribute, remembering something on the basis of how it looks.
3. Affective attribute, remembering the feelings associated with some thing or event.

4. Context attribute, remembering the context in which the original learning took place.
5. Verbal attribute, remembering learned material by associating it with words or related words (Klausmeier & Ripple, 1971, 594–98).

Retrieval of learned information is another process that has been studied. The results of a study by Kiess (1968) suggested that new verbal items are incorporated into the individual's language system and that this organization according to language form facilitates the retention of these items. Gellman (1969) concluded that individuals organize material into clusters. This process of storage in clusters improves recall. In addition, evidence indicates that certain types of retrieval are superior to others. A key word often assists the individual to remember the information for which she has been searching. Gagné (1970, p. 471) notes that ". . . Remembering is markedly affected by retrieval at the time of recall, more than it is, perhaps, by events taking place at the time of learning."

Transfer

Knowledge that has been learned, stored, and retrieved must still be applied, or transferred, to other situations. Transfer may be positive or negative, vertical to higher-level situations or lateral to related situations at similar levels of difficulty. The question that has occupied much research has to do with what is transferred. Bruner holds to the lateral transfer of general principles of knowledge and strategies for learning. Gagné believes that only behaviors that are basically similar can be transferred to new situations. Ausubel supports the thesis that it is subject-matter knowledge which is transferred (Shulman & Tamir, 1973). In a study conducted by Rychlak et al. (1974), evidence was found for both positive and negative "nonspecific" transfer.[3] Too, the results revealed transfer of affective factors for which there were no common stimuli or responses.

After reviewing the literature, Overing and Travers (1966) concluded that the "knowledge of a principle" facilitates transfer to situations in which that principle may apply. In their own study, the "verbalization of knowledge" prior to application improved its transfer. In a review of the research, Klausmeier and Davis (1969, p. 1489) cite studies that found that helping the students to identify rules, assisting in stimulus organization, having the students verbalize principles while solving problems, and having the students verbalize a generalization after solving a problem are approaches that facilitate transfer. The authors conclude, "In summary, the major concepts and princi-

---

[3]In other words, it was found that knowledge had been transferred from one context to another. "Specific" transfer would be transfer of identical elements.

ples in a subject field show greater positive transfer to later tasks than does specific information. Abilities, including strategies and learning to learn, facilitate positive transfer to subsequent tasks of the same class and to other classes of tasks."

Wittrock (1963, p. 184) conducted a study in which there were three factors: rule—given or not given; order—example first, rule second, or rule first, example second; and answer—given or not given. There were also four treatments: rule given, answer given; rule given, answer not given; rule not given, answer given; and rule not given, answer not given. The results indicated at a significant level that, "When retention of learned rules or transfer of learned rules to examples is the criterion, giving rules appears to be more effective than either less direction (not giving rules) or more direction (giving rules and giving answers to examples)."

Skanes et al. (1974) report a high correlation between intelligence and transfer. High intelligence makes possible a high level of learning, more meaningful learning, and broader generalizations, which in turn facilitate transfer. However, personality variables such as positive attitudes, strong self-concept, appropriate amount of anxiety, and willingness to participate in new experiences regulate to a large extent the individual's receptivity to learning, his likelihood of retaining information, and his using it in new or related situations (Mouly, 1973). Obviously, the student must have a positive set for learning, remembering, and applying the material being presented.

SPECIFIC STUDIES

Stressing Oral Language Skills

Audio-lingual proponents stressed that language is primarily speech. Therefore, initial and continued emphasis should be placed on listening and speaking. The ear was to be trained before the students were permitted to see the written representations of these sounds. Seeing the printed page prevented the students from developing native-like pronunciation due to the negative influence of the written word.

Listening training   Tezza (1962) found that students who received listening training did not do better than those who read or practiced audio-lingual drills. A related topic is auditory discrimination training. Based on the results of his research, Henning (1966) concluded that students who had been given discrimination training without repetition practice had better pronunciation than those who had imitated a model without discrimination practice. The implications of Henning's findings were expanded by Cook (1965). He hypothesized that in order to prevent errors in the initial learning stages, the teacher should not permit the students to "encode," i.e., to pronounce the sounds they hear. Asking them to pronounce the sounds that they are unable to process mentally necessitates their giving native-language interpretations to these sounds. The author extends this principle to include syntax as well as phonology. He suggests that it may be that students should be given much practice in "decoding" syntax before requiring them to "encode."

The effect of the written word on student pronunciation   In 1956, Richards and Appel reported the results of their study focusing on this aspect of second-language teaching. In both the experimental and control groups, the instruction was the same except that the students in the experimental class saw no written Spanish. They found that the experimental group had higher oral production and pronunciation. The outcome of Muller's study (1964) in Portuguese was similar. He found that being exposed to the written word adversely affected the students' pronunciation.

Two other studies reached an opposite conclusion. Sawyer et al. (1963) reported that having a text was a "slight benefit" in the development of student pronunciation. Estarellas and Regan (1966) contended that the simultaneous presentation of the sound and its graphemic representation helped the students in learning and probably in retention and recall.

Transfer of learning across sense modalities   Related to the insistence upon oral presentation prior to visual, i.e., the natural order of first-language learning, is the problem of transfer of learning across sense modalities. Dunkel (1948) examined a large number of studies and concluded that results of studies comparing transfer as a result of visual versus auditory presentations did not seem to vary greatly, but he indicated that visual presentation was superior in teaching grammar. Later studies on the subject have seemed to divide fairly evenly. Pimsleur, et al. (1964) found that the amount of transfer depended upon the language being learned, the learner, and her stage of development in the process of learning the language. Asher (1964) concluded that, even though there was transfer in both directions in the case of the so-called phonetic languages, in general transfer was greater from visual to auditory.

Prereading period   Lange (1966) studied the effects of a prereading period in beginning French in secondary schools. There were two groups, prereading and ordered introduction to all four skills, in two different schools. After twelve weeks, the prereading group was significantly better in speaking. There was no difference between the two groups in listening, reading, and writing. At the end of a year, there were no differences.

Motivation in classes stressing oral skills   The contention that students are more highly motivated in classes that emphasize listening and speaking has been widely accepted. Agard and Dunkel (1948) stated that, notwithstanding claims to the contrary, the "relentless regularity" of the drills often tires the students. In two studies on the problem of attrition in audio-lingual classes, Mueller and Leutenegger (1964) and Mueller and Harris (1966) concluded that the "drop-out" rate is higher in classes in which the students are forced to rely on only one sense modality in learning and who "have to talk so soon."

Acquiring and Using Structure

Audio-lingual proponents supported the use of pattern drills as a means of conditioning automatic language habits. They also favored an inductive approach to teaching the structures drilled in pattern practice. This position was taken and defended even though ". . . hardly any empirical research can be cited either to support the use of pattern practice drills as contrasted with other variables of teaching grammar, or to indicate what variables control the successes of particular types of drills" (Carroll, 1963, p. 1072).

Since that statement was made, some research involving pattern drills has been done. Torrey (1965) found students taught inductively through pattern practice to be superior to students taught rules and vocabulary. McKinnon (1965) conducted an experiment with two relevant factors: (1) method of practice, and (2) an inductive versus a deductive presentation. The results indicated that active practice before listening to the master tape was superior to listening prior to practice, that practice in which pictures indicated "situational meaning" was superior to no pictures, and that both methods were superior to normal "pattern practice." In addition discovery learning was not as effective as deductive presentation of structure.

McKinnon's findings suggested that active composition prior to hearing the correct answer was important in language practice. In other words, type of practice was found to be more important than mere rate of repetition. An experiment by Lim (1968) produced similar results. The conclusion was that conformation (practice in which the students respond to a stimulus prior to being presented with the correct response) was superior to prompting (practice in which the stimulus and response patterns are presented together).

Often, pattern drills have been viewed as a means of conditioning structural patterns in the language. Meaning was not considered to be important. The drills were not part of a communicative context, nor were they meant to be. In two separate studies, Oller and Obrecht (1968, p. 173) obtained results that contradicted the validity of this conception of pattern practice devoid of any communicative context. In their words, "The data indicate that the separation of 'manipulative-skill' from 'expressive use' in the FL classroom is, at best, highly undesirable." Those students practicing drills in context responded 40 percent faster and scored 17 percent higher in pronunciation.

The findings of a study by Jarvis (1970) support the conclusions of Oller and Obrecht. Jarvis compared two groups of students. In one group, the students practiced with pattern drills in which the object was to manipulate structural forms without reference to particular people, places, or things. In the other group, the students referred to real people, places, and things during the practice periods. They talked about specific rooms, specific classes, specific activities, etc. At the end of one semester, there were no significant differences between the two groups in listening and reading, but the students in the contextualized practice groups had significantly higher achievement scores in speaking and writing. In other words, those students who had practiced using language in communicative contexts were better able to originate needed language utterances to express meaning.

In a study dealing with the functionalization of structure as a vehicle for communication, Savignon (1972) examined the effects of three treatments: one hour per week learning to communicate in French, one hour per week studying aspects of French culture in English, and one hour per week practicing French structure in the language laboratory. During the other class periods the students were involved in similar activities. At the end of the study there were no differences among the three groups in listening, reading, or final course grade. The students who had spent one hour per week communicating in French were significantly superior on the instructor's evaluation of oral skill and on a test of communicative competence. Savignon also suggests that a distinction should be made between communicative competence and linguistic competence.

In a recent study that has far-reaching implications for the acquisition of structure, Hosenfeld (1973) asked students to think aloud while doing exercises for their French class. The solicitation of learner strategies by means of retrospection and introspection indicated that often a great disparity exists between what teachers think the students are learning from doing a specific exercise and what is actually going through their minds. Often neither the entire sentence nor its meaning is even considered while an exercise is being completed. Instead the students, in a typically human fashion, seem to search for some insight that will allow them to complete the task with the minimum amount of information and effort.

METHODOLOGICAL COMPARISONS

Broad comparisons between methods of teaching in all academic areas are criticized due to the fact that so many of the results indicate no significant differences. Surveys have confirmed that few studies find significant variations among groups. There are at least two plausible explanations for this state of affairs. First, experimental design is not sophisticated enough at present to control all the variables involved. Until educational research reaches a higher level of development, conservative interpretations of trends may have to suffice as indicators of superiority or inferiority of different teaching methods. Additional support for favoring differences can be gained by replicating the original study. Second, in some problem areas, such as sense modality preference, no significant differences should be expected. If some students prefer to learn with their ears and some prefer to learn with their eyes, a random sample should distribute these two preference groups equally into the experimental and control classes. Other factors being equal, the effects of this preference for learning equally distributed in both groups should counterbalance the effects of the other. A plausible and more productive alternative would be to place all those students preferring visual learning in a given section and teach them via visual materials. All those students favoring auditory learning should be placed in another section and taught by procedures emphasizing aural learning. For example, Chastain (1969) found that results, although tentative, of a statistical analysis indicated that on the basis of selected predictors it would be possible to select those students who would be more likely to succeed in an audio-lingual class and those who would be more likely to do better in a cognitive class. Of course, in such a situation there might still be no difference in achievement between groups, but one would suspect that overall achievement would be much higher. (For a description of studies on audio-lingual teaching, see chapter 5, pages 124–26. For a description of studies on cognitive teaching, see chapter 6, pages 157–59.)

In short, methodological comparisons occupy an important, although not unique, position in research in second-language education. Such studies are needed for several reasons:

1. Teachers in the classroom can identify more readily with the procedures and results that relate directly to the classroom situation.
2. Comparisons of different classroom methods in their descriptive forms can be used to survey emphases in the classroom.
3. Methodological comparisons can temper the exaggerated claims of over-zealous supporters of innovative materials and procedures and provide an objective perspective to a subjective task.
4. Although the problems of language teaching can be approached by examining selected variables in isolation, the researcher can also begin with broad methodological studies and vary selected factors in subsequent tests. Approaching the questions confronting second-language education from both angles seems preferable to the exclusive use of one or the other.

APTITUDE-TREATMENT INTERACTION

As was implied in the research conducted by Chastain (1969) and discussed in the preceding section, the important question is not which method of teaching is better, but which method is better for which students. Education should concern itself with determining the most efficient fit between the teaching-learning situation and the learner. In line with this need, a major focus in recent classroom research has been on the interaction between the instructional program and learner characteristics. An aptitude-treatment interaction occurs when one type of student achieves more in one approach while another type does better in another approach. Obviously, the ideal situation would be to place students, by means of diagnostic tests, into programs that correspond most closely to their abilities, needs, and interests.

In addition to the several instances of aptitude-treatment interaction that have been mentioned previously in this chapter in relation to other topics, additional cases of interaction have been, and are being, found. Gage and Berliner (1975) refer to a comparison by McNeil in which boys learned better by machine than girls, but girls learned better in the regular classroom taught by a woman teacher. The authors also summarize results of an investigation of beginning reading instruction conducted by Stallings and Keepes that indicated that students with high auditory ability learn to read better using a linguistic method. Students low in auditory ability learned more in a whole-word method.[4] This study also revealed that students beginning with higher scores for vocabulary and concepts achieved more with a linguistic approach while students having lower scores on vocabulary and concepts did better with the whole-word method. Dowaliby and Schumer (1973) found that students high in anxiety did significantly better in teacher-centered classes while students low in anxiety did significantly better in student-centered discussion groups. The results of this study suggested two types of students: (1) independent achievement motivation and (2) conforming achievement motivation. Each type of student preferred a teacher of her own type. Rhetts (1974) obtained results indicating that impulsive learners respond more quickly and make fewer errors on easy tasks while reflective learners respond more slowly but make fewer errors on difficult tasks. Kirkpatrick (1974) reported that introverted students tend to do better in IPI and that extroverted students tend to do better in lecture-discussion classes.[5]

Wood and McCurdy (1974) investigated the achievement of students with varying degrees of "skills of self-direction" as they participated in a science

---

[4]In a *linguistic* approach, students study parts of words as a means of learning to read, while in the *whole-word* method they learn to read words.

[5]IPI (Individually Prescribed Instruction) is a highly organized and complex type of individualized instruction developed at the University of Pittsburgh by Glaser et al.

program characterized by continuous progress and self-pacing through eighty LAPs containing behavioral objectives. The results of the study indicated that success in such a program depends upon the ability of the students to direct their own learning, i.e., to operate independently of the teacher, to use class time effectively, to plan a work schedule, to use study skills, to use the curriculum materials, and to work up to the level of their abilities. Ramey and Piper (1974) studied the effect of open and traditional classrooms on student creativity. They mention two other studies, one by Haddon and Lytton and one by Stuckey and Langevin, which concluded that students scored higher on creativity scales after having studied in a traditional classroom or in informal discussion situations than in an open classroom. In their own study, students in an open classroom situation scored higher on all measures of figural creativity, while students in a traditional classroom did better on all measures of verbal creativity. Allen et al. (1974) reported that students with an external locus of control contracted for and received lower grades, began their work more slowly, were more anxious, and performed less well on written exams than their internal locus of control classmates.

Aptitude-treatment interactions have been obtained in studies comparing the audio-lingual and cognitive methods in second-language education. Studies by Chastain (1969), Chastain and Woerdehoff (1968), Kelly (1965), Mueller (1971a), and Mueller (1971b) have indicated that high-aptitude students have higher achievement scores in a cognitively based instructional system while low-aptitude students have higher achievement in a audio-lingual system. Such results lend strong support to the need to provide different types of learning material and learning situations for different types of learners.

FUTURE RESEARCH

Past research has not provided definite answers for solving classroom learning difficulties. However, it has established a more realistic basis for future research, and it has broadened our vision and indicated paths that might profitably be explored. Studies in the future may well center around the following:

1. Individual differences in the cognitive, affective, social, and psychomotor domains.
2. Interaction among the various learner characteristics in each of these domains with a wide range of teaching-learning materials and situations.
3. Development, selection and implementation of programs designed to provide instruction best suited to meet individual needs, i.e., seeking

maximum efficiency and achievement in learning based on the knowledge obtained in points 1 and 2.

4. Innovative programs to which the students can relate and for which they can see a purpose.
5. Establishing and maintaining a positive self-concept during the time needed to learn a second language.
6. Applying meaningful learning and practice principles to second-language learning.
7. Ways and means of developing language skills at the "real" language level.
8. Improving methods of evaluation and measurement, especially in the area of "real" language skills.

CONCLUSION

In spite of the fact that the results have often been inconsistent, inconclusive, and even controversial, a great deal of progress has been made in educational research. However, research that broadens the vision also reveals new questions remaining to be answered. As the search for the one best teaching method has given way to the search for the most suitable method for particular students or types of students, the numbers of questions have multiplied. Moving into the area of learner characteristics in the affective-social domain has opened up a vast new territory for exploration. The problems in need of answers continue to be more and more complex, but the fact that more questions have been envisioned expands the opportunities for encountering hidden answers and for developing subsequent solutions to current problems. In this sense, future researchers have a more solid and extensive base from which to originate their investigations than those of the past, and education has much to gain from the positive results.

REVIEW AND APPLICATION

DEFINITIONS

1. advance organizers, p. 79
2. affective variables, p. 68
3. aptitude-treatment interaction, p. 91
4. cognition, p. 74
5. cognitive style, p. 75
6. discovery learning, p. 78
7. feedback vs. reinforcement, p. 82
8. intelligence, p. 74
9. meaningful learning, p. 77
10. overt vs. covert responses, p. 80
11. self-concept, p. 69
12. subsumption, p. 79
13. transfer, p. 85

DISCUSSION

1. How did you feel when you first started learning a second language? How did your friends feel? Did any of you have problems with shattered self-concepts?
2. What are the basic student personality characteristics? Which are most important in second-language learning?
3. What motivates students? Which are internal and which are external motivators?
4. What are the various components of the affective-social and cognitive domains?
5. Discuss the individual differences in the affective-social and cognitive domains. Include any others discussed in other classes.
6. Summarize in three or four sentences the general trend of research relating to learning in each of the following: meaningful learning; practice; feedback and reinforcement; acquisition, retention, and recall; and transfer.
7. Is it better to start second-language learning with the written word or with the spoken language?
8. What is the objective of aptitude-treatment interaction? What are some of the findings to date?
9. What additions would you add to the list of suggested emphases in future research?

ACTIVITIES

1. Survey some of the journal articles listed in the Selected References section of this chapter to determine what new research information has been uncovered since the publication of this text.
2. Identify and examine some prepared materials for determining and assessing individual cognitive, affective, and social differences. Discuss how each might be used as a basis for developing teaching-learning strategies.
3. List existing problems in second-language teaching and learning that need to be researched.

SELECTED REFERENCES

Agard, F. B., and Dunkel, H. B. (1948) *An Investigation of Second-Language Teaching.* Boston: Ginn.

Alegre, C., and Murray, E. J. (1974) Locus of Control, Behavioral Intention, and Verbal Conditioning. *Journal of Personality,* 42:668–81.

Allen, G. J., et al. (1974) Locus of Control, Test Anxiety, and Student Performance in a Personalized Instruction Course. *Journal of Educational Psychology,* 66: 968–73.

Alvord, D. J., and Glass, L. W. (1974) Relationships Between Academic Achievement and Self-Concept. *Science Education,* 58:175–79.

Anderson, R. C. (1970) Control of Student Mediating Processes During Verbal Learning and Instruction. *Review of Educational Research,* 40:349–69.

Asher, J. J. (1964) Vision and Audition in Language Learning. *Perceptual and Motor Skills,* 19:255–300.

Ausubel, D. P. (1968) *Educational Psychology: A Cognitive View.* New York: Holt, Rinehart & Winston. Pp. 137, 276, 291, 316, 319, 497, 504.

Ausubel, D. P., and Fitzgerald, D. (1961) The Role of Discriminability in Meaningful Verbal Learning and Retention. *Journal of Educational Psychology,* 52:266–74.

Ausubel, D. P., and Robinson, F. G. (1969) *School Learning: An Introduction to Educational Psychology.* New York: Holt, Rinehart & Winston. Pp. 216, 251, 357–59.

Baker, P. J.; Bakshis, R.; and Tolone, W. (1974) Diversifying Learning Opportunities: A Response to the Problems of Mass Education. *Research in Higher Education,* 2:255–57.

Bernstein, B. E. (1974) Tailoring Teaching to Learning Styles. *Independent School Bulletin,* 34:50–52.

Birkmaier, E. M. (1960) Modern Languages. In C. W. Harris (Ed.), *Encyclopedia of Educational Research.* New York: Macmillan. Pp. 861–88.

Birkmaier, E. M. (1973) Research on Teaching Foreign Languages. In R. M. W. Travers (Ed.), *Second Handbook of Research on Teaching.* Chicago: Rand McNally. Pp. 1280–1302.

Blumenthal, A. L. (1967) Promoted Recall of Sentences. *Journal of Verbal Learning and Verbal Behavior,* 6:203–6.

Blumenthal, A. L., and Boakes, R. (1967) Prompted Recall of Sentences. *Journal of Verbal Learning and Verbal Behavior,* 6:674–76.

Borden, R., and Hendrick, C. (1973) Internal-External Locus of Control and Self-Perception Theory. *Journal of Personality,* 41:32–41.

Briggs, L. J., and Hamilton, N. R. (1964) Meaningful Learning and Retention: Practice and Feedback Variables. *Review of Educational Research,* 34:546.

Brinkman, E. H. (1973) Personality Correlates of Educational Set in the Classroom. *Journal of Educational Research,* 66:221.

Brown, J. A., and MacDougall, M. A. (1973) Teacher Consultation for Improved Feelings of Self-Adequacy in Children. *Psychology in the Schools,* 10:320–26.

Brown, R. K., and Richard, W. C. (1972) Social Responsibility and Its Correlates Among Normal and Behaviorally Disordered Children. *Psychology in the Schools,* 9:52–55.

Bruch, C. B. (1971) The Gifted Child. In D. W. Allen and E. Seifman (Eds.), *The Teacher's Handbook.* Chicago: Scott Foresman. Pp. 119–30.

Carroll, J. B. (1963) Research on Teaching Foreign Languages. In N. L. Gage (Ed.), *Handbook of Research on Teaching.* Chicago: Rand McNally. Pp. 1060–1100.

Carroll, J. B. (1966) Research in Foreign Language Teaching: The Last Five Years. In R. G. Mead, Jr. (Ed.), *Language Teaching: Broader Contexts.* Modern Language Association of America. Pp. 12–42.

Carroll, J. B. (1969) Modern Languages. In R. L. Ebel (Ed.), *Encyclopedia of Educational Research.* (4th ed.) New York: Macmillan. Pp. 866–78.

Carroll, J. B. (1974) Learning Theory for the Classroom Teacher. In G. A. Jarvis (Ed.), *The Challenge of Communication.* Skokie, Ill.: National Textbook. Pp. 113–49.

Chalmers, D. K., and Rosenbaum, M. E. (1974) Learning by Observing Versus Learning by Doing. *Journal of Educational Psychology,* 66:216–24.

Chastain, K. (1969) Prediction of Success in Audio-Lingual and Cognitive Classes. *Language Learning,* 19:27–39.

Chastain, K. (1975) Affective and Ability Factors in Second-Language Learning. *Language Learning,* 25:153–61.

Chastain, K., and Woerdehoff, F. J. (1968) A Methodological Study Comparing the Audio-Lingual Habit Theory and the Cognitive Code-Learning Theory. *Modern Language Journal,* 52:268–79.

Clark, L. L., et al. (1960) Repetition and Associative Learning. *American Journal of Psychology,* 73:22–40.

Clouse, B. B. (1969) The Effect of Selected Cues in the Acquisition and Retention of Four Meaningful C-V-C Trigrams. *Dissertation Abstracts,* 29:3867-A.

Cofer, C. N., and Appley, M. H. (1964) *Motivation: Theory and Research.* New York: Wiley. P. 808.

Cook, H. R. (1965) Pre-Speech Auditory Training: Its Contribution to Second Language Teaching and Motivation for Continuous Broadcasting. Ph.D. diss., Indiana University.

Crum, B. C., Jr. (1969) The Effects of Set, Awareness, and Reinforcement on the Acquisition and Extinction of a Conditioned Response. *Dissertation Abstracts,* 29:3479-B.

Davis, W. L., and Davis, D. E. (1972) Internal-External Control and Attribution of Responsibility for Success and Failure. *Journal of Personality,* 40:123–36.

Dawson, M. E. (1967) Human GSR Classical Conditioning and Awareness of the CS-UCS Relation. *Dissertation Abstracts,* 28:1705-B.

Della-Piana, G. M., and Endo, G. T. (1973) Reading Research. In R. M. W. Travers (Ed.), *Second Handbook of Research on Teaching.* Chicago: Rand McNally. Pp. 908–9.

Denny, D. R. (1974) Relationship of Three Cognitive Style Dimensions to Elementary Reading Abilities. *Journal of Educational Psychology,* 66:702–9.

Dowality, F. J., and Schumer, H. (1973) Teacher-Centered Versus Student-Centered Mode of Classroom Instruction as Related to Manifest Anxiety. *Journal of Educational Psychology,* 64:125–32.

Dubois, E. A. C. (1967) Induction and Deduction. *Dissertation Abstracts,* 28:492-A.

Dunkel, H. B. (1948) *Second Language Learning.* Boston: Ginn. P. 119.

Egan, D. E., and Greeno, J. G. (1973) Acquiring Cognitive Structure by Discovery and Rule Learning. *Journal of Educational Psychology,* 64:85–97.

English, R. A., and Kinzer, J. R. (1966) The Effect of Immediate and Delayed Feedback on Retention of Subject Matter. *Psychology in the Schools,* 3:143–47.

Estarellas, J., and Regan, T. F., Jr. (1966) Effects of Teaching Sounds as Letters Simultaneously at the Very Beginning of a Basic Foreign Language Course. *Language Learning,* 16:173–82.

Estes, W. K. (1960) Learning Theory and the New "Mental Chemistry." *Psychological Review,* 67:207–23.

Farnham-Diggory, S. (1972) *Cognitive Processes in Education: A Psychological Preparation for Teaching and Curriculum Development.* New York: Harper & Row. Pp. 256–85.

Flanders, J. P. (1968) A Review of Résearch on Imitative Behavior. *Psychological Bulletin,* 69:316–37.

Francis, E. W. (1975) Grade Level and Task Difficulty in Learning by Discovery and Verbal Reception Methods. *Journal of Educational Psychology,* 67:146–50.

Frederick, W. C., and Klausmeier, H. J. (1970) Cognitive Styles: A Description. *Educational Leadership,* 27:668–72.

Gage, N. L., and Berliner, D. C. (1975) *Educational Psychology.* Chicago: Rand McNally. Pp. 183–87.

Gagné, R. M. (1970) Some New Views of Learning and Instruction. *Phi Delta Kappan,* 51:470–71.

Gellman, E. S. (1969) Clustering as a Factor in Recall. *Dissertation Abstracts,* 29:3504-B.

Getzels, J. W., and Dillon, J. T. (1973) The Nature of Giftedness and the Education of the Child. In R. M. W. Travers (Ed.), *Second Handbook of Research on Teaching.* Chicago: Rand McNally. P. 696.

Glaser, R., and Cooley, W. M. (1973) Instrumentation For Teaching and Instructional Management. In R. M. W. Travers (Ed.), *Second Handbook of Research on Teaching.* Chicago: Rand McNally. P. 837.

Goor, A. (1974) Problem Solving Processes of Creative and Non-Creative Students. *Dissertation Abstracts International,* 35:3517-A.

Gordon, I. J. (1969) Social and Emotional Development. In R. L. Ebel (Ed.), *Encyclopedia of Educational Research*. (4th ed.) New York: Macmillan. Pp. 1221–30.

Guthrie, J. T. (1967) Expository Instruction Versus a Discovery Method. *Journal of Educational Psychology,* 58:45–49.

Hancock, R. R. (1975) Cognitive Factors and Their Interaction with Instructional Mode. *Journal for Research in Mathematics Education,* 6:37–50.

Hauptman, P. C. (1971) A Structural Approach vs. A Situational Approach to Foreign-Language Teaching. *Language Learning,* 21:235–44.

Henning, W. A. (1966) Discrimination Training and Self-Evaluation in the Teaching of Pronunciation. *International Review of Applied Linguistics,* 4:7–17.

Hosenfeld, C. (1973 and 1974) Learning about Learning: Discovering Our Students' Strategies. Revised and expanded version of a paper presented at the 1973 and 1974 ACTFL Conventions.

Jarvis, G. A. (1970) A Comparison of Contextualized Practice with Particularized Referents vs. Practice with Generic Meaning in the Teaching of Beginning College French. Ph.D. diss., Purdue University.

Johnson, D. W., and Johnson, R. T. (1974) Instructional Goal Structure: Cooperative, Competitive, or Individualistic. *Review of Educational Research,* 44:214.

Johnson, M. G. (1968) The Distribution Aspects of Meaning Interaction in A-Grammatical Verbal Contexts. *Dissertation Abstracts,* 29:1859-B.

Johnson, N. F. (1965) The Psychological Reality of Phrase-Structure Rules. *Journal of Verbal Learning and Verbal Behavior,* 4:469–75.

Johnston, M. C. (1961) Foreign Language Instruction. *Review of Educational Research,* 31:188–96.

Kagan, J. (1971) Controversies in Intelligence: The Meaning of Intelligence. In D. W. Allen and E. Seifman (Eds.), *The Teacher's Handbook.* Glenview, Ill.: Scott Foresman. Pp. 655–57.

Kelly, L. (1965) *A Comparison of the Monostructural and Polystructural Approaches to the Teaching of College French.* Ph.D. diss., Purdue University.

Kiess, H. O. (1968) The Effects of Natural Language Mediation on Short-Term Memory. *Dissertation Abstracts,* 28:3494-B.

Kirkpatrick, D. A. (1974) The Relationship of Personality Structure and Methods of Instruction to Academic Achievement. *Dissertation Abstracts International,* 35:3483-A.

Klausmeier, H. J., and Davis, J. K. (1969) Transfer of Learning. In R. L. Ebel (Ed.), *Encyclopedia of Educational Research.* (4th ed.) New York: Macmillan. Pp. 1483–93.

Klausmeier, H. J., and Ripple, R. E. (1971) *Learning and Human Abilities: Educational Psychology.* (3rd ed.) New York: Harper & Row. Pp. 50, 445, 591, 594–99, 610–12.

Kohn, M., and Rosman, B. L. (1974) Social-Emotional, Cognitive, and Demographic Determinants of Poor School Achievement: Implications for a Strategy of Intervention. *Journal of Educational Psychology,* 66:267–76.

Krovetz, M. L. (1974) Explaining Success or Failure as a Function of One's Locus of Control. *Journal of Personality,* 42:159–74.

Lambert, W. E. (1963) Psychological Approaches to the Study of Language Part II: On Second Language Learning and Bilingualism. *Modern Language Journal,* 47:114.

Lambert, W. E., and Jakobovits, L. A. (1960) Verbal Satiation and Changes in the Intensity of Meaning. *Journal of Experimental Psychology,* 60:376–83.

Lampron, D. R. (1967) Cognitive Qualities of the Reinforcing Features of Response Contingent Stimuli. *Dissertation Abstracts,* 8:1709-B.

Landry, R. G. (1973) The Relationship of Second Language Learning and Verbal Creativity. *Modern Language Journal,* 57:110–13.

Lange, D. L. (1966) An Evaluation of Pre-Reading Instruction in Beginning French in Secondary Schools. *Dissertation Abstracts,* 27:1710-A.

Laughlin, P. R. (1969) Selection Versus Reception Concept Attainment Paradigms as a Function of Memory, Concept Rule, and Concept Universe. *Journal of Educational Psychology,* 60:267–73.

Lawler, J., and Selinker, L. (1971) On Paradoxes, Rules, and Research in Second-Language Learning. *Language Learning,* 21:27–43.

Levenson, H., and LeUnes, A. (1974) Students' Evaluation of an Instructor: Effects of Similarity of Attitudes. *Psychological Reports,* 34:1074.

Levie, W. H., and Dickie, K. E. (1973) The Analysis and Application of Media. In R. M. W. Travers (Ed.), *Second Handbook of Research on Teaching.* Chicago: Rand McNally. Pp. 876–77.

Lim, K-B. (1968) *Prompting vs. Confirmation, Pictures vs. Translations, and Other Variables in Children's Learning of Grammar in a Second Language.* Princeton, N.J.: Educational Testing Service.

Lipe, D., and Jung, S. M. (1971) Manipulating Incentives to Enhance School Learning. *Review of Educational Research,* 41:253.

McClelland, D. C., and Watson, R. I., Jr. (1973) Power Motivation and Risk Taking Behavior. *Journal of Personality,* 41:121–31.

Machr, M. L., and Sjogren, D. D. (1971) Atkinson's Theory of Achievement Motivation: First Step Toward a Theory of Academic Motivation? *Review of Educational Research,* 41:155.

McKinnon, K. (1965) An Experimental Study of the Learning of Syntax in Second Language Learning. Ph.D. diss., Harvard University.

Mahmoudi, H. M., and Snibbe, J. R. (1974) Manipulating Expectancy in the Affective Domain and its Effects on Achievement, Intelligence, and Personality. *Psychology in the Schools,* 11:449–57.

Mascolo, R. P. (1967) Key Conceptual Schemes and Inquiry Training: Some Effects upon New Learning. *Dissertation Abstracts,* 28:1345–A.

Meinke, D. L.; George, C. S.; and Wilkinson, J. M. (1975) Concrete and Abstract Thinkers at Three Grade Levels and Their Performance with Complex Concepts. *Journal of Educational Psychology,* 66:154–58.

More, A. J. (1969) Delay of Feedback and the Acquisition and Retention of Verbal Materials in the Classroom. *Journal of Educational Psychology,* 60:339–42.

Mouly, G. J. (1973) *Psychology for Effective Teaching.* (3rd ed.) New York: Holt, Rinehart & Winston. Pp. 166–67, 222, 257, 312–13, 338.

Mueller, T. (1971a) Could the New Key be a Wrong Key? *French Review,* 44:1085–93.

Mueller, T. (1971b) The Effectiveness of Two Learning Models: The Audio-Lingual Habit Theory and the Cognitive Code-Learning Theory. In P. Pimsleur and T. Quinn (Eds.), *The Psychology of Second Language Learning.* London: Cambridge University Press. Pp. 113–22.

Mueller, T. H., and Harris, R. (1966) The Effect of an Audio-Lingual Program on Drop-Out Rate. *Modern Language Journal,* 50:133–37.

Mueller, T. H., and Leutenegger, R. R. (1964) Some Inferences About an Intensified Oral Approach to the Teaching of French Based on a Study of Course Drop-Outs. *Modern Language Journal,* 48:91–94.

Muller, D. H. (1964) A Study of the Effects on Pronunciation and Intonation of Accompanying Audio-Lingual Drill with Exposure to the Written Word. *Dissertation Abstracts,* 24:5414.

Murdock, B. B., Jr., and Babick, A. J. (1961) The Effect of Repetition on the Retention of Individual Words. *American Journal of Psychology,* 74:596–601.

Noar, G. (1972) *Individualized Instruction: Every Child A Winner.* New York: Wiley. P. 3.

Norland, F. H.; Lawson, A. E.; Kahle, J. B. (1974) A Study of Levels of Concrete and Formal Reasoning Ability in Disadvantaged Junior and Senior High School Science Students. *Science Education*, 58:569–75.

Nostrand, H. L., et al. (1962) *Research on Language Teaching: An Annotated International Bibliography for 1945–1961*. Seattle: University of Washington Press.

Oller, J. W., Jr., and Obrecht, D. H. (1968) Pattern Drill and Communicative Activity: A Psycholinguistic Experiment. *International Review of Applied Linguistics*, 6:165–74.

Oller, J. W., Jr., and Obrecht, D. H. (1969) The Psycholinguistic Principle of Informational Sequence. *International Review of Applied Linguistics*, 7:117–23.

Ornstein, J., and Lado, R. (1967) Research in Foreign Language Teaching Methodology. *International Review of Applied Linguistics*, 5:11–25.

Overing, R. L. R., and Travers, R. M. W. (1966) Effect upon Transfer of Variations in Training Conditions. *Journal of Educational Psychology*, 57:179–88.

Pimsleur, P., et al. (1964) Further Study of the Transfer of Verbal Materials Across Sense Modalities. *Journal of Educational Psychology*, 55:96–102.

Pines, H. A., and Julian, J. W. (1972) Effects of Task and Social Demands on Locus of Control Differences in Information Processing. *Journal of Personality*, 40:407–16.

Posner, M. I., and Keele, S. W. (1973) Skill Learning. In R. M. W. Travers (Ed.), *Second Handbook of Research on Teaching*. Chicago: Rand McNally. Pp. 805–25.

Prawer, F. H. (1974) The Self-Concept as Related to Achievement in Foreign Language Study. *American Foreign Language Teacher*, 4:7–10.

Ramey, C. T., and Piper, V. (1974) Creativity in Open and Traditional Classrooms. *Child Development*, 45:557–60.

Ramirez, M., Jr., and Price-Williams, D. R. (1974) Cognitive Styles of Children of Three Ethnic Groups in the United States. *Journal of Cross Cultural Psychology*, 5:212–19.

Rest, J. R. (1973) The Hierarchical Nature of Moral Judgment: A Study of Patterns of Comprehension and Preference of Moral Stages. *Journal of Personality*, 41:86–109.

Rhetts, J. E. (1974) Task, Learner and Treatment Variables on Instructional Design. *Journal of Educational Psychology*, 66:339–47.

Richards, S. E., and Appel, J. E. (1956) Effects of Written Words in Beginning Spanish. *Modern Language Journal*, 40:129–33.

Rock, I. (1957) The Role of Repetition in Associative Learning. *American Journal of Psychology*, 70:186–93.

Rohrman, N. L. (1968) The Role of Syntactic Structure in the Recall of Sentences. *Dissertation Abstracts*, 28:3905-B.

Rosenfield, J. B. (1968) Information Processing: Encoding and Decoding. *Dissertation Abstracts*, 28:3065-B.

Rosenthal, T. L., and Zimmerman, B. J. (1973) Organization, Observation, and Guided Practice in Concept Attainment and Generalization. *Child Development*, 44:606–13.

Rutherford, W. E. (1968) Deep and Surface Structure, and the Language Drill. *Teachers of English to Speakers of Other Languages*: 71–79.

Rychlak, J. F.; Tuan, N. D.; and Schneider, W. E. (1974) Formal Discipline Revisited: Affective Assessment and Nonspecific Transfer. *Journal of Educational Psychology*, 66:139–51.

Salomon, G. (1972) Heuristic Models for the Generation of Aptitude-Treatment Interaction Hypotheses. *Review of Educational Research*, 42:329.

Sassenrath, J. M., and Yonge, C. D. (1969) Effects of Delayed Information Feedback and Feedback Cues in Learning on Delayed Retention. *Journal of Educational Psychology*, 60:174–77.

Savignon, S. J. (1972) *Communicative Competence: An Experiment in Foreign-Language Teaching*. Philadelphia: Center for Curriculum Development.

Sawyer, J. (1964) Foreign Language Instruction. *Review of Educational Research*, 34:203–10.

Sawyer, J., et al. (1963) The Utility of Translation and Written Symbols During the First Thirty Hours of Language Study. *International Review of Applied Linguistics,* 1:157–92.

Sax, G. (1969) Concept Formation. In R. L. Ebel (Ed.), *Encyclopedia of Educational Research* (4th ed.). New York: Macmillan. P. 198.

Schwartz, L. L. (1972) *Educational Psychology: Focus on the Learner.* Boston: Holbrook Press.

Scott, N. C., Jr. (1973) Cognitive Style and Inquiry Strategy: A Five-Year Study. *Journal of Research in Science Teaching,* 10:323.

Shuell, T. J., and Keppel, G. (1970) Learning Ability and Retention. *Journal of Educational Psychology,* 61:59–65.

Shulman, L. S., and Tamir, P. (1973) Research on Teaching in the Natural Sciences. In R. M. W. Travers (Ed.), *Second Handbook of Research on Teaching.* Chicago: Rand McNally. Pp. 1098–1148.

Skanes, C. R., et al. (1974) Intelligence and Transfer: Aptitude by Treatment Interaction. *Journal of Educational Psychology,* 66:563–68.

Slock, J. A. (1975) Evaluation of the Effectiveness of Advance Organizers in a Medical Microbiology Course. *Dissertation Abstracts International,* 35:4274-A.

Smith, F. J. (1968) Rule Learning in a Miniature Linguistic System. *Dissertation Abstracts,* 28:4784-B.

Stiles, J. A., and McCandless, B. (1969) Child Development. In R. L. Ebel (Ed.), *Encyclopedia of Educational Research* (4th ed.). New York: Macmillan. P. 121.

Temple, J. G. (1974) Information Processing Preference and the Learning of Motor Tasks. *Dissertation Abstracts International,* 35:3496-A.

Tezza, J. S. (1962) The Effects of Listening Training on Audio-Lingual Learning. *Dissertation Abstracts,* 23:2035.

Thorsland, M. N., and Novak, J. D. (1974) The Identification and Significance of Intuitive and Analytic Problem Solving Approaches Among College Physics Students. *Science Education,* 58:245–64.

Torrey, J. W. (1965) *The Learning of Grammar: An Experimental Study.* Washington, D. C.: Public Health Service Research Grant No. 07167.

Walker, H. M., and Buckley, N. K. (1972) Effects of Reinforcement, Punishment, and Feedback Upon Academic Response Rate. *Psychology in the Schools,* 9:186–93.

Walters, L., and Sieben, G. (1974) Cognitive Style and Learning Science in Elementary Schools. *Science Education,* 58:66, 73.

Weiner, B. (1969) Motivation. In R. L. Ebel (Ed.), *Encyclopedia of Educational Research* (4th ed.). New York: Macmillan. Pp. 878–88.

Weiner, B. (1972) Attribution Theory, Achievement Motivation, and the Educational Process. *Review of Educational Research,* 42:335.

Wertheimer, M., and Gillis, W. M. (1958) Satiation and the Rate of Lapse of Verbal Meaning. *Journal of General Psychology,* 59:79–85.

Wheeler, R., and Ryan, F. L. (1973) Effects of Cooperative and Competitive Classroom Environments on the Attitudes and Achievement of Elementary School Students Engaged in Social Studies Inquiry Activities. *Journal of Educational Psychology,* 65:402–7.

Witkin, B. R. (1969) Auditory Perception—Implications for Language Development. *Journal of Research and Development in Education,* 3:53.

Wittrock, M. C. (1963) Verbal Stimuli in Concept Formation: Learning by Discovery. *Journal of Educational Psychology,* 54:183–90.

Wolk, S., and DuCette, J. (1973) The Moderating Effect of Locus of Control in Relation to Achievement Motivation. *Journal of Personality,* 41:59–70.

Wood, F. H., and McCurdy, D. W. (1974) An Analysis of Characteristics of Self-Directedness as Related to Success in an Individualized Continuous Progress Course in Chemistry and Physics. *School Science and Mathematics,* 74:382–88.

Young, L. C. (1975) The Effects of Advance and Post Organization on the Learning and Retention of Prose Material. *Dissertation Abstracts International*, 35:4269-A.

Zimmerman, B. J., and Rosenthal, T. L. (1974) Observational Learning of Rule-Governed Behavior by Children. *Psychological Bulletin*, 81:29–42.

AUDIO-LINGUAL THEORY AND TEACHING

Antecedents to the Audio-Lingual Approach
>The Grammar-Translation Method
>Influences from Psychology
>Influences from Linguistics
>Resulting Theories of Language and Learning

Implications for Language Teaching
>Behavioristic Psychology
>Descriptive Linguistics

Basic Tenets of the Audio-Lingual Approach

Audio-Lingual Teaching
>Audio-Lingual Textbooks
>>Presenting New Material
>>Transformation Pattern Drills
>>Application Activities
>Proceeding Through the Text
>Classroom Procedures
>>The Dialog
>>Pattern Drilling
>>Application Activities

Research on Audio-Lingual Approaches to Second-Language Learning
>Favoring the Audio-Lingual Approach
>Containing Reservations
>Advantages for Both

INTRODUCTION

The audio-lingual movement, which was to revolutionize second-language teaching in the United States, originated among experimental psychologists trying to establish their discipline as an exact science and cultural anthropologists and linguists studying unwritten Indian languages. As the ideas of these developing fields became more widely disseminated and as the need for second-language speakers became more widely recognized, a widespread reaction against grammar-translation procedures occurred. Stimulated by favorable public opinion and readily available public monies, the audio-lingual approach rapidly assumed a position of favor in second-language teaching. However, even though the proposed techniques and classroom procedures were eagerly adopted by teachers anxious for a change, the basic tenets were little understood. The purpose of this chapter is to outline the basic philosophy underlying audio-lingual theory.

ANTECEDENTS TO THE AUDIO-LINGUAL APPROACH

The Grammar-Translation Method

The first step in comprehending the direction second-language teaching took in the fifties is to consider the grammar-translation method of language teaching that preceded it. The audio-lingual approach was the outgrowth of a swing away from the traditional methodology employed to teach Latin and Greek. Modern languages had been established in the curriculum under the guise of the classical approach to language teaching. The problem was that the profession later neglected to revamp its procedures to keep them in line with evolving objectives. The times and rationale changed, but the techniques did not change. Grammar-translation teaching satisfied the desires of the "mental faculties" school of thought and the traditional humanistic orientation, which placed primary emphasis on the *belles-lettres* of the country, but it did not prove to be entirely suitable to the world that emerged after World War II.

The primary purpose of the grammar-translation method of the thirties, forties, and fifties was to prepare the students to be able to explore the depth and breadth of the second language's literature. A secondary objective was to gain a greater understanding of the first language. An equally important goal was to improve the students' capability of coping with difficult learning situations and materials, i.e., to develop the students' minds.

In attaining these objectives, the students first had to learn grammar and vocabulary. Grammar was taught deductively by means of long and elaborate explanations. All the regularities and irregularities, all the rules and exceptions to the rules were described in grammatical terms. This presentation contained the prescription that the students were to apply in order to translate the readings and do the exercises. (Textbooks written in the grammar-translation format were easily identifiable: the explanations took several pages and the exercises were usually quite short.) Much class time was spent "talking about" the language. Normally, the vocabulary was listed somewhere in the chapter, and the students memorized these lists of words along with the native-language meanings.

Comprehension and assimilation of grammar and vocabulary were put to the test in translation. If the students could translate the readings to the first language and if they knew enough to translate especially selected and prepared exercises from the first to the second language, they were judged to have learned the language. In addition to translating, the students were commonly asked to "state the rule."[1]

During the entire process of going from complete explanations designed to teach the students the rules of the language through to the end of the translation exercises, there was a constant comparison of the native language and the second language. The goal was to be able to convert each language into the other, and the process was one of problem solving, the problem being that of puzzling out the correct forms assisted by the grammar rules and the dictionary. There was little concern with being able to communicate orally in the language. Consequently, there were few opportunities to listen to or to speak the language in class. Learning the grammar and vocabulary was achieved by reading and writing exercises.

Influences from Psychology

The roots of the psychological theories of learning most closely associated with the audio-lingual theory can be traced back to antiquity. Early philosophers mentioned from time to time the possibility that learning in humans might be similar to that in animals. However, these hints and suspicions were not considered seriously by most people until the middle of the nineteenth century. The event that influenced the widespread acceptance of these speculations was the publication in 1859 of Darwin's *Origin of Species*. The important implication of this book from the point of view of psychology was that "there may be a continuity between the human mind and the animal mind" (Munn et al., 1969, p. 640).

---

[1]This author once observed a class in which a student who was reading aloud misplaced the accent on a word in Spanish. Becoming confused, the best she could do was to sit in embarrassed silence until the teacher finally put an end to her ordeal telling her, "For tomorrow I want you to copy the rules for accentuation in the back of the book *fifty* times."

As Darwin's theories spread, an interest in animal psychology grew. Experimenters such as Thorndike and Watson studied the actions and reactions of animals in the psychological laboratories in order to determine how they learned. Naturally, observation of mental processes was impossible; therefore, this was not a factor in the scientific study of learning. Scientists had to limit their descriptions to the overt actions of the animals, i.e., to behavior.

The school of psychology that developed from these psychological studies based on experiments with animal behavior was called *behaviorism*. At first, behaviorism was more a method than an actual set of learning theories. The trend was away from introspection toward precise descriptions of observable behavior. These early experimenters wanted psychology to be as scientific as physics or chemistry. Therefore, they concerned themselves only with the behavior of the animals. However, the method became a theory of learning when Pavlov conditioned dogs to salivate at the sound of a bell. In the words of Broudy and Freel (1956, p. 86):

> This conditioned reflex gave behaviorism another powerful string to its bow. It provided a theory with which to account for learning.
> In later developments the conditioning method of Pavlov came to be known as *classical* conditioning. Conditioning is also used to describe other types of learning:
> 1. A rat runs to the left and finds food (positive reinforcement); runs right and gets an electric shock (negative reinforcement).
> 2. A rat runs left and gets food. When he runs to the right and nothing happens, the rat comes to regard the right turn as equivalent to the shock or disappointment.

Soon behaviorists concluded that all learning consisted of some form of conditioning. The organism was conditioned to respond in a specific way to a selected stimulus. Complex activities were nothing more than a complex collection of conditioned responses. Since all learning is conditioned and since human learning is similar to learning in animals, the next step was to conclude that human learning could be, and is, conditioned in the same way. The belief was that humans are reinforced by their environment in much the same way as the rat in a maze.

Behavioristic, mechanistic theories have occupied an important place in attempts to explain learning. Of course, experiments with learning in animals have continued, and results from these studies have continued to be the basis for much of the explanation of learning in humans. In discussing verbal behavior, Skinner (1957, p. 3) expresses this extrapolation in the following fashion:

> It would be foolish to underestimate the difficulty of this subject matter, but recent advances in the analysis of behavior permit us to approach it with a certain optimism. New experimental techniques and

fresh formulations have revealed a new level of order and precision. The basic processes and relations which give verbal behavior its special characteristics are now fairly well understood. Much of the experimental work responsible for this advance has been carried out on other species, but the results have proved to be surprisingly free of species restrictions. Recent work has shown that the methods can be extended to human behavior without serious modification.

The most recent behavioristic school is termed *stimulus-response (S-R) psychology.* The best known proponent of S-R psychology is B. F. Skinner. Based on his research in the animal laboratory, he uses the term *operant conditioning* to describe learning. As he teaches pigeons, he begins with some action that they are performing, an operant. For example, he may want the pigeon to turn a complete circle in a clockwise direction. Watching carefully, he reinforces the slightest move in the desired direction with some food. The next time the pigeon must turn a little more in order to be rewarded. This process continues until the pigeon learns to make a complete turn in order to receive food. This whole learning sequence takes only a short while, and complex variations can be added. In the film *Learning and Behavior,*[2] examples of conditioned learning include pigeons that respond only to certain lights or combinations and sequences of lights. Two even play ping-pong.[3]

Basically, operant conditioning is a mechanistic approach to learning. External forces select stimuli and reinforce responses until desired behavior is conditioned to occur. Learning is the result of external factors operating on and shaping the organism's behavior. Given the proper reinforcement, behavior will change. In simple terms, the theory says that learning occurs in the following manner: The learner, be it human or animal, responds to a stimulus. The response must be active. The connection between the stimulus and the response is conditioned by reinforcement. In the whole process the steps taken are extremely small in order to promote a satisfactory response.

Influences from Linguistics

As linguists studied among the Indians, they departed from the traditional point of view concerning languages. Up to that time, the stress in language study had been upon historical linguistics. The method used in studying the history of different languages was to examine extant manuscripts in order to detect changes in vocabulary and form. These researchers in language,

---

[2] *Learning and Behavior* is distributed by Carousel Films, 1501 Broadway, New York, N.Y. 10036.
[3] The reader may have seen additional examples of operant conditioning in zoos. Many have animals that perform tricks in return for an extra bit of food. The zoo in Indianapolis, Indiana, for example, used to have a rooster that played basketball and a rabbit that kissed a wooden dummy.

however, were forced to concentrate on oral language in conversational speech due to the fact that the Indians had no written alphabet. Their concern lay with what people said, not with what the learned scholars of society wrote. From their work came the basic tenets of descriptive, or structural, linguistics.

First, working with unwritten Indian dialects convinced the descriptive linguists that language was primarily an oral phenomenon. All native languages are learned orally before reading is begun. (In fact, in the 1920s the majority of the world's languages had no written form.) In their opinion, language was considered to be a stream of oral sounds. Written language was a secondary representation of speech.

Descriptive linguists made no attempt to try to force all languages into the classical mold. They felt that each language was a unique system and that each must be learned within the context of its own system, not in comparison to another. Brooks (1964, pp. 56–57) was reflecting this opinion when he asserted, "What he [the learner] does not know is that the sound system and the structural system of the new language are different in nearly every detail from those in his mother tongue, that meanings in the new language will never be identical with those in English, and that there is no more a universal grammar than there is a universal diet."

Rather than beginning with Latin grammar and searching for that system in the language being studied, the descriptive linguists began with the language itself and studied the recurring patterns. As they pursued this study of patterns, they concluded that each language system is a purely arbitrary one that is learned by the members of the speech community. In their study of language patterns, the major portion of their attention was focused on the phonology, phonemes, and the morphemes of the language.

Another idea of the descriptive linguists was that correct speech is what people say, not what grammarians decree they should say. The standard by which language was evaluated was not some formulation of abstract rules and regulations. Instead, proper language was to be based on descriptions of how the language is used by the speakers of that language.

The Indians themselves were not of any great help in studying their language. They spoke the language, but they could not describe it. The patterns of the language had to be classified on the basis of collected samples of speech. This led the descriptive linguists to the conclusion that native speakers cannot describe their own language system. At the same time, it was evident that language is overlearned to the point at which the speakers are able to focus their attention on what is being said rather than how. In his *Outline Guide for the Practical Study of Foreign Languages,* Bloomfield (1942, p. 12) stated, "The command of a language is not a matter of knowledge: the speakers are quite unable to describe the habits which make up their language. The command of a language is a matter of practice," and *"language learning is overlearning: anything else is of no use."*

Resulting Theories of Language and Learning

The influences of behavioristic psychology and descriptive linguistics were at their peak from World War I to shortly after World War II, when the foundations of the audio-lingual approach were being laid. In addition, the field of descriptive linguistics was profoundly affected by the theories of learning held by the behavioristic psychologists. Learning, as was stated earlier, was viewed basically as being a process of conditioning behavior. From this tenet came the definition of learning as "a change in behavior." Brooks (1964, p. 46), for example, defines learning as *"a change in performance that occurs under the conditions of practice."*

Language, although more complex, was no different from any other learning. Language, too, was composed of conditioned responses. Skinner (1957, p. 81) makes quite clear that language is no different from other learned behavior when he says:

> In all verbal behavior under stimulus control there are three important events to be taken into account: a stimulus, a response, and a reinforcement. These are contingent upon each other, as we have seen, in the following way: the stimulus, acting prior to the emission of the response, sets the occasion upon which the response is likely to be reinforced. Under this contingency, through a process of operant discrimination, the stimulus becomes the occasion upon which the response is likely to be emitted.

Other psychologists agree with Skinner. Broudy and Freel (1956, p. 86) summarize their feelings as follows:

> More complicated behaviors, including the learning of language meanings, also are described by conditioning. Thus, according to Mowrer, the meaning of a predicate is transferred by conditioning to the meaning of a subject. For example, the meaning "thief" is attached to the meaning "Tom" in the sentence "Tom is a thief."

These same tenets have also been accepted as valid in second-language learning. Morton and Lane (1961) concluded on the basis of laboratory experiments that the tasks involved in learning another language are "indistinguishable" from those required to condition desired behavior in the animal laboratory. In addition, Lane (1964, p. 250) has stated, "there is nothing extrapolative in the application of laboratory techniques and nothing metaphorical in the use of concepts gained from a functional analysis of behavior in the laboratory."

IMPLICATIONS FOR LANGUAGE TEACHING

Although neither the behavioristic psychologists nor the descriptive linguists were language teachers, their ideas have profoundly influenced the direction that second-language teaching has taken. First, descriptive linguistics accepted most of the basic tenets of behaviorism with regard to language and learning. Later, these ideas along with their own were put into effect in establishing the intensive language courses of the Army Specialized Training Program. The same basic principles were incorporated into the audio-lingual classes of the schools.

Behavioristic Psychology

Accepting the fundamental ideas of behaviorism also involved a shift away from beliefs commonly held prior to that time. Specifically, this viewpoint rejected the mentalistic (the mind is the center of learning) interpretations of learning that had prevailed for so long. Learning was not viewed as a mental process, but as a mechanical one. Teaching did not involve the proper arrangement of information to be presented, but the establishment of learned connections between selected stimuli and desired responses. Conditioning the desired responses depended upon providing immediate and appropriate reinforcement.

The implications for the classroom of this apparently simple explanation of learning were far-reaching and indeed revolutionary. No longer were learners supposed to sit passively in their seats soaking up the information presented by the teacher. Instead, the students were to respond actively, and the teacher's role was to reinforce the correct response.

The most complete description and application of these theories of learning were made in the preparation of linear programmed materials.[4] The basic principles of programming are (1) specification of desired behavior, (2) minimal steps in learning, (3) active response to presented stimuli, and (4) immediate reinforcement. The same tenets, applied to language teaching, produced a method that advocated the use of mimicry-memorization and pattern drills to teach language skills.

Descriptive Linguistics

Descriptive linguists had as much to say about the "how" of teaching second languages as about the "what." Their fundamental ideas were contrary to many

---

[4]The theoretical positions underlying programmed instruction of this type and audio-lingual teaching procedures and materials are basically the same.

of the practices common to the typical classroom in the first half of the twentieth century. Clearly a shift to their way of thinking involved basic changes in the approach to language teaching. The implications for revision and change revolved around the following points:

1. Traditional classes had begun with and emphasized written work. The new approach should begin with and center around oral practice. The ear and the tongue should be trained first. Oral language was not only more important; it also involved those skills that were prerequisite to gaining a satisfactory command of the written skills.

2. In grammar-translation classes, the students had learned the second language by comparing it to the native language. However, the rules of one language should not be used to learn another. Learning a second language should begin with that language, not another. All languages are different, and comparisons are not beneficial to the language learner.

3. At the same time, descriptive linguists believed that most errors in second-language learning were due to interference from native-language habits. Therefore, the focus of the activity in the classroom should center around these conflicting structures. The traditional approach had been to analyze these contrasts. The new approach should be to develop new habits to overcome the old ones.

4. The traditional method had stressed written forms. The new method should emphasize the sounds of the language. Language is a stream of sounds, and oral speech is basic to learning a language. Therefore, the sounds and oral patterns should be learned.

5. Modern languages should not be described in terms of Latin grammar rules. New descriptions of language based on scientific analysis of the spoken language should be substituted for the traditional grammatical terms. The descriptions included the oral aspects of language as well as the written.

6. The classical approach had been to learn by heart the rules of the language. The new linguistic approach recognized that the first-language learner is not aware of the rules he is applying. Therefore, the second language should be practiced, not studied. The learner should learn by analogy, i.e., the recognition of identical elements in recurring patterns, not by analysis of grammar per se.

7. The traditional approach had been to spend a considerable amount of time studying about the language. The new linguists stressed that language should be overlearned. Language consists of a set of habits, not knowledge about how the language is put together.

8. A common practice in the past had been to learn grammar in isolated sentences and vocabulary in lists. The newer methodology maintained that both should be taught in context. Language does not occur in isolated segments; it occurs as part of a communicative situation.

BASIC TENETS OF THE
AUDIO-LINGUAL APPROACH

Although various writers emphasize different aspects of this theory, five basic tenets of the audio-lingual approach emerge from the implications discussed in the preceding section.[5]

1. The goal is to develop in the students the same types of abilities that native speakers have. That is, the students should reach the point at which they can handle language at an unconscious level. As Brooks (1964, pp. 49, 62) puts it, *"The single paramount fact about language learning is that it concerns, not problem solving, but the formation and performance of habits."* He also states that *". . . the acquisition of nonthoughtful responses is the very core of successful language learning. . . ."*

2. In order to achieve their goal, audio-lingual proponents advocate teaching the second language without referring to the first-language system. The new language skills are to be developed in the contexts in which they occur in that language. Brooks (1964) regards the grammar-translation method as being "compound" teaching: i.e., the two languages are constantly associated with each other. Instead of this approach, he proposes that a "coordinate" system be developed in the students. That is, the new language system is to be established separate from that of the first language. In order to accomplish this separation of languages, the first language is banned from the classroom, and a "cultural island" is maintained.

3. The desired skills are acquired basically by setting up teaching-learning situations in which the students are conditioned to give correct responses to oral or written stimuli. They must not be allowed time to think about their answers. If there is any hesitation, the teacher should turn to another student or have the entire class repeat the correct answer. The basic task boils down to one of establishing automatic, nonthoughtful responses to language stimuli. For example, if the teacher greets her students with "Good morning. How are you?", they do not think to themselves, "Gee, she used an irregular verb in the second person plural of the present tense. Now we must answer with the same verb in the same tense, but in the first person singular," before replying, "I'm fine, thanks." They have learned to talk without paying attention to the way language is put together. Their native language is a habit with them. They must learn to use the second language in the same manner. The very core of audio-lingual teaching is to condition the same types of responses by means of dialog memorization

---

[5]The aural-oral method has evolved considerably since its inception. For additional comments regarding these changes, the reader should consult the articles by Barrutia, del Olmo, and Ney listed in the Selected References at the end of this chapter.

and pattern drills. In these drills, the students are given a stimulus, they respond chorally or individually to the stimulus, and then they are immediately reinforced by hearing the correct reply. Gradually they are conditioned to supply the appropriate form of the verb to correspond to *Yo, Je, Ich* or whatever without consciously making that selection based on some grammatical explanation.

4. Pattern drills are to be taught without explanation. That is, the students practice the patterns before having the structure explained to them. The purpose of the drill is to establish a nonthinking response. Knowledge of the rule, according to audio-lingual proponents, only impedes the students' progress. Experience with the native language has proven that one cannot use a language and think about its constructions at the same time. Therefore, the generalization is given only after the students have been thoroughly drilled in the pattern, and then only in brief terms. The complete explanations of the grammar-translation method are not used.

5. In developing the four language skills, the teacher follows the "natural sequence" that the students followed in learning their own language. That is, the students first learn to understand, then to speak, later to read, and finally to write. In the elementary levels, the pupils are to say nothing that they have not heard, read nothing that they have not spoken, and write nothing that they have not read. Thus, many audio-lingual classes begin with a prereading period, and most try to maintain the sequence of language skills throughout the year. Of the four skills, the oral skills are more important than the written. However, the written skills are not omitted. They are simply taught later, and less importance is attached to them.

AUDIO-LINGUAL TEACHING

Prior to the evolvement of the audio-lingual approach, some leaders in the field of second-language teaching had advocated mimicry-memorization of set phrases as the basis for language acquisition activities. Others had preferred practice of structure as the fundamental component of language instruction. The audio-lingual approach that grew out of behavioristic psychology and descriptive linguistics is a combination of these two techniques. Basically, in the audio-lingual approach the teacher and/or the tape recorder act as external agents to connect certain linguistic responses to selected language stimuli.

The basic tenets of the audio-lingual approach were reflected in the textbooks published, in the manner in which teachers proceeded through the text, and in the types of classroom activities used in audio-lingual teaching. In the following sections, each of these components of audio-lingual methodology is described.

Audio-Lingual Textbooks

The first audio-lingual textbooks consisted of chapters or units divided into three principal sections: a dialog, pattern drills, and some type of application activity. There was little grammatical explanation (none in some) and what there was was presented after the drills as a summary of the grammar involved in the preceding oral drills. Linguistically, the structures included were based on a scientific linguistic analysis of the two languages involved. Primary attention was given to structure rather than to vocabulary in order to spend more time in the development of automatic responses to oral or written stimuli.

Tapes for use in the classroom and the language laboratory accompanied the textbooks. Usually these tapes contained all the dialogs and most of the oral exercises. Sometimes there were take-home records for student use in memorizing the dialogs. Audio-visual aids to demonstrate the meaning of the dialogs and to serve as stimuli for conversation practice often were prepared to supplement the text itself. Many of the texts also had exercise manuals for improving writing skill.

The typical text was arranged in a polystructural format: i.e., several structures were introduced in the dialog as they would occur in a normal conversational situation. All texts did not necessarily follow this arrangement: some authors preferred to sequence their texts one structure at a time. Such monostructural texts as *A Structural Approach to Spanish* by Wolf, Hadlick, and Inman and *Active French Foundation Course*, Book I, by Marty did not incorporate dialogs at all. Another monostructural text, *Spanish for Secondary Schools* by Franco, Mueller, Vargas, and Woodward, placed the dialog after the presentation of structure and the follow-up drill.

Second and third edition audio-lingual texts have changed somewhat from the early editions. Although some texts can be identified as basically audio-lingual, the trend has been toward an eclecticism that combines elements of cognition and meaningful learning. Three of the major changes in approach have been to: (1) include grammatical explanations before the pattern drills, (2) give more complete descriptions of the grammar being presented, and (3) deemphasize the natural sequence of language learning. However, the use of dialogs to introduce new vocabulary and new structures, the use of pattern drills, the stress on habit formation, the emphasis on oral skills, the desire to avoid and to eliminate student errors, and the reinforcement of student response by the teacher and/or the tape continue to be the basic elements in any text favoring the audio-lingual approach.

Presenting new material The first component of any text deals with the problem of presenting new material to the students. In texts favoring the audio-lingual approach, new material is introduced in dialogs. While studying the dialog lines, the students learn the language in the dialog. The next step is to focus on the sounds, structures, or vocabulary to be learned. This material is drilled in simple pattern drills requiring no change of structural forms or patterns.

DIALOGS

The *dialogs* contain the basic content of the unit or chapter. Dialogs are chosen as the principal means of introducing new content because audio-lingual theorists place primary emphasis in elementary courses on the oral aspects of language.

Another characteristic of the dialogs in early audio-lingual texts was that they were to be linguistically and culturally authentic. Linguistic authenticity meant that the utterances in the dialog were to be true to native speech. Thus, any structure might occur in any given dialog. However, only selected structures were to be learned in each unit. Cultural authenticity meant that the conversation was to take place in the second culture and be appropriate to the dialog situation. Some recent audio-lingual texts have departed from this quality in order to select simple language geared to the students' level of language learning.

NO-CHANGE PATTERN DRILLS

The language elements to be learned in the unit are isolated from the dialog for additional conditioning in *no-change pattern drills*. First, the teacher recalls the related dialog sentences to the students' minds before proceeding with two principal types of drills. The initial drill is the *repetition drill*. In this drill the teacher, or the tape model, gives the forms of the structure to be learned, and the students repeat, focusing on the structure. Following is an example of a repetition drill:

Répétez

Michel marche dans le parc.
Il reste dans le jardin.
Annette travaille dans la cuisine.
Maman donne l'argent.

Je marche sous les arbres.
Je travaille avec maman.
Je donne l'argent.

Tu travailles à la maison.

Tu prépares le dîner.
Est-ce que tu prépares le dîner?[6]

After having the students repeat the forms to be acquired, early audio-lingual authors proceeded to a *substitution drill*. This type of drill starts with a model sentence repeated by the students. The students are then given another word to incorporate into the model sentence. This type of drill is slightly more difficult for the students than the repetition drill in that it requires the students to remember the basic sentence as they continue with the drill. This is the first time in the sequence of going from dialog to conversational stimulus that the students go beyond simple repetition of the model. However, the students are required to make no structure changes in the sentence, so to this extent it is still a fairly simple task. The object of such a carefully controlled sequence is to keep the students practicing correct language rather than making all sorts of errors during the language learning sequence. The purpose of the substitution drill is to present examples of the linguistic variations possible with each pattern. Following are examples of substitution drills:

Vocabulary	*Structure*		
Bist du im Haus?	Mme Duval		
im Keller?	Il		
im Hof?	Maman	prépare le dîner.	
im Wohnzimmer?	Elle		
	La fille		
Wir sind in der Küche.			
in der Schule.			
in der Stadt.[7]	Le garçon	marche	dans le jardin.[8]
		travaille	
		reste	

In some early audio-lingual texts, structure and vocabulary were supposed to be acquired during practice with the dialog lines and with repetition drills and substitution drills. In other texts, a *summary* of the grammar was added after the students had already thoroughly practiced the structures involved.

---

[6]Helstrom & Metz (1972, pp. 18–29). Reprinted by permission.
[7]From A-LM GERMAN, Level 1, New Second Edition, by George Winkler, copyright © 1974 by Harcourt Brace Jovanovich, Inc., and reprinted with their permission.
[8]Helstrom & Metz (1972, p. 28). Reprinted by permission.

This generalization normally consisted of a listing of the forms followed by a short explanation of the important features of the structure. For example:

	Present Progressive	
subject pronoun	verb *to be*	*-ing* form of the verb
I	am	
You	are	
He, She, It	is	talking, eating, etc.
We	are	
You	are	
They	are	

1. The present progressive is made up of a form of the verb *to be* and an *-ing* form of the verb.
2. Forms of the verb *to be* change to agree with the subject. The *-ing* form of the verb never changes.
3. To make the *-ing* form of the verb, remove the infinitive sign, *to,* and add *-ing* to the end of the verb.

Since the first editions of the audio-lingual texts were published, various changes have been incorporated into the audio-lingual approach, many of which have centered around measures to improve student comprehension of the material being presented. There is much less reluctance now than in the early days of audio-lingual teaching to use the first language. Some texts give first-language translations or use pictures to assist in student understanding of the dialog. The other major change regarding comprehension is that the newer editions have tended toward earlier and more complete presentations of structure.

Transformation pattern drills   The next portion of a text favoring the audio-lingual approach consists of pattern drills in which the students are required to make some change in form or pattern. (This characteristic habit formation type drill has changed only slightly in the intervening years since its initial introduction in *Modern Spanish.*) The purpose of these drills is to condition the same linguistic skills into the second-language learner as those of the first-language speaker. The format of the drills is a direct application of S-R psychology to second-language teaching. The student receives a linguistic stimulus, he responds, and this response is reinforced immediately either by the teacher, the tape, the record, or the text.

By the time the students reach the level of transformation pattern drills, they are expected to be able to make the changes in structures they have been repeating in the dialog lines and simple pattern drills. At this level, the students are asked to respond with a proper choice of forms or patterns. However, the response, due to the amount of drill with each prior to this selection of forms, is still to be an automatic, unconscious one, free from analysis.

The following are examples of transformation pattern drills:

PERSON-NUMBER SUBSTITUTION DRILL

Model	Students
Wo ist Jochen?	Wo ist Jochen?
———er?	Wo ist er?
———wir?	Wo sind wir?
———ich?	Wo bin ich?
———ihr?	Wo seid ihr?
———du?	Wo bist du?
———Sie?	Wo sind Sie?
———Jochen?	Wo ist Jochen?[9]

PATTERNED RESPONSE DRILL

When are you leaving?	I'm leaving now.
When is he leaving?	He's leaving now.
When are they leaving?	They're leaving now.
When are we leaving?	We're leaving now.
When is she leaving?	She's leaving now.
When am I leaving?	You're leaving now.

CHANGING NUMBER: SINGULAR ⟷ PLURAL

Tu discutes tout le temps!	Vous discutez tout le temps!
Je regarde un documentaire.	Nous regardons un documentaire.
Il manque toujours les informations.	Ils manquent toujours les informations.
Je prépare le petit déjeuner.	Nous préparons le petit déjeuner.
Vous présentez Philippe à Marie.	Tu présentes Philippe à Marie.
Nous dînons tout de suite.	Je dîne tout de suite.
Elles goûtent toujours le dessert.	Elle goûte toujours le dessert.
Nous déjeunons dans une heure.	Je déjeune dans une heure.[10]

---

[9]From A-LM GERMAN, Level 1, New Second Edition, by George Winkler, copyright © 1974 by Harcourt Brace Jovanovich, Inc., and reprinted with their permission.

[10]From A-LM FRENCH, Level 1, New Second Edition, by Marilynn Ray, and Katia Brillié Lutz, copyright © 1974 by Harcourt Brace Jovanovich, Inc., and reprinted with their permission.

CHANGING TENSE: PRESENT TO FUTURE

Er nimmt den Kuchen.   *Er wird den Kuchen nehmen.*

1. Sie essen den Apfel.   6. Du bringst das Obst.
2. Wir kaufen Gemüse.   7. Sie tanzt gern.
3. Ihr trinkt ein Glas Wasser.   8. Er isst Nachtisch.
4. Sie zahlt die Rechnung.   9. Du übst Trompete.
5. Ich mache nichts.   10. Wir spielen Tennis.[11]

In the earlier editions the answers to all these drills were given in the text. In the later editions the answers are presented in the first drills and gradually eliminated as the students progress through the various drills.

Another addition in recent texts favoring the audio-lingual approach has been the increased use of realistic drills. These are also transformation drills. However, they differ from the drills described previously in that they resemble a language exchange that could very well occur in a real language situation.

DIRECTED DRILL

Pregúntele al señor si habla español.
Pregúntele a la señorita si canta bien.
Pregúntele a la señora si compra la bolsa.
Pregúntele al señor si toca la guitarra.
Pregúntele a la señorita si nada en el mar.[12]

DIRECTED DIALOG

Pregúntele a Pepe si él está en la   ¿Estás en la foto?
   foto.
Pepe, diga que sí, y a ver si   Sí, a ver si adivinas cuál soy yo.
   adivina cuál es usted.
Diga que claro: ése que está   Claro: ése que está sentado en el
   sentado en el sofá.   sofá.
Pepe, diga que no, que ése es   No, ése es Camilio.[13]
   Camilio.

CUED RESPONSE

Was ist das?   (Saft)   Das ist der Saft.
                    (Milch)
                    (Lappen)
                    (Café)
                    (Illustrierte)[14]

---

[11]Moeller et al. (1970, p. 114). Reprinted by permission.
[12]Schmitt et al. (1972, p. 22). Reprinted by permission.
[13]From A-LM SPANISH, Level 1, New Second Edition, by Barbara Kaminar de Mujica, and

TRANSLATION DRILL

Although not so commonly used as repetition drills, substitution drills, and the various types of transformation pattern drills previously mentioned, *translation drills* are used in some texts. The cues are given in the first language, and the students are asked to respond in the second language. These drills are used to practice structures in which the forms are completely different from the first language. The teacher should be aware that these exercises are still pattern drills. They are not the typical translation exercises of a grammar-translation text. There are only minimal changes from one sentence to the next, and the students are to give automatic responses.

Model	*Students*
Me gusta el libro.	Me gusta el libro.
I like the class.	Me gusta la clase.
I like the parties.	Me gustan las fiestas.
I like the school.	Me gusta la escuela.
I like the teachers.	Me gustan los profesores.

Application activities   Even though the students are approaching a functional ability to use language forms to communicate, audio-lingual proponents are conscious of the students' tendency to create incorrect language forms in spite of the large quantity of drills undertaken to condition new language habits. Therefore, great care is taken to control, as far as possible, what the students may try to say. At this stage the students are beginning to select language responses, but the teacher and the text attempt to keep them within the bounds of their linguistic capabilities in order to avoid language error.

DIALOG ADAPTATION

In this activity, questions are asked about the dialog that require answers directly from the dialog or answers that require only minor changes in the appropriate dialog line.

Johnny: What's your name?
Jane: My name is Jane. What's yours?
Johnny: Mine is Johnny.

Questions based on the dialog structures:
What's your name?

Guillermo Segreda, copyright © 1974 by Harcourt Brace Jovanovich, Inc., and reprinted with their permission.

[14]From A-LM GERMAN, Level 1, New Second Edition, by George Winkler, copyright © 1974 by Harcourt Brace Jovanovich, Inc., and reprinted with their permission.

RESPONSE DRILLS: NONDIRECTED ANSWER
What time do you get up?
What time do you go to bed?
What time do you eat lunch?

RECOMBINATION NARRATIVES
More difficult than the preceding activities are the *recombination narratives.* The structures and vocabulary are recombined in short readings. The students should be familiar with all the semantic and syntactical forms in the narrative, but the context is new to them. These recombination narratives give the students an example of how the parts of language are put together in a combined whole. The chief purpose of these narratives is to provide reading practice, but they also serve as the basis for question-and-answer practice over the content.

GUIDED PRESENTATION
However, the time comes when the students must be given more freedom to talk. Guidelines are still maintained, but more freedom of answer is permitted. In many texts, for example, at the end of the unit the students are expected to give very short oral or written reports in which they are to use the vocabulary and structures learned in that unit. By answering the guiding questions, the students can construct short paragraphs. Naturally, these reports become longer and more complex as the semester progresses.

Your Family
What's your name? What are your parents' names? What is the name of your brother? Sister? Where do you live? Where do you go to school? Where does your father work? Where does your mother work?

CONVERSATION STIMULUS
You see a new girl in the hall. You walk up to her, introduce yourself, and find out her name and where she lives.

All during the process of building up the students' abilities to the point where they can really use the language, one of the basic principles is to have the students practicing correct forms. Creative use of the language in which incorrect forms might be derived by the students is to be avoided. The students are to be carefully guided in order to be kept from making mistakes. Models are provided for many of the activities. Most of the others guide the students by limiting their answers to structures with which they should be completely familiar.

Proceeding Through the Text

The typical approach in the classroom was to begin with a "prereading" period during which the books were withheld from the students. It was felt that seeing the written word interfered with the development of proper habits of pronunciation. The length of the recommended prereading period varied from a few days or weeks to an entire semester, or perhaps even a year or more in the elementary and junior high schools. The language being taught also influenced the length of time that teachers felt was necessary for an adequate initiation of proper habits of pronunciation. Obviously, there is less interference from the written word in a more phonetic language like Spanish than in a language like French. The tendency recently seems to be to shorten the prereading period considerably, or to eliminate it entirely.

After the students received their books, the class maintained a natural sequence of language skills. At any given time the teacher might be covering oral work in one chapter and assigning reading and writing material from preceding chapters. The class progressed through the book by memorizing the dialogs, practicing the pattern drills until the students could give automatic responses to the stimuli, and then, using the learned vocabulary and structure, talking about some topic in a carefully controlled context.

Within the units themselves, the teacher might choose to proceed by studying each unit separately. In this fashion, she had the students memorize the dialog, do the drills, and then practice. Another possibility was to partition the book horizontally rather than vertically. In this procedure, the students learned the first few lines of the dialog, drilled the structures in these specific lines, and then applied these learned structures and vocabulary to a communicative situation. The students progressed in a similar fashion through all the lines of the dialog. Using this organization of the materials, there were a few days in which the students were beginning the next unit while finishing the preceding one. Thus, the units as well as their content were integrated into a continuous sequence.

Classroom Procedures

Early audio-lingual classes were prime examples of teacher-centered classes. The teacher, or the tape, served as the language model. The students listened to the model before repeating sounds, words, phrases, dialog lines, or no-change pattern drills after the model. As they progressed in the language sequence, they began to make changes in the forms or patterns of the sentence. The students' role was to respond orally, or occasionally in writing, to language stimuli. The students performed chorally, in small groups, and finally individually. The teacher's role was to serve as a model, give the stimuli, listen with a critical ear, provide the language reinforcement to the stimuli presented, i.e., the correct response, and correct student errors. She was the agent to condition correct second-language habits.

As the students repeated the lines of the dialog and passed on to the structural drills, they were engaged in active responses that required them to practice the very structural and semantic elements they were to learn. They were occupied speaking the language rather than talking about it. Very little English was used in the classroom. Resorting to the mother tongue was not necessary, except for the occasional need to clarify meaning by means of the first language, when all visual aids, gestures, and explanations in the second language failed. Pattern drills were conducted without continually equating meaning with the first language. During this whole process of drilling the dialog and the structures, the students were carefully led in minimal steps through a series of drills in which the possibility of error was almost eliminated, and the opportunity for practice of forms was expanded to the fullest. The students were not supposed to analyze and search for answers but to respond immediately to the stimulus of the teacher, whether it be a line from a dialog that she was asking them to repeat or a pattern drill that she was asking them to perform. Classroom time was spent practicing correct forms rather than puzzling out answers based upon some little understood and perplexing language code.

The teacher who uses a text favoring the audio-lingual approach and who chooses to convert to an individualized program is faced with the problem of how to provide immediate reinforcement to the pattern drills. How is it possible to condition automatic responses to the drills when the students are at various points in the text? One possibility is to abandon the audio-lingual goal of automatic responses and to use the drills as a basis for the study of language patterns. If the teacher prefers to work toward automatic responses, the students can use tapes, practice with each other, do the drills orally while looking at the cues given in the text, or find an opportunity to practice individually with the teacher.

The dialog   The students' first task is to master completely all the sounds and intonation patterns contained in the dialog. As the students study the dialog by mimicking the model provided by the teacher, tape, or record, they are learning to distinguish and to pronounce the sounds of the language. At the same time, they are learning to place these sounds in proper intonation patterns. Most important of all, they are growing accustomed to the sounds of the language, i.e., they are developing the ability to hold these strange new sounds in their minds and to process them. Until they can increase their capacity to receive sentences of several syllables in length, they have little chance of ever being able to use the language orally.

While learning the sounds and intonation patterns of the language and improving their auditory memory, the students are also faced with the task of acquiring new vocabulary and new structures. Both are used in subsequent drills over the important language patterns. The important consideration from the audio-lingual point of view is that both are being learned in context as opposed to the more traditional word lists and the study of isolated examples of grammatical structures.

Depending upon the setting of the dialog situation, the students may also gain new insights into the people and their culture. This information may range from the historical to the political, from the economic to the social. The point is often made that such social practices as using the polite or familiar *you* in the second language is certainly a cultural concept and that a contextual situation is the best method of demonstrating and clarifying such cultural differences.

The students' task as they practice with the dialog is much more difficult and complex than seems apparent to the novice teacher. Learning the dialog completely is basic to their performance in the latter parts of the unit, and they have many different aspects of the language to absorb. Therefore, the teacher must be continually aware of her responsibility to model carefully and sufficiently before asking the students to repeat after her. Also, she should continue to practice and review the material until it has been thoroughly assimilated by the students.

Pattern drilling After becoming thoroughly familiar with the dialog lines, the students begin to manipulate these same semantic and structural elements in pattern drills. Pattern drills do not attempt to simulate communication. Their purpose is to enable the students to overlearn the structure involved to the point of automatic, nonthoughtful response. It is evident that the first-language speaker has an unconscious and automatic control of the various elements of his own language, and the objective of these drills is to develop a similar control of the basic structures in the second language. The students must necessarily reach this skill level, at which point they can respond unconscious of the way in which they are putting words together, before they can successfully converse with a native speaker.

As they perform these drills, the students are learning the grammar point being practiced. By the process of analogy, i.e., perceiving identical patterns in similar structural relationships, the students are able to progress from one example to another. This placing of similar or identical structures and vocabulary items in related contexts also helps to demonstrate to the students the almost infinite number of possibilities of each. The correct answers are to be supplied after each active response in class in order that the students be immediately reinforced. They are to learn correct forms from the beginning.

Application activities   After the students have met the structure in context as part of the dialog to be practiced and drilled the same grammar point in pattern drills, they move on to some type of activity in which they have an opportunity to use these same forms which they have been practicing. These activities are more difficult than the previous drills. The students at this level are rather close to the goal, i.e., to be able to use the structure under consideration to communicate with someone else using these same grammatical forms. The purpose of these activities is to provide opportunities for the students to employ what they have been studying in practical situations and to assist them in transferring these learned forms to new contexts.

The unit ends with the students, hopefully, having the ability to use the content of the introductory dialog in a communicative context. In each unit there is a careful sequencing of activities in a continuously increasing level of difficulty. The students are led through minimal steps in order to avoid error as completely as possible. The object is to practice the correct forms until there is an automatic connection between the stimulus and its associated form. Throughout the sequence, the teacher is in control of all language practice as he seeks to condition correct language habits.

RESEARCH ON AUDIO-LINGUAL APPROACHES TO SECOND-LANGUAGE LEARNING

Favoring the Audio-Lingual Approach

Delattre was one of the first to report the outcomes of the "aural-oral" approach in the teaching of modern languages. In his two articles (1947a, 1947b) he stated that with this method ". . . results of high quality—such as private instruction alone has generally produced—can be attained with students working *en masse*. Yet it is effort-saving to the teacher (it has machines to do the tedious work), and labor saving to the student." Later he added, "Students came so well prepared to class, their answers were so sharp, that it took only a few minutes to cover the assignment or check that it was done in the right manner. No excruciating effort on the part of the embarrassed students." Working with records, the "aural-oral" students ". . . acquired grammatical habits with unexpected ease. . . . As they applied them without knowing them, they applied them more completely, for their application of rules did not depend on and was not limited by their understanding of them." The author was "amazed" at the results that had "conclusively proven" to him that the "aural-oral" approach is best, not only for oral French, but for any French class. He concluded that emphasizing oral skills produced superior results in written as well as in oral work, that students preferred the oral method and worked harder, and that poorer students learned better, thus unifying the class with regard to ability.[15] (See chapter 4, pages 86–89 for studies on research in audio-lingual teaching.)

Containing Reservations

Enlisting the aid and cooperation of volunteer schools, Agard and Dunkel (1948) undertook a major investigation of the outcomes of the "aural-oral" methods of teaching foreign languages. The report of this study was published in 1948. From the beginning of their report, the authors admitted the lack of sufficient controls to conduct a proper experiment. However, the results of this survey did not substantiate the earlier claims of the protagonists of the "aural-oral" approach, and the authors listed a need for greater modesty of claims. Specifically, the study did not support the theory that oral training improves reading ability. Furthermore, students receiving "aural-oral" instruction did not demonstrate a superior ability in listening comprehension. The authors concluded by calling for additional research in more carefully controlled situations.

Hamilton and Haden (1950) reported on a three-year study at the University of Texas. In this investigation, three problems of teaching second languages were examined: (1) Do achievement results reflect oral or reading skills in proportion to the extent that the skill was emphasized in the classroom? (2) Is it necessary that grammar be taught? (3) What methods are best for teaching pronunciation? Their major finding was that instruction in the specifics of grammar seemed to have very little effect upon the students' knowledge of morphology and syntax. No definite conclusions were drawn with respect to teaching pronunciation, but it was inferred that (1) descriptions of speech production were helpful; (2) phonetic symbols were beneficial in French, but not in Spanish; and (3) imitation alone was not sufficient to develop a proper pronunciation. The authors also concluded that differing emphases in presentation of material may not necessarily produce corresponding differences in achievement results.

Advantages for Both

Scherer and Wertheimer (1964) compared the results of audio-lingual versus traditional teaching procedures. In this study, the authors included 165

---

[15]It should be noted, as Delattre admitted, that ". . . some problems did come up. First, two students registered objection to the Dean in the very beginning and were allowed to transfer. Then twice during the first semester, some students campaigned to abandon the system and return to the book method of instruction."

audio-lingual students and 124 traditional students in elementary German classes over a two-year period. The achievement test scores indicated that the students in the audio-lingual classes were significantly superior in listening and speaking at the end of the second semester. The students in the traditional classes received significantly higher scores in translating, reading, and writing. During the second year of the experiment, students from both groups were mixed in the typical second-year class. At the end of the second year, the audio-lingual students were better in speaking; the traditional students were better in writing and in translating from German to English. There were no differences in the other skills.

CONCLUSION

Proponents of the audio-lingual approach aim to duplicate first-language habits in the second-language learner. The theoretical bases for their approach come from two other fields, descriptive linguistics and behavioristic psychology. Politzer (1964b, p. 149) states, "Thus, behaviorism and formal analysis of language were the chief features of the linguistic impact on language instruction in the 1940s." Since behaviorism is not specifically a linguistic theory, this statement serves to reflect the influence of behavioristic psychology on descriptive linguistics. Valette (1966, p. 132) recognizes the contribution of behaviorists to modern-language teaching when she states, "The new curriculum materials have been devised on the assumption that foreign-language learning is basically a mechanical process of habit formation."

Textbooks based on the audio-lingual theory have been quite widely used since the inception of the NDEA language institutes, which popularized this approach. Second and even third editions of these original texts are now on the market. As they have evolved, the direction has been toward including more grammatical explanation and using the first language more to insure comprehension. Too, in keeping with the present stress on eclecticism, teachers are more inclined to modify audio-lingual tenets as they seek to find the most efficient approach to use with their students. Of course, dialog practice and pattern practice drills under the external control of the teacher and/or the textual materials of the stimuli and reinforcement underlie the major portion of the classroom activities. The goal is to condition in second-language learners the same types of automatic speech habits they have in their native language. The process is a very tightly controlled one in which the students are conditioned to give predetermined responses in order to avoid the errors typically made by students who create non-native forms as they attempt to communicate. Since the students typically spend so much time listening to a model and repeating after the model or making minor changes in the model sentence, the strengths of this approach are the students' pronunciation, their auditory memory, their ability to process sounds at native speed, and their speed of speech during drill practice.

REVIEW AND APPLICATION

DEFINITIONS
1. analogy, p. 110
2. behaviorism, p. 105
3. mimicry-memorization, p. 112
4. operant conditioning, p. 106
5. pattern drill, pp. 114–19.
6. stimulus-response psychology, p. 105

DISCUSSION
1. Discuss the implications of the behavioristic model of learning as the concept relates to establishing teaching-learning situations. In what sense is it external and mechanistic? Describe the role of the learner and of the teacher.
2. From your perspective, were the reactions of the audio-linguists against grammar-translation procedures valid or invalid?
3. Summarize the basic concepts of behavioristic psychology and descriptive linguistics. Relate each to goals and practices in contemporary education.
4. Discuss the relationships between behavioristic psychologists, descriptive linguists, and audio-lingual teachers.
5. Outline the guiding principles you would follow and the kinds of activities you would employ in an audio-lingual class.
6. For what types of students and what types of teachers do you think an audio-lingual approach is best suited?
7. Discuss the concept of external choice of stimuli and the reinforcement of desired responses. What types of classroom activities would be utilized to change behavior?
8. What are the characteristics of pattern drills? How and for what purpose are they used in language teaching?
9. Delineate the teacher's responsibility and the text's function in the establishment of second-language habits in an audio-lingual class. What is the student's role?

ACTIVITIES
1. Choose examples of additional audio-lingual drills and bring them to class.
2. Make up some of your own audio-lingual drills.
3. Teach some structure, vocabulary, or phonology to your classmates according to S-R principles for changing behavior.
4. If possible, view and analyze the films *Audio-Lingual Techniques for*

Teaching Foreign Languages French, German, and *Spanish* produced by Yale University pursuant to a contract with the U. S. Office of Education, 1962, Pierre J. Capretz, Project Coordinator.

SELECTED REFERENCES

Agard, F. B., and Dunkel, H. B. (1948) *An Investigation of Second-Language Teaching.* Boston: Ginn.

Barrutia, R. (1966) Some Misconceptions about the Fundamental Skills Method. *Hispania,* 49:440–46.

Blindert, H. D. (1971) The Science of Behavior, Behavior Modification, and Verbal Behavior. *International Review of Applied Linguistics,* 9:53–62.

Bloomfield, L. (1942) *Outline Guide for the Practical Study of Foreign Languages.* Baltimore: Linguistic Society of America. P. 12.

Brooks, N. (1964) *Language and Language Learning: Theory and Practice.* (2nd ed.) New York: Harcourt, Brace & World. Pp. 46, 49–53, 56–57, 62, 96.

Broudy, H. S., and Freel, E. L. (1956) *Psychology for General Education.* New York: Longmans, Green and Co. P. 86.

Brown, T. G. (1969) In Defense of Pattern Practice. *Language Learning,* 19:191–203.

Carroll, J. B. (1966) The Contributions of Psychological Theory and Educational Research to the Teaching of Foreign Languages. In A. Valdman (Ed.), *Trends in Language Teaching.* New York: McGraw-Hill. Pp. 93–106.

Chastain, K. (1969) The Audio-Lingual Habit Theory Versus the Cognitive Code-Learning Theory: Some Theoretical Considerations. *International Review of Applied Linguistics,* 7:97–106.

Cook, V. J. (1968) Some Types of Oral Structure Drills. *Language Learning,* 18:155–64.

Delattre, P. (1947a) A Technique of Aural-Oral Approach: Report on a University of Oklahoma Experiment in Teaching French. *French Review,* 20:238–50.

Delattre, P. (1947b) A Technique of Aural-Oral Approach: Report on a University of Oklahoma Experiment in Teaching French, (Continued). *French Review,* 20:311–24.

Del Olmo, G. (1968) Professional and Pragmatic Perspectives on the Audiolingual Approach: Introduction and Review. *Foreign Language Annals,* 2:19–29.

De Mujica, B. K., and Segreda, G. (1974) *A-LM Spanish, Level One.* (New 2nd ed.) New York: Harcourt Brace Jovanovich.

Hall, R. A., Jr., et al. (1962) Linguistics and Language Teaching. Northeast Conference. In W. F. Bottiglia (Ed.), *Current Issues in Language Teaching.* Pp. 3–17.

Hamilton, D. L., and Haden, E. T. (1950) Three Years of Experimentation at the University of Texas. *Modern Language Journal,* 34:85–102.

Helstrom, J., and Metz, M. S. (1972) *Le Français à Découvrir.* New York: McGraw-Hill.

Hilgard, E. R., and Atkinson, R. C. (1967) *Introduction to Psychology.* (4th ed.) New York: Harcourt, Brace & World.

Hok, R. (1966) Principles and Techniques Characteristic of the Oral Approach. *Language Learning,* 16:87–92.

Jakobovits, L. A. (1968) Physiology and Psychology of Second Language Learning. In E. M. Birkmaier (Ed.), *The Britannica Review of Foreign Language Education.* Chicago: Encyclopaedia Britannica. Pp. 191–92.

Lado, R. (1964) *Language Teaching: A Scientific Approach.* New York: McGraw-Hill.

Lane, H. (1964) Programmed Learning of a Second Language. *International Review of Applied Linguistics,* 2:249–301.

Moeller, J., et al. (1970) *German Today, One.* Boston: Houghton Mifflin.

Morton, F. R., and Lane, H. L. (1961) Techniques of Operant Conditioning Applied to Second Language Learning. An address to the International Congress of Applied Psychology, Copenhagen.

Moulton, W. G. (1961) Linguistics and Language Teaching in the United States 1940–1960. In C. Mohrmann (Ed.), *Trends in European and American Linguistics 1930–1960.* Antwerp, Belgium: The Hague. Pp. 82–109.

Munn, N. L., et al. (1969) *Introduction to Psychology.* (2nd ed.) Boston: Houghton Mifflin. P. 640.

Ney, J. W. (1968) The Oral Approach: A Re-Appraisal. *Language Learning,* 18:3–13.

Paulston, C. B. (1970) Structural Pattern Drills: A Classification. *Foreign Language Annals,* 4:187–93.

Politzer, R. L. (1964a) Some Reflections on Pattern Practice. *Modern Language Journal,* 48:24–28.

Politzer, R. L. (1964b) The Impact of Linguistics on Language Teaching: Past, Present, and Future. *Modern Language Journal,* 48:149.

Politzer, R. L., and Staubach, C. N. (1961) *Teaching Spanish: A Linguistic Orientation.* Boston: Ginn.

Ray, M., and Lutz, K. B. (1974) *A-LM French, Level One.* (New 2nd ed.) New York: Harcourt Brace Jovanovich.

Rivers, W. M. (1964) *The Psychologist and the Foreign Language Teacher.* Chicago: University of Chicago Press.

Sacks, N. P. (1964) Some Aspects of the Application of Linguistics to the Teaching of Modern Foreign Languages. *Modern Language Journal,* 48:7–17.

Scherer, G. A. C., and Wertheimer, M. (1964) *A Psycholinguistic Experiment in Foreign-Language Teaching.* New York: McGraw-Hill.

Schmitt, C. J., et al. (1972) *Español: A Descubrirlo.* New York: McGraw-Hill.

Skinner, B. F. (1957) *Verbal Behavior.* New York: Appleton-Century-Crofts. Pp. 3, 81.

Staats, A. W. (1961) Verbal Habit-Families, Concepts, and the Operant Conditioning of Word Classes. *Psychological Review,* 68:190–204.

Valette, R. M. (1966) Evaluating the Objectives in Foreign-Language Teaching. *International Review of Applied Linguistics,* 2:131–39.

Winkler, G. (1974) *A-LM German, Level One.* (New 2nd ed.) New York: Harcourt Brace Jovanovich.

COGNITIVE THEORY AND TEACHING

Antecedents to the Cognitive Approach
> The Reaction Against the Audio-Lingual Approach
> Influences from Psychology
> Influences from Linguistics
> Processing Thought to Language
> Resulting Theories of Language and Learning

Implications for Language Teaching
> Cognitive Psychology
> Transformational-Generative Linguistics
> Processing Thought to Language

Basic Tenets of the Cognitive Approach

Basic Characteristics of a Cognitive Class

Cognitive Teaching
> Cognitive Textbooks
>> Comprehension
>> Exercises
>> Application Activities
> Proceding Through the Text
> Classroom Procedures
>> Introduction of New Material
>> Exercises
>> Application Activities

Research on Cognitive Approaches to Second-Language Learning

INTRODUCTION

In *The American Heritage Dictionary of the English Language* the meaning of *cognition* is given as "the mental process or faculty by which knowledge is acquired." There are several basic characteristics of cognition. First, cognition is a process. Second, this process is mental. Third, this process is purposive. Fourth, by implication this process is internal. And fifth, by implication this process is ultimately under the control of the learner, even if one is coerced into learning by external pressures. Thus, the term *cognitive processes* refers to the individual's internal mental operations, whether they be nothing more than "day dreaming" or as involved as the manipulation of abstract symbolic concepts to solve some complex problem. Cognitive processes may involve conscious attention to some point the teacher is making, conscious reorganization of material to understand better the concepts being learned, or conscious attempts to recall previously learned information. They may be momentary, such as the instantaneous flash of revelation experienced by Einstein which led to the theory of relativity, or they may endure for long periods of time as in the case of the patient young suitor who spends hours, days, and even months making plans for capturing the affection of his chosen lady.

In cognitive theory the mind is viewed as an active agent in the thinking-learning process. As such, it is a mentalistic, dynamic theory. Mouly (1973) states that the cognitive process is best represented by a dynamic system such as a whirlpool or a hurricane. Knowledge is acquired, not implanted by the teacher. In this sense there are no passive learners. By definition, conscious learning requires active mental participation on the part of the learner. Given this cognitive view of learning, the conception of language gains additional dimensions. First, the individual becomes an active participant in the language acquisition process. Afterwards, the mind continues to be engaged actively in the production of language, i.e., the mind can create needed language combinations for specific occasions.

ANTECEDENTS TO THE COGNITIVE APPROACH

A substantial segment of the second-language teaching profession subscribes to cognitive approaches to second-language teaching. In order to understand the cognitive position, the practicing teacher and the prospective teacher should be acquainted with second-language teaching prior to the development of audio-lingual techniques, audio-lingual theory and teaching, the reaction against audio-lingual theory and teaching, and the new directions that have been taken by cognitive psychologists and transformational-generative linguists. These recent cognitive theories are more complex than their predecessors, and they accord the individual a central role in learning in general and in the acquisition and use of language in particular.

In both learning and language, the emphasis is on the internal, mental processes of the individuals and their contributions to what they learn and how they use what they have learned. The purpose of this present chapter is to outline the basic principles of cognition related to learning and language and to examine how these theories may be adapted to second-language teaching and learning.

The Reaction Against the Audio-Lingual Approach

The original enthusiasm with which second-language teachers in general embraced the audio-lingual approach subsided in the latter half of the sixties. As Hanzeli (1967, p. 42) described the situation in 1967 at the annual meeting of the American Council on the Teaching of Foreign Languages, ". . . Our craft has been stagnating for the last five or six years, and there are signs that the audio-lingual method, approved by the majority of American applied linguists, has been losing momentum." Bolinger's (1968, p. 30) description was even more graphic: "If an applied linguist of the mid-1950s had gone to sleep in his cave, say around 1956, and awakened yesterday, the sight that greeted him would have sent him hurrying back to his dreams. Virtually every tenet that he had proclaimed in his heyday would have been returned to him upside down. . . ." Since these two addresses, the reaction against the audio-lingual approach seems to have increased rather than diminished.

This rejection of principles previously accepted with little or no questioning has occurred in psychology, in linguistics, and in second-language teaching itself. The new movements in psychology and linguistics are discussed later in this chapter. The focus of attention in this section is limited to criticisms that practitioners have had of audio-lingual teaching. In general, the major complaints have been as follows:
1. Claims that "New Key," i.e., audio-lingual, procedures would produce bilingual graduates are not being realized.
2. Reliance upon only the ear in beginning language work may hinder some students who are more eye oriented.
3. Teachers find it impossible to eliminate English from the classroom; nor do they feel that such a practice is desirable.
4. Avoiding any discussion of grammar until the structure has been overlearned is time-consuming and frustrating to the students.
5. The continuous repetition required for overlearning is monotonous to the students and places considerable physical strain upon the teacher (Childers, 1964).

6. Students want to know what they are learning and why.

7. Eliminating the native language from the students' minds is impossible.

Unfortunately, the criticism of audio-lingual procedures has created considerable disagreement within the profession. For example, Gefen (1967, p. 192) represents many teachers who reject the heavy reliance on conditioning-type exercises:

> . . . Many linguistically oriented drills are deadly dull and so intent on avoiding the distractions which a meaningful content to the pattern might offer that the learner sees little or no connection between these boring exercises and that promise of wider cultural horizons or of communicative facility which originally motivated his learning. . . . In general, one might list the results of the "audio-lingual" or "fundamental skills" schools' over-indulgence in pattern practice as (1) the neglect of other language-learning techniques, (2) the loss of motivation and interest through overlearning, and (3) the disregard for meaningful contexts.
>
> In such circumstances, the learner may utter the pattern perfectly, substitute in exactly the right slot and yet not understand a word. He will complete the course without a mistake and still not know the language—performance without competence, or not even performance. There will be no interference by the mother-tongue, but none by the thought processes either! Graduates of the "new school" will suffer from the same faults as the traditionalists: knowing the patterns (where the traditionalists know the paradigms) but not knowing the language.

Other writers, such as del Olmo (1968, pp. 19, 22), defend audio-lingual teaching, saying that such criticism ". . . fails to do justice to enlightened audio-lingual practitioners." In their opinion, ". . . The critical scrutiny audio-lingualism is being subjected to stems from new developments in psychology and linguistics rather than from mere awareness of wrong practices and poor results."

Influences from Psychology

Behavioristic psychology views all learning as a process of acquiring new behaviors through conditioning and reinforcement. The basic factors in conditioning behavior are the stimuli and reinforcements that determine which reponses are learned. The mind is a *tabula rasa* upon which are stamped associations between stimuli and responses. Such a conception of learning is an external, mechanistic viewpoint. The process is external in that forces and/or factors outside the learner determine the stimuli and reinforce selected responses to a predetermined level of proficiency. It is mechanistic in that the process of choosing and reinforcing stimuli is a mechanical process. Mouly (1973, p. 38) quotes Hebb as saying, "Psychology's only hope of remaining scientific is to assume man is basically a mechanism." He adds that behavioristic, mechanistic theory is best represented by a "physical machine with parts, gears, and levers." And it is appropriate to add that the machine is controlled by the operator, not by the machine itself. It was on the basis of this conception of learning that early audio-linguists claimed that intelligence was an unimportant factor in language learning.

Cognitive psychology, however, does not accept the behavioristic point of view. The term *cognition* implies mental activity, mental processes. Cognitive psychologists emphasize the role of the mind in acquiring new information. They say that learning is controlled basically by individuals and not by their surroundings. Cognitive theory stresses perception of experiences and organization of knowledge. The mind is not a passive plastic glob to be molded by environmental forces, but an active and determining agent in the acquisition and storage of knowledge. Such a viewpoint of learning is considered to be mentalistic.

The emphasis in psychology prior to behavioristic theories was mentalistic. Gestalt psychological theories, which are considered to be mentalistic, were recognized even during the years dominated by behaviorism. The newer cognitive theories are also mentalistic interpretations of learning. However, present cognitive theory should not be confused with earlier formulations based on "mental faculties" interpretations of learning, on scientific introspection, or on insightful behavior of animals. Cognitive psychology is a relatively new development.

One of the leading cognitive psychologists is Ausubel. The discussion here is based on ideas set forth in his book, *Educational Psychology: A Cognitive View* (1968). In the introduction to this book he says, "Some kinds of learning, such as rote learning and motor learning, are considered so inconsequential a part of school learning as to warrant no systematic treatment in a textbook on educational psychology. . . . And still other kinds of learning, for example, animal learning, conditioning, instrumental learning, and simple discrimination learning, are considered irrelevant for most learning tasks in school, despite the fact that wildly extrapolated findings in these areas quite commonly pad the learning chapters of many educational psychology textbooks." Later in his preliminary remarks he decries ". . . the prevailing tendency, over the past three or more decades, for educational psychologists to extrapolate findings from animal, rote, and perceptual-motor learning experiments. . . ." (pp. viii, ix).

In his discussion Ausubel states that there are two types of learning: rote learning and meaningful learning. Based on student activity during the learning process, he also makes a distinction between reception learning and discovery learning. He points out that either reception learning or discovery learning may be meaningful, or either may be rote. It is not true that discovery learning is always meaningful and reception learning is always rote. The crucial factor in determining whether learning is rote or meaningful is the manner in which the material is learned. Rote learning is a process in which the material is learned arbitrarily and verbatim. Material learned in a meaningful way is acquired in a nonarbitrary and a nonverbatim fashion.

The key concept in Ausubel's cognitive theories of learning is that learning must be meaningful. The learner must understand what is to be learned. In fact, Ausubel (1968, p. 61) makes the statement that, "The acquisition of large bodies of knowledge is simply impossible in the absence of meaningful learning." The primary responsibility of the teacher, then, is to assist his students in learning meaningfully. As Ausubel (1968, p. 89) maintains, "A central task of pedagogy, therefore, is to develop ways of facilitating an active variety of reception learning characterized by an independent and critical approach to the understanding of subject matter." The implication of the preceding quotes is that learning must involve *active* mental processes in order to be meaningful and that only through meaningful learning can students acquire significant amounts of knowledge.

In *School Learning: An Introduction to Educational Psychology,* Ausubel and Robinson (1969, p. 51) explain the concept of meaningful learning as depending on three factors. First, they maintain that the most important factor influencing learning is the "quantity, clarity, and organization of the learner's present knowledge . . . which consists of facts, concepts, propositions, theories, and raw perceptual data." This collection of knowledge constitutes the learner's cognitive structure. The second important factor in influencing learning is the extent to which new information being received or considered is relatable to the learner's existing cognitive structure. Third, the learners must approach the learning task with the intention of relating it in a meaningful way to what they already know. In short, meaningful learning takes place when the learners comprehend the material; can relate it to their present knowledge system in a nonarbitrary, nonverbatim manner; and consciously intend to integrate the material being learned into their own cognitive structure.

To summarize the discussion to this point, cognitive psychologists maintain that the mind processes information to be learned. In order for this processing to be maximally efficient, the material must be meaningful. The mind is not a computer. It does not simply absorb information in bits and pieces that it never forgets. The indications are that it organizes the material into meaningful chunks, which it relates to information already contained in the individual's cognitive structure. This material is then stored for future use. The fact that meaningful relationships enhance learning does not imply that rote learning is impossible, but that it is less efficient and less productive. The schema on page 136 represent graphically what happens when the individual meets a learning situation.

Meaningful learning then, involves the integration of newly learned material into the learner's cognitive network. As the figures indicate, material that has been organized into meaningful units is more easily learned. Such

Figure 6.1:   Schema showing the knowledge bits that can be associated with an existing concept are accepted and "subsumed" to enlarge and strengthen this concept (meaningful learning). Nonsubsumable knowledge bits are not accepted by the learner or are learned independently (rote learning).

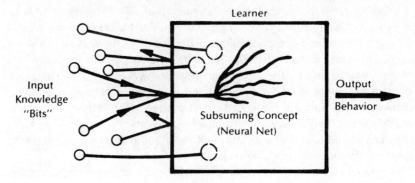

Source: (Novak, 1970, p. 778). Used by permission.

material also is more easily retained for longer periods of time. Too, it is much more valuable to the learner since the possibilities for application to new learning tasks and to acquiring new knowledge are much greater.

Figure 6.2:   Schema showing that appropriate knowledge sequences can serve as "organizers" to facilitate subsequent meaningful learning.

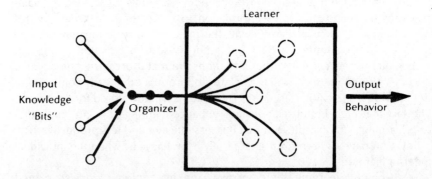

Source: (Novak, 1970, p. 778). Used by permission.

Influences from Linguistics

In 1957 Chomsky published *Syntactic Structures,* and in 1959 he reviewed Skinner's *Verbal Behavior.* These two publications have had a tremendous impact upon the conceptions regarding what language is and how language is learned. In both his works, Chomsky argues forcefully and logically that language is more complex than it had originally been considered. He, in effect, rejects prior behavioristic theories concerning both language and language learning as being too elementary and simplistic and adopts a mentalistic, rationalist view of learning and language closely related to the basic premises of cognitive psychologists.

Chomsky's ideas gave rise to a new school of linguistics. Those holding to this "new" branch of linguistics are usually referred to as transformational, generative, or transformational-generative (T-G) linguists. The name derives from the transformational-generative conception of language upon which their theories are based. Although many linguists do not accept the explanations given by T-G linguists, their theories have risen to a position of prominence since they were first proposed. In fact, after a review of the literature, Di Pietro (1968, p. 19) concluded, "The transformational-generative theory of linguistics continued its rapid development in 1968, with published works by its developers far outnumbering those of its adversaries."

Currently the transformationalists are primarily concerned with developing additional theoretical insights. The field is new and promising. As Di Pietro (1968, p. 19) states: ". . . The transformational-generative theory is far more productive than any alternative yet suggested." And Saporta (1966, p. 88) feels that ". . . there seems to be little question that the recent investigations by Noam Chomsky and others on the nature of language and grammar provide the most coherent view thus far proposed. . . ."

Green (1972) summarizes the innovations in the field of linguistics since 1965, saying that most of the new developments have grown out of Chomsky's conception of the goals that linguistic theory should seek to achieve. Although there is little disagreement with regard to aims, some controversies have arisen with regard to ways and means of achieving these objectives. The first is a proposal by Fillmore in 1968 that the study of case is a more productive approach to comprehending the basic relationships in deep structure than the more typical subject-verb organization.[1] Case categories, such as agentive, instrumental, and dative can be used to explain the difference between sentences such as *John broke the window,* and *A hammer broke the window.* In both sentences the subject is clear, but based on that analysis the

---

[1] See page 140 for further discussion of *deep structure.*

relationships within the sentences are not clear. Fillmore handles this problem by saying that *John* is agentive and that *hammer* is instrumental. Case grammar is not a major departure from the theories proposed by Chomsky. However, the second innovation, generative semantics, does differ somewhat from Chomsky's formulation. Chomsky holds that meaning resides in syntactical relationships and is expressed in semantic and phonological components. Those linguists adopting the generative-semantic viewpoint maintain that meaning resides in the semantic elements of language and is expressed in syntactical and phonological components.

Under the influence of Chomksy and his followers, the science of linguistics has taken on a new dimension. The objective in descriptive linguistics is to describe the language. The purpose of transformational-generative linguistics is more than a description; it is an understanding of the total language process. Ohmann (1969, p. 31) explains T-G objectives as follows:

> But in addition to describing the facts of language, a generative grammar tries to explain them; in this it differs from grammars of other kinds. To explain the facts of language is to link a description of them to what we know about human mental capacities. So a generative grammar is actually a theory of a particular language—more precisely, a theory of the knowledge that any fluent speaker has of that language. Herein is another sharp difference between generative and other grammars; what a generative grammar describes and explains is not merely the linguistic "output" of speakers but their *understanding* of language. In brief, a grammar of this sort attempts to describe part of human mentality. In the view of generative grammarians, grammar is a part of human psychology.

T-G linguists, then, hope to delve into the very basic elements of the human mind and thought processes through the study of language. They feel that language and mental processes are inextricably related and therefore must be studied together. In fact, in a more recent book, *Language and Mind*, 1968, Chomsky views the study of language as being a part of the larger context of cognitive psychology.

One of the basic characteristics of T-G linguists has been the emphasis that they have placed on syntax. As they have sought to understand language more completely, they have focused their attention not on streams of sounds but on the syntactical arrangement of words. The problem has been to determine how the component parts of language are put together. They have been interested, for example, in what determines the order in which words are placed in context to express meaning.

As early as 1957, Chomsky rejected the view that sentences are composed of strings of words formed in an ordered sequence from beginning to end.

Instead of explaining sentence structure on the basis of mathematical processes, he turned to rules, to the grammar of the language. In doing so, he initiated a return to the importance of rules in the study of languages.

In T-G theory, a grammar must be able to "generate" all sentences, but *only* those sentences that are acceptable to a native speaker.[2] At the same time, a grammar must be finite. Otherwise, no human would be able to acquire the system necessary for understanding and speaking a language.

From this view of grammar and study subsequent to its delineation by Chomsky, the following important concepts have emerged:

1. The use of language is controlled by rules. In other words, the speakers' knowledge of a language is based on a finite set of rules, which they activate in order to understand and to produce an infinite variety of language.
2. Language is infinitely varied. Native speakers are continually creating new utterances which they have never heard previously. To illustrate the complexity of language, Ohmann (1969, pp. 31–32) gives as an example the results of asking twenty-five native speakers to describe a drawing of a tourist waiting outside a telephone booth for a bear, who is inside, to finish using the phone. All the descriptions were different, yet contained basically the same information. A computer analysis of the varied descriptions revealed that they contained sufficient linguistic data for ". . . 19.8 billion sentences, all describing just one situation." He adds, "When one reflects that the number of seconds in a century is only 3.2 billion, it is clear that no speaker has heard, read, or spoken more than a tiny fraction of the sentences he *could* speak or understand, and that no one learns English by learning any particular sentences of English.
3. The view of language as being infinitely varied leads to another basic concept of the transformationalists. Since native speakers cannot possibly say everything they could say, a distinction must be made between that which they say and that which they know how to say. They refer to the ability as *competence* and to the expression of that ability as *performance*. In their opinion, competence is achieved prior to performance. It is a

---

[2]*Generate* in no way implies that the speaker can state the rule. Normally, native speakers cannot describe their own language. In the introduction to *Genesis of Language,* Smith and Miller explain, "By a *generative grammar* Chomsky means simply a system of rules that in some specific and well-defined way assigns structural descriptions to sentences. Obviously, every native speaker of a language has mastered and internalized a generative grammar that constitutes his knowledge of his language. Nevertheless, a generative grammar is *not* a model for a user of the language, either a speaker or a listener. The construction of a performance model based on the generative competence of the language user is a further task for the theorist and one that linguists share with their colleagues in psychology. The term *generative grammar* does not mean that actual sentences are produced by the abstract generative system of rules; actually producing the sentences according to the rules is not a matter of generative competence but of productive performance."

prerequisite to and a basis for the performance, i.e., the productive expression of the native speaker. Chomsky's contention is that the linguist and psychologist must first understand the native speaker's competence before they can begin to undertake the problem of explaining performance. In studying competence, the generative linguist asks native speakers to distinguish between those sentences that are grammatical and those that are ungrammatical. For example, the following sentence, *Colorless green ideas sleep furiously,* is immediately recognized by a speaker of English as being grammatical, although little meaning can be attached to it. Scrambling the words to read, *Furiously sleep ideas green colorless,* renders the sentence ungrammatical as well as nonmeaningful. However, the same order of grammatical forms in the sentence, *Friendly young dogs seem harmless,* is grammatical and meaningful (Lenneberg, 1967, pp. 273–74).

4. The analysis of sentences and their grammaticalness leads to the formation of another basic concept, that of surface structure and deep structure. Surface structure is what we hear and read; yet meaning is connected with the deep structure of a sentence. Although on the surface the structure of the two sentences *John is easy to please,* and *John is eager to please,* is identical, anyone who speaks English immediately knows that the meaning is different. In the first, the meaning is that it is easy to please John. In the second, John is eager to please someone else. Ohmann has described three abilities that a native speaker possesses. First, he is able to derive different meanings from sentences that are exactly the same. For example, the native speaker knows *I had three books stolen,* may mean either *I had three books stolen from me, I had three books stolen for me,* or *I had three books stolen when someone interrupted my burgalarizing.* Second, he is able to detect differences in sentences that seem to be the same. For example, a speaker of English is aware of the difference between *The cow was found by the stream,* and *The cow was found by the farmer.* Third, he is able to see similarities in sentences that do not look the same. For example, he understands that *The cow was found by the farmer,* and *The farmer found the cow* express the same idea (Ohmann, 1969, p. 32).

5. The problem of explaining the existence of deep and surface structure is solved by utilizing two types of grammar rules. The first, generative rules, are applied to explain the formation of base sentences such as *The students write the exercises.* This, of course, is a typical sentence consisting of a subject, a verb, and a direct object. Rules of transformation are then applied to account for the transformation of these sentences into additional, more complex, but related sentences. An example often given is that of the passive voice. The conversion of the base sentence to *The exercises are*

written by the students, is explained on the basis of rules of transformation. The same types of rules are employed to explain the fact that native speakers have the ability to recognize deep structure meanings even though they hear or see only the surface structure.

6. T-G linguists disagree as to whether meaning resides in semantics or in syntactical structure. However, they do tend to agree that the meaning, i.e., the deep structure, does originate with one or the other and that the total communication is then developed through the other two components of language, either semantics or syntax plus phonology.

7. The fact that children learning their mother tongue hear only surface speech, yet learn deep structure poses another problem. How do they learn something to which they have not been exposed? The answer given by transformationalists is that all humans are born with an innate capacity to learn languages. This ability is universal.

8. Another universal, according to transformational theory, is grammar itself. The hypothesis is made that there are certain basic elements of grammar that are common to all languages. In other words, although the model is not that provided by Latin grammar, the concept of a universal grammar is now accepted by the transformationalists.

Processing Thought to Language

Although little is known for sure about the process of going from thought to language, cognitive psychologists and transformational-generative linguists accept the existence of this process. If they are right and if the goal in second-language learning is to attain a level of proficiency at which learners can convert their thoughts into the second language, more information regarding this process needs to be acquired and more activities in which second-language learners participate in this process need to be provided.

In an insightful essay dealing with this topic, Vigotsky (1961) describes thought as a subword process carried out at the sense level. External speech does not coincide with inner speech. When one talks to a good friend, a great deal of abbreviation is possible due to the close bonds that exist between the two people. Speaking to someone who is not so close requires more words to convey exact meaning. Oral communication with someone who has a distinctly different background would require even more words. Writing does not have the advantages of intonation patterns, facial expressions, and hand signals, and, therefore, requires an even more precise and complete use of words. The point is that the farther one goes from thought the more complete use of word descriptions of thought is necessary.

Thoughts, then, are a series of sense impressions, and the conversion of thoughts to language is a process of going from thoughts consisting of sense images through inner speech to external speech consisting of words more or less concise depending upon the person to whom one is talking. The next question is, "What is the stimulus for thoughts?" Vigotsky's answer is that they arise out of our desire and needs. Vigotsky (1961, p. 533) summarizes his discussion as follows:

> Thought and words do not coincide. Thought, unlike speech, does not consist of separate words. If I want to communicate the thought that today I saw a barefooted boy in a blue shirt running down the street, I do not see everything concerning that separately: the boy, the shirt, its blue color, his running, the absence of shoes. I see all this in one act of thinking, but in transferring it into speech I put it in separate words. A speaker very often unfolds one and the same thought in the course of several minutes. In his mind the thought is there simultaneously, but in speech it has to be developed successively. A thought can be compared to a cloud which sheds a shower of words. Thought fails to coincide not only with words but also with the meanings of words in which it is expressed, yet the way from thought to words leads through meaning. In our speech there is always hidden thought, an "under-text."
>
> We now have to take the final step in the analysis of the inner planes of thinking-in-words. Thought is not the last instance in this whole process. Thought itself is not born out of another thought—but out of the sphere of motivation which comprises our desires and needs, our interests and emotions. Behind thought stands the affective and volitional tendency. It alone can give an answer to the last "why" in the analysis of thinking. If thought may be compared to a cloud shedding a rain of words—the motivation of thought might be compared to wind which sets the clouds in motion. A true and full understanding of another person's thought becomes possible only when we understand its real affective-volitional basis.
>
> Thinking-in-words appeared as a complex dynamic whole in which the relation between words and thought revealed itself as a development and transition from one plane to another. . . . In the actual thinking-in-words the development takes place in the opposite direction—from the motive which brings forth a thought, to the formation of this thought, to its materialization in inner speech—then in the meanings of external words, and finally—in words.

Resulting Theories of Language and Learning

New theories of learning have shifted away from the conditioning models of the behaviorists. Cognitive psychologists do not accept the results of experiments with animal behavior as valid models for human learning. Instead, they have turned to neurophysiological and information-processing models as a basis for trying to understand the learning process. They are attempting to go beyond earlier solutions to problems regarding learning. In the words of Harper et al. (1964, p. v), ". . . Another stage of development is essential, consisting of a more systematic and vigorous attack on the thought processes." The behavioristic definition of learning stressed behavior; the cognitive definition stresses the role of the mind in processing the information acquired. A cognitive definition of learning is similar to the following: Learning is the perception, acquisition, organization, and storage of knowledge in such a way that it becomes an active part of the individual's cognitive structure. In this view of learning, the central component in the learning process is the learner, not the agent in the environment controlling the stimuli and the reinforcers.

This same trend away from behavioristic definitions of learning is equally apparent with regard to language. Recent theoretical models reflect a conception of language that is much more complex than that accepted by behavioristic psychology and structural linguistics. In *Language Teaching: Broader Contexts* (1966, p. 44), Chomsky, one of the prime movers in more recent linguistic studies, says, ". . . It seems to me impossible to accept the view that linguistic behavior is a matter of habit, that it is slowly acquired by reinforcement, association, and generalization. . . ." Just as cognitive definitions of learning stress mental processes so, too, do cognitive definitions of language. The definition of language as conditioned verbal responses to previously met stimuli does not seem adequate to explain the infinitely vast repertoire of a native speaker. Language is now considered to be creative, rule-governed behavior. As is true in the cognitive definition of learning, this definition of language assigns the central role to the learner.

IMPLICATIONS FOR LANGUAGE TEACHING

Neither cognitive psychologists nor transformational-generative linguists are interested in second-language pedagogy as such. Their chief concern lies in the realm of learning and language in general. In fact, the generative linguists maintain that at the present state of knowledge they have nothing to say to the second-language teacher. Ausubel does discuss language teaching from an overall point of view, but he offers no outline of classroom techniques nor practical classroom applications of his theories. Perhaps this situation is a healthy one. After all, theory and practice should complement each other, and the teachers are the ones who should concern themselves with the application of theory to the classroom instead of expecting to be told by the linguists and the psychologists how they should teach.

Cognitive Psychology

Cognitive interpretations of learning assign a central and dominant role to the mental processes that are subject to the individual's control. The individual's knowledge does not consist of conditioned behavior but of assimilated information within her cognitive resources that makes her behavior possible and controls it. Rote learning and motor learning are considered to be relatively unimportant in the explanation of basic and higher mental activity. The extrapolation of learning outcomes from animal to human subjects is rejected.

The role of the teacher is to recognize the importance of the students' mental assets and mental activity in learning. In the final analysis, learning resides within the learner. The teacher's task is to organize the material being presented in such a manner that what is to be learned will be meaningful to the learner. To do this, he is obligated to consider the students' existing cognitive structure. What do they already know? What information do they bring with them to the learning situation? His next obligation is to try to couch the material in such a fashion and in such a context that the learners can relate the content to their existing fund of knowledge. The new information, if learning is to be meaningful, must be relatable by the students to their past knowledge and experience. By his teaching and testing procedures, the teacher should demonstrate to the students that he does not expect rote learning in order to return a verbatim regurgitation of the material. In addition, he should encourage an active, questioning attitude on the part of the students, which helps them to understand and relate what is being learned to what they already know. Periodic application sessions in which the students are expected to demonstrate an ability to recall what they have learned and to "use" it are basic to insuring that the information is functional and can be utilized to further additional learning or to solve problems.

Transformational-Generative Linguistics

Although T-G linguists disclaim any insights into second-language teaching itself, language teachers would do well to consider some of their ideas, such as the following:
1. Teaching all the sentences and expressions that students may need to know is impossible. Language is too complex and too varied to anticipate all the varied situations that may be encountered at some time in the future.

2. Since the whole of language cannot be taught, the teacher should concentrate on teaching the students the system that makes language production possible. Language competence precedes language performance. Before asking the students to perform, the teacher should establish the basic foundation or foundations that make performance possible.

3. Using language implies combining the building blocks of language in novel ways as new situations arise. Therefore, the teacher should provide opportunities for the students to create language as they seek to function in language-demanding situations. In order for the resultant expressions of language to be creative, the opportunities must be linguistically unique as far as the students are concerned. For example, preparing a dialog may provide practice in the creative recombination of language.

4. Teachers should keep in mind that language consists of both competence and performance as they direct the learning sequences in their classes. They should not forget to provide for the establishment of a system and subsequent opportunities to invoke that system.

5. The teacher needs to be attentive to this distinction between generative and transformational rules as she plans her teaching activities. As soon as the students can form basic sentences involving the material being learned, she should initiate additional exercises in which they practice the many variations and transformations possible. They must learn that with only a small amount of linguistic data they can create hundreds of sentences. Such insight is not automatic, and the teacher bears a great deal of the responsibility for seeing that it does take place.

6. The grammar of a language does contain elements that are universal. At present, linguists are concentrating their efforts on determining just what these universals are. *If* they succeed in their task, their conclusions will be most helpful to textbook writers and to teachers. (Hopefully, they will be able to ascertain additional similarities of forms and structures that perceptive teachers have not already determined on the basis of their own experience!) Until that time arrives, teachers should remember that there are common structures in the first and second languages, and they should focus upon these similarities as a means of utilizing the grammatical knowledge that the students have of their own language in order to facilitate their learning of the second language.

7. The stress placed on phonology, semantics, and syntax may well vary depending upon whether one accepts Chomsky's theories or the tenets of generative semantics. Those holding to Chomsky's conception of language will stress syntax with semantics and phonology playing secondary roles, while those favoring the generative-semantic viewpoint will place primary emphasis on semantics as the basic building block of language learning.

Processing Thought to Language

Although highly speculative, Vigotsky's (1961) postulated model of thinking and speaking, which he readily admits may be only one of several procedures the individual has of going from thought to a linguistic manifestation of that thought, is acceptably logical and corresponds quite closely to the introspective experience of most, if not all, language speakers. His interpretation of the thought to language process implies the following:

1. *Productive language skills,* i.e., speaking and writing, develop from thoughts through inner speech to the external expression of these thoughts in words. The *receptive language skills,* i.e., listening and reading, are the reverse of the productive.
2. Second-language learners must be given opportunities to participate in this type of process if they are to be expected to develop "real" language skills.
3. Language originates out of some need or desire. The second-language teacher, then, must be concerned not only with the learners' ability to communicate; she must also be concerned with their willingness and desire to communicate. The establishment of some reason to communicate and of an atmosphere in which communication is encouraged, expected, and rewarded is also necessary. Second-language teachers should attempt to avoid conducting classes in which the students with the greatest skills at the communicative competence level do not receive the best grades. They should attempt to avoid conducting a class in which the determining factor in course grades is rote memory, whether it be of dialogs and pattern drills or of verb paradigms and grammar rules. Such a class will certainly not encourage students to concentrate on linguistic expression of thoughts.

BASIC TENETS OF THE COGNITIVE APPROACH

Cognitive theory supports the thesis that learning in general and language learning in particular are internal, mental operations controlled by the individual. The second-language learner is seen as consciously acquiring *competence* in a meaningful manner as a necessary prerequisite in the acquisition of the *performance* skills. The teacher assists learning but does not assume full responsibility for it. Following are some basic tenets of the cognitive approach to second-language learning and teaching:

1. The goal is to develop in the students the same types of abilities possessed by native speakers. The goal is the same as that proposed by audio-lingual

theorists, but the conception of what language is differs. The objective according to cognitive proponents is to develop the students' ability to the point at which they have a minimum control over the rules that allow native speakers to create the language necessary to communicate. That is, they should reach the point at which they can formulate their own replies to previously unmet language situations.

2. In developing the students' language ability, the teacher proceeds from competence to performance. First, he must establish in the students' cognitive structure the necessary prerequisites that enable the students to perform. That is, they must know the rules of the language before being asked to apply those rules. The foundation comes first. This base is made up of the grammar of the language.

3. As soon as the students comprehend the underlying structure, they must be required to perform. Since language is basically a creative activity, they need to activate their competence in order to create the specific utterances required. Textual materials and the teacher introduce situations that promote the creative use of language.[3] The primary concern is that the students have active practice in going from thought to performance by means of competence.

4. The infinitely varied and innovative nature of language necessitates teaching of the language rule system, not language per se. Attention to and acquisition of the basic aspects of the language system cannot be omitted. Otherwise, what does the second-language learner have to guide him as he creates the language needed to express his thoughts? However, this language system must be learned not as an endless series of abstract rules and exceptions to these rules but as a functional system which can be applied to communicative contexts.

5. Learning should be meaningful. The students should understand at all times what they are being asked to do. They should understand what they are saying, writing, reading, and hearing. New material should be organized to relate to knowledge that the students already have about their own language, the second language learned to that point in the course, and their concepts about the world about them. Since not all students rely on the same senses to learn, the teacher should appeal to both the eye and the ear through written and oral exercises in order to teach the language.

---

[3]*Creative*, in the sense the word is being used here, does not connote artistic, aesthetic originality. The point is that the students shoud be given the opportunity to create needed language communications. Nor should the word "creative" be confused with the students' tendency to create language which is neither his native language nor the second language. They should be learning to create needed language for communications, not to create nonexistent language forms.

BASIC CHARACTERISTICS OF A
COGNITIVE CLASS

Classroom procedures based on cognitive theories of learning emphasize understanding rather than habit formation. The task of the teacher in a cognitive classroom is to facilitate student acquisition, organization, and storage of knowledge rather than to develop automatic, nonthoughtful responses through reinforcement procedures. The goal of the teacher in such a classroom is to expand the students' ability to create meaningful replies to any given circumstance rather than to emit a conditioned response.[4] The teacher recognizes a hierarchy of tasks in developing language skills. In preparing to lead the students from initial presentation of new material through to the use of that material in communicative contexts, she selects appropriate activities and arranges them in a sequential order of increasing difficulty, each nearer the goal of "real" language usage than the preceding one.

The students should always be aware of what they are learning. All learning is to be meaningful. In order to foster student comprehension, the teacher presents all new structures and concepts in such a way as to maximize student understanding of functional patterns and relationships in the language. In these introductions she does the following:

1. Builds on what the students already know.
2. Helps the students relate new material to themselves, their life experiences, and their previous knowledge.
3. Avoids rote learning (except perhaps in the case of vocabulary).
4. Uses graphic and schematic procedures to clarify relationships.
5. Utilizes both written and spoken language in order to appeal to as many senses as possible.
6. Attempts to select the most appropriate teaching-learning situation for the students involved.
7. Employs the first-language, visuals, or demonstrations as a base from which to build conceptualization of meaning and form in the second language.
8. Uses inductive, deductive, or discovery-learning procedures as the situation warrants.
9. Distinguishes between the various backgrounds and potentials of each student.
10. Stresses the functional use of grammatical patterns, not abstract rules per se.
11. Attends to student attitudes as well as to comprehension of content.

---

[4]The author gratefully acknowledges the contribution of Professor Gilbert Jarvis, of the Department of Modern Language Education at Ohio State University, in preparing the following lists.

12. Gives students a chance to queston and practice.

As the students progress in acquiring the necessary competence, they should:

1. Realize that using a language involves combining component elements.
2. Know the building blocks of any sentence or phrase being studied as well as the total meaning.
3. Be conscious of which structure is being studied and comprehend its relationship to the other parts of the utterance.
4. Practice with exercises that force them at first to make conscious selections of appropriate forms and to choose between and/or among related structures.
5. Attempt to relate the various components of language to each other.

As the students progress in acquiring the necessary performance skills, they should:

1. Be given opportunities to go from language to thought either by listening or reading and from thought to language either by speaking or writing.
2. Be given both assistance and encouragement as they participate in these processes.

This outline of classroom procedures and guidelines designed to implement cognitive interpretations of learning and language can only point out indicated directions. The psychologist and the linguist can do little more than give general guidelines to second-language teachers. It is the teacher herself, not the psychologist or the linguist, who is responsible for the adaptation of theory to practice. Theory without practice is incomplete, but so, too, is practice without the support of theory.

COGNITIVE TEACHING

Cognitive teaching is a direct application in the classroom of the classroom procedures previously outlined in this chapter. In cognitive teaching, the major emphasis is placed on meaningful learning, meaningful practice, and expression of meaning. In the following sections, attention is focused on textbooks containing cognitive exercises and activities, on organizing the material in a cognitive text, and on procedures used to teach cognitive materials.

Cognitive Textbooks

The materials in a cognitive textbook are sequenced in such a manner that the learner progresses from comprehension to a state of competence and then to a level of functional performance skills. In addition, the materials are so arranged that the learner is first exposed to the parts to be learned and then to the total communicative picture. Throughout the text, the emphasis is on meaningful learning and meaningful practice and application activities. If all four skills are to be stressed in the course (and all four are considered to be complementary in the learning process), each is coordinated in the course sequence and activities to reinforce acquisition of competence and performance in each of the other skills.

Comprehension   The most important task of the writer of a cognitive text is to present the material, whether it be some phonological, semantic, or syntactical aspect of the language system or culture, in such a way that the second-language learner can comprehend the concepts involved. The author may attempt to address his material to (1) a given level of knowledge, or he may attempt to (2) teach all the information needed to understand the concept being presented. The most common approach, which is often difficult for the learner to comprehend given the diversity obviously present in any class larger than one, is the former. The burden for the selection and preparation of meaningful presentations is the responsibility of the teacher. An excellent example of the latter approach is *Spanish for Communication* by Bull et al. (1972). Using a frame format, the authors present all the information the students need to know in a self-teaching approach to the comprehension of the language system. They begin by establishing comprehension of the English system and then relate it to the Spanish. For example, the forms of the singular indefinite articles are presented as follows:

Forms of the articles and plurals

1 The sounds represented by the letters *a, e, i, o,* and *u* are called (a) consonants (b) vowels.

vowels

2 All the other letters, such as *p, c, b, g, m,* etc., stand for sounds which are called ‿‿‿‿‿.

consonants

3 All English words must begin either with a vowel or a consonant sound. This tells us when we must use *a* or *an,* the two forms of the indefinite article. Look at these two columns of words and notice the sound with which each noun begins.

a pen	an apple
a book	an eagle
a cow	an iceberg
a girl	an ocean
a man	an umbrella

The indefinite article form *a* goes with words which begin with a ‿‿‿‿‿ sound; *an* goes with words which begin with a ‿‿‿‿‿ sound.

a goes with consonant sounds; *an* with vowel sounds. (When a consonant letter is not spoken, you use *an:* an hour.)
4 Do *a* and *an,* in *a pen* and *an apple,* have different meanings?
no (Two forms having the same function may have the same meaning.)
5 Spanish, like English, has two forms of the indefinite article. You have
already learned them. They are *un* and *una.* But Spanish is just the
opposite of English. The *last* sound of a word (with very few exceptions)
tells the Spanish speaker when to use *un* or *una.* Look at these two
columns of words and notice the last sound of each noun.

un libro	una mesa
un rodeo	una silla
un santo	una casa

The indefinite article form *un* goes with nouns which end in the vowel
~~~~~~ ; *una* goes with nouns ending in the vowel~~~~~~.
un with *o; una* with *a* (The few exceptions have to be memorized.)[5]

Mueller and Niedzielski in *Pratique de la Grammaire: Basic French,*
Second Edition (1974) also base their arrangement of materials on the establishment of initial comprehension of structure prior to practice. First, they
acquaint the student with the related English concepts and patterns. This
introduction is followed by a complete explanation with examples of the
French concepts and patterns. The students then complete a self-checking test
of their comprehension before proceeding to pattern drills or application
exercises, depending upon how much practice they need to acquire a
functional mastery of the structure.

Exercises   Cognitive exercises differ from audio-lingual drills. The purpose of
a drill is to condition automatic responses into the learner's repertoire of
verbal S-R connections. The purpose of a cognitive exercise is the comprehension of forms, the conscious learning of forms, and the conscious selection of
forms to fit the context. The following are selected examples of cognitive type
exercises:

STRUCTURE SIGNALS
The learner demonstrates comprehension without actually manipulating
language forms.

Listen to the following sentences. After each sentence write **M** if the
adjective you hear is masculine or **F** if the adjective you hear is feminine:

---
[5]Bull et al. (1972, p. 20). Reprinted by permission.

1. Je suis grand.
2. Je suis française.
3. Vous êtes américain?
4. Tu es petit.
5. Je suis américain.

6. Je suis petite.
7. Tu es français.
8. Tu es grande.
9. Vous êtes grand.
10. Je suis française.[6]

PRODUCTION OF FORMS

At the next step the learner either chooses or gives the form required in the sentence.

a. Complete the following sentences with the appropriate reflexive pronoun to agree with the subject and the verb: myself, yourself, himself, herself, ourselves, yourselves, themselves

1. He hurt_____.
2. They see _____.
3. I cut _____.

4. John, did you hurt _____?
5. We treat _____.
6. She dressed_____.

b. Complete the following sentences with the correct form of the verb given in parentheses.

1. (to hurt oneself) Did she _____?
2. (to free oneself) Can they _____?
3. (to see oneself) No, we did not _____.
4. (to dress oneself) Yes, you can _____.
5. (to treat oneself) Yes, I often _____.
6. (to fool oneself) No, he never _____.

ESTABLISHING A CONTEXT OR SITUATION

The student's response will reveal whether or not he comprehends the concept and whether or not he can choose the correct form or forms to demonstrate the proper language usage. The first exercise checks the distinction between the formal and the familiar forms of address in Spanish.

Ask the indicated questions in Spanish.

1. You are talking with your teacher, and you want to know where he is from. You ask. ¿ _____?
2. You are talking with your friend, and you want to know where she is from. You ask. ¿ _____?
3. You are talking with your friend María, and you want to know if she is from Madrid. You ask. ¿ _____?
4. You are talking with Mr. Sánchez, and you want to know whether he is Mexican. You ask. ¿ _____?

---

[6]Coulombe et al. (1974, p. T83). Reprinted by permission.

Answer the following questions by using the information in parentheses together with the appropriate preposition from the list below. NOTE: There is *only one* sensible answer to each question.

ausser	gegenüber	seit
bei	mit	zu

1. Wohin möchten Sie denn, Fräulein? (das neue Kunstmuseum)
2. Geht Frau Köhler allein einkaufen? (nein; ihre kleine Tochter)
3. Wo wohnt der Amerikaner? (die nette Frau Möller)
4. Wo ist Georgs Büro? (das neue Theater)
5. Seid ihr schon lange hier? (ja; der erste Januar)
6. Wer weiss die Antwort? (Max; keiner)[7]

"REALISTIC" PRACTICE

A step closer to "real" language skills is the type of exercise Stevick (1971) refers to as "realistic" practice. This is a simple communicative exchange used to practice grammatical structure.

Question-answer patterns of verbs:

1. Are you a student?   Yes, I am a student.
2. Am I a student?   No, you are not a student.
3. Are we students?   Yes, you are students.
4. Is he a student?   Yes, he is a student.

Practice of idiomatic expressions:

1. ¿Van a comer?   No, acaban de comer.
2. ¿Vas a abrirlo?   No, acabo de abrirlo.
3. ¿Van ustedes a comer?   No, acabamos de comer.
4. ¿Va a salir?   No, acaba de salir.

A grammar point, *there,* practiced in a conversational exchange:

Je vais au magasin.	J'y vais avec vous.
I'm going to the store.	I'm going with you.
Vous n'y êtes pas allé hier?	Non, je n'y suis pas allé.
Didn't you go there yesterday?	No, I didn't (go there).

Je vais à l'école.   J'y vais avec vous.
  Vous n'y êtes pas allé hier?   Non je n'y suis pas allé.
Je rentre à la maison.   J'y rentre avec vous.
  Vous n'y êtes pas rentré hier?   Non, je n'y suis pas rentré.

---

[7]Excerpt from an exercise to appear in *Deutsch: Stimme und Bild* (Chicago: Rand McNally). In preparation. Used by permission.

Je reste à l'hôtel.	J'y reste avec vous.
Vous n'y êtes pas resté hier?	Non, je n'y suis pas resté.
Je travaille à l'usine.	J'y travaille avec vous.
Vous n'y avez pas travaillé hier?	Non, je n'y ai pas travaillé.[8]

Since cognitive exercises are not designed to trigger automatic, non-thoughtful responses and therefore do not require immediate reinforcement, they can be completed in independent study situations. The correct answers can be included in the text itself, as in the case of *Spanish for Communication* and *Basic French,* or the correct answers can be supplied during the following class period either by the students themselves or by the teacher. One advantage of employing cognitive exercises is that given a successful meaningful learning preparation more class time is freed for application activities.

Application activities   The final portion of the chapter or unit in the text is designed to provide the students with opportunities for incorporating what they have learned into a communicative whole. Students should be asked to participate in activities in which the material they have been working with plus previously learned vocabulary and grammar is combined into listening comprehension and/or reading passages. The purpose of these activities is to provide practice in utilizing consciously acquired competence in receiving oral or written messages. At the same time, the learners should have the opportunity to produce messages intended to communicate their thoughts to someone else.

Most textbooks provide for performance in reading, but often they do not provide sufficient practice at the performance level in listening comprehension. Also, there should be sufficient time for speaking and writing during the language-learning sequence. Written language can be completed independently, but class time should be spent on speaking in the second language. In the more recent texts, authors and publishers are attempting to include more ideas for getting the students to participate in activities in which they practice the productive language skills at the communicative level. Following are some examples of types of activities that stimulate production of oral and/or written language:

1. Answering questions over reading or listening comprehension passages.
2. Asking and/or answering personalized questions.
3. Completing sentences to give one's own opinion or feelings: i.e., I like (don't like) television because. . . . I like (don't like) exams because. . . .
4. Describing pictures.
5. Interviewing, demonstrating, explaining.

---

[8]Mueller & Niedzielski (1974, p. 139). Reprinted by permission.

In all these activities the learners should be converting their thoughts into the second language. They should be using their acquired competence to generate the language needed. Needless to say, as the beginners create language appropriate to the situation with an interim grammar that does not correspond exactly to the second-language grammar, their utterances will never be masterpieces of expression, and in fact they will often contain inaccuracies. This period, according to cognitive theories of learning and language learning, cannot be avoided. Indeed, it is a necessary preliminary to the development of second-language skills. In fact it is this very process of hypothesis testing that the learner uses to reach the native grammar level.

In addition to preparing presentations of concepts that are consistent with the students' previous knowledge and providing practice manipulating and choosing appropriate forms in cognitive exercises, the author and/or teacher needs to demonstrate the applicability of these concepts in contexts that the students can relate to their present and past life experiences. For example, can they relate to what they are reading or to what they are doing with the language? Have they ever had any experiences similar to those taking place in the dialog or the reading? Is the vocabulary related to concepts that are important to their life and interests? Are the materials interesting in their own right, or are they presented merely to use the grammar and vocabulary in the unit? Two factors are involved in the relatability of content to the learner. The first, the ability to relate to the materials, is cognitive; the second, the set to learn the materials and to integrate them into the cognitive structure, is affective. Both are quite obviously closely interrelated.

Proceeding Through the Text

The book is introduced at the very beginning of the course, since all four language skills are introduced at approximately the same time. There is no prereading period, and the students can be expected to prepare written homework as early as the first day of class. Nor is it axiomatic that the four skills be introduced in the so-called natural sequence. Admittedly, children learn their native language orally before they are introduced to reading and writing. However, it does not necessarily follow that a similar sequence is most effective in learning a second language. A sequence in which the written skills are learned prior to the oral might be just as effective. Decoding activities, such as those the students perform in listening and reading, must precede encoding activities, i.e., speaking and writing. Listening and reading—the receptive skills—are in effect the means of developing and expanding "competence." This statement in no way implies that receptive skills are passive. They are not. Active mental processes are involved.

The students proceed through the book in its arranged order, studying the structural presentations, the exercises, and then the application activities. Since most texts contain several new structures in each chapter or unit, the teacher needs to decide upon the amount of new material that he feels the students can assimilate, and then follow the sequence for each structure. For example, if a chapter includes a new verb form plus agreement of adjectives, on the first day the teacher introduces one of the grammatical topics, beginning a sequential progression for that point. The next day a sequence involving the other structure is started. The implication of progressing through the book in this manner is that each day the students have some new material, some exercises, and some application activities.

Classroom Procedures

Introduction of new material   The first step in the classroom is to present all new sounds, vocabulary, and structures in a manner meaningful to each student. New sounds and their symbols are practiced as they appear. This practice with sounds resembles that of the audio-lingual classes very closely except that descriptions of mouth and tongue positions would most likely be given, and the symbol would be introduced along with the sound. New words and forms can be introduced in various ways. New vocabulary can be presented with visual aids, by means of native-language or second-language definitions, or through context. New structures can be presented by means of visuals, contrastive comparisons, explanations, examples, or, in the case of concrete examples such as prepositions of place, by demonstrations. The introduction of new material serves as the basis for all future exercises and application activities. During this part of the class, the purpose is to establish a cognitive base from which language skills can be developed.

Exercises   The exercises completed by the students in a cognitive class are designed to complete the understanding process begun during the introduction of new material, to help the students learn to manipulate and to remember these forms, and to demonstrate comprehension of usage. Usually, these exercises are written at home as part of the homework assignment, and they require the students to make a conscious selection of word or form. As far as possible, these exercises are written entirely in the second language, but occasional clues in the first language are sometimes given.

Application activities   The students by this time in the sequence should be able to conceptualize the structures being taught and to manipulate the forms. Their competence with regard to the grammar introduced should have reached a level at which they can begin to activate slowly and consciously these concepts in order to begin to express themselves. They are now ready to undertake performance activities.

The teacher can now assign the reading or listening comprehension passage for the students to study. In these passages, of course, the students have an opportunity to see the learned forms used in context. Such activity helps them to comprehend how what they have learned can be fitted together to communicate.

After having practiced the reading and listening comprehension passages, the learners should also engage in producing their own thoughts in the second language orally and in writing. At this point their proficiency will not challenge that of their teacher, but they and the teacher should focus on understanding and making themselves understood in the second language. The attainment of performance skills depends upon early and continued participation in such activities.

RESEARCH ON COGNITIVE APPROACHES TO SECOND-LANGUAGE LEARNING

In a series of studies from 1966 to 1969, Mueller (1971) compared the achievement of students studying audio-lingual materials and cognitive materials. Achievement scores in listening, reading, and writing were much higher for those students working with cognitive materials.

A series of studies, called the GUME project, were conducted in Sweden comparing the "implicit" method, consisting of drills but no analysis or explanation, and the "explicit" method, consisting of analysis, explanations, and practice in the manipulation of forms. For fourteen-year olds in their fourth year of English there was no significant difference between the two methods (Levin, 1969). Another study by Levin and Olsson (1969) with advanced students also found no significant difference between the two approaches. In a later comparison by von Elek and Oskarsson (1972) with adults, the explicit method was superior on class achievement scores and on an oral test, at all age levels, and at all proficiency levels. In addition, the authors concluded that once the students understand the language, structure pattern drills are of only limited value. In general, these studies seemed to concentrate on the acquisition of grammatical concepts rather than language skills.

During the 1966–67 academic year, Chastain and Woerdehoff conducted an investigation comparing the audio-lingual habit theory and the cognitive code-learning theory as applied to teaching first-year Spanish at the college level. The authors defined the audio-lingual approach as having three basic characteristics: (1) the use of pattern drills, (2) the inductive presentation of new structure, and (3) the introduction of the four language skills in the natural order of listening, speaking, reading, and writing. The cognitive classes were taught (1) using traditional exercises, (2) presenting deductive grammatical explanations, and (3) utilizing all four language skills from the beginning of the course. At the end of the first year, the audio-lingual students received significantly higher scores in repeating sentences after a native speaker; the cognitive students received significantly higher scores in reading. There was no difference in the students' ability to answer questions and describe pictures. Achievement scores in listening and writing favored the cognitive students, although the differences were not significant. The authors concluded that the results favored cognitive teaching procedures.

The most extensive study to date in the general area of methodological comparison of audio-lingual versus traditional teaching procedures was the Pennsylvania Project.[9] This study was conducted at the high-school level and included classes in French and German from various high schools throughout the state. Although careful preparation attempted to control important variables in the project, and although it was well done in this respect, certain weaknesses are inevitable in a project of such vast scope. The Pennsylvania Project was no exception. Nevertheless, the outcomes present important information with regard to conditions as they exist in the schools. In this sense, the study is more correctly viewed as a descriptive study than as a truly experimental one. The important conclusions at the end of the first year were as follows:

1. "Traditional" students exceeded or equalled "functional skills" students in all measures.[10]
2. The language laboratory systems (employed twice weekly) had no discernible effect.
3. There was no "optimum" combination of strategy and system.
4. The best combination of predictors of success were the MLA *Cooperative Classroom Listening Test,* the *ML Aptitude Test,* and language IQ as measured by the *California Test of Mental Maturity* (Short Form).
5. Females achieved better than males.
6. Student attitude was independent of the strategy employed.
7. "Functional skills" classes proceeded more slowly than "traditional" classes.
8. There was no relationship between teacher scores on all seven portions of the MLA *Teacher Proficiency Tests* and the achievement of their students in foreign-language skills.

---

[9] For critical reviews of this project the reader should consult the *NALLD Newsletter,* 3 (March 1969); *Modern Language Journal,* 53 (October 1969); *Foreign Language Annals,* 3 (December 1969).

[10] In this report, "functional skills" refers to the audio-lingual approach and TLM to the traditional approach.

After another year of investigation and replication, the following conclusions were reached:

1. No significant differences existed among strategies on all skills except reading (TLM<) as measured on contemporary standardized tests after two years.
2. The language laboratory of any type, used twice weekly, had no discernible effect on achievement.
3. The best over-all predictors of success are prior academic success and a modern-language aptitude test.
4. Student opinion of foreign-language study declines throughout the instruction, independent of teaching strategy employed.
5. Published test "norms" and implied in text layout progress were more than most of the experimental population achieved.
6. Within the functional skills strategies students utilizing Holt, Rinehart and Winston materials did significantly better than students using the *Audio-Lingual Materials.*
7. Neither teacher experience in years and graduate education nor scores on the MLA *Teacher Proficiency Tests* are related to mean class achievement after one or two years (Smith & Baranyi, 1968).

CONCLUSION

Proponents of a cognitive approach have as their first goal the development of *competence* (as the term is used in T-G linguistics) in the second-language learner. The means employed to achieve this goal are based on mentalistic interpretations of learning. A cognitive teacher accepts the fact that the native speaker does not have to think about language as such during the communicative process, but she does not agree that the language was learned in the same fashion. As Chastain (1969) said in an article in the *International Review of Applied Linguistics:*

> They [cognitive proponents] feel that the fact that a habit is an action which can be performed without conscious thought in no way negates a process of conscious, continued application in developing the skill. For example, the fact that a man ties a tie or drives a car without conscious awareness of individual actions in no way signifies that this skill was attained without thinking through each step in the beginning stages of learning. Thus, these instructors place primary emphasis on student comprehension of structure. With further practice, the student can perfect his ability to use these same structures unconsciously, leaving his mind free to concentrate on the content of the speech.

The second goal is to give the students opportunities to develop functional, not necessarily perfect, performance skills. The students need to be placed in situations in which they can activate their interim learner language and compare the product with native language. They need to be given many and continued opportunities to convert their thoughts into the second language, both in writing and in speech, independently and in conversational interchanges.

Cognitive presentations of material and cognitive exercises are outgrowths of the belief that new material must be presented in such a manner that the students are learning meaningfully. Exercises are designed to give the students a chance to demonstrate comprehension as they consciously select correct forms. The latter portion of any learning sequence contains materials and activities in which the students are given the opportunity to communicate using what they have learned. During the entire sequence, learning is viewed as primarily an internal process assisted by the text and the teacher.

REVIEW AND APPLICATION

DEFINITIONS

1. competence vs. performance, p. 140
2. comprehension activities vs. exercises vs. application activities, pp. 150–55
3. deep structure vs. surface structure, p. 140
4. exercise vs. drill, p. 151
5. generative vs. transformational rules, p. 140
6. inner speech, p. 141–42
7. language universals, p. 141
8. productive vs. receptive language skills, p. 146
9. "real" language, p. 147
10. rote vs. meaningful learning, p. 134

DISCUSSION

1. From your perspective, were the criticisms of the audio-lingual approach valid or invalid? If you were a student in an audio-lingual class, what did you like about the class? What did you dislike?
2. Summarize the basic concepts of cognitive psychology and T-G linguistics.
3. Summarize the relationship and similarity of concepts held by cognitive psychologists and generative linguists.
4. Outline the guiding principles you will follow and the kinds of activities you will employ in a class if you teach cognitively.
5. Discuss the implications of the concept of meaningful learning. In what ways would the classes you have had be affected? In what ways would there be no changes?
6. Explain the differences between cognitive exercises and audio-lingual drills.
7. Delineate the teacher's responsibility and the text's function in presenting meaningful learning tasks. What is the student's role?
8. For what types of students and what types of teachers do you feel a cognitive approach is best suited?

ACTIVITIES

1. Prepare a presentation of a grammar point that would be meaningful to the average student at the level you expect to teach.
2. Choose examples of additional cognitive exercises and bring them to class. You can make up some of your own.
3. Check for additional research studies on cognitive teaching/and or learning.
4. Generate some application activities in which the student gains practice converting thought to language or language to thought.

SELECTED REFERENCES

Anisfeld, M. (1966) Psycholinguistic Perspectives on Language Learning. In A. Valdman (Ed.), *Trends in Language Teaching.* New York: McGraw-Hill. Pp. 107–20.

Ausubel, D. P. (1968) *Educational Psychology: A Cognitive View.* New York: Holt, Rinehart and Winston. Pp. viii, ix, 61, 89.

Ausubel, D. P., and Robinson, F. G. (1969) *School Learning: An Introduction to Educational Psychology.* New York: Holt, Rinehart, and Winston. Pp. 51–53.

Bolinger, D. (1968) The Theorist and the Language Teacher. *Foreign Language Annals,* 2:30–41.

Brown, H. D. (1972) Cognitive Pruning and Second Language Acquisition. *Modern Language Journal,* 56:218–22.

Brown, T. G. (1972) Cognitive Pruning in Foreign Language Teaching. *Modern Language Journal,* 56:222–27.

Bull, W. E., et al. (1972) *Spanish for Communication, Level 1.* Boston: Houghton Mifflin. P. 20.

Carroll, J. B. (1966) The Contributions of Psychological Theory and Educational Research to the Teaching of Foreign Languages. In A. Valdman (Ed.), *Trends in Language Teaching.* New York: McGraw-Hill. Pp. 93–106.

Chastain, K. (1969) The Audio-Lingual Habit Theory Versus the Cognitive Code-Learning Theory: Some Theoretical Considerations. *International Review of Applied Linguistics,* 7:97–106.

Chastain, K., and Woerdehoff, F. J. (1968) A Methodological Study Comparing the Audio-Lingual Habit Theory and the Cognitive Code-Learning Theory. *Modern Language Journal,* 52:268–79.

Childers, J. W. (1964) *Foreign Language Teaching.* New York: Center for Applied Research in Education. P. 60.

Chomsky, N. (1957) *Syntactic Structures.* The Hague, The Netherlands: Moulton and Co.

Chomsky, N. (1959) Review of *Verbal Behavior* by B. F. Skinner. *Language,* 35:26–58.

Chomsky, N. (Ed.) (1968) *Language and Mind.* New York: Harcourt, Brace & World.

Cook, V. (1969) The Analogy Between First and Second Language Learning. *International Review of Applied Linguistics,* 7:207–16.

Corder, S. P. (1967) The Significance of Learner's Errors. *International Review of Applied Linguistics,* 5:161–70.

Coulombe, R., et al. (1974) *Voix et Visages de la France.* Chicago: Rand McNally.

Cox, J. L. (1975) Dream to Reality: Towards a Psycholinguistically Based Methodology. *Canadian Modern Language Review,* 31:326–31.

Del Olmo, G. (1968) Professional and Pragmatic Perspectives on the Audio-lingual Approach: Introduction and Review. *Foreign Langue Annals,* 2:19, 22.

Di Pietro, R. J. (1968) Linguistics. In E. M. Birkmaier (Ed.), *The Britannica Review of Foreign Language Education.* Chicago: Encyclopaedia Britannica. Pp. 15–36.

Ewing, W. K. (1972) The Mentalist Theory of Language Learning. *Foreign Language Annals,* 5:455–62.

Gagné, R. M. (1965) *The Conditions of Learning.* New York: Holt, Rinehart and Winston.

Gagné, R. M. (1970) Some New Views of Learning and Instruction. *Phi Delta Kappan,* 51:468–72.

Gefen, R. (1967) "Sentence Patterns" in the Light of Language Theories and Classroom Needs. *International Review of Applied Linguistics,* 5:185–92.

Green, J. (1972) *Psycholinguistics.* Middlesex, England: Penguin Education.

Hanzeli, V. E. (1968) Linguistics and the Language Teacher. *Foreign Language Annals,* 2:42–50.

Harper, R. J. C., et al. (1964) *The Cognitive Processes: Readings.* Englewood Cliffs, N. J.: Prentice Hall. P. v.

Hilgard, E. R. (1956) *Theories of Learning.* (2nd ed.) New York: Appleton-Century-Crofts.

Hilgard, E. R., and Atkinson, R. C. (1967) *Introduction to Psychology.* (4th ed.) New York: Harcourt, Brace & World.

Ingram, E. (1971) A Further Note on the Relationship Between Psychological and Linguistic Theories. *International Review of Applied Linguistics,* 9:335–46.

Jakobovits, L. A. (1968a) Implications of Recent Psycholinguistic Developments for the Teaching of a Second Language. *Language Learning,* 18:89–109.

Jakobovits, L. A. (1968b) Physiology and Psychology of Second Language Learning. In E. M. Birkmaier (Ed.), *The Britannica Review of Foreign Language Education.* Chicago: Encyclopaedia Britannica. Pp. 181–227.

Jakobovits, L. A. (1969a) Research Findings and Foreign Language Requirements in Colleges and Universities. *Foreign Language Annals,* 2:436–56.

Jakobovits, L. A. (1969b) Second Language Learning and Transfer Theory: A Theoretical Assessment. *Language Learning,* 19:55–86.

Kimpton, J. R. (1973) For a Conservative Methodology. *French Review,* 46:762–65.

Krech, D. (1969) Psychoneurobiochemeducation. *Phi Delta Kappan,* 50:370–75.

Krohn, R. (1970) The Role of Linguistics in TEFL Methodology. *Language Learning,* 20:103–8.

Lenneberg, E. H. (Ed.) (1964) *New Directions in the Study of Language.* Cambridge, Mass.: M.I.T. Press.

Lenneberg, E. H. (1967) *Biological Foundations of Language.* New York: Wiley.

Levin, L. (1969) *Implicit and Explicit—A Synopsis of Three Parallel Experiments in Applied Psycholinguistics.* Gothenburg, Sweden: Gothenburg School of Education, Department of Educational Research.

Levin, L., and Olsson, M. (1969) *Learning Grammar.* Gothenburg, Sweden: Gothenburg School of Education, Department of Educational Research.

Lewis, K. R. (1972) Transformational-Generative Grammar: A New Consideration to Teaching Foreign Languages. *Modern Language Journal,* 56:3–10.

Miller, G. A.; Galanter, E.; and Pribram, K. H. (1960) *Plans and the Structure of Behavior.* New York: Holt, Rinehart and Winston.

Mouly, G. J. (1973) *Psychology for Effective Teaching.* (3rd ed.) New York: Holt, Rinehart and Winston.

Mueller, T. H. (1971) The Effectiveness of Two Learning Models: The Audio-Lingual Habit Theory and the Cognitive Code-Learning Theory. In P. Pimsleur and T. Quinn (Eds.), *The Psychology of Second Language Learning.* Cambridge, England: Cambridge University Press.

Mueller, T. H., and Niedzielski, H. (1974) *Pratique de la Grammaire: Basic French.* (2nd ed.) Quebec, Canada: Intermedia.

Newmark, L., and Reibel, D. A. (1968) Necessity and Sufficiency in Language Learning. *International Review of Applied Linguistics,* 6:145–64.

Noblitt, J. S. (1972) Pedagogical Grammar: Towards a Theory of Foreign Language Materials Preparation. *International Review of Applied Linguistics,* 10:313–31.

Northeast Conference on the Teaching of Foreign Languages (1966) In R. G. Mead,

Jr. (Ed.), *Language Teaching: Broader Contexts.* New York: Modern Language Association of America. Pp. 43–49.

Novak, J. D. (1970) Relevant Research on Audio-Tutorial Methods. *School Science and Mathematics,* 70:778.

Ohmann, R. (1969) Grammar and Meaning. In E. Morris (Ed.), *The American Heritage Dictionary of the English Language.* Boston: Houghton Mifflin. Pp. 31–32.

Reid, C. L. (1973) Discovery of Latent Structure as the Major Process in Language Acquisition: Implications for the Second Language Program. *Foreign Language Annals,* 6:481–86.

Reinert, H. (1969) Guided Learning for Foreign Languages. *NASSP Bulletin,* 53:90–96.

Saporta, S. (1966) Applied Linguistics and Generative Grammar. In A. Valdman (Ed.), *Trends in Language Teaching.* New York: McGraw-Hill. Pp. 81–92.

Smith, F., and Miller, G. A. (Eds.) (1966) *The Genesis of Language.* Cambridge, Mass.: M.I.T. Press.

Smith, P. D., and Baranyi, H. A. (1968) *A Comparison of the Effectiveness of the Traditional and Audiolingual Approaches to Foreign-Language Instruction Utiliz-* ing Laboratory Equipment. Washington, D. C.: U. S. Department of Health, Education and Welfare.

Stern, H. H. (1974) Retreat from Dogmatism: Toward a Better Theory of Language Teaching. *Canadian Modern Language Review,* 30:244–54.

Stevick, E. W. (1971) *Adapting and Writing Language Lessons.* Washington, D. C.: Foreign Service Institute.

Stevick, E. W. (1974) The Meaning of Drills and Exercises. *Language Learning,* 24:1–22.

Van Ek, J. A. (1971) Linguistics and Language Teaching. *International Review of Applied Linguistics,* 9:319–34.

Vigotsky, L. S. (1961) Thought and Speech. In S. Saporta (Ed.), *Psycholinguistics: A Book of Readings.* New York: Holt, Rinehart and Winston. Pp. 509–37.

Von Elek, T., and Oskarsson, M. (1972) An Experiment Assessing the Relative Effectiveness of Two Methods of Teaching English Grammatical Structures to Adults. *International Review of Applied Linguistics,* 10:60–72.

Wardhaugh, R. (1971) Theories of Language Acquisition in Relation to Beginning Reading Instruction. *Language Learning,* 21:1–26.

THE STUDENT

Environmental Influences
    Society
        Permissiveness
        Mobility
        Television
        Counterculture
        Family Life
        Anomie
    School
    Students

Factors in Student Action, Reaction, and Interaction
    Affective
        Phenomenology
        Student Attitudes and Feelings toward School
        Attitudes and Feelings toward Second-Language Study
    Cognitive
    Psychomotor
    Personality
    Other Factors

Student Needs
    Self-Concept
    Self-Actualization
    Socialization
    Values

INTRODUCTION

The purpose of this chapter is to consider the students, their world, their characteristics, and their needs. The goal of this chapter is to make teachers or prospective teachers aware of the existence of these various student characteristics and of the significant role each plays independently and collectively in facilitating or impeding student achievement in the classroom, to tune their senses to the multitudinous individual and group signals that are generated daily in class. Ways and means of meeting student needs are treated in chapter 9.

ENVIRONMENTAL INFLUENCES

Some years ago in an interview over the Purdue University radio station, a former vice-president of the university stated that the major problems with which he had to deal involved people, finances, people, facilities, and people. Anyone in a leadership position has a multitude of problems to meet, but the principal one is always the people with whom one is associated. Teachers are no exception. They have accepted the responsibilities of leadership and are duty-bound to fill this role to the best of their capabilities. Their students' appreciation, now or in the future, will correlate rather highly with the conscientious exercise of the obligation to lead them toward optimum levels of achievement. What complicates their problem even beyond that of the aforementioned vice-president is that they operate in a situation containing a captive, at times disinterested and perhaps even hostile, group of young people attempting to make their way successfully through the physical, cognitive, psychological, emotional, and social mazes separating childhood from adulthood.

The complexity and difficulty of the problems facing teachers in the classroom further emphasize the importance of their task. Given the proper amount of food, rest, exercise, and medical attention, the student will develop physically; but psychologically, emotionally, socially, morally, and intellectually desirable growth requires encouragement, guidance, and support. And it is that student (or students) in class exhibiting the greatest need who requires the greatest amount of attention. The teacher's task is to recognize the symptoms, analyze the problem, and devise a plan for fostering improvement, personally, socially or academically as the case may be. However, accomplishing the goal is vastly more complicated than stating what should be done. Often the relationship between cause and effect in student actions is not obvious. In fact, a student's actions, such as the insecure student lacking in self-confidence who dons a behavior pattern of extreme aggressiveness to mask her true inner feelings, may have little or no apparent correspondence to her actual basic inner feelings.

One often hears the question, "What do you teach?" In response to a reply naming the subject taught, the questioner states smugly, "*I* do not teach a second language; *I* teach students!" As appealing as this distinction may be, the dichotomy is inherently false. A teacher teaches (1) a second language, or any other subject, (2) to students with cognitive and affective needs (3) in a social situation. In establishing his instructional program, the teacher should keep all three factors and their interrelationships in mind as he selects appropriate teaching-learning situations for the class and as he evaluates the results of those activities.

Teachers should also remember that they cannot learn the material for the students. Learning is the students' responsibility. One of the positive influences of "individualized" instruction is that an attempt is being made to place the responsibility for learning on the students themselves. For too long the educational system has struggled under the unwritten assumption that the teachers must bear the burden for learning. The students were excused from shouldering their share of the task. This generally accepted belief contained three basic components. (1) If the students are not interested, they cannot be expected to learn. (2) If they are not interested, it is the teacher's fault. (3) The resultant corollary is that there are no failing students, only failing teachers. Hopefully, the present trend will lead to the quiet burial of this debilitating premise.

A word of caution is appropriate at this point. Placing the responsibility for learning on the student, where it justifiably belongs, does not sanction any degree of a "take-it-or-leave-it" teacher attitude. The teacher's role includes not only teaching but also the promotion of learning. Effective teaching in contemporary schools, with their stress on the individual, can only occur when the teacher is sensitive and responsive to the students and their attitudes and feelings as well as to the content of the subject matter.

The major focus of this book is on the cognitive factors in second-language teaching. The reader may even get the impression that the primary concern is with the teacher and what the teacher does. Such is not the case. If most of the discussion seems to be teacher-centered or subject-centered, the purpose of such an emphasis is to provide guidelines for developing teaching-learning activities for student participation that lead to functional language skills. Indeed, the author could not do otherwise. All the research points to the learners themselves as being the single most important variable in the success or failure of any instructional method. As early as 1963, Carroll listed five component factors in school learning. Three of these, aptitude, ability to understand instruction, and perseverance, are student factors! Therefore, recognition of the crucial student contribution to learning is necessary. Equally essential is the realization that students are more than just minds. They are also living, feeling human beings, filled with doubts, likes and dislikes, ambitions, etc. Their psychomotor abilities and affective states play as important a role in their academic work as their cognitive abilities. Although the psychomotor, the affective, and the cognitive student factors are inseparably interrelated, the major focus of this chapter is on the affective.

Society

A satisfactory description of contemporary society is understandably rare. In the first place, the degree to which any given member of that society can divorce himself from the confinement of his culture is severely limited because of his own membership in the group. Even if he does manage to divest himself somewhat of the restrictions of his cultural heritage, he is still bound by his own subjective interpretations of what he sees. Will Durant reflects the extent of this cultural and contemporary myopia when he states that history is 95 percent opinion and 5 percent fact. Another factor is that most modern societies are so pluralistic that generalizable characteristics of the society are difficult to determine. The industrialized societies of the Western world are somewhat like a cracked pane of unbreakable glass: immediately observable are the innumerable fissures. The multitudinous elements are held together by some connecting factors, but the relationships involved and the strength and importance of each are not directly apparent. During periods in which the emphasis is on the pluralistic nature of society and the importance of the individual, society places importance on the multitudinous components of its various parts. At other times greater emphasis is attached to the connecting fibers, i.e., to the overall characteristics of society itself, and the process of socialization assumes a major role in the educational process.

The fact that all teachers are products of some culture or subculture makes it difficult for them to comprehend entirely the world of those students who are from a different cultural environment. The fact that the students are products of their own culture places a responsibility on the teacher to consider the students' world and to attempt to understand it. The fact that the culture of each student is a product of a unique background makes it imperative that the teacher distinguish among the students and be sensitive to their individuality.

Permissiveness   In addition to the general trends and movements in society discussed in chapter 1, other pertinent factors have played influential roles in the students' world in recent years. Overall, students have been nurtured in a society characterized by advanced technological systems of production and consumption. The possession of things has been the primary goal in the lives of many people. The high degree of purchasing power attained by the vast majority from the end of World War II to the early 1970s quickly converted luxuries into necessities. Too, the affluence of society made it possible for people to satisfy material desires and brought about a situation in which the gratification of desires was expected. Consequently, there arose among the population a low level of tolerance for frustration. The term *permissive*, usually associated with the rearing of children, applies equally well to society as a whole. Suppression of desires, whether they be material, social, or physical, is not characteristic of the 1970s. The expectation of instant gratification of wants and of solutions to personal or societal problems is almost universal.

Mobility   The mobility of contemporary society has been a major influence on the life experience that many students bring with them to the classroom. Any given student may have gone through the necessity of adjusting to several different school systems. They will have been through the experience of leaving past friends and familiar landmarks to move into unfamiliar circumstances. This movement from one area and one situation to another is unquestionably broadening, if the student has the personality type to benefit from the experience, but the breadth of experience may be counterbalanced by a certain lack of development in other aspects of personality created by the severing of ties with the familiar past. The outcome is that the students may be more knowledgeable but less comfortable and less sure of themselves and their surroundings. They may have an intellectual maturity that is not matched by their psychological or emotional development.

Television   Television has been praised and panned. Whatever one's opinion regarding program content and the viewing habits of children, the impact of television and the general mass communications media on the lives of everyone is undeniable. Just as a second-language learner's world expands into another culture as a result of language study, so the child now grows up in a world vastly different from that experienced by the preceding generations. On-the-spot reporting brings the entire planet and even the universe directly into the home every day. The breadth of knowledge and vision of today's student is vastly superior to that of their parents when they were students. Children today are exposed to a multitude of information at a rate and to a degree unimaginable only a few decades ago. At the same time, they are subjected to an infinitude of ideas and stimuli that make their growth as individuals more complex and more difficult than was true in the past. Another characteristic of the television generation with which the teacher must deal is the competition television presents for the classroom. Television entertains as well as informs. Experts, supported by almost limitless facilities and huge budgets, prepare programs of a quality with which the classroom teacher simply cannot compete. It is quite a challenge for the teacher to attract and retain the attention for fifty minutes or more, day after day, of thirty students accustomed to television programming.

Counterculture   Society seems to be characterized by a cyclical repetition alternating between "activism" and "quietism." "Activism" was dominant in the late 1960s. Katz (1974) explains the student unrest during that period as being due to three social factors: (1) The affluence of society gave youth the material security needed and the necessary time to expand their outlook and to consider other aspects of their world. (2) The liberality of child-rearing practices during and immediately after World War II created a group of youth disposed to question society's actions and to participate in seeking solutions to perceived problems. (3) During that same period society as a whole was involved in self-examination and in reform movements.

In the early 1970s there has been a period of relative "quietism." After the period of rapid change and social protest has come a trend toward a renewed interest in the past. A national nostalgia has turned interest back to country music, folk dancing, antiques, etc. As many members of society have turned to the past, substantial numbers of youth have turned inward to escape from or to avoid seeking solutions to society's problems. Discredited by the results of the activist movement of the late 1960s, political radicalism has given way to cultural radicalism. Many young people are occupied with introspection, self-analysis, and personal encounter as productive alternatives to "satisfy the social needs of people disaffected from the structure of American society" (Larkin, 1974, p. 29). The counterculture groups seek to substitute their brand of humanism for the puritanism of the past. Their beliefs reflect a blend of Rousseau of the West and Zen Buddhism of the East. They question marriage, the nuclear family, authority, religion, work, money, careers, and sexual morality. They are seeking answers to the problems they see in their technological society: decline of community, increased rationalization, impulse repression, and personal isolation (Larkin, 1974).

One outgrowth of living in an age of mechanical marvels has been the increased amount of "free" time that adults have to spend with their families and to pursue leisure activities. As a result, middle-class youths spend a great deal of their time in activities supervised by adults. Whether at home, in school, or participating in some extracurricular activity, they frequently perform in situations in which adults determine the rules and define success or failure. This state of affairs has definite advantages for youngsters, but they must also be content to operate under constraints established by adults. This type of child rearing creates in individuals a certain ambivalence toward the societal structure. Society can help them, but society is also the agent to blame when their expectations are thwarted. Young people used to rebel against parents. Now much of that rebellion is directed toward society as a whole and toward society's institutions (Larkin, 1974).

A characterization of all youths as being either active or potential participants in the counterculture would be erroneous. Neither the counterculture nor the so-called generation gap is universally applicable to all young people. Not all youths seek alternative life styles. Many are earnestly striving for the same security and financial rewards as their parents. Discussions of activist, humanistic youths largely ignore the "Middle Americans," who are generally satisfied with their society, and lower-class groups, who are actively seeking to improve their standard of living. Both the "Middle Americans" and the lower class are chiefly vocationally or domestically oriented, and they are quickly assimilated into the realities of the adult, working world (Spady & Adler, 1974).

Family life   Some young people have never been told no, while others have never been told yes. Some students are totally bored with an existence in which someone caters to every whim but in which they feel no sense of accomplishment or success. Some burn with the desire to achieve and to move up the social and economic ladder. Others dwell in a world of despair and hopelessness.

Some students have been reared in a permissive family atmosphere, some are accustomed to a democratic relationship, while others have learned to operate in an authoritarian climate. Thus, their expectations and methods of social relationships are already different when they enter school for the first time. In general, middle-class students are more likely to have been reared in a permissive or democratic environment, but they are also more likely to be dependent upon others than the lower-class child. Middle-class children are used to being helped when they have problems. Too, they are likely to be more frustrated than the lower-class student due to the fact that they have had to operate in a situation in which adults have supervised a major portion of their activities. On the other hand, lower-class children are usually more independent, since they have been left to their own devices more often. They are less likely to understand the democratic process or to be able to cope with a permissive classroom situation. Types of incentives and disciplinary procedures may have to vary depending upon the background of the student.

Many students come from family units that are far less cohesive than was true in the past. Few, if any, have other relatives living with the family, and, in fact, the family may have only limited contact with any of their relatives. If the mother works, her job prevents her from spending much time with the children outside the necessary routine. The father's job now takes him out of the home and in many cases out of the community (Coleman, 1965). In many instances children are reared by only one parent.

Anomie   The net result of having lived in a modern, industrialized, technological society is that the students come to the school already having been exposed to a much greater variety of information and experiences than was true prior to World War II. They are much more experienced and knowledgeable about what goes on in the world. At the same time, the changes in society have produced an environment in many cases in which the students are deprived of the security and the roots characteristic of their predecessors in the schools. They not only lack the close family support which they formerly had, but religious faith and church attendance have suffered a simultaneous decline. With no other readily available substitute in a society characterized by bigness and impersonal relationships, an increasing tendency toward anomie and alienation from society in general, and from school specifically, has occurred. Fischer (1975) reports that anomie has increased from the 1950s to the early 1970s. This trend is especially noticeable among whites under thirty-five. Anomie has increased at all educational levels.

School

The comprehensive American high school is unique in the history of education. For the first time, an educational system was established to educate everyone, not just a select minority. In order to accomplish this all-encompassing goal and to handle the increasingly large enrollments, the schools have sought ways and means of streamlining the system and of making it more efficient. In so doing, larger and larger buildings have been constructed as schools have been consolidated and students bussed to more central locations. This trend in schools is a direct reflection of society itself, which has emphasized size and efficiency. One unfortunate consequence has been to develop a system that at times resembles an assembly line more than an educational institution. Schools that were the pride of the nation in the 1960s have become the object of mounting criticism. Critics decry their curriculum, procedures, organization, purposes, and failure to accomplish their selected goals.

Dissatisfaction with the schools is not limited to a small group of writers attacking the system from a philosophical point of view. The general public is also upset. Rising costs are a primary consideration, but public concern goes beyond the pressure for funds. The public harbors doubts as to the amount of learning that is being obtained in exchange for the money being spent. They believe a gap exists between what the schools have promised and what they have delivered (Manning, 1972). A general public questioning of the state of affairs in the schools and with student achievement persists, in spite of efforts by the schools to improve education and to improve communication with parents and the public.

Just what is wrong with the schools? Critics present many different opinions. The only point of agreement seems to be that the present situation is serious and that needed changes should be instituted immediately. Spady and Adler (1974, p. 145) state: "The major source of student hostility and unrest lies in the school's preoccupation with the custody, control, certification, and selection of students rather than its instructional effectiveness." Spady (1974) quotes Seeman, who identifies five sources of student frustration. First, in many cases the students feel *powerless* in the school situation to control their own fate. Second, they are forced many times to attempt to cope with a situation that is *meaningless* to their personal life situation and experience. Third, Spady perceives a breakdown in the norms that govern behavior and interpersonal relationships, and an ensuing *normlessness* results. Fourth, students feel *isolated* from their peers. Fifth, students participate in activities selected for them and for which they see no need. This continued behavior of seeking utilitarian goals to the exclusion of intrinsic goals can lead to *self-estrangement*. Dobay (1973, pp. 44–45) disagrees, affirming that the current crisis is caused by "the absence of hierarchy, the negation of the concept of authority, and the distortion of ideals." She goes on to say, "No young person is born arrogant. Accepting less than the best from the few lowers the level of excellence for the many. This is the real tragedy of our educational crisis today."

What does the public see as the major problems in the schools? The sixth annual Gallup Poll (1974) of public attitudes toward education provides a summary of student and adult opinions. The adults listed the following as being major problem areas, in order of decreasing importance:

1. Lack of discipline.
2. Integration/segregation problems.
3. Lack of proper financial support.
4. Use of drugs.
5. Difficulty of getting "good" teachers.
6. Size of school/classes.
7. Parents' lack of interest.
8. School-board policies.
9. Poor curriculum.
10. Lack of proper facilities.

It is interesting to note that three of the first four problems listed deal with student behavior and that the students list the same three problems. The first four on the student list were:

1. Lack of discipline.
2. Integration/segregation problems.
3. Pupils' lack of interest.
4. Use of drugs.

Automatic promotion to the next grade was rejected by 90 percent of the adults and 87 percent of the students. Seventy-four percent of the adults and 82 percent of the students favored having industries provide practical training in job skills. Surprisingly, there was rather solid agreement between students and adults on measures to be followed to handle students who cause trouble.

Suspension or expulsion was favored by 31 percent of the adults and 41 percent of the students. Adults were more prone to punish misbehavior (11 percent to 4 percent) or to paddle (7 percent to 3 percent), while students would prefer to give detentions (8 percent to 4 percent). Students felt that the major outcomes of school were making friends and learning to get along with other people. Less commonly mentioned were a general education, preparing for a job, and preparing for college.

The congruence between adult reactions and opinions and those of the student population hints that the "generation gap" may not be quite the unbridgeable crevice once suspected. Too, the results seem to indicate that students are as desirous of establishing an atmosphere conducive to learning as the adults. In this sense, they may be more mature and more serious than the adult population has recognized. In both polled groups the major concern lay in the realm of people problems as opposed to curricular problems.

The recommendations for measures to alleviate these problems are far-ranging: from the return to an authoritarian, teacher-centered class; to a permissive, student-centered classroom; to deschooling the educational process. An examination of the experience gained from previous educational programs would lead one to suspect that specific situations and circumstances will require varying approaches. The ability of the administrators and teachers to solve current difficulties depends upon their flexibility in determining productive procedures in response to particular aspects of each problem rather than insisting upon a certain predetermined program as the answer to all concerns and to all needs.

Perkinson (1974) suggests that current dissatisfaction with the schools lies not so much in the realm of what the schools are and what they are doing as in society's expectations of the schools. Confronted by a complex array of social, political, and economic problems, the public's reaction has been to turn to education to solve these problems. When the educational system was unable to produce immediate results to the problems of the sixties, such as the population explosion, pollution, drug use, the reaction was to look for defects in the schools. Perkinson recommends that educators be honest with the students and with the public. Problems should be brought into the open and discussed with them, and it should be pointed out that the recognition of difficulties is a different matter entirely from solutions to these problems. A tradition of critical analysis of the existing system and its functioning, with an objective of improvement and refinement, should become an integral component of the educational experience. Perkinson (1974, p. 395) summarizes his discussion by stating: "Because our present education now lacks such critical encounters, the young do not understand the existing social, political, and economic arrangements, and they do not know how to use them to protect themselves. They feel alienated from, and victimized by, the present system, which they see as unchangeable—except perhaps by force."

Students

This section is entitled "Students," not "Student." The plural form of the noun was selected consciously and purposefully to contrast with the stress on the individual in the other sections of this chapter. Coping with individual differences in the cognitive and affective domains can be achieved, to any substantial degree, only by emphasizing the individual, but the group cannot be ignored. The old saying is that the forest cannot be seen for the trees. In the classroom, the problem may be viewed from both perspectives. The teacher faced with conducting five classes of thirty students each day may fail to see the individuals for the group. Focusing on both the group and the individual, while attempting to keep up with her many duties and responsibilities, certainly presents the teacher with a challenging assignment. The teacher is confronted with the task of determining how each student is unique and how each is similar to, yet different from, the general student population as a whole and how each functions within the group and relates to his peers. Each student is a separate entity operating in a distinguishable set of circumstances.

What are some of the general characteristics of adolescence? How is adolescence different from childhood and adulthood? First, this is a period of transition from one stage of development to another, a period of emergence from the cognitive, emotional, and social world of the child to that of the adult. The outward physical and sexual changes are obvious. Too, the stress on social acceptance and the importance of the peer group are easily identifiable. Parents, teachers, and other adults readily recognize, at times painfully and not too sympathetically, the questioning of adult values and the increasing attempts of the maturing youth to establish independence. Not so obvious are the qualitative cognitive changes that are occurring simultaneously in the individual's mental makeup.

The nature of the individual's internal and external pressures during this phase of life creates tensions within and without, often resulting in psychological and emotional turmoil. What is needed, both by the individual and significant people in his life, is a tolerance for vacillation, searching, insecurity, and questioning. The single most important consideration is that the lines of communication with the adult world be kept open. In dealing with them, the adult should keep in mind their egotistical, idealistic perspective on the world and their impatience for solutions to problems. These are all direct results of their lack of experience rather than an intentional rejection of the values of their cultural heritage. Questioning and/or disagreement are not necessarily permanent, nor do they necessarily reflect rejection of the cultural past. Tempted as they may be to overreact to youthful attitudes, adults should keep in mind these characteristics of the maturation process.

Some people view adolescence as a period of alienation. Hill (1971) states that there is a commonly held belief that there is a separate adolescent society with a distinct culture, but that the available evidence does not support the existence of a separate youth society or culture. He says, "The continuities that bind adolescence to the childhood that preceded it and to the adulthood that will follow it are more impressive than the discontinuities" (p. 105). He attributes the prevailing attitude concerning a separate subculture to the fact that many of our impressions have been created by the mass media, by studies of psychiatric patients, and by cases of juvenile delinquency. By the time the teacher enters the classroom, he arrives complete with a predisposition to expect either "the ruminating, painfully self-conscious, affectively unpredictable, upper-middle-class neurotic" or "the uncommunicative, tough, and, above all, threatening, lower-class delinquent" (p. 105). The question that immediately occurs is the extent to which the teacher's expectations and subsequent actions serve to promote the fulfillment of these preconceived notions. To what extent do such preconceptions affect the teacher's desire or ability to interact with the students and to treat each as a separate and distinct individual? To what extent do such feelings promote an initial defeatist attitude that causes the teacher and the schools to settle for minimum rather than maximum standards, for "baby-sitting" rather than education?

The previous discussion is not intended to deny the existence of problems as youths pass through adolescence nor to dismiss their importance. Disagreement is certain to occur, but the resultant discord at times is not unhealthy, *if* the conflict does not grow out of proportion or reach a stage of permanent rupture. During this period of rapid physical and mental growth, increased social participation, and heightened self-awareness, the adolescent is likely to be insecure, impulsive, self-conscious, lacking in self-control, and overly idealistic.

Part of the generally held belief in the generation gap can be traced to apparent lack of understanding of the changes taking place during the maturation process and to a misconception between adults and adolescents as to what opinions and attitudes the other group actually holds. One trait, which may seem surprising, is that adolescents tend to idolize adults. Not so unexpected is the adolescent belief that the average adult has a low opinion of teen-agers, and the feeling of parents that teen-agers have a tendency to underrate adults and to overrate themselves (Klausmeier & Ripple, 1971). This problem of perception of the attitudes and opinions of others also plays a significant role in the school situation. Dropouts, for example, see themselves as being treated poorly by teachers as well as other students. They say that the teacher is not interested in them or their problems (Schreiber, 1969).

In the years between childhood and adulthood young people go through some rather profound changes. This is a period of intense socialization and strong peer group relationships. At the same time, adolescents have the problem of establishing their independence from their parents and of establishing their own identity. They are helped in these adjustment processes by their increased cognitive ability to handle abstract, conceptual thought. All in all, although growth may be more rapid, maturity progresses from one level to another just as in the other phases of life. Their basic drives, "the drive to understand and the drive *to be understood*," differ little from those of any other person at any other stage of development (Brown, 1974, p. 26).

FACTORS IN STUDENT ACTION, REACTION, AND INTERACTION

In the classroom, students act, react, and interact with others. The teacher needs to concern himself with student factors that determine what students do, to what they respond, and with whom they interact.

Affective

The affective component includes those feelings and attitudes individuals hold toward themselves and their environment. *Affective* refers to the individuals' emotional characteristics as opposed to their intellectual and social traits. The question involves not what or whom they know, but how they feel about the information they have and the feedback they receive from their interpersonal relationships. Needless to say, each factor in an individual's total framework is formed in conjunction with and is influenced by the development of all other aspects of her person. Dividing these aspects into categories is impossible, but the consideration of each is important in the development of a total teaching-learning environment.

In the discussion of factors influencing student action, reaction, and interaction, affective variables will be presented prior to a consideration of the cognitive for several reasons. First, some psychologists are now saying that the influence of attitudes and feelings is a greater contributing factor in determining student achievement and success than the cognitive. This assumption may be true on practical as well as theoretical grounds due to the reluctance of many members of the "new" generation to concentrate on learning to the exclusion of feelings. Second, the current stress in education is to educate the whole individual, not just the mind. The modern-day tendency toward anomie requires that the students' emotional development and socialization be given equal status with their academic preparation. Third, in the past the affective domain has not received the attention it deserved. The assumption was that the students would automatically develop emotionally and socially as they developed intellectually. The results indicate that such is not the case. Students need assistance in growing emotionally and socially just as they do intellectually.

Phenomenology   One problem in dealing with attitudes and feelings is the multitude of intangibles involved. This lack of specificity causes some educators to shy away from a serious consideration of the affective domain. As valid as this reaction may be from a truly scientific view, circumstances in the schools emphasize the necessity of investigating the affective and social realms. In seeking solutions to educational problems, phenomenologists attempt to take these factors into consideration.

Phenomenology is related to existentialism and to humanistic psychology. Its focus is on the inner universe of feelings, attitudes, emotions, meanings, and purposes of the individual. Although cognitive psychology and phenomenology are both internal theories of learning, the attention of cognitive psychologists is directed more toward meaningful learning. Phenomenologists are more interested in the development, or self-actualization, of the person as a total thinking, feeling, social being. Obviously, cognitive learning and growth affect self-concept and self-actualization and vice versa (Mouly, 1973). The basic premises of phenomenology are the following:

1. Behavior is the result of the individual's perception of reality. Reality is psychological rather than objective. It exists in the mind of the individual.
2. Perceptions are the result of the individual's interpretation of the present situation.
3. Behavior is the result of the present situation and must be dealt with from that point of view.

A major implication of these premises is that people act the way they do because they see the situation the way they do. From this point of view, the student who is a behavior problem, however much he may depart from the teacher's conception of proper decorum, is merely doing what seems best to him in that particular situation (Mouly, 1973).

These premises serve to explain behavior, not to justify it. Phenomenology is an attempt to comprehend behavior, not to condone misbehavior. As a conceptual framework for understanding the why of student action, the tenets presented can provide insight into the motives behind what the student may do. However, the theory should not be used as a guise to justify the adoption of a permissive, *laissez faire* classroom atmosphere in which self-actualization for the students and for the teacher would become haphazard and inefficient, if not impossible. Such an atmosphere is, in effect, contrary to the primary goal of phenomenology, which is self-actualization.

Student attitudes and feelings toward school   Concurrent with the diminishing influence of the home and the church on the life of the individual has appeared a seeming lack of ability on the part of many individuals to cope in our complex technological, industrialized society. The students' reaction has been to question the ability of the schools to prepare them for participation in society. In this sense, perhaps the charge of irrelevancy has a certain amount of justification. However, a more accurate appraisal would be that the scope of the teaching-learning experience has been inadequate. Relevancy may be related more closely to failure to deal effectively with the often neglected affective and social areas of education than to the inapplicability of the cognitive. At any rate, it would appear that either the home, the church, or the educational system will have to fill the current void in the background of many individuals in our society.

The students' attitudes and feelings toward school are affected by several variables, such as their own personalities and backgrounds, those of their classmates and teachers, the curriculum, and the methods of teaching. Figure 7.1 presents a schematic outline of the relationships and interrelationships influencing the affective domain in the classroom. It is interesting to note those relationships that are reciprocal and those that are not and to consider the implications of each on individual growth and on the teaching-learning atmosphere of the class.

Figure 7.1: A Schematic Representation of Various Effects on School-Related Attitudes (SES-Socioeconomic Status; Pers-Personality; Ach-Achievement).

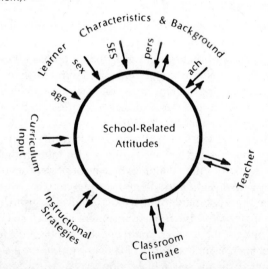

Source: Kahn, S.B., and Weiss, J., "The Teaching of Affective Responses," In R. Travers (Ed.). *Second Handbook of Research on Teaching* (Chicago: Rand McNally, 1973), p. 770. Copyright 1973, American Educational Research Association, Washington, D.C.

Attitudes and feelings toward second-language study   Attitudes and feelings play important roles in the prestige and importance of any academic subject in the curriculum, and this influence is strongly felt in the field of second-language study. The fact that enrollments in second-language classes have declined steadily since the late sixties seems to be of little concern to those not directly involved. Except in times of crisis, such as the unexpected launching of the first Sputnik, second-language study is not valued highly by many people in the United States. This attitude is partly the result of the large numbers of immigrants who have been concerned with becoming Americanized, partly the natural consequence of being relatively isolated from speakers of other languages, and partly the outgrowth of living in a country with such a vast financial and political influence throughout the world that large numbers of people from other countries learn to speak English. The readiness with which people of other nations have learned English in order to reap the financial benefits has led some Americans to the mistaken conclusion that there is no need to learn second languages.

Second-language study is also handicapped by the negative attitude with which many adults and students alike view second-language classes, which for some were and are a traumatic experience. These people feel that it is a "hard" subject, that they do not get anything out of the class, and that they shortly forget what little they do learn. In part, this attitude is due to a general lack of public relations sensitivity on the part of many second-language teachers. However, the nature of the subject matter itself must also be considered in attempting to identify the causes of the negative reaction facing second-language teachers from some, but not all, quarters.

What is this quality inherent in second-language study that may result in negative student reactions? Discomfort is one answer. Second-language study requires the student to tread new linguistic and cultural territory. This use of new, partially mastered language patterns and vocabulary, as well as the exposure to different culture patterns and customs, can be just as psychologically uncomfortable to some as it is exhilarating to others. Learners tend to avoid that which produces discomfort and to seek out and repeat that which makes them feel good. The teacher may either be oblivious to the students' emotional straits or may tend to react as negatively to the student as the student has to the second language.

Both the profession as a whole and individual teachers can promote efforts to improve the image of second-language learning in the United States. The profession can continue to foster community and public awareness of the need for people with second-language skills. Teachers can do their part by sensitizing themselves to the psychological comfort-discomfort threshold of each of their students. They can seek to devise ways and means of reducing or eliminating the causes of discomfort when reactions indicate that the discomfort zone has been reached and that the result is affecting student attitude and achievement.

Also, second-language teachers in the United States should not overlook the considerable reservoir of support that exists for second-language learning among the public and among the students. Rivers (1974a) reported the results of a survey of student attitudes towards second-language study conducted at the University of Illinois that refuted commonly held myths about how much students dislike language classes. Similar data were obtained in a questionnaire administered to the students enrolled in the first four semesters of language study at the University of Virginia. In this study almost 70 percent rejected the statement that students see no reason for studying a foreign language. Over 75 percent answered no to the statement that there is no need to study a foreign language because everyone else speaks English. Nor are the students isolated from the influence of second languages. More than 15 percent had parents who spoke a second language, and more than 60 percent had friends who spoke a second language. Many of the students were planning careers in fields such as journalism, foreign service, government work, social work, etc., for which they felt a second language might be useful. The student response to the beginning language courses was surprisingly favorable. The percentages of electives for each of the languages were 13.8 percent (F), 35.2 percent (G), and 17.0 percent (S). The response to "I enjoy language even if it is required," was positive by 51.8 percent (F), 61.2 percent (G), and 50.0 percent (S). Even if language was not required, 43.6 percent (F), 63.4 percent (G), and 42.6 percent (S) said they would study a language anyway, and 31.3 percent (F), 54.2 percent (G), and 39.0 percent (S) of the students said they planned to take courses beyond the requirement. Although the grade-point average of some students may suffer, a situation which would most likely be true for any academic subject, large numbers of students received higher grades in second languages than in their other subjects. In fact, the percentage of A's and B's received by students in second-language classes at the University of Virginia was more than 20 percent higher than their overall grade-point average. An even more revealing survey is the one referred to by Savaiano (1974) in which the members of a 1969 graduating class were asked what courses they wish they had taken that they did not take. The most frequent reply was foreign languages.

Cognitive

Cognition refers to internal, mental operations. (Obviously, cognition affects and is affected by the individual's attitudes and feelings.) The emphasis in cognition is on what is occurring within individuals as they react to the stimuli impinging upon them. Cognition includes not only the individuals' mental capacities, but also the intellectual network into which they have organized their previous experiences, their learning style for acquiring, organizing, perceiving, and storing new information, their learning skills, and their set for learning. A person's ability to learn is affected by many factors, including previously acquired knowledge, learning aptitude, and various affective factors.

"Undoubtedly, the most comprehensive view of development is the cognitive-developmental (stage) theory formulated by Piaget . . . , the top child psychologist living today" (Mouly, 1973, p. 130). For many years Piaget's work was rejected by psychologists in the United States due to the fact that many of his conclusions were based on research procedures that did not conform to the strict scientific approach followed by American psychologists. His approach was qualitative, while prior to 1960 the dominant approach in American psychology was quantitative. Too, ". . . most Americans were behaviorally oriented and did not treat with much respect Piaget's attempt to examine the child's internal thought processes" (Gorman, 1972, p. 4). However, as the pendulum in psychology began to swing back in the 1960s from a strict behaviorist approach toward a more cognitive and personalistic view of the child, Piaget's ideas have been more readily and widely received and accepted.

In Piaget's model of cognitive development there are five stages, encompassing the qualitative changes in cognitive processes as individuals learn, grow, and mature. The first stage lasts from birth until around the age of two. This is the *sensori-motor* state in which reflexes and habits are developed. Children become aware of permanent objects and learn how to use means to gain ends. They begin to organize their previously undifferentiated world. The next stage, *symbolic thought,* lasts from two to four. During this period children learn to use language and to participate in symbolic play. From four to seven, the period of *intuitive* thought, children progress to the level of syncretism[1] of understanding and transductive reasoning.[2] The stage of *concrete operations* begins at approximately age seven and continues to around age twelve. In this phase, the children's mental and perceptual processes are beginning to be organized into a logical system. They grow beyond the rather simple trial-and-error learning system which has dominated their thinking up to this point. Finally they enter the stage of *formal operations.* At this stage of cognitive maturity they can handle abstract, conceptual thought without reference to concrete objects and examples. They are now ready for hypothetico-deductive thinking at the highest and most abstract level (Gorman, 1972).[3]

---

[1]*Syncretism* is the tendency to combine or reconcile differing beliefs.

[2]*Transductive reasoning* involves the ability to transfer concepts from one example to another.

[3]*Hypothetico-deductive thinking* implies the ability to formulate hypotheses and to test their validity with deductive reasoning powers.

Piaget's model of intelligence contains two basic components: assimilation and accommodation. The term *assimilation* refers to the mental processes involved in incorporating new information from the environment into the individual's existing mental organization of reality. As the individual's acquired knowledge changes, he *accommodates* himself to this new experience. Piaget "assumes that higher mental processes organize thought and keep it adaptive, coordinated, and efficient" (Kagan, 1971, p. 657).

Two major implications for teaching are attributable to Piaget's theories. The first is that the stages of cognitive development are hierarchical and progressive. That is, the child must complete one level before she can move to the next. The second is that teaching and learning materials should be geared to the student and her level of cognitive development, not vice versa. (It should be kept in mind that these differences in cognitive processes as the child develops from one stage to the next are qualitative as well as quantitative.) The areas with which the educational system must concern itself are (1) the extent to which children from underprivileged backgrounds with deprived learning environments have failed to proceed through the various stages of cognitive development, and (2) ways and means by which the individual's cognitive abilities can be improved.

Psychomotor

Psychomotor skills, as the term itself implies, involve more than simple motor abilities. Muscular coordination and dexterity are basic components, of course, but these skills depend upon underlying mental processes similar to those more commonly associated with so-called intellectual and academic endeavors. In fact, recent research has uncovered an unexpectedly strong cognitive influence in the acquisition of psychomotor skills. Fitts has postulated three phases in the development of a skill. The first is the *cognitive* phase, during which the learner benefits from instruction in the form of description and/or demonstration. The second phase, *fixation,* is characterized by the formation and refinement of motor coordination. The third and final phase is that of *automation*. At this stage, the various components have been internalized, the intervening symbolic props have been eliminated, and the act has become automatic (Mouly, 1973).

Given the relationship between psychomotor and cognitive abilities, positive correlations obtained between psychomotor skills and educational achievement come as no surprise (Klausmeier & Ripple, 1971). Handwriting, eye movement, hand-eye coordination, etc.—all influence the acquisition of cognitive material. Nor is a strong connection between psychomotor abilities and social and personal adjustment at all unexpected. The individual who is so uncoordinated or different in his physical movements that his lack of prowess attracts the attention of his peers is likely to be keenly aware of that disparity. Often the student with such a handicap begins to suffer from difficulties in social or emotional adjustment (Klausmeier & Ripple, 1971). One would suspect that the effect of psychomotor skills on individuals and their status in the group is even greater than is true in the area of cognitive development. If students are not accepted by their classmates, their social growth is surely diminished. Consequently, their self-concept may be damaged.

Personality

Personality is such a common term that a definition appears unnecessary. Yet using a term like this without clarifying the meaning intended often leads to confusion and misunderstanding. For example, when referring to *personality,* the average person tends to refer to the individual's skill in relating to others and in evoking a positive response in the people with whom he comes in contact. The psychologist, on the other hand, is accustomed to following a more specified, organized approach to the definition of *personality.* Some stress "social interaction" and a predisposition to behave in a consistent pattern. Others focus on the "integration" of specific actions with the total behavior pattern, the "total adjustment" of individuals with their physical and social environment, and the "unique aspects of behavior" that give the person her individuality (Ausubel & Robinson, 1969).

The variety of definitions for *personality* arises from the many-faceted aspects of this concept. Various groups select differing components of personality as the focus of their attention. As a result, the meanings reflect varying emphases on cognitive, affective, and social considerations. Those who stress cognitive aspects are interested in the internal processes with which the individual perceives and organizes his life situation into a meaningful, comprehensible (to him) whole. Those who focus on the social components in their definition of personality are most aware of the interrelationships occurring in the social matrix in which the individual is operating. Those who place primary emphasis on the affective components are concerned with the person's attitudes and feelings as he draws meaning from his interaction with the physical world and his social circumstances. In defining *personality,* the affective-social variables normally receive more stress than the cognitive, although it is obvious that the individual's cognitive structure plays a determining role in the development of the affective-social aspects of personality and that there is a decided interaction among all three components.

Klausmeier and Ripple (1971) outline some milestones of ego development (which they adapted from Loevinger and Wessler) that are pertinent to personality development. As was true in the case of cognitive development, any individual may be at any given level. It cannot be assumed that someone of a particular age will have reached a certain ego development stage. Some individuals (perhaps many) will never reach the highest ego state. A knowledge of the hierarchical stages of ego development provides the teacher with greater insight into the general stage at which the student or students may be at a particular point in their growth and gives a framework for attempting to comprehend and interpret individual and group behavior. The following list summarizes the succeeding stages in ego development:

1. *a. Presocial. b. Symbiotic.* In this stage infants are primarily concerned with themselves and with making a distinction between self and the non-self parts of their surroundings. At first they do not distinguish between animate and inanimate objects. At the beginning of the symbiotic stage they are able to identify "mother." This stage ends with the onset of speech.

2. *Impulsive.* Children are conscious of their separate existence from mother and are concerned with body feelings and functions. They have acquired few, if any, restraints on their impulses. An act is bad only if they are punished for it.

3. *Self-protective.* This is an intensely competitive period. Growing out of dependency on parents, the youngsters seek to gain control over other people and/or things. They want to get the best of everything, to be first, to have the most, etc. Following rules is desirable if one gains an advantage by doing so, and behavior is wrong only if one gets caught.

4. *Conformist.* During this period of development an intensely high premium is placed on appearance, possessions, and reputation, especially as each compares and relates to one's peers. Certain people, things, and acts which are "in" dictate an outward conformity. Rules are followed simply because they are rules, and the person is ashamed of breaking the rules.

5. *Conscientious.* The individuals reach a stage of internal direction and personal responsibility for their actions. They now have the capacity for self-evaluation and self-criticism. They are more capable of forming true and meaningful personal relationships based on feelings rather than group-sanctioned conformity. They can envision goals and ideals and plan for means of achieving them. When they fail to "live up" to their expectations, they suffer guilt rather than shame.

6. *Autonomous.* On this level individuals gain two abilities. They learn to cope with conflict, whether it be inner-conflict or inter-conflict. They become more tolerant of differences in others. They emphasize the desirability of self-fulfillment for each individual.

7. *Integrated.* Individuals reaching the highest possible level of ego development are able to reconcile the conflicts going on within themselves and around them. They value individual worth and achieve a sense of their own integrated identity.

It goes without saying that personality is a major factor in determining student success or failure in school. The position of the student on the adjustment-maladjustment continuum furnishes the student with, or deprives her of, the security and confidence needed to grow cognitively, emotionally, and socially. The student who lacks confidence in herself is likely to be low in achievement motivation, high in anxiety, and low in achievement. Knowing where the student is on the ego-development scale will enable the teacher to ascertain more specifically what steps might be beneficial in overcoming student problems. However, a word of warning must be inserted here. Teachers usually lack sufficient training and experience to handle severe emotional problems, and they must distinguish between those situations in which they are capable of assisting and those in which they are not. As Disick and Barbanel (1974, p. 213) state the situation: "Although a sensitive teacher can contribute to the positive emotional development of his students, there are limits to what he can accomplish. Since most teachers lack extensive psychiatric training, there *must* be limits on what is said and done in the classroom."

Other Factors

Other variables affecting the student's actions, reactions, and interactions are social adjustment, socioeconomic status, and sex. The student cannot disassociate himself from the influences of his personal relationships at home and in the school during classroom activities. The atmosphere of the classroom situation itself imposes its effects on the student's willingness and perhaps even ability to participate in the group activities. The student who is socially well adjusted has a definite asset in learning, while the student burdened by social adjustment problems labors under a decided handicap. The need for social recognition is a basic component of human behavior, and as such it must be satisfied if complete social adjustment is to be attained (Mouly, 1973).

Socioeconomic background not only plays a major role in the student's current circumstances but also determines to a great extent the quality of learning skills and quantity of knowledge that the students bring with them when they enter the classroom. The student who comes from a deprived environment is likely to be deficient in language development and reading skills, two basic building blocks upon which successful academic achievement rests. As a consequence of an inadequate background, the underprivileged student suffers from year to year, thereby creating an ever widening gap between her learning and abilities and those of students having more fortunate circumstances.

Sex is a significant determinant of student activity and an undeniable focal point of student interest. Learning to establish healthy sexual attitudes and relationships continues to be a primary goal and a major accomplishment for students from the age of middle school and junior high school on to the university level. To date, general differences have characterized the two sexes, although the women's liberation movement may effect change in certain sex roles and attitudes. Physically and linguistically, girls mature earlier than boys. Girls tend to be more social and more conforming. They tend to get along better with teachers and to receive better grades. They, more than boys, seem to prefer courses such as English and foreign language, which involve a great deal of reading and writing.

STUDENT NEEDS

Mouly (1973) divides human needs into two categories: physiological and psychological. The physiological needs are the needs for food, water, sleep and rest, activity, and sex. The psychological needs are the needs for affection, belonging, achievement, independence, social recognition, and self-esteem. Mouly (1973) also refers to a hierarchical classification of human needs proposed by Maslow. Maslow's taxonomy of needs includes (1) physiological (2) security, (3) love, (4) esteem, (5) self-actualization, and (6) the need to know and to understand. The achievement of each higher-order need rests upon the prior satisfaction of supporting, lower-order needs. The following discussion deals with some aspects of the student's basic needs.

Self-Concept

Lecky proposed a definition of *self-concept* in 1945 of which the "basic premise is that all of an individual's values are organized into a single system, the nucleus of which is his valuation of himself. The fundamental need of every individual is to develop and maintain a unified mental organization. As he undergoes new experiences, he accepts or rejects them in terms of their compatibility with his present self. He thereby maintains his individuality and avoids conflict" (Mouly, 1973, p. 85).

Several implications are readily apparent from the preceding definition of self-concept. The first is that the individual must begin by liking himself. However, Maslow's hierarchy indicates that self-love must be supported by and developed from the satisfaction of physiological needs and from having received the necessary security, love, and esteem from the other significant people in his environment. The individual's view of himself is influenced by the self-view reflected from his surroundings as he interacts within his life situation. Normally, the most influential people in each individual's life are the members of his family, and the most important single component in the development of the self-concept is the home. Therefore, although new dimensions can be molded into the student's self-concept, he brings his basic self-concept with him when he comes to school for the first time.

The individual's self-concept encompasses his entire person. It is a product of all the physical, cognitive, social, economic, moral, and emotional factors that have gone into his makeup. The acquired self-concept is a prerequisite for all subsequent endeavors that the individual may undertake. Until he has developed a unified mental organization of his world of reality, maximally satisfactory participation in his life situation is unlikely. This cognitive network of information determines to a large extent not only how he perceives the external world but also how he reacts to it. Lacking an adequate self-concept, the individual is reluctant to accept himself or others. He will also shy away from any and all activities that threaten him.

As well as a conception of what she is as a person, each individual has a vision of what she would like to be, an "ideal self" (Ausubel & Robinson, 1969). The closer the perceived self approaches to the desired self, the better the individual's adjustment and the more adequate her self-concept. If the distance between the two is small enough to permit the individual to like herself, the disparity serves as a strong motivating factor. If the gulf is discouragingly wide, psychological maladjustment may arise (Klausmeier & Ripple, 1971). Most, if not all, of her thinking and resultant actions arise from her desires to maintain her self-concept, to narrow the gap between the "I" she sees and the "I" she would like to be, and/or to avoid psychological damages to her self-image and self-esteem. As Anderson (1952, p. 236) describes the process, "The pattern of life of every individual is a living-out of his self-image; it is his road map for living. People can be counted on to behave according to their own patterns."

Schwartz (1972) has identified five stages in self-concept development:
1. From birth to one-and-one-half or two, children acquire a sense of trust or distrust in and for their surroundings and the people in their surroundings.
2. From two to four, they develop a sense of autonomy or feelings of shame and doubt.
3. From four to seven, their self-concept is characterized by a sense of initiative or of a sense of guilt.
4. Between the ages of seven and eleven or twelve, they progress to a sense of industry or feelings of inferiority.
5. The final stage occuring during adolescence is the arrival at a state of self-identity or the failure to do so, which results in an identity diffusion.

The extremes postulated in the various stages are not either-or descriptions, but general tendencies. The same individual might demonstrate varying tendencies in given situations or at different stages of development. For example, a student might have a strong academic self-concept while at the same time be quite insecure socially. Too, individuals can be expected to differ with regard to the age at which they may move from one stage to another.

As was mentioned previously, one of the problems with which contemporary schools have to deal is the feeling of alienation being experienced by substantial numbers of the student body. This anomie is due partially to an inadequate self-concept. The search for personal identity, or the failure of many young people to be able to answer the question "Who am I?", has become an increasing problem as growing portions of society have moved away from the family unit as the basic socializing agent. As the family has failed to fulfill its traditional role, the responsibility has fallen increasingly on the schools. Many parents now expect teachers to concern themselves with areas of individual development that were previously relegated to the home and family (Finkelstein, 1973).

The child with a positive self-concept accepts himself and is confident of his ability to deal with others and with his environment. The child with a negative self-concept is plagued by feelings of two inadequacies. First, he is unable to accept himself as a person, seeing himself as being unlovable. Second, he is insecure in his relationships with his surrounding circumstances, feeling a lack of ability to cope with his situation. The individual who has a negative self-concept may attempt to compensate for this by turning to some form of deviant behavior, such as drug addiction, crime, etc. (Ellsworth, 1967). A person handicapped by a low self-image has difficulty expressing himself freely, undertaking new and different tasks, and participating in new and different situations (Brothers, 1973).

Self-concept is such a basic component of one's personality that it affects not only how one thinks and feels but also what one attempts to undertake. Furthermore, it affects one's expectations and performance. Individuals' ability to learn, their capacity to grow and change, their choice of friends, mate, and career are all determined to a greater or lesser extent by their vision of themselves (Brothers, 1973).

The individual's self-concept is stable, but not static. Each person seeks to maintain a relatively high degree of harmony within himself and between himself and his environment. As he does so, a gradual evolution of his self-concept occurs as a result of his adjustment to the image of himself that he is receiving from his experiences. To promote change in a person's self-image, one must first take into account the defense mechanisms built into the ego. The ego must be protected from uncomfortable damage, and most individuals are more concerned with protection than change. Therefore, the crucial factor in attempting to change a person's self-image is to establish a nonthreatening atmosphere (Mouly, 1973).

Self-Actualization

Self-concept is fundamental to self-actualization. Actually, self-actualization begins with self-concept and develops into other facets of the person's total self. In this sense, *self-actualization* is a broader, more encompassing term. Mouly (1973, p. 34) describes *self-actualization* as follows: "The humanist sees the human person, not as the defenseless victim of stimuli, but rather as a purposeful being geared to such concepts as self-determination, self-fulfillment, and self-actualization. The role of education, for example, is to foster individuality by helping each child actualize his potentialities to the fullest, not to turn out identical, interchangeable 'pieces' on an assembly-line basis." The first step in the self-actualization process is to answer the question, "Who am I?". The second step is to answer the questions, "What can I do?" and "What would I like to do?". The individual is responsible for finding her own answers to these questions.

Existentialism has provided the general philosophical orientation from which self-actualization has developed. Specific emphases in this orientation, however, have been passed down through related disciplines encompassing personality and learning. The concept of the wholeness and uniqueness of each individual has been promoted by the organismic view of personality. The stress on the importance of the individual's input in using his capacities to cope with his situation has been the principal tenet of theories proposed by Gestalt psychologists and the phenomenologists. The concept of anticipatory activity, i.e., the principle of becoming, has been supported in the work of Adler, Jung, and Rank. The trend away from concentration on biological factors and toward the socioeconomic environment has been fostered by the fields of cultural anthropology and sociology (Cofer & Appley, 1964).

What are the characteristics of self-actualizing persons? First, they have learned to accept themselves and to live with themselves. They have no need to follow the lead of others or to reject their own basic values in order to be an "in" member of some group. Second, they have developed a guiding moral and social system which permits them to live relatively free from conflict and feelings of guilt. Third, they have reached a level of emotional control at which they have an effective behavior pattern and at which they can pursue worthwhile and meaningful goals. Fourth, they have determined exactly what their abilities are and have developed an acceptable degree of competence in these areas. Fifth, they have chosen a life style appropriate to their capabilities, personality, and situation. Sixth, they have accepted a process of continuous growth in life. Seventh, they have achieved a level of social sensitivity at which they can integrate personal needs and goals with those of the group and at which they can relate meaningfully and effectively with others. Eighth, they have progressed to a point of being able to derive satisfaction from altruistic endeavors while maintaining their own self-interests. Ninth, they have formulated a positive outlook on life, and have learned to laugh at life in general and at themselves in particular (Mouly, 1973).

Socialization

Socialization is especially important today due to the emphasis on individuality. Few would question the desirability of focusing on individual abilities, interests, and needs. That which individuals perform in their own way and on their own initiative is usually done with greater dispatch, with more enjoyment, and at a higher level of quality than that which is done at someone else's bidding. Ayn Rand has even gone so far as to discount the desirability of altruism. However, in order to operate within the limits of a culture, individuals must become acculturated and socialized to some functional extent.

The process of socialization involves both social and cultural learning. As children grow and interact with their social groups, they gradually acquire a cultural heritage. From contact with people in their environment, for example, they learn the language, and language influences the way they view the world around them. Learning the cultural intricacies of society is a prerequisite for membership in that group due to the restrictions society places upon acceptable behavior patterns. At the same time most of the individual's secondary needs are culturally determined. Therefore, participation in society becomes a major means of satisfying needs.

Everyone belongs to some social group and acquires a basic cultural heritage. This socialization occurs as a result of the obvious dependent state of the young child and continues throughout the individual's lifetime. If at any time one chooses to "drop out" of a certain culture and society, one normally "drops into" another culture and society more in keeping with one's self-actualization needs. In this new society the pressure to conform is equally as strong as in the former. As Taba (1962, p. 131) states the situation: "Generally speaking, man conforms to culture, and even his deviations occur only within certain limitations. . . ." The influence of one's culture is so total that it is "difficult to understand either behavior or learning except in relation to the particular culture in which it occurs." McDonald (1965) asserts that an adjusted person is a socialized person, i.e., she satisfies her own needs by learning the acceptable social behavior patterns.

Taba (1962) lists seven principal tenets of social learning.

1. Anthropologists and sociologists define the goal of learning as the acquisition of socially acceptable behavior. What is absorbed includes not only external behavior patterns but also basic beliefs and concepts held by the culture. Each person learns the cultural patterns of his social group.
2. The individual's functional capacity to learn is determined by cultural expectations, and by self-expectations, which have been acquired as a result of socialization.
3. For the most part individual behavior is acquired.

4. Individual behavior, thinking, and feeling are closely associated with those of the social and cultural group.
5. Learning is primarily a social process. The individual learns the culture and the social standards of behavior.
6. Socialization occurs at home, in school, among peers, etc.
7. Individual actions are controlled by motives, which are largely culturally determined.

While it is true that all individuals pass through a continuous socialization-acculturation process, the experiences they have and the information they receive may be quite varied. Since many subgroups, including social classes and ethnic and racial groups, exist in society, there is a tremendous variation among individuals in their acquired social and cultural experiences, which in turn affects their abilities and expectations.

This variation in the socialization process presents difficult problems for the schools to solve. Difficulties occur in communication and understanding when a member of one cultural-social group interacts with a member of another group. The necessity of having some common ground upon which to establish a meaningful exchange becomes a significant factor in the social atmosphere of the school and of the class as the students interact with each other and with the teachers.

Another problem is that the behavior patterns of different families and different groups may contain conflicting and opposing predispositions toward certain types of action and interaction. For example, students who are accustomed to varying systems of reward and punishment will, in all likelihood, react in diverse manners to any set of rules and expectations the teacher attempts to establish in the classroom.

A further problem is the one dealing with academic achievement in the schools. Students from a low socioeconomic class often lack the background support to achieve their academic desires. In the first place, deficiencies in past achievement have left them in the position of being unable to cope with the cognitive material being presented at each succeeding level. Consequently, their achievement motivation suffers. They have been exposed to the same aspirations and desires as students from upper socioeconomic levels, but their backgrounds have not stressed the necessity of perseverance and acquisition of supportive abilities in order to attain these aspirations. As a result, their attitude toward success, school, authority, and their own ability to rise to the level of their aspirations does little to motivate them in the direction of maximum participation and effort in school (Ausubel & Robinson, 1969).

On the other hand, some students are consumed by such a fierce determination to succeed in school that their achievement rises far above what one would suspect from examining their academic credentials. Other students are so blessed innately with intelligence that their deprived sociocultural background does little to affect achievement. The latter two types represent the kind of student all teachers like to have in class because of the positive effect their achievement has on the teachers' egos. This reaction is natural and to be expected, but it does point out vividly the extreme difficulty of establishing "person" goals in education in which the teachers' satisfactions can be derived not from how high the students fly, but how much teachers have helped them. Setting a goal of self-actualization for students in their academic work, their personal growth, and their social adjustment presents a Herculean task to education, and its attainment will require much more than good intentions. Continued, conscious effort is the least teachers can bring to their work.

Practically all aspects of individual personality are learned through socialization. The individual's location on the adjustment-maladjustment continuum is a most influential factor in prediction of the probability of successful acclimatization to the school and classroom social situations (McDonald, 1965). How well each student is assimilated into the school and class social system, her resultant social status in the group, and her relationship with the teachers play a major role in her ability not only to feel a part of the school and to enjoy the experience, but to benefit from it.

Values

A values crisis seems to have struck in contemporary, industrialized society. The deterioration of the family, the community, and the church has weakened the channels through which the cultural heritage has traditionally been transmitted. The failure of many young people to acquire a satisfactory values system has been speeded up by the negative influence of world events, the effects of the mass media which popularized the "generation gap" and glamorized the new life styles, and the disconcerting effects upon youth of being exposed to varying and often inconsistent value systems. In their book, *Values and Teaching,* Raths, et al., (1966, p. 7) ask, "Could it be, we wonder, that the pace and complexity of modern life has so exacerbated the problem of deciding what is good and what is right and what is worthy and what is desirable that large numbers of children are finding it increasingly bewildering, even overwhelming, to decide what is worth valuing, what is worth one's time and energy?" The same authors (1966, p. 7) contend that "few would deny that there are far too many children in the schools today who do not seem to learn as well as they might because they simply are not clear about what their lives are for, what is worth working for."

Raths et al. (1966) have proposed a values continuum. At one end are those individuals who can be classified as "becoming" or "self-actualizing" people. They can be labeled as being positive, purposeful, enthusiastic, and proud. On the other end are those other individuals who, due to their inability to cope with their surroundings, have adopted quite different behavior patterns. They are characterized as being (1) apathetic, (2) flighty, (3) uncertain, (4) inconsistent, (5) drifters, (6) overconformers, (7) overdissenters, and (8) role players. Obviously, many people fall somewhere between the extremes. However, the point the authors make is that the positive group has very clear-cut values while the others do not.

Values are acquired during the course of the socialization process. If they are not, special programs must be instituted to insure that a functional, harmonious values system is developed. The basic approaches to values acquisition are summarized as follows by Rest (1974):

1. *Socialization or Indoctrination.* In this approach, youths are told what is right, what is to be valued.
2. *Behavioristic.* Youths are conditioned to react within certain predetermined patterns.
3. *Humanistic.* Humanistic psychologists stress experience and transitory states of feeling.
4. *Values Clarification.* This approach is essentially neutral. The goal is to give youngsters an insight into the process of clarifying exactly what their values are.
5. *Developmentalist.* Developmentalist psychologists focus on the development of conceptual frameworks, problem-solving strategies, and structured competencies which can be transferred to other situations and which serve to enhance and enrich later life. They hold that the individual's cognitive structure is the basis for comprehending and interpreting her affective experiences. They do not accept the ethical relativity and the value neutrality of the values clarification approach.

Raths et al. conceive of values as being an outgrowth of three processes: choosing, prizing, and acting. According to their viewpoint it is essential that each individual be allowed to choose "freely," "from alternatives," and "after thoughtful consideration of the consequences of each alternative." After choosing, individuals indicate the extent to which they prize their choice by "being happy with the choice," and by being "willing to affirm the choice publicly." If they prize the choice, then they will confirm their values in action by "doing something with the choice repeatedly, in some pattern of life." Individual's values are revealed by their goals and purposes, aspirations, attitudes, interests, feelings, beliefs and convictions, activities, and worries and problems (Raths, Harmin, & Simon, 1966, p. 30). The teacher interested in pursuing "person" education should sensitize herself to the various manners in which individuals express their values. Based on her observations and analysis of the students' strengths and/or weaknesses, she can institute procedures to take advantage of the strong aspects of each student and to build up those areas in which growth and development would be beneficial to each personally, socially, and academically.

CONCLUSION

The reactions and attitudes of many students in the "new" generation sound a warning to educators that all is not well. In one or more areas of student needs, i.e., self-concept, self-actualization, socialization, and values, some needs are apparently not being met. Few would disagree as to the need for helping the students, but the number of solutions as to how to help them rivals the number of problems in need of attention. The trend at the moment, however, is to emphasize the individual and the affective state. This trend is commendable as long as teachers do not neglect the cognitive and social components of the total student in the process. In the first place, educators must consider student attitudes in light of what they know about the maturation process and student needs. In the second place, educators must resist the tendency in education to jump from one approach to another in search of a single answer to all problems. A total program for the total student will not fail to consider all facets of the student: the cognitive, the affective, the social, the personality, and the psychomotor. Educating the nation's youth is a complex undertaking, and simple or one-sided models do not meet the need.

REVIEW AND APPLICATION

DEFINITIONS
1. adolescence, p. 174
2. anomie, p. 171
3. counterculture, p. 169
4. "democratic" vs. "authoritarian" vs. "permissive," p. 170
5. generation gap, p. 173
6. "person" education, p. 192
7. phenomenology, p. 176
8. psychomotor, p. 182
9. self-actualization, p. 188
10. values clarification, p. 192

DISCUSSION
1. Describe examples of instances in which affective variables influenced academic achievement. In what ways? How have affective variables influenced your own learning?
2. Discuss the dichotomy of "teaching a subject" or "teaching students." What effect would each have on classroom activities? On teacher-student relationships? How does a teacher-centered class relate to these two?

3. What is your reaction to the statement, *There are no failing students, only failing teachers*? Upon what basis is this statement made?

4. Discuss the relationship between socialization and cognitive and personality variables. What effect does socialization have on each?

5. Is there a generation gap in your family? To what extent? How does it influence the relationship between you and your parents? Between you and the other members of your family?

6. What are some general characteristics of adolescence? What effect do these characteristics have on students and their relations with others?

7. Discuss why the affective domain is receiving so much stress in contemporary society, and give your opinion as to the appropriateness of such an emphasis.

8. How do self-concept, self-actualization, socialization, and values relate to each other and to the basic needs of every student in the classroom?

ACTIVITIES

1. Invite a school psychologist or a school counselor to talk to your class about current student worries and problems as a teenager and as a student.

2. Read and discuss the latest polls regarding student and public attitudes toward the schools.

3. List and compare your ten major problems with those lists of the other students in class.

4. Visit a student-centered, a subject-centered, and a teacher-centered class. Which do you prefer? What are the distinguishing characteristics of each?

SELECTED REFERENCES

Anderson, C. (1974) Reaching the Student. *ADFL Bulletin,* 5:5–7.

Anderson, C. M. (1952) The Self-Image: A Theory of the Dynamics of Behavior. *Mental Hygiene,* 36:236.

Aronson, H. I. (1973) The Role of Attitudes About Languages in the Learning of Foreign Languages. *Modern Language Journal,* 57:323–29.

Ausubel, D. P., and Robinson, F. G. (1969) *School Learning: An Introduction to Educational Psychology.* New York: Holt, Rinehart and Winston. Pp. 388–90, 405, 432–34.

Brothers, J. (1973) Learning to Like Yourself: Self-Image. *Good Housekeeping,* 176:74–78.

Brown, C. T. (1974) Communication and the Foreign Language Teacher. In G. A. Jarvis (Ed.), *The Challenge of Communication.* Skokie, Ill.: National Textbook. P. 26.

Callas, H. (1974) A Survey of Student Attitudes at the University of Texas at Austin. *ADFL Bulletin,* 6:52–56.

Carney, H. (1973) Students Make the Scene. *Modern Language Journal,* 57:335–40.

Carroll, J. B. (1963) A Model of School Learning. *Teacher's College Record,* 64:729.

Carter, I. M. (1971) Early Adolescent Characteristics, Limitations, Problems, and Desirable Attitudes. *Education,* 92:90–94.

Cofer, C. N., and Appley, M. H. (1964) *Motivation: Theory and Research.* New York: Wiley. Pp. 655–68.

Coleman, J. S. (1965) Social Change: Impact on the Adolescent. *NAASP Bulletin,* 49:11.

Disick, R. S. (1972) Developing Positive Attitudes in Intermediate Foreign Language Classes. *Modern Language Journal,* 56:417–20.

Disick, R. S., and Barbanel, L. (1974) Affective Education and Foreign Language Teaching. In G. A. Jarvis (Ed.), *The Challenge of Communication.* Skokie, Ill.: National Textbook. P. 213.

Dobay, C. M. (1973) A Look at What Lies Behind the Crisis in Our Schools. *The Education Digest,* 39:44–45.

Ellsworth, S. G. (1967) Building the Child's Self-Concept. *NEA Journal,* 56:54–56.

Finkelstein, B. J. (1973) The Search for Identity: An Institutional Problem. *Intellect,* 102:150–51.

Fischer, E. M. (1975) Change in Anomia in Detroit from the 1950s to 1971. *Dissertation Abstracts International,* 35:4697A.

Gallup, G. (1974) Sixth Annual Gallup Poll of Public Attitudes Toward Education. *Phi Delta Kappan,* 56:21–29.

Gorman, R. M. (1972) *Discovering Piaget: A Guide for Teachers.* Columbus, Ohio: Merrill. Pp. 4–6, 109–10.

Gross, N. (1973) Critical Questions for Contemporary Education. *Intellect,* 102:26.

Hancock, C. R. (1972) Guiding Teachers to Respond to Individual Differences in the Affective Domain. *Foreign Language Annals,* 6:225–31.

Hanzeli, V. E. (1972) Foreign Language Teachers and the "New" Student: A Review Article. *Modern Language Journal,* 56:15–21.

Heard, L. E. (1972) Foreign Language and the Group Context: Expanding Student Roles. *Foreign Language Annals,* 5:313–20.

Hill, J. P. (1971) Adolescence. In D. W. Allen and E. Seifman (Eds.), *The Teacher's Handbook.* Glenview, Ill.: Scott Foresman. Pp. 105, 115.

Kagan, J. (1971) Controversies in Intelligence: The Meaning of Intelligence. In D. W. Allen and E. Seifman (Eds.), *The Teacher's Handbook.* Glenview, Ill.: Scott Foresman. Pp. 656–57.

Katz, J. (1974) The Psychology of Student Unrest. *Uses of the Sociology of Education.* The Seventy-third Yearbook of the National Society for the Study of Education, edited by C. W. Gordon. Chicago: University of Chicago Press. Pp. 4–10.

Kahn, S. B., and Weiss, J. (1973) The Teaching of Affective Responses. In R. M. W. Travers (Ed.), *Second Handbook of Research on Teaching.* Chicago: Rand McNally. Pp. 760–70.

Klausmeier, H. J., and Ripple, R. E. (1971) *Learning and Human Abilities: Educational Psychology.* (3rd ed.) New York: Harper & Row. Pp. 106, 528–29, 558, 562, 567–70.

Kleine, P. F. (1971) Preadolescence. In D. W. Allen and E. Seifman (Eds.), *The Teacher's Handbook.* Glenview, Ill.: Scott Foresman. Pp. 100–1.

Lafayette, R. C. (1972) Diversification: The Key to Student-Centered Programs. *Modern Language Journal,* 56:349–54.

Larkin, R. (1974) Protest and Counterculture: Disaffection Among Affluent Youth. *Uses of the Sociology of Education.* The Seventy-third Yearbook of the National Society for the Study of Education, edited by C. W. Gordon. Chicago: University of Chicago Press. Pp. 19–20, 29–31.

McDonald, F. J. (1965) *Educational Psychology.* (2nd ed.) Belmont, Calif.: Wadsworth. Pp. 443, 445–47.

McNamara, J. (1973) Nurseries, Streets and Classrooms: Some Comparisons and Deductions. *Modern Language Journal,* 57:250–54.

Manning, W. (1972) The Credibility Gap That Is Neutralizing the Public Schools. *Interchange,* 3:31–32.

Maslow, A. H. (1970) *Motivation and Personality.* New York: Harper & Row.

Miller, J. (1973) Schooling and Self-Alienation: A Conceptual View. *The Journal of Educational Thought,* 7:115–16.

Mouly, G. J. (1973) *Psychology for Learning*. (3rd ed.) New York: Holt, Rinehart and Winston. Pp. 33–34, 43, 53–59, 85, 96–97, 104–05, 130, 212–13, 331, 466.

Mueller, T. H. (1971) Student Attitudes in the Basic French Courses at the University of Kentucky. *Modern Language Journal,* 55:290–98.

Northeast Conference Reports (1970) J. A. Tursi (Ed.), *Foreign Languages and the "New" Student.*

Northeast Conference Reports (1974) W. C. Born (Ed.), *Toward Student-Centered Foreign Language Programs.*

Papalia, A. (1970) A Study of Attrition in Foreign Language Enrollments in Four Suburban Public Schools. *Foreign Language Annals,* 4:62–67.

Perkinson, H. J. (1974) How Schools Can Make a Difference. *Intellect,* 102:395.

Raths, L. E.; Harmin, M.; and Simon, S. B. (1966) *Values and Teaching.* Columbus, Ohio: Merrill. Pp. 6–8, 30–33.

Rest, J. (1974) Developmental Psychology as a Guide to Value Education: A Review of "Kohlbergian" Programs. *Review of Educational Research,* 44:242.

Rivers, W. M. (1974) A Pleasant Surprise: Students Like Foreign Languages! *Modern Language Journal,* 58:124.

Rivers, W. M. (1974) The Non-Major: Tailoring the Course to the Person, Not the Image. *ADFL Bulletin,* 5:12–18.

Rogers, C. R. (1969) *Freedom to Learn.* Columbus, Ohio: Merrill.

Savaiano, E. (1974) The FL Requirement, a Liberal Education, and You. *ADFL Bulletin,* 5:13.

Schwartz, L. L. (1972) *Educational Psychology: Focus on the Learner.* Boston: Holbrook. Pp. 152–53.

Schreiber, D. (1969) Dropout—Causes and Consequences. In R. Ebel (Ed.), *Encyclopedia of Educational Research.* New York: Macmillan. P. 314.

Scriven, E. G., and Westerman, J. E. (1974) Traditional vs. Emergent—A Study of Value Change. *Intellect,* 102:398–400.

Smith, A. N. (1971) The Importance of Attitude in Foreign Language Learning. *Modern Language Journal,* 55:82–88.

Spady, W. G. (1974) The Authority System of the School and Student Unrest: A Theoretical Explanation. *Uses of the Sociology of Education.* The Seventy-third Yearbook of the National Society for the Study of Education, edited by C. W. Gordon. Chicago: University of Chicago Press. P. 71.

Spady, W. G., and Adler, C. (1974) Youth, Social Change, and Unrest: A Critique and Synthesis. *Uses of the Sociology of Education.* The Seventy-third Yearbook of the National Society for the Study of Education, edited by C. W. Gordon. Chicago: University of Chicago Press. Pp. 141, 145, 155–56.

Taba, H. (1962) *Curriculum Development: Theory and Practice.* New York: Harcourt, Brace & World. Pp. 130–31, 147.

Thogmartin, C. (1974) A Survey of Attitudes Toward Foreign Language Education Among First-Year Students. *ADFL Bulletin,* 3:39–45.

DIVERSIFYING INSTRUCTION

The Rise of Individualized Instruction

Characteristics of Individualized Instruction

Characteristics of a Totally Individualized Program

Reactions to Individualized Instruction

An Examination of the Basic Assumptions of Individualized Instruction
  Aptitude
  Behavioral Objectives
  Interests
  Goals
  Taxonomy
  Social Interaction
  Self-Pacing
  Mastery Learning
  Continuous Progress
  Criterion-Referenced Examinations

Ways and Means of Diversifying Instruction
  In Traditional Classes
  Two Types of Courses
  Deciding to Offer an Individualized Approach
  Alternatives to Individualized Instruction
    The Three-Stage Model of Instruction
    Group-Based Individualized Instruction

INTRODUCTION

The major educational movement of the early seventies has been without question the trend toward "individualized" instruction. This is not a methodological, but a curricular approach to teaching, emphasizing the organizational framework of the class. In fact, few changes have occurred during the seventies in basic methodological principles or in the types of classroom activities employed to accomplish chosen goals. With individualized instruction, each student proceeds through the materials at his own rate. As is commonly true of innovations in education, the "individualized" movement began with a great deal of fanfare. Although the number of individualized classes is still growing, individualized classes have been in existence long enough for the preliminary evaluations to be in and for the first criticisms to begin to appear. The purpose of this chapter is to examine the principal characteristics of individualized instruction and to explore alternative ways of meeting the needs of individual students.

THE RISE OF INDIVIDUALIZED INSTRUCTION

Crucial to the comprehension of individualized instruction is a familiarity with the conditions, reactions, and goals that provided the impetus for change in the types of instruction students were receiving. What were the criticisms of contemporary education? (For more information, see chapter 2, "Perspectives," pages 26, 30–34, and chapter 7, "The Student,", pages 171–73). What were the reasons for the rise of individualized instruction? Following is a selective list of these reasons, some of which are interrelated:

1. There was a need to increase learning for all the students in the schools. Block (1971, p. 2) is speaking for many of the critics when he says, ". . . The schools continue to provide successful and rewarding learning experiences for only about one-third of our learners."

2. In order to improve the education of the majority of students who were having unsatisfactory learning experiences, the emphasis was shifted to this group of students. Walker (1973, p. 191) states, "Major concern for individual differences has centered on low-achieving students and has significantly influenced the direction of public school education within the last fifteen years."

3. As the ideas of the critics have become widespread, the public has come to expect an educational system responsive to the needs of all the students. The public would like to see a higher ratio of success among the student population than in the past (Cohen, 1972).

4. If the purpose of education is to prepare students for constructive, productive adult lives, the educational system should try to promote the development of productive habits and sound emotional character. Block (1971) maintains that the requirement of having to spend a large percentage of their childhood in failure may lead to mental and emotional problems for up to 20 percent of the students in the schools.

5. One of the goals in individualized instruction is the avoidance of failure. In theory, at least, the outcome of this approach is to have no failing students. If their needs are met, all students will be able to succeed. If their needs are not met and they are not successful, they simply do not receive credit. However, no failing grades are recorded.

6. Individualized instruction reflects the recent stress on the individual and a pluralistic society. Individualized instruction is an application to the classroom of the contemporary "do-your-own-thing" philosophy.

7. Individualized instruction attempts to avoid the dehumanized aspects of society in general. The enrollments in the schools have grown to the point that maintaining individual contact is difficult. The object of individualized instruction is to create a classroom organization in which the teacher and the student have more occasions for one-to-one interchanges. A large number of people feel a strong sense of urgency to increase efforts to humanize the educational system.

8. Individualized instruction is seen as a practical means of establishing an educational program which can react to the tremendous variety of ability levels in the comprehensive American high schools. Grouping, tracking, etc. have been incorporated into the school program in the past, but grouping according to ability levels does not seem to be in keeping, in the minds of many people at the present time, with a democratic, pluralistic society.

9. As a result of the interest in providing a successful educational experience for all students, there has been a trend away from the competitive classroom and from the comparison of one student with another. In fact, some critics condemn the competitive nature of American society and insist that we should stress competition with self and group cooperation instead. Grades, for example, are supposed to indicate achievement based on capability, not some normative ranking of the student's ability compared with other students in the class. The result of this philosophy is to abandon the system of grades entirely.

10. In one sense, individualized instruction is an application of the mass-production, technological model of industry to education. As the organization becomes larger, efforts are made to streamline and to make the system more efficient by specifying discrete job tasks to be accomplished.

11. Carroll's (1963) definition of *aptitude* is a major tenet in the philosophy

behind the recent popularity of individualized programs. He defines *aptitude* as "how long the learner takes to learn a given amount of material rather than the amount of material he can learn."

12. To some extent, the popularity of individualized instruction is due to the promotion of this approach by administrators as a means of meeting the call for accountability in the schools.

13. Accustomed to the variety of television presentations and lacking self-discipline for long-term concentration, many students are unaccustomed to sustaining attention during a traditional classroom period. Individualized instruction does not require the students to sit for long periods of time.

14. The world is changing at a dizzying pace. What is learned today may be out of date before the students have the opportunity to apply what they have learned. Therefore, the most important outcome of education is not the information learned, but the skills acquired.

Most, if not all, of these reasons apply to second-language classes. Following are a few special factors affecting second-language education.

1. The application of individualized instruction in second-language classes is to a certain extent a reaction to the lock-step, choral repetition of audio-lingual techniques.

2. Individualized instruction is seen as a way of increasing and maintaining enrollments. Some teachers talk of second languages for everyone. The image of being a difficult subject for the elite academic students who are planning to continue with a university education should, in their minds, be eradicated.

3. One problem that has always presented major obstacles to second-language teachers is the fact that there seems to be no normal curve in most second-language classes. For one group of students language study is apparently fairly easy; for the remainder of the class the same subject is impossible. The large middle group usually found in other classes is often almost nonexistent. Individualizing instruction is one way of attempting to compensate for this variability of aptitude in the class.

CHARACTERISTICS OF INDIVIDUALIZED INSTRUCTION

Discussing *individualized instruction* is complicated by the wide variety of meanings attached to the term. The term may mean "independent study"; "team teaching"; "the use of programmed materials"; "having more than one text for the class to use"; "assigning different exercises to the brighter students"; "adding supplementary, duplicated materials"; etc. (Coppedge,

1974). Nor does agreement as to the definition of the concept insure that the classroom applications will be identical or even similar. At times, a great gulf separates the philosophy a teacher purports to support and the activities in which her students are expected to participate. Travers (1975, p. 1) states, rather cynically, that the term has a "Madison Avenue flavor about it" and that "Educational programs are described as individualized, for the purpose of marketing them, much as breakfast cereals are described as a source of energy."

Travers (1975, p. 1) delineates two distinct types of individualization. Type 1 individualization refers to those programs in which all students are working toward the same objectives, but each is permitted to work at his own pace. According to Travers (1975, p. 1) type 1 individualization "provides individualized standardization of the educational product." In type 2 individualization the objectives may be different for each student. Consequently, the learning materials may also have to be different. The crucial difference between type 1 and type 2 individualization is that in type 2 the student either sets the objectives alone or in consultation with the teacher. That is, type 2 individualization is student-centered.

Block (1973) also speaks of two different types of individualization, but his distinction is based on the organization of student activities more than on choice of objectives. According to Block, the objectives would be chosen by the teacher, who would then provide individual assistance in the attainment of those preselected goals. In the first approach the students study individually for mastery. In the second approach the students work together in a group-based class. In either type of individualization the students are expected to achieve a predetermined level of mastery.

It goes without saying that the objective of individualized instruction is to provide for individual differences in the classroom. How have most proponents set up a program geared to meet individual needs? Although most established programs have been developed by individual teachers in response to specific situations, and although many variations are in existence, the following components seem to be basic to the majority of existing programs:
1. *Self-paced.* The students proceed through the materials at their own rate, for only they can judge for sure when they are ready to learn.
2. *LAPs.* LAPs may be more or less complex. However, the essential elements are as follows:
    a. Behavioral objectives. Everything that the student is to learn is expressed at the beginning of the LAP in behavioral terms. Behavioral objectives specify exactly what the student is to be able to do after completing the activities designed in the LAP. For example: "To demonstrate your comprehension of the story (pp. 27–28) by reading it aloud, answering the

questions (p. 33) orally or in writing, and providing an explanation in English of any part of it" (Valette & Disick, 1972).

b. Activities. All the required exercises and/or activities are listed. Each is then completed and checked off the list provided for keeping track of the work that has been done. In progressing toward the acquisition of the stated behaviors, the students may be asked to work with the text (or texts), the lab or tape recorder, a learning center, or other students who may be studying the same material.

c. Criterion-referenced tests. Attainment of behavioral objectives is evaluated by means of criterion-referenced tests. These are tests designed specifically to test the behaviors that the students have been told to be able to demonstrate at the end of the LAP. As such, they are related to the specific, predetermined behaviors listed at the beginning of the LAP rather than language proficiency per se. They are designed to ascertain the achievement of specific goals.

3. *Mastery learning.* The material in each LAP is to be learned to a level of mastery, normally set by the instructor at 80–85 percent. Before the students are permitted to proceed to the next LAP, they must demonstrate that they have mastered the material in the preceding LAP by making a grade of 80–85 percent or above on the criterion-referenced test accompanying the LAP. The assumption is that they are then ready to move to the next LAP in the learning sequence.

4. *Continuous progress learning.* One of the basic characteristics of this organization of learning activities is that the students are to progress steadily through the materials. There is to be no jumping forward before they are ready just to keep up with the remainder of the class. There are to be no interminable, bored, wasted interludes while some students wait for the remainder of the class to "catch on and catch up."

5. Normally, all students study the same materials. The objectives, the activities, and the criterion-referenced tests are for all the students. The only difference among students is that they may pace themselves through the materials.

6. The teachers' responsibility in this curricular organization of classroom instruction is twofold. First, they have the responsibility of preparing the LAPs. (They do this for two reasons. First, few commercial LAPs are available. Second, if the term *individualization* holds true to its name, the teachers practically by definition must prepare materials themselves for their particular situation. In fact, some insist that this is a crucial factor in individualization.) Second, they have the responsibility of administering the program. Both responsibilities require a great deal of time, energy, and expertise.

7. The teacher's role in the classroom is to serve as a "resource person." She is available to give assistance to those students if and when they encounter difficulties that they are unable to solve for themselves. In the new terminology, the teacher is a "facilitator of learning." She assists students in their learning process when they want help, not when it fits into her class sequence.

CHARACTERISTICS OF A TOTALLY INDIVIDUALIZED PROGRAM

The preceding section was a description of the type of individualized program that has been implemented in many schools. The term *individualized*, which has been used throughout this chapter, refers to the generally accepted definition of instructional programs set up to teach individuals as opposed to instruction geared toward the group. The next question to be considered is how closely this standard application of individualized instruction corresponds to the ideal goal of providing instruction that is the most appropriate for each individual in the class. In other words, if the ideal program were developed, what would be its characteristics? Saying that most programs fall short of being truly individualized, Coppedge (1974, pp. 273–76) gives the following essentials of a program of totally individualized instruction involving "the interaction between teacher, student, and learning experiences."

1. "Students are expected to perform commensurate with their ability and previous learning." In a truly individualized program students do more, not less. They learn more, not less. They are not allowed to work as "the spirit moves them." Self-pacing is not permitted to become a guise for procrastination. As Coppedge expresses this theme so well, "To permit a student to 'get by' with doing less than he is capable of is a waste of human potential, as well as a poor development of character." The implication, of course, is that in a program designed for him and his abilities the student is able to achieve more, and he is rightly expected to do so.

2. "Evaluation of student effort is based primarily on individual ability." The capabilities of each student are diagnosed to ascertain exactly what they are capable of achieving. Their efforts and work reflect these capabilities. Rather than rank each student in relation to other members of the class, the teacher is primarily concerned with the development of individual potentials. Standards are instituted for each individual. Otherwise, the students may allow themselves to become dependent upon the group's average for their sense of achievement and progress. At the same time, standards are raised, not lowered. Comparisons are put into perspective, not abandoned.

3. "There is more contact between teacher and student on a one-to-one basis." Class time is to be given to helping the students on a one-to-one basis. If the teacher becomes so busily involved preparing LAPs, taking care of routine chores, keeping administrative details in order, and correcting tests that no time remains for the students, the program becomes self-defeating.

4. "The student must become a full partner in the learning process." The implications of this statement are far-reaching. First, in this context the word *partner* signifies student participation in the entire spectrum of the learning sequence. Equal decision-making power is invested in the students. Their desires, interests, opinions, etc. are to be considered in making joint decisions about objectives and learning activities. The amount of independent study may vary with the student, but the students are never to study in isolation. Both they and the teacher are to be involved in the learning process at all times.

5. "The teaching-learning process is a cycle of diagnosis, prescription, and evaluation." The first step in establishing a truly individualized program is to determine the characteristics of each student. What are his abilities and the extent of his present cognitive structure? Before a series of learning activities can be selected for him, both he and the teacher are to be informed as to what he knows and what he is capable of learning. The second step is for the teacher and the student to decide together just where the student is and where he is going. At that point materials and learning exercises and activities can be determined. This material falls into three categories: (1) *required* material consisting of the basic essentials, (2) *expected* work encompassing material that contains suitable learning material for the majority of the students, and (3) *enrichment* content providing additional information and/or activities for the brightest and most highly motivated students. The author states that required material constitutes from 25–50 percent of the course, depending upon the student. Expected work makes up 30–60 percent of the course, again depending upon the student. And 25–50 percent of the content can center around enrichment materials and/or activities.

6. "Instructional planning is designed to promote student learning through continuous progress." LAPs are prepared so that the student may begin working at her present knowledge level and proceed through the course at the pace most suitable to her. Under the teacher's supervision and limited only by her own ability and interest, the student is to progress steadily. In addition to those components mentioned previously in this chapter, Coppedge feels that a LAP should (1) make provisions for a diagnosis of the student's capabilities, (2) list the major concepts, and (3) provide "quest" activities to stimulate additional exploration in breadth or in depth.

One of the basic goals of a humanized program of instruction entails placing the person or the individual in the center of the instructional process.

Frymier and Galloway (1974) emphasize this aspect of education in their discussion of an individualized program. First, they warn that curricular changes in classroom organization do not insure individualization of instruction. In their opinion, the primary requisite of an individualized program rests upon the teacher's willingness and ability to relate individually to the student, not whether the class works as a group or individually with LAPs. Since each child learns in his own way, each child should be taught in a manner that takes his individuality into consideration. Individualization occurs as the teacher, based on observation and analysis of each student, responds to the needs of each.

Wood (1973) suggests that the first step in individualization is to determine exactly how students differ both in the cognitive and the affective domains. The next step is to ascertain which of these factors most affect the student's learning and which have been sufficiently researched and explored so that the teacher can adapt instruction to these differences. Individualization entails applying the results of Aptitude-Treatment Interaction (ATI) research to the individual student. (See chapter 4, "Research," pages 91–92.) In order to meet the needs of all students, in most cases a rather wide variety of teaching-learning materials and situations should be made available to the students. Wood presents the following chart as a means of organizing an individualized program:

Individual Differences	Instructional Components				
	A. Objectives	B. Content	C. Learning Experiences	D. Media	E. Evaluation Techniques
1. Learning Style					
2. Learning Skills					
3. Motivational Styles					
4. Reading Skills					
5. Need for Direction					
6. Interests					
7. Achievement Level					

Source: Wood (1973, p. 27). Used by permission.

REACTIONS TO INDIVIDUALIZED INSTRUCTION

Since the early seventies, many leaders in second-language education, as well as in education in general, have been promoting individualized instruction as the solution to current problems in education. The major professional journals have contained a steady stream of articles highly supportive of this approach, and administrators have encouraged teachers to experiment with and to establish individualized programs.

What are some of the reactions on the part of both teachers and students to individualized instruction? Some teachers wax eloquent and enthusiastic, recounting how the new approach has revitalized their teaching. This is the type of teacher who appears at local, state, and national meetings. Teachers who have negative reactions or who have had unsuccessful experiences with individualized instruction have not made their feelings and opinions so widely known. Student reaction parallels that of the teachers. Some are fired up; others are turned off. In this sense, the early years of individualized instruction are similar to the initiation phases of most other movements. The appearance of negative reactions follows a few years behind the initial promotion.

At the present time, even the most avid proponents of individualized instruction are cautious. Griffin (1974) candidly admits his surprise at the "unbridled hostility" toward individualized instruction of teachers taking his graduate class of applied linguistics. He summarizes their negative reactions to concepts of individualized instruction as follows:

Proponents of individualized instruction were unfair in making the following statements:

1. "Individualized instruction is a new and improved approach." In the teachers' opinions, good teachers have always responded with concern and extra help for the individual in each of their classes.
2. "Teaching to the middle of the class is wrong." The teachers' response is that the teacher should teach to the middle of the group while at the same time providing for extra help for the slower students and extra credit work for the faster students. They say that most of the students can follow a middle-of-the-road pace. Provision should be made for those students who cannot.
3. "The total stress in the classroom should be placed upon the individual." The teachers' reaction is that both the individual and the social aspects of second-language learning should be emphasized in the classroom. In other words, although the individual should not be ignored, neither should the social interaction among and between students and students and teachers.
4. "Mediocrity and failure should be eliminated from the classroom." The teachers' position is that failure is a part of life and should be recognized as such. Too, they point out that failure can have beneficial effects upon the individual.

Proponents of individualized instruction were unrealistic in making the following proposals:

1. "Teachers should prepare behavioral objectives for every learning activity in the classroom." The teachers' reaction was that the implementation of such a requirement would take too long to be practical.

2. "Teachers should prepare individual learning programs corresponding to the interests and goals of each student." The teachers said that attempting to implement this goal would involve an enormous amount of repetitive effort on the part of the teacher. Implementing individual learning programs that foster learning in isolation would also seriously impair the needed communicative exchanges in the second-language classroom.
3. "Learning should be student-centered, permitting the students to decide upon their own goals and learning procedures as well as to evaluate their own progress and achievement." As highly desirable as such a situation might be, the teachers described the students in their own schools as lacking "the maturity, ambition, and willpower to embark on such a self-propelled project."
4. "Anyone can individualize." The teachers replied that new programs require (a) appropriate physical facilities, (b) flexible scheduling, (c) additional personnel, and (d) extra funds. All or some of these may be unavailable to the teacher.
5. "The teacher's role is to act as a 'resource person' or a 'learning facilitator.'" The teachers replied that all the outstanding teachers in their own backgrounds had been warm, humane individuals as well as superb organizers of classroom activities. They felt that teachers should be able both to relate to individuals and to manage group situations.

Overall, these teachers considered that individualized instruction was inappropriate for the average teacher in the average school district. They were also afraid that such a do-it-yourself climate might lead to a state of confusion, disorganization, and later to discipline problems. On the other hand, the teachers agreed that it was a good idea to provide for individual differences among students.

Following are additional criticisms of individualized instruction not mentioned in Griffin's summary. (It must be recognized that many of these criticisms are refuted by proponents of individualized instruction.)

1. LAPs are satisfactory for drill and reinforcement, but not for the presentation of concepts. It should be recognized that LAPs do not constitute a total program of instruction, although they have been used in this manner. Too, the preparation of a LAP for every topic is impossible (Krulik, 1974).
2. Serving as a "resource person" may not be acceptable to a "center stage" teacher (Miller & Gonyar, 1974).[1]
3. Using LAPs as a means of instituting an accountability program may cause concern among teachers (Miller & Gonyar, 1974).[2]
4. Grading and the granting of credit present new and difficult problems to

[1]A "center stage" teacher is one who insists upon being the center of all classroom activity.
[2]Accountability means that the teacher is held responsible for student achievement of objectives stated at the beginning of instruction.

solve for teachers, students, parents, and schools long accustomed to the traditional procedures (Miller & Gonyar, 1974).

5. Individualized instruction is almost impossible to implement without a resource center (Miller & Gonyar, 1974).

6. Individualized instruction supposes that the students have the ability to make wise decisions. There is some evidence to indicate that students choose grading systems rather than learning processes (Baker, Bakshis, & Tolone, 1974).

7. If, as the proponents suggest, the students choose their own goals and activities, their choices may merely correspond to present strengths and continue to overlook weaknesses. (Baker, Bakshis, & Tolone, 1974).

8. In individualized programs many students do not become a part of the learning process just as many do not in a traditional class. These uninspired students need more help and more direction. Giving them the responsibility for structuring what they are to do makes them uncomfortable (Walters & Sieben, 1974).

9. Teachers do not have the time to prepare the LAPs. Too, the preparation of good LAPs is no easy task even if the teacher has the necessary time (Groff, 1975).

10. Although individualized instruction has been characterized by a preponderance of A's and B's, there has also been an increase in the number of withdrawals, an increase in the tendency toward procrastination, and a trend toward low scores on comprehensive examinations (Newman et al., 1974).

11. Much of the organization of programmed materials and individualized programs implies that second-language learning is a linear process. This assumption may not necessarily be a valid one.

AN EXAMINATION OF THE BASIC ASSUMPTIONS OF INDIVIDUALIZED INSTRUCTION

The criticisms presented in the preceding section of this chapter stem from reactions to individualized instruction. What do theorists have to say about the basic tenets of this widely discussed and implemented movement in education? Reviewing the data that has been collected regarding individualized instruction, Travers (1975, p. 3) sums up his general conclusions saying, "The results are disappointing, perhaps because the whole problem of individualizing instruction is much more complicated than naive enthusiasts believe it to be."

This comment leads to the first weakness of the movement as a whole—

the insufficient information available to educators regarding the immense complexity of individuality. In what specific ways are individuals different from each other? Once this problem has been sufficiently explored and empirical answers found, the question of how best to gear instruction specifically to these differences still remains. Neither question can be answered satisfactorily at the present time. Recent studies have made great strides in delineating various ways in which students are unique, and the ongoing research on aptitude-treatment interactions is beginning to uncover preliminary information as to the types of learning situations that seem most propitious for the vast number of individual differences in the cognitive and affective-social domains. (See chapter 4, "Research," page 91.) However, until that time when research is able to specify a more complete and total description of how learners are different and how best to handle these differences, efforts to deal with individualization of instruction can only be viewed as initial steps in the direction of a totally individualized program. On the other hand, the concept of individualization may be a self-destructing one as far as education is concerned. Suppose the investigations lead to the conclusion that each student is indeed completely different and must be given a unique, specially prepared teaching-learning program. Just how far are educators prepared to go with this process? Might the profession not reach the conclusion that the classroom can accommodate only a limited number of different types of learners and set a reasonable and workable limit on that number? At any rate, the knowledge available to education at the moment falls far short of either alternative.

The point being made here is that some educators have attempted to individualize in the absence of a sufficient body of data to delineate adequately the total range, breadth, and depth of individuality. The leaders in the movement did recognize that individualization involved at least three aspects of the learning process: (1) self-pacing, (2) mode of learning, and (3) goals (Altman, 1971). However, for the most part, self-pacing is the one component that has received attention as individualized programs have been implemented in the classrooms.

Prior to proceeding to an examination of the basic assumptions of individualized instruction, it should be made clear that as presently constituted individualized programs based primarily on behavioral objectives and mastery learning are external and mechanistic in nature. The objectives are prepared by the teacher, and the learner is to acquire the behaviors the teacher specifies. The teacher, via the LAP, outlines the objectives and attempts to shape selected student behaviors. Only in the area of the speed with which they complete the work do the students have any say in the learning process. Speed is the only aspect that is student-centered, or internal. The other components are external. Traditional, self-contained classrooms with a humane, considerate, sympathetic teacher may be just as student-centered, and perhaps more so, if the teacher in an individualized program becomes so busy with the program that he has no time to devote to the students. The terms *humanization* and *student-centered* are not synonymous with *individualized instruction*. The description of Travers (1975, pp. 6–7) falls far short of being either humanistic or student-centered:

> Much of it [individualized instruction] represents a drab mechanization of learning. Although the term may conjure up an image of one teacher interacting with one student, the more realistic image is that of one student interacting with one worksheet, his own, in the absence of the teacher. Although individualization of instruction has the potential for enhancing education, if enough money is available to provide an individualized teacher-pupil relationship, economic realities typically reduce individualized instruction to the worst form of mechanized routine.

The next important consideration underlying current practice in individualized instruction after that of external theories of learning is based on a behavioral, external view of aptitude. In his article, "A Model for School Learning," Carroll (1963) proposed a new working definition of *aptitude.* Prior to Carroll's revelation, *aptitude* had been defined as the student's facility or capacity for learning in any given area. Instead of stressing the amount of material learned, Carroll emphasized that aptitude is the "amount of time" required by the learner to attain mastery in a given learning situation. The underlying theory behind this definition is that learning is not based on internal processes and capabilities, but on the selection of behaviors, activities, and proper reinforcement of student response. That is, external factors are the crucial variable in learning, not the learner himself. The implication is that almost anyone can learn anything *if* he is given the time to do so. (Carroll does state that there may be some students who never learn the material.) The potential of such a proposal opens up the possibility of tremendous change in the instructional process. The first immediate classroom implication is that given the validity of this tenet most students can earn an A in any course. The obvious implication for curricular organization is that enough time be allowed for *each* individual to learn the material. This definition of *aptitude* has become the basic building block for individualized instruction as it is commonly implemented at present in the school situation.

The remainder of this discussion of the basic assumptions of individualized instruction will be devoted to an examination of Carroll's definition of *aptitude,* the component parts of LAPs, and the manner in which LAPs are used in the classroom. In order to permit the individual student to spend as much time as necessary to learn the material, most individualized programs utilize some form of LAPs. A LAP may be more or less elaborate, but the essential elements are (1) a listing of behavioral objectives, (2) specified activities for the student to follow in order to attain the listed objectives, and (3) posttests to evaluate the student's success in achieving the objectives (Krulik, 1974).

Aptitude

Normally, the LAP contains a list of activities. Although there is some selection, the choice involves mostly the amount of material and/or supplementary material. The implication of this practice is that the only characteristic of aptitude is the time factor as postulated by Carroll. However, previously cited references to the difference in cognitive style and the affective-social domain indicate that such an assumption is not justified on the basis of available evidence. (See chapter 4, "Research," pages 68–77.) In fact, as early as 1957, Cronbach, in his American Psychological Association (APA) presidential address, urged educational researchers to "design treatments not to fit the average person, but to fit groups of students with particular aptitude patterns" and to "seek out aptitudes that correspond to modifiable aspects of the treatment." He believed that "treatments should be differentiated in such a way as to maximize their interaction with aptitude variables" (Boutwell & Barton, 1974, p. 13). Research goals have shifted from the illusive dream of the one best method to the best method for the particular student. Much recent research has dealt with aptitude-treatment interactions in an attempt to ascertain which students learn best by which methods. (See chapter 4, "Research," pages 91–92.)

Another aspect of Carroll's postulate is that given enough time most learners can learn most material. Carroll assumes that the learner either has (or will be given) the necessary prerequisite skills to complete the given learning task. Currently, most neobehaviorists and cognitive psychologists support a hierarchical model of learning. Gagné's (1965) model contains eight types of learning, each more complex than the preceding and each depending upon the preceding. Piaget conceives of the development of cognitive skills as occurring in five stages, each growing out of and being at a higher level of complexity and abstraction than the previous (Gorman, 1972). If hierarchical models are appropriate, the assumption must be made that in order to learn anything the learner must know, or be taught, all the necessary prerequisite knowledge and skills in order to complete the designated learning task itself. In some cases this necessity would lead to a point of diminishing returns, although the accomplishment of such a procedure is theoretically possible. Even this theoretical possibility is rather slight in some contexts since one can easily postulate that the individuals' inherent intellectual capacities place some limit upon the heights of abstraction, conceptual thought, and symbolic processes to which they can attain.

Behavioral Objectives

In spite of the popularity of behavioral objectives and in spite of the insistence with which many educators urge teachers to use them, opinion is by no means unified as to the desirability of their use. In fact, behavioral objectives are the center of a growing storm of controversy. Those who favor external control of the learning process are wholeheartedly in support of the use of behavioral objectives. They view their use as a means of lifting education to the level of a scientific, quantifiable approach to learning. In addition, they see behavioral objectives as the principal cog in the application of the technological efficiency of the industrial system to education. Only by the delineation of discrete behaviors can the educational process be quantified and made accountable. Since learning is a change in behavior, both the behavior and the means for conditioning the change must be specified.

Henson (1974) lists the following advantages of a learning program based on accountability and performance-based objectives:

1. Behavioral objectives, or performance objectives if the reader prefers, clarify the teaching goals, thus assuring a purposeful teaching process directed toward specific goals.
2. Stating the behavioral objectives for the students enables them to work toward predetermined goals. They know exactly what they are to do at the end of the learning sequence, thus making their learning more meaningful and more enjoyable.
3. By basing their organization of the course on behavioral objectives, the teachers are better organized and more efficient. As a result, they have more time to spend with the students.
4. When the behavioral objectives are prepared commercially by experts, the content of the course is not subject to the variability of teacher competency. The quality of the course can be maintained in spite of the teacher's inadequacy. Thus, learning can be made not only external to the student, but also external to the teacher and the local school situation. In this fashion it would be possible to eliminate the extremes that currently exist in the quality of education offered in different schools and in different areas.
5. Performance-based teaching, i.e., teaching based on behavioral objectives, is the only way to identify and to reward excellence in teaching. Using behavioral objectives provides a quantifiable basis for specifying what the teacher should be doing and comparing that model with what he is doing.
6. Gearing learning to behavioral objectives makes the students more active participants in their own learning and provides more motivation than a teacher-centered class.

7. The use of behavioral objectives is a concrete means of exposing incompetent teachers and motivating them to improve.
8. The practice of including behavioral objectives enables all faculty members as a group to meet, to discuss, and to make joint decisions concerning the curriculum.
9. The use of behavioral objectives frees the teacher for more time to plan for more creative student activities.
10. Behavioral objectives have so great a potential that they will significantly improve education.

As valid as these arguments for the use of behavioral objectives may seem to some, they are strongly rejected by others. For the most part, those who oppose the use of behavioral objectives hold in some way to an internal focus as the central concept to be maintained in the learning process. Cognitive psychologists stress internal mental processes at a highly complex and abstract level of operation. Many of these mental processes cannot be specified in behavioral terms. Humanists stress the individual's internal psychological states, i.e., feelings and emotions, rather than the acquisition of either behaviors or knowledge as such.

The chief criticisms of behavioral objectives include the following:

1. Behavioral objectives deal primarily with behaviors and do not take the entire emotional and social growth of the student into consideration.
2. Basing the learning of all students on the same stated behavioral objectives makes the task quite difficult for some learners but especially easy for others.
3. If the teachers in a system of accountability become concerned primarily with how they appear in the eyes of the administration, this vested interest may lead to a dehumanization of the classroom and of the learning process.
4. The selection of behavioral objectives and activities outside the classroom, even if done by experts, may be unrelated and meaningless in the local situation.
5. It is possible that the stress on efficiency may result in stressing time factors to the detriment of learning.
6. Basing all learning on stated behavioral objectives may lead to an overemphasis on facts, rote memorization, and superficial teaching and learning.
7. It might be possible for the administration to use behavioral objectives as a means of penalizing or dismissing teachers if their students are not accomplishing the stated behaviors.
8. The use of behavioral objectives makes it possible for materials developers to specify exact behaviors without input from the local teachers and administration.
9. Stated behavioral objectives at the beginning of a learning sequence may actually inhibit learning in the sense that desired gains are limited to

teacher-selected objectives. There is no room provided for student imagination and creativity.

10. The use of behavioral objectives is a fad that will be overused and misused to the harm of the educational system (Henson, 1974).
11. Teachers can rarely state their goals in terms of precise behaviors.
12. Stating objectives in specific behavioral terms is more difficult and time consuming than stating general course objectives.
13. Planning in advance specifically how the learner is to behave after learning is undemocratic and manipulative.
14. Those objectives easiest to state in behavioral terms are usually trivial, low-level goals.
15. In certain subject matter areas, such as fine arts and humanities, the goals are difficult to specify in behavioral terms.
16. Predetermination of goals and activities may deter spontaneous interchanges between teacher and students in class (Waks, 1973).

In a paper related specifically to second-language instruction, Valdman (1975) questions the validity of using behavioral objectives as a basic device in the development of communicative competence, or as he terms it, "communicative performance." First, he states that "competence" cannot be acquired solely by acquiring specific linguistic elements. Nor can the acquisition of a certain number of discrete linguistic behaviors guarantee the ability to function in a communicative situation. In short, there seems to be no meaningful relationship between behavioral objectives specifying linguistic behaviors and the linguistic concepts of "competence" and "performance." Behavioral objectives and classroom drills based on these objectives deal with the manipulation of linguistic elements, not communication. He later adds that the specification and control of linguistic behaviors may in fact keep the learner from formulating hypotheses about the language system and discovering important regularities and irregularities in the language, both of which are basic components of internal theories of first- and second-language learning. The author also maintains that the conception of language learning as an internal process, actively participated in by the learner, in effect relegates behavioral objectives and their associated drills to a secondary role. He concludes that behavioral objectives have contributed little to the improvement of second-language instruction.

The National Council of Teachers of English has passed a resolution urging restraint in the use of behavioral objectives. In 1972 the American Historical Association was opposed to behavioral objectives. The Texas chapter of the AAUP has expressed concern over their use in the competency-based program in Texas. The board of directors of the NEA "recently resolved to fight simplistic approaches to accountability in our schools" (Day, 1974, pp. 305–6).

Some studies to determine the effectiveness of the use of behavioral objectives have been conducted. Levine (1972) found that knowledge of "criterion-referenced instruction" did not produce significant differences in achievement. Effective practice was the significant variable. Stedman (1972) concluded that objectives had no significant effect on posttest performance. After examining the influence of objectives on the acquisition of complex cognitive learning, Yelon and Schmidt (1973) stated that giving objectives to the student had no positive effect on learning, and, in fact, that there was an apparent negative effect on both achievement and attitude. The results of a study by Webb and Cormier (1972, p. 95) indicated that objectives, criterion evaluation, and remediation produced positive results in the case of "disruptive adolescents." Duchastel and Merrill's (1973) review revealed five comparative studies which indicated that students achieved more with behavioral objectives and five with no significant difference on immediate retention. On long-term retention two studies favored giving the students behavioral objectives with one showing no significant difference.

Interests

If the activities outlined in the LAP are to be maximally effective, attempts must be made to accommodate the variability of student interests. The implication here is that the content of the materials should be relatable to the student's life. Thus, not only will different students in the same class be more interested in and stimulated by certain content than by other types of material, but students in different schools and different areas of the country will have different backgrounds which will necessitate the selection of content dealing with vocabulary and situations with which they are familiar.

Goals

To a great extent, the content of the classroom activities and the materials selected will depend upon the student's objective in studying a second language. If he is primarily a reader who wants to enjoy the literature of a foreign country, he will desire a course emphasizing literature. If she is a young soprano hopeful of a career in singing, she will be most interested in perfecting her pronunciation and enunciation. These goals and many more place an obligation upon teachers to search for a variety of course content in an attempt to reach all interests. If they have the energy and facilities, teachers may want to establish a variety of courses or mini-courses to attempt to reach all these individuals.

Taxonomy

Not only is there a hierarchy of cognitive development, there is also a hierarchy of content and skill development in second-language learning. If the teachers prepare their own LAPs, they must be extremely careful to incorporate provisions for all the various steps in the language acquisition sequence. Chastain (1971) has outlined a model of language acquisition in which the student must proceed through three steps: (1) understanding, (2) manipulation and production, and (3) communication. Another variation is the taxonomy of subject-matter goals presented by Valette and Disick (1972). The five-stage model consists of (1) mechanical skills, (2) knowledge, (3) transfer, (4) communication, and (5) criticism. Whatever model is chosen, the activities in the LAP should be so arranged as to require the student to proceed through all the steps necessary to reach the skill level of language usage. Practice at the skill level in listening comprehension and speaking requires interaction in the class. In order to provide learning at all levels of the taxonomy student activity must include more than isolated study with a LAP.

Social Interaction

One of the perplexing problems in individualized instruction has been how to incorporate class and small-group activities into a system based on the use of LAPs. Directly or indirectly, language involves social interaction through linguistic exchange. The socialization of the individual is a learning process, and learning includes many social components. Social interaction seems to be an indispensable component of the learning situation, especially in language learning. At the communication level the students must interact with each other.

James (1974, p. 54) sees a classroom in which students are "set apart from each other to work on carefully systematized assignments" as a "stagnant form of education—a bore." Duane (1974) maintains that LAPs are not a total instructional system and that the teacher must be cognizant of the need to maximize the amount of human interaction in the classroom. Johnson and Johnson (1974) believe that this curricular organization is appropriate for cognitive materials and skills, but the approach may produce feelings of loneliness and isolation and fail to develop interpersonal and group skills.

Self-Pacing

The most widely recognized and implemented tenet of the typical individualized program is self-pacing. This procedure allows students to learn when they are ready to learn and to assume responsibility for their own learning. For some students, self-pacing permits a certain degree of autonomy, which appeals to their sense of independence. However, the research on personality types and large-group and small-group instruction implies that not all students respond favorably. In a research project concerning pacing in programmed materials there was no significant difference between group instruction and self-paced instruction (Schramm, 1964). Although the attention of the investigation was focused on a slightly different approach, results of another study found that students in a teacher-structured class progressed through the material faster and had significantly higher achievement scores than those in a student-structured class (Humphreys, 1974). Describing the reaction of his college-level students to individualized instruction, Aschermann (1974, p. 241) laments that his "original enthusiasm has almost been washed away by the tide of his students' tears." The fault was due to the inability or unwillingness of the students to assume the responsibility for directing their own learning. The teacher's role in a self-paced class is to monitor student progress and to determine that each student is progressing at an optimum rate. Nor is the association between rate and degree of learning as simple as it may at first seem. Altman and Politzer (1971, p. 162) state, "Simply allocating more time is a highly inefficient way of increasing the rate and degree of learning. More essential is what the learner is doing in whatever time is available."

Noblitt (1975) examines the concept of self-pacing and systematization as they are interrelated in the learning process. The assumption is made that learning requires the organization and systematization of information being learned. The author outlines two problems associated with self-pacing. Both are related to those students who fail to maintain an adequate pace through the materials. If the learner proceeds too slowly, progress may be hindered by an inability to relate discrete linguistic elements, separated as they may be by rather lengthy periods of time, into a meaningful interrelationship necessary for systematization. Another problem which may accompany a slow pace is related to the model of language learning as being characterized by a series of interim grammars, which learners update periodically as they move toward the native language system in the second language. There is a tendency for this interim grammar to crystallize if movement through the materials becomes too sluggish. Thus, a certain speed seems to be necessary in order to remember the material, to relate it to other structures being learned, and to avoid a tendency toward crystallization of incomplete linguistic knowledge. Noblitt concludes that self-pacing cannot be the sole determinant of progress through the course materials. The teacher also bears a responsibility for helping the student maintain a satisfactory pace.

Mastery Learning

Before proceeding to new material, the student is to score 80–85 percent or above on a criterion-referenced test over the material covered in the LAP. The assumption underlying this requirement is that subject matter is hierarchical and that the material at each level must be mastered before undertaking subsequent course content. Such an assumption is certainly logical, and one would expect research to substantiate mastery learning. Bloom (1968) gives no comparative statistics, but he does state that under the guidance of mastery learning procedures 20–80 percent of the students receive an A. In addition, he maintains that the students have more confidence in their ability to learn the material, they like the subject better, and they have a more positive self-concept. The percentage of A's given in a course is not synonymous with academic achievement, but the positive outcomes in the affective domain are desirable pluses to any approach.

The concept of mastery learning is an outgrowth of behavioral objectives and Carroll's definition of aptitude. The goal is to insist that each student achieve mastery of a small segment of material before moving on to a more complex level of work. On the surface, the concept of mastery learning appears to be the solution to all those difficulties encountered by students who get farther and farther behind because they are pushed into grappling with new concepts and new material before having mastered prerequisite information. Yet, mastery learning is subject to the same criticism as that directed at behavioral objectives and Carroll's definition of aptitude. Groff (1975) affirms that mastery learning underestimates the enormous complexities of the learning process. Too, he insists that forcing students to attempt to reach a level of mastery while studying materials beyond their capabilities may be dangerous to their mental health. Noblitt (1975) points out that if the time needed to attain mastery involves a period of time sufficiently lengthy to hinder the students' likelihood of being able to systematize their knowledge, then in actuality the language system is not being acquired.

Valdman (1975) views behavioral objectives, mastery learning, and the "obsession with error-free performance" which characterized programmed instruction and audio-lingual teaching as being interrelated. If the learner is viewed as a passive agent in which linguistic responses are to be conditioned, errors can be eliminated by careful selection of stimulus and response. However, the view of the learner as an active agent in learning postulates a model in which the errors made by the second-language learner are important, productive, and beneficial components of language learning.

Continuous Progress

With individualized instruction the students are to progress steadily through the course content. There are to be no delays caused by waiting for other students to catch up. Nor will they be forced to take bewildered leaps over needed, basic material, frantically trying to keep up with the other students in the class. In any instructional sequence, however, review must be incorporated into the materials. Too, spaced practice is an important variable in increasing retention. As the teacher prepares the instructional sequence, he should keep these two factors in mind while arranging content and practice in such a way as to enhance both short-term and long-term retention.

Criterion-Referenced Examinations

The final component of a LAP is an evaluation based on the behavioral objectives given to the students at the beginning of the LAP. Of course, criterion-referenced examinations are subject to the same criticisms as those directed toward behavioral objectives in general. The major difficulty in implementing this type of examination is that most teachers are more familiar with norm-referenced examinations,[3] and they may have problems switching to the new type. The teacher should keep in mind that the purpose of the test is to determine to what extent the students have mastered the material, not to rank them in comparison with their classmates.

Criterion-referenced examinations do have certain disadvantages. They return results that are meaningful only when examined in relation to the behavioral objectives prepared for the material to be learned. They are difficult for the teacher to change. They increase problems of storage and handling. They may create a situation in which instruction is based on the tests rather than vice versa. They may not be appropriate for learning tasks that cannot be broken into small, discrete units. And they are not geared for testing goals other than those encompassed in behavioral objectives (Esler & Dziuban, 1974).

Criterion-referenced tests also have certain advantages. The results give direct information as to which behavioral objectives have been attained and which have not. They give a score indicating amount of learning acquired. They permit the teacher to make a profile of the objectives attained by each student. They can be taken by the students when they are ready. And they have a more direct relationship to the classroom itself, when prepared by the teacher, than do standardized, norm-referenced examinations (Esler & Dziuban, 1974).

WAYS AND MEANS OF DIVERSIFYING INSTRUCTION

Contemporary teachers face a dilemma. On the one hand they are expected to respond to individual differences; on the other hand, not enough is known about individuality and ways and means of providing individualized instruction. Individualized instruction is widely supported in the literature and education meetings. However, a close examination of teacher reaction and of

---

[3]The purpose of norm-referenced examinations is to rank students, i.e., to place them in some relationship to other students.

the basic theoretical assumptions causes second thoughts as to the general acceptability of this approach—both from a practical teacher perspective and from a theoretical point of view. Teachers must seek ways and means of diversifying instruction, ways and means that are acceptable both to them and to the students. Today's students are looking for diversification and alternatives to traditional classroom learning procedures.

In Traditional Classes

Many aspects of responding to individual differences have always been part of the traditional class structure. Students should be treated as individuals in the quantity of work expected and in the quality. Research indicates that some students learn better by cognitive procedures while others learn better by conditioning drills. Some students may prefer oral work while others prefer written or visual materials. Some students may prefer to respond a great deal in class while others, who are learning equally well, are quieter. Some students prefer to participate in social exchanges while others prefer to study alone. Some students may well be expected to complete more work or longer assignments than others. Some students may well be put on their own while others should be given extra help.[4] Some students may demand more attention from the teacher than others. Some students need individual help while others manage very well in the group-conducted class. In homework assignments (which have always been self-paced) and on tests, the teacher should be conscious of including some work at a level appropriate for those students who need stimulation and challenge.

Two Types of Courses

If the teacher does decide to individualize, provisions should be made to offer both traditional and individualized classes. In other words, students should not be placed arbitrarily in an individualized class, and if at all possible, teachers should be allowed to teach the type of class that is most in keeping with their philosophy and capabilities. As old-fashioned as it may sound, research indicates that the most appropriate type of classroom structure for some individuals is a traditional, teacher-centered class. Individualized instruction is no more suitable to all teachers and to all students than is any other approach.

Based on research evidence, another distinction in approach to learning is

---

[4]For example, when this author was teaching in high school, the brighter, more self-reliant, and more highly motivated students were always allowed to participate in the class discussion or to study material that they felt would be more interesting and helpful to them. If at any time they wanted to participate in the class, they were free to do so. The only stipulation was that they were expected to take the tests with the rest of the class. Frankly, there was not enough time to prepare special examinations for these students. The purpose of this setup was to refrain from holding back any students who had the ability and the inclination to go ahead on their own.

also possible. Several studies, both in second-language learning and in other areas, have obtained results supporting the existence of at least two types of learners. One type learns more using a cognitive approach, while the other learns better using a behavioral approach. In general, researchers have found that higher aptitude students do better using a cognitive approach, while lower aptitude students do better in the stimulus-response, drill type of learning situation. To some extent these differences can be taken into consideration in the regular classroom situation by varying assignments and by providing a variety of activities for all students. In schools with sufficient enrollment, both types of approaches might well be offered, if the department members and the administration are amenable. The success of such a division would depend largely on having a knowledgeable and enthusiastic teacher for each type of course. Students, parents, and administrators would also need to be made aware of the reasons for such a division.

Deciding to Offer an Individualized Approach

Before deciding to prepare an individualized course, teachers should pause to take inventory. First, they should consider the amount of time, energy, and expertise needed to carry out the project once it is begun. They should ask themselves if they would like to use this approach. Are they willing to initiate a long-term project that will require a continuing commitment to change and revision over a period of years? Do the students need and want such a course? Will there be support from the administration, the parents, and the students? Are the needed funds and facilities available? Some resource persons should be available for consultation prior to beginning the project and often thereafter. Before making the final plunge, they should visit a teacher who has an *ongoing* individualized program to see for themselves how it functions, to discuss the program's good and bad points with the instructor, and to gain insights into pitfalls to be anticipated and avoided.

As soon as the teacher has made the decision to individualize, he needs to occupy himself with procedures for implementing this decision. Just how does one individualize a class? He may be thoroughly familiar with the reasons for and convinced of the desirability of individualized instruction, but how to do it is another question. For the reader who needs assistance in planning step-by-step procedures for preparing an individualized program, the best descriptions of the "nuts and bolts" of putting an individualized program together are *Individualized Foreign Language Instruction* by Grittner and La Leike (Skokie, Ill: National Textbook) and *Individualized Foreign Language Learning: An Organic Process* by Logan (Rowley, Mass.: Newbury House). If at all possible, the teacher should have some lead time to prepare as large a percentage of the needed paper work as possible. Putting himself in a situation in which he must teach as well as prepare materials is less than desirable for various obvious reasons which need not be listed here.

Even after reaching a decision and fortifying the likelihood of success with reading, consultation, and visitation, the advice of most teachers with experience is to begin slowly and in a reasonable fashion. At first, for any given class a segment of the text or a selected number of class periods can be individualized. If the initial reactions to individualized instruction are favorable and the results seem to justify an expansion of initial efforts, the teacher can make plans to expand the number of individualized segments. One possibility, especially since students seem to like variety, is to reserve part of each week for individualized activities. For example, part of each class period might be set aside for this type of activity, although a longer period of time would normally seem to be called for. Another variation is to have regular class meetings for the major part of the week, but to let the students work on individualized materials for one day, or two days, if they prefer. The number of days might eventually be expanded if the results warrant increased use of individualized materials.

The next step is to individualize an entire class. Two possibilities exist at this point. The teacher may either individualize the lowest level course or the highest. If she decides on the lowest, she has the obligation to take the students through the other levels following the same procedures (given a reasonable amount of success with the program). Beginning at the beginning commits the teacher to a great deal of work over a period of years. The advantage of starting with beginners is that they are accustomed from the start to working with individualized materials. On the other hand, many experienced teachers recommend beginning with the highest level. Individualized instruction at the lower levels can be implemented in subsequent years. The latter approach would not involve as strong a commitment as the former.

Establishing an individualized program of study for certain groups of students within a class is also a possibility. The teacher may want to identify groups of students with certain abilities or interests for which special materials can be individualized. For example, those students with a special interest in conversation and travel might be offered materials covering these two interests.

Another obvious possibility is to individualize parts of the course. With a text like *Spanish for Communication* (Boston: Houghton Mifflin, 1972), the grammar might well be treated through an individualized approach. *Sounds of French* (Chicago: Rand McNally, 1974) is a self-instructional program that gives the students the responsibility for learning on their own. Readings have long been assigned as independent study projects. With a little extra preplanning, readings can be individualized by giving students the choice of what to read and at what pace. With time and ingenuity, LAPs focusing on culture can be prepared for the students to do when convenient to the class schedule. In addition to reading and culture, individualized LAPs can be prepared in each of the other language skills. Tapes and/or records can be the basis of listening comprehension projects. Students can be asked to prepare oral reports, to discuss some topic with selected classmates, and to give an oral report on the conclusions reached, etc. LAPs can be prepared in which the final product is a composition or a dialog written by the student. Obviously, various combinations of the language skills can be included in any given LAP. For example, students can listen to a dialog on a tape and then give a written or oral summary of the contents, or they can react orally or in writing to the content of the tape.

The purpose of the preceding discussion is not to convey the impression that an individualized program must be established piecemeal. The concern is that the teachers experiment with this curricular approach to ascertain how it works for them and for their students. They should determine how much time and energy the preparation of LAPs will take; gain experience and expertise in the writing of LAPs and in administering the program in the classroom; and have some free time for themselves and for their family and friends. No innovation should require more of teachers than they have the time, the energy, and the knowledge to accomplish.

Alternatives to Individualized Instruction

The preceding discussion presumes that the teachers either have decided to individualize, that they would like to experiment with certain aspects of a typical individualized course structure, or that they would like to respond to individual differences in the classroom. However, the individualized instruction commonly outlined in the literature dealing with second-language teaching is not the only approach to individualizing instruction. The following descriptions are of two alternative models developed in other fields. Both of these models include group instruction as well as individual study, thus incorporating social interaction and components normally associated with a more traditional class.

The three-stage model of instruction   Feldhusen et al. (1974) designed a three-stage model of instruction for use in their classes. This model grew out of their goals for the course, the recent trend toward individualization of instruction, the present interest in simulation and gaming, the need to teach higher cognitive abilities, and the calls for relevance.

The objectives of Stage I are for the students to learn the basic facts and concepts being presented and to become self-directed learners. To help the students accomplish these goals the instructor may suggest the use of texts, programmed materials, taped lectures or lessons, audio-tutorial units, or drills.[5] The students study the materials on their own, preferably materials they

_____
[5]*Audio-tutorial units*, originated at Purdue University by Professor Postlethwait, are self-teaching materials containing taped explanations.

can take home rather than having them in a resource center or in a laboratory. The instructor's role is to (1) select material to be used, (2) help develop new materials, (3) write self-instructional guides for the students, and (4) work with other instructors in developing the content and structure of the course. The basic content of the materials is tested at the mastery level in "multiple guess" tests. The purpose of this stage is to insist that the students learn the basic information of the unit before going on to higher level tasks.

The purpose of Stage II is to develop higher cognitive abilities. During the instructional process the instructor works with small groups of students asking them to analyze, reorganize, consolidate, and integrate the material previously learned. By means of questions and comments the instructor encourages the students to recall the facts and to consider this knowledge as it relates to current problems in education. The instructor's task is to anticipate the meaningful applications of the learned material and to assist in drawing discussions of these relationships out of the students. Evaluation at this stage is informally based on student participation in the small groups.

At Stage III students are expected to apply the knowledge acquired during Stage I and the cognitive abilities gained during Stage II to a practical problem. There are two major types of activities employed: small-group and independent projects. Group work takes place in or out of class under the guidance of the instructor. The group selects a problem and attempts a solution based on their learning in the unit. The independent project is a follow-up to the group work. During this project individuals follow the same general approach of the group, but are allowed to select an angle or a topic of special interest to them. Evaluation is based on the quality of the group and individual projects.

The principles involved in the preceding model, which applies to an educational psychology class, can be derived for use in second-language classes. In a second-language class, Stage I would involve the presentation and mastery of sounds, vocabulary, and structure. Stage II would be devoted to the application of the material learned to test comprehension and to practice the manipulation of forms, either in the language laboratory or in the classroom. During Stage III, the teacher and the students would concentrate on the use of the learned material to express themselves in each of the four language skills, both in groups and individually.

Group-based individualized instruction   Based on Carroll's definition of aptitude, his model of school learning, and the concept of mastery learning, Bloom has developed a group-based approach to individualized instruction. (See the article by Bloom [1968] and the description by Block [1973] listed in the Selected References section of this chapter.) Bloom offers an alternative to the typical individualized course usually described in second-language learning literature.

In the normative class grading system based on the bell-shaped curve, students in a class in which all receive the same instruction receive a normal distribution of grades. However, Bloom maintains that if students in a normally distributed class are given differential instruction so that the time allowed and the quality of the instruction vary according to student needs, up to 95 percent of the students can be expected to reach a level of mastery in the class (mastery being defined as scoring about 80–85 percent on the summative examination). In other words, students receiving uniform instruction who make C's, D's, and F's are provided compensatory materials and activities to help attain mastery.

The basic components of Bloom's model are as follows:

1. The teacher makes the assumption that all students can learn to a level of mastery and that he can teach them to learn to this level. In his introduction to the class at the beginning of the course he makes those assumptions clear to the class and tells them that they will be given all the help they need to learn to a level of mastery and to receive either an A or a B in the course.

2. Grades are based on the students' performance and achievement rather than their rank in class.

3. The teacher selects the course objectives and makes them known to the students.

4. In choosing the objectives, the teacher also establishes the expected level of achievement.

5. The teacher makes plans for evaluating the students' success in acquiring the stated objectives.

6. The next step is to compare the students' achievement with the mastery level. Mastery is normally defined as receiving an equivalent to an A or a B on the teacher's traditional tests. A lower grade indicates nonmastery of the material and means that additional compensatory work is in order.

7. In preparation for teaching the material in the course, the teacher divides the material into units of approximately two weeks.

8. Given the material to be covered in the two-week units, the teacher can plan to use the tests he already has or to prepare new tests over the content of these units. These tests are termed *formative* tests or *diagnostic-progress* tests. These tests are given at the end of each unit as the class progresses through the material. The purpose of the tests is to determine which students have reached a level of mastery and which have not. No grade is assigned on the basis of these test scores. However, those students scoring below 80–85 percent must do additional work to bring their knowledge up to the mastery level.

9. In order to accommodate those students who have not achieved mastery, the teacher develops *unit feedback/correction procedures* to help them reach a mastery level over the content of the unit. These procedures consist of alternative instructional materials and activities based on the

content of the formative tests. At this point, instruction is provided to meet the needs of each student who did not achieve mastery. Since group-based instruction did not accomplish the goal, the students now work with peer and cross-age (advanced-student) tutoring, small-group study sessions, alternative textbooks, programmed instructional materials, academic games and puzzles, and selected "affective" educational exercises. The goal is to present the material in different sensory modes and in different forms and to get the students to interact in different ways with the instructional materials.

10. The final component is the preparation of summative examinations. These tests are given periodically to evaluate achievement, and grades are assigned to the student scores. Those scoring at the mastery level receive an A or a B.

Bloom does not discuss what happens to those students who achieve mastery on the formative test. In this author's opinion, these students have a terrific opportunity at this point to have some variety and a little fun while they take advantage of this pause in the linear continuity of the course to pursue supplementary enrichment activities in breadth. These broadening activities might include additional reading, preparation of visuals or bulletin board displays, creative writing, conversation, skits, a language newspaper, projects, etc. What is important is that they are given the opportunity to continue learning and to do something they are interested in and that they enjoy.

Although the obtained results are tentative, Bloom and his followers report more positive learning outcomes from the group-based, individualized approach to instruction than in traditional classrooms. First, two or three times as many students receive A's and B's in the courses and fewer students make lower grades. Second, the students seem to have better attitudes and to be more interested in their work. Third, the students seem to have a greater confidence in their ability to learn. And, fourth, the adherents of this model feel that it helps students learn to learn. These conclusions are similar to those of many innovations at the present in which grades, feelings, attitudes, etc. are stressed instead of comparative achievement scores.

There are several apparent strengths of group-based, individualized instruction. First, opportunities for study in breadth as well as in depth can be incorporated into the language learning sequence. Second, the procedures are most like the instructional process of the traditional classroom with which teachers are already familiar. Third, since the approach does not involve a completely new class setup, it would be easier for the teacher to adopt and adapt. Fourth, the preparation for and the administration of the program would most likely be less time consuming and less of an adjustment for the teacher. Fifth, the approach includes group processes as well as individual study, basic material as well as supplementary material. Sixth, it would be easier for the average teacher to maintain control of the class and the progress of the class. Seventh, a steady rate of progression is built into the program which will discourage the type of procrastination often reported in self-paced, individualized courses. Eighth, the described group-based instruction is more adaptable to individual differences in some respects than the typical individualized program, although the approach is not totally individualized. The instructor still chooses the objectives as there are very close connections between Bloom's model of mastery learning and external theories of learning. Ninth, since so many different types of organization are utilized in the approach, it will accommodate different types of students in one general approach to instruction. Tenth, the concept of formative and summative testing is an interesting alternative to the diverse positions of tests which are considered as being of little or no value and the crucial, traumatic, all-or-nothing tests of some traditional classrooms.

CONCLUSION

At least three dangers are likely to accompany any educational innovation. The first is that proponents will create the impression that they have finally achieved the solution to all problems. If individualized instruction is to last, its believers must recognize that for some students, and for some teachers, the traditional classroom system of instruction may be infinitely preferable and superior. The same is true for some aspects of language learning. If past experience with innovations can serve as a guide, individualized instruction will make a greater contribution if what it can do best is incorporated into a total instructional program developed to accommodate the individuality of all the teachers and students.

The second danger is that the description of the proposed program will be so appealing that enthusiastic support for and adoption of the approach will occur prior to the appearance of any empirical evidence to support the basic tenets of the innovation. In the past, the sequence seems to have been to sell a program first, leaving the collection of supportive research evidence to others. Unfortunately, the results of research studies often do not support the basic assumptions upon which the innovation rests. Even more unfortunate is the subsequent disillusionment following such revelations and the eventual abandonment of the program.

The third danger is that the initial, developmental phases of the movement will be accepted as the final version, thus stagnating efforts to improve and expand preliminary programs as new insights are gained in practice. As experience accumulates, amplification of original concepts and assumptions should be disseminated so that improvements in existing programs can be made. Both leaders of and participants in innovative programs should realize that a decision toward change requires a continuing commitment to evaluate results and to remain receptive to indicated procedures for improving the original program.

Like many terms coined in previous movements in education, *individualized instruction* is subject to similar misinterpretations and misapplications. To date, the majority of the programs in second-language education have been characterized by a self-pacing format in which the student works through a teacher-prepared LAP. Practice seems to indicate that individualized instruction is being defined in the classroom as students studying individually. However, the objective of individualizing instruction is to match instructional programs and materials with individual interests, goals, and styles in order to maximize efficiency of learning and achievement.

In other words, individualizing instruction means gearing the learning to the needs of the individual, not learning in an isolated context. The implementation of this goal will necessitate classroom interaction between students or between the students and the teacher in large or small groups. Students need to work together for social, psychological, and emotional development. In the language classroom, interaction is essential if the student is to learn to participate at all in the rapid-fire repartee of the conversational context. Individualized instruction characterized by a continuous series of classes of supervised homework in which everyone is given the same assignment bears slight resemblance to the promised package inherent in the term individualization.

Nor is a self-paced class, in and of itself, a complete individualized program. Modes of instruction should be varied to accommodate individual cognitive styles. Content and types of instruction need to be chosen to reflect student interests and goals. The classroom organization itself may vary in conformity with the multitude of personality types enrolled in the classes. All these factors will need to be considered separately and in relation to each other. Individualized instruction that fails to incorporate the entire spectrum of individuality cannot hope to achieve its stated objectives. Once the scope of cognitive abilities and styles, personality types, and social structure is brought into focus, the ways and means of implementation will be much clearer.

"Diversifying Instruction" was chosen as the title of this chapter, in preference to "Individualized Instruction," for several reasons. On the negative side, this title was used because many have confused individualized instruction with individual study. Individualized instruction, as commonly practiced, is closely associated with a particular theoretical approach to learning, i.e., the external. On the positive side, the title was used because it embodies the trend in society and in education to diversify and to permit diversity. "Diversifying instruction" can encompass a wide range of practices geared toward meeting this characteristic of contemporary society without being tied to any particular theory. It can incorporate the same philosophical approach to instruction without being subject to the misinterpretation of the term *individualized*. Diversification can be made a part of any class curricular organization. The present participle was used intentionally to specify a continuing process, not a completed, all-or-nothing, instantaneous conversion to the final format.

REVIEW AND APPLICATION

DEFINITIONS

1. accountability, p. 208
2. aptitude, p. 211
3. behavioral objectives, p. 202
4. continuous progress learning, p. 203
5. criterion-referenced tests, pp. 203, 220
6. formative vs. summative tests, pp. 226, 227
7. mastery learning, p. 203
8. norm-referenced test, p. 220
9. performance-based teaching, p. 213
10. student-centered vs. teacher-centered, p. 208
11. unit feedback/correction procedures, p. 226

DISCUSSION

1. Compare and contrast individualized instruction with a totally individualized program.
2. Outline the reasons for the lack of totally individualized programs at the present time. Discuss the likelihood of achieving totally individualized programs.
3. What are the strengths and weaknesses of individualized instruction?
4. Discuss the type of classroom organization that you and your classmates prefer.
5. What is a LAP, and why are LAPs so commonly used in individualized instruction?
6. What theoretical criticisms are being leveled at the basic assumptions of individualized instruction?
7. What is student-centered learning? To what extent can, or should, learning be student-centered?
8. Would you or would you not use stated behavioral objectives? Why? Summarize the pros and cons of their use.
9. Discuss the implications of the concept of systematization with regard to second-language learning.
10. What would you do if you were planning to individualize?
11. Compare and contrast the "three-stage" model and the "group-based"

model of instruction. What are the advantages and disadvantages of each? How is each different from and similar to individualized instruction? Which would you prefer and why?

12. Outline what your past teachers have done to diversify instruction and to deal with individual differences in the classroom.

ACTIVITIES

1. Complete Wood's chart for totally individualizing material based on your preferences for learning.
2. Examine some LAPs and point out their similarities and differences.
3. Prepare your own LAP over some segment of an elementary text.
4. Survey the latest journals for the most recent insights into individualizing instruction.

SELECTED REFERENCES

Altman, H. B. (1971) Some Practical Aspects of Individualized Foreign Language Instruction. Paper presented at the Seventh Southern Conference on Language Teaching, Atlanta, Georgia, October 21–23.

Altman, H. B. (1974) Individualized Destruction? Process Doesn't Have To Be That! *Accent on ACTFL*, 4:12–14.

Altman, H. B. (1975) Demythologizing Individualization: Some Common Assumptions About Implementing an Individualized Language Program. *Canadian Modern Language Review*, 31:234–39.

Altman, H. B., and Politzer, R. L. (Eds.) (1971) *Individualizing Foreign Language Instruction: Proceedings of the Stanford Conference*. Rowley, Mass.: Newbury House.

Aschermann, J. R. (1974) Learning Activity Packages Don't Work for Everyone. *American Biology Teacher*, 36:241.

Baker, P. J.; Bakshis, R.; and Tolone, W. (1974) Diversifying Learning Opportunities: A Response to the Problems of Mass Education. *Research in Higher Education*, 2:251–63.

Berwald, J.-P. (1974) Supervising Student Teachers in Individualized Foreign Language Classes. *Modern Language Journal*, 58:91–95.

Block, J. H. (1971) *Mastery Learning: Theory and Practice*. New York: Holt, Rinehart and Winston.

Block, J. H. (1973) Teachers, Teaching, and Mastery Learning. *Today's Education*, 63:30–36.

Bloom, B. S. (1968) Learning for Mastery. *Evaluation Comment*, Los Angeles: University of California, Center for the Study of Evaluation.

Boutwell, R. C., and Barton, G. E. (1974) Toward an Adaptive Learner-Controlled Model of Instruction: A Place for New Cognitive Aptitudes. *Educational Technology*, 14:13.

Carroll, J. B. (1963) A Model of School Learning. *Teacher's College Record*, 64:723–33.

Chastain, K. (1971) *The Development of Modern Language Skills: Theory to Practice*. Philadelphia: The Center for Curriculum Development. Pp. 245–48.

Cohen, E. G. (1972) Sociology of the Classroom: Setting the Conditions for Teacher-Student Interaction. *Review of Educational Research*, 42:441–52.

Coppedge, F. L. (1974) Characteristics of Individualized Instruction. *Clearing House*, 48:272–77.

Day, J. F. (1974) Behavioral Technology: A Negative Stand. *Intellect*, 102:305–6.

Disick, R. J. (1973) Guest Editorial: Individualized Instruction: Promise Versus Reality. *Modern Language Journal*, 57:248–50.

Disick, R. J. (1975) *Individualizing Language Instruction*. New York: Harcourt Brace Jovanovich.

Duane, J. E. (1974) Let's Not Forget the Human Aspects When Individualizing Instruction. *Educational Technology*, 14:32.

Duchastel, P. C., and Merrill, P. F. (1973) The Effects of Behavioral Objectives on Learning: A Review of Empirical Studies. *Review of Educational Research*, 43:54.

Esler, W. K., and Dziuban, C. D. (1974) Criterion Referenced Test: Some Advantages and Disadvantages for Science Education. *Science Education*, 58:171–73.

Feldhusen, J. F., et al. (1974) Designing Instruction to Achieve Higher Level Goals and Objectives. *Educational Technology*, 14:21–23.

Frymier, J. R., and Galloway, C. M. (1974) Individualized Learning in a School for Tomorrow. *Theory into Practice*, 13:65–70.

Gagné, R. M. (1965) *The Conditions of Learning*. New York: Holt, Rinehart and Winston. Pp. 31–61.

Gorman, R. M. (1972) *Discovering Piaget: A Guide for Teachers*. Columbus, Ohio: Merrill. Pp. 109–10.

Gougher, R. (1975) *Individualizing Basic German Texts*. Detroit, Mich.: Advancement Press of America.

Gougher, R., and Smith, P. (1975) *Individualizing Basic Spanish Texts*. Detroit, Mich.: Advancement Press of America.

Gougher, R., and Wolfe, D. (1975) *Individualizing Basic French Texts*. Detroit, Mich.: Advancement Press of America.

Griffin, R. J. (1974) Individualized Instruction: Another Point of View. *Modern Language Journal*, 58:115–17.

Grittner, F. M. (1972) Behavioral Objectives, Skinnerian Rats, and Trojan Horses. *Foreign Language Annals*, 6:52–60.

Grittner, F. M., and La Leike, F. H. (1973) *Individualized Foreign Language Instruction*. Skokie, Ill.: National Textbook.

Groff, P. (1975) Some Criticism of Mastery Learning. *Education Digest*, 40:26–28.

Henson, K. T. (1974) Accountability and Performance-Based Programs in Education: Some Pros and Cons. *Intellect*, 102:250–52.

Humphreys, D. W. (1974) The Effects of Teacher- and Student-Selected Activities on the Self-Image and Achievement of High School Biology Students. *Science Education*, 58:298.

Hunter, M. (1971) The Learning Process. In D. W. Allen and E. Seifman (Eds.), *The Teacher's Handbook*. Glenview, Ill.: Scott Foresman. Pp. 158–66.

Hunter, M. (1971) The Teaching Process. In D. W. Allen and E. Seifman (Eds.), *The Teacher's Handbook*. Glenview, Ill.: Scott Foresman. Pp. 146–57.

James, C. (1974) Developments in the Education of Adolescents: A Critique. *Urban Review*, 7:54.

Jarvis, G. A. (1971) Individualized Learning—Where Can We Risk Compromise? *Modern Language Journal*, 55:375–78.

Johnson, D. W., and Johnson, R. T. (1974) Instructional Goal Structure: Cooperative, Competitive, or Individualistic. *Review of Educational Research*, 44:214.

Kalivoda, T. B. (1972) An Individual Study Course for Facilitating Advanced Oral Skills. *Modern Language Journal*, 56:492–95.

Krulik, S. (1974) Learning Packages for Mathematics Instruction—Some Considerations. *Mathematics Teacher*, 67:348–51.

Lafayette, R. C. (1972) Diversification: The Key to Student-Centered Programs. *Modern Language Journal*, 56:349–54.

Levine, M. G. (1972) The Relationship Between Knowledge, Practice, and Pupil Achievement in the Use of a Criterion-Referenced Instructional Model. *Journal of Experimental Education*, 41:49.

Logan, G. E. (1973) *Individualized Foreign Language Learning: An Organic Process*. Rowley, Mass.: Newbury House.

Miller, J. R., and Gonyar, P. A. (1974)

Learning Activity Packages. *Social Studies,* 65:120–25.

Newman, F. L., et al. (1974) Initial Attitude Differences Among Successful, Procrastinating, and "Withdrawn-From-Course" Students in a Personalized System of Statistics Instruction. *Journal for Research in Mathematics Education,* 5:105–13.

Noblitt, J. S. (1975) Pacing and Systematization. Paper presented at the Symposium on Individualized Instruction at the Kentucky Foreign Language Conference, Lexington, Kentucky, April 25.

Papalia, A. (1975) Using Different Models of Second-Language Teaching. *Canadian Modern Language Review,* 31:212–16.

Papalia, A., and Zampogna, J. (1972) An Experiment in Individualized Instruction through Small Group Interaction. *Foreign Language Annals,* 5:302–6.

Rosenthal, B. (1973) Developing a Foreign Language Learning Activity Package. *Modern Language Journal,* 57:195–99.

Schramm, W. (1964) *The Research on Programmed Instruction: An Annotated Bibliography.* Washington, D.C.: U. S. Government Printing Office.

Stedman, C. H. (1972) Is Providing Students with Behavioral Objectives Incorporated into Programmed Materials Efficient? *Journal of Experimental Education,* 41:75.

Steiner, F. (1971) Individualized Instruction. *Modern Language Journal,* 55:361–74.

Travers, R. M. W. (1975) Individualized Instruction: Panacea or Plague (carbon copy).

Valdman, A. (1975) On the Specification of Performance Objectives in Individualized FL Instruction. Paper presented at the Symposium on Individualized Instruction at the Kentucky Foreign Language Conference, Lexington, Kentucky, April 25.

Valette, R. M., and Disick, R. S. (1972) *Modern Language Performance Objectives and Individualization.* New York: Harcourt Brace Jovanovich.

Waks, L. J. (1973) Re-examining the Validity of Arguments Against Behavioral Goals. *Educational Theory,* 23:133–43.

Walker, W. E. (1973) The Slow-Progress Student in Graded and Nongraded Programs. *Peabody Journal of Education,* 50:191–210.

Walters, L., and Sieben, G. (1974) Cognitive Style and Learning Science in Elementary Schools. *Science Education,* 58:65–74.

Webb, A. B., and Cormier, W. H. (1972) Improving Classroom Behavior and Achievement. *Journal of Experimental Education,* 41:95.

Wells, G. T. (1974) How About a Compromise Toward Individualization? *Accent on ACTFL,* 4:24–25.

Wood, F. H. (1973) Individual Differences Count. *NASSP Bulletin,* 57:23–31.

Yelon, S. L., and Schmidt, W. H. (1973) The Effect of Objectives and Instructions on the Learning of a Complex Cognitive Task. *Journal of Experimental Education,* 41:95.

Conclusion to Part One

The purpose of part 1 of this book has been to relate current theory in both the affective and the cognitive domains to second-language teaching. First, the reader's attention was directed toward a consideration of the reasons for including second-language study in the curriculum. Obviously, a rationale acceptable to the public and to the students must be developed if second-language study is going to continue to be an important educational component in this country, or in any other country. In the next chapter, "Perspectives," the currents in society, education, and related disciplines that influence second-language teaching were examined in order that second-language teachers would be aware of the forces affecting their profession. As the title of the chapter indicates, the purpose of this discussion of historical events and movements was not meant to be a history of second-language teaching, but an attempt to provide the reader with a perspective on the interrelationships existing between the classroom and the surrounding world. This author is not so much concerned with what has happened in the past as he is with teachers' comprehension of the present and their ability to anticipate and prepare for future movements and changes.

Following this initial introduction to second-language teaching, attention turned to two areas to which second-language educators have gone to find support for recommended classroom methodology—first-language learning and research. Although the circumstances surrounding first- and second-language learning are unquestionably dissimilar, the study of the former may lead to insights into the latter. In fact, the latest studies indicate more similarity between the two processes than had been previously suspected. Research, which had until recently concentrated principally on the cognitive processes, has now begun to branch into the affective domain. Investigators seem to be turning away from studies attempting to prove the one best way of doing things to initial inquiries into which methods are best for which students under the guidance of which teachers. This prospect holds forth the potential of employing obtained knowledge about individuality to prepare instructional programs geared to individual differences.

With this background, the reader examined the theoretical bases of the principles and procedures employed in audio-lingual theory and cognitive theory. In order to simplify and clarify the presentation, the discussion was separated into opposing theoretical positions similar to the division in contemporary psychology and linguistics. For second-language educators to derive benefit from these related disciplines, both positions need to be understood. Unless teachers comprehend the various viewpoints being proposed, they will be unable to select intelligently those tenets most applicable to the teaching of second languages. This division was made consciously in spite of the current preference for eclecticism because it was felt that only in this manner can practicing or prospective teachers comprehend the various blends found in some textbooks. Too, it was felt that this methodological distinction must be understood in order to arrive at valid curricular decisions with regard to the selection and organization of classroom teaching-learning activities.

Chapters 7 and 8 surveyed the students, their world, and curricular approaches that have been advocated as a means of accommodating individual student differences. The first question explored was the contemporary world of modern-day students and how it may affect their attitudes and needs in the classroom. (It goes without saying that any subject that does not satisfy student needs and fails to promote positive student attitudes is in danger of losing its place in the curriculum.) Chapter 8, "Diversifying Instruction," dealt with what has been done to develop individualized instruction and with the basic assumptions underlying this curricular approach. Many objections to and criticisms of the principal tenets of individualized instruction were encountered. Alternatives for diversifying instruction as a means of accommodating the wide variability of interests and talents in the classroom were outlined.

Too often, theory is considered irrelevant to the classroom situation, but such a conclusion is not valid. Theory does influence instruction in the second-language class whether or not the teacher is cognizant of this influence. The teacher who ignores present-day theoretical positions has no alternative but to follow blindly the dictates of others. The teacher who is acquainted with theory can select instructional procedures that are solidly based on currently accepted positions of learning theory.

In addition to being familiar with current theory, teachers should also keep informed about the latest research findings as a means of substantiating the theoretical contentions being proposed. In general, there are two common misinterpretations of research. The first is to accept all research findings as proving the conclusions of the author. The second is to refuse to accept the findings of any research, except those agreeing with one's own preconceived conclusions. Obviously, both types of reactions are incorrect. Research, especially given the number of variables involved, never conclusively proves a theory. Research support is needed. All teachers wear rose-colored glasses that let them see what they want to see, but they ignore research at the risk of losing an important source of objectivity. This loss of perspective blinds them to the potential benefits that may be derived from innovations in other areas and in second-language education.

In psychology, contemporary thinking has tended to place greater emphasis on cognition rather than habit formation. Generative linguistics, which follows a cognitive interpretation of language, has challenged the conception of language formulated by descriptive linguistics, which adheres to a behavioristic interpretation of language. The pendulum of opinion that formerly supported the behavioristic view of learning and language has shifted dramatically in the last decade toward cognitive models.

It is appropriate at this point to inform the reader that some writers in the field of second-language education do not support the dichotomy presented in this text. These writers say that the distinction between audio-lingual theory and cognitive theory is a false differentiation. Others feel that the basic elements of the two theories condense to the difference between inductive and deductive learning.

While this author has never intended to imply other than a continuum connecting the two extremes, the differences between the two poles of the continuum are fundamental. They are not false differences, and they cannot be reduced to the differences between inductive and deductive learning. Bruner is a cognitive psychologist; yet he advocates discovery learning, which means that learners are to induce their own principles and rules. On the other hand, Ausubel advocates deductive presentations of rules and principles. Both inductive and deductive learning depend upon internal mental processing of information for learning. Both, therefore, are cognitive processes. The crucial factors separating the two models are the role of the learner in the learning process and what controls his subsequent actions.

For years the dominant position in psychology was that of behaviorism. The emphasis has now shifted from external shaping of behavior to internal, mental processing by the individual of information perceived. Do these recent developments carry with them the obligation to develop all teaching-learning situations along cognitive guidelines? Undoubtedly, recognition of the individual's role in the learning process and the concept of the learner as an active, performing agent in learning are productive concepts in the educational model. However, the results obtained in the initial investigations into aptitude-treatment interaction indicate that various types of learners must be recognized. Just as educators cannot assume that all students learn by the conditioning model, neither can they assume that all learners are ready to benefit from cognitively based teaching-learning situations.

Ideal learners can easily be described. First, they are intrinsically motivated. They have reached the development level in which they are capable of directing their own learning. Their feelings and attitudes are positive and productive. Second, they are socialized to the point at which they are accepted, functioning members of the group and of the group processes. They contribute to rather than detract from the ongoing learning process in the classroom. Third, they have reached an intellectual level at which they have the capacity for formal mental operations and the necessary learning skills to complete the learning tasks being presented in the class. (Have such individuals not been alluded to for years in educational literature, but rarely found?)

In all the developmental models presented in chapter 7, "The Student," a definite hierarchical sequence is postulated in which the individual progresses from the more elementary and simple stages to the more complex, from the more directed to the more self-directed. In the various areas of intellectual growth, ego development, moral development, social maturity, etc., the apex of each is the emergence of an internally directed, self-sufficient, autonomous individual. That is the ideal. Unfortunately, neither the world nor the classrooms are peopled by ideal individuals. The point is that the conception of student-centered learning is appropriate for the student who is capable of benefiting from such a program. If the individual is capable of self-direction, she should have that opportunity. However, many students have not reached the level of cognitive and affective-social development at which they are capable of self-direction. To the extent that the student deviates from the desired autonomous learner, the truly individualized program will be forced to deviate from the ideal envisioned in student-centered learning.

Student-centered learning must first of all be built around the needs and attitudes of the students. For those students who have matured to the self-sufficient stage, student-centered learning may mean self-directed learning. In this sense, learning is centered *within* the student. For those students who are incapable of self-direction, external organization, assistance, and even control must be introduced into their teaching-learning experiences to provide the discipline and direction that they lack at their current stage of development and maturity. In this sense, learning is centered *on* the student's capabilities and needs. For example, self-pacing is a valid concept only as long as it facilitates student learning. When it serves to impede progress, when the students become victims of their own procrastination, self-pacing must be discarded immediately. If a student is a "level 1" (external) learner, she should not be expected to manage abstract, deductive presentations. If he is a "Level 2" (internal) learner, he should not be subjected to a frustrating, for him, series of mechanistic, conditioning drills. Other students are at a stage where a tightly controlled teacher-centered class best meets their needs. Obviously, adjustments must be made depending upon each student. In any case, the teacher is responsible for finding the best fit between the student's internal-external profile and the appropriate internal-external, teaching-learning situations. As the students grow, develop, and mature, they should be progressing toward the internal ideal. However, one must recognize that deadlines are set because many never attain or maintain that ideal, internally directed state, which is much easier to conceptualize than to actualize.

Finally, what choices does the teacher make among the alternatives? Mechanistic or mentalistic classroom procedures? Inductive or deductive presentations? Conditioning drills or reasoning exercises? Extrinsic motivation or intrinsic motivation? Teacher-centered, subject-centered, or student-centered classes? First, teachers should understand what types of practices are outgrowths of which theories. For example, as currently practiced individualized instruction is in general an external approach to learning, not student-centered, in the strict sense of the word, nor humanistic. Yet the terms *student-centered* and *humanistic* are used in conjunction with the individualized approach as if they were synonymous. Second, they should avoid the temptation to say, "*This* is the right method." If anything has been learned to date, it is that there is no single best method. Third, they should seek to develop teaching-learning activities that are appropriate, both affectively and cognitively, to the various types of learners in class. Students are different, and they learn in different ways. Teachers are different, and they teach in different ways. Fourth, they should stay abreast of new developments in and related to second-language teaching, especially in the area of aptitude-treatment interaction.

Part Two: Practice

Once teachers have a sufficient theoretical background to support their decisions concerning their approach to the teaching-learning process, the time has arrived to direct their attention toward the classroom. Neither theory nor practice alone is sufficient; each should complement the other in order to blend the teachers' philosophy and practice into a unified, rational whole. Given a theory of learning and of language, teachers can begin an examination of the art of the teaching process itself. Fortified with the armor of their understanding of theory, they can continue to prepare themselves for the day in which they sally forth to do battle (intellectually) with their first class.

In the classroom, teachers present content to students operating in a social system. In order to do their job well they should first of all know the material they are attempting to teach to the students. Second, they should be familiar with various methodological and curricular approaches to establishing appropriate teaching-learning situations. And third, they should have matured to the level at which they can develop a productive rapport with each student personally and with the class as a whole. They should like young people, be willing to take them for what they are, and most of all, maintain their commitment to helping them learn and grow to higher levels of intellectual, emotional, and social maturity. As important as knowledge of subject matter and methodology and curriculum are to becoming a successful teacher, the most important factors are personal qualities which the teachers bring to the classroom. Unless they can relate to the students and vice versa, other factors will be insufficient.

Aside from the myriad of personal relationships existing in the classroom, the teacher's tasks fall into three major categories: (1) establishing objectives, (2) preparing learning activities geared toward the attainment of the aforementioned objectives, and (3) evaluating the outcome of task 2 to determine whether the objectives of task 1 were indeed obtained. Teaching, then, becomes a continuous process of the formulation of hypotheses, hypotheses which are subsequently put to the test in the classroom. As teachers evaluate the results, they receive evidence as to the validity of their hypotheses. Modifications and revisions are then incorporated into teaching procedures. As they receive feedback on their hypotheses, teachers have an obligation to learn and to grow. Unless teachers continue to learn and grow, they will undoubtedly not rise to the height of their potential.

The purpose of part 2 of this book is to relate the theory discussed in part 1 to the classroom situation and to examine with the prospective and/or practicing teacher various aspects of teaching a second language. The goal is to present a sufficient amount of information, insight, and examples, so that the reader can become an internally directed, creative teacher, not an imitator of incompletely understood models and techniques. Chapter 9 focuses on meeting student needs in the classroom. Chapters 10, 11, 12, and 13 treat separately each of the four language skills. Chapter 14 is a discussion of teaching culture. Chapter 15 outlines general guidelines the teacher should keep in mind. Chapter 16 discusses lesson planning. Chapter 17 summarizes various classroom procedures appropriate to each phase of the class hour. Chapter 18 gives an overview of evaluation along with some specific examples and suggestions. A short summary concludes part 2.

MEETING STUDENT NEEDS

Classroom Management
>Environment for Learning
>>The Physical Environment
>>The Emotional Environment
>Planning and Scheduling
>Keeping Student Records
>Handling Materials

Self-Concept
>Damaging Self-Concept
>Improving Self-Concept
>Self-Concept and Second-Language Teaching

Self-Actualization
>Values
>Achievement Motivation
>>Theories of Motivation
>>Types of Achievement Motivation
>>Conditions of Motivation
>>Improving Motivation
>>Improving Motivation in Second-Language Classes
>Discipline
>>Classroom Discipline Patterns
>>Approaches to Discipline
>>Types of Behavior Problems
>>Discipline in the Classroom

Classroom Climate
>Aspects of Classroom Climate
>Improving Classroom Climate

What Do Students Want?
>Sources of Student Satisfaction and Dissatisfaction
>Student Evaluation of Teachers
>Student Opinions About Second-Language Classes

INTRODUCTION

The premise upon which this chapter is based is that students have basic needs and that the teacher is responsible for helping to meet these needs, most of which revolve around the need to be sustained, encouraged, guided, and nurtured in growth. Obviously, the teacher's major responsibility lies in the area of intellectual growth, but often psychomotor or affective-social factors render the teacher's best efforts to teach academic content ineffective or even useless. The contemporary scene is such that the teacher is being asked to attend to these affective-social factors in order to promote student learning. Thus, the teacher's role is expanded beyond the covers of the textbook and the confines of her academic preparation to the realms of student attitudes and social adjustment.

The preceding paragraph is not intended to imply that the teacher is concerned about her students only as a means of improving academic achievement. Her guidance in the affective-social areas may well have beneficial effects that will in the present or in the future far surpass those of the subject matter itself. Growth in one area tends to affect growth in other areas, and all aspects of the total student are important to that student now and in the future and to the classroom learning atmosphere.

Of course, no teacher can be expected to shoulder all the students' problems. He is no amateur psychologist in white coat who comes running at the first sign of trouble. He has neither the training nor the time to assume such responsibility. However, he should be committed to fostering student cognitive, affective, and social growth as far as possible within the confines of the classroom situation and the limited contact he may have with any given student. Too, he should be prepared to refer any student needing specialized assistance to someone who can provide those services.

Chapter 7 treats the students and their world and closes with an examination of student needs. Chapter 8 focuses on the variability of individuality. The reader should keep the contents of both the aforementioned chapters in mind while reading this chapter. The primary purpose of chapter 9 is to discuss ways and means of meeting student affective-social needs in the classroom. (Ways and means of meeting student cognitive needs in the second-language class are dealt with in the remaining chapters of part 2.)

CLASSROOM MANAGEMENT

The teacher role is a multifaceted one requiring a variety of skills, many of which are not limited to instruction alone. Although teachers might prefer to confine their activities to the more creative and interesting aspects of teaching,

---

The organization and basic content of this section are from the following source: Alexander (1971, pp. 177–88).

they do have other obligations that must be fulfilled. The first step toward meeting student needs is to learn to manage the classroom situation. Classroom management includes those bookkeeping and housekeeping chores that provide the basis for establishing all teaching-learning situations and activities. These everyday chores are an integral part of teaching, and a successful teaching career requires that teachers learn to handle them promptly and efficiently. Teachers' records are the principal cornerstone of the entire administrative-counseling system of the school, and handling the housekeeping routine is vital to the ongoing classroom activities.

The following outline of the various housekeeping and bookkeeping chores is being presented as a guide to the classroom management responsibilities the teacher has to meet. Limited space precludes detailed discussion of ways and means of handling each. In fact, how these chores are to be managed is not so important as the necessity for the teacher to have some plan or system for doing so. The point is that the teacher needs to anticipate these responsibilities and find ways to meet them. He may develop his system individually, with the cooperation and input of the students, or in consultation with experienced teachers. (The latter method is so common that beginning teachers are often assigned an experienced "buddy" who serves as a resource person to answer questions and to provide general support during the first few weeks of classes.) Preschool meetings for new teachers also serve as orientation sessions in which many questions are answered.

Environment for Learning

Obviously, the environment for learning encompasses much more than the classroom itself. Students are products of the entire community and school social system, and the teacher should be familiar with the neighborhood and the school prior to entering her specialized domain within that environment. Too, teachers should be acquainted with school policy and procedures before classes begin.

The physical environment Teachers also have the responsibility for overseeing their classroom and its contents. Following are some areas that will need attention.

Preparation for the coming school year is the fall room cleaning of the school. Shelves are cleaned, materials are organized, inventories are prepared, and all supplies needed are acquired or ordered.

Teaching aids, both auditory and visual, need to be located, put in good working order, and placed in a convenient spot in the room. In the case of those teaching aids not kept in the room, teachers should know what the school has available and how and where to get them for use in their classes. Teachers may also plan to ask students to assist in the preparation of new teaching aids.

The *bulletin board* can be a valuable asset in the classroom. A good bulletin board display requires considerable attention and a great deal of work. Students can relieve teachers of much of the work of preparing the bulletin board display while at the same time learning from and enjoying the experience. The materials on the bulletin board should be changed regularly, they should be relevant to class content, and they should make a contribution to learning. Bulletin board displays should be filed and saved for future use. Also, commercial materials are available, and handbooks containing numerous ideas and suggestions can be found in educational libraries.

The *seating arrangement* is normally the teacher's prerogative, although it is determined to a large extent by the physical facilities and the prevailing types of activities to be employed in the class. Seats may be arranged in rows, circles, U-shapes, or in small groups. The current preference seems to be toward having the students face each other in order that they may relate better to each other during recitation sessions, in small groups, or individually in order to break down the feeling of rigidity prevailing in some classes. As helpful as these different arrangements may be, teacher attitude probably has more to do with class tone than does the seating arrangement. The important point is that teachers may feel free in most schools to experiment with the seating flexibility needed to implement their particular type of classroom activities.

Within the limits of teacher control, the *temperature* of the room should be comfortable. Students who are uncomfortable cannot be expected to concentrate on their studies. For those days on which the temperature cannot be kept within comfortable limits, teachers should try to include some occasional special activities to stimulate student interest.

The teacher should also be cognizant of the *noise level*. It may be necessary to close the door or ask for quiet if there is too much noise in the hall. Similarly, it may be necessary at times to decrease the volume of noise in the classroom itself if it reaches the level of disturbing the teacher or the learning activities of the other students. Sometimes the students themselves will ask those creating a disturbance to be quiet. If they do not, the teacher should not hesitate to do so. Noise must not be permitted to exceed a permissible productive level.

The emotional environment   New buildings and unlimited facilities in and of themselves are no guarantee of a productive learning environment, and teachers should recognize that productive learning situations can be developed within the contexts of almost any physical environment. The more important part is the sum of the emotional elements present in the classroom.

Voices play an important role in the classroom. As they speak, both teachers and students indicate the purposiveness of what they are doing and the respect they have for each other. All verbal exchanges should have a learning objective in view, and all members of the class should be kind and courteous to all other members. Silence may also be desirable at times, depending upon the objective of the student activity, and teachers should not hesitate to insist upon silence at those times. However, students who are always silent normally reflect some problem, which teachers should seek to resolve and eliminate.

Expectations are important in any class. The teacher knows what to expect from each student, and each student knows what to expect from the teacher. Teacher assignments are realistic, but high quality work is expected. Both the teacher and the students regard themselves and each other highly and expect high returns on efforts put into the course.

Tempo refers to the pace of the class. Some teachers speed through the activities and the materials; others follow a more leisurely pace. The tempo itself is not so important as whether or not the teacher and the student can adjust to each other's style. In this sense, homogeneous grouping may permit a certain degree of matching of teacher and student styles. Teaching tempo may need to be adjusted to varying conditions, such as different types of students, different hours of the day, different seasons of the year, different climatic conditions, and even different days of the week.

Humor, if it is not made the objective of the course and occurs naturally in teaching-learning activities, can enhance the emotional environment of the class. If the teacher and the students can learn to laugh together often and even at themselves occasionally, chances are they will be able to work together better.

Planning and Scheduling

Within the physical and emotional environment the teacher plans for instruction and schedules teaching-learning activities. She asks herself how maximum learning may be achieved, how classroom procedures may be handled more efficiently and more smoothly, and how trouble spots may be avoided. In this process the class develops systematic routines that enable the teacher and the students to work together harmoniously and productively.

Some problems are *recurrent.* Students seem always to need to sharpen a pencil or to dispose of a piece of paper in the wastebasket. However, pencils can be sharpened and paper discarded without disrupting the class. At no time should such trivia be allowed to impede or interfere with ongoing teaching-learning activities, and the teacher and/or the class should develop a system, known to everyone, for handling such small matters.

No teacher can expect to teach without the *interruptions* that accompany the school scene. He must be prepared for school programs, absences, irrelevant comments by students, changes in the daily schedule, etc.

Passing in papers is such a common class activity that the novice may tend to overlook the potential for disruption and inefficiency. Where are students to write their names? How are papers to be folded? There is no reason that the passing in or return of papers should become a disorderly melee. As with other matters relating to classroom conduct, there should be a system that can be accomplished with a minimum of time and noise. One tested procedure is to ask the students to pass the papers to the front of the room where one student can collect all the papers and give them to the teacher. They can be returned by a similar system, except in the case of examinations.

The teacher should have her *lesson plans* and all *teaching materials* ready prior to the beginning of each class. Otherwise, the flow of the class activities will come to an unnecessary halt, and the students will tend to lose their concentration on and interest in the subject matter at hand. In individualized classes, all materials including new LAPs and tests should be ready for student use, and they should be systematically filed and clearly labeled. The students should be familiar with how to use LAPs and the materials available in the classroom. They should be familiar with the system for indicating progress and the system for taking tests and recording test scores.

The teacher should have a system for giving the *assignment.* During what part of the class hour is it given? How is it given, orally or written on the chalkboard? Do the students know exactly what they are to do? When is the assignment due? Is it to be oral or written?

Keeping Student Records

Records are kept for present and future reference by teachers, administrators, counselors, parents, students, and prospective employers. They are useful not only to record what has happened but to provide insights into quality and trends of the educational program.

Formal records include *attendance records, grade books,* and *report cards.* Attendance records are required by law, tax-funds being allocated on the basis of the number of students attending the school. Calling the roll is too time-consuming to be used in class. The teacher can either check the attendance at the bell or designate a student to do so. The names of those absent are then relayed to the principal's office. The teacher records absences, grades, and other information related to grades in his grade book. The material in the grade book should be legible, systematic, and comprehensible. Report cards are the measure of student class progress that the teacher gives to the students and the parents. In this sense, the report card is the student growth report. Formerly, the report card concerned itself primarily with conduct and academic record. Presently, especially in elementary grades, many aspects of the affective-social domain are also reported.

In many schools, *informal records* are kept continuously or as the occasion requires. These informal records include everything from lunch money, to money received from receipts of a money-making project, to anecdotal records of student behavior. In some cases, folders are prepared for each student. With an individualized program, for example, a folder in which each student records her progress facilitates the record-keeping chores associated with this approach. The students indicate work done, and the teacher can add additional, informal information.

Handling Materials

Most teachers maintain an ever-growing collection of materials useful in their classes. However, to be usable, these materials must be organized, cataloged, and stored in such a manner that the teacher knows what he has and where it is. Some of this responsibility is shared by the *central resource center,* of course, and the teacher should have a list of relevant materials and teaching aids contained there. However, most of the *textbooks* and *teaching materials* that the second-language teacher uses are in his own classroom or that of a colleague. (Teachers, especially beginning teachers, should remember that sharing is an excellent way of increasing the amount of teaching materials at one's disposal.) The problem of handling classroom materials in an efficient manner is multiplied in an individualized program. Not only must the teacher know what he has and where it is, but the material must also be readily available to students at various points in the course outline. Such a program requires extra storage space, an operable system understood by all the students, and student assistants or monitors, or an aide, to see to it that everything is returned to its appropriate location.

SELF-CONCEPT

Once the administrative and logistic classroom chores have been taken care of, the teacher can begin to concentrate on each individual student in class and on each student's self-concept. One's opinion of self is the single most critical factor in determining attitudes, values, social relationships, academic achievement, and goals. Thus, the development of a positive self-image is important in the school setting and for a productive adult life. Since self-concept is derived to a considerable degree from the feedback the individual receives from relationships with others, a change in the treatment the individual receives can over a period of time modify his opinion of himself. The question for the classroom is whether or not teachers can develop attitudes and behaviors that improve student self-concepts. Brown and MacDougall (1973) found that, with training, teachers were able to modify their classroom actions in ways that did result in students regarding themselves more positively.

Damaging Self-Concept

Teachers do not intentionally plan to diminish a student's self-concept. However, they may at times do so simply by teaching as they were taught without seriously considering the consequences of their actions. Tolar (1975) lists three major ways in which teachers may hinder student emotional development. The first is the use of *threat* to coerce students into classroom conformity. This practice may be counterproductive in that students may reach the point at which they are dependent upon external authority for direction. Too, this practice may produce feelings of fear and anxiety, and these feelings can lead to psychological and social maladjustment problems. The second is the practice of appealing to *guilt* feelings. Students are made to feel that their self-worth is dependent upon classroom achievement, and they are shamed in order to elevate performance. The third is the classroom that places students in the position of a captive audience participating in *unchallenging classroom experiences.* Tolar (1975, p. 72) states that teachers contribute to "students' sense of inadequacy by offering classroom experiences which are not challenging. Some teachers unwittingly confuse respectful empathy with sympathy, and invite self-pity by offering sympathy." He adds that self-reliance and independence are crucial to healthy emotional development.

Another way in which teachers may damage a student's self-concept is by using him in various ways as a scapegoat for their own inadequate self-images. Many of the articles listed in the Selected References section of this chapter refer to the widely held belief that the teacher must have an adequate self-concept in order to develop positive self-esteem among students. Oliva (1972) maintains that teachers should be aware of the importance of a positive self-concept both in themselves and in their students. He gives examples of teachers with low self-concepts as being those who see students as monsters or vegetables, who avoid controversial issues, who think students are opposed to their subjects, who are afraid to try new ideas, and who talk about the students in the teachers' lounge.

Teachers may also fail to take steps toward improving student self-concepts because they are not informed as to what the problems and the signs of the problems are. In an interesting study by Sack and Sack (1974), teachers and mental hygienists were asked to rank, in order of importance, the fifty greatest student behavior problems. Teachers tended to select acts, while mental hygienists chose undesirable emotional or social traits. The top five selected by the teachers were: (1) stealing, (2) destruction, (3) cheating, (4) lying, and (5) defiance. The top five chosen by the mental hygienists were: (1)

unhappiness and depression, (2) fear, (3) unsocial and withdrawing behavior, (4) cruel and bullying behavior, and (5) domineering behavior.

Improving Self-Concept

Schwartz (1972) believes that self-concept is based on four factors: competence, significance to others, virtue (doing the right thing), and power (influence in the individual's social structure). Ellsworth (1967) lists two types of negative self-concept: feeling of inability to cope and feeling of being unlovable. The importance of each of these factors on self-concept, of course, depends on the individual. In some cases, significance to others will be most influential, while in others competence will be, and so forth. From the teacher's point of view, the important consideration is what she can do in her class to improve self-concept.

As the teacher attempts to supplement her regular classroom behavior with ego-enhancing procedures and techniques, she should keep in mind that modification of the self-concept is a slow metamorphosis rather than a sudden conversion. Too, she should be aware that the self-image of her students is influenced as much by her actions and her manner as by what she says. Mattocks and Sew (1974) suggest specific ideas for shaping self-concept.

1. The teacher is sensitive to each student.
2. She attempts to promote consistency of self-concept.
3. She focuses on the promotion of student confidence and the integration of each [student] into classroom activities.
4. She is aware of the student's body image and self-acceptance.
5. She selects teaching-learning activities that involve learning by doing as well as thinking.
6. She makes clear to the students that mistakes are not tragedies.
7. She is tolerant, understands student limitations, and avoids unreasonable demands.
8. She takes advantage of natural student curiosity.
9. She dishes out generous quantities of reward and judicious amounts of punishment.

Piaget feels that growth develops from egocentric limitations and that each step in this process is dependent upon the successful completion of the previous step. What can be done in the case of those students who have gotten stuck in the process of developing a healthy self-concept? How can the teacher help the student bridge the gap between failure or stagnation and success? First, he must be willing to accept the student as a worthwhile person. Second, he must get the student to talk about the problem. Together they should identify exactly what the problem is. Third, he should try to get the student to understand that other students have similar problems. Fourth, he needs to try to get the student to accept himself as he is. Together they can find the student's strengths and build upon them. Next, he should attempt to encourage the student and to build up his confidence. And last, he should involve the student in some activity at which he can be successful (Gowan, 1974).

In relation to the fourth point in the preceding paragraph, the teacher should realize that only self-images based on realistic self-appraisal can in the long run be beneficial to the student. Self-esteem means that the student knows his capabilities and accepts himself as he is. In fact, the greater the gap between the student's capabilities and his self-image and self-expectations the more likely he will be subject to psychological problems. According to a practicing clinical psychologist who works with adolescents, one of the most common problems of adolescents is that they have not been told the truth. They do not know what are their strengths and weaknesses, their potentials and limitations. Tolar (1975, p. 73) stresses that student mental health depends on frank and genuine appraisal by teachers. He criticizes teachers in general saying, "It is common for students to go without accurate feedback, because some teachers are not genuine enough to provide a realistic picture of students' performances. Sometimes they lack courage enough to carefully confront inconsistencies or provide constructive criticism." Therefore, teachers should not misinterpret teaching for self-concept as meaning that students are always patted on the back whether or not the praise is justified.

As she works with those students who have self-concept problems, the teacher needs to develop a problem-solving attitude. She should be objective, help students realize their potential, consider student goals, permit freedom of expression, develop a flexible stance toward student problems, and encourage any evidence of response and growth. Above all, she should not expect stupidity and failure (LeBaron, 1974). In short, the teacher commits herself to assisting student affective-social growth in ways that seem to be productive. Exact procedures develop out of the specific circumstances surrounding each individual student.

Self-Concept and Second-Language Teaching

The self-image that is weak but adequate in other classes in first-language exchanges may become uncomfortably fragile in the second-language class. For this reason, second-language teachers, more than teachers working with students in their first language, should be sensitive to self-concept and to its effects on the students and their work in class.

Stern (1975) mentions three problems common to students in initial stages of second-language study, each of which may create problems with student self-concept. First, the learner must learn to tolerate the frustration of being unable to express himself. Second, he has to learn to deal with the necessity of accepting the new sounds, forms, and structures of the second language. And third, he must learn how to operate linguistically in a system in which momentarily he is disoriented, in which he does not know what to expect. Nor do these three constitute all the emotional strains that second-language study places on student self-concept. Brown (1973, p. 233) states that any language acquisition process that results in meaningful learning for communication involves some degree of identity conflict regardless of the age and motivation of the learner. (Classroom culture shock is discussed in chapter 14, page 387.) Stevick (1973) mentions the fact that second-language learners are forced temporarily to operate at an infant linguistic level and to accept corrections from someone else. Too, students may feel that they are not learning as rapidly as other students or as fast as they had anticipated, and they may not see the relationship between second-language study and their career plans. (This latter problem is discussed in chapter 1, pages 9–11.)

Second-language teachers should become sensitive to the insecure emotional state of their students, especially in the initial stages of second-language study. They should consider what they expect of their students and how they correct student errors. They should become familiar with procedures for building student self-concept and practice them in their classes. They should seek to establish a supportive, encouraging atmosphere for second-language acquisition. Curran is of the opinion that the teacher must abandon his natural questioning, doubting manner toward the learner and replace it with unconditioned positive regard and try to respond in a warm, secure, reassuring way that will convey a deep understanding of the learner's anxious, insecure state (Stevick, 1973, p. 262).

The acceptance of "person" education entails a much broader spectrum of responsibilities than those previously associated with the classroom. "Person" education with regard to self-concept means that the teacher commits himself to the goal of helping students grow in self-esteem and self-awareness. In working toward this objective, the teacher should realize his need for and the difficulty of obtaining objectivity in dealing with his students. He should not expect students to reward him, for instance. Willis and Brophy (1974) state that students who do not reward teachers are avoided and/or rejected by them. Friedman (1973) found that teachers are much more likely to praise student responses to teacher initiated interchanges than student originated comments. Neither should he fail to remember that students are individuals, and some do not need the teacher as much as others. Too, he should realize that ascertaining student feelings and attitudes may be practically impossible in many cases. For example, Ducette and Wolk (1972) found that, in general, teachers are not very good judges of student attitudes. They assume that students making good grades have good attitudes and vice versa. However, this feeling does not correspond with data collected on student attitudes. Thus, teachers tend to overestimate the attitudes of good students and underestimate the attitudes of poor students. As they become better acquainted with the students, their assessments become more valid. The crucial factor affecting student self-esteem seems to be the teacher himself rather than the curricular organization of the class. Harvey (1974), Black (1974), and Humphreys and Townsend (1974) report that types of classroom organization apparently have little effect on self-concept.

SELF-ACTUALIZATION

Once the individual has reached a functional level in self-concept development he can begin to work toward the realization of his potential. The actualization of inherent capabilities on an individual basis requires a productive values system, motivation to grow, and discipline.

Values

In chapter 7, page 193, five different approaches to values acquisition are mentioned: socialization, behavioristic, humanistic, values clarification, and developmentalist. To a greater or lesser degree all these approaches are present in any given classroom situation whether or not the teacher consciously chooses to incorporate them into the teaching-learning activities. Each student absorbs values from the class social structure. In the normal course of conducting the class, each teacher reinforces some values and inhibits others. The varying psychological and emotional states of the students cause them to accept some values, reject others, and change those they already have. Values are clarified during discussion sessions, and problem-solving strategies and cognitive skills that lead to an increasingly mature and complex values system are acquired as part of the educational process.

However, more can and should be done. All students need to develop a personal values system, and classroom activities can help meet this need. The position taken in this book is that the values clarification approach offers the greatest potential in education at the moment. In the first place, proponents of this approach seek to clarify values, not teach them. This is probably the only approach acceptable to the various elements in a pluralistic society. Therefore, values clarification is a practical and acceptable classroom procedure as long as the teacher does not use clarification procedures to pry into personal and sensitive matters. In the second place, techniques developed for clarifying values in recent years permit students to examine their own values in respect to the values of others without feeling obligated to take certain positions or be ashamed of their choices. In the third place, this approach serves very well as a vehicle for examining cultural similarities and differences without threatening the students' own cultural values. (See chapter 14, page 387.) And in the fourth place, values clarification techniques can be used in second-language classes as the basis for meaningful communicative activities. (See chapter 10, pages 300–2; chapter 11, page 322; and chapter 12, page 349.)

The main tenets to be followed in including values activities in class are restraint and freedom. The teacher must limit the topics selected in order that delicate and inappropriate subjects can be avoided. An anything-goes philosophy might be damaging to the emotional health of individual students. Values activities are not substitutes for sensitivity sessions or psychological counseling. Too, the teacher must put values activities in perspective with other class needs and activities. Values clarification can be an important asset in the class, but it should not be allowed to dominate classroom activities. Once the questions or activities have been selected, any member of the class including the teacher should feel free to participate or not participate. An atmosphere of tolerance and nonjudgment is essential if values activities are to be successful.

Before the teacher undertakes values clarification activities, she should make the ground rules clear to all students. They should understand that there are *no* correct answers, that they are *free* to answer or not to answer any questions, and that they have the *right* to ask the teacher any question she asks them.

Simon et al. (1972) have prepared a handbook containing seventy-nine values clarification strategies. One example is the "proud whip" (pp. 134–35). In this activity, class members consider what they are proud of regarding some specific area or issue. The point is made that "proud" in this activity refers to things they really feel good about. The authors also stress that skipping questions is all right, since one cannot be expected to have values concerning all questions.

Achievement Motivation

Students may be motivated in numerous ways. They may, for example, be motivated to do well in class or do poorly. As Mouly (1973, p. 358) puts it, "The child is always motivated." Generally, when teachers talk about motivation, they are referring to students' efforts to learn. Thus, in this section the term *motivation* is used to mean "achievement motivation."

Motivation does not imply fun and games. Motivation does not necessarily imply interest in the task itself. Motivation is not synonymous with either noise or silence. Motivation, such as in those cases in which motivation is so high that extreme and debilitating anxieties are produced, is not always beneficial. Poor motivation is not necessarily the fault of the teacher, since influences on motivation are not limited to the classroom. Teacher enthusiasm, for example, may not be a motivating influence on all students. Motivation is not a cure-all for all instructional problems and difficulties. Motivation is not achieved by a bag full of tricks. Motivation is not generated in isolation. Motivation cannot convert any and all students into superior students. Factors that enhance motivation are not the same for all students. Motivation is not expressed in the same way by all students. Any given teacher does not motivate all students equally well. Neither student nor teacher motivation is equally high all the time.

Motivation does imply some incentive that causes the individual to participate in activity leading toward a goal and to persevere until the goal is reached. Motivation is affected by student self-concept, values, needs, and goals. Motivation is influenced by success or failure in past classroom activities, by the social environment of the class, and by teacher behavior. Motivation may be intrinsic as in the case of anxiety, need to achieve, self-concept, and aspirations, or extrinsic as in the case of sociocultural influences and social reinforcers (Schwartz, 1972). Sustaining classroom motivation requires continuous attention and effort. Motivation is an outgrowth of attending to both cognitive and affective-social variables. In order to achieve and maintain high motivation in class the teacher should be sensitive to individual differences in motivational influences and in the ways in which each student demonstrates his motivation.

Theories of motivation   Basically, there are two theories of behavior. In the first, the external, motivation is not a factor (Gage & Berliner, 1975). External theorists emphasize "more direct control of student behavior through the systematic manipulation of relevant incentives along Skinnerian lines of selective reinforcement of progressively more adequate behavior" (Mouly, 1973, p. 355). That is, given the appropriate reinforcement the act will be repeated in response to the activating stimulus. In the classroom, students participate because they receive selected, positive reinforcement. In the second theory, the internal, motivation is an important factor in prompting and controlling behavior. Internal theorists conceive of individual action as being the result of internal drives. Actions are planned and purposive. In the classroom, students participate because they conceive of any given activity as being enjoyable in and of itself or as a means of achieving a goal.

Types of achievement motivation   Students may be motivated by a *desire to know*. For these students, learning is a goal in and of itself. No additional incentives are needed. They seek to understand and to acquire new information simply because it is there. Other students are motivated as a means of *enhancing* their *self-concepts*. Thus, they strive for success, however that may be defined. Alternatively, ego-deflating failure is avoided just as vigorously.

Students may be motivated by *goals*, either short-term or long-term. Short-term goals range from a gold star, to a party in class on Friday, to a desired grade on a quiz. Long-term goals range from wanting to be able to speak a second language to wanting to graduate from college. Students may also be motivated by *social factors*. They are trying to please their parents, they are responding to peer group standards important to their social standing in the class, or they are working to attain a certain power status in the group (Ausubel & Robinson, 1969; McClelland & Watson, 1973).

Individual students may be activated to participate by any or all types of achievement motivation. The teacher should be aware of each type with regard to each individual student and use any or all with each student to maximize classroom effort and perseverance.

Conditions of motivation   One of the major problems of contemporary education is to motivate students. What are the conditions that enhance motivation? Oliva (1972, p. 269) lists the following:
1. Students learn when they conceive of themselves as capable individuals.
2. Students learn when they are dealing with materials geared to their level.
3. Students learn when they see purpose in their activities and study.
4. Students learn when they see their studies as important.
5. Students often do not like easy or trivial work. They grumble at difficult class work, but they respect demanding education.
6. Students are motivated if they live in a secure environment.
7. Students are motivated if they have the opportunity to express their psychological needs for success, recognition, and approval.
8. Students are motivated if they feel the learning is for them and not for the teacher.
9. Students are motivated when the subject matter is interesting.
10. Students are motivated when they have some opportunity to make decisions, enter into the planning, and feel responsibility for participating.
11. Students are motivated when they experience more success than failure. If they feel incapable, they will give up.

Improving motivation   Within the context of the conditions of learning and within the context of the class itself, what can be done to promote achievement motivation? The teacher should recognize that to improve motivation she will be dealing with cognitive, affective, social, and perhaps even psychomotor variables. The following recommendations are being offered as positive suggestions for improving student achievement motivation:

COGNITIVE
1. Clarify for the students what the goals of the course, the unit, and the class are.

2. Assist each student to set and achieve goals related to those of the rest of the class.
3. Give the students feedback as to their progress (Klausmeier & Ripple, 1971, pp. 328–29).
4. Summarizing important content of each class at the end of the period will help the students to focus on what they should be learning.
5. Résumés and review sessions help students organize the material in their minds (Oliva, 1972, p. 272).
6. Use examples familiar to the students. That is, learning of new material should begin with what the students already know.
7. If used appropriately, tests and grades do motivate students to do better work academically.
8. Classwork should require the use of previously learned material (Gage & Berliner, 1975, pp. 338, 347, 348).

AFFECTIVE

1. Avoid practices that produce temporary stress or continued anxiety.
2. Take advantage of each student's need to achieve in some area.
3. Give the students the opportunity to talk about their concerns.
4. Develop a system of rewards for good work or good conduct. Be prepared to punish poor work or misconduct as necessary (Klausmeier & Ripple, 1971, pp. 328–29).
5. Try to make the content of the course as close to existing student interests as possible.
6. Use audio-visual aids whenever possible within reason and within the teacher's available time and expertise to prepare.
7. Plan for a variety of activities during the class period.
8. Give assignments that appeal to the students, that they can accomplish, and that will improve their class performance the following day (Oliva, 1972, p. 271).
9. Use praise both during the class period and when grading papers.
10. If used inappropriately, tests and grades may create attitude problems with regard to the course.
11. Take advantage of any and all opportunities to arouse suspense and curiosity.
12. Do the unexpected sometimes.
13. When applying concepts, use contexts that are interesting to the students.
14. Simulations and learning games may be used in appropriate situations to enhance learning and heighten motivation (Gage & Berliner, 1975, pp. 335–48).
15. Success breeds success (Mouly, 1973, p. 359).

SOCIAL

1. Discuss desired "prosocial" behavior with the class (Klausmeier & Ripple, 1972, p. 329).[1]
2. Try to establish an environment in which desired social behavior is the accepted norm. Desired behaviors are rewarded and undesirable behavior ignored or punished. If the teacher can gain the cooperation and good will of the class social leaders, their social power and prestige will do a great deal to assist in this goal.
3. Examine the social climate of the class, the school, and the community. The teacher must operate within the limits imposed by these climates.
4. The teacher should comprehend the power relationships operating in the classroom. He has various powers inherent in his position as the teacher: reward power, coercive power, legitimate power, referent power, and expert power. These powers give the teacher the advantage over the students. At the same time, he should realize that the students have a degree of social power also that can be employed individually and collectively to influence teacher behavior (Gage & Berliner, 1975, pp. 349–54). Obviously, the teacher should be responsive to student attitudes without being subject to manipulation by them.
5. Competition can be a motivating force in class. Classes can compete with other classes or with themselves, and students can compete with other students or themselves. Competition with self offers the greatest potential. Competition with others should not be allowed to reach the point at which it has a debilitating effect on some students.

The preceding recommendations are all concerned with what the teacher should attempt to do. There are also things that should not happen to participating students if high levels of motivation are to be maintained. Gage and Berliner (1975, pp. 350–51) offer the following list of warnings:

1. Students should not be made to suffer a loss of self-esteem as a result of trying to understand a concept or complete an exercise.
2. They should not be subject to physical discomfort such as prolonged periods of sitting, being unable to hear what is going on in the front of the room, being unable to see a visual located at the chalkboard, etc.
3. They should not be told that the content is uninteresting, that the book is no good, or that they will not be able to understand new material being introduced.
4. They should not be continually asked to put effort into work at which they are not achieving any success.

---

[1]*Prosocial behavior* refers to actions that promote cooperative, productive social relationships.

5. They should not be asked to take tests over material that has not been taught.
6. They should not have to take tests containing trivial or incomprehensible questions.
7. They should not be asked to learn material that is beyond their present capability level.
8. They should not be asked to continue without complete and clear indications of how well they are doing in the class.
9. They should not be asked to keep up with students who are superior learners.
10. They should not be grouped in a section of inferior students.
11. They should not be asked to compete in a class in which only a few students have the possibility of getting an A or a B, i.e., in a class graded on a curve.
12. They should not have to sit through repetitive, boring, unchallenging teacher presentations. For example, having the teacher read material out of the text is not likely to arouse student enthusiasm.
13. They should not be expected to be interested in and learn material in which the teacher herself is uninterested.
14. They should not be expected to behave differently from the teacher or the class social leaders.

Improving motivation in second-language classes   Second-language educators have also focused their attention on ways and means of improving motivation. In many instances their suggestions parallel those previously outlined in this chapter. However, they do have additional points to offer. The following recommendations have been put forth as being beneficial in improving motivation in second-language classes:

COGNITIVE
1. Students remember the material better if it is based on a real-life situation.
2. Language instruction is better if language is considered to be a creative process (Grittner, 1974b).

AFFECTIVE
1. Enjoyable classroom learning activities increase motivation (Grittner, 1974b).
2. A positive attitude toward the speakers of the second language, toward learning a second language, toward the second-language class, and toward the second-language teacher improves motivation. Integrative motivation, i.e., motivation to get to know members of the second-language community and perhaps to become a member of that community, is said to be a

stronger motivator than instrumental motivation, i.e., the desire to complete second-language study as a means toward an unrelated goal (Gardner & Smythe, 1975).

3. Students tend to participate more in those activities that are under their own control, at least to some extent. The following are some tactics that can be used in the classroom.
   a. Let the students ask the questions.
   b. Ask brighter students to lead the class in some activities.
   c. Have students prepare their own questions over a reading assignment and ask them in class.
   d. Let students generate and give stimuli for drills (Jarvis, 1973, p. 12).
   e. Discuss your goals and methods with the students. Try to get a continuing reading on their attitudes and reactions.

4. Students prefer activities that permit them some degree of individuality in completing the task.
   a. Ask question that lend themselves to a variety of answers. Asking student preferences is one possibility.
   b. Teach pattern variations, and encourage individual choice of response.
   c. Ask students to bring conversational stimuli to class and to talk about them.
   d. Recognize individuality in class (Jarvis, 1973, p. 12).

5. Activities should be relevant to the real language world. As Disick (1972) points out, first-language speakers do not go around reciting passages and asking the listener to pick the correct answer from A, B, or C choices.

SOCIAL

1. The use of small groups in class increases participation and improves student attitude (Disick, 1972).

   In achievement motivation, as in cognitive learning, the desired model is an internally directed individual. However, this is a goal, not an educational prerequisite. After all, if all the students already possessed all those qualities and knowledge hopefully promoted by the educational program, the educational system would be forced either to adopt new curricula or to admit that their services were unnecessary. For those individuals who have not reached the stage of the self-starting, internally directed student, external procedures must be utilized. In fact, the teacher should be prepared to teach in the absence of motivation while applying external motivators to arouse interest. However, steps to promote internal tendencies should be undertaken for student personal and social growth. One interesting recommendation is that the teacher discuss the various causes and consequences of motivation with students. One theory is that getting the student to think about motivation and to understand it will improve his motivation (Gage & Berliner, 1975).

One goal for each student should be participation and perseverance to goal completion. Any and all means available to the teacher for fostering this goal should be explored and implemented. Needless to say, he will not always succeed with every individual, but the effort should be made. By arousing and sustaining motivation, the teacher can increase enrollments and decrease the attrition rate in second-language study.

Discipline

The word *discipline* has been misused and abused to the point at which the mere mention of it conjures up frightening images of unruly students and methodical repressive measures on the part of the teacher and the administration. In the minds of many, *discipline* is synonymous with punishment of some type. As used here, the word *discipline* refers to those rules and measures that promote and maintain "learning-appropriate behavior" in the classroom specifically and to those rules and measures that promote and maintain appropriate behavior in society in general (Gnagey, 1971, p. 193). Ideally, this behavior is self-directed. Whenever self-control is lacking, however, external measures and regulations must be imposed. An internal approach to discipline results in inner growth and self-discipline. On the other hand, inappropriate use of external measures results in dependency on authority, coercion, restraint, and punishment (Carnot, 1973).

The acquisition of disciplined behavior is an absolute essential in the educational process both in and out of the classroom. In the first place, discipline is necessary if the individual is to learn the social group's cultural standards of conduct. Second, without discipline the individual cannot develop such adult personality characteristics as dependability, self-reliance, self-control, persistence, and the ability to tolerate frustration. Third, discipline is the basis for the development of conscience. Fourth, discipline is an important factor in promoting children's emotional security (Ausubel & Robinson, 1969). Fifth, social order is dependent upon mutually accepted rules of social relationships. And sixth, intellectual growth cannot rise to its maximum potential in the absence of mental discipline. Spock (1974, p. xi), often accused of being the father of the permissive generation, says, ". . . that parents should stick by their ethical convictions and feel no hesitation in showing them to their children; that they should ask their children for cooperation and respect; that children who are held up to high ideals and considerate behavior are not only a lot pleasanter to live with but they are happier themselves." There is no reason to expect a different reaction in the classroom. Discipline is indispensable in learning, personality development, and productive social interaction.

Classroom discipline patterns Based on his philosophy, the teacher may adopt one of the following general approaches to discipline. If he chooses to go in to class with the tough guy attitude to show the students who is boss, he is following the *authoritarian* approach. If he assumes the philosophy that kids will be kids and that anything goes, he is assuming the *permissive* approach. If he prefers to establish a classroom organization in which the students help formulate and enforce the rules and regulations, he is taking a *democratic* approach. What are the effects of each? The authoritarian approach tends to produce outward quiet, acquiescence, and conformity, but may lead to inner resentment and rebellion. A permissive atmosphere not only disrupts learning-appropriate behavior for many students in many instances, it also may create feelings of insecurity and resentment toward the class and the teacher. The goal of the democratic approach is to cultivate internal self-discipline (Carnot, 1973).

Approaches to discipline As is true in learning, language, and motivation, teachers may take one of two basic approaches to establishing a disciplined, productive atmosphere in their classrooms. They may take the internal approach, in which students are responsible for their behavior. Or they may take the external approach, in which teachers are responsible for student behavior. With the internal approach, teachers outline the ground rules to be followed in class along with why each is desirable. Both teachers and students may work together, however, to select the rules and regulations they feel necessary to establish a learning atmosphere in class.

With the external approach, teachers decide what behaviors they want in the classroom and attempt to condition those behaviors in the students by means of selective reinforcement. This approach, called *behavior modification* or *contingency management,* is highly recommended by Skinnerian psychologists and others, and it is appropriate at this point to describe the basic procedures employed by its proponents. Using behavior modification techniques, teachers first choose an example of desired behavior. Second, they determine how common the behavior is. Third, they choose a system for reinforcing this behavior. Fourth, they plan how to administer the reward or reinforcement. Fifth, they begin to reinforce any actions in the direction of the desired behavior. This procedure consists of reinforcing actions closer and closer to the goal until desired behavior has been conditioned to insure proper student actions. Reinforcement may be any type of reward from a nod of approval to some tangible token such as a candy bar or a package of gum. Behavior modification practitioners believe that permanent changes in behavior are best induced by positive reinforcers. Undesired actions are ignored, within reason, and goal behavior is obtained by means of positive reinforcers

(George, 1973). Mouly (1973) feels that behavior modification techniques are promising with students who do not have behavior patterns suited for learning behavior in the classroom and who are accustomed to immediate and tangible rewards.

Types of behavior problems Gage and Berliner (1975) divide behavior problems into two major categories: those involving too much undesirable behavior and those involving too little desirable behavior. Too much undesirable behavior includes physical aggression, being overly friendly during the class period with other members of the class, attention seeking, challenging the teacher's authority, and critical dissension. Too little desirable behavior includes failure to pay attention, failure to show interest in work or to prepare assignments, failure to become a member of the class social group, failure to follow rules about attendance and promptness, and failure to develop independent behavior. The authors recommend following a behavior modification pattern in order to eliminate or reduce too much undesirable behavior. The teacher is advised to ignore the behavior, to get the other students to ignore it, to promote desirable behavior through reinforcement, to avoid those situations that seem to encourage such behavior, and as a last resort to punish the offending student. The opposite approach is taken to encourage and stimulate increased instances of desirable behavior.

Discipline in the classroom Good discipline is not synonymous with absolute quiet. Often students, especially those in a second-language class, must be actively involved in using the language to be learned. Nor should the teacher expect the staid, stilted atmosphere of the Latin grammar schools. Although she may not be interfering with the progress of the class, a quiet student may not be learning anything. In fact, the quiet student may be mentally miles or hours away from the classroom. Good discipline may or may not be related to the noise level in the classroom. The classroom is a place to learn. Any study behavior that disrupts the learning process, her own or that of other students, can be considered a discipline problem. This behavior may be quiet or noisy; it may be malicious and sly or open and unintentional. In either case, the teacher's job is to reestablish and maintain the learning situation.

Before the prospective teacher enters the classroom, he should realize that rapport is not a matter of being able to entertain the students or of being their "buddy." In spite of what they may say, students need a teacher they respect rather than an overgrown adolescent with whom to clown around. Rapport implies a classroom atmosphere in which learning is taking place. It is this establishment of learning situations that is the teacher's prime task. Unless he can assume that responsibility, he should not become a teacher. He may sympathize and empathize with the students but always from his position as a teacher. Crossing the line to become, in effect, a student again destroys his image as a teacher and neutralizes his potential effectiveness. The teacher must admit that, in the words of Thomas Wolfe, "You can't go home again."

Before entering the classroom, the prospective teacher should also determine to expect courtesy at all times in the classroom. Much undisciplined behavior is simply a matter of bad manners, and the teacher should emphasize respect for the rights and feelings of others. In addition to courtesy, he should also determine to establish and maintain certain standards of work and behavior in the classroom that will encourage the students to be and do their best at all times. Permissiveness and lowered standards aggravate and magnify discipline problems rather than solve them. The students may forget all the language they learn, but they should remember the importance of courtesy, self-discipline, and sincere effort to do one's best.

The first order of business with regard to discipline is to make the rules clear to everyone in the class. Establishing the guidelines for the class to follow is not a matter of "laying down the law," but one of making concise statements comprehensible to all. However, stating the rule is only the beginning. After this comes the process of establishing the validity and applicability of the rules. Within a short period of time the teacher can expect to face the first test case. The classroom is a social situation, and the students must determine in practice the limits of behavior (Ausubel & Robinson, 1969). Stenhouse (1967, p. 52) describes this process in the following fashion:

> The class explores the situation by a process which might be called "testing the limits." There are inevitably areas of uncertainty in their relationships with a new teacher, areas in which the practice of teachers diverges. The class sets about clearing up these uncertainties by confronting the teacher with test cases. One might say that the class experiments with the teacher. It may not do this consciously and in planned fashion, but every experienced teacher will recognize the process we have in mind. It is almost as if the teacher were the subject of an experiment in social psychology in which the class plays the role of the experimenter, seeking to discover the laws which will help them to predict, and perhaps even to control, their teacher's behavior. Only in the light of these laws can they shape their own reaction. Thus the class seeks to discover, for example, under what circumstances the teacher is prepared to allow them to talk to one another, to walk about the room, or to read their own books. It may also try to find out whether it can seduce him from his purpose by introducing red herrings, whether it can embarrass him by introducing sexually loaded questions, or whether it can make him lose the thread of a mathematical explanation by interrupting him with questions.
>
> By its very nature this experiment turns into an attempt to discover the limits to which the class can go: the lowest standards of work the teacher will accept, the extremes of disorder which he will tolerate. The class "tries to get away with things," because this is the only way in which it is possible to trace the boundary line between what is acceptable and what is unacceptable.[2]

---

[2]Stenhouse (1967, p. 52). Reprinted by permission.

In addition to these natural testings of teacher authority there may be threats to the teacher's self-esteem. These threats can come in many forms. For example, they may be positive comments about other classes and other teachers with the direct implication that the class of the teacher in question falls far short of the others. They may be direct and cutting remarks about the class or the teacher, or a nickname designed to embarrass the teacher. As shattering as these may be to the teacher's ego, the teacher has no adequate means at her disposal for combatting these tactics. In fact, overt reaction can only worsen the situation. The best approach is to ignore the remarks and assume that they are of a temporary nature, which they likely are (Ausubel & Robinson, 1969).

The first few weeks of the school year are especially important in establishing the classroom atmosphere that the teacher desires. During this period, the teacher should eliminate all possible discipline problems before they become established habits. The teacher may relax somewhat her strict discipline later in the year if she so desires, but "cracking down" is almost impossible. Students can accept a teacher who expects proper discipline in the classroom, but they resent a teacher who turns out to be a lion in sheep's clothing. The opposite situation, i.e., a teacher who eases up once the desired classroom discipline pattern has been established, creates no problems for the pleasantly surprised students, but the teacher has to suffer the consequences if she relinquishes control to the students.

The best approach to discipline is to avoid circumstances that create discipline problems. The following suggestions concern ways of preventing the occurrence of discipline problems during the class hour:

1. Start the class promptly and with a spirit of enthusiasm and vigor.
2. Get everyone's attention before starting the recitation.
3. Have all possible material that may be needed written on the chalkboard before the bell rings.
4. Have your plan and all teaching aids ready.
5. Learn to "ride the class with your eyes." The teacher should be able to see all the students all the time.
6. Talk to all the students and ask them to talk to the entire class. The class recitation period is not appropriate for a series of private conversations between the students called upon and the teacher.
7. Call on those students who are beginning to lose interest.
8. Emphasize a "we" feeling of class responsibility for all that transpires.
9. Encourage all students to attempt to answer the questions silently whether they have been called on or not.
10. Study the seating arrangement of the students. Those who affect each other adversely may need to be moved.
11. Be businesslike.

12. Watch your voice. Be expressive, and speak loudly and clearly.
13. Stand in class and move around.
14. Keep the pace moving.
15. Learn to "feel the pulse" of the class, so that changes can be made as the class progresses. For example, there is no need to spend ten minutes on an activity if the students obviously do not need the practice. At other times, the teacher may need to spend ten minutes on some exercise that he had expected to do more quickly.
16. Hold every member of the class responsible for all that takes place during the period.
17. State the question before calling on the student.
18. Call on students in a random fashion rather than by rows.
19. Have a variety of activities.
20. Use examples in preference to abstract explanations.
21. Keep those students at their seats busy during chalkboard exercises.
22. And last, but certainly not least, know the material before attempting to teach it.

In addition to the positive practices presented in the preceding list the teacher should not do the following:

1. Use sarcasm.
2. Play favorites.
3. Insist on apologies.
4. Make threats.
5. Give overly difficult assignments.
6. Punish the entire class for the misbehavior of one or a few students.
7. Appeal to fear.
8. Get sidetracked by irrelevant questions.
9. Tie herself to the textbook.
10. Use vocabulary over the students' heads.
11. Talk too rapidly or nervously.

If discipline problems do occur, the teacher should first ask himself if his teaching merits the attention he expects. Second, he should try to find out more about the student causing the problem. Misconduct may have nothing at all to do with the class itself. Economic and social status, physical health and development, mental ability, problems at home, community conditions, group influence, emotional stability, etc.—all influence class conduct. A private conference with the student may help to determine the problem and to improve conduct in the class. If not, a counselor or a dean may be able to help in solving the problem.

If the student does not respond to a personal chat, the teacher may be forced to discipline him in front of the class. The teacher should attempt to do so in a dignified manner which will preserve the respect the students have for him. At the same time, he should be ever conscious of the student's own worth as a person and never do anything that may cause the student to lose his self-respect.

When correcting inappropriate behavior, the teacher should be conscious of the "ripple effect" her actions may have. For example, if she corrects one of the class leaders for some act or in such a way that the goodwill of the high-prestige student is lost, the ripple effect among the class members will be negative. Focusing on appropriate behavior rather than negative will have a positive ripple effect. A program so set up that any student can earn approval and privileges will have a positive ripple effect. Punishment that is restitution will have a positive ripple effect; punishment that is retribution will have a negative ripple effect. Reprimands that are clear have a positive ripple effect: for example, "John, please stop rattling that magazine and do your algebra problems." Reprimands that are unclear do not have a positive effect: for example, "Now you cut that out back there and get busy." Reprimands that are firm, delivered with an I-mean-it tone of voice, will have a positive ripple effect: for example, "It is time to start the homework now." Tentative reprimands will in all likelihood not accomplish the teacher's wishes: for example, "I wish we could be more quiet this morning" (Gnagey, 1971).

Continuous, conscious disruption of classroom activities cannot be permitted. Nor should the teacher ignore his responsibility to help each student develop productive behavior patterns. Glasser (1975) offers a plan of action to foster learning appropriate behavior to be used in those instances in which special attention is needed. First, the teacher makes friends with the student. Second, the questionable behavior is specified. Third, he and the student evaluate the results of the student's actions. Fourth, a plan to improve is formulated. Fifth, the teacher gets a commitment from the student to change his behavior. Sixth, the teacher accepts no excuses for not following the plan of action. He asks the student when he is going to do what he said, and he insists that the student take responsibility for his actions. Seventh, the teacher expects the student to continue following the rules. The student must learn that the rules and regulations are to be obeyed and that the teacher will not accept anything else. At no time does the teacher ridicule the student or make fun of him. He helps him formulate a definite plan and to make a commitment toward improved conduct. If progress is not demonstrated, the student is asked to spend some time alone in a teacher-designated area to think about taking steps to improve.

In conclusion, a productive learning atmosphere in the classroom requires a disciplined, responsive class. The teacher should not shrink from this responsibility of establishing a learning-oriented rapport with the students. Often those with whom he has the most difficulties later become his most ardent supporters. Far from resenting his standards and his efforts, they respect him for these very qualities.

CLASSROOM CLIMATE

In addition to self-concept needs and self-actualization needs, students also have social needs. Edwards (1974) says that every child desires to be accepted, to be with a group, and to be a part of that group. Thus, the assumption can be made that a class characterized by congenial, supportive, harmonious social relationships is more conducive to academic achievement than one in which this atmosphere is missing. If students like each other and work together in a productive manner, they not only like the class better, they accomplish more. Of course, the importance of social interaction varies from individual to individual, but a positive *esprit de corps* has beneficial effects among all students as long as they feel a part of the group. Needless to say, feeling a part of such a group is much easier than in the case of an antagonistic group, and given the right circumstances and teacher encouragement many students can be won over in spite of their initial reluctance to participate.

Just what this desirable classroom climate consists of and how to achieve it are not easily determined, but the experienced teacher is aware of its reality and importance. Any visitor can walk into a classroom and recognize whether or not it is present. A teacher may be able to establish such a climate with one class and not with another. It may be present for a period of time and disappear due to problems that appear in the class. A class that seemed unresponsive may suddenly achieve that cohesiveness sought for by the teacher but not predictable earlier in the year.

Aspects of Classroom Climate

Trickett and Moos (1973) have developed a classroom environment scale that can be used to measure classroom climate. The nine categories measuring the social environment in junior high and high school classrooms are as follows:

1. Involvement—student attention and interest.
2. Affiliation—extent to which students know each other and work together.
3. Support—teacher interest in and concern for the students.

4. Task orientation—orientation of class activities toward the accomplishment of academic objectives.
5. Competition—stress on academic competition.
6. Order and organization—organization and orderliness of classroom procedures.
7. Rule clarity—clarity of rules and student comprehension of the rules.
8. Teacher control—amount and extent of rules governing student conduct.
9. Innovation—different types of learning activities and classroom interaction.

Improving Classroom Climate

What are the conditions that foster an energetic relationship among the members of the class? First, the teacher must like students and like to teach. She must want to help the students grow and be willing to interact with them in teaching-learning situations. Second, she must be able to handle the classroom management chores efficiently. Third, she must be willing to help each student develop a positive, functioning self-concept. Fourth, she must be helpful in assisting each student to actualize his own potential cognitively and in the affective-social domain. Fifth, she should include opportunities in the class for the students to get acquainted. And sixth, she has to be flexible as she attempts to achieve a productive relationship with each group of students. For example, classroom environments may be competitive, cooperative, or individualistic. She may try any or all of these environments in various combinations with different students seeking the right combination for each particular class.

Moskowitz (1973) takes a more scientific approach to developing a positive, productive learning atmosphere in the classroom. Basing her suggestions on interaction analysis, she urges second-language teachers to consider their classroom behavior. By using an interaction matrix, the teacher can quantify the different types of behavior employed during the class hour.[3] Teacher talk may be of two types: direct or indirect. Direct teacher talk includes lecturing or giving information, giving directions, and criticizing. Indirect teacher talk includes accepting students' feelings, praising, encouraging, joking, using students' ideas, and asking questions. The premise upon which interaction analysis rests is that indirect teacher behavior results in more positive student attitudes. Too, by limiting the amount of teacher talk, the teacher can get more students involved in the class for a larger portion of the class hour.

---

[3]An *interaction matrix* is a grid used to record and later to quantify direct or indirect teacher behavior in the classroom.

Rogers (1968) makes two recommendations for improving classroom climate that are of special interest. First, the teacher's actions should demonstrate trust in and respect for students. And second, the teacher should be sensitive to the need for keeping the psychological climate of the class in the comfort zone.

WHAT DO STUDENTS WANT?

Most of this chapter has focused on students' affective-social needs. To what extent do these needs coincide with what students want? To what extent do students' wants coincide with what teachers think they want? Is the teacher's primary responsibility to keep the students happy or to satisfy their growth needs? Is it possible to satisfy needs and keep the students happy? Is it possible to keep students happy without satisfying growth needs?

This author thinks that, in the final analysis, it is impossible to keep the students happy without satisfying growth needs. This dissatisfaction may not be expressed overtly, but it is reflected in student attitudes and actions. The following quotes from student letters to the editor of a newspaper support this opinion. To the teachers at his school a high school senior writes:

> Discipline was often very bad in your classes, but as I observed your own lack of self-discipline from the manner in which you dressed, wished to be called by your first name, and sat on top of your desk, I knew that it was not all the fault of the class for such an atmosphere of unlearning.
>
> Many days were spent in doing things to entertain me and I finally got bored of being entertained.[4]

A student school board member evaluates the open classrooms in a middle school as follows:

> I would say that at the most there were five students who looked in any way like they were doing history; I must say that I can't fault the rest for just sitting around, because it was too noisy to hear yourself think, much less study. This seemed to be the pattern for just about all the classes in the open areas, some worked, most didn't, and the teachers were too busy trying to quiet down the unruly that they would give none of the individual aid that this system was to so miraculously make possible.
>
> They [the students] are being lulled into the deception that school is a place where you do—or don't do—what you want.[5]

A survey conducted by Megiveron (1975) produced surprising disparities when he compared student opinions regarding selected aspects of the school

---

[4]Reprinted from *The Charlottesville Daily Progress*, Charlottesville, Virginia, April 30, 1975.
[5]Reprinted from *The Charlottesville Daily Progress*, Charlottesville, Virginia, April 9, 1975.

program with how teachers believed the students felt. The results with regard to school rules, grades, and homework, for example, were as follows:

**Table 9.1: Student Opinions vs. Teachers'
Views of Student Opinions**

	No Complaints	Occasional Complaints	Many Complaints	Disagree Often	Never Pleased	No Answer
School Rules						
Students	14.7%	59.2%	14.4%	6.2%	3.6%	1.9%
Teachers	7.5%	47.5%	40.0%	5.0%	0.0%	
Grades						
Students	18.4%	49.5%	17.7%	5.8%	6.4%	2.2%
Teachers	15.0%	27.5%	40.0%	12.5%	5.0%	
Homework						
Students	21.0%	46.2%	16.8%	5.4%	8.1%	2.5%
Teachers	10.0%	25.0%	40.0%	22.5%	2.5%	

Source: Megiveron (1975, p. 46).

Megiveron (1975, p. 48) states that the student attitudes were much more positive than the teachers gave them credit for, and he poses two questions. "Are teachers becoming more negative than their students?" "Can student attitudes become more positive if staff attitudes are more positive about students?"

A survey of what students want in the future indicated little change from the desires of past generations. Overall, students are cautiously optimistic. Most of all, they want to be happy. Both boys and girls want to achieve their goals, and they express a willingness to work hard to achieve those goals (Cromer, 1975).

Sources of Student Satisfaction and Dissatisfaction

Beelick (1973) identified scholastic achievement, personal recognition, school activities, and interesting schoolwork as sources of satisfaction to students. On the other hand, students were dissatisfied with teachers' behavior, interpersonal relations with other students, and school policy and administration. The author also points out that some students may have a psychological set for dissatisfaction.

Student Evaluation of Teachers

Student evaluation of instruction has become increasingly common in recent years. Although more commonly practiced at the university level, some students at the high school level also have the opportunity to rate the work of their teachers. The rating sheets for evaluating teachers and instruction are of many varieties. However, many of the same factors are included in a sizeable portion of the forms. By means of factor analysis, Greenwood et al. (1973) identified the eight most important factors in student evaluation of college teaching practices. They were: facilitation of learning, obsolescence of presentation, commitment to teaching, evaluation, voice communication, openness, currency of knowledge, and rapport. Field (1973) states that students consider skill, rapport, and interaction as the three most important teacher qualities. An examination of these factors reveals that students are aware of cognitive, personal, and social factors affecting the quality of education. An objective reaction to this data compels teachers to recognize that students are rather knowledgeable regarding the teaching-learning process.

Student Opinions about Second-Language Classes

Walker (1973) lists the opinions of university students about language teaching. Although obtained from a sample of university students, the results appear to be typical of second-language students in general. The following is a summary of what the students want. First, they want opportunities to use the language in situations of interest to them. They do not believe that the goal of the course should be learning grammar. Second, they do not want to be corrected for every minor grammatical error. They feel that constant correction causes them to lose confidence and to be unable to keep their minds on what they are trying to say. Third, they want teachers to use the second language more in class and to cover less material. Fourth, they want to study with teachers who are interested in them as individuals, who are trying to help students learn and enjoy second-language study, who are well prepared, and who are trying to teach a living language. They do not want teachers who treat students with contempt. Fifth, they want more study of culture.

CONCLUSION

As teachers interact with their students, they should remember that education is not synonymous with entertainment. In the past, learning was supposed to be disagreeable; now many seem to be of the opinion that learning should be one continuous sequence of fun and games. Learning may be almost anything as long as growth is present and students are gaining some educational goals. This philosophy is reflected on a plaque to the memory of William Holding Echols on the lawn at the University of Virginia that states, "By precept and example, he taught many generations of students with ruthless insistence that the supreme values are self-respect, integrity of mind, contempt of fear, and hatred of sham." Mr. Echols's image hardly corresponds to that type commonly portrayed in contemporary educational literature, but those of his former students responsible for the plaque obviously felt he helped them grow.

To meet student needs, teachers need to make a commitment to themselves and to each student to help that student grow. Some will grow more than others. Many will need different kinds of help, and all will grow in different ways. Teachers will need to be flexible in seeking means to help and persistent in assuring that their efforts bear dividends.

The purpose of education is student growth. Basically, teacher responsibility entails intellectual growth. However, in recent years the importance of affective-social variables in learning and the role teachers play in fostering personal and social growth have received increased attention. Optimum growth in desired directions is enhanced by helping each student achieve a feeling of self-worth, success, and acceptance in the class social structure. If teachers can help in these three areas, they will be helping meet student needs.

REVIEW AND APPLICATION

DEFINITIONS
1. achievement motivation, p. 253
2. classroom management, p. 242
3. discipline, p. 260
4. external vs. internal motivation, p. 254
5. interaction analysis, p. 268

DISCUSSION
1. In what ways might classroom management affect values, motivation, discipline, and learning?
2. Summarize the various aspects of classroom management.
3. What types of teacher behavior might damage student self-concept?
4. Discuss the threat of second-language study to student self-concept. How might students react to this threat? What can be done to overcome the threat?
5. What can the teacher do to improve student motivation? Name some ideas of your former teachers.
6. Which type of classroom environment do you prefer? As a teacher? As a student? Should students help formulate the rules?
7. How important is psychological climate?
8. Evaluate the disparity between student opinion and what teachers think they believe.
9. Discuss the difference in classroom techniques between internal and external approaches to motivation and discipline.

ACTIVITIES

1. Simulate motivation and discipline problems and discuss measures to take in each case.
2. Prepare a list of rules you would institute in your class. Compare your list with that of the other members of the class.
3. Prepare a student evaluation form for your students to use in evaluating your second-language class.
4. Visit at least three junior high or high school classes. In each class notice (a) classroom management practices, (b) motivation techniques of the teacher, (c) discipline, and (d) classroom climate. (If you are interested in establishing an individualized class, you should pay special attention to the handling of materials.)

SELECTED REFERENCES

Alexander, P. (1971) Classroom Management. In D. W. Allen and E. Seifman (Eds.), *The Teacher's Handbook.* Glenview, Ill.: Scott Foresman. Pp. 177–88.

Aronson, H. I. (1973) The Role of Attitudes About Languages in the Learning of Foreign Languages. *Modern Language Journal,* 57:323–29.

Ausubel, D. P., and Robinson, F. G. (1969) *School Learning: An Introduction to Educational Psychology.* New York: Holt, Rinehart and Winston. Pp. 357–58, 467, 470–71.

Beelick, D. B. (1973) Sources of Student Satisfaction and Dissatisfaction. *Journal of Educational Research,* 67:19–22.

Beniskos, J. M. (1971) The Person Teacher. *Education Digest,* 36:34–36.

Black, M. S. (1974) Academic Achievement and Self-Concept of Fourth Grade Pupils in Open Area and Traditional Learning Environments. *Dissertation Abstracts International,* 35:3323-A.

Brothers, J. (1973) Learning to Like Yourself: Self-Image. *Good Housekeeping,* 176:74–78.

Brown, H. D. (1973) Affective Variables in Second Language Teaching. *Language Learning,* 23:231–44.

Brown, J. A., and MacDougall, M. A. (1973) Teacher Consultation for Improved

Feelings of Self-Adequacy in Children. *Psychology in the Schools,* 10:320–26.

Buchholz, E. S. (1974) The Proper Study for Children: Children and Their Feelings. *Psychology in the Schools,* 11:10–15.

Carnot, J. B. (1973) Dynamic and Effective School Discipline. *Clearing House,* 48:150–53.

Cohen, E. G. (1972) Sociology and the Classroom: Setting the Conditions for Teacher-Student Interaction. *Review of Educational Research,* 42:441–52.

Cooke, M. A. (1973) Social Psychology and Foreign-Language Teaching. *Foreign Language Annals,* 7:215–23.

Cromer, J. (1975) Students Look Ahead: A Cautious Optimism. *Education Digest,* 40:32–35.

Diamond, S. C. (1974) A School Designed for SELF-ESTEEM. *Clearing House,* 48:342–46.

Disick, R. S. (1972) Developing Positive Attitudes in Intermediate Foreign Language Classes. *Modern Language Journal,* 56:417–20.

Disick, R. S. (1973) Teaching Toward Affective Goals in Foreign Languages. *Foreign Language Annals,* 7:95–101.

Ducette, J., and Wolk, S. (1972) Ability and Achievement as Moderating Variables of Student Satisfaction and Teacher Perception. *Journal of Experimental Education,* 41:12–17.

Edwards, W. J., Jr. (1974) Examining Classroom Behaviors. *School and Community,* 61:28–29.

Ellsworth, S. G. (1967) Building the Child's Self-Concept. *NEA Journal,* 56:54–56.

Field, T. W. (1973) Teacher Differences as Perceived by Students. *Improving College and University Teaching,* 21:64–66.

Finkelstein, B. J. (1973) The Search for Identity: An Institutional Problem. *Intellect,* 102:150–51.

Friedman, P. (1973) Relationship of Teacher Reinforcement to Spontaneous Student Verbalization Within the Classroom. *Journal of Educational Psychology,* 65: 59–64.

Gage, N. L., and Berliner, D. C. (1975) *Educational Psychology.* Chicago: Rand McNally. Pp. 209, 300, 315–16, 335–54, 662–68.

Gardner, R. C. (1968) Attitudes and Motivation: Their Role in Second Language Acquisition. *Foreign Language Annals,* 3:141–50.

Gardner, R. C., and Smythe, P. C. (1975) Motivation and Second-Language Acquisition. *Canadian Modern Language Review,* 31:218–30.

George, P. S. (1973) Good Discipline Through Contingency Management. *Clearing House,* 48:145–49.

Getzels, J. W. (1975) Images of the Classroom and Visions of the Learner. *Education Digest,* 40:6–9.

Glasser, W. (1975) Discipline (part of a series entitled) *Human Relations and School Discipline.* Kentucky Educational Television, April 24.

Gnagey, W. J. (1971) Classroom Discipline. In D. W. Allen and E. Seifman (Eds.), *The Teacher's Handbook.* Glenview, Ill.: Scott Foresman. Pp. 189–95.

Gowan, J. C. (1974) Effecting Change in Self-Concept. *National Association for Women Deans, Administrators, and Counselors,* 37:103–6.

Greenburg, J. S. (1975) Behavior Modification and Values Clarification and Their Research Implications. *Journal of School Health,* 45:91–95.

Greenwood, G. E., et al. (1973) Student Evaluation of College Teaching Behaviors Instrument: A Factor Analysis. *Journal of Higher Education,* 44:596–604.

Grittner, F. M. (Ed.) (1974a) *Student Motivation and the Foreign Language Teacher.* Skokie, Ill.: National Textbook.

Grittner, F. M. (1974b) Motivating Students in the Foreign Language Classroom. Paper presented at the Southern Conference on Language Teaching, Atlanta, Georgia, November.

Hancock, C. R. (1972) Guiding Teachers to Respond to Individual Differences in the Affective Domain. *Foreign Language Annals,* 6:225–27.

Harvey, S. B. (1974) A Comparison of Kindergarten Children in Multigrade and Traditional Settings on Self-Concept, Social-Emotional Development, Readiness Development, and Achievement. *Dissertation Abstracts International,* 35: 3340-A.

Humphreys, D. W., and Townsend, R. D. (1974) The Effects of Teacher- and Student-Selected Activities on the Self-Image and Achievement of High School Biology Students. *Science Education,* 58:295–301.

Jarvis, D. K. (1973) Student Initiative: Key to Motivation and Meaningful Practice. *ATSEEL Newsletter,* 15:12.

Kelly, E. W., Jr. (1974) Classroom Discussions for Growth and Democratic Problem-Solving. *Education Digest,* 40: 26–28.

Klausmeier, H. J., and Ripple, R. E. (1971) *Learning and Human Abilities: Educational Psychology.* (3rd ed.) New York: Harper & Row. Pp. 328–29.

Kohn, M., and Rosman, B. L. (1974) Social-Emotional, Cognitive, and Demographic Determinants of Poor School Achievement: Implications for a Strategy of Intervention. *Journal of Educational Psychology,* 66:267–76.

Krueger, K. G. (1974) Inner-Big-City Classroom Plan Integrates 4 Skills Immediately. *Accent on ACTFL,* 4:6–8.

LeBaron, M. T. (1974) The Marginal Student: Development or Decay. *Improving College and University Teaching,* 22:24–26.

McClelland, D. C., and Watson, R. I., Jr. (1973) Power Motivation and Risk-Taking Behavior, *Journal of Personality,* 41:121–31.

Mattocks, A. L., and Sew, C. C. (1974) The Teacher's Role in the Development of a Healthy Self-Concept in Pupils. *Education,* 74:200–4.

Megiveron, G. E. (1975) Relevancy and Morale of Students. *NASSP Bulletin,* 59:46–49.

Moskowitz, G. (1968) The Effects of Training Foreign Language Teachers in Interaction Analysis. *Foreign Language Annals,* 1:218–35.

Moskowitz, G. (1973) Don't Smile Till Christmas. *Accent on ACTFL,* 4:20–23.

Mouly, G. J. (1973) *Psychology for Effective Teaching.* (3rd ed.) New York: Holt, Rinehart and Winston. Pp. 355, 358–59.

Mueller, T. H. (1971) Student Attitudes in the Basic French Courses at the University of Kentucky. *Modern Language Journal,* 55:290–98.

Nachtmann, F. W. (1973) Let the Student Have the Last Word. *French Review,* 47:62–65.

Oliva, P. (1972) *The Secondary School Today.* New York: Intext. Pp. 240, 269–70, 272.

Papalia, A. (1970) A Study of Attrition in Foreign Language Enrollments in Four Suburban Public Schools. *Foreign Language Annals,* 4:62–67.

Papalia, A. (1973) An Assessment of Attitudes and Behaviors of Foreign Language Teachers. *Foreign Language Annals,* 7:231–36.

Papalia, A. (1974) Characteristics of Successful Language Programs. *Language Association Bulletin,* 26:7–8.

Reinert, H. (1970) Student Attitudes Toward Foreign Language—No Sale! *Modern Language Journal,* 54:107–12.

Rogers, C. (1974a) Can Learning Encompass Both Ideas and Feelings? *Education,* 95:103–14.

Rogers, C. (1974b) Questions I Would Ask Myself If I Were a Teacher. *Education,* 95:134–39.

Rogers, H. E. (1968) How's Your Classroom Climate? *Instructor,* 78:96.

Sack, R. T., and Sack, K. S. (1974) Attitudes of Teachers and Mental Hygienists about Behavior Problems of Children. *Psychology in the Schools,* 11:445–48.

Schwartz, L. L. (1972) *Educational Psychology: Focus on the Learner.* Boston: Holbrook. Pp. 153, 164.

Simon, S. B., et al. (1972) *Values Clarification: A Handbook of Practical Strategies for Teachers and Students.* New York: Hart.

Simpkins, W. S., et al. (1973) Teacher Differences as Perceived by Students. *Improving College and University Teaching,* 21:64–66.

Smith, A. N. (1971) The Importance of Attitude in Foreign Language Learning. *Modern Language Journal,* 55:82–88.

Spock, B. (1974) *Raising Children in a Difficult Time.* New York: Norton. P. xi.

Stanton, H. E. (1973) Teacher Education and the "Good Teacher." *Educational Forum,* 38:25–30.

Stenhouse, L. (1967) *Discipline in Schools.* London: Pergamon Press. P. 52.

Stern, H. H. (1975) What Can We Learn from the Good Language Learner? *Canadian Modern Language Review,* 31:304–18.

Stevick, E. W. (1973) Review Article. Counseling-Learning: A Whole Person Model for Education. *Language Learning,* 23:259–71.

Stevick, E. W. (1974) Language Instruction Must Do an About-Face. *Modern Language Journal,* 58:379–84.

Swartz, R. (1974) Education as Entertainment and Irresponsibility in the Classroom. *Science Education*, 58:119–25.

Tolar, C. J. (1975) The Mental Health of Students. *Journal of School Health*, 45:71–75.

Trickett, E. J., and Moos, R. H. (1973) Social Environment of Junior High and Senior High School Classrooms. *Journal of Educational Psychology*, 65:93–102.

Trowbridge, N. (1972) Self-Concept and Socio-Economic Status in Elementary School Children. *American Educational Research Journal*, 9:525–37.

Walker, J. L. (1973) Opinions of University Students About Language Teaching. *Foreign Language Annals*, 7:102–5.

Willis, S., and Brophy, J. (1974) Origins of Teachers' Attitudes Toward Young Children. *Journal of Educational Psychology*, 66:520–29.

Wolfe, D. E., and Howe, L. W. (1973) Personalizing Foreign Language Instruction. *Foreign Language Annals*, 7:81–90.

LISTENING COMPREHENSION

INTRODUCTION

Listening comprehension might well be called the forgotten skill in second-language learning. This tendency can perhaps be partially explained by the fact that what the learner hears is somewhat analogous to the stimulus received by a learner. Although the importance of the stimulus is not questioned, it is the response that has been the focal point of attention among learning theorists. Too, authors and teachers have apparently assumed that listening comprehension is an inevitable by-product of learning to speak.[1] Another factor is that teachers have a product in speaking and writing that allows them to correct specific errors in the use of grammar or vocabulary.

This neglect of listening comprehension certainly is not justified. Listening comprehension is at least as important as any of the other skills, perhaps more so. The phonological system of the language is acquired by listening, and oral communication is impossible without a listening skill that is much more highly developed than the speaking skill. Listening skills serve as the basis for the development of speaking. In addition, past experience clearly indicates that second-language learners are not acquiring the listening skill level necessary to function in a second-language communicative situation. The purpose of this chapter is to examine several aspects of listening comprehension and to outline an example sequence for developing listening comprehension.

The four language skills are all based on the same language system, which seems to be acquired in a series of definitely sequenced operations. First, the learners perceive a certain segment of the language and discriminate among what they consider to be the important linguistic aspects of the language. Second, they comprehend the distinctions involved and begin to formulate their own language system. Third, based on their hypotheses about the language, they develop a personal competence. Fourth, once they have the competence, they begin to use their performance skills. Fifth, as they activate the performance skills, they make adjustments, moving their language competence into line with that of the language they perceive around them. Sixth, the performance skills consist of both the receptive and the productive skills. The receptive skills are put into operation before the productive skills.

INTRODUCTION TO THE FOUR
LANGUAGE SKILLS

This book contains a separate chapter dealing with each of the four major language skills. The present chapter treats the ability to understand the spoken language. However, the fact that listening comprehension is placed first in the

---

[1]An exception is Paul Pimsleur's *Le Pont Sonore: Une Méthode Pour Comprendre le Français Parlé* (Chicago: Rand McNally, 1974), designed to teach students to understand spoken French.

series implies no priorities. Audio-lingual proponents have advocated the natural sequence in learning a second language: listening, speaking, reading, and writing. They say that this is the order in which the first language is learned. However, the hypothesized transfer from oral to written skills has not occurred in actual practice. Learning the oral skills first has not automatically improved the students' reading or writing ability.

There are two reasons why the failure of initial stress on oral skills to improve reading comprehension accordingly should not be surprising or disappointing. First, the extrapolation of theory from the first-language acquisition process to second-language teaching techniques is somewhat tenuous. (See chapter 3, page 45.) Second, present knowledge indicates that the amount of transfer across sense modalities varies depending upon the language, the learner, and the learner's level of language study. (See chapter 4, page 87.)

Relevant research and accumulated teacher experience seem to point in the direction of appealing to as many of the senses as possible rather than insisting upon a single approach for all students regardless of their predisposition toward oral or visual means of learning. Teachers need to broaden their scope of activities to include all the language skills and all student abilities. In this case, oral and written presentations can complement each other even though the transfer from one to the other may not be so great as was originally supposed. In other words, the students who do not pick up the structures and vocabulary presented orally may do so visually and vice versa. If the initial introduction is comprehended, additional study in the other mode serves to reinforce the concepts being studied.

The decision to include a prereading period at the beginning of the language-learning sequence no longer seems to merit the relative importance that it used to have. On the other hand, it is logical to assume that the receptive skills, listening and reading, precede the productive skills, speaking and writing, in the language-learning process. Thus, the problem seems to be one of determining the most efficacious procedures for developing the receptive skills and of delineating the types of knowledge and abilities within the receptive skills that are most beneficial to the students as they proceed to the productive skills.

In Chomsky's theory of generative linguistics, language learners first acquire a language "competence," which by some means, unknown at the present time, they activate to perform in the language. "Competence" is what native speakers know about their language, intuitively, not analytically. "Performance" encompasses the activation of what they know about the language to communicate. "Competence," which underlies all four language skills, is an internally stored set of language rules and must be acquired prior to "performance." Communication in any of the four language skills is an active, not a passive, process in which the native speaker's language system is activated either to decode an incoming message or to encode an outgoing one.

SEQUENCING THE FOUR LANGUAGE SKILLS

Once the receptive skills have been established by means of listening and reading, speaking and writing can be undertaken and developed toward communicative fluency. Often teachers focus on the goal of language production and forget the prerequisite importance of the receptive skills. Listening and reading provide the means for acquiring additional vocabulary and new language structures. Therefore, the teacher needs to be most careful that the students have the means before he asks them to continue in language learning toward speaking and writing. Without having made the first step, they will be unable to take the second. Unless they have the ability to decode an incoming message, they certainly cannot be expected to encode an outgoing one.

The component parts of language are the same for the receptive and the productive oral skills and for the receptive and the productive written skills. These components, i.e., phonology, semantics, and syntax, provide the basis for interrelating the four languge skills. The students' knowledge of vocabulary and structure can be deepened by studying vocabulary and structure in all four language skills. In this fashion each language skill can complement the other. Encountering new words and grammar to be learned in both listening and reading exercises and practicing the same forms in each of language's productive manifestations enable the students to achieve a greater degree of language mastery than could ever be accomplished by insisting upon either oral or written activities alone.

The fact that the components of language are the same for the receptive and the productive skills has led many teachers to assume that the step from comprehension to usage or from oral skills to written skills or vice versa is a small one. Such is not the case. Even though the building blocks are identical, each skill has to be practiced separately. Students, for example, who can understand vocabulary and structure when used by someone else have not necessarily incorporated them into their own speech. Students who can do a pattern drill orally with no errors and little hesitation may not be able to write the same forms correctly. Students who can read an assigned story with ease and almost total comprehension may not be able to discuss the content in class afterwards. Therefore, teachers need to be constantly aware of their obligation to provide practice in all four language skills.

In all facets of language learning and teaching, one of the key concepts is sequencing. The preceding discussion emphasizes the sequential relationship existing among the four language skills. Listening comprehension precedes and serves as a basis for speaking. A similar relationship exists between reading and writing. The teacher should be aware that it is the students' knowledge of the phonology, semantics, and syntax in listening that is activated to produce speech, and that it is the students' knowledge of semantics and syntax in reading that is activated to produce written communication.

Cognitive Processes Involved

In language learning, there seems to be a sequence of increasingly difficult and complex cognitive processes as the students progress toward the ability to use another language. First, the students must go through an initial stage of acquiring an elementary familiarity with the content of the material they are to learn. This initial competence is attained by means of the receptive skills, listening and reading. The next step is to practice production of this material in exercises and/or drills in order to facilitate its incorporation into the students' repertoire of available language. Only after the achievement of a basic ability in manipulating the words and forms can the students be expected to use this same content in a communicative context.

On the surface, the cognitive processes involved in each phase of language acquisition seem to be different. The first step requires an inductive or deductive mental grasp of concepts that may be quite abstract and unfamiliar. The second phase requires an application of the previously acquired understanding in various exercises and drills. And finally, the students are expected to attach meaning to the learned structural forms as they communicate in a "real" language situation.

The stumbling block seems to be the final phase. Most motivated students gain some insight into the structural manipulations to be undertaken and some facility in performing the exercises and/or drills satisfactorily. They fail, however, in their attempts to attach meaning to the forms of which they have partial control. Students who have memorized perfectly the dialog and who can respond automatically to the related structural drills will slow down considerably and perhaps even come to a frustrated mental halt when asked to talk to someone else using these same words and structures. Learning the vocabulary is not so difficult; learning to manipulate the structures is not impossible; but combining the two to express their own ideas presents almost insurmountable difficulties to many students.

More research and experimentation need to be undertaken with regard to facilitating "real" language activities. Are there exercises that might narrow the gap between manipulation and expression of personal ideas? Would it be possible to combine practice and meaning and to eliminate this present weakness in the sequence toward language usage? The preceding questions were asked in the 1971 edition of this text. Since that time, progress has been made toward the evolution of such exercises, practice, and activities. The combination of form and meaning in situational, meaningful contexts is more prevalent. Normally, the fusion of practice of form with expression of ideas in a meaningful context is accomplished by giving the students the structure and/or vocabulary they will need or by supplying them with the needed vocabulary as the occasion arises during the activity and structuring the activity around some situation familiar to the students.

Combining the students' cognitive knowledge of the language with their affective interests is one way of getting the students involved in an activity and of creating a situation that stimulates them. As Christensen (1975, p. 4) puts the case for this type of activity, "Although there is no evidence yet to support the hypothesis, I surmise that as students enter the creative process of producing original language content along affective lines, their learning is intensified, so that grammatical structures are internalized quicker than they are by means of lengthy repetitions of the same language structure, using conventional text-book sentences."

Affective Reactions Involved

As has been stated previously in this text, the student's affective side exerts a tremendous influence on the cognitive and vice versa. Positive feelings and attitudes can compensate to a certain extent for a certain lack of cognitive capabilities, just as negative attitudes and feelings can diminish the most gifted academic potential. Otherwise, the nation's classes would not be filled with vast numbers of so-called overachievers and underachievers. (Actually, given what is known at the present time, one is led to the conclusion that there is no such animal. Everyone achieves in accord with his cognitive, affective-social, and psychomotor capabilities. The problem is to free the cognitive and psychomotor potential from the debilitating effects of any negative affective-social factors.) The influential role played by affective-social characteristics on academic achievement is especially important in second-language classes. In these classes the student is taken into new and unfamiliar territory in which positive student attitudes—confidence, cooperation, participation, and perseverance—are of critical importance.

Some students come to the second-language class replete with a negative predisposition toward the class itself. This attitude is especially prevalent among those students who are forced by one means or another into taking the class. Add to this the hesitation and misgivings many people have about treading new waters as they move into a different linguistic and cultural world, and it is clear that the first task of the second-language teacher is to try to make the students feel *comfortable.* She will encourage them as they attempt to comprehend new linguistic structures, and she will support them in their initial and subsequent halting, stumbling attempts to create sentences to express themselves. Second, she has an obligation to make the content of the course *interesting* to the students. Third, she should seek ways to make the material *intellectually stimulating* to the students. That is, the content should be such that the students feel there is something in the course that is worth the time and effort to learn. And last, the students should feel a *sense of accomplishment* as they proceed through the materials.

A positive attitude toward the course is especially important in acquiring the productive skills. In the performance of the productive skills (speaking and writing), language is generated internally. Thus, achievement of a functional level of proficiency in these two skills is dependent upon student incentive as well as cognitive ability. (In this author's opinion, the fact that some students learn to speak a second language while others do not can be explained by a lack of the needed internal incentives required to generate creative language utterances.) In dealing with the productive skills, the teacher is obligated to pay as much attention to affective-social factors as to cognitive factors.

Vigotsky (1961) points out that productive skills originate out of the individual's feelings, needs, and emotions. One can well postulate that communication in the receptive skills is also influenced by affective-social factors. The point being made is that communication divorced from the students' feelings and attitudes is in all likelihood not very meaningful to them. Since the purpose of language is to communicate, and since communication seems to involve affective as well as cognitive aspects, teaching-learning activities that incorporate both aspects appear to be the most promising in the second-language class.

LISTENING COMPREHENSION

Goals

The goal in listening comprehension is to be able to understand native speech at normal speed in unstructured situations. This statement does not imply an ability equal to that in the students' first language, although certainly their ability in the receptive skills needs to be closer to first-language level than that of the productive skills. The implication is that they reach a level at which, in ungraded contexts, they can concentrate on the message without conscious attention to component elements of that message. At times, the students may not know the meaning of all the words being used, but they should be able to guess some meanings from the context. At times, in the excitement of spirited conversational exchanges, the speaking rate may be much faster than normal, and in these situations the students need much additional practice. At any and perhaps all times, the students should expect to hear occasional words and phrases that they do not understand. Instead of becoming flustered and losing the thread of the conversation, they need to learn to concentrate on the general content. Total comprehension at all times and in all situations is impossible even in the first language. The students should be made aware of their tolerance for such situations in their native tongue in order to overcome the feelings of insecurity that they likely feel initially in the second language.

Listening comprehension does not normally receive the amount of attention in the classroom that it deserves. Generally, listening is treated as almost incidental to the goal of speaking. The students listen to the dialog and repeat the lines after the teacher. Later, they respond to oral cues in the pattern drills and perhaps even to questions that the teacher has prepared. Yet, rarely do they listen to language in a continuous conversational exchange in which previously learned materials are recombined in slightly different contexts.

The students need practice in listening to the second language in communicative contexts so they can tune their "language ears" to the rhythm and sounds of the language. They need to be made aware of the many aspects of "vocalic communication": rate of speech, volume, characteristic and relative pitch, type and frequency of juncture and vocal quality (Pearce & Mueller, 1975). They need to be provided sufficient experience so that they can begin to anticipate and to expect "what is coming next." They need to learn which aspects of the language are important and which aspects are redundant or unnecessary as far as decoding the message is concerned. Such practice should be provided by the texts and by the teacher. Without practice in decoding new messages using familiar vocabulary and structure, the students will be unprepared for the unrehearsed situations that a native speaker must face every day.

The greatest weakness of students who go abroad is not their inability to speak, but their inability to understand the native's answer. They are not accustomed to meeting unstructured oral situations. This is not to say that the students can speak better than they can understand. Certainly, their productive skill can never surpass their receptive ability. The point is that students can limit their speech to language that they can control, but they must be prepared to understand the unstructured language encountered in the replies.

The second-language students' inability to function well at first in the foreign country should come as no surprise. For many of them, this experience is their first attempt to comprehend "real" conversation in the second language. Second-language teachers should make efforts to eliminate this weakness in the second-language experiences of their students by continuous efforts to provide classroom activities in which the students are asked to participate as users of the language, not only as learners. They should be given as many experiences as possible that are similar to those needed to function in the foreign country.

In reading, students are given clues that will make reading easier and more enjoyable. They are taught to look for word families, to practice sensible guessing, etc. The students are assisted in making the jump from carefully controlled materials to less structured readings. However, in listening comprehension, little assistance and very few guidelines are provided. The assumption is made that the students will automatically understand the spoken language without specific exercises and practice in that skill. The results in most classrooms would indicate that such is not the case. The point being made is that many of the aids normally given in promoting reading comprehension can also be used to facilitate the improvement of listening comprehension skills. (See chapter 11, pages 315–18.)

Problems

The first hurdle that the teacher must overcome in developing auditory memory and in promoting the acquisition of listening skills is the short attention span and poor listening habits that many students have. The teacher should impress on the students the importance of careful and constant listening in class. They must be aware of the need to listen more attentively in language class than in other classes. Brooks (1964) states that they must hear three to five times as much in a language class as in the normal class. The reason for this extra concentration lies in the fact that in their own language they do not need to listen so carefully. Their ability in the language has reached the point at which they know what to expect from the language. Therefore, they know how to discard the redundant and unnecessary elements of the message and even to fill in those parts that they may have missed. Of course, this is the goal in the second language also, but at the beginning levels that ability in unstructured situations is quite far away. In the introduction to language and in subsequent introductions to new sequences, the students must pay complete attention to all the components of the code before attaining true listening comprehension.

While the teacher is stressing to the students the importance of improving their listening habits and explaining why they must concentrate more fully in language class, she should also contrast the language class, in which listening plays such an important role, with other classes in which most of the learning may be visual. She should make the students realize that both auditory and visual learning play a large role in language classes and that both the eyes and the ears can be learning and memory aids.

In the introduction to a class in which a great deal of emphasis is placed on listening, the teacher should also spend a few moments discussing the discomfort and uneasiness that such a class may cause. There is no reason to become frustrated while reading because the opportunity of turning back, rereading a section, or pausing to meditate is always present. Such is not the case in listening. Whether it is understood or not, the stream of speech continues. Therefore, the students should expect to feel a certain strain in the early stages of language learning as they strive to cope with this problem. They should be encouraged not to pause to reflect on any given phrase, but to stay with the speaker even if they do not understand everything. Just as the water skier hopes to stay with his skis, they should try to stay with the stream of speech. The teacher should encourage the students to voice their feelings of frustration if the need arises during the course of the semester. She can make adjustments in her expectations, and she can make arrangements to provide additional listening comprehension activities to help them improve their listening skills. This additional practice can be provided by the teacher, by the students themselves, or by commercially prepared materials in the classroom or language laboratory.

As desirable as it may be to get the students to listen, the question of how to listen remains. Following are some pointers the teacher should keep in mind in order to stimulate student attentiveness in class. At the risk of duplicating advice given in chapter 15, "General Guidelines for Teaching a Second Language," some of those, in no specific order of importance, are being listed here:

1. Tell the students why they need to listen.
2. Explain the frustrations that may accompany attempts to comprehend the spoken second language.
3. Call on students in random order. Keep them guessing as to who is next.
4. Expect and encourage participation. They must listen to participate.
5. Keep the pace moving at a clip sufficient to maintain interest.
6. Be interested yourself in what is going on.
7. Have fun. Occasional laughter will do as much as anything to keep some students involved in class activities.
8. Select content to which the students can relate.
9. Provide a variety of activities.
10. Be responsive to student ideas and input in the class. Nothing is so interesting as to see one's own idea incorporated into some future class.
11. Give them material worth listening to and at a level consistent with their capabilities.
12. Do not permit students not to listen. Students who spend day after day in your class wandering listlessly through a dream world of their own cannot be successful second-language learners.

Components of Listening Comprehension

Being able to understand the spoken language is not an automatic, concomitant outcome of language study. The teacher should realize that this often
overlooked skill must also be stressed and that, as in all the other skills, a
sequential arrangement of activities should be provided in order to develop it.
Listening comprehension can be divided into at least five sequential components, each dependent upon the preceding one. The first is the ability to
distinguish all the sounds, intonation patterns, and voice qualities in the
second language and to discriminate between them and similar sounds in the
native tongue. The second is the perception of an entire message produced by
a speaker. The third is the ability to hold that message in one's auditory
memory until it can be processed. Fourth, the listener decodes what the
speaker has said. Comprehension of the message, however, is not synonymous with the ability to discuss content in the second language. The fifth and
last stage is the ability to use the message and/or store it in the second
language.

Discrimination When presented sounds unlike those of their own language,
speakers tend to give those sounds first-language interpretations. In other
words, the hearers perceive the new sounds in terms of the nearest equivalent
in their own language. Students, for example, who are asked to imitate a line of
a dialog in a second language may be confronted for the first few days with
several sounds that they have never heard before. In such a situation, the
students most likely do not even hear the distinctions which they will be called
on to make in the second language. They translate the unfamiliar sounds into
familiar ones in order to be able to process what they have heard. Especially if
they are being asked to imitate these utterances, they are inclined to interpret
the new language in terms of first-language sounds. Some research has
indicated that second-language students learn more rapidly if they are not
asked to produce language immediately in the early stages of second-language
learning. This conclusion fits with the postulated need to establish the
receptive skills prior to the productive.

The first task facing the teacher, then, in the process of building up the
students' listening comprehension ability, is to teach the students to perceive
and to distinguish those sounds that are not found in the first language from
familiar sounds that may be somewhat similar. These distinctions should be
taught prior to asking students to imitate any lines containing those sounds.
One way of teaching these differences between the sounds of the two
languages is to contrast the first-language and the second-language sounds in
minimal pair drills.

The sounds in French that should be carefully distinguished prior to any active imitation on the part of the students are the vowels and the consonant sounds represented by the following letters: *t, d, l, r, p, b,* and the *s* sound as in the English word *pleasure,* which may occur at the beginning of a word.

In German, the most troublesome sounds are the vowels, especially the long *e* (*geht* versus *gate*) and the long *o* (*Boot* versus *boat*), and the consonant sounds of *l, d, t,* and the *ts* sound, which occurs in English but not initially as it does in German.

The problem sounds in Spanish are the vowels and the consonant sounds of *g* (between vowels), *j, t, d, l, p, k,* and the fricative *b.*

All the sounds (including the schwa) that may be misinterpreted and thereby mispronounced should be contrasted with the English sounds until the students can hear the difference. Before the students can eliminate the typical English vowel glide, for example, they must be made aware of that glide. With a little practice, they can readily discriminate between the Spanish words, *me, le,* and *se,* and the English words, *may, lay,* and *say.* Once there is no hesitation about which sound belongs to which language, pronunciation practice can begin. Similar minimal-pair comparisons should be made with the other vowels and consonants. The same is true for the schwa, i.e., the tendency in English to pronounce vowels in unstressed syllables as "uh."

As the students learn more sounds in the language, instances may arise in which important phonemic distinctions must be made between sounds in the language itself that are quite similar. In order to communicate in the oral aspects of the language, either listening or speaking, the students must be able to distinguish these phonemic differences. Before they are asked to make these distinctions as they occur in contextual situations and certainly before they are expected to make these distinctions in their speaking, these important contrasts should be isolated and studied in minimal-pair drills. The students should first be made aware of the problem, and then sufficient practice should be provided to insure that they can hear these often slight variations.

This problem is not so great in French and Spanish as it is in German. In German, the students need practice distinguishing between the long and short umlaut vowels *ü* and *ö* and the front and back *ch* sound. For example, *Hüte* means "hats," but *Hütte* means "hut." There is considerable difference between *Höhle,* which means "cave," and *Hölle,* which means "hell." In the word *ich,* the *ch* is pronounced in the front of the mouth. In the word *ach,* it is pronounced in the back.

After the students have learned to distinguish isolated sounds, these same sounds should be placed into words to determine whether or not the students can identify the differences within the context of a word. The sounds and words should then be incorporated into sentences and communicative contexts to provide listening discrimination practice and to demonstrate the importance of these distinctions.

Nor can the students stop with individual sounds. Diphthongs, triphthongs, and various consonant clusters often create problems in student comprehension. The position in which a letter occurs may alter its pronunciation. For example, the voiced quality of a consonant may affect the pronunciation of an adjoining consonant. The joining of words in rapid speech may lead to the omission of certain sounds or to altered pronunciation of sounds.

In addition to the sounds and combinations of sounds, other speech characteristics, such as pitch, stress, and juncture, provide valuable linguistic clues to the meaning of the utterances. The voice quality characteristics mentioned earlier in this chapter also play an important role in the affective aspects of the communicative situation due to the emotional response they create in the listener. For example, if a speaker drops the intonation pattern sharply at the end of a sentence, he will appear curt and perhaps even rude. The listener reacts predictably, although perhaps subconsciously, to these cues. Children are the best examples of these voice quality characteristics. They very quickly learn to indicate with tone of voice when they are unhappy about something.

Perception of message   After acquiring the ability to distinguish between and among the sounds, intonation patterns, and voice qualities common to the language, the students are ready to listen to sentences for meaning. (The assumption is being made, of course, that they have also been learning the accompanying vocabulary and grammar contained in the text.) The first problem is simply to get the students to listen and concentrate on what is being said so that the stream of sounds registers on their consciousness. They obviously must hear what is being said, with the intent of doing something with what they hear.

The problem of getting students to listen has both cognitive and affective components. First, the students need to feel that it is possible for them to comprehend what they hear. This implies that they have sufficient preparation in phonology, semantics, and syntax. Second, for maximum concentration, the students should be aware of the purpose behind the activity. What is the objective? How will it help them? How does it fit into second-language learning specifically and language usage in general? Third, they should *want* to hear what is said and to understand the content.

Since listening to the second language requires a higher level of concentration and as a consequence a greater expenditure of energy, the teacher should not expect to spend a long time in any one class period on this skill. If he would like to provide the students with additional practice, he can switch to a different activity and return later to listening comprehension.

Auditory memory   Once the students are able to discriminate the various linguistic cues and perceive oral messages, they are ready to begin to develop their ability to retain sentences. The students face an insurmountable obstacle in second-language learning if they cannot remember what they have just heard. Most oral activities in the classroom, from repetition to question-answer practice, are based on the necessity of remembering the message. Even kindergarten children are asked to repeat a lengthy sentence in their native tongue to determine whether their auditory memories are developed sufficiently to profit from classroom learning activities.

In order to develop the students' auditory memory, the teacher should see to it that they hear as much language as possible. This means that most of the class will be conducted in the language being taught. However, the speed of presentation and difficulty level of the content must be geared to the students. Advanced language exchanges are little more than nonsense sounds to beginning students, and listening to language which is not understood does not provide satisfactory practice. Conversely, students at advanced levels soon tire of language that is beneath their capability level.

A proper sequencing of activities and difficulty levels, which challenges but does not defeat, needs to be maintained even in developing auditory memory. In the early stages of language learning, the sentences should be quite short. The students cannot cope if the sentences contain too many syllables and too much information. The sentences should not only be short; they should also be presented at a speed which permits the students to comprehend what is being said. Initially, native-speed renditions are not the most efficient manner of presentation. The fact that the goal is to comprehend a native speaker does not require that native-speed conversations be employed from the beginning of the course. Speech should always be normal, i.e., with native stress, pronunciation, intonation, liaisons, and elisions, but not so fast as to be incomprehensible. The reduction in speed can be accomplished primarily by speaking in phrases and lengthening the pauses between phrases. Too, the linguistic level of the sentences should be within the range of the student's previous language experience. However, both the teacher and the textual materials will need to lengthen the utterances, speed them up, and increase the linguistic complexity during the course of the year.

Minimal-pair drills are used to teach sound discriminations, but connected phrases must necessarily be the basis for increasing auditory memory. With the audio-lingual approach, a great deal of emphasis is placed on developing auditory memory. The students spend much of their class time in mimicry-memorization of the dialogs or responding to cues in pattern drills. In spite of the fact that this aspect of the audio-lingual approach is one of its most important strengths, teachers need not limit their classroom activities to dialog memorization and pattern drills. Other techniques such as reading aloud, dictation, question-answer practice, listening to the second language in context, classroom expressions, etc. are also beneficial in developing auditory memory. In short, all language activity that is understandable promotes increased auditory memory. As the students progress through the course, their ears become attuned to the second-language sound system, and auditory memory expands. The important point to remember is the idea of progress. The progression from simpler to more complex and lengthy sentences must be slow, but continuous. During this progression, the speed of delivery should be increased in direct proportion to the students' ability to comprehend.

Comprehension in the first language With the ability to distinguish the sounds of the language, the ability to perceive strings of words, and the capability of remembering them, the students are in a position to comprehend incoming messages provided they have acquired the necessary semantic and syntactical bases for understanding what is received. Once the message is made available for processing, factors other than hearing and retention become involved. It is the students' conscious attention to these factors which severely limits listening comprehension ability in the early stages of language learning. There are simply too many elements with which to contend. The mind has difficulty coping simultaneously with both the code and the message.

Teachers should be aware of this stumbling block and attempt to prevent their students from becoming discouraged because of it. They should point out to them that comprehension of each single element is not necessary, desirable, or even possible. Psychologists find that information is processed in chunks. The students' listening skills will be much greater if they concentrate on absorbing chunks of information rather than bits and pieces. Mueller (1974) postulates separate processes in comprehending a message. The first process is termed *sensing.* During this process the listener gets a general idea or sense of the content of what he is hearing. In the second, called *segmenting,* the hearer begins to segment the content into simple linguistic units consisting of subject, verb, and object. Dividing the content into what Mueller calls *skeleton sentences,* the listener is able to decode the message in greater detail. Mueller emphasizes that there is more to the listening comprehension skill than merely learning the phonology, the words, and the structure. The students must also be given practice in the actual process of comprehending what they hear in the second language.

The teacher should be careful to develop listening comprehension activities that encourage the students to practice listening comprehension at the communication level. The teacher should not emphasize vocabulary building, knowledge of grammar, translation of individual words, speaking in individual words, repeating to the point at which students can concentrate on individual words or structures, or asking for the first-language meaning of words (Mueller, 1974). In addition, the teacher should be extremely careful not to expect comprehension of minute details in any of the follow-up activities.

Otherwise, he will be indirectly forcing the students to practice what they must avoid doing if they are to learn to understand a native speaker.

Comprehension in the second language   In the early stages of second-language learning and during initial exposure to new material the students will in all likelihood convert an oral communication into their first language in order to remember it, or sense the meaning at a subword level. This type of comprehension means that they will not be able to discuss the content in the second language at this stage of their development. As they make progress in listening comprehension, they will gradually develop the ability to receive the message in the second language itself. (In fact, in some respects this conversion of the message into a form for storage may in itself be a productive process rather than a receptive one.) After much practice, the students will be able to concentrate on the content of familiar dialogs and readings without being consciously aware of the manner of expression. In order to reach this level, the students must have practice listening to the spoken language in extended contexts. In sound discrimination, single words were used. In auditory memory, phrases and sentences were employed. Now, short conversations and oral readings become the bases for developing greater listening comprehension. At some time, all dialogs and readings should be heard in their entirety.

The ability to comprehend familiar material without the obstructing awareness of individual grammatical and vocabulary elements, i.e., getting the message without conscious attention to the code, is indeed quite a psychological accomplishment. This is difficult to achieve and its importance should not be underestimated by the teacher or the students. However, even this level of comprehension is still short of the goal—comprehension of native speech in *unstructured* situations. The students have not truly learned to understand the spoken language until they can understand it as it is spoken in "real" situations. In order to anticipate such situations, practice should be provided in the classroom.

As is always true, the teacher must teach for transfer. The students cannot make the leap alone. Students needs practice in listening to unstructured situations in which they cannot anticipate immediate comprehension of all the content. Material at this level will provide practice in transferring known forms and words to new contexts, in applying listening guides to increase comprehension, and in adjusting to similar situations that they will encounter with native speakers. Such practice is essential in order to be able to cope successfully with experience in the foreign culture.

Material for listening comprehension exercises can, and should, be of various types. Most important is to remember that conversational interchanges should be included as well as longer narratives. The students themselves can provide each other with a considerable amount of listening comprehension practice. For example, with games, impromptu conversations, dialogs prepared with classmates, short plays, descriptions, oral reports, etc., they have the opportunity to listen to other students. Listening to classmates stimulates motivation and provides an opportunity to relate to a live situation. The limitation of students listening to other students lies in their restricted language ability. Therefore, the teacher should provide additional listening activities, such as descriptions of customs, plays and scenes from plays, songs, lectures, radio broadcasts, movies, etc. These activities are essential to the development of a true listening comprehension ability. (Teachers can alleviate their task by sharing listening comprehension materials with other teachers.)

Sample of a Listening Comprehension Sequence

Following are examples of types of activities that might be used in a listening comprehension sequence. The purpose of presenting this sample is to help the teacher gain insight into ways and means of developing her own sequences in listening comprehension. Any teacher will need to create additional types of activities to fit her own particular students and situation.

While contemplating this selected sequence, the teacher should keep three points in mind. First, since listening and reading are both receptive skills, the sequence for both will be quite similar. Second, the success or failure of the sequence depends upon the active participation of the students. Third, second-language work at the intermediate and upper levels is not distinctly different from that at the elementary levels. In more advanced courses there is still an obvious sequence involved. The primary difference is that such elementary tasks as discrimination, dictation, etc., if they have been mastered previously, can be eliminated in favor of a greater portion of real language activities in the class.

Discrimination   Early in the second-language course the normal procedure is to teach the sounds of the language. The general approach is first to teach the sounds in isolation as well as in context. Prior to asking the students to produce the sounds, the teacher verifies that they can hear and distinguish the sounds. The following are sample sound discrimination exercises.

   I. Hearing the Sounds
     A. First vs. Second Language
       1. Explanation

Spanish vowels are short, single sounds. They do not have the diphthongized quality of English "long" vowels.

2. Examples

Pronounce for the students the sounds of a diphthongized English [ey] as in *day* and a one-sound Spanish [e] as in *de.*

3. Discrimination

In the following exercise you will hear either an English [ey] sound or a Spanish [e] sound. If you hear the English sound, write E in the blank; if you hear the Spanish sound, write an S. (The teacher then proceeds with the discrimination exercise.)

___le ___lay ___day ___de ___me ___may

B. In the Second Language

1. Explanation

In French there are four nasal vowel sounds: [ɛ̃] [ɑ̃] [ɔ̃] [œ̃]. The lip and tongue positions for each are illustrated on the chalkboard.

2. Examples

Pronounce each nasal vowel sound several times for the students, and point out the lip and tongue positions for each.

3. Discrimination

In the following exercise you will hear the four French nasal vowels pronounced in random order. Indicate (with phonetic symbols) which of the vowels you hear in each case.

II. Hearing the Sounds in Context

A. In Words

1. Explanation

Vowel sounds in German differ from each other in the length of the sound and in the tenseness or laxness with which the vowel is pronounced.

2. Examples

Pronounce a word containing a long *a* sound [a:] in German and one containing a short *a* sound [a]. Then ask the students to choose which is which until you are sure that they can distinguish the difference: for example, *Saat* versus *satt.*

3. Discrimination

In the following exercise you will hear three words pronounced. Choose the word that does not have the same vowel sound as the other two, and write the word and the phonetic symbol for the vowel sound being pronounced.

a. Staat   statt   statt
b. kam   Kamm   kam
c. Bahn   Bahn   Bann[2]

B. In Sentences
   1. Explanation
   You have learned that an English *k* sound is followed by a puff of air. A Spanish *k* sound is not. An American who "puffs" the *k* sound is speaking Spanish with an accent.

   2. Examples
   Give the students two Spanish words, one containing a *k* sound pronounced as in Spanish and one with a *k* sound pronounced as in English. Repeat, asking the students to tell which *k* sound is Spanish.

   3. Discrimination
   In the following exercise you will hear six sentences containing the *k* sound. If the speaker uses an American pronunciation of the *k* sound, write A. If she uses the Spanish pronunciation, write S.

   (S) a. ¿Qué hay de comer?
   (S) b. No sabe que hacer hoy.
   (A) c. ¿Cómo se llama ese chico?
   (S) d. Mi casa está en la calle catorce.
   (A) e. No me gusta el queso.
   (A) f. ¿Quién es Quico?

III. Stress and Intonation Patterns
   A. Stress
      1. Explanation
      In English, emphasis is indicated by accenting the word or phrase that the speaker wants to stress.

      2. Examples
      Repeat the following sentences and ask the students to demonstrate comprehension by indicating normal or emphatic before going on to the discrimination exercise.

      Normal sentence stress—He studies French.
      Emphasis on the subject—*He* studies French.
      Emphasis on the action—He *studies* French.
      Emphasis on the object—He studies *French.*

---

[2]These words were taken from Kadler (1970, p. 142).

3. Discrimination

Listen to the following sentences. Write N if the intonation pattern is normal and E if it is emphatic.

(N) a. I listen to the news every evening.
(E) b. *He* doesn't listen to me.
(E) c. We *walked* home.
(N) d. The family watched TV and talked.
(E) e. Mrs. Jones told *Michael,* not his *brother.*
(E) f. *I* don't know. That's for sure.

B. Intonation
1. Explanation

The speaker often indicates by the rise or fall of his voice whether he is asking a question or making a statement. In English a rising intonation pattern indicates a question and a falling intonation pattern is used with a statement.

2. Examples

Give the students examples of the statement pattern and the interrogative pattern with regular word order and with inverted word order. Be sure the students can distinguish between the two patterns before doing the exercise.

Statement—John is leaving now.
Interrogative—John is leaving now?
Is John leaving now?

3. Discrimination

Listen to the following sentences. If the speaker is asking a question, write Q. If he is making a statement, write S.

(Q) a. Am I going with you this afternoon?
(S) b. The guests will be here soon.
(Q) c. Have we eaten all the ice cream?
(S) d. Mr. Brown has a new car.
(Q) e. Do the students arrive before eight in the morning?
(Q) f. Jim is dating Becky?

The preceding examples are not, of course, the types of exercises that would be used throughout the course. They deal with the discrimination of important elements of the phonological system of the language, and they would be used primarily in the early lessons.

In addition to sounds, the students need practice perceiving and discriminating among various structure and vocabulary clues. These language elements may be small in relation to the total number of sounds and/or words in the sentence, but they are basic to comprehending the message of the sentence. The following are sample exercises giving the students practice listening for vocabulary or structure signals.

IV. Structure Signals and Vocabulary
   A. Structure Signals
      1. Explanation (From this point on the explanations will not be included.)
      2. Examples (From this point on the examples will not be included.)
      3. Discrimination
         Listen to the following sentences. If the speaker is talking about the past, write PAST on your paper. If she is talking about the present, write PRESENT.

         (past)   a. We helped him to finish on time
         (present)   b. They know she is at school.
         (present)   c. She goes downtown on the bus.
         (past)   d. I hated the thought of leaving so early.

   B. Vocabulary
      Discrimination
      Based on the content of the following sentences write H if the girl is at home and S if she is at school.

      (H) a. Mary is sitting on her bed.
      (S) b. Mary is eating in the cafeteria.
      (S) c. Mary is with her friends at a convocation in the auditorium.
      (H) d. Mary is watching TV in the living room.

Perception and auditory memory In addition to learning to discriminate among sounds, words, and structures, students need to gain gradually the ability to remember longer phrases and sentences. Auditory memory skill must precede comprehension because comprehension is made possible by the students' ability to remember what they have heard. Primarily, auditory memory is developed with other skills. In fact, auditory memory seems to lend itself best to growing and expanding as the students work with all other oral aspects of the language. However, for those students who need special help with this important component of language learning, special auditory memory exercises can be prepared. The following is a sample auditory memory exercise.

   A. Auditory Memory—Listening Only
      Discrimination
      Listen to the following pairs of sentences. If they are both the same, write S on your paper. If they are different, write D.

      (D) a. Ese chico se llama Miguel.
            Ese chico llama a Miguel.
      (S) b. La otra es una amiga mía.
            La otra es una amiga mía.
      (D) c. Hablo con el profesor.
            Habló con el profesor.
      (S) d. Sí, van a salir esta noche.
            Sí, van a salir esta noche.

The sentences for exercises similar to the preceding can be taken from dialogs, narratives, or drills in the book. This type of exercise is appropriate only for the first few weeks of the course. It should quickly be replaced by exercises that require an active response on the part of the student just as soon as the teacher determines that the students have the ability to remember typical sentences in the text.

Comprehension What the student hears consists of sounds, words, and structure. Obviously, he should be taught these elements before he is asked to attempt to comprehend sentences, conversations, or monologues in the second language. However, as many teachers know, students may know all three language components and still be unable to glean anything from what they hear in the second language. Although they have all the elements, they still need abundant opportunities to use the code to decipher incoming messages. They have to learn what to look for, what to expect. They have to learn what to do when they fail to understand, what to do when they get lost. They need to learn to listen for the meaning of the sentence.

The first step here is to get the students to listen and to attempt to comprehend or "sense" the meaning. Exercises can be prepared that require the students to demonstrate their comprehension without forcing them to use the language in their responses. If he is asked to discriminate, perceive, remember, understand, and prepare to answer in the language all at the same time, his ability to comprehend may be diminished. In other words, he will understand less if he is trying to store the information in the second language at the same time he is attempting to understand what he is hearing. The following exercises require the students to demonstrate comprehension without forcing them to try to recall the appropriate answers in the second language.

    A. Physical Response
      The teacher gives a series of commands that individual students act out to demonstrate comprehension. (An alternative is to ask each student to pretend she is acting out the command.)

1. Close your eyes.
2. Stand up.
3. Put your book under your chair.
4. Write your name on the chalkboard.
5. Take out a sheet of paper.
6. Fold your arms.

B. Selection of visuals

The teacher arranges six numbered visuals illustrating present progressive verbs at the front of the room. He then reads six descriptions, which in this case treat present progressive verbs. The students write the number of the corresponding visual for each of the descriptions.

1. The girl is reading.
2. The girl is swimming.
3. The girl is studying.
4. The girl is walking.
5. The girl is eating.
6. The girl is running.

C. Selection of Lines from a Dialog

The teacher gives the lines of a dialog orally in a random order. The students either select the corresponding visual associated with the dialog line or choose one of three alternatives in their native language as being what was said.

D. Definitions

The teacher gives simple oral definitions of some of the vocabulary words in the lesson. The students write down the word from a list given on the chalkboard.

student   father
teacher   child

1. This person is older. She works in a school. There she teaches classes and helps her students to learn.
2. This person is younger. He has a great deal of homework in the winter and looks forward to summer vacation. He is serious about the future, but he also wants to have a good time in the present.

E. Multiple-Choice (oral)

Listen to the following, and write on your paper the letter of the correct answer.

1. Sentence completion
When I am thirsty, I get a drink of _____.

   a. bread   b. fountain   c. cold   d. water

2. Logical Inference (oral)
Bobby plans to go to college.
a. His tooth has been bothering him recently.
b. He wants to continue his academic studies.
c. They need him there to support their program.

3. Rejoinder (oral)

When are we eating? I'm starved.
a. In about twenty minutes. Dinner is almost ready.
b. With our neighbors, the Waltons. They invited us last week.
c. Downtown. We're having a big celebration this evening.

F. True-False or perhaps something a little more extreme such as logical vs. ridiculous (oral)
Listen to the following statements, and write L if it is logical or R if it is ridiculous.

1. Cars should be driven backwards so the driver can see where he has been.
2. Small cars use less gas than large cars.
3. Large cars are more comfortable on the highway than small cars.
4. The minimum age for obtaining a driver's license should be set at thirty.

G. Using English
1. To Answer Questions
Early in the course, or even at later stages with some individuals, it may be appropriate in some cases to permit students to answer second-language questions in their first language. Later they should be expected to advance to the next stage at which they can store information in the second language and to recall it in order to answer questions or to give summaries of the content.

2. To Summarize the Content
A quick, simple, and effective way to check the comprehension of those students who have not reached the level of storing information in the second language is to ask them to give a summary of the details they remember from a conversation or a monologue in their native language. Permitting them to do so in the early stages of second-language learning will enhance their listening comprehension ability and ease the trauma that may accompany being forced to comprehend and to remember at the same time.

Affective exercises   A great deal can be done during the early stages of the students' acquisition of second-language skills in terms of real language practice by combining cognitive knowledge with the affective dimension. The following examples (which may be used as receptive exercises) demonstrate how student feelings and attitudes may be incorporated into meaningful practice.

What adjective best describes the following people?
1. Jean-Claude aime être seul dans sa chambre. Quand ses amis vont au cinéma, Jean-Claude préfere rester à la maison pour écouter la radio ou lire un livre. C'est un garçon . . .
   a. solitaire   b. agressif   c. extroverti
2. Marie écrit une composition pour sa classe de français. Elle examine chaque détail parce qu'elle veut donner à son professeur un travail parfait, sans aucune faute. Marie est . . .
   a. impatiente   b. méticuleuse.   c. indifférente
3. Pierre donne toujours des ordres à ses amis, et à ses frères et sœurs. Cela indique que Pierre a tendance à être . . .
   a. patient   b. docile   c. autoritaire[3]

In another type of exercise the students consider what their reactions would be in a number of given situations.

Avez-vous du sang-froid? (Can you keep your cool?) Si vous voulez le savoir, faites le test qui suit. Les situations que suivent sont susceptibles de provoquer une réaction de peur plus ou moins violente chez certains individus. Utilisez les nombres de I à 5 pour indiquer votre réaction à chacune de ces situations. Écrivez le nombre à côté de chaque phrase.

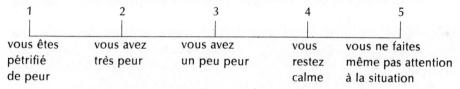

1	2	3	4	5
vous êtes pétrifié de peur	vous avez très peur	vous avez un peu peur	vous restez calme	vous ne faites même pas attention à la situation

_____ 1. Vous êtes dans un tunnel. Brusquement le train s'arrête et il n'y a plus de lumière.

_____ 2. C'est le soir. Vous êtes seul. Vous entendez un bruit étrange dans une autre partie de la maison.

_____ 3. Vous êtes dans un avion, au-dessus de l'Atlantique. Deux des quatre moteurs s'arrêtent de fonctionner.

Interprétation
1.00–1.49: Faites attention! Vous risquez de mourir d'une crise cardiaque.

---

[3]From *Connaître et se Connaître: A Basic French Reader,* Gilbert Jarvis, Thérèse Bonin, Donald Corbin, Diane Birckbichler. Copyright © 1976, Holt, Rinehart & Winston. Reprinted by permission of Holt, Rinehart & Winston.

1.50–2.49: Vous êtes très conscient du danger mais malheureusement vous n'avez pas assez de contrôle de vous-même.

2.50–3.49: Vous êtes conscient du danger mais vous savez voir les choses dans leur propre perspective.

3.50–4.49: Votre sang-froid est admirable—mais est-ce que votre sang-froid vient du contrôle de vous-même ou d'une certaine indifférence?

4.50–5.00: Ce n'est plus du sang-froid, c'est de l'apathie![4]

DIFFICULTY LEVEL OF MATERIAL

During the process of developing listening comprehension skills, not only is the student task becoming more and more complex and difficult but also the material which is selected should become increasingly complex and difficult. This hierarchical sequence applies to each chapter or unit as well as to the text as a whole. First, the students are given phrases and sentences. Second, they are presented material in the text in connected discourse, i.e., paragraphs and dialogs. After they learn to understand content directly from the material they are learning, they are asked to listen to material which they have already learned, but in new combinations of structure, vocabulary, and subject matter. The students should be ready at this point for graded material at essentially their level of linguistic comprehension. The students then proceed to material that was meant for native speakers, but which is typified by a linguistic simplicity. At the final stage, the students are able to comprehend the general sense of unstructured material that has not been selected specifically for them.

USING THE SECOND LANGUAGE FOR
REAL COMMUNICATION

Perhaps the single most productive procedure for developing the students' listening comprehension skills is to make the second language the means of communicating with the students. Kalivoda (1972b) makes a very valid point when he rightly asserts that second-language students quickly learn that second-language study is a game that they play with the teacher during part of the class hour in order to get a passing grade. However, when there is

---

[4]From *Connaître et se Connaître: A Basic French Reader*, Gilbert Jarvis, Thérèse Bonin, Donald Corbin, Diane Birckbichler. Copyright © 1976, Holt, Rinehart & Winston. Reprinted by permission of Holt, Rinehart & Winston.

something important to be said, it is said in the first language. All second-language teachers should take inventory to see if the "shoe fits" their classes. If it does, they should make immediate plans to turn over a new leaf for the sake of their students. Kalivoda gives the following suggestions for making the class a place where the second language is used for real communication:

1. Both the teacher and the students should learn the basic questions with which they can ask each other for information.
2. The teacher should make requests and/or give commands in the second language.
3. Both the teacher and the students should consistently use all the language they have had. If they have had the material, or if they can be expected to understand it, the use of the first language is unjustified.
4. The teacher should not limit himself only to the material the students have had. They can be expected to make intelligent guesses sometimes. If not, the teacher can define, draw a picture, etc. to make the meaning clear.
5. The teacher can often dramatize the meaning of what he is saying.
6. Both the teacher and the students should learn to be more selective in their speech in the second language than in the first.

If teachers follow these suggestions faithfully, the students will get the idea that the purpose of second-language study is to communicate, and they will have ample opportunity to communicate with a real purpose.

ANALYZING LEARNING PROBLEMS

For those students who have difficulty comprehending the spoken language, teachers should attempt to determine the students' problem areas by means of diagnostic tests or individual conferences. Is the student unable to hear the sounds and intonation patterns? Has her capacity for remembering sounds not developed sufficiently? Once the teacher knows what aspects of listening comprehension are causing the students' problems and how they are attempting to solve their problems, suggestions can be made as to what kinds of activities they need to engage in and how they might alter their approach to the task of mastering these activities and skills involved. Most likely the students need to hear more spoken language, and they need to be taught how to listen and what to listen for.

PROVIDING DIVERSIFIED PRACTICE

Ideally, the teacher will have a variety of listening comprehension materials available for the students to listen to on their own. These materials should be at various levels of difficulty, on different topics of interest to the students, and related to the content of the text. Some tapes should be geared for remedial work and others geared for supplementary activities for faster students. The tapes can be placed within access of the students along with accompanying practice sheets and suggested activities.[5]

CONCLUSION

At present, inadequate attention is given to the listening skills in most second-language classes. Students should be exposed to situations similar to those they would encounter in the real language setting. To improve this situation, the teacher should be aware of the importance of listening comprehension, its relation to the other language skills, and the sequencing necessary in the development of listening. The next step is to begin to collect materials for practice in listening comprehension. The school's stock of both graded and nongraded materials for listening should be at least equal to what is available for reading. Both records and tapes should be acquired. In addition to purchasing professionally prepared materials, the teachers can, and should, begin to make and save tapes of visiting speakers, dramatizations, readings, descriptions of cultural topics, guessing games, anecdotes, radio and short-wave broadcasts, etc., to use with their classes. Too, teachers can give their students a tremendous assist in developing their listening comprehension skills simply by conducting their classes in such a way that *whatever* they want their students to know (that they have the knowledge to understand) they give to them in the second language. Listening comprehension ability must be stressed.

REVIEW AND APPLICATION

DEFINITIONS
1. auditory memory, p. 289
2. discrimination exercise, p. 293
3. vocalic communication, p. 284

DISCUSSION
1. Discuss the underlying similarities, differences, and interrelationships among the four languge skills.
2. Compare and contrast the strengths and weaknesses of audio-lingual and cognitive teaching with regard to listening comprehension.

---

[5]Teachers can organize these diversified materials into independent study activities (Kalivoda, 1972a).

3. Discuss the importance of sequencing activities and content in developing the listening comprehension skills.

4. For how long would discrimination type activities be valuable exercises to use in the second-language class? What types might be used longer?

5. How did your teacher help your classes to develop their abilities to comprehend the spoken language? Share any good ideas with your classmates.

6. What kinds of things would you do in class to stress and to develop listening comprehension skills?

7. Discuss the internal and external aspects of listening comprehension.

ACTIVITIES

1. Using a second-language textbook of your choice, create your own listening activities over material in the text (a sound discrimination exercise, a structure signal exercise, a vocabulary exercise, an auditory memory exercise, and a comprehension exercise.)

2. Fit these exercises into an outlined sequence to teach some structure.

3. If time permits, practice conducting one, some, or all of these exercises in your class.

4. Critique the exercises and teaching techniques of your classmates.

5. Select a listening passage that you feel would be interesting and comprehensible to a beginning second-language class.

SELECTED REFERENCES

Allen, E. D., and Valette, R. M. (1972) *Modern Language Classroom Techniques.* New York: Harcourt Brace Jovanovich. Pp. 137–59.

Angelis, P. J. (1973) The Importance and Diversity of Aural Comprehension Training. *Modern Language Journal,* 57:102–6.

Belasco, S. (1965) Nucleation and the Audio-Lingual Approach. *Modern Language Journal,* 49:482–91.

Belasco, S. (1967) The Plateau, Or the Case for Comprehension: The 'Concept' Approach. *Modern Language Journal,* 51:82–88.

Belasco, S. (1969) Toward the Acquisition of Linguistic Competence: From Contrived to Controlled Materials. *Modern Language Journal,* 53:185–205.

Belasco, S. (1970) C'est la guerre? Or Can Cognition and Verbal Behavior Co-exist in Second Language Learning. *Modern Language Journal,* 54:395–412.

Belasco, S., et al. (1963) The Continuum: Listening and Speaking, In W. F. Bottiglia (Ed.), *Language Learning: The Intermediate Phase.* Northeast Conference Reports. Pp. 2–21.

Bodier, M. A. (1945) Aural Comprehension. *Modern Language Journal,* 29: 282–89.

Brisley, L., et al. (1959–61) Good Teaching Practices: A Survey of High-School Foreign-Language Classes. *Reports of Surveys and Studies in the Teaching of Modern Foreign Languages.* New York: Modern Language Association of America. Pp. 219–43.

Brooks, N. (1964) *Language and Language Learning.* (2nd ed.) New York: Harcourt, Brace & World. P. 74.

Cables, V. (1966) How Do We Teach Comprehension? *Modern Language Journal,* 50:141–44.

Christensen, C. B. (1975) Affective Learning Activities (ALA). *Foreign Language Annals,* 8:211–19.

Delattre, P. (1965) Comparing the Phonetic Features of English, French, German, and Spanish: An Interim Report. Philadelphia: Chilton.

Dreher, B., and Larkins, J. (1972) Non-Semantic Auditory Discrimination: Foundation for Second Language Learning. *Modern Language Journal,* 56:227–30.

Ehrmann, E. L. (1963) Listening Comprehension—In the Teaching of a Foreign Language. *Modern Language Journal,* 47:18–20.

Jarvis, G. A., et al. (1976) *Connaître et se Connaître: A Basic French Reader.* New York: Holt, Rinehart and Winston.

Jolly, Y. S. (1975) The Use of Songs in Teaching Foreign Languages. *Modern Language Journal,* 59:11–14.

Kadler, E. H. (1970) *Linguistics and Teaching Foreign Languages.* New York: Van Nostrand Reinhold. P. 142.

Kalivoda, T. B. (1972a) An Individual Study Course for Facilitating Advanced Oral Skills. *Modern Language Journal,* 56:492–95.

Kalivoda, T. B. (1972b) Let's Use Foreign Language for Real Communication. *American Foreign Language Teacher,* 2:14–15, 36, 39.

Kalivoda, T. B., et al. (1971) The Audio-Motor Unit: A Strategy That Works. *Foreign Language Annals,* 4:392–400.

Léon, P. R., and Martin, P. (1972) Applied Linguistics and the Teaching of Intonation. *Modern Language Journal,* 56:139–44.

Libhart, B. R. (1970) A Neglected Challenge: The Aural Comprehension of Unfamiliar Material. *French Review,* 43:800–4.

Mathieu, G. (1961) On the Anatomy of Listening Comprehension. *French Review,* 35:50–53.

Mueller, T. H. (1974) Another Look at How to Teach Listening and Reading Comprehension. *Modern Language Journal,* 58:19–23.

Nelson, R. J. (1972) Electronic Media in Foreign Language Education: A Report on Applications. *Foreign Language Annals,* 46:330–41.

Nord, J. R. (1974) Why Can't I Just Learn to Listen? *American Foreign Language Teacher,* 4:4–6.

Pearce, W. B., and Mueller, T. H. (1975) Vocalic Communication in Second-Language Learning. *French Review,* 48:856–63.

Pimsleur, P. (1974) *Le Pont Sonore: Une Méthode pour Comprendre le Français Parlé.* Chicago: Rand McNally.

Politzer, R. L., and Bartley, D. E. (1970) *Practice-Centered Teacher Training: Spanish (French).* Philadelphia: Center for Curriculum Development.

Postovsky, V. A. (1974) Effects of Delay in Oral Practice at the Beginning of Second Language Learning. *Modern Language Journal,* 58:229–39.

Rivers, W. M. (1966) Listening Comprehension. *Modern Language Journal,* 50:196–204.

Rivers, W. M. (1968) *Teaching Foreign-Language Skills.* Chicago: University of Chicago Press. Pp. 135–57.

Rivers, W. M. (1975) *A Practical Guide to the Teaching of French.* New York: Oxford University Press. Pp. 58–104.

Savignon, S. J. (1972) À L'Écoute de France—Inter: The Use of Radio in a Student-Centered Oral French Class. *French Review,* 46:342–49.

Taggart, G. (1973) Obtaining Lexical Information in Conversation: Strategies for the Advanced Language Learner. *Canadian Modern Language Review,* 29:8–15.

Therrien, M. G. (1973) Learning French Via Short Wave Radio and Popular Periodicals. *French Review,* 46:1178–83.

READING

INTRODUCTION

Prior to the revolution in second-language teaching in the direction of the audio-lingual approach, the major objective in language study was reading. Students, in general, studied a second language for only two years, and this objective seemed realistic. Teachers either used a reading approach per se or a grammar-translation method as a means of teaching students to read. The audio-lingual approach came about as a reaction against these past methods, which placed almost exclusive emphasis upon the written aspects of language while virtually ignoring the oral skills. These past methods, however, did not seem to be consistent with a world characterized by increasing international trade and travel and connected by almost instantaneous communication networks. In the ensuing enthusiasm for the oral skills, some teachers began to ignore reading and writing in their classrooms. Others believed that the term *audio-lingual* implied an exclusive concentration on listening and speaking. Because of this misunderstanding, another term, the fundamental skills method (FSM), was coined. FSM stressed that such an imbalance was not the intention of the early proponents of the audio-lingual approach.

Reading is the skill in which the students will have the greatest ability at the end of their language study. It can be a basis for individual learning about the country and its people. It can serve as a vehicle for entering into the *belles lettres* of the country's present and past civilization. The ability to read will stay with them longer than the other skills, and it is the skill that will be most convenient to use. Reading remains a valid goal in the second-language classroom.

THE READING PROCESS

Reading is a receptive skill. In this respect, the cognitive processes involved are similar to those employed while listening. In both, the students are engaged in decoding a message rather than encoding. Both require a passive knowledge of the vocabulary and structure of the language. Reading, however, is a written skill as opposed to an oral one. Reading employs the visual sense while listening utilizes the auditory sense modality. Another difference lies in the fact that reading is a more solitary experience. Listening requires that one be able to hear someone else, but one may read alone. Thus, reading and writing are less social than the oral skills.

The preceding paragraph indicates that, as far as the mental processes and the underlying language knowledge required are concerned, the shift from listening to reading should be quite simple. Although the gap between listening and reading is not so great as that between the receptive and the productive skills, there are differences that necessitate separate practice with reading. First, the fact that a different sense modality is employed makes practice with the written word necessary. Of course, a rather phonetic language like Spanish poses fewer problems in this respect than a less phonetic language like French. Second, most other subjects in the curriculum require that much of the knowledge be gained from books. Therefore, students are more accustomed to reading than to listening, and many feel more comfortable in this phase of language acquisition than in the oral. Some have difficulty knowing what to do with their hands and eyes while concentrating on listening. Third, some students are more at ease reading a book than listening to someone speak. This reaction may be due (1) to the fact that they can reread sections they did not understand and (2) to the fact that reading can be done in relative peace and quiet as compared with listening. Too, reading allows the students to control the speed (if not the level of linguistic complexity) at which they process the content of the passage.

THE READING OBJECTIVE

The goal in reading is to be able to read comfortably in the second language. The word *comfortably* implies that the students should reach a level at which they do not feel a conscious strain while reading. Naturally, students who spend most of their time thumbing through the dictionary while preparing an assignment have not attained a reading level consistent with the aforementioned objective. This implies that the students should acquire the ability to read, processing the content in the second language rather than immediately converting everything into their native tongue. They should not be expected to comprehend each individual element in the sentence or paragraph, but they should understand the message the writer is attempting to convey. Certainly, the content of intermediate and advanced courses should *not* be viewed as primarily a vehicle for forcing the students to memorize endless lists of words. Enlarging the learner's vocabulary is not synonymous with increasing reading fluency.

In order to attain this objective, the teacher has the responsibility, as in the other language skills, of leading the students from their state of knowledge at the beginning of the sequence to the desired goals. As with the other language skills, this objective is both overall and specific. The goal of the course is to be able to read without concentrating on structure or translating into their own language. The goal at the end of each chapter is to be able to handle the content of that particular chapter in the same manner. The sequence, then, proceeds in a stair-step fashion with the students always working to attain a short-range objective in the process of achieving the long-range goal.

READING ALOUD

The teacher must first make the distinction between reading aloud and reading for comprehension, since the term *reading* is often used for both. Practice in reading aloud is a preliminary step to both reading for comprehension and writing. Before the students can do either very well, the connection between the sound and its written symbol (or symbols) needs to be firmly established. The importance of this relationship must not be underestimated, and sufficient practice to establish this sound-symbol relationship should be provided. Without this practice, the students are not likely to be very successful in the typical language class stressing the four language skills. (It is important, too, to emphasize here that the sound-symbol objective of reading aloud is separate and distinct from the objectives of pronunciation and auditory memory focused upon in choral practice, dialog memorization, and pattern practice.)

The relationship between sounds and their graphemic representations should receive major stress as soon as the written word is introduced.[1] Early in the beginning course, a great deal of time should be spent on reading aloud and dictation practice. The language laboratory or the tape recorder can be a valuable asset in this respect. The students can listen to the text on tape or a record. Then they can read the same or similar material aloud, recording it on tape, and later listen, while looking at the written text, to confirm their pronunciation of the written word.

When their reading indicates that the students are having little difficulty pronouncing the words that they see on the printed page, the teacher should relegate this activity to a minor position and employ it only periodically in order to reinforce prior knowledge. Student boredom is a problem which the teacher faces after a few weeks of asking the students to read aloud. Listening to someone else read is not a very stimulating or challenging exercise. Even at the elementary school level, reading aloud is one of the least liked activities. The teacher, therefore, should be careful not to employ this technique too much. Once the students demonstrate a facility in reading aloud, the time has arrived to initiate more challenging types of activities in the classroom. The students should subsequently be encouraged to read aloud at home in order to improve their pronunciation and intonation and to increase their speaking speed.

The teacher should identify the pronunciation problems of those students who continue to have problems reading aloud and specify what their weaknesses are. Subsequently, they should undertake additional practice with the teacher or with better students who have the time and the interest to listen to them read and to help them. They can also spend time in the language laboratory on special drills selected to improve their weaknesses. Obviously, a successful experience with second-language study requires that the students learn how to read aloud from the printed page. Equally obvious is the fact that the problems are not going to disappear simply by ignoring them. By facing the problems and delineating them for the students, the teacher can help them overcome their weaknesses.

Reading aloud to establish the connection between the pronunciation of a sound and its written symbol should be limited to the initial stages of second-language learning for the majority of the students. Reading aloud for

---

[1]Actually, some teachers prefer to correlate the oral and written aspects of the language from the very first day of class. The argument is made that writing is also an important aspect of language learning and that its introduction should not be delayed. In addition, these same people feel that seeing the written word is going to influence the pronunciation anyway, so why not tackle the problem from the very beginning? The teacher's choice in this matter will likely be influenced by two principal factors: (1) the degree to which the language is phonetic, and (2) the importance placed on the oral and written aspects of the language. The reader should see chapter 5, page 121, for a discussion of the prereading period.

other purposes, however, may well be included later in the students' experience. There are times in any class in which reading aloud can be a very productive activity. For example, in advanced classes the students may benefit a great deal from reading aloud the parts of a play, a poem, a conversation, a description, etc. However, at this level the purpose of the activity is to heighten comprehension, empathy, and feeling, not to improve pronunciation.

Specific Procedures

Until the students can read aloud from the printed page with acceptable pronunciation and intonation patterns, the teacher should read aloud in class any homework material before it is assigned. Asking students to read material that they cannot pronounce weakens students' pronunciation and hinders follow-up classroom activities in which the reading is discussed. As the students gain proficiency in reading aloud and as the reading assignments become longer, this introductory preparation for reading lessons can be considerably shortened and even dispensed with entirely.

Students who have spent considerable time repeating the dialogs have less difficulty reading aloud from the printed page with an acceptable pronunciation. In fact, one danger with audio-lingual students is that, cued by the initial word in the sentence, they will repeat the line from memory rather than read the words. This reliance on memorized knowledge may enable them to bypass learning the connection between the oral sounds and their written representations, and the teacher should make sure that they are actually reading the words. Students who do not memorize or repeat dialog lines need to spend more time reading aloud. However, in both cases certain errors consistently occur. All students have a tendency to read words as isolated entities rather than in phrases and breath groups. The teacher should emphasize that words are not produced one at a time but in a stream. Many students, whether they have drilled orally or not, mispronounce words that are not spelled phonetically. With the French, German, and Spanish word for *general* (*général*, *General*, and *general*), for example, the students are likely to mispronounce the *g* sound until they learn that the pronunciation of that letter varies depending upon the following vowel. Often, audio-lingual students are simply amazed at the appearance of words, and it is not unusual for the word to be so different that they do not recognize it unless they see it in exactly the same context. Even then, the mere sight of it may cause them to mispronounce it. Most students are not able to overcome the effects of first-language habits in a few hours of repetition practice. Once they see the word, there is a tendency to revert to their old habits and give a first-language interpretation to the letter or combination of letters. This tendency is especially strong in the case of cognates. For example, students seeing the word *continent* in French, German, or Spanish (*continent, Kontinent,* and *continente*) for the first time usually give the first vowel the *ah* sound that it has in English. When they do, contrasting the pronunciation of the English and foreign word in a minimal-pair drill helps them hear the difference.

In teaching the students to read aloud, the teacher provides a model. First, he may read the whole dialog or passage while the students look at their books. Then, he breaks the lines into sense groups for the students to repeat chorally as they look at the words and attempt to make a connection in their minds between the sounds and their written forms. Since he is the model, the teacher should read as he would have the students read, i.e., in phrases and breath groups with expression in his voice and stressing proper pronunciation and intonation. His model will be much improved if he listens to the tape prior to modeling for the students and if he marks the phrase groups and elisions in his own text. Also, he should be careful to divide the lines into phrases that are not too long. Otherwise, the choral repetition disintegrates into a chaotic jumble of sounds, and he is unable to judge the students' response. The students should imitate the model immediately. Too often, the teacher reads an entire paragraph before asking the students to read. In the beginning stages, their auditory memory is not sufficiently developed to remember how to pronounce the words. While the students are repeating, he should be alert to catch pronunciation or intonation errors. Any sounds which are being mispronounced should be isolated and drilled before asking individuals to read.

The procedure for reading aloud first chorally and then individually is quite similar to the audio-lingual techniques employed in dialog memorization and pattern practice. However, there are two basic differences. First, the audio-lingual practice of repeating the latter portion of the sentence first is not necessary since the students are not asked to repeat whole lines, only breath and sense groups. Second, since the students are looking at their books, the speed at which they say the lines is likely to deteriorate. Therefore, the teacher should emphasize that they not slow down to the point where the words are not being combined as they would be by a native speaker. At the same time, the teacher should not expect the students to read at the same pace possible in reciting a line of a dialog from memory. If they do proceed rapidly, they are probably not making the association between the sounds and their written representations which they should, and the goal of the activity is being bypassed.

There are various ways in which the teacher can give the students specific feedback as to which sounds they are pronouncing correctly and which sounds are still causing them difficulties. One procedure is to keep a chart indicating their progress. Another is to record errors as they read individually. In this activity, the teacher asks them to read aloud out of his book while he indicates their mispronunciations in their books. The manner in which their mistakes are indicated and relayed to them is not so important as the fact that they know exactly those points of pronunciation on which they need to concentrate.

READING FOR COMPREHENSION

Although reading comprehension is one of the basic skills to be acquired during the language course, it may be the least teachable of the four language skills. By its very nature reading is solitary. The teacher cannot play an active role while the students are practicing reading comprehension. If she does, reading becomes some other related activity. Her responsibility is to select content that appeals to the students and is at a suitable linguistic level. She provides guidelines for reading in general and for each particular lesson, and she plans follow-up activities that encourage the students to read and prepare for class.

In comprehending a written passage, the reader first senses the overall meaning, then segments the passage into smaller units of specific information, and finally reaches a level of knowledge in the second language. Just as in teaching listening, the teacher should stress reading as a communicative skill. In doing so, classroom activities focusing on grammar or vocabulary as ends rather than means are to be avoided. (See chapter 10, "Listening Comprehension," pages 291–93, 298–302.) Too, it goes without saying that the students must have the necessary linguistic knowledge of phonology, semantics, and syntax before attempting to read for comprehension. Students who progress to the point of reading literature reach a level beyond that of acquiring the content in the language. They are ready to begin to examine and analyze the content of the literary selection for its meaningfulness in their own lives and for its aesthetic qualities.

Difficulty Level of Reading Materials

Obviously, students cannot jump from reading aloud to total reading comprehension. They must progress through a series of increasingly difficult levels of reading material. On the first level, they read materials in their own texts. The purpose of these readings is to give them an opportunity to encounter in context the structures and vocabulary they have been studying. Most students do not have a great deal of difficulty with reading and understanding at this level even though they may be unable to discuss the content in the second language.

Some texts now have accompanying reading materials that provide additional practice in reading. If these are not available, the teacher can acquire graded readers. Although the vocabulary may be new, these readers are very carefully graded to include only certain language structures. By examining the preface and the table of contents, the teacher can choose texts that are within the range of his students' language ability. To some students, readers of this type are a welcome relief from the normal classroom routine in which they are concentrating on the materials in their own text.

At a more advanced level, the students should be exposed to unstructured material. The implication here is not that they should be expected to read linguistically complicated books, but that they be given the opportunity to read material in which any structure is likely to occur. Unless students are assigned unstructured reading, they are not likely to do so on their own, or to be able to do so. The result is that the goal of reading comprehension is not attained at all and that, consequently, few students in later life ever have the ability or the interest to read in the foreign language.

In the development of the reading skill, the danger that must be avoided is the almost universal practice of requiring students to read material that is linguistically too complicated for their level of language ability. Reading assignments that degenerate into "thumbing" exercises serve no purpose except to convince the students of the impossibility of what they are being asked to do. Students who must look up twenty to thirty words per page in order to understand the content of the story cannot possibly absorb all this material, and the enjoyment of such an assignment is rather unlikely. Reading can be so much more. Who knows? If it were enjoyable, the students might even be motivated to read in the langue after they officially terminate their language study, a most uncommon practice at present.

Introduction to Reading For Comprehension

The first thing teachers must do to develop reading comprehension is to determine their own goals. The assumption is being made here that their goals are for the students to (1) read with enjoyment; (2) read for the message, not the code; and (3) appreciate what they read. If these are the goals, teachers will not insist upon translations during the discussions of the material read. The only discussion of structure will be to clarify those points absolutely necessary for comprehension of meaning.

Once the teachers have decided exactly what their goals are and the most effective activities for achieving these goals, they are prepared to initiate assignments geared toward a reading comprehension objective. (This is different from reading designed primarily as a reinforcement of vocabulary and structure included in the chapter.) As a preliminary to introducing specific techniques for reading while focusing on the content, teachers should explain these goals and activities to their students. Students should be aware that they are to read for appreciation and enjoyment of the content. They should also be aware that the purpose is not to decipher the code as they concentrate on what the author is saying. Told what is expected of them, the students are able to prepare more completely, and the ensuing classroom activities are much more rewarding and beneficial to them and much more satisfactory to the teacher.

Even if the students understand the goals of reading for comprehension, pleasure, and appreciation, they may still not have a definite idea of how to proceed to accomplish these goals. One of the most difficult tasks facing them as they begin a new activity is the development of a learning strategy. They must formulate some method of attack if their efforts are to be efficient and successful. Undoubtedly, many fail to arrive at a working system and thereby do poorly in the course. Therefore, the teacher should give them some hints as to the "how" as well as an explanation of the "what" and "why." Before they read any outside materials (and perhaps also in reading textual materials as well), students should be given some hints for improving their approach to reading for comprehension.

Specific suggestions   The teacher should suggest that before they look up any words, the students read the entire paragraph two or three times in order to get some idea of the total meaning. Too often students turn to the bilingual dictionary at the back of the book at the first sight of an unfamiliar word. Much of this dependence on the dictionary is unnecessary, and the students should be encouraged to do as little thumbing as possible. At this level they must begin to be attentive to larger units, i.e., the sentence and the paragraph, if they are to begin to enjoy and appreciate reading. Looking up each word robs them of this overall picture and leaves them instead with an overwhelming and disconnected mass of information that is both uninteresting and impossible to absorb.

The teacher should also encourage the students to make every effort to eliminate the first language from their minds while they are reading. In the beginning, thinking directly in the second language is difficult and frustrating. The tendency is to slip into the practice of attempting to convert all elements in the reading into equivalent forms in the first language. Persistence does pay off, however. Those students who continue in their efforts to read directly in the language soon find that the barrier is not so difficult to surmount as they had imagined, and they are pleased at how much more quickly their assignments can be completed. Reading directly in the language also has two other advantages. First, it enables the students to begin to grasp the totality of meaning. Second, it improves their capability to discuss the reading in the second language. Occasional reminders in class stimulate continued efforts toward attaining this necessary plateau in reading.

In short, the students need to be encouraged to read for the content of the material as they do in their own language. Meaningful reading requires concentration upon the important elements conveying the message. Constant attention to each word presents such an overwhelming amount of information that the mind cannot process it all, even in the native language. Just as in listening comprehension, the students must learn to focus their attention on message-carrying, manageable units of language in order to avoid being bogged down in a mass of detail. An analogy with boating may better describe the point being made here. As the boat leaves the dock, it must get up on top of the water in order to acquire any speed. Similarly, the students must rise to the point in reading where they are above the drag of all but the necessary information if they are to achieve any speed and enjoyment in reading.

Even after reading the entire paragraph two or three times while attempting to think in the language, the students still may not be sure of certain parts, some of which may contain ideas that are crucial to the total comprehension of the paragraph. Therefore, they often cannot avoid a more careful examination of some difficult phrases, but they should not resort to the dictionary until all other possibilities have been tried. The secret is to get them to exhaust all their own devices before "turning" for help. Often they fail to realize that the typical dependence upon the dictionary not only prevents them from really learning to read but also slows their reading. They need to be convinced that any kind of speed at all is impossible while they are dictionary-dependent "cripples." At the same time, they should be encouraged to read using the shortcuts that they commonly practice in their own language.

Reading shortcuts   One shortcut that they can carry over from their native language is the practice of guessing the meaning of words. Reading in their own language, they have acquired the almost unconscious habit of making a logical inference as to the meaning of words based on the context. Twaddell (1963) gives the following example to illustrate this point: "The clouds parted momentarily, and the snow on the mountain-top coruscated in the rays of the rising sun." All English-speaking students who understand the remainder of the sentence would automatically classify *coruscated* as being a synonym for *sparkled, shone, glistened,* etc. and proceed with their reading without even considering the use of a dictionary. The students should be encouraged to carry this shortcut into second-language study, and the teacher should make it a point each day to include a few examples from the assigned reading of vocabulary words easily understood by means of sensible guessing.

As well as applying their knowledge of the world around them to infer contextual meanings of words, the students' knowledge of language structure can also be exploited to simplify their task in reading comprehension. Some parts of speech are necessarily more important in grasping total meaning than others. Since students know their own language, they should have little difficulty in deciding which are the most important elements in any given sentence in the second language. Twaddell (1963) uses this sentence from Carroll's *Jabberwocky*, "Twas brillig and the slithy toves did gyre and gimble in the wabe," to illustrate students' grammatical awareness. Even if they do not know the meanings, the students still should recognize that *brillig, toves,* and *wabe* are nouns, that *gyre* and *gimble* are verbs, and that *slithy* is an adjective. Knowing the function of the word in the sentences helps the students to guess meaning. Even if this knowledge does not provide them with any illuminating clues, they still have an advantage in that they know which words to look up in the dictionary. The fact that they can concentrate on nouns and verbs makes the task more realistic and decreases the amount of time spent in consulting the dictionary. In short, it is important that they realize that a dictionary definition is not necessary for each word in the reading, and that normally nouns and verbs are the key words in the process of unlocking the meaning of difficult passages.

It is appropriate here to point out that students may not be aware of this ability to guess the meaning of seemingly incomprehensible sections of assigned reading based on their knowledge of native-language grammar and the world around them. Therefore, it is up to the teacher to assist them in fully developing these abilities in the second language. He should first of all give them examples similar to those given here during the introduction to reading for comprehension. Later, he should not forget to give examples of these skills in each of the reading lessons. For some time, he might point out a few before the students read the lesson and afterwards ask them for additional examples. Thus, he can teach them to be aware of and to practice this shortcut.

Other clues There are other clues that may be used as an aid in guessing meaning, and most students do not automatically practice them without some initial encouragement from the teacher.

1. The teacher should, for example, point out the fact that certain classes of endings in the second language are similar to words with a corresponding set of endings in English. For example, nouns in German ending in *heit* and *keit* correspond generally to nouns ending in *ness* in English; French nouns ending in *é* are similar to many English nouns ending in the letters *ty*; and Spanish nouns ending in *tad* or *dad* usually end in *ty* in English.
2. Cognates should always be mentioned until the students learn to look for them on their own.
3. The students should be made aware of word roots and how the roots of words and their meanings may be related. For example, if a student studying Spanish is stumped by the word *carne* ("meat"), the teacher can ask her to consider the meaning of the English words *carnivorous* and

carnal. Another example is the Spanish word *sonar* (to sound), which can be related to the English term meaning "sound" in such expressions as a *sonar system* or a *sonic boom*.

4. Word families require special and constant attention. Demonstrating to the students an awareness of similarities among words in the second language can assist them greatly in increasing their vocabulary. For example, point out the similarities among such words as *baigner, baigneur,* and *baignoire* in French; *essen, das Essen,* and *das Esszimmer* in German; and *comer, comida,* and *comedor* in Spanish.

5. At times, pronouncing the word aloud may give a clue to the meaning of the word. It is not uncommon for the sound to be closer to the English word than its appearance.

6. As a final test before resorting to the dictionary, the students should ask themselves if their version makes sense. If it does not, then the time has arrived to seek precise meanings of the key words, i.e., nouns and verbs.

Looking up Words

Students also need to be given suggestions with regard to looking up words. The most common, and most harmful, practice is for the students to look up the meaning of the unknown word in a bilingual dictionary and immediately write the first-language equivalent of the second-language word directly above it in the text. The problem with this whole process is that the next time the material is read, the foreign-language word fails to register. The eyes, taking the path of least resistance, glide jerkily in a roller coaster fashion along the known track, thereby unintentionally avoiding the problem of learning new words in the foreign language. Some students even go to the point of writing complete translations above the line. These copies, especially those of the better students, have been known to command premium prices in the marketplace.

Obviously, new vocabulary cannot be learned by avoiding the issue. A much superior method is to ask the students to make footnotes. They should place a number above the word they do not know and write the definition of the word beside that number at the bottom of that same page in the book. Thus, the meaning is there for ready reference, but not in a place that will prevent the students from first thinking about the meaning before seeking the precise definition. Another plan is to refrain from writing the meanings anywhere on the page. In this system, the students place a dot by the word in the dictionary each time they look up the word. Those words with several dots are then studied more carefully.

At a slightly more advanced level, the teacher should initiate a change from a bilingual to a monolingual dictionary. Definitions can be handled in a manner similar to that described above. The switch to a monolingual dictionary encourages the students to define the words in the language rather than depending upon the nearest native-language equivalents. At the same time, the students have much less difficulty thinking entirely in the second language if they eliminate the first-language clarifications of words. Thus, keeping both the classroom discussion and the reading process itself entirely in the second language is much easier than translating into the first language.

Introducing the Reading Assignment

Teachers have three principal responsibilities as they introduce a reading assignment. First, they should try to interest the students in the material they are to read. Second, they should anticipate and clarify any new vocabulary and structures that may present undue difficulties. Third, they should facilitate their reading with comprehension by giving them guiding questions that help them to read with a purpose. Too often the teacher ignores all three of these responsibilities. The typical approach to a reading assignment is to ask that the students read certain pages and write the answers to the questions in the book. Such an assignment, often without the benefit of an overall introduction to reading comprehension, leaves the students bewildered and confused. Except in the case of superior students, there is little chance of gaining any appreciable pleasure or benefit from the reading.

Motivating interest in the reading assignment boils down to the fact that the teacher must express enthusiasm for the material to be read. If she is not able to generate some excitement with regard to the assignment, the students are unlikely to look forward to the material. Obviously, she cannot tell them the content without spoiling the fun of reading, but she can outline the general topic and tell them what they should learn.

In addition to enthusiasm, another important component of motivation is confidence. The students need to know what the task is and to feel that they can do it. One of the best methods of indicating what they are to do is to ask them to look for the answers to questions that the teacher has prepared beforehand. These answers should summarize the important facts of the reading assignment. The teacher can give them confidence in tackling the reading by anticipating difficulties in vocabulary and structure. She should provide the students with necessary meanings through audio-visual aids, definitions in the language, synonyms or antonyms, contextual clues, word families, cognates, etc., or as a last resort, first-language translations.

In actuality, what the students do in preparation for the next day's class activities over the assigned reading depends largely on their past experience, which in turn is an important factor in determining the students' class attitude. If teachers do not require that students be prepared to participate in class activities dealing with the reading, or if they do the reading for them after they get to class, the majority will do nothing. If they are asked to translate the reading or sections of it, or if they are expected to know everything about the reading down to the minutest detail, they will spend their time looking up words. In neither case will they be learning to read in any true sense of the word. The teacher's attitude and selected classroom activities are the key to what the students expect and what they do.

In giving the reading assignment, the teacher should specify what the students are to do during the homework preparation and what they should be prepared to do when they come to class the following day. (This statement is not intended to imply that exact behaviors should be specified.) For example, he might say to the class that he wants them to read for meaning the story that he has just introduced and be prepared to answer twenty multiple-choice questions over the content.

One problem facing students is that they have the task of studying a reading or a story in order to answer questions that someone else thinks important. Such a procedure is not conducive to an excited and critical examination of a reading. To help eliminate the negative effects of such procedures, the teacher might say something like the following: "What words do you think are necessary to an understanding of this reading? Learn them. What words do you think you would need and use most if you were to go to the country where the second language is spoken or if you were to continue to read more in the language? Learn them." Vocabulary is a personal matter, and one would suspect that students will learn more words more readily if they are given the opportunity to select the words they think most beneficial and useful to them. The same goes for content of the story. "What did you like and/or dislike about the story? What kind of a person was the main character? Do you know anyone like that?" Allowing the students to approach the reading assignment with some freedom as to what they will learn and what they will contribute to the coming class discussion of the assignment will encourage creativity, interest, efficiency, and personal responsibility *if* the teacher sees to it that each student does indeed make a contribution.

If the purpose of assigned reading is to develop reading skills, the students should read for who, what, when, where, why, and how in order to get the basic content of the reading. If the purpose of assigned reading is to gain insights into a literary selection, the students should answer the five Ws and an H plus try to gain elementary insights into significant cultural and literary content of the selection. At this level, one step beyond knowledge of the content in the second language, the students should be familiar with setting, characterization, plot, use of symbols, theme, and the reader's personal opinions and conclusion.

Except for the early stages, the teacher spends very little time reading aloud. The typical assignment geared toward reading comprehension is made after a solid foundation in sound-symbol association has been established. Until that time, the students should, naturally, be given some practice in pronouncing all the words before they are required to read them.

Follow-Up Activities in the Classroom

All reading assignments should be treated in class as an important part of the day's activities. Otherwise, the students do not feel the necessity of preparing as they should outside of class. The teacher must choose activities that best reinforce the students for having read the lesson and that will further develop their understanding and appreciation of the content.

The first item of business in undertaking the reading lesson is to clarify all points of difficulty that the students encountered while doing the assignment. These problems of comprehension should be handled quickly and without using the first language except as a last resort.

Early in the course the students should be taught to ask specific questions, like "I do not understand line 10 on page 36." This kind of question aids clarification and indicates exactly where the problem is. As far as possible, questions raised should be answered by other students in order to foster a feeling of group responsibility for classroom activities.

Above all, the teacher should refrain from reading the assignment in its entirety, thus enabling many of the students to get by without diligent preparation. If the students are encouraged to indicate in the margin the passages that they do not fully understand, they will be able to locate them easily when the teacher calls for questions on that particular page. At no time should the teacher even hint that he is surprised or displeased with a question. The students should be given every opportunity to understand all phrases that were incomprehensible to them, even if they should have known the answer. While he is going through the reading lesson with the students, the teacher should make it a continuing practice to point out examples of the reading aids outlined earlier in this chapter. Providing additional examples of these reading shortcuts with each lesson will help the students to incorporate these desirable habits into their own reading skill development.

Since both listening and reading are receptive skills, the same types of exercises are used to check listening and reading comprehension. (See chapter 10, pages 298–302.) The major difference is that in this case the questions are written rather than oral. Obviously, the format of some exercises is such that they can only be completed in written form. One example is a ranking exercise such as the following:

En Prison
Vous êtes condamné à cinq ans de prison pour un crime que vous n'avez pas commis. Comment allez-vous occuper votre temps? Dans la liste suivante, choisissez les projets qui vous intéressent et mettez-les dans l'ordre de vos préférences. Si vous avez d'autres suggestions, n'hésitez pas à les ajouter à cette liste.

Projets	*Ordre de Préférence*
reconstruire mentalement tous les événements importants de votre vie	_____
apprendre une langue moderne	_____
écrire vos mémoires ou un roman	_____
contempler le passage des saisons	_____
faire le plan de votre maison idéale	_____
lire le plus grand nombre de livres possible	_____
apprendre la Bible mot à mot	_____
etc,[2]	

The purpose of using written exercises is to determine the students' level of reading comprehension. The teacher assumes that if the students fail to answer the written questions correctly, they have not or cannot read the assignment. If comprehension of the assignment is based on questions in any of the other skills, such as an oral discussion of the content, incorrect answers may be due either to an inability to read, to understand the questions, or to formulate the spoken answers. These activities can be used as a classroom exercise or as a short quiz over the content of the reading. Once the students' ability to read the material has been ascertained, subsequent activities can, and should, involve the other three language skills. After the students demonstrate the ability to discuss content in the language, the class can, in the case of literary selections, move on to consider the meaning and significance of the content and to relate it to their own lives.

In covering the reading lesson, teachers must be constantly alert to the danger of invalidating all their careful preparation for developing reading comprehension by including insignificant details and facts of minor consequence in the follow-up exercises. Once they begin to expect total translation

[2]From *Connaître et se Connaître: A Basic French Reader,* Gilbert Jarvis, Thérèse Bonin, Donald Corbin, Diane Birckbichler. Copyright © 1976, Holt, Rinehart & Winston. Reprinted by permission of Holt, Rinehart & Winston.

of all the vocabulary, their stated objectives lose their significance entirely. Almost immediately, the students become frustrated, and the goal of reading for content, pleasure, and appreciation is forgotten. The questions in the textbook itself often contribute to the students' dilemma by asking questions over unimportant details. It is not uncommon for the teacher to have to reread certain sections in order to answer these questions. A more suitable approach is to ask the students to answer only those questions in the book that the teacher can answer after one reading. If additional questions are needed to cover all the basic content, the teacher should prepare them or have the students do so.

There are two practical means of getting students to read for meaning without looking up unnecessary words. One way is to give speed readings in class. Students are given short passages to be read in two or three minutes. When the time is up, the content is summarized by the class in the first or second language. In this fashion the class reads the entire passage together in a very short time. Also, the class learns to read for the general meaning of the material without looking up individual words. Once the students have become accustomed to this type of exercise they can be given homework of such length that they do not have sufficient time to read the assignment intensively. (In order to avoid the problem of conscientious students struggling to look up and memorize all the words, teachers should be sure to state the type of preparation they expect and make its purpose unmistakably clear. They must be careful also to include only major points of the reading in the follow-up reading comprehension exercises and activities.)

SUPPLEMENTARY READING

Supplementary reading materials should be made available to the students. They should be able to find newspapers, magazines, and books in the language they are studying, both in the classroom and in the library. Since the librarian is probably not familiar with the sources for such materials, the responsibility for ordering them is left to the teacher. Usually, a direct correlation exists between the teacher's enthusiasm and initiative and the library holdings in each particular academic area. Second-language teachers need to see to it that their subject matter is not slighted. The best sources for new books are the MLA *Selected List of Materials* and its *Supplement,* advertisements in the pedagogical journals, catalogs from book companies, advanced language classes in college, and conversations with other teachers.

These reading materials should be of various levels of difficulty. The teacher can then assign materials to the students consistent with their language ability. The school should acquire readings on a difficulty level ranging from that of small magazines or papers prepared especially for junior high and high school classes, to graded readers, novels and stories which are at a rather simple level linguistically, to reading material of average difficulty.

With a sufficient store of supplementary reading materials, the teacher can begin to incorporate them into the language-learning sequence. Supplementary reading can serve as the basis for listening comprehension, speaking, and writing activities. Supplementary reading can be used to introduce the students to the foreign culture in greater variety and depth than is possible with the textbook alone.

Supplementary reading can provide a means for diversifying instruction at intermediate, advanced, and even lower levels. The students can read materials in which they are particularly interested at their own speed and at a difficulty level that they feel they can manage. Even if the class is kept together, superior students can choose the books, magazines, or papers that they would like to read as a supplement to the class program. Superior students can normally prepare their lessons more quickly than the other students and should be expected to do some additional reading each grading term or semester. In fact, most bright students are eager to do so *if* they can find material in which they are interested at a manageable linguistic level. These reading materials can introduce the students to the *belles lettres* of the language. They can provide a stimulating change of pace from the normal classroom routine. And magazines and newspapers can be a valuable asset in maintaining an attractive, up-to-date bulletin board.

These reading materials should cover all topics of interest to students. Teachers should attempt to acquire all the culture books possible, especially those which describe the everyday activities, customs, opinions, and life styles of the people. Teachers should also search for reading materials related to youth activities in general. The teacher can cut out newspaper and magazine articles and file them for future student use. For the slower students, teachers may suggest books in translation which would be beneficial, if not ideal.

Once the students have passed the elementary levels of language acquisition, the basic means for the second-language student in the classroom of learning more about the language and the people who speak that language is reading. The students should be encouraged to read as much as possible in order to broaden their understanding of the people and to increase their contact with the language.

IDENTIFYING STUDENT DIFFICULTIES

As is true in any learning situation, some students quickly learn to read with few, if any, difficulties. Others need assistance and guidance in order to develop the skills necessary to read and comprehend an article or a story in the second language. The teacher's role is to help these students identify their problems and to provide exercises and activities to help them overcome their weaknesses. At the same time, she should be providing additional reading materials for those students who are capable of reading more. First, the teacher should talk to the students and try to determine their learning strategies. From their descriptions (and she may even want to let them describe aloud what they are doing as they begin to prepare their homework), she may get some clue as to what they might do to improve their reading ability. If possible, she should try to ascertain whether the problem is in their knowledge of grammar, their knowledge of vocabulary, their pronunciation of the written words, their comprehension of the general meaning of the passage, or their inability to remember in the second language.

Diagnostic tests can provide insights into student problems and needs. Allen (1975) describes two such instruments—the reading miscue inventory and the cloze test procedure—and how they may be used to discover student reading problems. The reading miscue inventory gives information concerning the student's ability to answer questions of three types: factual, interpretative, and vocabulary recognition. The cloze test examines the student's ability to supply every n^{th} word which has been deleted from a running narrative. Having identified the problem, the teacher and the students can begin a program of specialized exercises to help them advance in reading comprehension. They may have to review the grammar, spend extra time on the vocabulary, read for the general sense of the passage, or practice coding the content in the second language.

CONCLUSION

Whether the teacher prefers the audio-lingual approach or the cognitive, he should not neglect reading. The point of difference between the two methods lies not in the goal, but in the approach to the goal. Audiolinguists maintain that establishing the oral skills first improves reading ability later. Therefore, students in audio-lingual classes, in general, spend a great deal of time in oral repetition of dialogs in which new vocabulary and new structures are introduced. Later, these same words and forms are recombined into narrative form. This procedure allows the teacher to spend much less time reading aloud when written materials are introduced. Students in cognitive classes, who do not have this background in repetition, require more practice in learning to pronounce the sounds of the language.

The principal problem (comprehension) that audio-lingual students encounter occurs at the point when they begin to read unstructured materials. Cognitive students have their main problem (pronunciation) earlier in the sequence as they are learning to read aloud. Achievement in reading has been one of the strengths of the more cognitively based approach, and most of the studies have found that these students comprehend better than audio-lingual students.

The ability to read for comprehension is a most important component of "knowing" a second language. In the sense that, along with listening, it is the major means of learning more about the language and its people, reading is basic to the improvement of other language skills and the expansion of knowledge. In the sense that the students are unable to control the complexity and difficulty level of reading material that they may encounter, their reading skill should reach a level of proficiency at which they can read unedited materials similar to those read by native speakers. Even though reading is a receptive skill, a definite sequence must be followed in helping the students reach a performance level that will enable them to read comfortably in the language.

REVIEW AND APPLICATION

DEFINITIONS
1. cloze test, p. 325   4. reading, p. 313
2. fundamental skills method, p. 307   5. reading miscue inventory, p. 325
3. inference, p. 316

DISCUSSION
1. How important is the ability to read aloud with good pronunciation and fluency in second-language learning? Discuss ways to practice.
2. What are the components of reading comprehension?
3. Summarize what you would like for your students to be able to do with regard to reading when they finish your class. What would you do and tell them in class to help them realize this goal? What did your teachers do to help you learn to read for comprehension?
4. Do you think a literary goal is still valid today? If so, why? If not, what types of materials do you think modern-day students should be reading? What do you think they would prefer to read?
5. Compare and contrast the strengths and weaknesses of audio-lingual and cognitive students with regard to the reading skill.
6. What were some of the follow-up activities that you found most interesting and most profitable when you were in junior high or high school?
7. What are some interesting activities for relating reading content to the students?

ACTIVITIES
1. For your second language, list the major instances for which there is more than one sound for a written symbol and those instances in which there is

more than one written symbol for a sound. Due to a lack of space and due to the fact that this problem is one to be dealt with in an applied linguistics class, this information has been omitted in this text, but each teacher should be familiar with the lack of fit between the sound system of the language and the written system.

2. Pretend that you are preparing your students for their first introduction to reading. What hints and examples would you give them to help them with their reading assignment?

3. Outline a hierarchical reading sequence in terms of the types of activities that could be used in class to teach each of the components of reading comprehension.

4. Prepare a minimal-pair drill on a cognate pronunciation problem.

5. Collect some samples of reading materials that you feel would be of interest to students at the age level you expect to teach.

6. Prepare examples of some reading shortcuts: inference, grammatical clues, suffix similarities, root similarities, and word families.

7. Select a reading passage from an elementary text. If time permits, in front of the class (a) present and assign the reading, and (b) conduct follow-up activities over the same passage. Ask your classmates for their reactions and suggestions.

SELECTED REFERENCES

Allen, E. D. (1975) Requisite Knowledge for Individualizing Instruction. (Paper presented at the Kentucky Foreign Language Conference, April 25).

Allen, E. D., and Valette, R. M. (1972) *Modern Language Classroom Techniques.* New York: Harcourt Brace Jovanovich. Pp. 189–215.

Blayne, T. C. (1945) Building Comprehension in Silent Reading. *Modern Language Journal,* 29:270–76.

Blayne, T. C. (1946) Results of Developmental Reading Procedures in First-Year Spanish. *Modern Language Journal,* 30:39–43.

Brisley, L., et al. (1959–61) Good Teaching Practices: A Survey of High-School Foreign-Language Classes. *Reports of Surveys and Studies in the Teaching of Modern Foreign Languages.* New York: Modern Language Association of America. Pp. 219–43.

Burling, R. (1968) Some Outlandish Proposals for the Teaching of Foreign Languages. *Language Learning,* 28:61–75.

Coleman, A. (1931) A New Approach to Practice in Reading a Modern Language. *Modern Language Journal,* 15:101–18.

Donati, R. (1970) Using Quotations to Encourage Careful Reading. *French Review,* 43:630–33.

Finstein, M. W., and Thomas, E. (1967) Reading Center Techniques for Second Language Reading Skills. *French Review,* 41:377–82.

Frechette, E. A. (1975) A Critical Survey of Elementary and Intermediate Level French Readers, 1968–73. *Modern Language Journal,* 59:3–7.

Grittner, F. M. (1969) *Teaching Foreign Languages.* New York: Harper & Row. Pp. 252–71.

Hagboldt, P. (1926) On Inference in Reading. *Modern Language Journal,* 11:73–78.

Huebener, T. (1965) *How to Teach Foreign Languages Effectively.* (rev. ed.) New York: New York University Press. Pp. 48–74.

Jackson, M. H. (1974) The Play's the Thing. *American Foreign Language Teacher*, 4:15, 32.

Jarvis, G. A., et al. (1976) *Connaître et se Connaître: A Basic French Reader*. New York: Holt, Rinehart & Winston.

Johnson, L. B. (1931) Oral Work as a Prerequisite to Reading. *Modern Language Journal*, 15:490–500.

Lado, R. (1972) Evidence for an Expanded Role for Reading in Foreign Language Learning. *Foreign Language Annals*, 5:451–54.

Mollica, A. (1973) The Reading Program and Oral Practice. *Canadian Modern Language Review*, 29:14–21, 46–52.

Mueller, T. (1974) Another Look at How to Teach Listening and Reading Comprehension. *Modern Language Journal*, 58:19–23.

Nacci, C. N. (1966) Realizing the Reading Comprehension and Literature Aims Via an Audio-Lingual Orientation. *Hispania*, 49:274–81.

Politzer, R. L., and Bartley, D. E. (1970) *Practice-Centered Teacher Training: Spanish (French)*. Philadelphia: Center for Curriculum Development. Pp. 123–30.

Purcell, J. M. (1974) Teaching the Short Story. *American Foreign Language Teacher*, 4:13–15, 28.

Reichmann, E. (1962) An Active Approach to Second Year Reading. *German Quarterly*, 35:79–84.

Reichmann, E. (1966) Motivation and Direction of Reading Assignments on the Intermediate Level. *Modern Language Journal*, 50:256–60.

Rivers, W. M. (1968) *Teaching Foreign-Language Skills*. Chicago: University of Chicago Press. Pp. 213–39.

Rivers, W. M. (1973) Reading for Information. *American Foreign Language Teacher*, 4:7–9, 38.

Rivers, W. M. (1975) *A Practical Guide to the Teaching of French*. New York: Oxford University Press. Pp. 171–235.

Scherer, G., et al. (1963) Reading for Meaning. In W. F. Bottiglia (Ed.), *Language Learning: The Intermediate Phase*. Northeast Conference Reports. Pp. 22–60.

Scherer, G., et al. (1963) Reading for Meaning. In W. F. Bottiglia (Ed.), *Language Learning: The Intermediate Phase*. Manchester, N.H.: Northeast Conference Report. Pp. 22–60.

Scott, C. T. (1966) The Linguistic Basis for the Development of Reading Skill. *Modern Language Journal*, 50:535–44.

Seelye, H. N., and Day, J. L. (1971) Penetrating the Mass Media: A Unit to Develop Skill in Reading Spanish Newspaper Headlines. *Foreign Language Annals*, 5:69–81.

Seibert, L. C. (1945) A Study on the Practice of Guessing Word Meanings from a Context. *Modern Language Journal*, 29:296–322.

Sparkman, C. F. (1930) Teaching Students to Read a Foreign Language *Versus* Letting Them Learn How. *Modern Language Journal*, 15:163–75.

Twaddell, F. (1963) Foreign Language Instruction at the Second Level. *Teacher's Manual: Espanol: Hablar y Leer*. New York: Holt, Rinehart & Winston. Pp. 1–25.

West, M. (1931) The Problem of "Weaning" in Reading a Foreign Language. *Modern Language Journal*, 15:481–9.

Young, E. C. (1963) The Effect of Intensive Reading upon Attitude Change. *French Review*, 36:629–32.

Young, E. C. (1969) Vitalizing the Reading Skill. *French Review*, 42:578–81.

SPEAKING

12

INTRODUCTION

Second-language educators have long espoused speaking as a major objective in second-language classes. A large percentage of students enrolled in second-language classes are there because they want to learn to speak the language. In general, when the statement is made that so-and-so "knows French," the remark refers to that person's ability to speak French. Yet it is the second-language student with some functional degree of speaking competence who stands out and attracts attention. In spite of the stated goal of speaking in second-language classes, a close observation of many classes reveals only a small percentage of time devoted to activities in which students are communicating with each other in the second language. Too, a casual observation of second-language classes indicates that a majority of students cannot or will not speak the second language.

This failure to produce graduates of second-language courses who can use the language accounts for some of the dissatisfaction with second-language learning among the students and the general public. Admittedly, miracles cannot be achieved in a year, or even two, but given the appropriate classroom activities, one has to hypothesize that many students (not all) can learn to communicate about those topics covered in their texts. The task is to enlarge the vision of second-language educators to the possibilities that exist, to change unproductive activities for those that are more promising.[1] Allen (1974, p. 4) describes an interesting and revealing contrast between the typical second-language class and a real second-language situation:

> Johnny can walk into a French shoe shop, ask for a pair of shoes in excruciating French, and get rewarded; he walks out of the shop with a pair of shoes. His same performance in an American classroom results in some sort of punishment—a low grade, a frown from the teacher, and even a reprimand. Little wonder that our students remain silent! They soon realize that their teacher is not interested in what they have to say, but in how they say it.

Second-language educators have spent countless hours attempting to condition linguistic habits into their students and correcting them for making the same errors they themselves made when they were learning both their first and second languages. The implication from the perspective of research and theoretical models is that second-language educators have fallen into the same trap as the mother who insisted that her child not go near the water until he

---

[1] An analogy as to how potential is limited by past experience and expectations can be drawn from the high jump in track. Apparently the limit to how high an individual could jump had been reached until someone got the crazy idea of jumping backwards over the bar. Now who would think of such an absurd way to jump? Since that time, the heights being jumped have risen.

had learned to swim. Second-language educators should be concerned with steps they can take to produce more positive results in their students.

The purpose of this chapter is to examine the cognitive, affective, and social aspects of speaking and to outline a few activities that might be used to help students learn to speak the second language.

LEARNING A LANGUAGE

Even a minimum amount of contact with someone learning a first or a second language is enough to show that the entire process is beset with incorrect sounds, forms, and patterns. Errors continue to crop up from time to time throughout the speaker's lifetime. The process of learning a language, especially in the area of vocabulary, is never completed. If the language system were ever perfectly mastered, dictionaries would be unnecessary, and writers would not have to keep a grammar book close by to consult as the need arises. In this sense, learning to speak is no different from any other skill. Tennis players, golfers, bowlers, etc. arrive close to the pinnacle of perfection only after sustained practice and improvement over a period of years. No player achieves maximum potential without a process of gradually eliminating errors and inconsistencies, and no player can ever say that there is nothing else to learn. A person does not have to be a star to be a player. Some second-language learners will have the ability and the perseverance to become stars. Others should be given the opportunity to enjoy being players.

With regard to errors, teachers should remember that many theorists believe errors are an important and productive part of the language learning process. Too, the occurrence of an error in nowise means that the learner does not know the grammar. The slip may simply mean that with all the other things he had to think about in formulating the message he was unable to incorporate a point or two.

Although learning a language is a process that is never completed, a functional level is attained in a fairly short period of time. By age three or four the child can communicate most of what he wants to say. However, it is not until around age eight that the majority achieve the ability to produce all the sounds of adult speech. Furthermore, it is not until around age ten that the speech of the majority reaches the syntactical level of adults. It is almost certain that second-language students will never reach the native level in their second language, at least not in class. A more realistic goal would be to expect a functional ability to make themselves understood.

Speech is somewhat like an iceberg. Most of the act of speaking is not directly observable. What we hear is the culmination of a series of internal processes. First, people's thoughts are an outgrowth of their feelings, desires, and needs. They have something to say and are motivated to communicate their thoughts to others. Second, speech involves the conversion of thoughts to language. Third, the sounds, words, and forms used are stored in internal cognitive networks. Fourth, the speakers' competence is brought into play as they begin the conversion of thoughts to speech. And finally, the listeners can hear the result, the performance skill, in action. In short, the speaker's cognitive network contains the motivating force behind the thoughts, content of speech, and knowledge of the language system by means of which thoughts are converted into speech. All except the overt oral message itself are internal processes.

Speech is an affective-social process as well as a cognitive one. The origin of the thoughts, the direction they take, the situation in which they are uttered, and the person to whom they are spoken are the result of both affective-social and cognitive variables.

Another basic characteristic of speech is that its purpose is to convey meaning. The message may be unclear to the listener. It may be poorly expressed and even grammatically incorrect, but the intent is always the motivating force behind speech. In fact, it is probably true to say that there is no true communication without meaning, and no real meaning without both cognitive and affective support underlying the message.

Some speech acts, however, are set phrases in language that seem to be purely stimulus-response reactions to linguistic stimuli. A good example is the formality of greeting someone. The speaker smiles and asks, "How are you?" The person greeted smiles and replies, "Fine, thanks." The person responding will in all likelihood give the same answer no matter how she feels. In fact, she may have a splitting headache due to the multitude of problems facing her at that moment. However, the truthfulness of the answer in this kind of exchange makes very little difference because the person who asks the question in the first place does so out of habit. Few people expect, or want, an honest answer from other than family or close friends. Although these are speech acts in one sense of the term, in another sense they are not because there is no intention of communicating true feelings or ideas.

LEVELS OF SPEECH

One of the difficulties in improving classroom activities selected to develop communicative competence is that the term *speech* is not always defined in the same way. Definitions of *speech* may range from "making sounds" to "communicating in the second language with a native speaker of that language in a social situation." Are the students in a second-language class speaking when they imitate sounds modeled by the teacher? Are they speaking when they repeat lines of a dialog? Are they speaking when they are reciting a dialog from memory in front of the class? Are students speaking when they are doing pattern drills?

Second-language teachers often conceive of speech as being a process of making sounds in the language. On the other hand, most students think of speech as communicating their thoughts to someone else by means of language, in this case the second language. When the students cannot speak, by their definition, they begin to question the practicality of second-language study. Imitating sounds, mimicking a model, and practicing with pattern drills do involve making sounds, but they are not speech, and the teacher must distinguish between making sounds and expressing thoughts and ideas.

There are several reasons why this conflicting situation exists in many second-language classes. First, having one's vision of the goals obliterated by the obsession with the means of achieving those goals is a common malady afflicting all teachers from time to time. Second, in the past the possibility of getting students to communicate with each other in the second language was not part of the model of second-language learning. Third, for those teachers who are insecure in their own language skills, emphasizing communicative activities may be beyond their linguistic or psychological capabilities. Fourth, keeping the class working on material in the book makes it easier to control the students. Fifth, second-language teachers cannot seem to endure the trauma of hearing incorrect grammar in their classrooms. Sixth, audio-lingual theorists have felt that the students should not be permitted to create language in uncontrolled situations. And last, as professionals, second-language educators have stressed linguistic competence more than communicative competence, at times almost to the exclusion of the latter. (One would hope that in the future both will be stressed and that the pendulum will not swing to the other extreme.)

The term *levels of speech* also refers to the many dialectal distinctions, social registers, and levels of expertise that exist in any language. At advanced levels, or perhaps even intermediate, the students may be introduced in their listening comprehension and reading activities to dialects and social differences in pronunciation, intonation, vocabulary, and speech patterns. Basing the students' own speech on one common dialect is the preferable approach, however. As the students progress in second-language study, their own knowledge of the language should grow, but the goal for the majority will be the ability to function in a real language situation.

THE SPEAKING SKILL

Speaking is a productive skill. As such, its development is undertaken after the receptive skill of listening comprehension, and perhaps of reading, and is always somewhat behind that of the receptive skill. How far the productive skill lags behind the receptive depends upon the learner, how far he has advanced in his language learning, and the linguistic complextity of the material. Learning to speak is obviously more difficult than learning to understand the spoken language. More effort is required on the part of the students, and more concern for sequential arrangement of activities is required on the part of the teacher. The entire process covers a greater period of time to develop than does listening comprehension and is more taxing on the students' energies.

Listeners catch certain key elements that enable them to understand the message. For example, in the sentence, *He is a great player,* there are four words that indicate that the message concerns one person. They do not have to concentrate on each single element. However, the native speaker provides all these clues. The encoding process at the native level requires a complete and readily accessible knowledge of sound, vocabulary, and structure. The second-language learner, of course, does not have to be able to generate all the correct forms in order to be able to communicate. The listener can fill in some of the omissions. The point is that functional communication can, and does, occur at various levels of proficiency.

Native speech combines both a code and a message. The code is composed of the sounds, vocabulary, and structures of the language. These components, along with various kinesic elements,[2] are organized into appropriate combinations in order to convey the speaker's ideas and opinions. The arrangement of the parts of the code into speech occurs at an unconscious level and in an almost instantaneous manner. The objective, then, is to develop the students' speaking ability to the point at which they can concentrate on the message rather than on the code. When they can speak in this manner, the desired skill level has been reached.

It is appropriate to emphasize here that this goal can, and should, be divided into small steps. The tendency in the past has been to delay speaking until the advanced courses. However, delaying work until second year or even second semester causes an unnecessary gap in the sequence of learning to speak and is discouraging to the students. The students should be able to use the content of lesson 1 to express themselves orally before going on to lesson 2. By insisting on complete mastery of each section of the book, the teacher builds a more solid foundation for later, more complex lessons and enables the students to experience the satisfaction of attaining short-term goals.[3] As

---

[2]The term *kinesic elements* refers to bodily movements during speech.

[3]The implication here is not that *all* the students learn *all* the material. That just does not happen. The idea is that *all* students have an opportunity to approach as closely to the "real" level of language usage of that material as their ability will take them before continuing to another chapter. It seems that *all* should reach the level of answering questions in which they communicate their ideas even if they cannot supply a long, sustained reply.

the authors say in the introduction to *Learning French the Modern Way*, Second Edition, "No one truly acquires language skills until he uses them to express himself—such self-expression is not only possible from the outset, it is essential" (Evans et al., 1967, p. 1).

The goal in learning to speak a second language is to be able to communicate orally with a native speaker. Realistically, teachers cannot, and should not, expect their students to be able to speak like natives. The rate of speech will be slower than that of a native. The pronunciation and intonation will not be perfect. The syntactical usage will be at a simple level and most likely will include carry-overs from the native language. There will be many needed words that they will not know. But if they can make themselves understood in the language, they and their teacher can be quite proud of their achievement. Although they may not wish to accept such a modest goal, honest second-language teachers must admit that most students do not attain this level of proficiency in speaking. Perhaps achievement would be higher if the goals of the profession were set at a more realistic level.

STUDENT ATTITUDE

Attitude and previous preparation are more important in developing the speaking skill than in the development of any of the other language skills. Speech is generated internally and, therefore, depends upon active participation on the part of the students. Speech cannot occur unless the students have actively incorporated the components of language into their cognitive network. In addition, they must have something to talk about and must be interested in communicating their ideas to someone else. Second-language teachers need to consider the total student as they plan activities to increase speaking proficiency. The teacher's role in acquiring competence is one of selection, explanation, and feedback. The teacher's role in assisting the students in perfecting their performance skills is one of fostering the proper student attitudes for productive participation in communicative speech activities and of providing opportunities for this type of practice.

Most students at the elementary, junior high school, and high school levels arrive at their first language class eager to learn to speak another language. Little do they realize the immensity of the task before them. Some time has elapsed since they learned their own language, and most are completely unaware of the complexity of the process that they are undertaking. The tendency to underestimate the language-learning task has been further complicated by the colorful advertisements claiming and proclaiming new methods of learning to speak a language. All that is necessary is for one to purchase a few long-playing records and to practice for a small number of hours at home. After that short, painless effort one will be sufficiently prepared to travel abroad, enjoying full benefits from the ability to speak a second language.

Most teachers realize the impossibility of learning a language in the fashion described in the preceding paragraph. The ability to speak a language, unfortunately, is not so easily acquired. Interest must be sustained over quite a long period of time if the students are to gain any measurable success toward their goal of learning a second language. It is important, therefore, early in the course and periodically thereafter, for the teacher to reassure the students with regard to their own progress and to remind them that learning a language is a lengthy process. One method of demonstrating how much has been achieved is to return once in a while to elementary chapters for some oral work. Normally, the students are amazed at how simple that material then seems. The teacher should also encourage the students to continue into third- and fourth-year courses.

In spite of the fact that the students want to learn to express themselves orally in a second language, they are often reluctant to participate in activities that will enhance their facility in oral expression. Why does this happen? First, speaking practice is more difficult than sitting back and listening to the teacher or wandering off into some dream world. Second, many feel uncomfortable in their first hesitant attempts at speech in the second language. Third, many students are self-conscious and do not like to make mistakes or to appear stupid in front of their peers. And last, they are afraid of failure, laughter, and ridicule. The desire to speak is real, but the physchological and social obstacles to speaking are just as real. The teacher should pay careful attention to the students' need for encouragement and support in overcoming these hurdles in the path to a functional speaking ability.

Enthusiasm in language study, especially in speaking, is related closely to success. If the course material is presented in such a fashion as to minimize error and maximize achievement, the students are normally diligent and interested. Speaking cannot be developed in a class in which the students are afraid to respond for fear of making a mistake. In successful classes, the confidence, uncertain at first, with which the students begin the semester is carefully nurtured by a competent teacher. In less successful classes, the number of active volunteers decreases in a direct proportion to the number of times the students experience the discomfort of being told they are wrong. After a few weeks, the class begins to wilt, and only a few continue to participate actively in the class recitation. Part of the teacher's success can be measured by the percentage of students who regularly recite.

Active class participation is important in all the language skills, but especially so in speaking. One does not learn to play a piano by listening, nor by studying sheet music. Any measure of skill is impossible without practice.

However, oral recitation is the most difficult activity to elicit from some students. They may not talk much even in classes in which their own language is used. For the shy, introverted student any oral answer in class is difficult. Answering in another language may seem next to impossible. Even those students who normally enter willingly into class discussions may hesitate to do so in a second-language class.

The development of a warm, friendly classroom atmosphere is a crucial prerequisite for a language class. Teachers should be receptive to, and encouraging of, the students' best efforts and should attempt to dispel the notion that they are constant evaluators of every response. Above all, they should refrain from the ever present urge to correct every single mistake. The students do not speak their own language perfectly, and the chances are that they will not speak the second language perfectly either. The important point is that they feel free to participate and to speak the language.

Both the teacher and the students should view errors as a natural, unavoidable, and even necessary part of second-language learning. The correction of errors should not become a "big thing" in the class. Correction of mistakes should be thought of in terms of feedback in which the proper sound, form, or structure is given to the student. Correction of errors should be limited to those portions of the class in which the students are concentrating on the acquisition of competence. Performance activities in which the students are concentrating on communicating some idea should not be interrupted to consider language forms or structures.

One way to prepare the students for individual participation and to give them confidence is to urge all students to answer all questions. First, the teacher explains to the students that they can learn just as much by answering mentally (covertly) as they can by reciting aloud (overtly). Second, he makes a practice of pausing just a few seconds after asking a question to give each of the students time to prepare the answer. With this procedure each student will have an opportunity to give each answer.

Sequencing is important in developing the speaking skill. The difficulty level of oral activities should be arranged in such a way that the students are usually asked to respond only to those stimuli for which they have been sufficiently prepared. Otherwise, they soon become discouraged and cease to be active participants in the class. Such students then wait patiently, or impatiently, until they are permitted to drop the class. The attrition rate in foreign-language classes at present is alarmingly high, and the teacher should strive to lower that mortality rate.

Individual variations are more noticeable in the productive skills than in the receptive. For psychomotor, affective-social, or cognitive reasons, some students do not speak so much, so often, so quickly, or so well as others. Teachers should be flexible in preparing appropriate activities and in establishing suitable proficiency goals for each student. In deciding what they should expect of each student in class, they should take the capabilities of each into consideration. Not many will be superstars, perhaps, but a large number can become players on their own level. Communication in the second-language class should not be an aesthetic process, but a practical one. The important point is that the teacher get everyone into the game.

ACQUIRING THE COMPONENTS OF SPEECH

Pronunciation

Perhaps too much attention has been given to proper pronunciation. Many students will not be able to make all the sounds, especially at first, and constant correction may discourage them. If they are successful in other aspects of the course, they may continue their study of language and improve their pronunciation in the advanced courses. Certainly, this process of successive approximation to adult pronunciation occurs regularly in first-language learning without constant criticism from parents or teachers. In addition, perfect pronunciation of all sounds is not necessary in order to communicate. It is quite common to communicate well with someone who has a noticeable accent. The goal should, realistically, be the ability to talk successfully with a native, not to have a native accent. Certain sounds, naturally, should receive greater stress than others. Those students who have the ability to achieve a near-native accent should not be denied the opportunity; but those who lack that ability should not be denied the opportunity to learn to communicate in the language. Of the two, pronunciation and communication, communication is the more important.

Any assistance that the teacher can give the students as they learn to make these strange new sounds should be provided. If the students are having difficulty with any given sound, the teacher should assist them by describing tongue and lip movements. At times, a diagram on the chalkboard may provide the clue necessary for improving their pronunciation. In focusing on intonation patterns, the teacher may use her hand to indicate the pitch level of the voice. The same is true of stress patterns in the language.

The first step is to teach the students to pronounce the sounds to the best of their ability. The second step is to get the students to repeat phrases and sentences they have just heard. (The teacher must not forget to teach sound discrimination prior to repetition exercises. Unless they can hear the sounds, students can obviously not be expected to repeat them correctly.) Repeating short sentences immediately after a model is not so easy for the beginner as it may seem to the teacher, and the ability to repeat is certainly an important stage in preparation for later, more difficult activities.

In French, German, and Spanish, the sounds that are more conspicuous in an "American" accent are those listed in the chapter on listening comprehension as being sounds that the students may not hear. (See chapter 10, page 288.) In addition, there are sounds that the students can hear but may have difficulty pronouncing. Both types of sounds need to be focused on in the beginning stages of pronunciation practice.

In French, the additional sounds that cause the most problems are (1) the sounds of the vowel *u* as in the pronoun *tu, eu* as in *deux,* and *œ* as in *sœur;* (2) the nasal vowel sounds; the sound similar to the *ny* of the word *canyon* in English, which is one phoneme in French; and (4) the semi-vowel *u* as it glides into the sound of the following vowel as in the word *lui.* In German, problem sounds, in addition to those listed in chapter 10, are the sounds of the umlauted vowels *ö* and *ü* and the sound of the consonant *r.* In Spanish, the additional sounds to be stressed are those of the consonants *r* and *rr.*

Also, in French and Spanish, various intonation patterns are different from English, and the students need to practice those patterns that contrast with their English counterparts. For example, those sentences beginning with an interrogative pronoun normally have a falling intonation pattern, while English often has a rising inflection at the end. Unless the students have practice with these differences in intonation, they normally place the second-language sentences in the native-language system.

In teaching pronunciation, the teachers' role is first to identify the differences and then to practice them in class. They can make the students' task easier by providing descriptions that will assist the students in pronouncing the new sounds correctly. For example, the students need to understand that the English *t* sound and the Spanish *t* sound differ because the tongue and lip movements are not the same. Asking them to pronounce the word *to* in English and *tu* in Spanish and then helping them to feel the difference between the position of their tongues in both cases is a good beginning. The teacher can then explain or diagram the two different tongue positions on the chalkboard. Given this basic understanding, the students need little more than continuing practice and occasional reminders to pronounce these sounds to the best of their capabilities. It may take some time for them to perfect some of the more difficult sounds.

Many students may never be able to pronounce the *r* in either French, German, or Spanish. They should not be penalized because of this inability. One thing the teacher can do is to give them hints that may help get them on the track toward an acceptable, if not native, pronunciation.

A good hint in French is to ask the students to pronounce a *ga* sound. In making this sound the tongue is in the same position as it is for pronouncing the French *r*. By releasing slightly the complete closing of the air as in the *ga* sound, the students can begin to shift to the French *ra* sound.

In German the *r* is also pronounced at the back of the mouth. A starting point is to ask the students to say the German word *rot,* substituting an English *w* sound for the German *r*. The next step is to have them hold the pronunciation of the *w* sound as they tilt their heads back. In doing so, the sound almost automatically approaches that of the German *r*, thereby giving them an idea of the exact feel of the points of articulation.

Although many students may never learn to trill the Spanish *rr* and initial *r*, almost all can learn to pronounce the *r*. A good exercise is to ask them to say butter, mutter, muddy, buddy, and then *pero*. If they have been conscious of tongue movement and position, they will feel the tongue movement and position are the same in both instances. The only difference is that they are pronouncing an *r* sound instead of a *tt* or *dd* sound.

The teacher's responsibility while the students are learning to pronounce the sounds is one of objective evaluator. He must identify for the students the sounds that they are mispronouncing, and he needs to point out to them the difference between what they are saying and the native sound. (Often they do not realize there is any disparity.) If possible, he should point out to them what they are doing wrong with their tongue and lips. And above all, he should proceed always with gentle encouragement rather than adamant insistence.

Vocabulary

Obviously, vocabulary is learned by means of the receptive skills. Elementary language students cannot be expected to generate words they have not seen or heard. Productive skills are not efficient means of learning words, but they are beneficial for practice in using them to the point at which they are readily available in the learner's active vocabulary. Repeating words that the learner does not know and does not understand is of little value as far as learning vocabulary is concerned.

Vocabulary is normally studied in dialogs and/or narratives. Although most authorities recommend the learning of vocabulary in context, some authors have adopted the practice of presenting words in lists. Generally, these words are unified around some theme or topic, and the purpose is to present to the students the vocabulary needed to talk about some aspect of their lives. For example, in order that the students talk about meals, the names of common foods might be listed along with a series of questions dealing with what they eat. As the students work with the dialogs, narratives, and lists, they gradually learn the words and begin to incorporate them into their own vocabulary. Undoubtedly, vocabulary that relates to the learner's life experiences and that can be used in meaningful communicative contexts will be internalized more quickly, will be more useful, and will be retained longer. Learners should be permitted to learn those words that seem to be most relevant to their lives. Affective variables play a major role in the acquisition of new words in the second language.

Meaning of the vocabulary is established by various methods. In some cases the context is sufficient. Visuals can establish the meaning while at the same time presenting an image that the learner can associate with the word. If the context is not clear and good visuals are not available, the teacher can give the definition of the word or paraphrase it in the second language. If this does not succeed, she can dramatize or demonstrate the meaning. As a last resort, she may give the meaning in the native language. As the learners progress with the language, they should become increasingly self-sufficient in determining the meaning of new words.

Acquiring words is not the only problem in vocabulary building. The learner also labors under the necessity of remembering the words previously learned while at the same time adding new words. The first step in maximizing the number of words learned is to ask the students to learn words they can use to talk about themselves. The second step is to promote the use of these words in communicative situations. The third step is to attempt to reintroduce these words at regular intervals so that they will not be forgotten.

Grammar

At various times grammar has been almost an unmentionable in second-language education. Few people wanted to talk about it; some pretended it didn't exist. Former students say it does not help in learning to use the language. Present students say they dislike it yet complain if it is not taught. Whatever one's opinion, there is one overriding fact that cannot be denied—the use of language is governed by rules, rules which the native speaker knows intuitively and which the second-language learner must acquire, either consciously or unconsciously. The difficulties associated with teaching grammar will not disappear by ignoring the problem, since grammar is inherent in the language skills being learned.

Grammar is generally introduced in one of two ways in most textbooks. Either the new grammar is incorporated in the dialog and/or narrative, or the new grammar is presented in example sentences at the beginning of the chapter or unit. Later, after the students have studied these initial presentations, the individual grammar points are isolated and practiced further.

Depending upon his philosophy, the teacher either drills the grammar into the students or introduces the concepts through meaningful explanations, examples, and exercises. The first procedure seeks to condition automatic responses, while the second seeks to help the learners incorporate the linguistic concepts into their cognitive structure. The first approach insists upon the ability to manipulate rapidly the grammar being learned prior to attaching meaning to form in order to communicate. The second approach stresses the acquisition of grammatical knowledge and concepts prior to using the grammar in a communicative context.

The acquisition of grammar seems to be affected by both cognitive and affective variables. First, learning grammar is primarily cognitive. Those learners who prefer conditioning-type drills would most likely do better in the first type of class. Those learners who are able to handle abstract concepts would most likely prefer and do better in the second type. Affective variables provide the motivation and perseverance to stick with the task of learning.

The liberties the teacher can take with varying the required standards with regard to grammar are less flexible than in the case of vocabulary. Too, individual differences in learning grammar, i.e., in the acquisition of competence, cannot be permitted to the same extent they can at the performance skill level in each of the four language skills. There is a certain basic knowledge of the language system that is necessary in order to attain even a minimal degree of functional language usage. In the case of grammar, the teacher should identify for the students a required core of grammar. Those students who have difficulty achieving this minimal level should be given specially prepared compensatory instructional materials that the teacher feels will help them overcome their difficulties.

DEVELOPING COMPETENCE

According to Chomsky, *competence,* the learner's knowledge of the language system, is the base upon which the four language skills are built. As second-language educators consider the question of how best to develop the learner's competence, the key word seems to be *meaningful. Meaningful* implies that the learners will understand the particular aspect of the language system being presented and that they will be willing and able to relate it to what they already know about their language or the second language. Just how this understanding may be best achieved depends a great deal upon the teacher, the learner, the amount of time available, and to some extent the language. Those concrete concepts that can be acted out and demonstrated for the class are perhaps best taught inductively. An example is teaching prepositions of place by putting a book on, over, under, etc. the teacher's desk. Those concepts that are more abstract and complex might best be taught deductively to some students and drilled into others. Followers of Gattegno (1963) refrain from talking and rely upon the perceptive powers of the learner to discover the linguistic patterns in his language charts. Advocates of the direct method favor putting the students in classes conducted entirely in the second language and letting them induce the language patterns, sounds, and vocabulary without explanation or linguistic organization.

For the average classroom, the following sequence of activities to be used to introduce new concepts of the language system would seem to be the most practical for the largest number of students.

Concrete Concepts	Abstract Concepts
1. Examples or demonstration	1. Explanation in terminology comprehensible to the students
2. Explanation in terminology comprehensible to the students	2. Examples
3. Discrimination to demonstrate comprehension	3. Discrimination to demonstrate comprehension
Example concept: comparatives	Example concept: subjunctive

Once comprehension has been established (and the teacher bears the responsibility for ascertaining whether or not comprehension has been attained on the basis of student reaction), the students are ready to practice with exercises containing these concepts. As far as possible, the exercises should convey meaning to the students while they work with the content. However, at this point the students should be asked to select, not produce, appropriate responses. Listening comprehension or reading exercises in which the students choose their replies are best for this stage of the sequence. Although conditioning drills used in audio-lingual classes and in language laboratories limit the possible answers to one which the authors have preselected, exercises may be prepared that permit student-generated answers.

Examples of the previously described exercises might be similar to the following:

1. In the evening I like to: a. watch television   b. do my homework   c. call a friend   d. help my parents   e. go downtown
2. When something is needed at your house from the store, who goes?
   A.   *B.*
   I   go, goes
   My mother
   My brother and I
   My brother and sister

3. Would you prefer to marry someone who is: a. rich   b. handsome or pretty   c. intelligent   d. religious   e. industrious   f. easy to get along with

Using this type of exercise to assist in the establishment of the learner's competence is a rather marked departure from the practice prevailing in recent years. Since the middle fifties, the accepted procedure for developing both competence and performance has been by means of oral stimulus-response drills. Prior to that time writing was the basic means of establishing competence. Performance skills were ignored for the most part in this era.

What is being postulated here is that the use of oral grammar drills is not the most efficient manner, for most students, in which to develop the learner's interim language system. Oral drills must be utilized, of course, to teach the students to pronounce the sounds of the language, and they may be used sparingly to produce and manipulate forms, but not to learn them. Relying upon meaning-carrying activities contained in either listening comprehension or reading exercises in which the students select responses would be more beneficial and more efficient than oral drills. The utilization of receptive exercises permits students to concentrate more effectively on one aspect of the language at a time in the beginning stages, and they have more opportunity to absorb the concepts if they do not have to concentrate on producing them in the early stages of the sequence. Exercises of this type can be found in the "Listening Comprehension" chapter in the discussion of practice that combines form and meaning in contexts dealing with feelings and opinions. (See chapter 10, pages 300–302.)

Developing competence by means of the receptive skills in general and written exercises in particular has several advantages over the oral stimulus-response drills. First, the exercises can be done outside of class. Second, they can be completed at the students' own pace with time out for pauses and reflection, or time out to return to the explanation and examples if the students find that they have become confused about some particular point. Third, working with a written exercise is not such a forced activity as the oral drill in class in which everyone must keep up with the rapid-fire pace. Fourth, the students do not have to be concerned with their classmates' reactions to their performance. Fifth, and most important, developing and confirming competency in written exercises at home can free much valuable class time for communicative practice, which must be carried out in a social context.

DEVELOPING PERFORMANCE SKILLS

As the students progress through a segment of the text, they will reach a point at which they should have an opportunity to practice the performance skills. Before they are asked to communicate, they should have the necessary cognitive knowledge of the sounds, the grammar, the vocabulary, and an interim knowledge of the language system to guide their efforts. In addition, they should have (1) a confidence in their preparation for and in their ability to communicate, (2) a supportive atmosphere to encourage their attempts, and (3) valid reasons for trying to communicate. Too, the students should have some opportunity to practice performance in the receptive skills prior to advancing to practice communicating with the productive skills. Although using pictures to stimulate conversation is a way of limiting oral practice to speaking, the major portion of speaking practice is in response to cues or messages received in listening or reading. The receptive skills not only support the productive skills in the language learning sequence, but in practice sessions as well. Limiting practice with the receptive skills to that one skill is fairly easy. The opposite is true in the case of the productive skills.

Second-language learners do not suddenly or automatically blossom into fluent speakers. They must be assisted in the process of acquiring the component parts of the system that makes language usage possible. At the same time, the ability to function in the language comes by functioning in the language. There is no other way. One learns to swim by swimming, to ride a bicycle by riding a bicycle, etc. What happens in the development of a skill such as swimming, according to physical education experts, is that the learners, through observation, gain an image of how to perform. By performing, they gradually bring their performance into line with the image. The same can be said for language performance. By means of their view of the language system, the learners, through practice in the performance skills, gradually bring their language system and subsequently their language performance in line with that of native speech. In order to learn to listen and comprehend what is being said the learners must practice hearing and understanding the spoken language. The same is true for each of the other language skills.

Performance skills involve the use of the language system to convey meaning. Competence exercises should be meaningful, but performance activities must convey meaning. Any practice devoid of meaning is merely preparation for later practice in performance skills and should never be considered an end in itself. In fact, the latest indications are that such practice may be of questionable value for many students in the development of communicative competence. The goal of second-language educators should be to seek ways and means to expand the proportion of class time spent in the exchange of meaning in the second language. Once comprehension has been established in meaningful presentations, the students can begin immediately to practice with activities in which meaning is conveyed. The students need to be given as many opportunities as possible to use their interim language system in order to create language appropriate for expressing themselves.

TYPES OF PERFORMANCE ACTIVITIES

Performance activities provide the students with opportunities to communicate in the language. At this stage both the teacher and the students should concentrate on the meaning and intelligibility of the utterance, not the grammatical correctness. With practice, grammar errors should gradually disappear.

Sub-Performance Drills

In the case of some students, and perhaps some grammatical points, it may be necessary to insert a drill between the comprehension activity and the use of the content of that activity to communicate to someone else. If such a drill (or drills) is necessary, it should entail the type of exchange that could occur in a real language situation, even though the drill is not being used to communicate. Too, the drill should require the students to make the same kinds of linguistic changes they would need to make if they were communicating. For example, the forms of a verb can be drilled in a realistic drill as well as in a mechanical drill.

Ich gehe zum Fussballspiel. Gehst du auch?	Nein, ich bleibe zu Hause.
Geht deine Freundin Maria?	Nein, sie bleibt zu Hause.
Geht Johann?	Nein, er bleibt zu Hause.
Gehen deine Eltern?	Nein, sie bleiben zu Hause.
Gehen deine Eltern und du zum nächsten Fussballspiel?	Nein, wir bleiben zu Hause.

The two chief weaknesses of such a drill, or of drills in general for that matter, are that the students are required to give answers that are not true and that they are required to give answers for which they have no referent, i.e., for which they have no conceptualized image or experience in their minds. Although such an exchange could occur in a conversational situation, in this context it is a drill of linguistic forms devoid of communicative meaning. (The reader should realize that these weaknesses are inherent in stimulus-response drills, which are based on a learning model in which a preselected response is reinforced. Diversity, creativity, and individuality are not accommodated in drills of this type.) This type of drill may be useful to condition linguistic habits in learners needing this type of practice. However, for other students it may not be very meaningful. Correction and choral repetition are still appropriate in these drills. Beyond this stage the teacher should refrain from interrupting student attempts to communicate except where assistance is necessary. The primary purpose of subsequent performance activities is to encourage second-language learners to activate their competence to create appropriate and needed language, not to interfere with the process or discourage them. The following activities combine practice and communication in meaningful contexts in which exchanges of meaning occur.

Discussion of Textual Materials

Textual materials, in this case, refer to both listening comprehension and reading passages. Discussion of the material in the text is so common that no examples are given here. For the most part, these questions deal with the who, what, when, where, why, and how questions over the basic content. These questions are beneficial for several reasons. First, going over them encourages the students to study the passages assigned, a necessary step in second-language acquisition in the classroom setting. Second, this type of question can be prepared carefully before class, giving those students who have less chance to succeed in the give-and-take of the class an opportunity to "get one right in class." Third, these questions are easier to answer in many cases than other types of questions because the students can often take the answer from the passage with only minor changes.

In asking questions over the textual materials the teacher should attempt to avoid two dangers. First, she should not negate her exhortations that force attention to minute details. And second, she should preview carefully the questions included in the text. Those that do not meet her qualifications should be omitted. If additional questions are needed, they can be prepared either by the teacher or by the students.

However, there are obvious disadvantages to asking questions about the textual material. In the first place, the activity is artificial. The teacher knows the answer, or should, when she asks the question. No genuine communication is taking place, although the students are communicating information when they answer. Too, for some students answering questions from the text over some portion of the assigned material may be less than challenging. For both these reasons questions over content of the text should not be counted on for a major portion of the performance skill activities in the class.

Using Language to Communicate in Class

At the beginning of their second-language experience, the students should be taught to understand and use those expressions necessary for conducting the class in the second language. From that point on, all exchanges that can be made in the second language should be. (See the reference to Kalivoda in chapter 10, page 302.)

Relating Material to the Students

For linguistic and cognitive reasons, teachers must take steps to teach the students to transfer what they have learned to other contexts. They should attempt to relate what is being learned to the students' lives. One of the problems in second-language classes is lack of interest. One reason for this has been the inability of second-language educators to relate second-language skills to student knowledge and experience at a manageable linguistic level. Activities that involve students' feelings and attitudes may give them the satisfaction of expressing themselves in the second language from the early days of second-language study. Certainly, the use of affective activities appears at the moment to offer great promise.

For example, what are the possibilities if the teacher wants to teach the students variations of the question, "What's your name?" One possibility is a mechanical drill like the following:

Model	Students
What's your name?	What's your name?
his	What's his name?
my	What's my name?

Another possibility is to use a realistic drill:

Model	Students
What's your name?	My name is Jim.
What's his name?	His name is John.
What's my name?	Your name is Martha.

The teacher can use this realistic pattern to combine language practice with a meaningful exchange of information and at the same time promote the development of positive-affective-social variables in the class. Obviously, asking the names of the students is a false activity if the teacher already knows their names. Therefore, the teacher may decide to get the students involved directly in the activity. He might start by saying, "My name is _____. What's yours?" After doing this for a time or two and responding with "Pleased to meet you" he asks the students to look around to see if there are other students they do not know. (Given the size of most modern-day high schools, there should be a few.) The activity is to get up, go to those persons, and introduce themselves. The activity need not last very long, but it does meet the requirement of talking with meaning for a reason, it does get the students actively involved, and it helps the students loosen up and begin to get acquainted. Afterwards, if the teacher wants to practice the third person singular forms of the expression, he can ask the students the names of those classmates they met during the activity.

Christensen (1975) has developed a series of "affective learning activities" for practice of the basic grammatical structures in Spanish. The following is an adapted outline format of how one of his ALA activities is organized.

Situation Model

The situation consists of four components: (1) the description or setting, (2) the matrix sentence, (3) the teacher's two examples, and (4) the basic set of questions. The following example in English and Spanish illustrates the structure of these four components.

Language Structure: single verb, future tense

Theme: personal experience or fantasy

1. *Situation Setting:* (given verbally)

   Let's suppose you have been overeating for several months. The doctor says it's time to cut down for your health's sake. Name five things you (the class) will not eat for a while.

   Vamos a suponer que últimamente usted ha comido mucho. El médico dice que Ud. tiene que comer menos para su salud. Nombren ustedes cinco cosas que no comerán.

2. *Matrix Sentence:* (written on the chalkboard)

I won't eat _____.	No comeré _____.

3. *Examples:* (given verbally)

I won't eat French fries.	No comeré papas fritas.
I won't eat pastries.	No comeré pasteles.

4. *Possible Questions:* (verbal practice)

What won't you eat?	¿Qué no comerá Ud.?
Who won't eat _____?	¿Quién no comerá _____?
X, what won't *Y* eat?	*X*, ¿qué no comerá *Y*?
Z, what does *X* say?	*Z*, ¿qué dice *X*?
Z, of these five things, what won't you eat?	*Z*, de estas cinco cosas, ¿qué no comerá Ud.?[4]

Those teachers who are interested in incorporating affective activities into their own classes should consult Allen (1974), Christensen (1975), Simon et al. (1972), Stoller et al. (1974) and Wilson and Wattenmaker (1973) in the Selected References section of this chapter. All have very good suggestions.

Cummings Device

Stevick (1971, pp. 143–44) makes a particularly insightful statement when, in discussing textual materials, he says, "Any fixed set of materials, however,

---

[4]Christensen (1975, p. 214). Reprinted by permission.

carries within it the seeds of its own rejection: irrelevant content, inappropriate length, or uncongenial format. Furthermore, it fails to tap the enthusiasm that comes when the users of a course feel that something of themselves is invested in its creation." One technique to relate the materials to the students, to get them actively involved in manageable communicative exchanges, and to give them an opportunity to create a variety of replies is to use the Cummings device.

Thomas Cummings, who taught missionaries in India, felt that the relatively few interrogative words in any given language could be used to elicit new vocabulary on a variety of topics of interest to students. The prime characteristic of the replies to the questions is that each learner gives a different answer depending upon her own situation. Stevick has found in his own work that (1) shorter dialogs are more profitable; (2) rate of learning was more homogeneous "when the material was true, important and, if possible, autobiographical"; and (3) content used to communicate seems to be remembered better (Stevick, 1971, pp. 310–12).

The Cummings device is basically an utterance initiating some possible interchange accompanied by a list of potential rejoinders and followed by practice. It seems to be a very practical technique of meeting some of the qualifications for communication activities outlined earlier in the chapter. It is a practical technique which teachers may prepare over almost any structure or content as long as they have the creativity to put it into some meaningful exchange which can be answered by individuals in a variety of ways. The format may be used for speaking or writing activities. The following is an example of a Cummings device:

Basic utterances:

Qu'est-ce que vous faites à 6 heures du matin?	What do you do at 6 A.M.?
Et après, qu'est-ce que vous faites?	And then what do you do?

Potential rejoinders:

Je me réveille.	I wake up.
Après je me lève.	Then I get up.
Après je me lave.	Then I wash.
Après je m'habille.	Then I get dressed.
Après je vais au réfectoire.	Then I go to the dining hall.
Après je prends un casse-croûte.	Then I have a bite to eat.
Après j'étudie le français.	Then I study French.[5]

[5]Stevick (1971, pp. 318–19).

DIFFICULTY LEVEL
OF SPEAKING ACTIVITIES

Most of the activities outlined earlier in the chapter consist of questions by the teacher and answers by the students. Question-answer practice is a most important part of the second-language class, and deservedly so. However, as the students develop in their ability to generate oral messages, they should progress from short responses to more complex answers, from short utterances to sustained speech over a period of minutes, from mini-dialogs to sustained monolog and back to sustained dialog. Answering a question is easier than maintaining a line of thought for more than a minute or two, but the most difficult speech activity is the action, reaction, and interaction of a sustained conversation. A related factor in the difficulty level of speaking is the amount of anticipation and preparation time the students have to prepare their responses. Extemporaneous speech requires a higher level of language proficiency than an assigned activity.

The difficulty level of the content also obviously varies. Practice with the material in the text is probably the most elementary. (This statement is certainly dependent upon the linguistic complexity of the textual materials. In some cases teachers may have to provide their own adaptations to put the text on a level appropriate to their students' capabilities.) As the students draw farther and farther away from the text itself, they will have to supply more and more of the content of the class activities.

Question-and-Answer Practice

Asking and answering questions is much more closely related to real-life language activity than drills or grammar exercises and, as such, is normally much more interesting to the students. They can readily see the purpose of this activity and relate it to actual speech. Therefore, motivation and participation are not as great a problem. At the same time the difficulty level is much higher than for drills and exercises, and the students may become discouraged if they cannot answer as readily and as easily as they would like. The teacher should be sensitive to this pitfall and be prepared to turn back to additional comprehension exercises if the students are not sufficiently prepared for such a difficult activity. Also, he should make them aware that this slowing down and groping for words is a natural and unavoidable reaction when the learner begins to attach lexical meaning to structural forms. He should assure them that as they practice true communication, their speed and ease of response will increase.

Once the students are ready to participate in question-and-answer practice, they should be expected to answer the questions truthfully. They have now passed beyond the comprehension stage and are ready for practice in attaching meaning to form. At some point, they must begin to combine code and message, to encode their ideas, to express their own thoughts; and this is the time. Each answer must have a referent in their life. For example, if they asked, "What is your friend's name?", they are expected to answer the question by referring to *their* friend. If they are asked, "How old are you?", they should answer the question by telling *their* own age.

Teachers should be aware also that a sequence of difficulty level exists within the question-and-answer practice at the "real" language level. Some questions are more difficult than others, and they should keep this fact constantly in mind as they ask the questions. For example, it is much easier for the students to answer the question, "Do you walk to school?" than the questions "How do you come to school?" or "Why do you come to school?" The easier questions should be given to the slower students, with the more difficult being saved for the brighter ones. During the question-answer session, the teacher should encourage other spontaneous comments in the language. After all, communication consists of continuous reaction and interaction. Therefore, the teacher should avoid, if possible, plodding through a monotonous list of prepared questions. Short conversational exchanges in reply to student answers at appropriate points will keep the students on their toes and enliven and expand the discussion.

Personalized questions for "real" language practice may not be provided in the textbook. If this is the case, responsibility for this activity falls by default to the teachers. They must prepare carefully in advance if they want to have rapid, smooth sessions. Teachers should avoid, at all costs, asking the same questions every day. The questions asked each day should be different from those of the day before. Language contains sufficient variety for the teacher to be able to formulate questions that practice the same structures but with different vocabulary and in different contexts. Admittedly, the preparation of these questions requires time and ingenuity. However, the questions can be put on cards and saved from year to year, and the results certainly justify the expenditure of time and energy. For the purpose of variety, the teacher can at times ask the students to prepare the questions. They can ask each other questions during the next class period.

Résumés

After having gained some facility in answering questions, the students should be given practice in going beyond simple, one-sentence answers. A good exercise with which to start is to ask the students to give an oral summary of a dialog or reading. This activity has the advantage of providing reasonable restrictions as far as vocabulary and structures are concerned while at the same time requiring the organization of more sustained communication. This practice is much more difficult than it may appear. If it is to be successful, it should be started at the beginning of the course. Holding the students responsible for the material from the first chapter will prevent superficial learning. If the students have truly assimilated the vocabulary and structure, they should be able to summarize, in an elementary fashion, the content. (Actually, at the elementary level it may be necessary at times to let the class as a whole summarize the dialog or reading. Summarizing in this fashion avoids putting too much pressure on a single student. Also, the teacher can begin with one student but switch to other students as the summary progresses. Whether done by one person, a few students, or the class as a whole, the important point to remember is that the main facts be kept in order and that no important facts be omitted.)

Semi-Controlled Oral Reports

At some time the students must, obviously, be given the opportunity to take the next step beyond the résumé—to practice sustained speech in which they are not summarizing material from the book but expressing their own thoughts. Just as in the question-and-answer practice when they went from questions over the content of the text to personalized questions, they now are ready to go beyond the summarization of the content of the text. In this type of activity students need to be given some idea of what to say, some point of departure to get them started. One way of solving this problem is to provide guidelines for them to follow. For example, they might be asked to prepare an oral report on their family by answering such questions as the following: "What is your father's name?" "What is your mother's name?" "How old are they?" "How many brothers and sisters do you have?" "What are their names?" "How old are they?" Of course, the number and complexity of the questions depend upon the material covered in the chapter, but the important point to remember is that unless the students have reached this stage before they continue, they do not have the functional control of the chapter that they should have.

Discussion of Selected Topics

Although many students may not progress beyond the level of guided reports, some students will hopefully have achieved sufficient control of the material in order to be able to discuss selected topics related to the content of the chapter. The brighter students should always be given an opportunity to operate at this level before proceeding to subsequent chapters. These students should be permitted to practice speaking in groups.

In asking the students to discuss a topic, the teacher should be careful to avoid a subject that may frustrate them by causing them to want to go beyond their language capabilities. For example, if she selects some literary or philosophical topic comparable to one the students discuss in their own language, they begin to think in complex terms far beyond the capacity of their language background. The focus should be simple, more like that of everyday conversations rather than serious discussions. Also, the focus should be on something with which the students are familiar and in which they are interested. Often, the students themselves can provide good ideas for stimulating topics.

One way to limit the general direction and to avoid complicated, philosophical answers is to base the oral work on audio-visual materials. The students may describe pictures, slides, posters, paintings, drawings, etc. or use them as a stimulus for short oral presentations. One interesting idea is to take slides of local points of interest and student hangouts and use them as stimuli for conversation practice or oral reports (Grittner, 1969). A related activity that eliminates the memorized oral presentations common to many classes is to allow the students to prepare an oral presentation based on a picture or drawing. The students are not to describe, but to amplify and create a situation. For example, in viewing a picture of a boy, the students may talk about what he is thinking, his mood, etc. as well as a simple description. While they are talking about their reactions to the picture, the teacher intersperses comments that elicit "real" language replies (Blomberg, 1969).

At a more advanced level (the teacher must be the judge of when the students are ready), more demanding questions can be incorporated into the question-and-answer practice. Sooner or later, the students must be expected to go beyond a simple answer, and this type of question is designed to do just that. Questions such as "What do you think of . . . ?" "What do you know about . . . ?" "How do you feel about . . . ?" are employed more to stimulate discussion than to extract a simple answer to a factual question. By this stage, the students should be capable of expressing opinions and making comparisons and contrasts that require more prolonged answers. They need to be given some practice in making sustained responses. For example, they can be asked to describe the difference between some aspect of a foreign culture as described in the text and their own, the typical after-school activities of high school students, their school, their reaction to a character in a story, and so on. The brave teacher may include discussion of opinions regarding school regulations, advantages and disadvantages of studying a foreign language, going to college, etc.

The better students should be provided opportunities toward the end of each chapter to operate beyond the guidelines and call up material from previous chapters in order to expand upon any topic related to the material in the chapter. Without such practice in going from thought to expression, the students never really learn to use the language, because language is essentially communication, and communication involves the exchange of thoughts or feelings with someone else. Although errors may occasionally crop up in their speech, the fact that they are getting additional practice expressing their own thoughts by means of another language is the essential factor if they are ever to gain the fluency necessary to communicate with a native speaker. Perfect language is only an abstraction at best, and the students will eliminate their own errors as they have more contact with the language.

Interaction

More difficult than answering questions or speaking a sustained number of sentences is participating in the normal interchange of a conversation. Each participant must be a listener as well as a speaker. In most conversations, people are forced to wait until the speaker stops before generating their own replies. It is this necessity of prompt replies that is most difficult for second-language learners.

For this reason, teachers should be alert and take advantage of all those situations during question-and-answer practice in which they can turn the students' answers into mini-conversations. If a student **answers** that he has a car, ask him what kind it is, if he drives it to school, and who buys the gas. In the discussions of selected topics, the students also have the opportunity to interact with each other as they exchange ideas and opinions.

Two ways of inducing the students to interact, which are quite popular at the present time, are role-playing and gaming. Zelson (1974, p. 34) gives an example of a role-playing situation that might be used in class to stimulate students to interact and create appropriate language responses. The following is a selected example.

> Ask your brother or sister to let you borrow some article of new clothing. He or she is somewhat reluctant to lend it to you, but you really feel that you need it today. He (she) brings up some of your past sins in that area, and you defend yourself, describing the circumstances, and making excuses, etc., and try to persuade him to change his mind.

A tendency in more recently published texts is to include games to promote student interest and interaction. One example is "Mais vous êtes ma femme!" ("But you are my wife!") from *Voix et Visages de la France, Level 1* (Rand McNally, 1974). In this game each student is given a card containing information about two people, himself and his wife. The object is to circulate through the class asking questions in the second language in order to find the person corresponding to the information given on the card.

REASONS FOR COMMUNICATING

Teachers must not only help the students acquire the necessary competencies to communicate; they are also responsible for establishing situations in which the students are stimulated to express themselves. Rivers (1972, pp. 30–32) lists fourteen reasons for using language that can be incorporated into interaction activities in the classroom. She mentions:
1. Establishing and maintaining social relations,
2. Expressing one's reactions,
3. Hiding one's intentions,
4. Talking one's way out of trouble,
5. Seeking and giving information,
6. Learning or teaching others to do or make something,
7. Conversing over the telephone,
8. Solving problems,
9. Discussing ideas,
10. Playing with language,
11. Acting out social roles,
12. Entertaining others,
13. Displaying one's achievements,
14. Sharing leisure activities.

ORGANIZATION OF STUDENT ACTIVITIES

Using language to communicate is influenced by affective, social, and cognitive factors. The class atmosphere and esprit de corps and the individual student's social position in the group become crucial variables in determining the success or failure of any given conversational activity in the class. Teachers should be aware of the social forces at play in the classroom and be sensitive to cultivating a productive and congenial atmosphere. Too, they should be ever mindful of the students' need for participation in group and social interaction in the second language. The preparations for and the inclusion of stimulating conversational activities in the class format will be the teacher's major contribution to the oral fluency that the students attain in class.

Teachers should pay careful attention to the lines of communication and take advantage of these as the students begin to get involved in communicative activities. On this positive basis, other productive conversational groups can be built. As the course continues, teachers should attempt to develop a helpful working relationship between and among all the students in class.

One way to build a cohesive group in class is to let students help each other during the conversation activities. Too, student input should be encouraged. Any ideas for types of activities or for content of discussions should be considered and used if at all appropriate.

Speaking, i.e., making sounds, in order to acquire competence is not, of course, a social activity and need not involve other people. Mechanical drills in which the students practice the sounds of the language and/or the structures of the language may very well be undertaken in isolation or in choral group repetition in the classroom or in the laboratory. Students may also read aloud at home or in the class, or they may do a pattern drill individually in the class. However, in neither case is the purpose a communicative one.

Speaking to send a message ultimately requires a listener. Therefore, all speaking activities at the performance level imply at least one listener. These communicative interchanges may involve the teacher, other students, and/or a native speaker who has agreed to work with the students. Ideally, the students will have all of these opportunities to converse, especially with their classmates. This author recommends most highly conversational practice in groups of three or possibly four students. Each student should have the opportunity to communicate at least once in every class meeting. One way to accomplish this goal is to let the members of the class talk to each other as many times per week as time allows and as the students themselves can do productively. (This is not to imply that conversation groups should be organized every day. There are other types of conversation activities and other language skills that must also be included in the class activities. The question of how much time the students can spend in beneficial activity of this type depends to a large degree upon the students themselves, the atmosphere of the class, and the ingenuity of the teacher in arriving at stimulating topics.)

Teachers should be mindful of the varying degrees of socialization and maturity levels in the class when they pursue these various types of social interchanges in the second language. As mentioned previously in connection with individual differences, it behooves teachers to be flexible and to permit the students a certain amount of leeway as to the areas and types of activities in which they choose to participate and make their maximum contributions.

CONCLUSION

Especially in speaking, students learn to do what they do. Repeating dialogs, drilling patterns, and memorizing rules, vocabulary, and verb endings are not expressions of language skill, but means to achieving a skill. Those students who drill constantly may become fluent in manipulating structure, but be unable to use that same structure to express their own ideas. Those students who memorize all the rules may be amazing grammarians but be unable to apply the rules to express their own ideas. Success in both cases depends upon the ability to transfer known grammatical forms and vocabulary to novel combinations used to express meaning in new situations. Such transfer is not automatic, unconscious, or easy; it must be premeditated. The person responsible for seeing that the students have opportunities to use all structures and vocabulary in new contexts is the teacher. Past practice seems to have been predicated on the premise that second-language acquisition is primarily a process of stuffing the memory or drilling habits. The emerging picture is one of activating the thought-to-language conversion process. In this process the learner is an active agent guided by the teacher who is responsible for establishing comprehension, for creating a productive affective state and social atmosphere, and for providing communicative contexts for language usage.

Before finishing a unit or chapter, the teacher should expect the students to be able to talk about themselves and their lives, using the content of the unit or chapter. The teacher should provide these opportunities but should stay in the background as much as possible. It is the students who need to practice. Too often, conversation sessions become listening comprehension sessions for the students as the teacher practices.

In evaluating this criterion, teachers should make it a practice to ask themselves before proceeding to a new chapter, "Do the students have the ability to communicate with a native on a topic or topics related to the content of the chapter?" The implication is that the students have a *functional* knowledge of the material. It is crucial in skill development that the teacher not confuse means and goals.

REVIEW AND APPLICATION

DEFINITIONS
1. affective learning activity, p. 349
2. Cummings device, p. 349
3. interim language system, p. 344
4. mechanical drill, p. 348
5. realistic drill, p. 348
6. role-playing, p. 355
7. speaking, pp. 331–35

DISCUSSION
1. Discuss the internal processes and the external influences in speaking.
2. Based on your present perspective and knowledge, describe your ideal class content with regard to speaking activities. What speaking goals would you select for the students?

3. Outline a sample sequence of increasingly difficult activities to be followed in developing the speaking skill for a particular unit.
4. Outline ways and means of accommodating individual differences in developing the speaking skill in second-language classes.
5. Discuss the importance of meaning in the process of developing speaking skills.
6. In any second-language class, the teacher must determine the proportion of time to be spent on developing competence and on practicing performance skills. What are some of the factors involved in this decision?
7. What role do errors play in second-language acquisition? How and when should student errors be corrected?
8. Formulate guidelines for keeping the class in the second language.

ACTIVITIES

1. In an elementary second-language text find examples of oral drills or exercises to develop both competence and performance skills.
2. Prepare an affective speaking activity, a game involving speaking, a role-playing situation, a stimulating discussion activity, and at least one speaking activity based on one of Rivers's fourteen reasons for using language. Present them to the class for student reactions and suggestions.
3. Visit a conversation class. Note (a) the types of speaking activities, (b) student reaction and classroom atmosphere, (c) the quantity and types of student errors, and (d) the teacher's role.
4. Plan a sequence of increasingly difficult speaking activities for some grammar point in the text you are using.
5. Using a dialog or a reading from an elementary second-language text, prepare some personalized questions relating the content to the students.

SELECTED REFERENCES

Allen, E. A. (1974) Communicative Competence. Paper presented at the ACTFL Convention.

Allen, E. A., and Valette, R. M. (1972) *Modern Language Classroom Techniques.* New York: Harcourt Brace Jovanovich. Pp. 43–63, 160–88.

Bashour, D. S. (1966) Teaching French Pronunciation to Beginners. *French Review,* 39:910–18.

Belasco, S., et al. (1963) The Continuum: Listening and Speaking. In W. F. Bottiglia (Ed.), *Language Learning: The Intermediate Phase.* Northeast Conference Reports. Pp. 2–21.

Blomberg, J. (1969) Give Them A Better Chance. *Hispania,* 52:881–84.

Bonin, T. M., and Birckbichler, D. W. (1975) Real Communication Through Interview and Conversation Cards. *Modern Language Journal,* 59:22–25.

Brisley, L., et al. (1959–61) Good Teaching Practices: A Survey of High-School Foreign-Language Classes. *Reports of Surveys and Studies in the Teaching of Modern Foreign Languages.* New York: Modern Language Association of America. Pp. 219–43.

Carton-Caprio, D. (1975) Learning by Doing: A Practical Foreign Language

Classroom Experience. *Modern Language Journal*, 59:97–100.

Chastain, K. (1969) A Proposal for Sharing. *Hispania*, 52:57–59.

Christensen, C. B. (1975) Affective Learning Activities. *Foreign Language Annals*, 8:211–19.

Cook, V. J. (1968) Some Types of Oral Structure Drills. *Language Learning*, 18:155–64.

Coulombe, R., et al. (1974) *Voix et Visages de la France, Level 1.* Chicago: Rand McNally.

Edgerton, M. F., Jr., et al. (1968) Liberated Expression. In T. E. Bird (Ed.), *Foreign Language Learning: Research and Development.* Northeast Conference Reports. Pp. 75–118.

Evans, J., et al. (1967) *Learning French the Modern Way.* (2nd ed.) St. Louis: McGraw-Hill. P. 1.

Freilich, J. S. (1973) Imagination—Let's Tap It. *Accent on ACTFL*, 4:26, 38.

Gaarder, A. B. (1967) Beyond Grammar and Beyond Drills. *Foreign Language Annals*, 1:109–18.

Gattegno, C. (1963) *Teaching Foreign Languages in Schools: The Silent Way.* Reading, England: Educational Explorers.

Grittner, F. M. (1969) *Teaching Foreign Languages.* New York: Harper & Row. Pp. 245–49.

Hammerly, H. (1973) The Correction of Pronunciation Errors. *Modern Language Journal*, 57:106–10.

Hartley, P. J. (1974) Dialing Data Diversifies Speaking Situations. *Accent on ACTFL*, 4:17–18.

Hok, R. (1964) Oral Exercises: Their Type and Form. *Modern Language Journal*, 48:222–26.

Hooper, A. C. (1973) Pictures Stimulate Conversation. *Accent on ACTFL*, 4:16.

Jarvis, G. (1968) A Behavioral Observation System for Foreign Language Skill Acquisition. *Modern Language Journal*, 52:335–41.

Jarvis, G. (1970) *A Comparison of Contextualized Practice with Particularized Referents vs. Practice with Generic Meaning in the Teaching of Beginning College French.* Ph.D. diss., Purdue University.

Joiner, E. G. (1974) Keep Them Guessing. *American Foreign Language Teacher*, 4:16–18.

Kalivoda, T. A. (1972) Let's Use Foreign Language for Real Communication. *American Foreign Language Teacher*, 2:14–15, 36, 39.

Keaton, R. (1974) Hola, ¿Cómo Estás? *Accent on ACTFL*, 4:27.

Knop, C. K. (1972) Toward Free Conversation. *American Foreign Language Teacher*, 4:5–9.

Lafayette, R. C. (1974) The Case for Student Creativity. *American Foreign Language Teacher*, 4:14–15, 17, 36.

Meiden, W. (1963) A Device for Teaching Pronunciation—The Reading of the Lesson of the Day. *Modern Language Journal*, 47:65–69.

Molina, H. (1968) Transformation Grammar in Teaching Spanish. *Hispania*, 51:284–86.

Nacci, C. N. (1965) Enriching the Audio-Lingual Activity in the Classroom. *Hispania*, 48:109–14.

Nachtmann, F. W. (1973) Let the Student Have the Last Word. *French Review*, 47:62–68.

Oates, M. D. (1972) Principles and Techniques for Stimulating Foreign-Language Conversation. *Foreign Language Annals*, 6:68–72.

Palmer, A. (1970) Teaching Communication. *Language Learning*, 20:55–68.

Parker, D. V. (1974) Effective Use of Questions. *Canadian Modern Language Review*, 31:75–78.

Politzer, R. L., and Bartley, D. E. (1970) *Practice-Centered Teacher Training: Spanish (French).* Philadelphia: Center for Curriculum Development. Pp. 101–22.

Potter, E. J. (1971) French Conversation for Young Adults. *Modern Language Journal*, 55:505–57.

Rivers, W. M. (1968) *Teaching Foreign-Language Skills.* Chicago: University of Chicago Press. Pp. 158–212.

Rivers, W. M. (1972) Talking Off the Tops of Their Heads. *Speaking in Many Tongues.* Rowley, Mass.: Newbury House. Pp. 30–32.

Rivers, W. M. (1975) *A Practical Guide to the Teaching of French.* New York: Oxford University Press. Pp. 3–57, 141–68.

Runte, R. (1974) A Definition of Goals in Teaching Conversation. *American Foreign Language Teacher,* 4:28–29, 36.

Simon, S. B., et al. (1972) *Values Clarification: A Handbook of Practical Strategies for Teachers and Students.* New York: Hart.

Sinnema, J. R. (1971) Rotation Drills in Teaching Conversation. *Modern Language Journal,* 55:269–71.

Stack, E. M. (1966) *The Language Laboratory and Modern Language Teaching.* (rev. ed.) New York: Oxford University Press. Pp. 83–144.

Stern, H. H. (1975) What Can We Learn from the Good Language Learner? *Canadian Modern Language Review,* 31:304–18.

Stevick, E. W. (1971) *Adapting and Writing Language Lessons.* Washington, D. C.: Foreign Service Institute.

Stevick, E. W. (1974) The Meaning of Drills and Exercises. *Language Learning,* 24:1–22.

Stoller, P. H., et al. (1974) *Real Communication in French.* Upper Jay, N. Y.: The Adirondack Mountain Humanistic Education Center.

Strain, J. E. (1968) Drilling and Methodology. *Language Learning,* 18:177–82.

Taggart, G. (1973) Obtaining Lexical Information in Conversation: Strategies for the Advanced Language Learner. *Canadian Modern Language Review,* 29:8–15.

Wilson, V., and Wattenmaker, B. (1973) *Real Communication in Spanish.* Upper Jay, N. Y.: The Adirondack Mountain Humanistic Education Center.

Zelson, S. N. J. (1974) Skill-Using Activities in the Foreign Language Classroom. *American Foreign Language Teacher,* 4:33–35.

WRITING

The Role of Writing in Second-Language Learning

Sequence in Developing the Writing Skill

Sequence of Writing Exercises and Activities
- Competence—Writing Words
  - Copying
  - Spelling Sounds
  - Dictation
- Competence Exercises—Writing Language Forms
  - Language Forms
  - Simulation Exercises
- Productive Performance Exercises
  - Explained Situation
  - Sentence Completion
  - Answering Questions
  - Originating Questions and Answers
- Sustained Writing
  - Summaries
  - Semi-Controlled Writing
  - Quality Versus Quantity

Combining Language Skills

INTRODUCTION

It was stated in chapter 10 that in the rush to attain speaking skills, listening comprehension often fails to receive the attention it deserves. Writing, too, is often slighted. Especially since the inception of the audio-lingual movement the oral skills have received major attention, and writing has been considered least important of the language skills. It seems somewhat strange that in the case of oral skills, less importance is attached to the receptive skill (listening), while in the other case, the written skills, less importance is accorded to the productive skill (writing). Whether or not the students need to learn how to express themselves in writing actually depends upon the individual students and their goals. As many may have opportunities to write to native speakers in the language as have the opportunity to talk to native speakers. Even if they do not need the writing skill for communicative purposes, writing is a valuable asset in the classroom as the second-language learner seeks to gain competence and to functionalize productive skills. The purpose of this chapter is to discuss the writing skill and how it may help the students in learning a second language.

THE ROLE OF WRITING IN SECOND-LANGUAGE LEARNING

Writing is a recognized objective among most language teachers, and as such, it should be emphasized in the classroom. Although the development of a true literary ability in the second language is extremely unlikely at this level, a situation may arise in which there is a need to communicate a written message in that language. If so, the students should be prepared to do so.

The ability to write is recognized in society and in the schools as an important objective of language study. A method in which there was no writing practice would be suspect from the traditional point of view. Traditionally also, the students associate homework with a written assignment. Beginning students who do not have homework often get the false, but exciting, notion that a second-language class requires no preparation. Even mature students at more advanced levels tend to treat oral assignments with less respect than written ones. At times, the only successful method of eliciting outside class preparation is to assign written work for the next day.

During the following class period, these written exercises are easily and quickly corrected in class and are an important means of determining true comprehension of the structures being studied. At the same time, changing the focus of the students' attention from oral to written activities during the class period can be a welcome relief. After a few minutes the students will be ready for some other activity, but the necessary change of momentum has by then been achieved.

Writing also helps to solidify the students' grasp of vocabulary and structure and complements the other language skills. Another factor is involved here also. Since writing and speaking are productive skills, they demand learning at a more profound level, thereby insuring greater retention of the receptive skills. One would expect that students who have spent a considerable proportion of their language-learning time in the productive skills would have a more complete knowledge of the language. Certainly, they have more facility in the performance of that knowledge.

In learning to control the use of the second-language system, learners must learn the bits and pieces of words as well as the words themselves and how the words fit together in sentences. They must, for example, learn to produce and manipulate the morphemes of the language.[1] One important characteristic of writing is that written exercises can be prepared in which the learner is asked to produce appropriate word endings or word changes according to the context of the sentence. It is the only type of practice in which the learner can realistically be asked to supply parts of words. In listening comprehension and reading, the learner must be able to recognize and comprehend the meaning carried by the morphemes, but not to produce them. In speaking, the learner must be able to produce words containing the appropriate word endings and changes, but not to produce them in isolation. Listening comprehension, reading, and speaking, then, provide valuable practice in using the morphemes in communicative situations, but how do the students concentrate on these parts of words and learn them? The most appropriate skill for such practice is cognitive writing exercises. In this sense, writing is the most valuable type of practice for developing the morpheme aspects of second-language competence.

The teacher can also use written exercises to evaluate student progress in concept acquisition as well as in writing ability. These exercises can be written so as to be easy to grade, and the results are easily interpreted by the students. Scores from such tests are tangible evidence of student achievement and are important components of the course grade. The goal in writing is twofold. The immediate goal is to develop the students' ability to write to the point at which written homework assignments can be given. Psychologically, students are more impressed by exercises that are to be written and handed in than by those that are to be "learned." Realistically, the teacher knows that writing homework exercises and other written activities help the students to acquire

---

[1]A *morpheme* is the smallest unit of meaning in a language. For example, in the word *books*, there are two morphemes: *book* and *s*. The morpheme *book* is a "free morpheme" in that it can stand by itself. The *s* is a "bound morpheme" in that it must always be joined to another morpheme.

the vocabulary and the grammar of the lesson. Practically, the students' minimum contact with the language in the classroom must be expanded as much as possible. The overall objective, of course, is to be able to write a message that a native speaker would be able to understand. Just as was true in the case of speaking, this aim does not imply native speaker proficiency. However, the important criterion is that they can express their ideas in written form, however elementary the fashion.

Students do not have to acquire as high a level of proficiency in speaking and writing as they do in listening comprehension and reading to be able to function in the language. This contention can be supported on three counts. First, the receptive skills provide the means for the students to absorb new vocabulary and structure. From this point of view, it is most important that these two skills be developed to the maximum. From this base, the students have limitless possibilities for expanding their knowledge of the language and its people. Second, the students have little control over the linguistic complexity of language which they may hear or need to read. Thus, it is most important that they be trained to anticipate complex forms which they are not able to use actively. Third, although correct speech is the goal, the native speaker can fill in the gaps and comprehend the message, *if* there are not too many errors. A point of incomprehensibility does, of course, exist.

The purpose of the preceding paragraph is not to deemphasize the importance of the productive skills but to stress the fact that the students can control the level of their speech and writing. Students should learn to speak and write in a manner that makes self-expression in both skills possible, but communication is possible and acceptable at a level below that of a native speaker. In the classroom, both the teacher and the students are much better satisfied if they keep in mind that the goal in the productive skills is not native speech, but the ability to communicate with a native speaker. On the other hand, the goal in listening comprehension and reading should be to comprehend native speech.

The many similarities between speaking and writing indicate that there is quite a bit of carry-over from one skill to the other. The mental processes involved in both give the students practice in going from thought to language. However, the differences are sufficiently important to require that practice be provided in each. Obviously, speech involves sound while writing does not. At the competence level, the purpose of speaking practice is to develop sound discrimination and auditory memory while writing practice stresses sound-symbol association, vocabulary, spelling, and structural forms. Speech is normally a social process carried out in the presence of other people while the written lesson may be completed alone. Speech requires almost instantaneous formulations of statements or questions followed by replies and reactions, while writing is a much slower process. In writing, the students have more time to search for words and forms. To some students, completing written exercises presents much less threat than giving responses to oral stimuli. The last two differences, then, may cause a psychological discomfort in speaking that is not a factor in writing.

SEQUENCE IN DEVELOPING THE WRITING SKILL

The sequence of classroom activities necessary to develop the writing skill resembles that of speaking except for the fact, of course, that the students write rather than talk. Too, writing exercises can be used to practice separate morphemic components of words. This is not the case in speaking. As in speaking, the students must first gain a certain degree of control over the underlying language competence before they can begin to move into the development of the productive performance skill of writing to communicate a message. The initial steps in the sequence are merely preparatory exercises, and the teacher should never regard them as ends in themselves. The teacher should also be aware of the fact that proper sequencing in the teaching of the productive skills cannot be ignored if the students are to develop the confidence necessary to use these skills. Unless the students are led, step by step, in activities of increasing levels of difficulty, they cannot be expected to have an active command of the material.

Attention to sequencing should begin as soon as writing is introduced, and performance skills should be actualized for each chapter as the material is being covered in class. At the end of the first chapter or unit in their text, the students should be able to express themselves orally or in written form about the topic or topics of that chapter.

Past approaches to second-language teaching have failed to develop complete sequences leading to writing. In the grammar-translation approach, the students were expected to translate complex sentences and even conversations or paragraphs from the first to the second language; however, there was little attention given to self-expression in writing. With audio-lingual materials, students were expected to leap from copying practice, sentence completion, and pattern drill practice to controlled responses in writing; however, there was still little emphasis on composing in the second language. An examination of such sequences is sufficient to explain the fact that in the past students have acquired only a quite limited facility in expressing themselves in writing. Too, some second-language educators have been guilty of wanting to wait until the next level to introduce written compositions.

Similar problems occur in teaching both speaking and writing due to the fact that both require the learners to activate their interim, incomplete grammar system by means of performance skills that are not sufficiently developed to put into practice all the structure and vocabulary that the learners know. In the beginning, what the learners say or write will not, in all likelihood, be a true representation of the total knowledge contained in their cognitive structure. As they attempt to create language to express their thoughts, both their speech and writing will contain various inaccuracies. The functionalization of the learners' language system involves bringing the learners' performance skills into line with their competence and of bringing their competence as close to that of the native speaker as their capabilities permit. The position taken in this text is that the learner's competence and performance will not coincide with that of the native, except in rare cases. The goal is to reach the point at which unavoidable individual deviations do not prevent communication.

Other problems in writing relate to the affective domain of student interests and attitudes. There are several things teachers can do to alleviate these problems. First, the student's confidence and motivation must be maintained during the competence acquisition stage. Second, topics should be selected that are stimulating without being highly complex and philosophical. Ideally, the writing assignment will center around some idea of interest to the students but not encourage them to attempt to utilize complicated sentence patterns beyond their level of language learning. One type of activity, which at the moment promises to fit these qualifications, combines language expression and affective content. (Please see chapter 12, pages 347–49, for examples.)

Accepting the goal of communication in writing is especially difficult due to the fact that by tradition more is expected of written than spoken language. Writing is more carefully prepared and more highly polished. Teachers generally tolerate errors in writing more readily than errors in speaking. However, teachers should not expect most students to write polished compositions in the second language under any circumstance, since they can rarely do that in their first language. Moans of surprise and displeasure also come from the classrooms of first-language teachers as they read student compositions.

SEQUENCE OF WRITING EXERCISES AND ACTIVITIES

Before being introduced to writing, the students should be able to hear the sounds of the second language and to pronounce them aloud when they see them. They should have a corpus of vocabulary, and they should comprehend the grammatical structures with which they will be working as they are writing.

In the writing sequence, writing consists of the completion of exercises that teach students to (1) write the sounds they can understand, pronounce, and read; (2) master the forms of the grammar being studied; and (3) proceed to activities in which they practice combining words and grammar to express themselves in writing. Many of the exercises and activities used in developing speaking abilities are also appropriate for developing writing abilities.

Competence—Writing Words

Copying   The first step in teaching writing is to develop the students' ability in the formation of graphemes and to acquaint them with all punctuation.[2] In the case of those languages using the Latin alphabet, few difficulties are encountered. Languages using other alphabets are, needless to say, much more difficult, and additional attention should be given to this first step in writing.

One of the recommendations of early audio-lingual proponents was to ask the students to copy each assigned line of the dialog five times. However, the results were not encouraging. Often the fifth version contained more errors than the first. Instead of improving, many students' work deteriorated during the course of what was supposed to be a learning activity. This is an example of high error rate due to low level of difficulty and its corollary, lack of sufficient challenge to stimulate student interest.

In order to avoid such errors of carelessness, teachers should watch carefully, and at the first sign that copying is not accomplishing its purpose of learning how to make the letters and to punctuate the sentences properly, they should abandon this technique. It is doubtful whether copying will hold the students' attention for more than a few weeks after writing is introduced. In fact, the teacher should consider the advisability of varying the ways of copying. One possible way is to scramble the words and ask the students to rearrange them in the proper order. Especially in those languages that have a similar alphabet many students can begin immediately to write answers to simple questions. For example, writing the answers to a question such as "Is the house big?" would provide identical practice in making the letters and punctuation but would be more stimulating than mere copying. Too, practice of this type would be more beneficial in developing competence and performance skills.

Spelling sounds   The first step that students should take in learning to spell what they hear is to learn the different graphemes possible for each sound and the context in which each occurs. The teacher should isolate these graphemes and present them one at a time in the early stages of writing. Doing one of

---

[2]A *grapheme* is the written representation of a sound.

these a day until all have been covered provides a needed preliminary to dictation and a variation from oral or reading activities. Needless to say, the students should be able to hear, pronounce, and read aloud these sounds before they are asked to write them. In fact, this activity correlates very well with practice in reading aloud.

The following are examples of sounds that have different spellings and, therefore, should be included in spelling practice. (The French words are from *Reading-Writing-Spelling Manual, A-LM French Level I,* 1964, p. 45.)

French

je	orange	gitan
bonjour	dommage	gisant
journal	gens	girafe

German

Pause	Dieb	Lippe
Papier	er gibt	Kappe
Professor	du lebst	Gruppe

Spanish

que	casa	culpa
queso	cama	cuna
quita	cosa	
quinto	como	

Dictation   The purpose of dictation practice is twofold. First, taking dictation provides additional reinforcement to the relationship between the sound and the symbol that was established in reading aloud. (The past tense was used in the preceding sentence because dictation would not precede practice reading aloud. If the students cannot look at a word and pronounce it, there is practically no chance that they will be able to spell it correctly during a dictation.) Second, the dictation, properly given, is an excellent test of the development of the students' auditory memory. In this sense, it is more a test of listening comprehension than of writing. It is a means toward an end, not a goal in itself.

At first, the students should be asked to write only language taken directly from their own text. Later, familiar vocabulary in new contexts or even unfamiliar material can be used to test whether they have really been hearing the sounds and spelling them or whether they have merely been memorizing the lines. In selecting the dictation, the teacher should choose only short sections with words containing the sounds being studied. Dictations can easily become long, drawn-out procedures if too many lines are dictated.

The teacher should be careful to read at normal speed and with the normal elisions. (Beginning teachers may profit tremendously by listening to the tape before giving the dictation!) Slowing down to the point of pronouncing each word separately negates the whole purpose of the dictation. Too, the teacher must not succumb to the pleas of some students to repeat just one more time. Phrases that are repeated over and over again are no longer tests of listening comprehension. While reading the dictation, the teacher should pay close attention to the students. By watching them, she can easily judge the length of the pauses. Obviously, she cannot wait for everyone to finish, but she can estimate the writing speed of most students in class. Except for quizzes, dictations should be graded by the students themselves.

In order to prepare for dictations, the students need to pay careful attention during the mimicry-memorization drill and reading-aloud practice. They should be encouraged to read aloud as they study for the dictation and to repeat the sentence without looking at the words. While practicing the pronunciation, they should also take special notice of all words or combinations of words that do not look the way they sound. Then, during the dictation itself, they should not be allowed to write any words until the teacher has completed the entire phrase being dictated. As soon as the teacher finishes the phrase or sentence, the students should repeat it to themselves and continue to repeat as they write.

Students who have difficulty taking dictations are often committing two serious mistakes. First, they think of a dictation as a spelling test. The teacher should make clear to them that a dictation also tests their ability to hear sounds and to hold these sounds in their minds while they are writing. Second, they begin to write before they hear all the dictated phrase. This "jumping the gun" causes them to miss much of the dictation.

As was mentioned earlier, dictation practice is a step, but only a minor one, in developing the ability to write. At the early levels of language learning, the students use dictation practice in each chapter as a means of putting the material in that chapter into writing. However, once they have had all the sounds of the language and have learned to spell them, constant attention to dictation is unnecessary and is no longer challenging to the students. Students who have no difficulty spelling what they hear should be allowed to progress to more stimulating exercises. For those who have not acquired this ability, additional practice should be provided during study time, while in the lab, or on occasions when the other students are engaged in other projects or activities. The point is that the abilities called for in dictation—sound discrimination, sound-symbol association, and auditory memory—are basic to language learning and must be developed before students can progress satisfactorily to more difficult activities.

Competence Exercises—Writing Language Forms

The students should now know how to spell at least some of the sounds of the language. They should also know the vocabulary words and comprehend the concepts being studied. They are ready at this stage to practice writing the grammar forms being learned. In a sense, these written exercises may be viewed as a means of verifying comprehension and of developing the ability to produce the grammatical forms. This kind of writing practice certainly serves the function of reinforcing structural concepts. Furthermore, practice in writing verb endings, adjectival forms, etc. gives the students valuable manipulation practice. Both conceptual understanding and manipulative facility are necessary if the students are to be able to use the language. Conceptual understanding and manipulative facility entail control of morpheme components of words as well as of words and phrases. Written exercises can be utilized to confirm the first goal and develop the second better than any of the other three language skills. (This statement should not be misconstrued to mean that writing language forms is the only means of checking understanding and practicing manipulation of forms nor that such exercises are the one and only purpose of writing.)

The type of exercise in which the students write in the appropriate form may range from asking them to write crucial word endings and/or changes to entire verb forms, from isolated words to words in sentences or in narrative or conversational contexts.

Language forms   In written exercises any key element in the word or in the sentence can be omitted in order to focus student attention on the particular grammar point being learned and to provide practice in gaining competence with these forms. Cognitive exercises emphasizing language forms may be similar to the following types.

MORPHEME COMPONENTS

In the following sentences the ending on the verb that indicates the person performing the action has been omitted. Write in the appropriate person ending. If no ending is required, write an X in the blank.

1. Mi amigo y yo nos ve _____ cada día.
2. María no habla _____ mucho en clase.
3. ¿Tienes _____ tú un examen mañana?
4. Los otros comen _____ en casa.

VERB FORMS IN ISOLATION

Write the forms of the verb that go with the subject.

1. Je (manger, habiter, demander, fumer, jouer)
2. Tu (écouter, raconter, visiter)
3. Jacques (jouer, aimer, travailler)

VERB FORMS IN SENTENCES
Complete the following sentences with the appropriate possessive to refer to the person indicated in the sentence.

1. Judy cut _____ finger.
2. We rented _____ apartment.
3. They painted _____ room.
4. He sold _____ car.

OBJECT PRONOUNS IN REALISTIC CONTEXT
Answer the following questions as in the model.

Model: Siehst du die Sterne?   Ja, ich sehe *sie*.

1. Isst du Fleisch?   (Ja, ich esse es.)
2. Liest du Bücher?   (Ja, ich lese sie.)
3. Siehst du Johann?   (Ja, ich sehe ihn.)
4. Kennst du Maria?   (Ja, ich kenne sie.)

VERB FORMS IN CONVERSATIONAL CONTEXT
Complete the following dialog with the appropriate forms of the verb *to be*.

Bob: How _____ you today?
Bill: I _____ tired and sleepy.
Bob: What have you _____ doing?
Bill: My cousin _____ visiting us, and he, Jim, and I have _____ having parties.
Bob: Where _____ he now?
Bill: He and Jim _____ home taking a nap.

Exercises and directions in which successful completion is dependent upon knowledge of grammatical terminology rather than the ability to produce forms should be avoided. For example: "Give the first-person singular of the following infinitives," or "Complete the following sentences with the present perfect tense, passive voice of the verbs given in parentheses."

Obviously, the students are not communicating as they complete the preceding kinds of exercises. As the research of Hosenfeld (1973) on learner strategies so vividly points out, students may be resorting to various tricks and shortcuts to arrive at the correct answers rather than learning both the forms of the words and the contexts in which they occur (see chapter 4, page 89). Too, this type of exercise does not force the same thought processes that might well be expected to take place in the generation of a sentence to communicate. Nor do some of them entail the expression of meaning, the key element in communication. However, given the proper teacher-prepared introduction to the exercises and the prerequisite student comprehension of the concepts involved prior to undertaking the exercise, all should be meaningful from a grammatical point of view.

Simulation exercises   Some exercises have been developed that seem to more nearly duplicate the mental processes involved in sentence production. In this type of exercise, students are still not communicating, but they process mentally most of the sentence elements. The purpose is to get the students to string together words and to put them into sentences as well as to give the appropriate forms of the words themselves. The following exercises require the students to pay attention to all the components of the sentence.

DEHYDRATED SENTENCES

Using the indicated words, plus any necessary additions, write a complete sentence. Do not change the order of the words.

1. boy/go/home/school
2. I/be/there/nine
3. students/eat/cafeteria
4. we/travel/car

SENTENCE PATTERNS

Using the words given in each column, write eight sentences of the same pattern as the model. Each word must be used at least once.

Pattern:	subject	verb	verb complement
	The dog	wags	his tail.
The teacher		know	cookies
My friends		see	the Jones
I		read	signs
You		bring	many books
Betty and I			them
			Jerry

Normally, writing practice is assigned as a homework activity. Since the students will be completing the drills or exercises on their own, it is essential that they be prepared for what they have been asked to do. The teacher should preview the assignment carefully in class, giving several examples of the structure involved. Then he should give a few sentences in which the class as a whole is expected to demonstrate their comprehension of what they are to do. Perhaps the first two or three sentences in each exercise can be done in class, just to be sure that they have indeed understood. An adequate preview of homework exercises enables the students to complete their task much more quickly and efficiently. Otherwise, they are often frustrated doing the homework as they search for answers; and if they decide upon incorrect forms, they must unlearn in class the next day as well as learn the correct answers.

Productive Performance Exercises

Having acquired a knowledge of the grammatical forms in the chapter and a facility in manipulating them, the students are ready for the crucial step in the sequence. At this point they must begin to attach meaning to these forms in order to communicate. This step is a difficult one because psychologically the load on the mental processes is suddenly doubled. Therefore, initial "real" language writing should be as simple as possible. At first, the students are limited to one-sentence answers. Later, they begin to put sentences together into sustained sequences of expression.

The teacher may be surprised to find that his students who had almost perfect control of the structures during prior writing practice begin at this stage to revert to "thoughtless" errors they should not be making. This rash of mistakes is not atypical, and if considered from the viewpoint of the mental load involved, quite to be expected. Therefore, the teacher should refrain from the urge to chastise the students and, instead, give them simple exercises to perform until they are more accustomed to expressing themselves in writing.

In the following exercises the students' internal mental processes are actively involved as they attempt to send a message via their newly acquired, yet incomplete, language system and developing performance skills. As the students progress and as their internalized language system becomes more firmly and more completely established, the need to practice the receptive skills prior to the productive becomes less and less pronounced.

Explained situation   In this exercise a situation is described and the students are asked to give an appropriate question or statement.

Give an appropriate question to fit the following situations.
1. You see your brother leaving the house and you are interested in his destination. You ask, _____?

2. You call a friend whom you have not seen for some time and you are interested in her activities. You ask, _____?

3. Father sees his young daughter with something in her hand and he is concerned. He asks, _____?

4. You have just been introduced to a person your own age. You say, _____.

Sentence completion   This kind of exercise gives the students the opportunity to express their own ideas.

Complete the following sentences truthfully.

1. I see _____.
2. I hear _____.
3. I smell _____.
4. I feel _____.

This same type of exercise can be combined with values situations.

Complete the following sentences using the appropriate form of the verb *to like.*

1. After school my friends and I _____.
2. On weekends I _____.
3. During vacation my dad _____.

Sentence completion exercises can be extremely interesting. First, the students are writing about something that relates to their lives and which they can visualize in their minds. Therefore, the exercise is meaningful as well as expressing meaning. Second, doing this exercise in class provides a great deal of variety and gives the students an opportunity to find out more about their classmates. Too, the format of the exercise gives them a chance to create language to talk about things important to them.

Answering questions   Students can be asked to write answers to questions based on the content of listening comprehension or reading passages, or they can be given personalized questions to answer. Questions over the content of the readings are easiest in that the answers (or a form of the answers) are contained in the readings. Answering questions over listening passages is slightly more difficult, and the students should have the opportunity to listen to the material until they are able to answer the questions. Personalized questions are the most difficult in that the answers involve transfer of knowledge and may include structures and vocabulary that do not come directly from the material being studied. However, relating the content of the material to the students and demonstrating to them that they can use what they have been learning to write about themselves is an extremely important aspect of each learning sequence and should not be omitted. As is true with speaking, teachers should keep in mind that the questions themselves are of varying levels of difficulty, from the simplest level, "Is John going?" to "How are you going?" to the most difficult, "Why are you going?" In this fashion, all students will have some questions that stimulate their best efforts.

Originating questions and answers   Practice in writing simple sentences need not be limited to responses to questions. The students may also be asked to write their own questions that they then ask the other students in class. The content and difficulty level of these questions can be limited in the same way the teachers limit their questions. First, they ask questions over the reading or dialog, and later, they should be expected to ask each other personalized questions using content words from the reading. One-sentence descriptions of persons, places, or events in the reading vary the procedure of asking questions. Also, the teachers can use lists of relevant vocabulary or visuals to cue sentence writing. They can ask the students to write sentences using teacher-selected words or to describe some aspect of teacher-chosen pictures. For variety, lists of vocabulary can be assigned to be completed as questions. These questions in turn become the basis for the following day's oral practice.

Sustained Writing

After the students have learned to write sentences to express meaning, they should be given the opportunity to take the next step in the sequence—combining these sentences into paragraph form.

Summaries   One of the best ways to give the students practice in writing a series of sentences is to ask them to write a summary of the reading or the dialog. Students who have prepared the lesson should know the vocabulary necessary to write a résumé without too much difficulty, thus developing performance skills and confidence at the same time. From the beginning of the course the students should be led to expect this activity for each chapter. The teacher can point out the importance of this activity and emphasize the fact that unless they can do it they have not really learned the material. Variety can be added by rewriting dialogs as narratives and vice versa.

Semi-controlled writing   The next step is *semi-controlled* writing, in which the students are given written, oral, or visual guides to assist them in composing as well as to provide ideas to stimulate their thinking. By following the guidelines, the students can compose a short paragraph. For example, students who are finishing a chapter on telling time might write a short description of their daily schedule by answering the following questions: "What time do you get up?" "What time do you eat breakfast?" "When do you leave home?" "What time do you get to school?" "When do you eat lunch?" "When are classes over?" "What time do you get home?" "What time do you have dinner?" "What time do you go to bed?" More talented students can, within the limits of their language background, easily expand on these questions and write more complete versions of their daily activities.

All students who are progressing well in the course should achieve the ability to write short, guided paragraphs on topics related to the content of the chapter before they proceed to the material of the next chapter. Each chunk of material needs to be digested, absorbed, and applied in its entirety before the students are ready to continue. Failure to attain this achievement level for each chapter only prolongs the development of the writing skill and makes its attainment more difficult. There are no shortcuts, and delays only add to the burden.

At the most advanced level, the students write *free compositions* on *selected topics*. Naturally, the selected topics should be in line with the students' language ability and the extent of their vocabulary knowledge. The guidelines are omitted, however, to permit them more freedom in organizing their own paragraphs. Writing at this level is more difficult in the sense that the students must draw upon their total knowledge of language rather than their familiarity with just one chapter. In this sense, free compositions serve as excellent practice in review and consolidation of knowledge. In assigning these compositions, the teacher should be careful to select topics that are interesting but simple, especially at the elementary levels. If he chooses topics requiring complex thoughts, the students are likely to attempt to write at a level consistent with their thoughts in the first language, and they are not ready to do so in the second language.

This incongruity between thought patterns in the first language and second-language ability should be pointed out to the students. The teacher should caution them to try to keep their compositions within the boundaries of language with which they are familiar. The implication here is that they should not write with dictionary in hand; nor should they write their composition in the first language and then attempt to translate it to the second language. If the students must use a dictionary occasionally, they should use one of the phrase and sentence dictionaries that are available.[3]

---

[3]In these dictionaries each meaning of the word is given and then used in a sentence in the first language followed by the translation of that sentence in the second language. Dictionaries of this type help the students to select the specific word they need to express their exact meaning.

As most former students fully realize, nothing is more deadening to the creative thought processes than to be forced to write on an uninteresting topic. Writing that is satisfactory to both teacher and students is the product of working with a stimulating idea. The teacher should not hesitate to solicit suggestions from the students. Nor should she be averse at this stage to allowing students to write on topics of their own choosing. Insisting that everyone write on the same topic is indefensible from anyone's point of view. The purpose of this kind of writing is to express thoughts in the second language. If the interest is not there, the thoughts will not be there either. And if the thoughts are not there, the writing exercise designed to practice converting thoughts to language has practically no chance of being a successful activity in either the cognitive or the affective domains.

Quality versus quantity   Unfortunately for the teacher, written compositions must be graded—or must they? In a study by Brière (1966) at UCLA, the results indicated otherwise. In this study, foreign students learning to write compositions in English were divided into two groups. One group followed the traditional procedure of careful preparation of compositions followed by a detailed analysis of their errors. The other group concentrated on quantity rather than quality. They were supposed to write as much as they could without paying special attention to language forms. At the end of the study, not only could the latter group write more, they could compose with fewer errors.

The study in the preceding paragraph was described not to convince the teacher that errors are unimportant but to suggest that practice in going from thought to expression in the second language is more important than concentrating on grammatical forms. No one learns to write without making errors. Students who have a genuine desire to learn to write in a second language are often discouraged from continuing their interest by the teacher's insistence upon unattainable standards. At the stage of expression the message is more important than the code, and the students should be encouraged to practice self-expression while concentrating on the total structure rather than on the building blocks of language.

To reinforce this objective and to stress the importance of writing as opposed to overconcern with correctness of language, the teacher can periodically give the students five minutes in which to write about some topic related to the textual materials. He should explain to them that the idea is to write as much as they can without recourse to the text or the dictionary. During the exercise, the teacher can circulate around the class to read and comment on what the students are writing. (This is also an excellent way of learning more about the students themselves.) Just as is true in the case of assigned compositions, he should remember to emphasize facility in expression rather than focusing on errors. The students should be urged to remember how much they can write in five minutes in order to be aware of their increasing facility to express themselves in writing.

COMBINING LANGUAGE SKILLS

In order to develop listening and reading skills the teacher and the students concentrate on each of these skills separately. However, in the case of writing and speaking, the normal pattern is to use one of the receptive skills to cue student written or oral responses. This combination of skills is common to a variety of communicative contexts. Except for the initial stages of second-language learning, when they are attempting to determine the acquisition of certain basic foundation competencies, teachers should select teaching-learning activities in which the students have the opportunity to combine the skills of listening, reading, speaking, and writing.

Elkins, Kalivoda, and Morain (1972) have addressed themselves to this topic. These authors outline an activity in which each student practices each of the four skills in a period of thirty to thirty-five minutes. In this activity two short stories are given to two subgroup leaders in a total group of six students. The subgroup leaders read the passage and tell it orally to the other two members of their subgroup, who write the story. The stories are then exchanged, and the other subgroup members read the second story and tell it to their subgroup leader, who writes it down. At the end all group members discuss the two stories.

CONCLUSION

In writing, as in speaking, a willingness to express themselves, and a confidence in their ability to do so, must be developed in the students. The constant reminders of errors can have only negative results. Tender language neophytes need a steady stream of positive reactions rather than a harrassing hail of criticism if their interest in language is to sprout to full bloom. Most students do not learn to write well, but they should learn to express themselves in an understandable manner. The skill level attained in writing will likely be the lowest of any of the four language skills, but writing is extremely valuable in the classroom as a means of establishing competence and developing productive performance skills.

REVIEW AND APPLICATION

DEFINITIONS
1. bound morpheme, p. 364
2. dehydrated sentences, p. 373
3. free morpheme, p. 364
4. grapheme, p. 368
5. morpheme, p. 364

DISCUSSION
1. What is the role of writing in the second-language class? Delineate what can be done better with writing than with the other language skills and what the limitations of writing are.
2. Compare and contrast writing and speaking from the point of view of (a) using each as a means of manipulating language forms, (b) developing the skill, and (c) practicing the skill.
3. Discuss the reasons for and/or against practicing the productive performance skills in writing prior to initiating speaking practice activities.
4. Discuss the difference between drills, exercises for verifying competence, and exercises for practicing productive performance skills. Give examples of each.
5. Discuss the need to correlate the level of difficulty of the various types of drills and exercises with individual student differences.
6. Discuss additional ideas for combining language skills in developing teaching-learning situations.

ACTIVITIES
1. Prepare a writing sequence based on the materials in the text you are using.
2. Prepare cognitive exercises to (a) produce morphemes, (b) practice spelling a sound, (c) write a language form, and (d) simulate the mental processes involved in producing a sentence.
3. For your second language, list all the sounds not spelled as they are pronounced.
4. Make a list of ideas to stimulate sustained writing. Try to make the activity both realistic and interesting.
5. Get examples of different types of drills and/or exercises and writing activities used in your text and rank them according to level of difficulty. Judge the sequence. Are there some exercises that should be rearranged, changed, added, or deleted in order to develop an appropriate sequence for the typical second-language learner?
6. Share some of the ideas of your former teachers for developing the writing skill which seem especially good to you.
7. Prepare a series of written questions and rank them in their order of difficulty.

SELECTED REFERENCES

Allen, E. D., and Valette, R. M. (1972) *Modern Language Classroom Techniques.* New York: Harcourt Brace Jovanovich. Pp. 216–41.

Barrutia, R. (1964) From Phoneme to Grapheme Audio-Lingually. *Hispania,* 47: 786–88.

Boeninger, H. R. (1949) A New Approach to Advanced German Composition and Conversation. *Modern Language Journal,* 33: 100–105.

Brière, E. J. (1966) Quantity before Quality in Second Language Composition. *Language Learning,* 16: 141–51.

Brisley, L., et al. (1959–61) Good Teaching Practices: A Survey of High-School Foreign-Language Classes. *Reports of Surveys and Studies in the Teaching of Modern Foreign Languages.* New York: Modern Language Association of America. Pp. 219–43.

Calvert, L. (1965) The Role of Written Exercises in an Audio-Lingual Program. *Hispania,* 48: 313–16.

Campbell, H. D. (1963) Teaching Composition in Secondary School. *French Review,* 36: 388–92.

Dykstra, G., and Paulston, C. B. (1967) Guided Composition. *English Language Teaching,* 21: 136–41.

Edgerton, M. F., Jr., et al. (1968) Liberated Expression. In T. E. Bird (Ed.), *Foreign Language Learning: Research and Development.* Northeast Conference Reports. Pp. 75–118.

Elkins, R. J.; Kalivoda, T. B.; and Morain, G. (1972) Fusion of the Four Skills: A Technique for Facilitating Communicative Exchange. *Modern Language Journal,* 56: 426–29.

Grittner, F. M. (1969) *Teaching Foreign Languages.* New York: Harper & Row. Pp. 271–78.

Hosenfeld, C. (1973–74) Learning about Learning: Discovering our Students' Strategies. Revised and expanded version of a paper presented at the 1973 and 1974 ACTFL Conventions.

Huebener, T. (1965) *How to Teach Foreign Languages Effectively.* (rev. ed.) New York: New York University Press. Pp. 75–85.

Politzer, R. L., and Bartley, D. E. (1970) *Practice-Centered Teacher Training: Spanish (French).* Philadelphia: Center for Curriculum Development. Pp. 123–25.

Prochoroff, M., et al. (1963) Writing as Expression. In W. F. Bottiglia (Ed.), *Language Learning: The Intermediate Phase.* Northeast Conference Reports. Pp. 62–81.

Rivers, W. M. (1968) *Teaching Foreign-Language Skills.* Chicago: University of Chicago Press. Pp. 240–60.

Rivers, W. M. (1975) *A Practical Guide to Teaching French.* New York: Oxford University Press. Pp. 236–309.

Valdman, A. (1966) On the Primacy of Writing in French: The Primacy of Speech. *Modern Language Journal,* 50: 468–74.

TEACHING CULTURE

Attitudes toward Other Cultures
    Society
    Teachers
    Students

Definition of Culture

Categories of Culture

Modes of Presenting Culture
    In Class
        The Students
        The Teacher
    Out of Class
        Pen Pals and Tape Exchanges
        Special Programs and Events
        Community Resources
        Travelogue Films
        Summer Camps
        Student Exchange and Travel/Study Abroad
        Regional and State Language Festivals

Incorporation of Culture into the Class
    In the Lesson Plan
        Daily
        Weekly
        Periodically
    At Different Levels

Diversifying Second-Language Goals with Culture

Problems and Dangers of Teaching Culture
    Problems
    Dangers

INTRODUCTION

In the ideal second-language class the teaching of culture is an integral, organized component of the course content. Fundamental aspects of the culture are incorporated into the ongoing class activities and included in the tests over the material covered. The students realize that cultural knowledge is one of the basic goals of the course, and they are aware that they will be tested over cultural information presented in class. As they begin the course, the students expect to gain some degree of functional ability in the culture as well as in the language. The students anticipate that they will "learn a people" as well as a language.

Why is the culture component so crucial in second-language teaching? First, the ability to interact with speakers of another language depends not only on language skills but also on comprehension of cultural habits and expectations. Understanding a second language does not insure understanding the speaker's actions. Successful cross-cultural communication entails a great deal more than language skills. Intercultural communication between speakers of different languages is rooted in language skills, but it blossoms as people relate to others.

Another fundamental reason for the inclusion of culture in the second-language curriculum is intercultural understanding itself. International understanding is one of the basic goals of education in the modern, interdependent world community of nations. Too, the understanding of cultural differences among the various subcultures within a pluralistic society is equally important. Peace and progress in a world of diverse elements placed in close proximity to each other depend upon understanding, tolerance, and cooperation. Second-language study can be one of the core educational components for fostering this widely recognized objective of intercultural understanding. Whether or not it is successful depends upon the degree to which second-language teachers give their students information about the basic similarities and differences between their culture and that of the language they are studying. Because intercultural understanding is emphasized in education and society, the culture goal is a major asset in justifying second-language study in the schools. (See chapter 1, pages 6–9, for a more complete discussion.) The importance of second-language teaching in the future will depend to a considerable extent on the success of second-language teachers in promoting the goal of intercultural understanding.

The third principal reason for stressing culture in second-language classes has to do with the students. On the one hand, they are extremely interested in the people who speak the language they are studying. They want to know about them—what they are like and how they live. On the other hand, they know very little about the basic aspects of their own culture, and certainly most of them are too young to have had the experiences necessary to gain more than a superficial knowledge about cultures of other countries or even of the subcultures within their own society. Cultural habits are like language skills: the native speaker operates within the system at a subconscious level. Some of those fundamental factors that invoke a subconscious response must be brought to the conscious level in order that the students may begin to realize their own cultural values and those of second-language speakers. Second-language teachers in general are forced to admit that at the present time many students are not gaining a basic familiarity with the second-language culture. In fact, many students do not even realize that culture is a course goal.

Anthropologists agree that individual behavior in any culture lies within the limits of an overall system of learned patterns. In this sense, the study of culture is comparable to the study of language. The basic components of the system need to be identified and presented to the students in a comprehensible manner. Culture is so complex that students cannot be expected to absorb the totality of the native cultural habits, but they should become familiar with those aspects that are most important in understanding the people and their way of life. The extent to which the students wish to familiarize themselves with the second culture depends a great deal on the students. For some, an acquaintance is sufficient. For those who wish to major in the language and/or study in the second-language community, a functional ability to participate at a somewhat less than native level is desirable. At the very least, these students should be given the insights that will enable them to acquire the necessary cultural knowledge to participate in the second-culture setting.

In considering the cultural goals in second-language classes, the teacher should have realistic expectations. Just as few students will become bilingual, few will become bicultural. In elementary courses, the teacher should be concerned with comprehension and familiarity. Affinity for and commitment to a second culture is a personal matter that should remain in the realm of the student's own prerogative. Classroom content and activities should revolve around the development of an insight into what to look for in the second-language culture and a sensitivity to and a tolerance for what is seen in the culture. Although specific content will be necessary to develop the desired cultural goals, the processes for comprehending cultural similarities and differences and the attitudes toward those differences should be stressed in the second-language class. The purpose of this chapter is to outline some of the types of activities that have been developed to teach culture and to discuss some of the problems associated with the teaching of culture.

ATTITUDES TOWARD OTHER CULTURES

One of the major hurdles to the successful implementation of culture goals in second-language classes revolves around attitudes. Before students can learn about culture, they must be receptive to the concept of learning about cultures other than their own. Often the teacher has to break down cultural barriers prior to initiating teaching-learning activities designed to accomplish culture goals. Cooke (1972) suggests that one way to begin teaching culture on a positive note is to emphasize similarities between peoples. From this beginning, the students can move to a discussion of differences between members of their family, between families, between schools, and between cultures. This approach stresses that similarities are present in all cultures and that differences in the expression of these similarities are natural.

Society

The students' environment exerts a tremendous influence on their receptivity to the learning of cultural concepts. Obviously, societies are different and have different characteristics. If the students are from a society that is cosmopolitan and they are familiar with cultural diversity, they will be more ready to study and benefit from cultural content. On the other hand, students who are products of a rather closed society will probably have less interest in other cultures and subcultures. The teacher should take societal factors into consideration when selecting culture goals and culture content for the second-language class. What can be done will be determined to a large degree by the local situation. The paradox is that those students most in need of developing cultural awareness and cultural sensitivities are normally those who are least disposed toward these goals.

Teachers

The attitude of the teacher is a crucial factor in determining the extent to which the cultural objectives are attained. If she expects all the students to love the second culture as much as she does, she is certain to be disappointed. If she attempts to indoctrinate the students with attitudes from the second culture, she will most likely be rejected by the majority of her students. If she attempts to criticize the students' own culture, she may arouse negative, counterproductive feelings in the students. In short, the teacher should not insist that the students emulate her own affinity for and commitment to the second culture, as much as she may be predisposed to do so. The teacher's task is to make students aware of cultural differences, not pass value judgments on those differences. She is to acquaint, not indoctrinate.

The preceding paragraph should not be interpreted to mean that the teacher should not be enthusiastic about second-language teaching and second cultures. Without enthusiasm, any course becomes dry and unpalatable for both teacher and students. However, the teacher's enthusiasm should always be moderated by the realities of the students' situation. They are young, inexperienced, and struggling to develop a self-identity within their own culture. The teacher's enthusiasm should not reach a level at which the students feel culturally threatened, a point at which they are forced to reject all or many aspects of the second culture in order to protect their image of the first. The teacher should seek to make the study of culture a broadening experience, not one of rejection and entrenchment. The students should be made to feel that studying the second culture does not in any way imply the abandonment of their own culture.

Students

Ethnocentrism is defined in *The American Heritage Dictionary of the English Language* as the "belief in the superiority of one's own ethnic group." Oswalt (1970, p. 19) gives the following example of ethnocentrism:

> Among many tribal peoples this attitude is well reflected in the name that they have for themselves. For example, we call a group of primitives in northern North America *Eskimos;* this name, originated by certain Indians to the south of the Eskimos, means "Eaters of Raw Flesh." However, the Eskimos' own name for themselves is not *Eskimos* but is *Inupik,* meaning "Real People." By their name they provide a contrast between themselves and other groups; the latter might be "people" but are never "real."

Ethnocentrism has often been painted in negative terms, but such a reaction is not entirely justified. In order to live, each individual must make choices as to the desirable behavior patterns by which his life is most comfortable and most productive. In modern society, most individuals do not maintain in unaltered form all the cultural patterns of their parents; but neither is it possible for any individual to divorce himself entirely from his cultural heritage. To exist as a sociocultural entity all cultures must, by definition, conform to some system of shared behavior patterns. The extent to which anyone deviates from the native culture patterns depends upon the individual. From both the individual and societal points of view, ethnocentrism has its good aspects and its bad. When the critics decry ethnocentrism, they are actually referring to the myopic extreme that refuses to consider any viewpoint other than that of its own culture. Oswalt (1970, p. 20) delineates the need for and the possible negative aspects of ethnocentrism in the following terms:

> To hold one's own cultural ways up as the norm for measuring those of others is to reflect a bias in favor of one's own. In some respects this is desirable, for it gives one a full and meaningful sense of identity and assurance. In other ways it is harmful because it encourages intolerance. . . . If, however, there are areas in which one might profitably learn from other peoples, then in the long run an ethnocentric stance may be detrimental to one's entire way of living. This underlies the anthropological recommendation to avoid hardening of the cultural arteries by at least sampling other ways of life . . . .

Most junior high and high school students operate from an ethnocentric point of view. Their cultural position arises not so much from a consciously chosen point of view as from a background of exposure primarily to one general sociocultural system. Even though they are a member of a subculture within a total culture system, as everyone is, they tend to see things from their own point of view as do most people. This tendency toward cultural conformity is magnified by the adolescent desire to be like the other members of their group. What they do know about other cultures is usually information based on stereotypes acquired in magazines, newspapers, movies, or conversations.

All second-language teachers are quite familiar with the psychological trauma associated with total immersion in another culture. An individual with a broad perspective on life can emerge triumphant after the initial debilitating effects of culture shock have dissipated; but no one would say that that period of adjustment is easy. The point is that exposure to a second culture in the classroom can also be a disquieting experience for some students. Certainly, a classroom situation will never produce the problems that may accompany study in a second-language community, but the culture component may still bother some students. The teacher should be sensitive to student feelings in this respect and be prepared to take steps to ameliorate any negative reactions that develop. Most of all, precautions should be taken not to threaten in any way the students' belief in their own cultural system. Given the appropriate cultural information, they will acquire a certain degree of comprehension of the people and their culture. Such knowledge should develop in them a higher degree of sensitivity to and tolerance for cultural differences than they had prior to second-language study. As they grow and mature, they can incorporate those behavioral patterns and values that they deem desirable into their own lives.

DEFINITION OF CULTURE

Culture may mean different things to different people. In the anthropological sense, *culture,* often labeled "small *c* culture," encompasses the "lifeway of a population" (Oswalt, 1970, p. 15). This definition of culture as the way people live is the one most commonly and most highly recommended as the basis for selecting cultural content for second-language classes. This definition encompasses the types of information that would seem to be of most interest and of most importance to the typical student enrolled in a second-language class. In addition, this definition most nearly satisfies the requirements for the type of material needed to satisfy the stated culture goals of intercultural understanding. Ideally, at the end of their studies, the students will have a functional knowledge of the second-culture system just as they have of the second-language system.

In stressing this approach to culture, the teacher should make clear to the students that each individual is a member of a subculture within a culture just as every individual in a language group speaks a dialect of a language. Both the overall population and the specific group conform to certain behavior patterns generally common to the entire population or group. Too, the teacher should emphasize that the student of a second culture should gain insights into his own culture just as the student of a second language gains insights into language. In fact, at times the teacher may find it necessary to introduce a cultural topic by first clarifying the students' own cultural behavior in a particular situation. Often, comparing the two cultural systems can be beneficial to comprehension of one's own culture.

Another definition of culture focuses on the major products and contributions of a society in general or of outstanding individuals in that society. With this approach, often referred to as "large *C* culture," the students study the economic, social, and political history and the great politicians, heroes, writers, artists, etc. of the country. Although inherently interesting in its own right to many teachers and students, materials of this type may not contribute significantly to the students' ability to function linguistically and socially in the contemporary culture nor to their intercultural understanding.

The stance taken in this book is that the anthropological definition should be followed in beginning language classes. This is true both from the point of view of student interest and from the point of view of importance of the information to the students. Students who take a language for several years and who wish to explore the society's contributions to world knowledge and civilization should be given the opportunity in advanced classes to probe large *C* culture in greater depth and breadth. Organized in this fashion, materials can be developed that are more in keeping with student interest and with student linguistic and intellectual capabilities.

Prior to the audio-lingual revolution, most texts and most classes stressed large *C* culture whenever culture was included in the course (which was not always). Early audio-lingual proponents viewed the study of language as a total cultural system. The tendency was not to include separate discussions of culture but to rely on the students' absorption of small *c* culture that was contained in the dialogs to convey the culture system. Since that time, the emphasis on small *c* culture has continued, but devotion of more class time to culture and including culture as a separate component of the class content have been stressed.

CATEGORIES OF CULTURE

Defining *culture* is a necessary prerequisite to the implementation of the culture goal in second-language classes. However, the definition merely provides guidelines for choosing the types of information that are to be included in the course content. The problems of what basic information is to be given to the students and how it is to be organized remain. What should students learn about the second culture in order to be able to function in that culture? Around what basic topics should this information be organized? How much do students need to be given as a basis for developing insights and sensitivities to other culture patterns?

Various authors have addressed themselves to the topic of how to organize culture into key themes that will provide insights into characteristic behavior patterns. Nostrand (1974) states that no culture seems to have more than twelve major themes and lists the twelve themes of French culture. Seelye (1968) refers to twenty-three "key ideas" for the comprehension of Latin American culture developed (for social studies teachers) at the University of Texas in Austin. Taylor and Sorenson (1961) outline eight general categories that should be considered in the study of a culture. Although not discussing culture per se, Raths et al. (1966) identify ten value-rich areas basic to each individual in any given culture.

Based on the anthropological definition of culture, the following list is one possible categorization of culture themes. The reader should not hesitate to add other topics and subtopics with which he is familiar and with which the students should become acquainted. This list has been prepared from an anthropological perspective, a values point of view, and from the students' point of view. Both similarities and differences between cultures should be included. Comparisons and contrasts are always implied.

    I. Typical student activities
      A. School days

        1. Before school
        2. During school
        3. After school
        4. After returning home
        5. During free time
    B. Days school not in session
        1. Saturdays
        2. Sundays
        3. During vacation periods
    C. With family
    D. With friends
    E. Alone
    F. During family vacations
  II. Typical conversations
 III. What does the typical student think about most?
 IV. Money
  V. Meals and drinks
 VI. Leisure activities
VII. Careers
VIII. Happiness
 IX. Success
  X. Parents
 XI. Youth view of parenthood
XII. Masculine and feminine roles in society
XIII. The family
XIV. Relatives
 XV. Youth
    A. How do young people become acquainted?
        1. Before attending school
        2. In elementary school
        3. In secondary school
        4. In the university
        5. After completing their studies
    B. Are they permitted to visit and to go out alone?
    C. What are some typical games?
    D. Do boys and girls attend the same schools? The same classes?
    E. What are the most important customs with regard to boy-girl relationships?
    F. Do young people go to parties alone, in pairs, or in groups?
    G. How are sex roles changing?
    H. How are the customs different in your country?

XVI. Courtship and marriage

XVII. Education

    A. How is the educational system organized?

        1. Public and/or private?

        2. Who attends school?

        3. How long do students attend school?

        4. How much does it cost to attend?

        5. How are the schools supported?

        6. Who controls the schools?

    B. Describe the discipline in the schools. Give examples.

    C. Describe a typical school day.

    D. Do the students have periods of talk and recreation every day?

    E. What are the standards for academic work? How are students graded?

    F. What are the social rules and standards?

    G. What are the dress codes?

    H. What is the feeling toward cheating and dishonesty?

    I. Are the students interested and studious?

    J. What courses are offered?

    K. What aspects of school do students like most?

    L. What aspects do they like least?

    M. What kinds of homework and tests do students have?

    N. What are the extracurricular activities in which students participate?

    O. What is the attitude of students with respect to their studies?

    P. What importance is attached to education?

    Q. Is attendance at a university necessary to obtain a good position in the work force?

    R. What type of job can one obtain with an elementary school education? A high school education? A university education?

    S. Is it possible for poor students to attend the university?

    T. Are trade schools and apprenticeships important?

XVIII. Friends

XIX. The social system

XX. The generation gap

XXI. Drugs

XXII. Youth participation in politics

XXIII. The economic system

XXIV. Patriotism

XXV. Women's liberation
XXVI. War and peace
XXVII. Change and progress
XXVIII. Ecology
XXIX. Population
XXX. Religion
XXXI. Crime
XXXII. Law
XXXIII. Humor
XXXIV. Good manners
XXXV. Advertising
XXXVI. The press
XXXVII. Individual liberty
XXXVIII. Death
XXXIX. Discipline
XL. Holidays
XLI. Clothing
XLII. Transportation
XLIII. Courtesy phrases
XLIV. Kinesics[1]

For those students who anticipate having contact with speakers of the second language in social situations, special emphasis should be given to courtesy phrases and kinesics. Students should be familiar with what to say in certain regularly occurring situations. They should be prepared to respond, for example, when being introduced to someone, meeting a friend, ordering in a restaurant, asking for information, or receiving a compliment. In addition, they should be acquainted with facial expressions, gestures, and tones of voice that are normally used in specific situations and that carry important social and psychological implications. All information about the second culture is important, but courtesy phrases and kinesics serve as extremely important bases for the establishment of comfortable intercultural relationships.

MODES OF PRESENTING CULTURE

The teacher must have a definition of culture to determine what aspects of a second culture to present, a thematical organization of basic components of the second culture, and at least an elementary knowledge of the second-

---

[1]*Kinesics* is the systematic study of nonlinguistic body motion as it relates to communication.

language culture. The teacher's next step is to develop teaching-learning procedures for conveying the chosen information to the students. Fortunately, as attention has turned to the growing need for including more culture in second-language courses and for developing greater expertise in ways and means of teaching a second culture, new ideas for presenting culture have been proposed.

In Class

Although certain limitations are inherent in the classroom situation, culture can be taught as a basic part of the class and of the homework assignments. Both the teacher and students can present information to the class to promote increasing familiarity with the second culture. Obviously, vicarious exposure of this type is not comparable to study in the second-language community, but it can serve as a valuable lesson for those who will never have the opportunity to visit another country. It will also serve as preparation for those who do eventually have contact with native speakers of the second language.

The students   As is true in other aspects of the class, the teacher cannot do all the work, nor does she need to. The students are capable of gaining a great deal of information on their own, under the teacher's guidance. Assigned reports and projects geared to promote cultural knowledge can be an important adjunct to the material that the teacher provides for the students. For example, early in their exposure to second-language study the students can prepare maps. Working with maps will help them to locate the country as well as the important cities and regions within the country. Subsequent to the map project, the students can begin to delve into other aspects of the country's geography and geographic location. What is the country's relationship with other countries? With whom do they trade and for what products? What are the staples in the people's diet? What are the principal occupations? The students can find the answers to many of these questions in the school or public library. The teacher should be ready to help them with answers that they cannot find, either by answering the questions or suggesting other sources of information.

Jenks (1974b) advocates an approach to teaching culture in which the teacher provides questions that the students are to answer. These are not questions to which the students already know the answers but are questions that require the students to use the library and perhaps other resource centers to find out the answers to the questions. For example, the teacher might ask the students what the exchange rate is between the dollar and the various currencies of Latin America and what is the average wage in each of the countries. Once this information is obtained, the students can be asked to determine by studying the advertisements in a Latin American newspaper how long the average worker must labor for a pair of shoes, a dress, a sewing machine, a television, a car, a dozen eggs, a gallon of milk, etc. The next step would be to compare the results with the cost of similar products in the students' own country. In order to avoid possible student frustration with difficult research questions, the teacher would need either to choose her questions carefully or make clear to the students that the answers to some of the questions may be unavailable in their library. The important secondary outcome of this approach is that students learn to find their own answers to the questions.

Another potential source of cultural information (often untapped by the teacher) is student knowledge or experience with particular aspects of the second culture. It is not uncommon for one or more of the students to have some information about the second culture that the teacher does not know. Many students take a second language because they have had prior contact with the people and the culture of the foreign country. A survey of the class members at the beginning of the year may reveal students who have collections of stamps, coins, jewelry, etc. from the second country, who have traveled in the country, who have studied some topic related to the second culture, or who have relatives or friends who might serve as resource persons for culture content. Such assets complement the teacher's own cultural knowledge and enable him to expand his cultural offerings to the class.

The teacher   The primary responsibility for culture content lies with the teacher and the textual materials. The cultural information of any text will need to be supplemented, but choosing a book that incorporates culture into its format is a helpful beginning. (Authors of recent second-language texts seem to be more conscious of the need for cultural information, and this welcome addition should make the teacher's task somewhat easier. Joiner [1974] has prepared a checklist for evaluating the culture content of second-language texts.)

The following paragraphs contain descriptions and examples of various methods teachers have used to present cultural information in second-language classes.

The *culture aside* is probably the most widely used approach to the teaching of culture. A culture aside is an unplanned, brief, culture comment. During the class, the teacher commonly takes advantage of relevant topics as they arise to give the students bits of cultural information. For example, if the students have the word *coffee*, the teacher can differentiate between the coffee drunk in their country and that of the second culture and when and where people normally drink coffee. The advantage of this approach is that the information is pertinent to class content. The disadvantage is that overall the cultural information received by the class may not be very well organized.

The teacher can also prepare *lecture presentations* in which he discusses some characteristic of the second culture. For example, at Christmas he might describe the similarities and differences between the two cultures in the ways in which the people observe this holiday season. These comparisons should be carefully prepared in advance, but they should not be so long as to lose student interest or to take too much time from the remainder of the class. Interspersed with other techniques, lecture presentations can give the students many facts in a short period of time.

Taylor (1972) describes a *"slice-of-life" technique* for teaching culture. Using this technique, the teacher chooses a small segment of life from the second culture that is presented to the students at the beginning or end of the class period. The point is made with a minimum of comment and a maximum of dispatch. The information is valuable and interesting without requiring a great deal of class time. For example, the teacher might bring a second-language calendar to class and point out to the students in what ways it is different from those they are accustomed to seeing.

Culture assimilators are another means of supplying cultural information in class. A culture assimilator consists of three parts: (1) a short passage demonstrating an intercultural exchange in which a misunderstanding occurs, (2) four possible interpretations of what transpired, and (3) feedback for the students as to the correct answer. Bals (1974) gives an example in which the afternoon visit of a young American to a German home does not turn out as well as he had anticipated. Knowing that a gift is appropriate, he presents the hostess with a bouquet of red roses. However, he is startled to notice that she reacts negatively to the gift. The interpretations are (1) the hostess is allergic to roses; (2) the hostess prefers to buy her own flowers; (3) flowers are appropriate only when the guest is having dinner; or (4) red roses are given to sweethearts, not to hostesses. The students finish by learning the correct answer, number 4, and discussing the implications. The focus on confusion caused by differences in cultural expectations is an excellent means of developing student insight into those differences between cultures that can cause misunderstanding and even hostility. This type of activity has the potential to help create insight into and tolerance of cultural diversity. The disadvantages of culture assimilators are that they require a high degree of familiarity with the culture and a great deal of time to prepare.

Culture capsules are also used to teach culture. A culture capsule is a brief description of one aspect of the second culture followed by a discussion of the contrasts between the cultures of the first and second languages. For example, the teacher might describe post-elementary education in the other culture.

This description would include types of schools, courses, and students. In the follow-up discussion, the students discuss and summarize the principal differences between the educational system of the second culture and that of their own country. Given the knowledge needed to describe the second culture, the teacher can prepare culture capsules without too much additional work. Another advantage is that the students become involved in the activity and have an opportunity to consider basic characteristics of their own culture.

Meade and Morain (1973) refer to a related series of culture capsules dealing with a central theme as a *culture cluster*. In this approach, the teacher incorporates a small number of separate, ten-minute culture capsules into the class format. Later, one thirty-minute segment of the class is spent acting out the cultural concepts introduced in the capsules and reviewing the content of the previous culture capsules. In their article, Meade and Morain give an example dealing with wedding ceremonies in France. The first capsule treats the civil ceremony, the second the religious ceremony, and the third the wedding banquet. On the fourth day the differences between a city and a country wedding are contrasted, and an enactment of a country wedding is presented.

Some teachers use *minidramas* or *miniskits* to help the students visualize culture content. In this approach to the teaching of culture, the students incorporate the culture being learned into their actions as they perform in selected situations. Behmer (1972) has worked with this technique. These skits deal with such phenomena as the *kiosque* in France, the *Gasthaus* in Germany, and *el reencuentao* in Spanish-speaking countries. With a little ingenuity, the teacher can think of other situations suitable for miniskits. Certainly, any time the students are acting out dialogs or role playing, the teacher should insist on the appropriate actions to fit the words being spoken. If a video tape recorder is available, the most interesting and informative student efforts can be preserved for use with future classes.

An interesting approach incorporating both the teaching of language and culture has been developed at the University of Georgia by Kalivoda, Morain, and Elkins (1972). An extension of the "total physical response" approach to the teaching of second languages,[2] the *audio-motor unit* is a technique in which students act out commands given by the teacher. By choosing culture-rich situations, the teacher can combine teaching of language with teaching of culture. For example, after having been told that they are in a restaurant, the students are asked to pick up their napkins, unfold them, put them on their laps, pick up their forks in their left hands, pick up their knives in their right hands, cut a piece of meat, put it in their mouths, put down their knives and

---

[2]Students learning with "total physical response" techniques either do or pretend to do whatever they say in the second language.

forks, leave their hands on the table, break off a piece of bread, etc. As the students perform these actions, first following the teacher's cues and later on their own, they are practicing important cultural differences in eating habits.

With visuals or realia the teacher may use either a *question-directed discussion* approach or an *inquiry* method to bring out important cultural facts. The teacher, for example, can show the students a picture of a typical dwelling in the second culture. Then, by asking the students questions, he can lead them into important observations as to the differences between the house in the picture and their own homes. On the other hand, he might bring in a hat from the second culture. After displaying the hat, the teacher assumes the role of a resource person, and the students must determine where this hat is worn and why it has come to have the style it does by asking the teacher questions that can be answered with a yes or a no (Taylor, 1972).

Taylor (1972) also describes an activity in which the *group solves a situational problem*. For example, a young student who has been in the foreign country less than two weeks is invited by a friend of the family to a birthday party for their son, who is the same age. The problem is the following: Would he use the polite or the familiar form in addressing the son and the other guests? An alternative technique is to describe a situation in which the visitor to the second culture commits a *faux pas.* The students are asked to identify the "blunder." More appropriate actions for the described situation should be discussed.

Newspapers and magazines are as important for their cultural content as for their factual content. Each and every class should have these materials available for the students, both for browsing and for assigned class projects. Browsing time does not have to be lengthy, and assignments do not have to require advanced linguistic skills. Asking the students to survey articles on currently popular clothing styles, movies, TV programs, and books would be interesting, informative, and relatively simple for each student to accomplish. The more capable students can do independent projects and prepare a report for the class. By planning activities based on the content of the newspapers and magazines and the abilities of the students, the teacher can make these supplemental reading materials an important addition to the teaching of culture. Without her guidance, however, the wealth of information they contain may lie useless and untouched in the back of the room. The students will benefit from such materials only if they are assisted in doing so. Schulz (1974) recommends that the teacher provide the students with a purpose, a topic, and specific questions before asking them to work with printed news media.

Bulletin boards can be a striking means of presenting cultural information while at the same time brightening up the classroom. Students often have a difficult time attempting to visualize the cultural element being described.

Carefully selected pictures and art work placed on the bulletin board can help eliminate this problem. Old magazines and newspapers are a rich source of pictures, cartoons, and articles for collection, organization, and display. If the teacher does not have the time to search for appropriate materials, faster students needing extra work or slower students seeking extra credit can look for interesting visuals dealing with certain cultural themes. Advertisements are interesting and contain a great deal of information about what people eat, wear, etc. (The best displays can be labeled and saved for other classes.)

Visual aids, such as films, filmstrips, slides, and photographs, can make a vital contribution to the stimulation of interest in the second culture and to a clearer perception of the way of life in the second culture. Telling students about outdoor markets, squares, and other points of interest only suffices if pictures are not available for student viewing. The teacher should acquaint herself with the holdings of nearby film libraries and order films each year for her classes. (Normally, the audio-visual director for the school will have these catalogues available for teacher use.) Slides taken by the teacher add a touch of personal authenticity to the teacher's credibility, and the teacher should show them to all her students varying the commentary to the students' linguistic level. All the slides may be shown at once, or the teacher can select them individually to illustrate specific aspects of culture. Drawings and models (for example, the Eiffel Tower) prepared by artistically talented students can be saved from year to year to add a visual dimension to teacher and textbook descriptions.

In the case of those teachers who have the ability and interest, *music* and *dance* of the second culture can be introduced. The words, the music, and the dance movements can all be related to the people, their moods, their interests, and their way of life. Not all students, of course, are interested in music or dance. With some classes, such activities are successful while with others they are not. Some teachers have the spirit and enthusiasm to get the students involved while others do not. For those teachers who can bring music and dance into the schools succesfully, activities in which the students participate in singing or dancing can be a tremendous morale builder among the students. Too, a program based on student talent is an excellent means of building interest in the second language both in the school and in the community. To be successful, however, the students need to become active participants in the singing and dancing. Simply listening to music or watching films of dancing does not hold adolescent attention for more than short periods of time.

Out of Class

Learning activities focusing on culture need not be restricted to the classroom. Many possibilities for extending student familiarity with the second culture exist beyond the classroom.

Pen pals and tape exchanges   Pen pals and tape exchanges give the students an opportunity to make personal contact with someone their own age from the second culture. Thus, they get to know a speaker of the second language from a personal point of view, and they can ask the questions in which they have an interest. If the teacher has time and if the students are willing, some of the most interesting and informative letters can be shared with the other members of the class. Besides the cultural advantage, just writing to the pen pal can often be a strong motivating factor in second-language study. Tapes, either between classes or between individuals, can be undertaken with advantageous results for the students in both cultures. Each tape can deal with a different aspect of culture, which over the period of a year can yield cultural information that might not be available to the students in any other manner. The exchange of tapes may even lead to the exchange of realia and other objects of interest to the class.

Special programs and events   Cultural touring groups from abroad afford special opportunities for the students to witness some of the representatives of the language and the culture they have been studying. Fortunately, the intercultural exchange programs have brought singing, dancing, and theater groups from other cultures within driving distance of most American students. The alert teacher will take advantage of these opportunities for students to attend programs of large *C* culture and to motivate student interest in the second culture.

Community resources   Many cultural resources in the local school district can be tapped to broaden the students' exposure to cultural information and activities. One way to make the culture come alive is to bring the students into contact with the living culture in the community. *Native speakers,* for example, can be invited to the class to talk to the students about life in the second-language community, both in the students' own country and abroad. (Prior to the day of the visit the teacher should be sure to focus the attention of the students and the native speaker upon the specific topics to be discussed.) In most of the larger cities and even in many of the smaller ones, specialty *restaurants* offer foods from many different nations. A class excursion for a meal at one of these spots can highlight a semester and give the students the experience of tasting food of the second culture. (If the waiters speak the second language, the students are treated to a linguistic as well as a culinary experience.) *Museums* and *art galleries* in the larger cities may have special collections or exhibits of interest to some or all of the students. These may be of interest and importance for the cultural implications of the work as well as for the fame of the artist. In some areas, *theaters* show feature films from the second culture and in the second language with subtitles. With careful screening and detailed student preparation prior to seeing the movie, the teacher may be able to take the students to a movie. Obviously, movies in commercial theaters are not prepared with students in mind, so the teacher should keep in mind that not all films will be suitable. Those that are, however, can help the students to visualize cultural differences.

Travelogue films   Many communities have individuals or groups who sponsor a series of travel films. These filmed glimpses into other countries and other cultures are produced by experts and are normally very well done. Whenever one deals with a country of interest to the class, the students can learn a great deal by attending the program. They will learn about the architecture and the tourist attractions, of course, but they will also learn some things about the people and their customs.

Summer camps   Although not numerous, some summer language camps exist. Under the guidance of native speakers, the students learn, play, and work in the second language during their stay at the camp.

Student exchange and travel/study abroad   For those students who have the linguistic ability, interest, time, and money, the opportunity to study in the second-language community is a definite asset to any second-language program. The most valuable type of experience is direct exposure to the customs and habits of the second culture. Students can learn more in less time than is ever possible in class. However, they must be carefully prepared before going abroad, and both they and the programs must be carefully selected if the results are to be satisfactory and worthwhile.

Regional and state language festivals   A recent innovation in second-language education has been the holding of regional and state language festivals. Second-language students in the area come together for a day of fun, games, programs, and activities in the second language. Although organized primarily to promote interest in second-language study, making purchases, playing games, attending programs, etc. in the second language can have cultural advantages as well.

INCORPORATION OF
CULTURE INTO THE CLASS

Given the culture content and a variety of techniques for presenting the information to the students, the next decision facing the teacher is how to coordinate culture with the other material to be learned in the class. Learning the language itself is a full-time task. How can room be made for more material? The answer to this question is certainly not an easy one, but it is hoped that the second-language teacher will recognize the need for developing a second-language course in which culture is a basic component. Techniques have been developed that can be inserted unobtrusively into the class without disturbing the remainder of the lesson plan. On those days in which more time is required for lengthy activities, the culture portion of the class can serve as a change of pace to the more typical language routine. Too, a deepening insight into the people can be a motivating stimulus that will enhance student interest in the course.

How much time should be spent teaching culture? In this author's opinion, the answer to that question depends upon the teacher and the students in the class. Too, the type of cultural material presented and the manner in which it is organized will influence the amount of time spent. The point is that the amount of culture introduced is not so important as the degree of familiarity the students have with the second culture at the end of the course. However, if a rule of thumb is desirable, this author believes that in the ideal second-language class some culture is included in each and every regular class.

In the Lesson Plan

The following paragraphs specify how the various culture techniques may be incorporated into the structure of the class.

Daily Daily culture topics should be short and concise. Dwelling on a particular culture item every day robs the class of time needed for the four language skills. Too, the teacher should not overdo a good thing, for this would most likely lead to a point of diminishing returns. Cultural asides, culture assimilators, and slice-of-life techniques can be used daily with a major cumulative effect on class culture goals without taking up huge amounts of class time. None of these activities should last more than two or three minutes.

Weekly On a weekly basis, the teacher may decide to deal with cultural topics requiring longer periods of time. Near the end of the week he may want to give a lecture presentation, prepare a culture capsule, use a question-directed discussion or the inquiry approach, work with an audio-motor unit, involve the students in a group solution to a situational problem, or give the students time to look for specified topics in newspapers or magazines. These activities may take from a minimum of five to a maximum of fifteen minutes, and they permit a more complete examination of a culture component than is possible on a daily basis.

Periodically Occasionally, the teacher may decide to spend even longer periods on some cultural activity. She can show a film, utilize visual aids or models, develop a culture cluster, have the students prepare miniskits, prepare a bulletin board display as a class activity, give the students time to present reports or the results of projects, play records, sing, or dance. Although too time-consuming to be used regularly in the class, activities of this type can be beneficial learning activities if not used to excess and if approached with a learning objective in mind. The students should not be given the impression that these are minivacations entirely separated from the more serious aspects of the class.

At Different Levels

What culture is to be included at the different levels of instruction? Answers to this question remain to be developed. The culture objectives and materials should be so arranged, of course, that content is not repeated. Since many students study a second language for only one or two years, the most important concepts should be introduced during the first two years. Another problem related to teaching culture at different levels has to do with whether to teach the culture in the first or the second language. Some elementary textbook authors prefer to write cultural material in the first language, while others choose the second. A major factor in the decision rests on the content of the materials, but it would seem that as soon as the students have the linguistic skills to comprehend, culture should be taught in the second language.

Brooks (1971) has proposed a sequence of cultural content for each of four levels of second-language study. At the first level, he proposes to treat the family table, the schoolroom, the playground, homework, chores, letters, games, parties, parades, and holidays. The second level would deal with "close-ups of thought and action" contained in proverbs and sayings and pictures and photographs of situations exemplifying typical aspects of the culture. The third level would center on the anatomy of the culture in which the "regrettable" and the "tragic" side of the culture is explored. And the fourth level would synthesize the culture in its entirety. Brooks stresses that during this entire sequence the students will continue to be a part of the first-language culture and that the success of the culture program depends upon a comprehensible and organized presentation of the second-language culture.

Brooks's division is a logical one that can serve as a model for second-language teachers to follow. Beginning with those cultural aspects that are most important to the individual and progressing to a more generalized overview of the total culture system is appropriate in view of the need to interest beginning second-language students and to give them the most basic information in the first two years of second-language study. However, if the teacher is contemplating a program in which he plans to gather and prepare cultural materials for use in his classes, it would be most efficient for him to collect information suitable for all levels in the first year of the culture project. In the second year, the materials prepared the first year can be used with first-year students with the new materials being used with all students above the first-year level, and so forth. At the end of the four-year period, a series of cultural materials would be available for each level in the school system. Using this sequence, all students would learn important cultural information and concepts each year without having to repeat the same material; and the teacher would have to prepare only one set of materials each year.

DIVERSIFYING SECOND-LANGUAGE GOALS WITH CULTURE

Teaching culture lends itself extremely well to the learning activity package format of individualized instruction. Having LAPs at their disposal permits the students to select those areas of the second culture in which they have the greatest interest. Of course, if the teacher feels that a certain core of the materials is essential to comprehension of the culture, he can specify that all the students must complete those LAPs. Cultural activities are still included in the class, but the LAP format provides additional content beyond that possible in the regular lesson plan.

Work with culture materials is different from that with the language skills and can serve to provide a measure of success to those students floundering with the language skills. This statement is not intended to support culture classes conducted in English. It is merely to suggest that with students of limited linguistic ability the emphasis might be shifted from possibly unattainable language skills to attainable culture knowledge couched in relatively simple language. Allowing those students having difficulty developing language skills to base a larger percentage of their grade on culture might discourage them from dropping second-language study at the end of the first semester or the first year. The other students would still learn the culture and as much language as their capabilities permitted. Although the language skill objectives would be altered in their case, the culture objectives would remain the same for all students. In this manner, the goal of cultural sensitivity and tolerance could be made a part of the educational background of most students.

PROBLEMS AND DANGERS OF
TEACHING CULTURE

If present trends in cultural pluralism and international interchange continue, future second-language teachers must learn to transmit basic information needed to gain an elementary comprehension of the second culture. The potential for improving the teaching of culture is tremendous, but the problems to be solved are imposing.

Problems

The number one problem to be solved in order to improve the teaching of culture is unquestionably that of how to provide the cultural information needed. Many teachers, through no fault of their own, are simply not equipped to teach culture. In this chapter, the missing element is the content. The goals, definitions, organization, and techniques are all listed. Given this information, teachers can incorporate teaching-learning activities geared toward the culture objectives into their classes, *if* they know *what* to teach. What do teen-agers in the second culture do on Saturday evening? What do they wear? What is expected, permitted, frowned upon, and prohibited? What do they like? What do they dislike? What concerns them? What do they read? What do they watch on TV? Teachers who have not spent a considerable amount of time in the second-language community probably do not know. Local native speakers either may not be aware of the answers to these questions, or they may have been away from the country so long that conditions have changed.

Even those teachers who have visited or studied abroad may have overlooked many basic customs among the people. Kalivoda (1974a) suggests that without previous preparation and direction in planning what to look for, the visitor may gain relatively few insights into the second culture during a stay in the second-language community. Guidelines need to be provided, and powers of observation must be sharpened in order to achieve maximum benefit from the study-abroad experience.

Second-language teachers need assistance in overcoming their lack of knowledge about the second culture. First, in the study of sociocultural systems they need help from experts who can identify for them the basic characteristics of the second culture. Second, they need help from commercial publishers who can produce materials containing much of the information they need to know. And third, they need help from the colleges and universities who can provide the training they need to overcome their lack of expertise in culture. Certainly, students of culture, publishers, and college and university professors are aware of these needs, and steps are being taken in some areas to alleviate the problem. The Department of Foreign-Language Education at the University of Minnesota, for example, has conducted "work-ins" in which second-language teachers develop culturally authentic materials and share the results with other members of the group. (The reader who is interested in either participating in such a work-in or in acquiring some of the materials developed can write to the address given in the Selected References. Other recently published works containing cultural information are also listed in the Selected References.)

Another major problem is how to devise ways and means of presenting culture in such a manner that the students can comprehend and relate to the information. Learning experts say that students must be able to relate to course content. How can a student in an affluent suburb of a major city relate to the *campesino* of Latin America or a student in a rather isolated farming community relate to European apartment dwellers? Culture content must be presented at a level and in a manner to which the students can attach some relationship between the information and their own background experiences. Accomplishing this task is far from simple. It is this need for relatability and comprehension that underscores the advantage of visuals and dramatization in teaching culture. In no other aspect of the second-language class are visuals and demonstrations so useful. The teacher can explain that people in other cultures often hold their knives and forks in a different manner, but only a visual or a demonstration can really get the point across promptly and completely.

Another problem is that of finding time in the class period to include culture. The first point regarding this problem is that many of the techniques developed by teachers take relatively little class time. The second point is that even if they do take more time than the teacher might desire, the ends justify the means in this case. Culture is such an important component of the language and vice versa that separating them is just not practical. Undoubtedly, more time can be spent on culture without seriously weakening the students' language skills.

Dangers

One danger in teaching culture is that second-language teachers may attempt to teach culture when they do not have the knowledge or expertise to do so. Such attempts may do more harm than good. If the second culture is presented in such a way that false impressions arise, the alternative of no culture is preferable. This author, for example, once asked a German student of English what impression she had received of Americans from her English teacher. She replied that Americans are "rich, crazy, and they eat out of tin cans!" Stereotypes perpetuated by second-language teachers can lead to results the very opposite of the culture goals expressed at the beginning of this chapter.

The second danger is the amount of work done in the first language in many classes in which the teacher stresses culture. While few second-language educators would currently recommend banning the first language from the second-language class, work done entirely in the first language obviously does not lead to second-language communicative skills. The question does not revolve around which language to use but how to use all the language skills acquired by the students. Anything they can do in the second language should be done in that language. Any content that can be altered to accommodate the students' second-language skills should be geared to their level. Too, the linguistic level of the activities should become increasingly complex as the students progress in their studies.

The third danger is that the culture content selected for the class may concentrate on the unusual, the bizarre, and the esoteric to the exclusion of the basic characteristics of the culture. Cultural activities should not be turned into some sort of circus freak show. Occasionally, the teacher may contribute to such a student reaction by concentrating only on the differences between the cultures rather than on the total picture of any given culture segment. In order to avoid confusion and misunderstanding, the teacher should describe all aspects of the situation. For this reason, films and dramatizations are excellent means of conveying culture.

CONCLUSION

Culture is one of the two major areas (the other being communicative competence) in second-language education in which the greatest need and the greatest potential for improvement exist. The profession must take steps to remedy its unenviable record in transmitting cultural sensitivity and cultural understanding to second-language students. The stress on small *c* culture is a rather recent innovation in second-language teaching. Great strides have been made, but the knowledge generated by anthropologists, sociologists, and other experts in the second culture must be disseminated to the teachers. As this growing body of information becomes available to teachers, culture objectives will become more realizable. As the teaching of culture improves, so will the image of second-language teaching.

REVIEW AND APPLICATION

DEFINITIONS
1. audio-motor unit, p. 396
2. culture, p. 388
3. culture aside, p. 394
4. culture assimilator, p. 395
5. culture capsule, p. 395
6. culture cluster, p. 396
7. culture shock, p. 387
8. ethnocentrism, pp. 386–87
9. kinesics, p. 392
10. large *C* culture, p. 388
11. minidrama and miniskit, p. 396
12. slice-of-life technique, p. 395
13. small *c* culture, p. 388

DISCUSSION
1. Why should culture be, or not be, included in second-language courses?
2. What are the goals in teaching culture?
3. What role do attitudes play in the teaching of culture?
4. Discuss the good and bad aspects of ethnocentrism.
5. What are your opinions about incorporating small *c* or large *C* culture into second-language classes? Would you choose either one or the other or a combination?
6. What do you think students should know about the second culture before going abroad?
7. Compare and contrast the various techniques for teaching culture.
8. Discuss how to incorporate culture into class and the amount of class time to be spent on culture.
9. Discuss the desirability of stressing culture with slow students.
10. Consider ways and means of solving problems and overcoming dangers associated with teaching culture.

ACTIVITIES
1. Examine an elementary text and discuss how culture is presented in it.
2. Take one culture category per student, and list the subtopics you consider important. Discuss them with the class.
3. Alone or with a classmate prepare to teach a culture point using one of the techniques for teaching culture and practice it with the class.

SELECTED REFERENCES

Bals, H. H. (1974) Using Programmed Cultural Assimilators in an Individualized Foreign Language Program. *American Foreign Language Teacher*, 4: 7–10, 37.

Beaujour, M., and Ehrmann, J. (1967) A Semiotic Approach to Culture. *Foreign Language Annals*, 1: 152–63.

Behmer, D. E. (1972) Teaching with Wayne State Cultural Miniskits. *American Foreign Language Teacher*, 3: 3, 38–39.

Benedict, R. (1934) *Patterns of Culture.* Boston: Houghton Mifflin.

Bourque, J. M. (1974) Study Abroad and Intercultural Communication. In G. A. Jarvis (Ed.), *The Challenge of Communication.* Skokie, Ill.: National Textbook. Pp. 329–51.

Bourque, J. M. (1975) *The French Teen-Ager.* Detroit: Advancement Press of America.

Bourque, J.; Allen, E.; and Briggs, S. (1975) *The Spanish Teen-Ager.* Detroit: Advancement Press of America.

Brooks, N. (1964) *Language and Language Learning.* (2nd ed.) New York: Harcourt, Brace & World. Pp. 82–96.

Brooks, N. (1968) Teaching Culture in the Foreign Language Classroom. *Foreign Language Annals,* 1: 204–17.

Brooks, N. (1971) Culture—A New Frontier. *Foreign Language Annals,* 5: 54–61.

Condon, E. C. (1974) Gestures Can Lead to Misunderstanding. *Accent on ACTFL,* 4: 21.

Cooke, M. A. (1972) Suggestions for Developing More Positive Attitudes Toward Native Speakers of Spanish. In H. N. Seelye (Ed.), *Teaching Cultural Concepts in Spanish Classes.* Springfield, Ill.: Office of the Superintendent of Public Instruction. Pp. 97–107.

Cooney, D. T. (1975) *German Culture Through Performance Objectives.* Detroit: Advancement Press of America.

Elkins, R. J., et al. (1972) Teaching Culture Through the Audio-Motor Unit. *Foreign Language Annals,* 6: 61–67.

Green, J. R. (1968) *A Gesture Inventory for the Teaching of Spanish.* Philadelphia: Chilton.

Green, J. R. (1971) A Focus Report: Kinesics in the Foreign-Language Classroom. *Foreign Language Annals,* 5: 62–68.

Hatton, R., and Jackson, G. (1975) *The Bullfight.* Detroit: Advancement Press of America.

Jarvis, D. K. (1975) Teaching Foreign Etiquette in the Foreign Language Class: Student Involvement Techniques. *Foreign Language Annals,* 8: 138–43.

Jarvis, G. A., et al. (1976) *Connaître et se Connaître: A Basic French Reader.* New York: Holt, Rinehart & Winston.

Jenks, F. L. (1974a) Conducting Socio-Cultural Research in the Foreign Language Class. In H. Altman and V. Hanzeli (Eds.), *Essays on the Teaching of Culture.* Detroit: Advancement Press of America. Pp. 95–123.

Jenks, F. L. (1974b) Socio-Cultural Projects for Students and Teachers. Presentation at the annual SCOLT conference, Atlanta, Georgia.

Jenks, F. L. (1975a) Fifteen-Year-Old Students Can Do Cross-Cultural Research: Basic Inquiry Strategies and Exercises for Teachers and Pupils. In F. M. Grittner (Ed.), *Careers, Communication and Culture in Foreign Language Teaching.* Skokie, Ill.: National Textbook. Pp. 65–71.

Jenks, F. L. (1975b) *Planning to Teach Culture.* Detroit: Advancement Press of America.

Joiner, E. G. (1974) Evaluating the Cultural Content of Foreign-Language Texts. *Modern Language Journal,* 58: 242–44.

Kalivoda, T. B. (1974a) An Approach to the Study of Culture in Overseas Programs. Studies in Language Education, Report No. 7. Athens, Georgia: University of Georgia, Department of Language Education.

Kalivoda, T. B. (1974b) A Project for Facilitating Cultural Expertise: Design for Implementation. *American Foreign Language Teacher,* 4: 23–28.

Kalivoda, T. B.; Morain, G.; and Elkins, R. J. (1971) The Audio-Motor Unit: A Listening Comprehension Strategy That Works. *Foreign Language Annals,* 4: 392–400.

Lado, R. (1957) *Linguistics Across Cultures.* Ann Arbor, Mich.: University of Michigan Press.

Ladu, T. T. (1975a) *What Makes the French French.* Detroit: Advancement Press of America.

Ladu, T. T. (1975b) *What Makes the Spanish Spanish.* Detroit: Advancement Press of America.

Lafayette, R. C. (1974) Culture: An Individualized Instruction Option. In F. M.

Grittner (Ed.), *Student Motivation and the Foreign Language Teacher.* Skokie, Ill.: National Textbook. Pp. 81–94.

Lewald, H. E. (1974) Theory and Practice in Culture Teaching on the Second-Year Level in French and Spanish. *Foreign Language Annals, 7:* 660–67.

Meade, B., and Morain, G. (1973) The Culture Cluster. *Foreign Language Annals, 6:* 331–38.

Miller, J. D. (1974) *USA-FRANCE Culture Capsules.* Salt Lake City, Utah: Culture Contrasts Company.

Miller, J. D., and Bishop, R. H. (1974) *USA-MEXICO Culture Capsules.* Salt Lake City, Utah: Culture Contrasts Company.

Morain, G. (1971) Teaching for Cross-Cultural Understanding: An Annotated Bibliography. *Foreign Language Annals, 5:* 82–83.

Nostrand, H. L. (1973) French Culture's Concern for Relationships: Relationism. *Foreign Language Annals, 6:* 469–80.

Nostrand, H. L. (1974) The "Emergent Model" (Structured Inventory of a Socio-cultural System) Applied to Contemporary France. *American Foreign Language Teacher, 4:* 23–27, 40.

Oswalt, W. H. (1970) *Understanding Our Culture: An Anthropological View.* New York: Holt, Rinehart & Winston.

Pindur, N. (1972) Reflections on American Culture. *American Foreign Language Teacher, 2:* 25–27, 40.

Pindur, N. (1975) *The German Teen-Ager in Profile.* Detroit: Advancement Press of America.

Raths, L. E., et al. (1966) *Values and Teaching.* Columbus, Ohio: Merrill.

Runte, R. (1973) Students Can Create Cultural Mini-Dramas from Class Materials. *Accent on ACTFL,* 4: 37–38.

Santoni, G. V. (1974) An Integrated Approach through Linguistic and Cross-Cultural Exercises to Advanced Composition. *Foreign Language Annals, 7:* 425–34.

Schulz, R. A. (1974) Comparative Culture Study: An Approach Through the Printed News Media. *American Foreign Language Teacher,* 4: 11–13, 33–35.

Seelye, H. N. (1968) Analysis and Teaching of the Cross-Cultural Context. In E. M. Birkmaier (Ed.), *Britannica Review of Foreign Language Education.* Vol. 1. Chicago: Encyclopaedia Britannica. Pp. 37–81.

Seelye, H. N. (1975) *Teaching Culture.* Skokie, Ill.: National Textbook.

Taylor, J. S. (1972) Direct Classroom Teaching of Cultural Concepts. In H. N. Seelye (Ed.), *Teaching Cultural Concepts in Spanish Classes.* Springfield, Ill.: Office of the Superintendent of Public Instruction. Pp. 50–54.

Taylor, H. D., and Sorenson, J. L. (1961) Culture Capsules. *Modern Language Journal,* 45: 350–54.

Wallace, M. K. (1973) Cross-Cultural Education and Motivational Aspects of Foreign Language Study. *Foreign Language Annals,* 6: 465–68.

Wight, A. R., and Hammons, M. A. (1970) *Guidelines for Peace Corps Cross-Cultural Training, Part II: Specific Methods and Techniques.* Washington, D.C.: Peace Corps, Department of State.

GENERAL GUIDELINES FOR TEACHING A SECOND LANGUAGE

Three Phases of Language Acquisition

Primary Guidelines

Secondary Guidelines

INTRODUCTION

The following guidelines are not principles in the sense that they are proven theories of teaching. Some, naturally, are more important than others. Some, as one might suspect before reading this chapter, are overlapping. Some, undoubtedly, will fail to elicit a positive response. However, they do constitute a core of ideas that should be kept in mind as the teacher plans for and directs her classes. Prior to considering these guidelines, the teacher should be familiar with the three phases of second-language acquisition, which serve as a basis for a complete understanding of many of the guidelines and of related material in all the chapters of part 2 of this text.

THREE PHASES OF LANGUAGE ACQUISITION

There are three phases through which the students must pass in the acquisition of language structures or concepts. The importance of sequencing of learning activities has previously been stressed. One cannot overemphasize the fact that students approach language mastery in a series of increasingly difficult complex steps instead of suddenly acquiring complete control.

The first stage in the language-learning process is *understanding*. The students need to be aware of the meanings and relationships involved in the material being introduced. If the students do not realize "what is going on," the class activities become little more than an attempt to memorize nonsense syllables. The teacher's task is to focus on understanding during the initial presentation of the new material so that subsequent assignments and classroom exercises will be more meaningful to the students. As a general rule, those who fail languages are those who are unable to organize the language code into any sort of meaningful system. The teacher should constantly be aware of her responsibility to assist the students in the task of finding meaning and relationships in all new material introduced in the class.

The second stage in language acquisition is *production and manipulation* of structures and patterns. Wherever and whenever possible, the manipulation of grammatical forms should be combined with the expression of meaning, such as in affective learning activities and other examples given in the chapters treating the four language skills. For level 2 learners, who have the ability to learn through practice with cognitive writing exercises, forms should be manipulated in written homework exercises. For level 1 learners, who seem to learn better practicing with conditioning exercises, either oral or written pattern drills should be made available. With both types of learners, the goal should be the ability to manipulate structure consciously rather than to respond automatically. The objectives of this activity are to determine whether the students do know how to apply the grammatical forms that have previously been presented, not to learn them, and to promote a better retention of the material.

The third stage is *communication*. There are many different names for this phase. (Belasco terms it *liberated expression*, Gaarder *control of the language*, Birkmaier *variation and free manipulation*, Jarvis *real language*, and Rivers *skill-using*.) Whatever the name, the meaning is the same—practice in actually using previously practiced sounds, vocabulary, and structure to communicate one's thoughts to another person. It is during this stage that the students arrive at the very essence of language. All prior activity has been nothing more than preparation for this stage of unifying the three components of language to express one's own ideas, i.e., to turn competence into performance skills. This is the stage in which the students and teacher finally accomplish their goal of being able to use the language to understand, to speak, to read, and/or to write. Unfortunately, this stage is never reached in many classes; the teacher must always guard against the temptation to omit such "real" language activity from the classroom in order to finish the book or to cover more material.

The class period can be divided into three parts corresponding basically to the three phases of language acquisition. For purposes of discussion and organization, these three parts are labelled *preview*, *view*, and *review*. As was stressed earlier, repetition and sequencing are two basic considerations in second-language teaching. Adding to these two ideas the concept of three stages in second-language learning enables the teacher to structure various types of activities into separate parts of the class hour, each part having its particular objectives.

The first step in initiating any given learning sequence is to *preview* the material to be covered in the next day's assignment. On the average, this activity, done well, will take approximately one fourth of the class period. The purpose of homework should be to practice doing exercises or readings that the students already understand. No assignment should be given without a careful introduction of all the new concepts involved, without relating these concepts to what the students already know, and without providing several practice examples to let the students find out whether or not they really understand the new concepts.

In addition to a meaningful presentation of the new material, the teacher has two other responsibilities in the preview. First, she should make clear what the students are to do in the assignment, and second, how they are to do it. She may assign homework to be prepared for the view or the review sections of the next day's class. (Long-range projects may also be assigned, of course.)

Too often teachers fail to allot a sufficient amount of time to previewing new material. They get behind in their lesson plan and frantically shout the assignment as the students leave the class. Consequently, the following day the class goes slowly due to the fact that the students either did not know the assignment or did not know how to do it. Each day the class becomes more and more lost until there is never the slightest possibility of covering the assignment in time for a proper preview. In this type of disorganized progression through the text both the students' learning and their attitudes suffer.

The *view* portion of the class hour, approximately one half the period, is to be spent primarily on three basic teacher responsibilities in the second-language acquisition sequence. First, whether or not the students have indeed understood the concepts involved in the lesson must be determined. Second, whether or not the students can produce and manipulate the assigned language forms must be verified. Any additional explanations should be limited to answering questions raised by the students. The teacher should avoid the pitfall of attempting to explain the same grammar over and over again. Explanation should be limited to the initial introduction of new material in the preview. Thereafter, the students should learn that unless specific and relevant questions are raised, further analysis will be omitted. If additional manipulation practice is needed, the teacher should be prepared to provide it either in the same class or in a later one. Proceeding in this fashion not only encourages more careful attention on the part of the students and the teacher but also enables the class to maintain its sequence from primary presentation through manipulation to language usage in an uninterrupted progression.

Third, as soon as the teacher is satisfied that the students comprehend the structures and have the ability to produce and manipulate the forms, she should begin to ask the students to use these forms to comprehend or generate messages. She may want to include an affective activity in which the students use the forms to communicate how they feel about something, or she may wish to ask the students to comprehend or to generate a message dealing with the content of the textual materials. Both types of activities are appropriate and both should be used.

The remaining part of the class hour is the *review*. The purpose of the review is to establish situations in which the students have the opportunity to practice using what they have learned in the second language to listen, read, write, or speak for the purpose of communicating information. The students should have a chance during this part of the class to put into practice what they have been studying, to use the language to talk about themselves and their interests. Performance skills related directly to the content of the text are improved during the view part of the class hour. The review portion of the class hour should be devoted to relating course content to the students and to giving them time to perfect their performance skills at an even higher level. All four skills or combinations of skills should be included. Nor should this portion of the class hour be slighted. Although class activities may vary from day to day, it would seem that no less than one fourth of the hour should be spent in some type of personalized, contextual practice.

The three parts of the class hour may be arranged in any order. The most logical order, in this author's opinion, is to proceed chronologically from old material to new. In this fashion, the class begins with the review, goes to the view, and ends with the preview of the next day's assignment. However, those teachers who never seem to have time for an adequate preview may decide to begin the class hour with that part. Too, the teacher may want to alter her normal order on any given day due to special circumstances. The amount of time allotted to each part is a general estimate and may vary from one day to the next depending upon the content of the class.

The two parts of the class hour most often slighted are the review and the preview. Without the preview, however, the teacher must devote too much time to the daily assignment, and the students must spend too much time muddling over exercises that they should be able to do quickly and easily. Without the review, without the "real" language work, the rest of the class work is in vain, because the students are being asked to do all the difficult work without ever having an opportunity to find out the purpose of all the exercises and drills.

In summary, dividing the class period into three parts is a way of structuring class activities in increasingly difficult and complex tasks in order to maintain an integrated, articulated progression toward the teacher's objectives. This division of classroom activities corresponds to the three stages in language acquisition that were discussed earlier. The preview concentrates on understanding. The view activities include the confirmation of competence, production and manipulation of forms, and "real" language activities over the content of the text. The review provides the students with activities that promote and require "real" language practice beyond the content of the text.

PRIMARY GUIDELINES

Consider the whole person   The goal of teaching is to help everyone to be a satisfied, successful learner. But how? Each teacher is different, and each student is different. Also, each class is different, a phenomenon that surprises most beginning teachers, who normally expect to teach all three elementary language classes the same way. Given the quantity of individuality present in any class, the teacher should be alert to student needs and flexible as to measures to take to meet them. Helping students achieve the success they expect seems to be as much a matter of attitude as of specific steps to follow. The one overriding factor seems to be having each student's best interests in mind. By some sixth sense a student seems to know which teachers are genuinely interested in him, and which are more interested in themselves, in the subject matter, or, as the case may be, in getting out of the building before the students in the afternoon. A teacher who may resemble a medieval tyrant can very well have the respect of his students, while one who maintains a less rigidly controlled class can still manage to establish a productive learning atmosphere. However, if the dictator is primarily interested in the image his class presents to the administration, the students will sooner or later come to realize this; and if the teacher playing buddy-buddy is primarily interested in her image among the students, they will realize this, too.

To help the students the teacher needs to know how they feel and what they are thinking. Obviously, the best way to determine their reactions is to observe them before, during, and after class. Another way is simply to ask them for suggestions and ideas. Pausing from time to time to talk about the class and the way it is being conducted can be quite helpful. Ideas may be generated, and attitudes can be improved. At the same time the students have a chance to participate in the democratic process and to have some input into classroom procedures and activities. Too, the teacher can make clear to the students that they should feel free to come to him for a chat if anything is bothering them concerning their progress or the class in general.

Keep the students involved   During the class period the teacher should constantly seek to involve as many students as possible in what is happening. Each student should be able to leave the class knowing that she not only got something out of the class but that she also made a contribution to it. Each student should have the opportunity to participate each and every day. The extent to which the class is meeting her expectations is an important factor in student participation. If actuality coincides with anticipation, the student will continue to come to class prepared to involve herself in the class activities. If not, she will gradually take a less active role in the class.

Group activities are excellent for involving a high percentage of the students. Not only do they involve students, they give the students opportunities to interact with other members of the class. Group activities also provide excellent communicative contexts for practicing performance skills.

Rapport and motivation   Many teachers associate rapport and motivation with being liked by the students, but rapport and motivation are more than playing games, singing songs, and having fun in general. Rapport involves establishing a classroom atmosphere in which students are stimulated to learn. They are cooperative and diligent. Having a good rapport with the students means that they are motivated to learn what is being taught. Rapport refers to the working relationship between the teacher and the students, and motivation entails the students' incentive to learn. Both are an outgrowth of effective teaching. Novak (1969, p. 7) describes motivation as "cognitive drive" which is "the positive motivation resulting from the learner's awareness that he is learning meaningfully." How is this cognitive drive acquired? The answer is found in the following paragraph by Christensen and Shaw (1968, p. 3):

> Generally, successful learner achievement in the classroom depends on three factors: (1) the presentation of a well-articulated sequence of language structures and concepts, (2) the ability of the instructor to help the learner "internalize" the structures of the language without the interference of sophisticated grammar analysis or undue communication in the learner's native language, and (3) the motivation of the learner. Often, if the third factor is not present initially, it may be induced as a result of applying the first two factors.

Analyze the learning task   The teacher is faced with three questions that he must answer as he and his students approach each new learning task: (1) What do the students already know? (2) What do they need to know in order to understand all the concepts involved? (3) How do I structure the learning situation so that they can learn the concepts?

For example, American students studying Spanish encounter a great deal of difficulty learning to express the idea of liking something. Instead of saying, "I like," Spanish speakers say, "It pleases to me." They, not unexpectedly, become entangled in the web of this new structure. The flow of their thinking simply runs in a different direction.

The teacher's responsibility at this point is to lend a helping hand in order to avoid as many pitfalls as possible. In the preceding example, the students should already know three important concepts in the second language that will help them to learn the new structure: they should already know the appropriate verb endings, the indirect object pronouns, and the use of noun indirect objects. In addition, they already have a functional knowledge of a similar structure in English, i.e., "It seems to me." The logical point of departure for teaching the verb *to like*, then, is to begin with another verb, *to seem*, and work toward the unfamiliar structure. Once these concepts and this relationship are made clear to the students, the teacher's task becomes one of providing sufficient practice in order to verify comprehension and to provide opportunities for the students to use the structure in creative, communicative utterances.

Task analysis in reality involves three steps: an analysis of the complexity of the concepts to be acquired, an analysis of the students' prior knowledge, and an analysis of possible procedures for presenting the concepts under consideration. Above all, the teacher should be aware of the hierarchy of the complexity of the learning tasks that he is asking the students to undertake. Otherwise, satisfactory and steady progress is impossible.

Tell the students the objectives   One reason for the disinterested attitude of many students is probably due to the fact that they have no idea why they are doing what they are doing in class. Each day the students should be aware of what the objectives are for that day, even if they cannot verbalize them in grammatical terms specifically. They should also be aware of how these daily objectives fit into the objectives for the course as a whole. Needless to say, the teacher should be aware of the objectives of *each* of the planned activities. Preferably, these are made clear to the students either orally or in writing. It is obvious that goals are attainable only to the extent that they are apparent to the teacher, but it is most likely equally true with regard to the students. Work without a goal is just not so efficient nor so interesting as goal-directed activity. Learning should be goal-oriented, and the goal should be more than passing the teacher's tests.

Make class activities reflect the objectives   Having decided upon the objectives, the teacher next turns her attention to ways of accomplishing them. The problem here is that the teacher often becomes confused while delineating steps toward the objectives. She becomes so involved in the means that she loses sight of the ends. If she concentrates on functional components of the language skills, she is less likely to devote the majority of the class hour to grammatical explanation or to pattern drill. She should go beyond both explanation and drill to help the students toward the objective of language usage in context. Classroom activities must of necessity include both means and ends, but the means should always be directed toward a final approach to the desired end, i.e., ability to communicate one's ideas to someone else.

Students learn to do what they do   There is no magical transfer from one language skill to another. Research has not indicated that students learn to read by concentrating on oral skills. If the objective is reading comprehension, the students must read for comprehension. If the objective is speaking to communicate, the students must express themselves in speaking. If the objective is to be able to use the language in a communicative context, the classroom should provide such activities. Naturally if the students spend all their time studying grammar, they learn structure, but little else. If they spend most of their time parroting pattern drills, they learn "patternese," but little else.

Teach all four language skills   From the point of view of producing language forms, at the elementary level there appears to be little transfer among the language skills. The fact that students can describe a certain structure in grammatical terms does not mean that they can apply that concept in context. Students may have memorized the present-tense verb endings but be unable to use present-tense verbs in conversation. Students may do the pattern drills beautifully in the language laboratory but be unable to write the same forms correctly. Students may comprehend certain structures in a reading passage but be unable to use the same forms to discuss the content.

On a conceptual level, however, the relationship among skills appears to be quite different. First, concepts learned in either of the receptive skills can be reinforced by working with them in the other and by practicing them in the productive performance skills. Second, competence is introduced by means of the receptive skills and strengthened through feedback from performance skills. Third, a student who has a poor ear for languages may not grasp the concept when it is presented orally, but may be able to understand when he has the opportunity to read and/or write these same forms.

Another important consideration here is that language is made up of the four skills. In order to teach students to communicate, the teacher must provide training in all the skills necessary for communication, which often involves various combinations of the four skills. Of course, there are special cases, such as graduate reading courses, in which students may desire not to concentrate on all four language skills. It is beneficial to the student and to the second-language program to accommodate these special interests as far as possible.

Sequence the learning tasks in order of difficulty   Too often, language is viewed as an all-or-nothing process. Teaching practices often seem to reflect the attitude that with enough pounding and threats of quizzes and tests, the frustrating barrier will be broken by the accumulated weight of the material presented in class, and the light of understanding will suddenly shine forth from the eyes of the students. Supposedly, miracles do happen, but the classroom is not the place to expect them.

Instead, language learning should be viewed as a continuous process of successive approximation to native speech. There is a hierarchy of steps of increasing difficulty that the students must tread as they approach language mastery. Omission of the elementary steps leaves them unprepared for classroom activities on a more difficult level. Omission of the last steps robs the students of an opportunity to put into practice what they have been learning. In sports, for example, a coach never sends a player into the game until the fundamentals have been drilled. On the other hand, it is difficult to get the players to practice the fundamentals faithfully unless there is some chance they can play. The same is true in the classroom. The teacher cannot expect students to study and do exercises unless it can be shown that their efforts will help them to use the language. In other words, it is naive to expect students to answer questions in the language unless they have been carefully prepared so that they have the abilities necessary for such activity. On the other hand, it is not fair to the students to ask them to be diligent in study and in doing exercise activities without letting them have some time to practice using the language.

Progress is by means of minimal steps   Although the great thinkers may proceed by means of giant intuitive leaps of the mind, most basic knowledge is gained as a result of a slow, difficult walk as the students acquire basic concepts. They cannot be expected to hurdle imposing difficulties. Progress is most sure and most agreeable to the students when they are guided carefully and in small steps up the ladder of language acquisition. New structures are more easily learned if they are presented one at a time. After the initial presentation, follow-up activities should become progressively more difficult until the students have reached the peak of the sequence or the ultimate objective, i.e., the ability to use the structure in context to communicate.

Learning involves much repetition of concepts   Once one has achieved some degree of mastery of a subject, it is quite common to forget the time and energy that was expended to attain that mastery. It is the teacher's responsibility to remember the importance of repetition in learning, but not to overemphasize it in class. (The meaning of the word *repetition* as used in this paragraph should not be confused with repeating after a model.) The teacher must provide for re-entry of concepts into the classroom activity, but each day the tasks involved should become increasingly more difficult. A common pitfall of inexperienced teachers is to repeat the same concept in the same drills and exercises day after day. Such repetition of identical activities fails to attain the desired objectives and usually creates serious motivational problems in the class. In short, learning involves a great deal of continuous repetition of concepts, but these concepts should be incorporated into new contexts in order to avoid boredom and in order to teach for transfer of knowledge.

Teach for transfer of learning There are various theories with regard to transfer of learning. The important consideration for the teacher is that he must assist in the process. He cannot relax and let fate take its course. It is the teacher who must place structures in different contexts for the students to see. It is the teacher who must emphasize all four language skills. It is the teacher who must provide opportunities through personalized questions and oral written compositions for the students to relate what they have learned, in perhaps a very abstract fashion, to their own lives. It is the teacher who must provide activities to stimulate the students to use learned structures in new and dissimilar contexts to communicate about either themselves or something or someone with whom they are familiar.

Provide a variety of activities The students' attention span is not very long. The teacher is obliged to provide as much variety of activities as possible. No activity should last more than ten to fifteen minutes, and drill should not last that long. In general, the teacher should provide approximately seven or eight activities during the class hour.

The language teacher has many possibilities at his disposal for providing variety. If he sequences the activities from simple to more complex, if he divides the class hour into three parts in which each section is aimed at a different stage of language acquisition, and if he remembers to teach all four language skills plus culture, the students are involved each class period in a variety of activities.

At times the teacher feels under pressure to surprise his students with something new each day. If he is gifted with such creativity, wonderful. However, most teachers are not. The important point to keep in mind is that variety is a necessity within the class hour. From class to class, daily innovations are not only impossible; they are undesirable. The students must have some idea what to expect in a general way as they enter the class each day. In other words, the key word within the class hour is variety; the key words for the course are continuity, consistency, and predictability.

Resist the tendency to correct each mistake   Teachers should refrain from demonstrating their own ability and intelligence at the drop of an error. More important than error-free speech is the creation of an atmosphere in which the students want to talk. Teachers may stifle the development of any enthusiasm for language simply by correcting the students each and every time some incorrect form slips past their lips. In the first place, the common practice of interrupting students while they are reading or talking is extremely discourteous. In the second place, it prevents them from concentrating on what they are saying. It is evident that students are not really using language to communicate unless they are thinking about what they are saying rather than how they are saying it. In the third place, students who are continually reminded of their mistakes are less than likely to be overjoyed at the experience of studying a language. Such constant correction is unheard of during childhood when the native language is being learned (except for stutterers, who suffer from the effects of parental criticism), so why use such a distasteful practice in second-language teaching?

Obviously, the students must be provided a correct model, and there is a proper time to correct student errors. First, it behooves the teacher not to interrupt students in order to make corrections. Second, he should attempt to develop the reaction among the students that such corrections are not forms of punishment but attempts to assist them in learning the language. Third, the teacher should limit his corrections to the production and manipulation portion of the class hour. During the preview, the students are given only a slight possibility of making errors due to the nature of the activity. During the review activities, the objective is to practice the receptive skills or to get the students to express themselves either in writing or in speech. The objective is expression and communication, not perfect speech. The ideal of perfect speech is impossible to attain, and insisting on such an ideal can only hinder the students' progress. As long as the teacher can decipher what the students are saying, he should not interrupt to correct or to clarify, but he should accept the message as understandable. He can then either reword the answer in an acceptable fashion, in such a manner as adults do with children, or at the end of the activity he may summarize and review the most common mistakes. The teacher must keep in mind that errors in usage are eliminated by the learner only when he gains control of the language.

Keep the pace alive   The teacher should begin the class promptly and vigorously. The impetus thus generated should be nurtured carefully (and the spark fanned into flame if possible) during the remainder of the class hour. Dead spots in the class hour are to be avoided by any and all means. It is the teacher's responsibility to have something up her sleeve in case the current disappears. She should be ready to encourage, to assist, to model, or to call on someone else anytime the students are unable to respond to the questions. She should not waste time monotonously repeating the same question at a slightly higher pitch, or fidgeting nervously during the embarrassed silence. The class movement may sway, regress, or progress, but always the focus of the activity and direction of emphasis is toward the attainment of the objectives of the class.

Teach from the known to the unknown   The teacher will have a larger following if he leads the students from the known to the unknown, the known being concepts in the native or second language with which the students are already familiar. For example, in introducing the concept of verb endings, the teacher can begin with an example of a verb ending in English. His explanation may resemble the following:

> In English we say "I talk" when we mean an action that takes place in the present or habitually takes place. Now, when we wish to mention this action in the past, when we wish to describe an action we did yesterday, how do we say it? (The students will normally supply the correct answer here.) Right! Notice that that *t* sound at the end of the word tells us that the action took place in the past. "I walk" is a present action. How would you change that to past? (The students answer.)

The teacher then continues with other examples in English until he is sure that the students understand the concept. He can then explain that the ending on some of our verbs tell us the time. In other languages this system is used much more, and it often tells the listener the person doing the action as well as when it is performed. At this point the students are prepared for the introduction of the new material in the second language.

If he is interested in emphasizing at the same time the different kinds of verbs, he can also introduce verbs such as *study, mow,* etc. for the *d* sound to express past tense. Later he may even introduce some irregular verbs in English to help the students anticipate irregular verbs in the new language.

If the teacher wants to introduce the concept of subject-verb agreement, he can introduce, with the students' assistance, the third person singular verb forms in the present tense. The concept is the same in French, German, Russian, and Spanish except that it is much more prevalent in these languages than it is in English.

There are four distinct and important advantages to planning the introduction of new material in such a way that the students proceed from concepts with which they are familiar to the new words and forms that they will be expected to learn. First, it permits the teacher to involve the students themselves in the introduction. Second, it serves often as a review of previously learned material. Third, it enables the teacher to teach new grammar without resorting to grammatical terms. Fourth, and most important, it provides a framework within which the students can assimilate the new structures and concepts being introduced.

Learning should not, and cannot efficiently, occur in a vacuum. The students who learn well must organize their knowledge. Moving from the known to the unknown helps them to relate and organize what they are learning.

Teach with examples   The old saying is that a picture is worth a thousand words. An example, then, in language teaching must be worth quite a few explanations. Unfortunately, the language teacher has often learned language as an abstract, prescriptive set of rules. She was the star of her class because she was able to visualize what her teacher meant. Therefore, she has a tendency to employ beautifully organized presentations replete with abstract grammatical terms but devoid of any substantive examples. The bright students can manage abstract concepts. The slower students, however, cannot, and they deserve an additional frame of reference upon which to anchor as they struggle for mastery of the language.

After using examples to introduce the new structures, the teacher should also provide a few additional sentences for the students to do as a test of their comprehension. Without this check, some students may be expected to do homework, for which they have been inadequately prepared in class.

The use of the first language   The teacher should use the first language in class when he feels it is the most efficient manner of presenting the point. The use of the first language by the students should be discouraged, but not to the extreme that students are unable to clarify points of difficulty. In fact, it is better to say that the teacher should encourage the use of the second language whenever possible.

The important thing to remember with regard to the use of the first language is not so much its use, but the timing of its use. (After all, the teacher cannot control the thoughts of the students in their first language.) It can be said that the use of the first language should decrease as the students' ability in the second language increases.

In the understanding phase, there may well be a great deal of first language used in the class. (The amount depends on the concept being introduced. Some structures lend themselves very well to inductive presentations and can be done entirely in the second language: i.e., learning to tell time or learning the weather expressions.) In the production and manipulation phase, there should be very little need for using the mother tongue. Examples can be given and exercises covered with instructions in the second language.

During the "real" language practice, the necessity of resorting to the first language should be practically nonexistent if the teacher has provided a realistic sequence in which the students have been brought from the initial knowledge level to the required skill level.

The same relationship applies to the various levels of language learning. One would expect to hear more first language in first than in second year. It seems that as soon as all the grammatical concepts have been studied, there is little reason thereafter for using any first language in the class.

The teacher may want to ban the mother tongue earlier, and may be quite successful in doing so. With the direct method, for example, the instructor conducts the class entirely in the second language from the first day of class. Obviously, the ingenuity of the teacher and the nature of the materials being used in class are important factors in making this decision. Also, it may be advisable to vary the presentation in class, depending upon the concepts being introduced and the type of classroom activity being utilized.

Figure 15.1 is a graphic representation of the use, on the average, of first language (and teacher talk) during language acquisition activity in each part of the class hour.

Figure 15.1:
Amount of First Language and Teacher Talk in Second-Language Classes

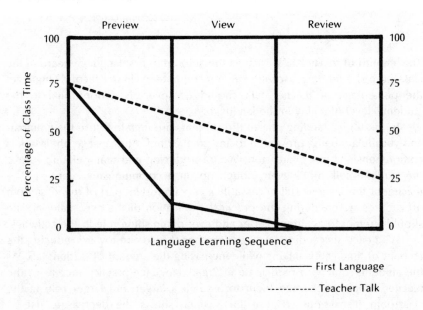

Figure 15.2, representing second-language use (and student talk), is the reverse of the preceding figure.

Figure 15.2:
Amount of Second Language and Student Talk in Second-Language Classes

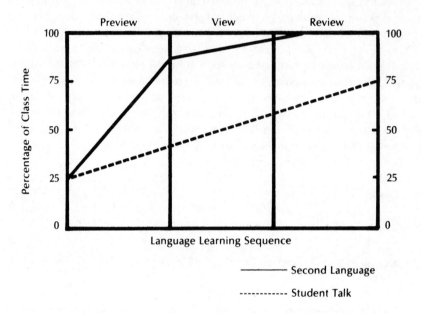

——————— Second Language

------------ Student Talk

The amount of teacher talk   Just as the amount of first language heard in the classroom should decrease with student competence in the second language, the percentage of teacher talk should be inversely proportional to the students' level of ability in the language.

In the understanding phase, the students are unable to use the grammar and vocabulary being presented to any great extent. At this stage, their task is comprehension, not expression. While producing and manipulating forms, the students talk more even though not in a communicative context. The teacher at this stage is still necessarily a very important part of the classroom procedures. Later, during the practical application of the new material, she should attempt to assume a lesser and ever diminishing role in the activities.

With each succeeding level, the teacher should aim toward reducing the amount of time she is talking while increasing the amount of student talk. As the students' ability to participate in "real" language practice increases, the teacher should encourage them to assume a larger and larger role in the classroom discussions. (Figure 15.1, which shows the decreasing use of the first language, also represents the decreasing amount of teacher talk in the class.)

Use life situations   One of the trends in the preparation of teaching materials and in teaching a second language is to make the exercises and drills as meaningful as possible. For example, in teaching verbs, the teacher can include drills similar to actual usage by concentrating on questions and answers. The easier drills are of the following type: "I am going to class. Are you?" Such a question is much more likely to occur in a conversation than the following: The teacher says, "I" and the students say, "I am going to class." The first example is also much easier, since the students have just heard the correct form. Similar sentences can be expanded to practice all the various pronoun possibilities and their corresponding verb forms. Another slightly more difficult activity is simply to ask questions. The teacher asks several questions such as: "Do you study a lot?" "Do you speak English?" This type of questioning gives the student a great deal of practice in answering "you" questions with an "I." Later, the teacher can reverse the procedure by asking questions about himself. Next comes the plural version of the same verb forms, preferably with different ideas attached. And last are questions employing the third-person singular and the third-person plural forms.

In order that there be as few errors as possible, the teacher should structure these questions carefully. At first, the verbs should be grouped according to type and person. Later, the types should be mixed. Last of all, the entire spectrum of verb forms and persons can be mixed in the test of the students' achievement. At this stage, the teacher can begin to ask the following kinds of questions: "Mary, do you speak Italian?" "John, does Mary speak Italian?" "Do you speak Italian?" "Do you speak it?" (if the students have had the pronouns) "Do you and Mary speak Italian?" "Joe, do they speak Italian?" "Do I speak Italian?" "Do we speak Italian?" This type of practice sets the abstract grammar in concrete form. The students can see how the idea of persons and verb endings combine to talk to and about others. The questions can later be expanded to other people, other contexts, and other structures. The point to be made is that the teacher should make language come alive by developing activities for practice that have some possibility of occurring in an everyday language situation.

Distinguish between abstract and concrete concepts   The teacher should be flexible in her approach. The complexity and abstractness of the concept may influence the approach. For example, it is quite easy to teach the word *chalk*, but the word *honesty* is more difficult. The subject pronouns are rather easily demonstrated merely by pointing, but the concept of reflexives is more complex.

Structures should be exemplified where possible, even the more concrete ones. The teacher can develop activities to demonstrate (even if somewhat artificially) contexts in which the topic under consideration may occur. For example, students who have been studying commands can be asked to carry out commands within the classroom as the teacher gives them. If the students have already studied present progressives, the teacher can combine the two activities by telling Jim to write his name. Then she can ask, "Joyce, is Jim writing his name?" "Jack, what is Jim writing?" "Who is writing his name?" "Where is Jim writing his name?" A great deal of oral practice can be generated from only a few commands.

The command forms can also serve as a basis for "concretizing" the subjunctive. For example, the teacher can tell Susan to write her name on the chalkboard. This command can be followed by the questions: "Does the teacher want Susan to write her name on the chalkboard?" "Who wants Susan to write her name on the chalkboard?" "What does the teacher want Susan to write on the chalkboard?" "Where does the teacher want Susan to write?" Then the teacher continues to more difficult questions such as "What does the teacher tell Susan?" "What does the teacher want?" "Why is Susan writing her name on the chalkboard?" "Is it true that Susan is writing her name on the chalkboard?"

Activities like those just presented help the students to comprehend more fully the way or ways in which the structure may be used. Later, this same type of practice can serve as a basis for review and for providing practical examples.

Structure the difficulty level of the questions   Obviously, some questions are more complex than others.[1] Equally true is the fact that the questions should be asked on a premeditated, selective basis. That is, good students should not be given easy questions, and poor students should not be given difficult questions. Questions can be divided, in general, into four levels of difficulty.

The easiest type of question, and the one that should be used only in the early steps toward mastery of the structure, is a question containing the answer. For example, "Is he a cowboy?" Such a question is quite valuable when the students have only a minimal skill level, for it requires little more than a restructuring of the word order.

More difficult for the students is the type of question in which some definite structural changes are required. For example, "Do you go to bed early?" "How many brothers do you have?" The latter questions also require more information as well as a more complex structural change.

[1]Many of the ideas for the present discussion come from Neale-Silva (1962, pp. 7–12).

Even more difficult for the students to answer are questions that require a more complete amount of information. Questions like, "What do you think of the new library?" "Why did you go to the theater?" or "What did you do last night?" are likely to discourage the students if they have not had a great deal of experience in answering simpler questions. The fault in such a case lies not with the students but with the teaching. The selective structure of questions also enables the teacher to gear the task required to the ability levels of the individual students in the class. Review portions of the class hour should include all types of questions directed toward those students most capable of handling a question at that particular difficulty level.

The most difficult questions are "reasoning" questions. An example is, "What do you think of aid to underdeveloped countries?" This type of question is designed to elicit a thoughtful response. The students may answer in several sentences rather than only one or part of one. In order to stimulate the better students, such questions should be interspersed with simpler questions. At the more advanced levels, these questions may constitute a majority of the items in any given day's questioning.

One of the problems facing teachers is where to obtain their questions. They may choose to use those in the text, to have students prepare questions, or to prepare their own. Their own questions are likely to be most consistent with the purposes in the lesson. However, questions from the text and student questions can be used to advantage. Those of the text may be used as a basis for homework preparation, and if so, they should be answered in class. Student questions often contain many errors and are vague and difficult to answer, but giving the students a chance to change the pace by asking questions either of other class members or of the teacher can be a highly motivating activity.

Do not teach a problem-solving class   The teacher who views teaching as nothing more than a repetition of grammatical explanations, at the end of which the students are supposed to understand grammatical terminology, is undoubtedly falling far short of the goal of skill development. Prescriptive grammar rules do not insure the ability to apply these same rules in any functional fashion. Focusing on structure and comparing similar concepts in the native and the second language may improve learning in the understanding stage of language acquisition. Continuing reference to the mother tongue, however, hinders skill development and stagnates the progress of the class. During manipulation of forms and contextual practice, explanations and comparisons with the native language are to be avoided. In order to use the language, the students must go beyond this level. The teacher should ask himself how much time he spends each day in explanation of structure either inductively or deductively and what proportion of his examinations deal with grammar as opposed to items testing the application of structure to communicate in the four language skills.

SECONDARY GUIDELINES

The preceding are major guidelines that should be given careful consideration by each teacher. The following guides are less important but certainly worthy of inclusion in this chapter for whatever help they may provide.

Have something to give the class   The teacher should ask himself each day as he enters his classroom whether or not the content of the lesson is worthwhile. Is the content interesting, and are the activities something he would like to do if he were a student? The teacher must have confidence in the material he is about to present and in the procedures he has outlined for learning the material. Such confidence is the result of careful planning. There are no shortcuts. Teaching is hard work.

Some teachers may disagree. Often student teachers are told that lesson plans are not necessary. Such statements are made because these teachers prefer a spontaneous-combustion type interchange in the classroom. However, adequate preparation in no way excludes spontaneity; it merely enables the teacher to maintain control of both the content and direction of the class discussion.

Assume your responsibilities   Often the beginning teacher recently graduated from the university remembers almost too well how the students feel. She may even share their discomfort to the point where she is apologetic for the work she asks them to do. Such apologies rarely do more than discredit the teacher in the eyes of the students; they may even negate her effectiveness in the classroom. Students are human, and most humans would rather play than work. Most students need to be stimulated and challenged to achieve their potential. The teacher is negligent in her duty if she fails to provide this stimulation. The students need to be assisted in developing self-discipline when confronted with tasks that at times may demand a rather large amount of effort and concentration. (At the same time, the teacher should be cognizant of the need to provide rewards and satisfaction for such work!)

Give the students a feeling of confidence and success   The teacher has achieved success if he can organize the sequencing of the classroom activities in such a way that the students feel sure of their ability to answer correctly and are given proof that they are actually learning to use the language. Student participation is primarily a question of being confident and feeling successful. Errors usually occur when the students are asked to perform tasks for which they have not been adequately prepared.

Insist that the students share the load   The old saying is that you can lead a horse to water but you cannot make him drink. That is true. The teacher's role is to teach. The students' task is to learn. Teaching begins with the teacher. Learning begins with the students. The teacher must not abdicate her responsibility for teaching, but she should not assume the responsibility for learning. That responsibility rests entirely with the students. The teacher may encourage, assist, prod, even demand that the students do certain work, but she should never remove that responsibility from the students.

The art of teaching   The art of teaching lies in teaching in such a way that the students know the right answers, not in telling them that they are wrong. Explaining errors is quite easy; preventing those same errors before they occur is quite difficult. When the teacher solves this problem (which he never does completely), he has unraveled the secret of the art itself. The proof of the teacher's success comes when the students enter the contextual practice stage. If they have sufficient command of the material to be able to express themselves, he has succeeded in that particular section of the book.

Encourage the students   Although the teacher has a perfect right to let the students know when he is displeased, he is at the same time obligated to compliment them when they deserve praise. He should not forget to reinforce good responses with a word of praise. However, reinforcement can become so common that a point of diminishing returns is reached. The teacher should also avoid falling into the habit of uttering stock phrases which soon become devoid of any meaning whatsoever. In short, praise should be used in appropriate circumstances, and then it should be a genuine expression of pleasure for a job well done.

   If the students become lethargic and listless, if they cannot seem to shake the doldrums, give them a pep talk. Remind them of all the reasons for studying a second language, and praise them for how far they have progressed. (Teachers need to learn to focus on accomplishments rather than shortcomings, on distance traveled rather than distance remaining to be covered.) Talk things over and try to get them back into the groove. If the students deserve a treat, take time out to have some fun once in a while. A special game, a film, or some other diversion from the routine may be just the needed pause that refreshes. It's not realistic to expect that junior high or high school students can keep their noses to the grindstone all the time.

Call on the students   Much classroom time is often wasted as the teacher decides upon whom she is going to call next. She should be making that decision while she is asking the question. Unless she learns to move the questions quickly around the room, the tempo slackens, and the pace gradually expires silently during the moment of indecision.

Do not do in class what the students can do for themselves at home   Classroom activities should be limited to those activities that must be done in the classroom and are most efficiently done with the assistance of the teacher or other students. For example, oral practice on the "real" language level is a classroom activity. On the other hand, writing exercises and readings can be assigned as homework.

A common complaint of the average teacher is that the students do not do their homework. There is no question but that students are often derelict in their duties. However, before condemning them, the teacher should inspect his own classroom procedures. He should ask himself, "Do I encourage this situation by permitting them to do their work in class?" If the teacher is going to do the homework in class for them, or if he is conducting the class on such a low level that preparation is not necessary for successful participation in the class, he should correct his own faults before casting accusing glances in the direction of the students.

Hold the students responsible for the material   The permission and acceptance of superficial learning is certain to have eroding effects on achievement in the classroom. The teacher should insist that the students know the assignment. They should be able to do more than merely read the answers off the paper. Of course, their papers should be checked with the correct answers, but eventually the teacher should determine whether they know the material well enough to do these same exercises without the benefit of a crutch. The same is true on the examinations. The tests should cover the application of what has been taught in the context of the four language skills. The students should be expected to apply their knowledge to contexts of language usage instead of regurgitating vocabulary and verb forms dutifully memorized but little understood.

Teach for respect   The teacher should resist the temptation to place primary importance upon being liked by the students. The important thing is whether she is respected. Respect insures cooperation and effort toward learning; personal affinity may not. The fortunate teacher is able to acquire both, but normally, respect comes before friendship. The teacher cannot be a pal, as much as she might like to be one, and the students really do not want, nor need, the teacher for a pal, as much as they may protest to the contrary.

Do not teach all you know   Admittedly, the truth of this statement depends upon the depth of the knowledge of the teacher. However, the teacher should keep in mind that too much new material presented at the same time may be impossible to assimilate. The students, especially at the beginning levels, are trying to learn the basics. The exceptions and nuances of the language can wait until they are in the advanced courses. For those who do not continue with the language, the finer points of syntax and style are unnecessary burdens anyway.

Do not strive for mastery in a single day   Learning takes place over a period of time. Skill development is the culmination of persistent practice. The teacher needs to accept the necessity of the repetition of concepts as a basic fact of teaching. He must learn to space his planned activities in a sequence of ever increasing difficulty over a span of several days. He has to learn to focus on heights of skill to be reached by the end of the week while concentrating on the initial means of attaining those peaks of performance at the beginning of the week.

Recognize individual differences   Each student is a unique individual. The teacher's task is to structure the learning situations in order to maximize the learning efficiency of each student. The teacher should not insist upon one approach for all students. Some learn better without the book; others may feel more comfortable with the book. Some may quickly grasp the concepts involved in any inductive presentation; others may require a deductive explanation. Some may want to learn to read; others may prefer to learn to speak. Some may be content to do oral drills; others may wish to practice written exercises. In other words, the ability levels, preferences, and habits of the students are all different. The teacher needs to provide as many varied procedures for learning as possible. The presentations can include both inductive and deductive elements as well as both oral and written examples. The exercises can include both pattern drills and cognitive exercises. The questions can be geared to the ability level of the individual students. The assignments can be varied for any given day to accommodate individual differences. Not all students have to complete the assignment. More difficult sentences can be given to the brighter students only. Nor do all the students have to complete the entire examination. A complete test includes the total range of abilities, i.e., easy questions for those struggling and more difficult items for those who need a challenge to prevent their becoming lethargic.

Use audio-visual aids whenever possible   Earlier in the chapter, the comment was made that a picture is worth a thousand words. In language teaching, visuals may give meaning to a thousand words. Visuals stimulate interest, provide variety, and promote understanding of structure, vocabulary, and culture. The teacher should never pass up the opportunity to incorporate visuals in the lesson plan at any of the three stages of language acquisition.

Maintain high standards   There seems to be a definite positive correlation between teacher expectations and student achievement, regardless of what method is used. Part of the teacher's responsibility is to maintain high standards of achievement, high standards that many young people are too immature to establish voluntarily for themselves. The teacher should always insist upon high quality performance by the students. Naturally, to expect performance beyond the students' capabilities is unrealistic and unjust, but the students should be required to produce to the limit of their potential.

CONCLUSION

Teachers, especially prospective teachers, often react negatively to a discussion of principles. Instead, they seek specific formulae that they may invoke to cope with any given classroom situation. The desire is to gather a store of reactions "guaranteed to work." If situation A occurs, they apply reaction B and get result C. If they learn all the proper responses, they are assured of success in teaching. While such feelings are understandable, they are quite unrealistic. The same lesson plan that produces gratifying results with the nine-o'clock class may be a tragedy at ten o'clock. The teacher who stimulates some students may be a failure with others. The procedures that work one year may be unproductive the next. Surefire formulae simply do not exist. If foolproof recipes were available, teaching would cease to be the exciting, stimulating profession that it is. The best that classroom teachers can do is to adopt a set of guidelines with which they can operate in a flexible fashion.

REVIEW AND APPLICATION

DEFINITIONS
1. abstract vs. concrete concepts, p. 425
2. learning task, p. 412
3. pace, p. 420
4. preview, p. 417
5. problem-solving class, p. 427
6. review, p. 418
7. view, p. 418

DISCUSSION
1. Relate the three phases of second-language acquisition to the concept of sequencing in learning.

2. Relate the three parts of the class hour to the three phases of second-language acquisition and sequencing.
3. Discuss the importance of task analysis prior to the selection of teaching-learning activities.
4. How can the teacher achieve variety of activity in the class? Name some different types of classroom activities.
5. Discuss ways and means of integrating the four language skills into the second-language learning sequence.
6. What can the teacher do to encourage students to prepare for class, participate in classroom activities, and persevere in second-language learning?
7. Compare and contrast homework and class work both as to purposes and types of activities.
8. How can visual aids be used in teaching? Would the types of visual aids and the ways they are used be different for the different phases of language learning? In which phase would they be most beneficial?
9. What was your reaction to the discussion of the amount of native language and teacher talk in the second-language class? To what extent did your past classes correspond to the suggested pattern?
10. Discuss the various components of individuality in relation to teaching the whole person. What are the variables involved?

ACTIVITIES

1. Prepare a sample task analysis as a basis for a meaningful presentation of a grammar point in the text you are using.
2. Prepare sample activities for understanding, manipulation, and contextual practice of this grammar point.
3. Prepare one or more audio-visual aids to use with an activity for understanding, manipulation, and contextual practice.
4. Give an example of a life-situation activity.
5. Prepare sample questions at the various levels of difficulty, and ask your classmates to rate them as you give them in random order.

SELECTED REFERENCES

Christensen, C. B., and Shaw, J. R. (1968) A Definition of Achievement Level II in the Control of Spanish Syntax. Unpublished doctoral dissertation, University of Washington, Seattle, Wash.

Neale-Silva, E. (1962) El arte de hacer preguntas. *The Wisconsin Spanish Teacher,* 15: 7–12.

Novak, J. D. (1969) Relevant Research on Audio-Tutorial Methods. Paper read at the Audio-Tutorial System Conference, Purdue University. P. 7.

LESSON PLANNING

INTRODUCTION

Having considered the internal-external dichotomy in learning and classroom organization, the student and student needs, ways and means of diversifying instruction, the four language skills and culture, the importance of sequencing learning activities in the development of each of the four language skills, and the general guidelines for second-language teaching, the teacher should now be ready to undertake the preparation of lesson plans. The time has arrived to "put into practice" what he has been learning. The background that he has acquired is applied toward the formulation of objectives and the selection of classroom activities to accomplish the desired goals. The purpose of this chapter is to focus on the planning of instruction.

THE IMPORTANCE OF PLANNING

Planning enables the teacher to organize classroom learning situations toward chosen goals. Only by delineating selected instructional objectives can she begin to arrange an appropriate sequence of classroom activities that progress in increasing levels of difficulty. Careful planning is crucial to successful teaching, and it is doubtful that anyone can be a good teacher unless she is aware of her objectives and plans the classroom activities accordingly. Certainly such preplanning is necessary to insure maximum effectiveness. Successful teaching activities do not suddenly burst into flame by a process of spontaneous combustion sparked by the inextinguishable enthusiasm of the teacher and her "charges." They result from much hard work and premeditation. During this premeditation period the teacher hypothesizes "what will work" in order to accomplish the objectives. Planning the work is what Huebener (1965, p. 118) calls "anticipatory teaching, for the learning situation is lived through, mentally, in advance."

The importance of careful preparation for each class period cannot be overstressed. Accidental accomplishment of unknown goals is extremely rare in any field, and teaching is no exception. Lesson plans involve two major portions of the actual teaching process—objectives and classroom activities. Without these essential components, teaching degenerates into a disjunctive array of nonrelated activities that lead nowhere in particular. Teaching is too complex for the teacher to make the right choices subconsciously and automatically in front of the class.

Plans do not insure a good lesson, of course. Often the teacher's hypotheses are incorrect and objectives or the resultant classroom procedures must be reevaluated. This constant reexamination of techniques and procedures constitutes one of the most exciting facets of teaching. Teaching should not be a static state but should progress toward the realization of the teacher's total capability. The teacher who ceases to learn from teaching has ceased to teach.

It is possible to have a vibrant class hour without a written lesson plan. There are times when unanticipated student reaction may cause the teacher to abandon the lesson plan in order to respond to the students. This type of interaction can be exciting and rewarding to both the teacher and the students. Teaching without teacher-student interaction is impossible, but the teacher should be in control of the overall direction this interaction takes. Lesson plans should be aids to productive teaching, not restrictive limits placed upon what can happen. The teacher should be flexible in following the anticipated guidelines. At the same time she needs always to keep in mind that she, not the class, should set the pace. The students may be quite content with a crawl, but the teacher's responsibility is to see to it that they cover as much ground as possible. In the long run, most students respond more agreeably to a feeling of satisfaction from a job well done than they ever do from wasting time in a state of semi-inertia.

As was stated in the preceding paragraph, lesson plans do not have to be written. An experienced teacher may be able to proceed quite well on any given day without writing a lesson plan. This does not mean that there is no plan, however. The experienced teacher has a sufficient background to be able to specify objectives and plan appropriate activities without writing them. The important thing is that she *must* be able to state them if the class is to have any continuity and direction. The ever-present danger is that she may simply follow the book without having any definite objectives. In such a case the teacher is undoubtedly placing severe limitations upon her teaching potential and effectiveness. The tragedy of such a situation is that it is entirely possible that she may not be aware of what her true capabilities are. She may succumb to the self-deluding egotism to which any teacher is susceptible, i.e., "I am conducting the class with relatively few problems; therefore, I am doing a good job." Such a situation is quite possible without any consideration of goals or objectives. However, good teaching is goal-oriented, requiring both goals and plans for their attainment.

PLANS AND THE BEGINNING TEACHER

The beginning teacher should prepare complete lesson plans. He is in the same situation as a student in mathematics who is learning a new problem-solving technique. At first, he must follow all the steps carefully in order to understand fully the entire process. Later, certain shortcuts may be taken that eliminate unnecessary minor details and make the work more efficient. The same concept is true in the preparation of lesson plans. The beginning teacher needs considerable practice in formulating specific objectives and correlating them with appropriate classroom activities. Establishing the connection between objectives and activities is not so easy as it might seem at first, and the beginning teacher must concentrate on working from objectives through classroom learning situations to testing procedures. Once he has acquired a certain expertise in lesson planning, the beginning teacher can justifiably shorten the written portions of the lesson plans. However, just as in a math problem, he should still be performing all the necessary steps in his mind, and he should always know what his objectives and planned activities are before the class begins.

During this initial stage of teaching, the beginning teacher hopefully learns several things about lesson plans. First, he should learn that careful preparation in advance helps him to feel more secure in front of a class. Second, he should realize that good teaching flows from objectives to teaching situations and that good planning is reflected in high student achievement and consequently in high student morale. Third, he should become aware that an efficiently run class period requires a systematic selection and arrangement of classroom activities. Fourth, he should comprehend the continuity necessary from one day's plan to the next as the class progresses toward the goals of the unit or chapter in the text. And fifth, he should understand that certain portions of the lesson plan require more complete preparation beforehand than others.

The drills and/or exercises, naturally, are in the book, although they may need to be supplemented. The major problem is selecting those activities that are consistent with the chosen objectives. In presenting new material or in contextualized practice, however, the teacher himself must assume most of the responsibility for clear, concise explanations, related examples, and stimulating "real" language activities related to the content of the course. No teacher, even one with many years of experience, can expect to "pull off the top of his head" everything needed in the entire class hour.

The beginning teacher should place portions of his lesson plans, such as "real" language practice of any kind and presentations of new material, on file cards that can be reused. These cards can be pulled very quickly, especially the "real" language cards, for review activities. Also, much of the same material can be incorporated into new lesson plans in subsequent years. The students and text may change, but many good ideas and questions continue to be applicable. In addition, teaching from cards is much easier than trying to locate needed references on a sheet of paper. Even slight hesitations while groping for the next question may break the pace of the class.

The beginning teacher should reconcile himself to the fact that plans are always necessary. New material must be presented in a comprehensible fashion accompanied by several examples in the second language to check for student comprehension. Providing satisfactory presentations requires much forethought and searching of other texts. Presentations of new material should *never* be taken directly from the text itself. Another explanation with additional examples can make the difference between understanding and incomprehension for some students.

Application activities must be structured toward specific objectives, and they must be numerous enough to attain those objectives. Providing adequate opportunities to communicate in the second language requires forethought and creative thinking. A good system for any teacher to follow is to have on his desk at the end of each day a sufficiently outlined and prepared lesson plan, so that in case a substitute teacher should need to conduct the class the next day, he would have a prepared plan to follow.

LONG-TERM OBJECTIVES

The first decision the teacher or the department must make is to choose the overall objectives of the course. If she plans to teach the whole person, she should keep both cognitive and affective-social variables in mind in choosing the course goals. If she plans to teach a general introductory course, the typical objectives in second-language teaching at the present time are normally stated as "the ability to use the four language skills plus an acquaintanceship with the culture." More specifically, at the end of the course the students should (1) be able to understand native speech; (2) be able to express themselves orally, although not at a native performance level; (3) be able to read for comprehension; (4) be able to communicate in simple written form, again not at a native level of proficiency; (5) have an initial insight into the people and the way they live within the limits of the material covered in the course; (6) have a positive attitude toward second-language learning in general and toward the class in particular; and (7) have a working relationship with the teacher and the other members of the class.

The choice of objectives, of course, depends upon many factors—the students, the teacher, the community, and/or the times. During the eighteenth and nineteenth centuries, the objective dealt primarily with memorizing grammatical rules. During the thirties, the reading objective was accepted, if not liked, by many second-language teachers. Since World War II, the stress has been placed on the oral skills. Currently, the ideal seems to be to develop courses in response to student interests and goals; the practice seems to be to work with all four skills and culture in the beginning courses. Given the context of her particular situation, the teacher may choose any, or all, of these objectives depending upon the students, the community in which she teaches, the facilities and materials available, and her own capabilities and energy. Ideally, teacher objectives will coincide with student objectives. In any given set of circumstances, the closer teacher objectives correlate with student objectives the more satisfactory the course will be to the students.

The teacher's next step is to select a text. Given her objectives and philosophy of learning and of language, she attempts to adopt textual materials that are consistent with both. If she feels that learning is primarily a matter of conditioning and that language is conditioned behavior, she chooses an audio-lingual book. If she thinks of learning as mental understanding and acquisition of concepts and language as rule-governed, creative behavior, she chooses a cognitive book. If she accepts portions of both viewpoints, she chooses a middle-of-the-road book or selects either an audio-lingual or a cognitive text with the idea of supplementing it with related materials from the other approach.

Two misconceptions related to textbook selection are common in the field. The first is that the text controls the relative emphasis that can be placed on each of the four language skills. Such is not necessarily the case. For example, the teacher can and should practice the reading and writing skills in an audio-lingual text. The only limitations are her own ingenuity and time. Conversely, the teacher can and should practice the oral skills with cognitive materials. The premise that students can learn oral skills only by means of mimicry-memorization practice and pattern drills is demonstrably false. Again, the only limitations are the teacher's ingenuity and time. Admittedly, audio-lingual texts have stressed the oral skills, and cognitive texts the written skills, but there is no theoretical basis for such a distinction. Nor is there any justification for the teacher blindly following the author's lead. Cognitive materials can be used to emphasize the oral skills just as stimulus-response materials have been prepared to teach reading and writing.[1]

Another misconception is that really using the second language must be put off for a long time. The students cannot speak the second language in second year; they must wait until third year. The teacher cannot use the second language in class the first year; she must wait until the following year. The implication seems to be that some magic moment exists beyond which the students suddenly become liberated and their tongues loosened. No such point exists. Listening, speaking, reading, and writing should be brought to the *skill* level by the end of *each* section of the book. Only in this way can the overall goal of being able to use each skill, within the limits of the vocabulary and structure covered in the course, be achieved. Waiting only thwarts acquisition.

---

[1]Most programmed materials are based on the same conditioning theories underlying audio-lingual materials, and several of these are designed to teach reading and/or writing.

The preceding two paragraphs state that almost any basic, introductory series can be adapted to the overall objectives of being able to understand, speak, read, and write the second language. Obviously, her personal preferences determine which text receives the highest rating in the teacher's own estimation. (See appendix 4 for a discussion of textbook selection.) More important than the objectives in determining which text to use is the approach to learning and language that the authors take.

SHORT-TERM OBJECTIVES

Once the textbook has been selected, the teacher begins to divide the academic year into units. Taking into consideration his goals, the amount of supplementary material that needs to be included in order to implement these goals, and the students in the class, the teacher makes a decision as to how much of the text he wants to try to cover during the course of the year. However, the teacher obviously cannot predict exactly at the beginning of the semester just how the class will progress through the materials, and he should be prepared to vary his schedule according to student response. Depending upon the caliber of students in his class and his ability to work with the group, he may need to speed up or slow down his schedule.

In general, although trying to finish the book for the sake of finishing is frowned upon by some practitioners in the field, such a practice is adopted in many cases. (Usually, the teacher is frustrated in the attempt!) Authors of early audio-lingual texts divided the material into twelve to fifteen units. Such a division meant that approximately three weeks were to be spent on each unit. Prior to this format, the majority of the texts contained thirty to thirty-six chapters, which meant that there was approximately one chapter for each week in the school year. Some authors have adopted a format of a lesson for every two class periods.

The beginning teacher should not interpret the preceding examples to mean that each section of the book will be covered in identical periods of time. Preparing each section of the text to be exactly equal in difficulty is impossible. The assimilation of the material in some chapters may take longer than in others. Too, as the year continues, the content usually becomes more complex, and the speed with which the chapters are covered diminishes. Therefore, the teacher may want to speed up in the beginning weeks in anticipation of this slowdown. An opposite view is that the class should proceed at an especially slow speed during the first few weeks in order to adjust fully to the process of learning a language, or to review past material.

Nor should the beginning teacher interpret the preceding discussion to mean that each division of the text is a separate entity. Each segment should merge with the previous one, if at all possible, and the teacher should attempt to interrelate the material from different units. However, the teacher may unconsciously contribute toward creating sharp dividing lines by the manner in which the class progresses from one unit to the next.

Each division of most texts has three sections: (1) a dialog or a reading, (2) a series of exercises or pattern drills designed to teach the structure, and (3) some elementary application activities. Just as the teacher has a tendency to separate each unit or chapter from preceding ones, he may even tend to separate the sections from each other by doing section 1, then section 2, and finally section 3. This is a tendency to be avoided. All sections of a unit should be welded into a whole. For example, important structures from the first few lines of a dialog or reading should be studied and practiced without delay. As soon as these same structures can be manipulated, they should be applied in communicative situations. No good excuse can be given for waiting to do the related activities until all lines of the dialog have been learned, and the same is true in relation to waiting to apply practiced concepts. The unit should be totally interrelated. The students can swallow material fed to them in a steady stream, but they may choke trying to gulp chunks.

The divisions themselves should also be interrelated. As the students are finishing the application activities of one unit of the text, they can be introduced to the dialog or reading of the next unit. The test can be given over the preceding unit as soon as all the "real" language practice for that unit has been completed. Either of the two procedures suggested in the preceding paragraph frees the teacher from having to spend (and the students from being asked to endure) entire class periods doing nothing but repeating dialog lines or reading or repeating pattern drills or doing exercises.[2] It also fosters a smooth progression through the book. Some grammar and some other content should, if possible, be included in each lesson plan.

The short-term objectives center around the content of the individual divisions of the book. Naturally, they should be related to and consistent with the long-range objectives of the language sequence and the course. Therefore, as the objectives were stated at the beginning of this chapter, the objectives of each section are to understand, speak, read, and write using the sounds, vocabulary, and structures of the particular segment of the book.

---

[2]The author once observed a student teacher drill four lines of a dialog for fifty-five minutes! Surprisingly enough, the students were admirably patient and well-behaved and possessed an incredible amount of endurance. When the need for variety of activity was broached in a post-class conference, the cooperating teacher rose quickly to her defense saying, "Well, you see, we are starting a new unit, and there is nothing else to do."

OUTLINE OF A WEEK'S WORK

Having decided upon the amount of time to spend on each unit, chapter, or lesson and having consciously considered the long-range objectives in terms of specific content, the teacher is ready to begin to divide these segments of the book into manageable units of work. Normally, a week's work is considered to be the basic unit.

The teacher looks at the material in terms of the amount the class can cover in a week's time. This content is then divided into daily work. Such a plan, in rough form, provides her with general guidelines to follow during the course of the week. This plan, of course, is quite tenuous, but without it the necessary continuity from one day to the next is a haphazard process at best. Each daily lesson plan must fit into some larger context for a smooth flowing progression toward objectives to be achieved. In addition, the teacher soon learns that preparing a rough draft of the week's work is less time-consuming than the preparation of individual daily plans without the benefit of a larger plan.

As the teacher outlines the material to be covered during the week, she should be conscious of the necessity of providing continuity of sequence and variety of activities. The students should know fairly well what to expect before they come into the classroom. The teacher's task is to provide enough variety of activities within the daily plan to guard against boredom. She needs to select and arrange the content in such a way that the students proceed over a period of days from the introduction of a new structure to the ability to use that structure in a communicative context. The implication here is that each day the activity selected should be on a higher level of difficulty than that of the day before. Also of concern is the need to provide practice in all four language skills and to manage to incorporate all these elements into as many varied activities as possible.

Following is an example of how a chapter designed to be covered in a week can be divided into a rough, overall daily lesson plan.

Friday:	Introduce new chapter in the latter portion of the hour.
Monday:	Do first part of reading and structural exercises plus "real" language review from previous chapter.
Tuesday:	Do second part of reading and structural exercises plus applying content of Monday's lesson.
Wednesday:	Do third part of reading and structural exercises plus applying content of Tuesday's lesson.
Thursday:	Do fourth part of reading and structural exercises plus applying content of Wednesday's lesson.

Friday: Apply content of Thursday's lesson the first quarter of the period. Give the test over the chapter the next half of the period. Preview the reading and grammar of the coming chapter to be assigned for Monday the last quarter of the hour.

Of course, the teacher lists the specific exercises and page numbers. With texts divided into longer segments, the principle is the same even though an entire unit cannot be covered in one week. In fact, with a program in which the units are longer and lengthy dialogs are given, there is even more need to overlap the end of one unit with the beginning of the next. A good idea to follow with those texts is to learn at least half the lines of the new dialog while finishing the latter part of the previous chapter. Too, in the case of longer units it is possible to wait until the end of the unit to give a comprehensive test. Such a test normally takes the entire class period. (The teacher who uses a text with shorter chapters may wait two or possibly three chapters and give a longer test of this type, but the general tendency is to give a test at the end of each unit or chapter in the book.)

Following is an example of a weekly plan in which one unit in an audio-lingual text is being finished while beginning a new one.

Friday: Introduce first four lines of dialog in new unit.
Monday: Do planned drills and application activities of previous unit and first four lines of dialog in new unit.
Tuesday: Do planned drills and application activities of previous unit and second four lines of dialog in new unit.
Wednesday: Do planned drills and application activities of previous unit and third four lines of dialog in new unit.
Thursday: Finish planned drills and application activities of previous unit and fourth part of dialog in new unit.
Friday: Give a test over previous unit, and preview the assignment for Monday.

THE DAILY LESSON PLAN

The Three Parts of the Class Hour

In the daily lesson, the teacher attempts to put his knowledge of theory, language, the student, and general guidelines for second-language teaching into practice. He knows that the students do not suddenly acquire skills, so he should plan to spend at least part of each period in review, in doing the assignment, and in introducing new material to be assigned for the next class period. Sequenced in this manner, the students are exposed to all assigned material in at least three consecutive classes. In attempting to build always from the old to the new, from the known to the unknown, he can organize his class period in the following sequence: review, view, and preview. Generally speaking, approximately one fourth of the class period should be spent in review, one half in viewing the assignment, and one fourth in previewing new material and making the assignment.

Formulating Instructional Objectives

Objectives are often mystifying and frustrating to the teacher, but they should not be. Objectives are ends, not means. Objectives are goals that the teacher expects his students to achieve, not activities for achieving them. In the weekly outline, the teacher is not overly concerned with specific objectives. His attention is focused on content matter. As he begins to write a daily lesson plan, he analyzes the task before him, first being attentive to specific objectives he wants to attain—what he wants his students to know and to be able to do at the end of the week. He next analyzes the task, beginning with what he thinks the students already know and proceeds to develop a series of steps that the students must take to reach this objective. These steps are, in effect, minor objectives that lead toward the end goal of being able to use the content of the chapter in a communicative context in any or all of the four language skills.

The following kind of statement is not an objective: "Go over exercise D on page 56." Nor is the following: "Explain the agreement of adjectives." Neither is such a statement as: "Have the students review for the test tomorrow." While all the above statements include activities or suggestions that might very well be a part of the class hour, they are not goals to be achieved.

Of course, exactly what an objective is depends upon one's definition of learning. If one adheres to an external, mechanistic definition of learning, objectives will be descriptions of abilities that the students will be able to demonstrate, i.e., behaviors that can be observed. Thus, the connection between behavioral theories of learning and behavioral objectives is clearly evident. On the other hand, internal, mentalistic theories of learning must be stated in terms of internal mental processes, i.e., competence, as well as what the students can do, i.e., production and manipulation of forms and performance skills. Thus, objectives prepared in line with internal theories will include understanding and knowledge as well as manifestations of that understanding and knowledge. The reader should also realize that in pure behavioristic theory, understanding is not a factor to be considered, since the goal of teaching is to condition desired responses to selected stimuli.

Although the more common terms found in the professional literature are either *behavioral* or *performance objectives,* the term being used in this chapter on lesson plans is *instructional objectives.* This term has been chosen because it has a broader, more inclusive connotation. It can be employed to cover all the classroom objectives: (1) the underlying knowledge and mental operations supporting performance skills as well as the performance skills themselves, (2) the values that cause people to act in certain ways as well as the actions themselves, and (3) the internal bases for external behaviors as well as the behaviors themselves.

There are at least three levels of instructional objectives. The first, understanding, involves cognitive objectives. The second, production and manipulation of forms, is both cognitive and behavioral. The ability to produce and manipulate the forms is predicated on a prior internal comprehension of the forms. The third, communication, combines cognition with performance skills to express knowledge and feelings. To cover the three stages of language acquisition, instructional objectives of different levels of difficulty encompassing internal and external factors and cognitive and affective-social variables must be included in the teacher's statement of instructional objectives.

In introducing new material, the teacher should ask himself how he can develop a meaningful learning situation for the students. His goal is to help the students to understand the structure and to be able to relate it to what they already know. This understanding need not necessarily consist of a formalized rule. The students may comprehend functional usage without being able to state a rule to support their knowledge. In this sense, the major objective of the preview section of the class hour is cognition, not behavior.

After the students understand the concepts involved, the teacher should seek to help them acquire the ability to produce and to manipulate these forms, to use the correct form in context. In audio-lingual classes, the procedure for accomplishing this goal is pattern drilling, and the objectives are behavioral. In cognitive classes, the objectives are cognitive and behavioral. What has been proposed in this text is to ask the students to learn to produce and manipulate forms in cognitive writing exercises that can be done as homework. This is due to the pressing necessity of putting the limited time available to the second-language teacher to its most efficient use. For those students who cannot learn to produce and manipulate forms by this means, habit-formation drills should be provided.

Once the students have acquired the ability to manipulate the structural forms correctly, they are ready to use these structures to express meaning. They are prepared at this stage to begin to attach meaning to form as they express their ideas. The goals at this level in the sequence obviously involve cognition, affective-social factors, and performance skills.

Examples of Specific Instructional Objectives

As was stated previously, the first phase of language skill development is understanding. The understanding phase corresponds to the preview part of the class hour because it is during this time that the teacher explains new material to be studied. During the preview, the teacher actually has two goals. She wants the students to understand the concepts involved and hopes to motivate them to do the assignment to be given at the end of the preview. (Giving the assignment is discussed later in this chapter.) Before undertaking the preview, the teacher should carefully analyze the task she is about to ask the students to tackle. She should begin by delineating what they already know and what they need to learn. The objectives of the preview reflect this analysis.

The purpose of the subsequent discussion is to provide examples of the types of objectives suited to the preview, view, and review portions of the teacher's lesson plans. The teacher should be aware of the hierarchy of instructional objectives as the students progress from initial introduction of material to its functional usage and be able to distinguish among the types of objectives appropriate to each phase of second-language acquisition.

Preview   The following objectives are designed to teach the verb *to be* to Spanish-speaking students. The lesson is for beginning students who know little English. The following objectives are representative of those appropriate for use in the preview portion of the class period.

A. Cognitive objectives
   1. Concepts and relationships
      a. Use of subject pronouns in English
      b. Use of *a* or *an* before a singular noun
      c. No plural adjectives in English
      d. Only one *you*-form in English
      e. Same person and number concepts with verbs in both languages
   2. Forms of the verb *to be* and the meaning of each in a sentence
B. Cognitive and behavioral objectives
   1. Ability to pronounce all the forms of *to be* with their corresponding pronouns
C. Affective-social objectives
   1. Wants to learn a second language

2. Confidence in ability to learn the material and to complete the exercises
3. Feeling that learning the material will help acquisition of second-language skills

The danger of such a preview as the one outlined above is the very fact that much of the mental activity involves reflection as opposed to recitation. Students may participate in overt response but take advantage of the emphasis here on covert response to slip away into some pleasant dream world of their own. Therefore, the teacher should be mindful of the students as she becomes involved in the complexities of her presentation. She should plan as simple a description as possible, avoiding all unnecessary grammatical terms. She should never completely turn her back to the class. By conscious attention to the fact that she is on stage, so to speak, the teacher can cultivate the art of writing on the chalkboard while talking *to* the students, not to the chalkboard. Also, she should involve them in the preview as much as possible. This can be done by asking them to recall what they already know, either from their first language or from previous lessons. Later in the presentation she may ask them to do a few examples to test their comprehension. Asking them to demonstrate comprehension is infinitely superior to asking if there are any questions.

View   During the homework assignment and in the following class period, the students take an additional step or steps toward being able to use the verb *to be* as they cover the assignment in class. This group of instructional objectives is designed to include (1) the confirmation of comprehension, (2) the production and manipulation of forms, and (3) the use of these forms to communicate with simple affective language activities or to discuss material in the text. The following are representative view objectives.

A. Cognitive objectives
   1. Confirmation of comprehension of concepts, i.e., competence
   2. Feedback as to appropriate language usage during contextual practice with the text
B. Cognitive-behavioral objectives
   1. Ability to associate subjects and verbs correctly
   2. Demonstrate when to use *a* and *an,* and when not to.
   3. Demonstrate use of singular adjectives in English to describe both singular and plural subjects.
   4. Ability to answer questions of the following type:

a. _____ you? — I _____.
b. _____ I? — You _____.
c. _____ you? — We _____.
d. _____ we? — You _____.
e. _____ he? — He _____.
f. _____ they? — They _____.

     5. Ability to write forms of the verb *to be*
     6. Ability to pronounce and read aloud a short paragraph with forms of the verb *to be*

C. Affective-social objectives
     1. Prepared for class
     2. Attentive in class
     3. Participating in class

D. Affective-social, cognitive, behavioral objectives
     1. Can use learned forms to communicate about content of the text or affective language activities
     2. Willing to try to communicate in the second language

These objectives are different from those of the previous class period. The grammatical content is the same, but the types of activities are different. In this phase, the teacher is trying to functionalize knowledge, to activate the concepts and relationships learned the previous day. One secret to success in teaching is repetition of concepts. The teacher realizes this and attempts to provide such practice. His mistake often lies in the fact that he repeats the material at exactly the same level of difficulty each day and expects the students to know the material. The important concept he needs to remember is to prepare objectives that enable him to repeat the same structures but in different contexts and at higher levels of difficulty. Nothing is worse than repeating the explanation given on the first day ad nauseum and then complaining because the students do not seem to listen attentively. There is no good reason for the students to listen if they know that the same thing is coming again tomorrow, and day after tomorrow, etc. Explanation is for the understanding phase. Another explanation has no place during production and manipulation. The students should be taken continually forward toward the end objective, not stalled in a daily rehash of past presentations.

One of the general guidelines to be followed is that not everything can be taught in a single day. In the example of objectives given above for the view, a slow class may not be able to progress so quickly, or a period may be too short to include all this work on structure and allow time for reading and other language skills. If so, the production-manipulation phase should be broken down into smaller sections and spread over more class days. For example, A, 1 and 2 and B, 1, 2, and 3 (listed in the preceding outline) can be handled easily in a short period of time, leaving B, 4 and 5, which are more difficult, for another day. The teacher may even decide to do A, 1 and 2, and B, 1, 2, and 3 on one day, B, 4 on the following, with the introduction of writing and reading delayed until some later day. However, some work with part D should be included. The most important considerations that the teacher should keep in mind are: (1) the fact that he must maintain a progression of activities, within the range of the students' capabilities, which become more and more similar to true language usage; and (2) that he must sustain student interest and participation.

Review After learning to manipulate the structures, the students should be asked to apply these forms to meaningful situations, first over the text and then beyond the text. The last stage in language-skill development is contextual practice in a communicative situation over content related to the text but applied directly to the students. The review part of the class hour corresponds to the third phase, or "real" language stage, of language acquisition as the content is applied to student interests and activities. The following objectives are appropriate for the review portion of the class hour.

A. Cognitive objectives
   1. Revision of interim language system
B. Cognitive-behavioral objectives
   There are no new cognitive-behavioral objectives.
C. Affective-social objectives
   1. Maintain confidence and interest as progress toward communicative competence
   2. Participate in communicative activities with other members of the class
D. Affective-social, cognitive, behavioral objectives
   1. Ability to understand an oral or written presentation with the verb *to be* on content related to themselves
   2. Ability to answer questions with all forms of the verb *to be* in order to communicate ideas regarding their own experiences
   3. Ability to talk briefly or write a short paragraph about themselves using the verb *to be*
   4. Ability to participate in a conversation using the verb *to be* in situations similar to those in the text and in objectives D, 1, 2, and 3

Review does not mean a restatement of the rules for the "umpteenth time." *Review* literally means to "view again." Discussion of rules and first-language equivalents should be relegated to their appropriate place, i.e., the understanding phase. The teacher who continually refers to rules and first-language equivalents traps the students in a problem-solving learning habit. By the review stage, the students should have understood the concepts and learned to manipulate the necessary forms. The purpose of the review part of the class hour is the internalization of concepts and relationships into the communicative processes. Here the teacher gives the students an opportunity to apply what they have been learning, to arrive at the goals rather than stagnate on the means of achieving those goals (i.e., grammatical explanations and drills). Too often the students never have a chance to express themselves in the language they are studying. The review part of the class should provide abundant "real" language practice. The students should be able to expect to practice using the language to talk about themselves and their lives at least one quarter of the class hour. Since the students learn to do what they do, the language teacher is not meeting his stated purposes and accepted responsibility if he provides less

APPLYING INSTRUCTIONAL OBJECTIVES TO CLASSROOM ACTIVITIES

With his objectives carefully delineated on the basis of a complete analysis of the students' task, the teacher begins to select appropriate activities to accomplish these objectives and to arrange them in a sequential order. Selecting the procedures to be followed is, in a sense, easier than deciding upon the objectives, since many of the objectives imply certain types of activities. Of course, some activities may accomplish more than one objective, but each activity should have at least one cognitive or cognitive-behavioral objective. In most cases, there is a separate activity for each objective. Affective-social objectives are not the result of any specific activity per se, but of all the activities and the class atmosphere in general. However, affective-social factors influence all student activities, especially the real language practice.

Also, since the objectives are different for each phase of language acquisition and for each part of the class hour, the activities for each objective will be different. It is especially important that the teacher keep these differences in mind, since the progression from one phase to another and the necessity to practice all four language skills provide her with a built-in variety of activities in her classes.

A word about variety is appropriate here. Variety should be considered from the students' point of view. Changing from a substitution drill to a transformation drill is still the same activity for them. Changing from an exercise involving one verb to one involving a different verb does not really provide much variety, either. The teacher should pay constant attention to selecting activities for the daily plan that are indeed varied. Normally, ten minutes is long enough for any one type of activity. Those students in upper-level courses probably have longer attention spans than the beginning students, and drill activities need to be changed more often than application exercises. The teacher should always be aware of the students' reaction as any activity progresses and be ready to proceed to a new activity before the "glassy-eyed" stage is reached. Blank stares usually indicate blank minds. In the following pages, representative lesson plans, based on the objectives previously outlined, are given for the preview, view, and review portions of the class period.

Preview   The selection and preparation of teaching-learning activities for this portion of the class hour require considerable preplanning. The teacher at times may not fully understand the concepts himself. Even if he does, understanding in and of itself does not guarantee an ability to explain any given structure to the class. (Student teachers are often amazed at how little they really know once the students begin to ask questions.) Just as important as the explanation are the examples chosen. They need to be geared specifically to the structure being presented and use vocabulary that the students can understand. These "just right" sentences sometimes are beyond the grasp of the teacher, and he needs to search through other textbooks until he finds what he needs. The preview is a basis for the sequence that is to follow, and it must *not* be slighted. Preparing a meaningful presentation is a crucial component in each learning sequence. Competence must precede "creative construction" of language, and the teacher should never rely solely on the text to provide meaningful presentations or to establish comprehension.

The preview should contain the following component parts: (1) explanation, (2) examples, (3) discrimination exercises or simple practice, and (4) assigning the homework. As was mentioned earlier in the text, the examples and explanation may be reversed depending upon the students and the concept being presented. This portion of the preview is followed by a comprehension check that the teacher structures into the preview to determine whether or not the students were able to understand the presentation. The assignment is given at the end of the hour when the students are involved in the presentation and interested in its content. Hopefully, the hour ends on a high point with the students looking forward to what is coming next. The lesson plan for Monday's preview would be similar to the following. (In this class the students are learning English as a second language. They have already learned the interrogative and negative forms in English. Since this is a class of Spanish-speaking students, some of what the teacher says is in Spanish.[3] In this sample, teacher comments are in English but enclosed in parentheses to indicate a translation.)

SAMPLE LESSON PLAN FOR MONDAY
   A. Review (15 minutes)
   B. View (25 minutes)
   C. Preview (15 minutes)
       Objectives: (See pages 446–47. The objectives for activities 1 and 2 are A, 1 and 2, page 446.)
       Activity 1 (1½ min.): This activity is conducted in the first language. It gets the students involved and indicates to them how the structures are used in context. As the students answer, the teacher writes their answers on the chalkboard, or asks another student to do so.

(Jim, are you tall?)   (Susan, are you and Jim tall?)
(Ann, is your uncle tall?)   (Arthur, are your parents tall?)
(Joe, am I tall?)   (Margaret, are my wife and I tall?)

       Activity 2 (3 min.): The teacher now tells the students that they are going to learn to say these same sentences in the second language (English). Next, he gives them the English equivalents for each answer, emphasizing the fact that the word *tall* is never plural in English. The English equivalents may be given orally or written next to the Spanish examples on the chalkboard. (This author prefers to write them, so the students can study them carefully and note the differences between the two sentences.) He also asks them in Spanish the difference in meaning between *Yo soy alto,* in which the subject pronoun is used and *Soy alto,* in which the subject pronoun is not used. He then explains that using the pronoun in English does not emphasize the person as it does in Spanish.
       Activity 3 (1½ min.): This is activity 1 repeated with a noun rather than an adjective. Again the answers are written.

---

[3]Arguments have been advanced for and against using the first language in the classroom. Obviously, the more the second language can be used with *understanding,* the more highly developed the students' listening comprehension is. The actual amount of first-language use depends a great deal on the concepts being taught and the teacher. Usually, if he keeps the language simple, the teacher can use the second language more than he may think. If he is careful to use only the second language during the production-manipulation and application phases of language learning, i.e., the view and review portions of the class, whether or not the first language is used in the preview probably makes little difference.

Teacher questions:

(Ed, are you a student?)	(Pat, are you and Ed students?)
(Mary, is your brother a student?)	(John, are your brothers students?)
(Frank, am I a student?)	(Jane, are Mr. Sanchez and I students?)

Activity 4 (3 min.): This is activity 2 repeated with nouns rather than adjectives. Again the English equivalents are given, and the differences between the two languages noted. These differences are focused upon without actually using grammatical terms such as *adjective, noun, pronoun,* etc. The students' functional knowledge of their native language should be sufficient to help them categorize the contrasts.

Activity 5 (3 min.): Repetition drill. (The objective here is B, page 446.) The teacher now leads the class in a repetition drill using both sentences.

Activity 6 (3 min.): The assignment grows logically out of the preview. At this time, specific exercises are assigned for the next day's class. The assignment normally should include some work from the reading or dialog as well as the exercises.

View   This portion of the class hour may require less teacher preparation than the other two because the text normally provides a sufficient number of exercises. If, however, some exercises in the book do not seem appropriate, the teacher should not hesitate to omit them or to supplement them with more productive practice activities. View activities involve the establishment of competence and initial, elementary practice of performance skills as in the sample plan presented here.

SAMPLE LESSON PLAN FOR TUESDAY
A. Review (15 minutes)
B. View (25 minutes)
   1. Structure
      Objectives: (See pages 447–48.)
      Activity 1 (5 min.): Giving answers to the cognitive writing exercises assigned for homework.
      a. (B, 1 and 5) Choose the appropriate form of the verb *to be* to agree with the subject.

I _____ an American.	He _____ old.
They _____ students.	_____ you a teacher?
We _____ young.	_____ she intelligent?

b. (B, 2) Complete the following sentences with *a* or *an* according to the context. If no word is necessary, place an X in the blank.

He is _____ actor.   We are _____ Americans.
They are _____ teachers.   She is _____ Mexican.
I am _____ student.   Are you _____ students?

c. (B, 3) Write the appropriate form of the adjective given in parentheses.

I am (young) _____.   We are (tall) _____.
She is (old) _____.   He is (short) _____.
They are (intelligent) _____.   You are (pretty) _____.

d. (B, 4) Write the answers to the following questions with a yes or no answer depending upon the question.

Are you a teacher?   Are you young?
Are you a student?   Are you tall?

The answers to these questions are put on the chalkboard either by the teacher, by a student, or by one student for each exercise. The students check their papers, ask questions about any errors, and turn their papers in to the teacher. If there is time and the teacher wishes additional practice, the teacher can ask the students some of the questions orally.

Activity 2 (5 min.): (A, 2; D, 1) Describe orally some students or other persons whom the students know and ask them to guess the identities of the persons from their descriptions. (Of course, the teacher needs to prepare these before class.)

Activity 3 (5 min.): (A, 2; D, 1) Two types of cards are prepared. On one the name of a profession is given. On the other a situation is described in simple terms or in English in which that person is seeking the aid of some professional person. For example, someone in your house is very sick. This person is looking for a doctor. The activity is for the students to get up and look for the needed person saying. "Pardon me, are you a doctor?" until he or she finds the person who can help.

There is no need to feel obligated to include both activities 2 and 3. If activity 2 is going well, save activity 3 until another day. Each may be varied to use other forms of the verb being practiced.

For those students who have at this point failed to learn the forms of the verb or who choose additional practice with habit-formation drills, the teacher should see to it that they have an opportunity to practice with him, with each other, with the tape recorder, or in the lab with drills similar to the following:

a. Repetition drill (Preview Objective, B, 1, page 446)
b. Substitution drill (Preview Objective, B, 1, page 446)

Model	*Students*
a student	I am a student.
old	I am old.
an American	I am an American.
short	I am short.

c. Person-number substitution drill (View Objective, B, 1, page 447)

Model	*Students*
I	I am young,
We	We are young.
He	He is young.
They	They are young.

d. Question-answer drill (View Objective, B, 4, page 447)

Model	*Students*
Are you young?	Yes, I am young.
Are you old?	Yes, I am old.
Are you an American?	Yes, I am an American.
Are you a Mexican?	Yes, I am a Mexican.

Activity 4 (10 min.): Other assigned work, preferably either reading or writing over material in the text to counterbalance the focus on structure in the previous activities.

C. Preview (15 minutes)
Objective: (See page 448, Objective B, 6.)
Activity: Reading aloud the following paragraph:

John is a student. He is young. His father is a lawyer. He is old. They are both tall and intelligent. They are Americans. His mother is strong. She is a doctor. (This paragraph is then made part of the assignment for the next day.)

Review   This portion of the hour requires extensive preplanning, since most textual materials do not provide sufficient amounts of "real" language practice and probably cannot due to the nature of the content. Planning interesting situations that encourage the students to talk or write requires a great deal of time, effort, and ingenuity. Searching for listening and reading materials with which the students can practice the receptive skills is no less demanding. There should be no reason for using the first language in this part of the class. During this period of time, the students should be using the second language within the limits of their language background in contexts similar but not identical to those in the text to talk about things that interest them and to which they can relate. The review should include practice in all four language skills. It should also include a large amount of interaction among the members of the class. Review activities would be on a functional, communicative level as in the following examples.

SAMPLE LESSON PLAN FOR WEDNESDAY
   A. Review (15 minutes)
       Objectives: (See page 449, Objectives D, 1 and 2.)
       Activity 1 (5 min.): Personalized questions

Are you a student?	Where am I a teacher?
Where are you a student?	Am I young?
Are you young?	Are you students?
Are you intelligent?	Are you old?
Is he (signaling a classmate) a student?	Are you tall?
	Are you Mexicans?
Where is he a student?	Are Mr. Sanchez and I Americans?
Is he young?	
Is he intelligent?	Are we tall?
Am I a student?	Are we young?
What am I?	Are we actors?

   Activity 2 (5 min.): Have the students ask similar questions of each other. Encourage them to include any other vocabulary words they know.
   Activity 3 (5 min.): One student chooses to portray a well-known personality. The other students try to guess who it is by asking questions that can be answered with a yes or a no. The teacher can supply needed vocabulary.
   B. View (25 minutes)
       Objective: (See page 448, Objectives D, 1 and 2.)
       Activity 1 (5 min.): Reading comprehension
       a. Clarify difficulties.
       b. Give a true-false test over the content.
       c. Ask the following questions over the reading:

Is John a student?	Are John and his father intelligent?

What is John?	Are they strong?
Who is a student?	Who is strong?
Is he young?	Is his mother a doctor?
Who is young?	What is his mother?
Is his father a lawyer?	Who is a teacher?
What is his father?	Is the family Mexican?
Who is a lawyer?	What nationality is the family?

Remainder of assignment (20 minutes)

C. Preview (15 minutes)

For the next day the students are to write a description of themselves and their families using the forms previously practiced.

The preceding samples are not complete lesson plans, only the portions related to the sequencing of activities involving the ability to use the verb *to be*. The plans need activities based on the reading or dialog to be well proportioned. Too, the sequence from introduction of the verb *to be* to the functional level in all four language skills has not been finished. On Thursday, the students should be prepared to write short descriptions of themselves, their friends, or their families. Friday would be spent either giving a sustained oral presentation about a similar topic or in conversation groups.

Using lesson plans of this type helps the teacher to keep track of the sequence of learning activities. Such a sequence also constantly reminds her of the importance of "real" language activity. In addition, the teacher should keep in mind that the students prepare for less than half of the class time. Approximately one fourth of the time (the preview) is the teacher's responsibility. The other fourth depends upon both the teacher and the students. If their jobs are done well, the teacher and the students should be prepared to enjoy the application activities because it is during this time in class that they both reap the fruits of their labors.

CHART OF SEQUENCE IN LESSON PLANNING

Once the planned progression is properly conceived, one day's activities flow into the next. Following is a chart that represents how the concepts introduced in one class period at one level of difficulty are incorporated into the next class period at a step closer to the communicative skill level. In order to make the chart simple, and hopefully comprehensible, the structure being presented is (1) subject pronouns, (2) first and second person singular of the verb *to be*, (3) first and second person plural of the verb *to be*, and (4) third person singular and plural of the verb *to be*.

	Monday	Tuesday	Wednesday	Thursday	Friday
Review	Personalize Friday's view	Personalize content of Monday's view	Personalize first 4 lines of dialog and subject pronouns	Personalize second 4 dialog lines and first and third person singular of verb *to be*	Personalize third 4 lines of dialog and first and third person plural of verb *to be*
View	Do the assignment given Friday	1. Do dialog lines 2. Do subject pronouns	1. Do second 4 dialog lines 2. Do first and third person singular of verb *to be*	1. Do third 4 lines of dialog 2. Do first and third person plural of verb *to be*	1. Do fourth 4 lines of dialog 2. Do third person singular and plural of verb *to be*
Preview	1. First 4 lines of dialog 2. Subject pronouns	1. Second 4 lines of dialog 2. First and third person singular of verb *to be*	1. Third 4 lines of dialog 2. First and third person plural of verb *to be*	1. Fourth 4 lines of dialog 2. Third person singular and plural of verb *to be*	Other new material in unit

ORGANIZING AND CHECKING THE PLAN

It is no simple task to select and organize the teaching-learning activities to be included in the lesson plan so that all the topics are covered and developed in a planned progression of cumulative difficulty leading from initial introduction to communicative competence. At first, making out lesson plans takes many hours and entails some degree of flexibility as the beginning teacher seeks to put all the pieces together in the most efficient and productive fashion. However, although practice in this case may not make the teacher perfect, it does enable him to accomplish his task much more quickly and with much greater expertise.

One way to insure coverage of all the points to be learned in the chapter is to make a checklist similar to the one below. By listing the days of the week, the teacher can keep track of when each is to be covered in the class at what level of difficulty. By writing in L, R, S, or W, he can also indicate in which of the language skills each of the topics has been practiced. Too, by giving the time spent on each activity, he can keep a record of how much practice the students have had with each topic.

Topic to be covered	Preview	View	Review
Subject pronouns	M: L (5 min.)	T: R, W (5 min.)	W: L, S (5 min.)
First four lines of the dialog	M: L (5 min.)	T: L, S (5 min.)	W: R, W, L, S (10 min.)
I and you forms of the verb *to be*	T: L (3 min.)	W: L, R, W (5 min.)	Th: L, S (5 min.)

After finishing the lesson plan, the teacher should take a few moments to go back over his work, checking for consistency, sequence, and balance of materials. Are the selected activities consistent with the objectives? Do the teaching-learning activities progress in a logical sequence toward the goals of the lesson? Have all the topics been included at all levels of difficulty, i.e., have all three stages in second-language acquisition been included? Have all four language skills been practiced? Is there a variety of activities, including large-group, small-group, and individual activities? Are the presentations meaningful to the students, and do the situations developed for the practice of each of the language skills involve the exchange of information and meaning related to student interest and life experience? The teacher should consider his prepared plans from the point of view of all these questions. He should also consider additional ideas from chapter 16, "General Guidelines for Teaching a

Second Language." As he takes an overview, he may very well see weaknesses of which he was unaware while preparing the various components of the plans.

THE ASSIGNMENT

The preview is in essence the part of the class in which the teacher prepares the students for the homework assignment for the next day. She should so prepare them that they are able to practice doing what is right rather than to have to sit and puzzle about how to do the assignment. If the teacher does her job poorly, they are certain to be frustrated trying to complete the assigned task and to be unable to perform as she wants during the next class period. Therefore, the shouted assignment after the bell has rung is not only useless, it is detrimental to all but the super-bright and extra-diligent because the others learn incorrect responses that they must then "unlearn" the following day before progress can continue. Even more detrimental are the negative attitudes that result. If the teacher has done her job well during the preview, by the end of the introduction the students should understand the concepts being presented, and they should be motivated to do the homework.

The appropriate time to make the assignment is at the end of the preview. Hopefully, the students' comprehension is clear and complete and their interest high. In making the assignment, the teacher should (1) be enthusiastic about what is to be covered the next day, (2) state the purposes of the assignment, (3) be sure that *everyone* understands the assignment, (4) be specific about what the students are to do and how, and (5) anticipate any difficulties. One way to insure against unforeseen difficulties and confusion is to practice doing the first two or three sentences in each exercise as an example of what is to be done. Another is to give a few minutes of study time in class. The teacher can then circulate around the class to see if the students are beginning correctly. In addition, the assignment is an excellent opportunity for providing for individual differences. The slower students may be permitted to omit certain sentences or even exercises. The faster students may be assigned extra sentences, exercises, or original work.

The assignment should *always* be a basic part of the following class hour. The students should prepare for the view part of the hour, and the class should be taught in such a way that they are rewarded for their efforts. In other words, the activities should always be based on the assumption that the homework has been prepared. (The teacher should be alert to those students who try to finish written homework in class by copying the correct answers as they are given.) The teacher should avoid doing work for the students that they can logically be expected to do for themselves. Too often she nullifies the necessity for study prior to class by, in effect, doing the homework for the students. This practice has a debilitating effect on student achievement.

All written homework, and there should be some each day, should be corrected in class by the students. (Saved, these corrected papers become valuable bits of information as the students prepare for examinations.) These papers should be collected by the teacher and returned the following class period. Naturally, the teacher does not have time to grade them again, but she can give the student a check for having done the work. Also, by making mental notes of the most common errors, she gains an insight into points with which the students are still having problems, and she can incorporate these bits of information into future lesson plans.

CONCLUSION

Inseparably associated with the concept of teaching is the concept of purposes, goals, and objectives. To teach, one must teach *something* to *someone.* The teacher may plan to develop conditioned responses as in the case of an audio-linguist, or he may plan to promote understanding as in the case of a cognitive teacher. Once he sets up goals, he must begin to develop plans for achieving his desired aims. Planning assists him in selecting and arranging the most efficient sequence of learning activities for arriving at the stated goals. From the point of view of time, the teacher may ask himself how he can afford to prepare sufficiently. From the point of view of student achievement, the answer is that he cannot afford not to.

REVIEW AND APPLICATION

DEFINITIONS
1. performance objectives, p. 445   2. instructional objectives, p. 445

DISCUSSION
1. Delineate the various types of instructional objectives that the teacher may have.
2. Discuss the relationship between type of text and classroom objectives. How can the text be adapted to the teacher's goals?
3. What would be your goals if you were teaching a beginning language class? How might these goals be altered depending upon student objectives?
4. Discuss the divisions of textual materials and dividing the text into teachable segments in the classroom.

5. Compare and contrast cognitive, cognitive-behavioral, affective-social, and combination instructional objectives. Give examples of each.
6. Discuss kinds of objectives appropriate for each stage of language acquisition.
7. Discuss types of activities appropriate for each stage of language acquisition.
8. Compare and contrast ways and means of previewing, viewing, and reviewing dialogs, readings, habit-formation drills, and cognitive exercises.

ACTIVITIES

1. With the text you have been using, prepare instructional objectives and select related teaching-learning activities to preview, to view, and to review a reading or a dialog and one grammatical concept in the chapter.
2. Prepare lesson plans for a chapter in the textbook you have been using. Begin with an outline of the week's work. For each day, divide the plans into the three parts of the class hour with objectives and activities for each. Be sure to give the time to be spent on each. Use visuals wherever possible. Include all materials needed to teach the plans.

SELECTED REFERENCES

Chastain, K. (1969) A Proposal for Sharing. *Hispania*, 52: 57–59.

Huebener, T. (1965) *How to Teach Foreign Languages Effectively.* (rev. ed.) New York: New York University Press. Pp. 118–31.

Mager, R. F. (1961) *Preparing Instructional Objectives.* Belmont, Calif.: Fearon.

Oliva, P. F. (1969) *The Teaching of Foreign Languages.* Englewood Cliffs, N.J.: Prentice-Hall. Pp. 60–98.

Rivers, W. M. (1968) *Teaching Foreign-Language Skills.* Chicago: University of Chicago Press. Pp. 371–77.

Seelye, H. N. (1970) Performance Objectives for Teaching Cultural Concepts. *Foreign Language Annals,* 3: 566–78.

Steiner, F. (1970) Performance Objectives in the Teaching of Foreign Languages. *Foreign Language Annals,* 3: 579–91.

CLASSROOM ACTIVITIES

INTRODUCTION

The purpose of this chapter is to outline the various types of classroom activities that the teacher may use. The teachers need to understand that the types of teaching-learning activities used at each stage of second-language acquisition are different from those used at other stages. They should also understand that audio-lingual and cognitive activities are different at the understanding and production and manipulation stages, but that they become somewhat similar at the real language stage.

Naturally, many procedures are not presented here, since the realm of possibilities is limited only by the teacher's inventiveness. Starting always with the formulation of specific objectives, he can begin to initiate a continual process of self-discovery of appropriate techniques that he has never seen used by other teachers, but that are suggested by the goals themselves. This process becomes the primary basis of an ever-expanding repertoire of classroom procedures, and the resultant techniques become the basic core of the teaching-learning situations employed in class. Thus, summarizing all the activities that may be used in class is impossible, but it is possible to focus attention on the separate categories and the basic principles in each.

The following discussion focuses on the types of activities usually employed in the three basic parts of the class hour. Since textbooks usually present new material either in dialogs or readings followed by conditioning drills or cognitive exercises, the procedures discussed in each part are further subdivided into activities related to structure lessons and those related to dialog or reading lessons.

PREVIEW ACTIVITIES

During the preview part of the class hour the teacher prepares the students to do the work for the next class period. If one of the objectives of the next class is to do transformation drills orally, she gives the students practice with pattern drills of low-level difficulty, i.e., repetition or substitution drills. (The objectives of this audio-lingual presentation are behavioral.) If one of the objectives is to do cognitive exercises as homework, she prepares a presentation of the concepts needed to do the exercises, either inductive or deductive, which the students can comprehend. (The objectives of this presentation are cognitive.) Neither in the audio-lingual nor in the cognitive approach are the students expected to do more than repeat new sentence patterns or comprehend new concepts. Demonstration of conditioned responses, ability to complete cognitive exercises, or use of the forms being presented to communicate are objectives for subsequent stages of the sequence being initiated.

Dialog

The objectives during the preview of the dialog are to establish the meaning of the lines being presented and to develop the ability to hear the sounds and to repeat parts of the lines correctly. Without additional practice, most students are unable to repeat entire lines rapidly, and they cannot be expected during the initial presentation to remember the sequential arrangement of the lines. The meaning is made clear to the students by summarizing in the first language the lines to be learned, by using visual aids, by acting out the lines, or in later lessons by paraphrasing in the language being learned. It is important in teaching the meaning of the dialog that the students know both the whole and the parts. Therefore, attention must be given to the meanings of words and phrases as well as entire sentences. Nor is a single presentation sufficient. Meaning should be kept before the students as they drill the lines.

After communicating the meaning of the selected portion of the dialog to be learned, the teacher breaks the dialog into manageable lengths to be drilled. He again brings the meaning to the students' attention as he models the phrase or line to be repeated. Then he drills the same phrase or line going from choral repetition by the entire class to smaller groups to individuals.

The dialog sample that is being used as the basis for the discussion in this chapter comes from unit 9 of *Modern Spanish,* Second Edition. Due to the limits of space, only a Spanish example is being given, but the English translation is presented too, so that teachers of other languages may understand the concept involved.

In a Café	En un Café
A. Álvaro F. Felipe C. Chalo	A. Álvaro F. Felipe C. Chalo
A. This is a first rate café! (What a good café this is!)	A. ¡Qué buen café es éste!
F. You're right. For good coffee there's no place like this one. Hey, pst, pst! Two black coffees, good and hot.	F. Tienes razón. Para café bueno no hay como este lugar. Mire, pst, pst! Dos cafés negros bien calientes.
A. There comes Carlos Francisco. What a glum look he has (bad face he brings)! What's new, Chalo? Sit down.	A. Ahí viene Carlos Francisco. ¡Qué mala cara trae! ¿Qué hay, Chalo? Siéntate.
F. Why didn't you go to school yesterday? We had an exam in philosophy.	F. ¿Por qué no fuiste al colegio ayer? Tuvimos examen en filosofía.
C. I meant to go, but I couldn't. I had a bad day. I was sick.	C. Quise ir, pero no pude. Tuve un mal día. Estuve enfermo.[1]

In addition to focusing on sounds, vocabulary, and structure in the dialog lines as a means of developing language skills, the teacher should also take advantage of each possible opportunity to foster cultural insights. The example dialog above offers several points for discussion: (1) the café in Spanish society, its appearance and its important cultural role; (2) coffee in Spanish-speaking countries; (3) the method used to attract the waiter's attention; (4) the school system in Spanish-speaking countries; and (5) such vocabulary points as the fact that in Spanish one says "you have reason" rather than "you are right," the difference between *ahí* and *aquí,* which can both mean "here," and the nickname *Chalo.* The explanation of cultural topics throughout the course helps the students to relate the often abstract sounds and forms of a foreign language to real people and places.

After the dialog lines have been drilled, they are assigned as part of the homework for the following class period. Preferably, the students have take-home records with their books or have access to tapes with which to

---

[1]Copyright © 1960, 1966 by Harcourt Brace Jovanovich, Inc. and reproduced with their permission from *Modern Spanish,* Second Edition, by D. L. Bolinger, J.E. Ciruti, and H. H. Montero.

practice. If not, the assigned lines should be drilled with the books open, after being drilled first orally, before they are studied outside of class.

The students should know exactly what their homework task is. The approach being taken here is that the benefits of actual memorization of the dialog do not justify the necessary expenditure of time. Therefore, the students are asked to be able to do three things by the next class period: (1) to have the ability to repeat any and all lines with appropriate speed, pronunciation, and intonation immediately after a model (this objective includes the development of auditory memory as well as proper habits of pronunciation and intonation); (2) to have the ability to give the first-language meaning of any sentence as soon as they hear the second-language equivalent; and (3) the reverse of number 2.

Reading

The objectives during the preview of the reading are to (1) anticipate any semantic or syntactical difficulties that the students may have reading for content, (2) form the necessary sound-symbol associations, and (3) develop the ability to read aloud with acceptable pronunciation and intonation. Any of the methods used to establish meaning in a dialog can be used with a reading, although typically the teacher uses first- or second-language definitions, the latter being preferable.

In introducing the reading, the teacher first reads through the entire reading assignment, pointing out and clarifying difficulties as she proceeds. (Once the students learn the necessary sound-symbol associations, the model and group repetition may be omitted except for occasional practice. At this point the stress turns to silent, rapid reading for comprehension.) Next, she asks the students to repeat the model while looking at the words. And last, individuals read without a model.

The reading sample given here is taken from lesson 7 of *Beginning Spanish: A Cultural Approach,* Third Edition. Again only a Spanish example is being used along with an English translation of the passage.

The Language of Mexico

The national language of Mexico is Spanish, since the great majority of the Mexicans speak this language. They speak and pronounce well, but the Mexican does not pronounce Spanish exactly like the Spaniards: he speaks with a different

La Lengua de México

La lengua nacional de México es el español, pues la inmensa mayoría de los mexicanos hablan esta lengua. Hablan y pronuncian bien, pero el mexicano no pronuncia el español exactamente como los españoles; habla con otro acento

accent and uses some words which the Spanish do not use. However, the differences in pronunciation and vocabulary are few.

The majority of the Mexicans have a mixture of Spanish and Indian blood, and they are called mestizos. There is a minority of pure Spanish blood and another minority of pure Indian blood.

The Indian who lives in the city speaks Spanish like the other Mexicans, but in the mountains and in the forests live some Indians isolated from the rest of the country due to a lack of communication. These Indians do not speak Spanish; they speak Indian dialects completely different from Spanish. There are almost a hundred different dialects.

However, in the regions where there are schools the Indian children learn the national language, and naturally, when they speak and read this language, they learn something about Mexico and the rest of the world.

y emplea algunas palabras que no usan los españoles. Sin embargo, las diferencias de pronunciación y vocabulario no son muchas.

La mayoría de los mexicanos tienen una mezcla de sangre española y sangre india. Hay una minoría de origen español y otra minoría de origen indio.

El indio que vive en la ciudad habla español como los otros mexicanos, pero en las montañas y en las selvas viven algunos indios aislados del resto del país por falta de comunicaciones, y estos indios no hablan español; hablan dialectos indios completamente diferentes del español. Existen casi cien dialectos diferentes.

Sin embargo, en las regiones donde hay escuelas, los niños indios aprenden la lengua nacional y, naturalmente, cuando hablan y leen esta lengua, aprenden algo de México y del resto del mundo.[2]

During the preview, the teacher should stress reading for comprehension and mention examples of all the aids to reading comprehension that are discussed in chapter 11. Since the two basic structures to be learned in this reading are the use of the definite article before the names of languages and the third person singular and plural verb forms, examples of each should be pointed out. Also, as the students read, the teacher must pay careful attention to their pronunciation of such words as *nacional* and *español,* because the tendency is to give an English pronunciation to the vowel *a.* In addition, all suggested cultural bits of information should be expanded upon. For example,

---

[2]Reprinted with permission from R. Armitage et al., *Beginning Spanish: A Cultural Approach,* 3rd ed. (Boston: Houghton Mifflin, 1972). P. 23.

in this reading the teacher can (1) distinguish between Spanish and Spanish-American pronunciations, (2) discuss the mestizo in Spanish America, (3) describe and explain the difference between the cultural life of the cities and the rural areas, (4) explain the importance of communication and transportation in a country's cultural development, (5) note the tendency in the Spanish-speaking world for the lifeblood of the country to gravitate toward the larger cities, (6) compare the dialectal differences in pronunciation with regionalisms in their own country, and (7) point out the difficulty Spanish speakers have pronouncing a word which has an initial *s* followed by a consonant.

The students should practice reading aloud outside of class, so that they are able to read in class the following day with acceptable pronunciation and intonation. They should write out the answers to the accompanying questions about the story and answer them orally in class without looking at their papers. In addition, they should be sufficiently familiar with the content, the vocabulary, and the structures to be able to give an oral or a written summary of the reading by the time they arrive in class.

Drills

The purposes during the preview of the drills to be assigned are to get the students to understand the meaning of the sentences and to be able to pronounce the forms. Normally, in the audio-lingual approach, conditioning of structure is accomplished in stages. First, the important structures occur in the dialogs. They are then recalled before the same forms are drilled and manipulated in pattern practice. Any explanation or generalization is given after the forms have been drilled thoroughly.

The forms to be used as a basis for this example are the irregular verbs in the past tense that are introduced in the dialog of unit 9 of *Modern Spanish,* Second Edition. In the dialog, the students learn a past tense form of the irregular verbs *to go, to have, to want, to be able,* and *to be.* In presenting this new structure, the teacher can assume that the students already know the regular past tense forms and that they understand the concept of past tense in their own language. Also, they should know the subject pronouns, the meanings of the verbs to be studied, and be familiar with the concept of verb endings. Therefore, the main problem in this case is one of establishing the meaning of the verb and of conditioning the relationship between the person and the corresponding verb ending. Since the students have only recently studied the dialog, the teacher can simply ask them to recall the meanings of these sentences and proceed to drill all the person endings by means of a repetition drill for each verb. Another approach is to begin with the same verbs in the present tense and to introduce the past tense forms by changing a time indicator word such as *now* or *today* to *yesterday* or *last night.*

The assignment is for the students to practice person-number substitution drills. For example, in the sentence, *I was sick,* substitute the following subjects, *they, he, we, you,* etc. and the corresponding forms of the verb *to be.* Then the students can practice a tense substitution drill. For example, change the tense of the following sentences from present to past: *I am sick. He has a date. You can eat.* The students should do these drills until they can respond orally and quickly in class the following day. The best way to practice these drills, of course, is with a tape recorder. In most high schools this type of practice is not available; therefore, the students must recite orally from the book or write the sentences as they practice.

Exercises

The purpose of the preview of exercises to be assigned is to establish a cognitive awareness of the concepts involved, and completing the exercises involves a conscious application of conceptual knowledge.

Two grammar points are to be learned in the sample lesson, chosen from lesson 7 of *Beginning Spanish: A Cultural Approach.* The students are to learn when to use, and when not to use, the definite article with the names of languages and the third person singular and plural verb forms for each of the three classes of verbs in Spanish.

In deciding how to introduce the use of the definite article with names of languages, the teacher needs to consider what the students already know in their own language and in the second language. By the time this topic is presented, they should already know the definite articles, and, of course, they know that they do not use the article with languages in English. In fact, a good place to start would be with the similarities between the two languages. In English one says, "He speaks Spanish," "They are talking in French," and "This is a book of Italian." Starting with these sentences, the teacher can simply give direct translations to let the students see that in these sentences the two languages use identical forms of expression. From this relationship, the teacher can lead to the dissimilar forms, "Spanish is an important language," and "The national language of Mexico is Spanish." In both these sentences, a definite article is required before the name of the language in Spanish.

The teacher asks himself the same questions before undertaking a preview of the verb endings to be learned. Given the students' background in languages at this point, the teacher may have to build mostly from the students' knowledge of their own language. Since the examples in the book are *to work, to read,* and *to exist,* it is a good idea for the teacher to select other verbs for his presentation. Taking the verbs *to talk, to learn,* and *to live,* he can begin by writing the three infinitives on the chalkboard. His next step is to get the students to understand that these are names of actions just as *desk* is the name of a thing. Following this point, he asks the students to use each of these verbs with two different subjects, *the teacher* and *the teachers*. Thus, the phrases *the teacher talks, the teachers talk, the teacher learns, the teachers learn, the teacher lives,* and *the teachers live* are written on the chalkboard. Now the teacher points out to them what they already know in a functional sense but what they may not have thought about, i.e., the form of the verb used with a singular subject and the form corresponding to plural subjects. (And he may do so without using the traditional grammatical terms such as *verb, subject, singular,* and *plural,* which were used here.) At this point the students are ready to consider these same structures in the second language. First, the teacher gives the three equivalent infinitives in Spanish, explaining that *hablar, aprender,* and *vivir* belong to different groups of verbs and that the letter before the last *r* indicates to which group each belongs. Then the teacher gives the forms of the first conjugation verb, pointing out the letter *a* used in the endings of an *a* verb and contrasting the singular and plural endings with the singular and plural forms in English. Also, in comparing the two, he should be careful to distinguish between the infinitive sign of a verb and the stem that names the action. With this information the students know enough to participate in completing the other Spanish equivalents. They should be able to give the third person singular and plural of an *e* verb using an *e* instead of an *a.* The fact that they will miss the *i* verb by putting an *i* in the endings only serves to emphasize that *i* verbs do not follow the pattern of the first two conjugations. (Since *i* verbs are the most irregular of the three, permitting the students to fall into a trap may help them to be more aware of these differences. At times, students can learn more by making an error.)

Next, the teacher asks the students to open their books and gives the assignment for the next class period. Together, he and the class complete two or three of the sentences in each exercise. This cooperative effort enables him to determine whether or not the explanation has really been understood and insures that the students know exactly what they are to do. Three exercises are to be assigned in this lesson: (1) (This boy speaks Spanish. These boys . . . .), (2) (The boys live here. The boy . . . .), and (3) (The Mexicans speak Spanish. The national language of Mexico is . . . .). These exercises are to be written, and the students should study them to the point that they are able to give the correct answers orally without looking at their papers.

VIEW ACTIVITIES

One of the three basic differences between the audio-lingual and cognitive approaches relates to the type of classroom activities employed during the view part of the class hour. Since audio-lingual proponents believe that language is conditioned behavior and that it can be learned only by a great deal of repetition, they spend most of this part of the class hour repeating dialog lines or practicing pattern drills, either written or oral. Since the cognitive advocates believe that language is creative, rule-governed behavior and that the students must acquire an underlying conceptual knowledge of what they are doing, they spend most of the view portion of the class covering cognitive-type exercises that have been prepared as homework or discussing material that has been read. With both types of texts, the latter portion of the view activities should include "real" language practice over the content of the dialog or reading.

Dialog

The objectives were stated in the preview. The teacher's purpose at this stage is to check on the attainment of the stated objectives. First, she models all the lines again. Next, she asks the students to repeat the lines together. Given this brief warm-up, the students should be ready to display the abilities they were supposed to acquire during the homework assignment. The teacher first calls on individuals to repeat the lines after her. While they are doing so, she should take note of the speed, pronunciation, and intonation. All weaknesses should be pointed out to the students and drilled. (The teacher may want to give grades for these repetitions.) Next, she gives the lines in the second language and asks the students for the first-language meanings. Following this exercise, the class proceeds to the more difficult task of giving the second-language sentence when cued by the first-language version.

After having drilled the lines in the fashion described in the preceding paragraph, the students should be able to discuss the content of those lines. The teacher now asks questions about what happened. For example, over the dialog lines studied the following questions can be asked:

1. (Where are the boys?)
2. (Who is in the café?)
3. (What are their names?)
4. (Is it a good café?)
5. (How's the coffee?)
6. (Do they order Cokes?)
7. (What do they order?)
8. (Who comes in?)
9. (Is he happy?)
10. (How does he look?)
11. (Why didn't he go to school yesterday?)
12. (What did they have at school?)
13. (Did he want to go?)
14. (Why didn't he?)
15. (How was his day?)
16. (How was he?)

Questions of this type are often not included in the text itself. If such is the case, the teacher should put these questions on cards and save them for future use.

At the point in the sequence where the students begin to talk about content of a dialog or a reading, they are beginning "real" language practice in the sense that they are using answers to communicate some information that they have rather than to answer questions merely to practice structural forms without regard to meaning.

Reading

The teacher's purpose is to check on the objectives stated in the preview. He checks the ability to read aloud from the printed page by asking randomly picked students to read a paragraph until he is satisfied with their pronunciation. Next, he asks if there are any phrases or sentences in the reading that are not clear. If there are none, he gives the correct answers to the questions while the students check their papers. While they are doing this, he encourages them to ask questions about any answers they do not understand. He then checks the objective of being able to answer the questions orally by asking them to answer the questions without looking at their papers. Once they can answer the questions, the students should be able to give an oral or written summary of the content of the reading. Since they have just answered the questions orally, he may ask them to spend five minutes writing a résumé of the reading.

Drills

The teacher spends this portion of the class hour doing the assigned pattern drills, first chorally and then individually. For maximum efficiency and effect, the pace must be brisk. Otherwise, the whole purpose of acquiring automatic responses is lost, and boredom quickly sets in. If the students cannot perform as desired, the teacher may do the person-number substitution drills as repetition drills. Then she can do the same drill again at a more difficult level. The important thing is that she should not hesitate to repeat the same drill until the students can perform at a satisfactory level. From time to time, she checks the meaning to be sure the students know what they are saying. If the students can do the drills well, the teacher at the end of the drill session can begin to insert some questions from a choice-question response drill. For example, "Did you do the lesson or didn't you want to?" Although this is still a drill in the sense that the purpose is to practice structural forms, this type of drill approaches very closely the format of "real" language questions. It is an important step toward being able to answer personalized questions. Students who can answer such questions well should be ready to take the step to attach meaning to structure.

To terminate the drill phase of the sequence leading toward a functional knowledge of the use of these irregular verb forms in the past tense, most audio-linguists describe briefly the grammar of what has just been drilled. The generalization is merely a summary rather than a complete explanation as given in a cognitive class. Here, it is sufficient to point out, with examples, that the endings are unstressed as opposed to the stressed endings of regular verbs, that the verb *to go* is completely irregular and must be learned separately, and that the other verbs have a systematized set of endings even though the stems are irregular.

Exercises

The objectives were to be able to choose the correct form of the verb to correspond to a third-person singular or plural subject and to be able to do the exercises orally without the use of their papers. Prior to asking the students to give the proper forms without referring to their papers, the teacher reads the correct answers. While he is reading, the students correct their mistakes and ask any questions pertaining to their errors. The teacher then goes over the same exercises again, asking the students to do them this time without looking at their papers. (This type of activity prevents the students from writing down answers without really learning the material.) If there is time remaining, the teacher can ask some structured questions similar to the following:

Answer the following questions with a yes answer:
1. (Does John work here?) *a* verbs, third-person singular (Does Mary speak Spanish?) etc.
2. (Does Joe live here?) *e* and *i* verbs, third-person singular (Is Carl learning a lot?) etc.

Answer the following questions with a no answer:
1. (Do they work a lot?) *a* verbs, third-person plural, etc.
2. (Are they learning well?) *e* and *i* verbs, third-person plural, etc.

REVIEW ACTIVITIES

The classroom activities of the review part of the class hour should all involve using "real" language activities to go beyond the content of the text. During this portion of the class the activities should resemble true language contexts as far as possible in the classroom. Before initiating any of the procedures in the review, the teacher should ask herself two questions: "Could such presentations, exchanges, interchanges, etc. occur in the second-language situation?" "Are the students combining structure and meaning to express their own ideas, opinions, information, and intentions?" The activities during this part of the class hour are at the highest level of skill development and approach quite closely to the true communicative situation. This level of language usage is the goal toward which the teacher and the students have been working. Now the goal is almost within their grasp. All that remains is to provide opportunities for practice. At this level the teacher should assume only a minor role as she urges the students to carry the major burden of maintaining the tempo of the class. As the students' skill increases, the teacher's *active* participation in the classroom activities should decrease in direct proportion to their abilities.

The long-range objectives and short-range objectives specify the ability to communicate in all four language skills. Therefore, all four must be practiced in the review. The review is more than just a warm-up. It is more than just a series of personalized questions. It is certainly more than a restatement of all the rules that the students should know, and it is more than one final repetition of the entire dialog before the test. The review is the time to use the language, i.e., to listen to it, to speak it, to read it, and to write it, in situations in which the object is not to practice sounds nor to learn vocabulary nor to focus on structures, but to communicate ideas, to focus on the message rather than on its form, to see whether the students can express themselves within the limits of their language experience.

During the review session the teacher should concentrate on establishing an atmosphere in which the students feel free to participate and use the language. Such an atmosphere cannot be maintained along with the almost constant criticism and correction that are common to many language classes. There should be continuous encouragement toward self-expression. As long as the teacher and the other students can understand, there should be no reference to correct pronunciation, words, or forms because the object is to concentrate on the message. Naturally, there is some overload on the students' mental processes when they begin to combine form and meaning. This may cause many additional mistakes to creep into their use of the second language, but this stage of faltering, hesitation, and committing errors is unavoidable in the language-learning sequence. There can be no automatization of language usage apart from the true-speech situation, i.e., speech production with meaning in a communicative context. Even students who have memorized dialogs at native speed slow down considerably when using the same vocabulary and structures in a real give-and-take language situation. The teacher should expect this period of language weakness, and she should warn the students to expect it. By concentrating on the fact that they are learning to communicate in the language, the teacher can make this a period of satisfaction and enthusiasm as opposed to a period of frustration, embarrassment, and deflated egos. No parent scolds a child learning to walk for being unable to run. Neither should the teacher scold students as they stumble taking their first halting, even clumsy steps in the language. Periods of uncertainty and insecurity are times for encouragement and praise, not criticism and correction.

In order to avoid impeding student progress in the review period, the teacher should discipline herself to refrain from the constant and almost overwhelming urge to correct immediately every single error. If the teacher demands perfect language prior to usage, she may just as well "close up shop." The students are not expected to be perfect in any other subject, but often they are expected to be in a second-language class. They did not learn their own language without making any errors, but they are expected to learn a second language in such a fashion. Thousands, even millions, of non-native speakers around the world can communicate very well even though their pronunciation and syntactical arrangements may not resemble in many aspects that of a native speaker.

Many students sincerely want to learn to use a language, but they are discouraged in their efforts by continuous criticism. To learn to use a language, the students must reach a point at which they can concentrate on what they are saying instead of how they are saying it. They often cannot reach this point, however, because the teacher places grammatical and phonological interruptions and stumbling blocks in their way. The language teacher tends to have an unwarranted obsession with perfection in the classroom. She should remember that the goal is not native speech, but the ability to communicate with a native. The time to correct is during the view portion of the class hour. During the review, the students must be permitted to focus on what they are saying. Significant errors that may hinder communication may be mentioned at the end of the review, but even then the stress should be placed on what the students were able to say rather than the weaknesses—on the positive rather than the negative.

Prior preparation is most important in the application phase of language learning. Creating effective classroom activities that indeed foster true language practice, as opposed to skill development activities, requires much anticipatory planning. The amount of "real" language materials varies from book to book, but with any text the teacher needs to supplement and expand these materials.

Dialog

As a follow-up to the content questions over the dialog, the teacher should personalize the material to the students' own lives. In succeeding days, he should provide listening comprehension practice, speaking practice, reading practice, and writing practice over this same material. For example, to practice the speaking skill he can ask the students the following questions:

1. (Do you know where there is a good café in town?)
2. (What's it called?)
3. (Where is it?)
4. (Is the food good?)
5. (How's the coffee?)
6. (Do you like coffee?)
7. (Do you like it black or with milk and sugar?)
8. (Do you like it hot?)
9. (Do you drink coffee for breakfast? At other times?)
10. (What do you drink with your meals if you do not drink coffee?)
11. (You look glum today. Are you sad?)
12. (Did you have a test yesterday?)
13. (Did you go to school yesterday?)
14. (Did you have a bad day?)
15. (Were you sick?)

As the teacher asks these questions, he should take advantage of every opportunity to turn each question into a conversational exchange, if possible. For example, when the questioned student answers that she did have a test yesterday, ask her what class it was in, whether it was easy or difficult, how well she did, etc. Thus, the teacher can find out whether the students are really communicating or merely manipulating structural forms, and he can also move away from the stilted activity that question-and-answer practice can become in the absence of true communication. Also, the possibility for conversational exchange and the normality of the situation are enhanced by grouping the questions around topics.

After asking these questions to the point at which the students can answer them fairly easily, the teacher can begin to provide practice in which the students carry more of the responsibility. He can divide the class into small groups with one of the better students to lead a discussion of the same topic. At the end of five or ten minutes, the discussion leaders can summarize what was said in their group for the rest of the class. On another day, the students can, if time permits, be asked to prepare short oral reports in which they tell about their favorite restaurant or discuss the refreshments they drink or discuss something that happened in the past. Or they may be asked to prepare questions based on the content of the dialog and then ask them of each other in class.

Listening comprehension practice can be provided very easily by the teacher himself. By answering questions similar to those listed above, he can prepare a short oral presentation that provides him with practice speaking for a sustained number of sentences. (The teacher often needs this practice also.) While he is talking, the students gain valuable listening practice. Comprehension can be checked in follow-up questions or by some type of self-checked quiz. For example, without too much difficulty, the teacher can prepare a short oral presentation similar to this:

> (Say, I know where there is a good café. Some of the other teachers and I go there often after school to rest a few minutes. It's called Smitty's and it's over on Tenth Street. I don't like coffee myself, but I have a Coke. Yesterday I didn't go. I wanted to, but I couldn't. I gave a test in class, and I had to go home to grade it.)

If the teacher does not have time to prepare listening comprehension materials, he can ask the students to prepare short oral reports. This gives them practice in doing more than simply answering or asking questions and provides listening practice for the other students, if the teacher provides a follow-up activity to check comprehension and to encourage them to listen.

Reading and writing practice can be prepared in the same way as the oral activities. By altering slightly the questions, the teacher can write short, original paragraphs that the students should be able to read and comprehend. Comprehension can be stressed with self-checked written quizzes such as true-false or multiple-choice, or with oral or written questions. Again if the teacher does not have the free time necessary to prepare materials for reading comprehension, he can assign written reports based on guiding questions similar to those used in the oral question-and-answer session and use the best ones for reading practice. There is a great deal of talent and originality in most language classes, and with a slight amount of editing here and there the teacher can take advantage of that talent to assist in the preparation of supplementary materials.

In addition to these structured materials related specifically to the content of the text, the students need to have related but unstructured materials available for further practice. The collection of such materials requires much time and patience, perhaps more than any teacher has. By being always on the look-out and by sharing with other teachers, however, he can gradually build a very respectable file.

In the subsequent considerations of reading, drills, and activities, the same principles apply and the same possibilities exist. Therefore, the discussion of the following topics is limited to examples of personalized questions that may be used. The art of asking personalized questions is one that the language teacher should practice diligently. Even a modern language can be a so-called dead language unless the teacher helps to keep it alive. He can do this by relating it to the students and showing them that learning a language involves much more than memorizing a never-ending series of dialogs or lists of words. Too often, means become ends in themselves. Personalization of content is extremely important because many students never even get this far in the language development sequence. The teacher should attempt always to take his students beyond this stage to practice in connected discourse and with nonstructured contexts.

Reading

In the application of the reading lesson the teacher can, and should, prepare questions similar to the following:
1. (What language do the Mexicans speak?)
2. (What is their official language?)
3. (What language do they learn in the schools?)
4. (What language do they read?)
5. (Do they speak Spanish exactly like the Spaniards?)
6. (What language do North Americans speak?)
7. (What language do they speak in England?)
8. (Do North Americans speak exactly like the British?)
9. (What other languages are spoken in the United States?)
10. (What other languages do they speak on the continent of North America?)
11. (What languages do they speak in Canada?)
12. (What language do the Chileans speak? The Bolivians? The Colombians? The Guatemalans? The Brazilians? Etc.)
13. (Is there a lack of communication?)
14. (Are there regions in the United States where there are no schools?)

(At this point, the personalization of content is very difficult because, with this book, the students do not know the first- and second-person verb forms. Questions such as "Does your family . . . ," and "Do your friends . . . ," could be included, but they have not had the possessives either. However, these forms are introduced later on, and from that point personalization is much easier.)

Drills

The irregular past tense verbs can be grouped around some topic such as the weekend or vacations. The following questions deal with vacations:
1. (Did you go away?)
2. (Did you want to go someplace?)
3. (Were you at home?)
4. (Who came to see you?)
5. (Who prepared dinner?)
6. (Did you eat a lot? Too much?)
7. (Did you have a good day?)

8. (Did you study?)
9. (Did you want to study?)
10. (Did you want to come back to classes?)

These questions could, of course, be expanded to include more regular past tense verbs in order to cover more completely the students' activities during vacation. The teacher should remember, during these personalized question sessions, that it is no crime to ask several students the same question or to ask all the questions of one student before going on to another. Variety can be added, attentiveness stimulated, and other verb forms practiced by occasionally asking another student about the answers that have just been given. For example, if Joe has just answered one or all of the questions, the teacher can then ask questions about Joe's vacation.

Exercises

Cognitive exercises can also be personalized to the students' lives. In applying the verbs taught in the third-person singular and plural, the teacher could ask questions similar to these:
(Talking about the teacher)
1. (Does she work in a factory?)
2. (Where does she work?)
3. (Does he speak Spanish?)
4. (What languages does he speak?)
5. (Is she learning Spanish?)
6. (Does she read Spanish?)
7. (What languages does she read?)
8. (Does he live in school?)
9. (Where does he live?)
10. (Is she in class?)
11. (What class is she in?)
12. (Does he have a lot of money?)

(Talking about the students)
1. (Do they have a lot of money?)
2. (Do they have a lot of books, time, work to do?)
3. (Do they go to class?)
4. (Do they work in mines?)
5. (Where do they work?)
6. (Do they use Indian words? Dialects?)
7. (Do they pronounce English well?)
8. (Do they talk a lot in class?)
9. (Do they speak Spanish a lot in class?)
10. (Do they live here?)
11. (Are they good?)

CONCLUSION

This chapter emphasizes the types of objectives and activities employed in each phase of language acquisition and distinguishes between the types of classroom procedures used at each stage by audio-lingual and cognitive teachers. In this sense the techniques presented in this chapter are slightly different from those presented in the detailed lesson plans of chapter 16, which outline a cognitive approach to second-language teaching.

The objectives of the understanding phase are different from those of the drill phase, and those of both are different from those of the application phase. Therefore, the activities included in the preview, view, and review portions of the class hour are all different. The activities in an audio-lingual class during the preview and view are different from those of a cognitive class. The review activities may be similar for both. At each level the achievement expected of the students is slightly greater as students progress from no knowledge to ability to use the language. During the whole process, no activity in any particular sequence is repeated except as a brief occasional reminder of some concepts met before. If teachers keep these parts of the class hour and the purposes of each before them as they teach, they should fall naturally into a teaching procedure that includes an interesting variety of activities and the sequencing necessary for success in developing second-language skills.

REVIEW AND APPLICATION

DISCUSSION
1. Discuss the differences between types of activities included in the preview, view, and review portions of the class hour.
2. Discuss the differences between the types of activities included in each portion of the class hour in an audio-lingual and in a cognitive class.

ACTIVITY
1. Prepare a list of activities appropriate for the preview, view, and review portions of the class hour.

SELECTED REFERENCES

Armitage, R., et al. (1972) *Beginning Spanish: A Cultural Approach.* (3rd ed.) Boston: Houghton Mifflin. P. 23.

Bolinger, J. E.; Ciruti, J.E.; and Montero, H. H. (1966) *Modern Spanish.* (2nd ed.) New York: Harcourt Brace Jovanovich.

EVALUATION

INTRODUCTION

Evaluation is inseparably related to both objectives and classroom procedures and must be given equal consideration as the class proceeds through the course. The teacher begins any given learning segment by establishing instructional goals. She then proceeds to plan activities that will enable the students to achieve these goals. In planning the lesson, the teacher is in effect hypothesizing that the planned procedures will foster and develop the desired learning by the students. She is anticipating what will work and what will not work with this particular group of students. Sometimes she anticipates correctly, and sometimes she does not. The important point, if she wants to improve her teaching, is not whether she fails to predict correctly in planning the lesson, but whether she evaluates the results in order to improve subsequent teaching activities.

The primary purpose of evaluation in the classroom is to judge achievement, both student and teacher. Evaluation of achievement is the feedback that makes improvement possible. By means of evaluation, strengths and weaknesses are identified. Evaluation, in this sense, is another aspect of learning, one that enables the learner to grasp what was missed previously and the teacher to comprehend what can be done in subsequent lessons to improve her teaching. It is the final step in the sequence toward mastery of content and accomplishment of objectives. At times, poor students are not learning because they have failed to develop a practical learning strategy for second-language study. A test may provide clues to them or to their teachers as to what their problems are. Certainly, the teacher should continually stress the importance of evaluation as a learning device. In addition to improving the opportunity for learning, evaluation serves as a prime source of motivation for many students. After all, like most humans, they need extra incentives to operate at maximum capacity. The fact that teachers should never cease in their efforts to instill intrinsic desires in their students is no reason to abandon all forms of extrinsic motivation in the classroom.

Teachers need to evaluate constantly their teaching on the basis of student reaction, interest, and achievement. The conclusions drawn from this evaluation constitute their main source for measuring the effectiveness of instruction. In this sense, their first pressing need is to judge themselves. Second, they must accept the basic, and often burdensome, responsibility of judging the students' performance and attainment. In addition to teacher evaluation, the students are also participants in the evaluation process. Although they may not be so concerned as the teacher (some may be more so), they do, consciously or unconsciously, judge teacher effectiveness as well as their own level of learning in the course. If they are satisfied that they are learning, individual motivation and class participation will be high. If not, both the teacher and the students need to consider adjustments that will improve the situation.

TYPES OF EVALUATION

The term *evaluation* is an all-inclusive one that encompasses both subjective estimates of student work and formalized testing procedures. The advantages of subjective estimates are that the feedback which the teacher and students receive is immediate, constant, and informal. The weaknesses are that the value judgments reached are highly subjective, may be based on short-term learning, and, if given daily, may be confusing and burdensome to record in the grade book. On the other hand, tests have the advantage of being more concrete and thereby more objective. They also measure more material over longer periods of time, thereby stressing a greater degree of retention, organization, and comprehension of the material. The weakness lies in the fact that tests cause such anxiety among some students that they are unable to perform to their capability. (It is appropriate here to add that such a reaction is rare in a class in which the teacher is maintaining a feeling of confidence and success among the students and in which his tests are a true reflection of his goals and classroom activities.) Too, the argument is made that the score on any given test cannot represent adequately what the students have learned.

Subjective Evaluation

Both subjective evaluation and tests should be component parts of the total picture of classroom performance. Each complements the other and provides information which the other may not, although the correlation between the two is normally quite high. The teacher should be especially aware of the effects of daily classroom activities because it is at this point that the whole process of evaluation begins. As she teaches, she can sense from the student response whether the students are adequately prepared for what they are being asked to do. In this way she has the feedback necessary to judge whether her sequencing of prior activities and her teaching have been adequate. The students' ability to participate in the classroom activities also demonstrates to them whether or not they have learned what they should.

The daily classroom work itself, then, is the crucial factor in the entire evaluation process. This is true from the teacher viewpoint because the alert teacher sensitive to student response receives more feedback during class recitation than from any test. In fact, the experienced teacher in a beginning language class usually knows in advance the approximate scores that the students will receive on any given test, even though she may not be able to predict which items will be missed. The above statement is also true from the viewpoint of the students, because their general attitude toward the class is based on the challenge offered and the success and confidence achieved during daily recitation.

The teacher may decide to assign specific grades based on daily work. Giving a class grade is indeed a nebulous judgment at the end of the grading period, but such a grade often has the effect of increasing participation in the class, especially in the case of shy students who are reluctant to speak in front of the group. Also, for the teacher who chooses not to give speaking tests, the class grade is the only definite evaluation made of the students' ability to speak the language. Giving a daily grade based on classroom recitation hardly seems necessary, and the paperwork can become quite a chore.

In addition to a grade based on classroom participation, a grade may be assigned on the basis of performance in the language laboratory. Certainly, if the lab is used regularly, part of the grade in the course should reflect the students' work there. This grade may range all the way from a single letter grade based on a global subjective estimate by the teacher to a structured grading system for monitoring, such as that suggested by Stack (1966).

The preceding paragraphs stress the evaluation of cognitive achievement by subjective means. Equally important are the teacher's subjective estimates of the affective-social factors influencing student progress in the class. The teacher should continually be sensitive to the total class atmosphere and individual attitudes within that social environment. From this subjective interpretation of the feelings within the group she can strive to enhance the positive and counter the negative. By keeping an eye open to student actions and reactions in class, the teacher can cultivate a positive, productive relationship with her class and among the students that will make the class more enjoyable for everyone and that will improve cognitive achievement and affective-social attitudes.

For two reasons, subjective evaluation is especially important in the area of affective-social variables. First, attitudes are rather difficult to determine by means of tests, even though self-reporting attitude inventories are available. (For example, see Jakobovits [1970].) And second, the teacher needs to make continuous adjustments during the course of the semester in response to the affective-social forces affecting the classroom teaching-learning situation. The completion of an inventory, as helpful as the results can be, is not sufficient to give the teacher the everyday feedback she requires to be responsive to student feelings and needs.

Objective Evaluation

Subjective evaluation may be more fundamental and more important for the teacher, both from a cognitive and an affective-social point of view, than objective evaluation. Specific testing procedures, however, carry more weight with the students in the areas of cognitive acquisition of knowledge and skills and in the affective domain also. Although the students already have a general feeling for how they are doing prior to the test, they need test items over the instructional objectives to indicate to them which goals they have failed to achieve and which weaknesses in their preparation should be strengthened. (Prior to the test, the astute teacher should already be aware of student progress, but he needs concrete information from the results of the tests to impress on the students what he knows beforehand.) In this sense, tests are merely another type of learning activity. For those students who lack the insight to evaluate realistically their achievement during the classroom teaching-learning activities, test results provide the hard facts that give them the feedback they must have to improve and which they are unable to supply for themselves.

Testing in the second-language class is often quite inadequate. The teacher is so preoccupied with classroom activities that he fails to maintain a comprehensive perspective of the flow of the language-learning sequence from plans to activities to testing. If he has failed to delineate clearly his objectives, he will not be in a knowledgeable position for preparing the test. The preparation of the test begins with the objectives. They, in effect, are the criteria upon which to judge student performance and from which to prepare test items.

The test should be a sampling of these performance criteria stated in the lesson-plan objectives. Unfortunately, the teacher often does not test the objectives of the material covered. At times, he may not even test the planned classroom activities. (Whether or not these activities reflect the objectives is another question.) In such a situation, the practical objectives of the course are set by the tests. No matter what the teacher states as the goals of the course, the students study for the tests. The tests, then, in spite of all protestations to the contrary, determine what the students emphasize in their study. Some of the dissatisfaction associated with the audio-lingual approach, for example, can be traced to this very problem. Teachers who had been re-trained in audio-lingual classroom techniques continued to administer traditional, paper-and-pencil tests. The result was predictably disastrous, and student achievement in oral skills was understandably lower than had been expected. If the teacher is to insure learning, his objectives, planned activities, and testing procedures must reflect his philosophy of learning and language.

TYPES OF TESTS

There are several types of classroom tests. The most common one, which is a favorite of many second-language teachers, is the *quiz*. The quiz is a compromise between short-term, subjective evaluation based on daily work and the unit, six-week, or semester examination. Quite often the threat of a quiz is used as a scare technique to stimulate the students to prepare their daily lesson. A more desirable situation is the positive approach in which they prepare in order to be able to participate in the day's activities. The quiz may be announced or unannounced. Both are intended to check short-term learning and to encourage daily preparation. There is no consensus on the value of periodic quizzes. Some teachers use them very effectively. Others feel that quizzes, especially the "pop" variety, frustrate students who are anxious and conscientious, and that such tension may actually hinder learning and create a negative reaction toward the class itself.

If she does decide to give quizzes, the teacher should be wary of three tendencies that may negatively affect learning. The first is to place such reliance on the threat of a quiz to motivate the students that she neglects to plan adequately for her own teaching. Quizzes may be used to give an extra incentive, but proper motivation cannot be maintained on the basis of quizzes alone. Second, the teacher should take care not to ask questions of the same difficulty level on a quiz that she would on an examination. The purpose is to check initial comprehension of any segment of material, not final mastery. Third, the teacher should not overtest. If she decides to give quizzes, she should not give one every day, at least not for a grade. Most of the time in class should be devoted to teaching-learning situations, not testing. A good rule-of-thumb is to limit *all* testing to a *maximum* of *10 percent* of class time.

The greatest amount of expertise has been developed with regard to testing and evaluation in second-language learning in the area of prediction. Carroll and Sapon (1958) and Pimsleur (1965) have published aptitude tests that correlate quite highly with student achievement in language classes. Other factors such as past academic record, verbal and quantitative ability, interest, sense modality preference for learning, etc. have been found to affect achievement. One study even indicated that it might be possible to determine which students would be most likely to succeed in an audio-lingual class and which students would prefer a cognitive type of class. At any rate, it now seems possible to predict the strengths and weaknesses of each student on the basis of information in the counselor's office and from the scores on an aptitude test (Chastain, 1969). In spite of the possibilities in this area for sectioning students to enhance their opportunities for learning the language, few schools do so at present. Perhaps a future trend in this direction may enable the teacher to anticipate and avoid, or at least minimize, student difficulties.

Periodically, the teacher should give an *achievement test* that covers a major segment of material. With the typical textbook, tests are given at the end of each unit, lesson, or chapter. Tests of this type encourage the students to organize their knowledge, to assimilate larger chunks of material, and to learn for long-term retention. They also present the students with objective evidence with regard to what they have and have not learned. (The teacher is usually more aware of this prior to the test than they are.) Some authors provide tests to be given after each major division of the book. These tests may or may not be appropriate for any given teacher's interpretation of the book. She should examine them carefully in light of her own classroom procedures. Teacher-made tests are likely to be more consistent with the individual classroom approach, but the teacher may not have the time or, in the beginning, the expertise to prepare them.

Standardized achievement or *proficiency tests* are also available. The *MLA-Cooperative Foreign Language Tests* (1965) are designed to be given at the end of second level and at the end of the fourth level in high school. These tests are obviously not correlated with any particular textbook, and they would be inappropriate for use as a final examination over the textual materials used in the class. However, they are a valuable asset in curriculum evaluation and for comparing any particular students with the norms on the national sample. By comparing the scores over a period of years, the department can obtain a more objective measure of the quality and focus of instruction.

Although they are not commonly used in most second-language programs in secondary schools, *diagnostic tests* could be used to advantage. Their major function is to ascertain what the students know and what they do not know. Since the study of second languages is a cumulative process, the results of a diagnostic test would enable the teacher to determine those areas that should be reviewed and those areas that can safely be assumed to be a part of the students' existing knowledge. Such tests could be used beneficially to facilitate student progress from one level to another.

One way to incorporate diagnostic testing and diversified instruction into intermediate and advanced classes is to use pretests over basic grammar points as a diagnostic tool. At the beginning of the week the students take a pretest over the grammar for that week. Those students who score above a teacher-selected percentage are free for the remainder of the week to concentrate on other work. Those students who need additional work or who desire to raise their scores are directed to work they can do to prepare themselves for a posttest to be given at the end of the week.

Classroom tests can also be categorized on the basis of the way the information obtained from the results is to be used. If the test scores are to be used to rank the students, the test is referred to as a *norm-referenced test:* that is, student achievement is related to some norm. In the case of *standardized tests,* the results are compared to those of a nation-wide random sample of students at a comparable level. In the case of a *teacher-prepared classroom test,* the assumption is made that the students in that class are a normal group, i.e., that there is a normal distribution of abilities in that class. As a result of this assumption, the student scores are listed on a sheet in order to find out the numbers of students who have received the various scores. Using this chart, the teacher "curves" the results, i.e., he decides what percentage of the students receive an *A,* a *B,* etc. for the test. In theory, approximately 10 percent of the students get *A*'s, 20 percent *B*'s, 40 percent *C*'s, 20 percent *D*'s, and 10 percent *F*'s. In practice the teacher gives grades that he feels to be consistent with the students' abilities in the class. The weakness of such a practice is that students may rank very high and learn very little, or they may learn a great deal and receive a comparatively low grade if they happen to be in an especially strong academic group of students. Too, the concept of a normal distribution of abilities is based on the total population. Determining the extent to which any particular group corresponds to that distribution is practically impossible. In addition, it is assumed that the teacher can prepare examinations that generate normally distributed student scores. Justifying this assumption is a tenuous proposition.

If the test is prepared on the basis of the instructional objectives to determine to what degree the students have learned the material presented and practiced in class, the test is called a *criterion-referenced test.* Although this term is primarily associated with the use of behavioral objectives, the concept can be used with any instructional objectives that the teacher may have for the students. Tests of this type give the students and the teacher information regarding what percentage of the content they have learned, not what percentage of their classmates are above or below their level of achievement. Using this method, the teacher does not curve the scores. He merely determines the percentage of correct answers on the test. Those students who have received a predetermined score receive an *A,* a *B,* etc. The emphasis in this type of test is not on comparisons, but on achievement. The advantage of this type of test is that the teacher is obliged to prepare tests that evaluate how well the students have learned. The stress is placed on learning, and the possibility exists for all students to do well or to do poorly, as the case may be.

Criterion-referenced examinations, which are prepared to test the acquisition of behavioral objectives, do have certain weaknesses. (These are discussed in chapter 8, page 226.) In response to the criticisms made against criterion-referenced tests, some writers are proposing *domain-referenced tests,* which purport to test an entire spectrum of behaviors needed to master some aspect of knowledge. (The interested reader is referred to *Educational Technology,* vol. 14, June, 1974.)

There are also *formative* and *summative tests.* (See chapter 8, pages 226–27.) A formative test consists of items designed to test student achievement of instructional objectives. The test is given at the end of a particular segment of material to give the students feedback on what they have or have not learned. Subsequently, compensatory exercises and activities are provided to help the students fill in the gaps in their learning. The students receive no grade on these tests. The purpose is to assist them in learning, not to grade their performance. Summative examinations are given less often over larger quantities of material. Grades are given on achievement indicated by the scores received on these tests. Both types of tests are intended to be geared toward instructional objectives, not toward student rankings.

Another type of test which has received a great deal of attention among teachers of English as a second language is the *cloze test.* In a cloze test, every n^{th} word is deleted from a written passage. The students complete the test by filling in the missing words or suitable equivalents. It has been suggested that cloze tests measure the learner's "grammar of expectancy," and the "learner's internalized grammar of expectancy" is the central core of language competence (Jorstad, 1974).

GUIDELINES FOR
CLASSROOM TESTING

1. Test objectives. The purpose of a classroom achievement test is to evaluate student attainment of objectives for any given segment of material. Any test, or any portion of a test, that the teacher cannot relate to specific objectives in his lesson plans needs to be carefully scrutinized and probably revamped. Time restrictions may make it impossible to prepare questions for all the objectives, but a representative sample should be covered. The important thing is to remember that any group of items should be thought of as a check on the attainment of goals.

2. Test what has been taught. Just as the test should reflect the objectives, it should also reflect the classroom procedures that were employed to accomplish those objectives. In other words, the test should only include items that are of the same type as the exercises used to teach the structures and vocabulary involved. Words and forms certainly should be recombined, but the types of exercises should be the same. Too often the language teacher is guilty of using certain procedures in class but testing with different techniques. If one were learning to play the piano, for example, the test should include various pieces that have been practiced. It is not uncommon in language classes for the teacher to ask the students to play a different piece, or perhaps even to write a composition, rather than play anything at all.

3. Test all four language skills. If the objectives in the course include all four language skills, all four should be tested. The implication here is that each test should include one section to test listening comprehension, one for speaking, one for reading, and one for writing. If the teacher customarily limits herself to pencil-and-paper tests, these types of exercises become, in effect, the practical goals of the students. She can correct this common fault by including some items involving each of the language skills on each examination.

The aforestated guideline also carries another implication—the word *skill*. As well as testing all four skills, the teacher should also be careful to test the material covered as a skill, not as a set of memorized vocabulary words and verb forms. Admittedly, language is made up of sounds, words, and structures. There is a great deal of difference, however, between testing concepts in some communicative context as opposed to regurgitating a word from a memorized list. Testing the students' ability to answer the question, "Are you a student?"

by writing, "Yes, I am a student," is entirely different from asking him to write the first-person singular of the verb *to be.* Asking the students to choose a word in the second language that correctly completes a series of statements such as the following does not involve the same skill as asking them how to say "get up" in the second language: *The sun was shining. The alarm was ringing. Slowly I realized that it was time to _____.*

4. Test one thing at a time. There are two considerations related to this statement. First, as far as possible each skill should be tested separately from any other skill. The answers to listening comprehension items, for example, should be given orally. Or the students might possibly choose from pictures or some other visual aid rather than read the answers in the language. There are limits to the implications of this guideline. It would be most difficult to prepare sufficient visual cues to elicit the desired responses in speaking. Therefore, and even though visual aids provide excellent stimuli to certain portions of the speaking test, many items on the speaking test will be cued in the language. This type of item does involve listening comprehension as well as speaking, but this practice can be defended on the basis that such a combination is the normal one in everyday conversational situations. The teacher should, however, remember that the primary function of the speaking portion of the test is to test the speaking skill and consequently to limit the oral cues to those that the students are certain to understand. The same relationship also exists between the written receptive skill, reading, and the productive skill, writing.

Second, within each of the language skill tests, the teacher should test only one point at a time. If he is writing an item to test vocabulary, the students should be aware that a word or words are to be tested and that syntax is not involved. For example:

> For their golden wedding anniversary my grandparents received many gifts and had many _____.
> a. weddings   b. visitors   c. new excuses.

If he is testing structural knowledge, all the distractors, i.e., the answers given, should involve forms of words rather than just words. For example:

> His sister is _____ the gifts.
> a. opening   b. received   c. looks for

Another case in point is the speaking test. When judging the students' pronunciation, the teacher should grade only one sound per utterance. When evaluating the use of grammatical forms, he should grade only the grammar and not focus upon the pronunciation and the vocabulary. Similarly, vocabulary should be graded independently of the pronunciation and structural manipulation. Only in this fashion is objectivity and identification of specific weaknesses possible.

5. Weight exam according to objectives. Since the test is to reflect the classroom objectives, it should be weighted according to the stress placed on each of the language skills. If the teacher wants to emphasize all four language skills equally and has endeavored to do so in his class activities, one fourth of the exam should test listening comprehension, one fourth speaking, one fourth reading, and one fourth writing. This is not to say that each portion of the exam should be equal in length, but that the weights assigned to each should be equal. On an examination graded according to a scale of one hundred points, each portion would be worth twenty-five points. (A test of any length may be converted to a hundred-point scale by multiplying or dividing.) Normally, a test of speaking and writing will include more separate factors to grade. Therefore, each might be worth fewer points even though the total score would be the same as on the listening and reading portions of the test. Conversely, the listening and reading sections will most likely have fewer points to grade, but each will be worth more.

6. Sequence the items from easy to more difficult. Most students enter an examination slightly apprehensive about their ability to answer the questions. Even though most of this anxiety can be extinguished in any given class before it becomes a real problem, the aura of testing remains. Therefore, one of the teacher's tasks in preparing the items is to include a few at the beginning which most students should be able to do fairly easily. This progressive introduction will help to reestablish their confidence and to set them at ease. Thus, the resulting score should be more representative of their true ability.

Another reason for arranging the items in each portion of the test in an order of ascending difficulty is to insure that some items are included that will challenge each student's ability level. There should be some items that each student can get fairly easily and some that challenge each student. In this sense, arranging the items from easier to more difficult is merely another way of acknowledging individual differences on the test. Slower students, for example, should not be expected to complete all the items if they do not feel capable of doing them. Faster students may be given extra-credit items, which will keep them occupied while the others finish the examination.

7. Avoid incorrect language. This guideline is obvious. The students make enough errors in the classroom without the teacher contributing some of her own. Equally obvious is the fact that, with some ingenuity, the teacher can test the common errors without actually committing them herself.

8. Make directions clear. The purpose of a test is to measure achievement, not cleverness in reading the directions. The students should be encouraged to ask questions if they fail to comprehend what is expected, and, if possible, the teacher should circulate through the class during the exam to check whether they did in fact understand. (Many beginning teachers are astounded to learn that asking, "Are there any questions?" is not sufficient. Many students do not know what kind of questions they should be asking. The teacher is always responsible for determining whether there indeed are questions; asking if there are any questions is usually an ineffective procedure.)

9. Prepare items in advance and prepare more than you need. The preparation of test items is a difficult and time-consuming task. Often the teacher is not aware of the weaknesses of his examinations. He can improve this situation by preparing the test in advance and by having more items than are needed. In a few days he can go over all the items again, eliminating the weaker ones. After the test, those questions which appear to be good ones can be placed in an item file for future reference. Categorizing these by structural topic will speed up location later on. The vocabulary associated with each item is easily and quickly changed.

10. Specify the material to be tested. Although the teacher may feel that the students should know what the examination will cover, and although he may have been extremely careful to convey the objectives of each class to them, he still should delineate exactly the material that will be tested. Such a summary motivates the students to study and focuses their attention on the most important concepts in the lessons while they are studying. Much time is wasted by students as they attempt to develop a learning strategy and to organize the basic knowledge to be assimilated. By outlining what should be reviewed, the teacher can assist them in spending their time more efficiently.

11. Acquaint the students with techniques. Normally there should be little difference between the normal classroom activities and test items. However, if the teacher does occasionally consider it necessary to include an innovative type of item distinct from classroom techniques, he should provide the students some practice with this type of item before counting the results as part of a grade. For example, if the teacher decides to ask the students to record their speaking tests in the language laboratory, they must first be well acquainted with the lab. Even then, he may want to consider the first test as a practice run.

12. Test in context. This concept was previously considered in the discussion of testing all four language skills. The teacher who tests vocabulary and structure has a tendency to revert to teaching a problem-solving class, i.e., one in which the teacher and the students focus on the means rather than on the ends, on the building blocks of language rather than on the application of these components to actual communication situations. He should always try to write items as similar as possible to language that would occur in actual usage. Furthermore, testing in context implies that often a contextual situation must be established clarifying for the students exactly what the correct answer would be. In distinguishing between the two past tenses in French and Spanish, for example, the teacher is almost forced to write an entire paragraph in order to establish a definite relationship between the two tenses. Even in testing a vocabulary item, a contextual situation may need to be established. For example:

Did you get the letter?
No, the _____ still has not arrived.
a. card   b. code   c. male   d. mail

13. Avoid sequential items. A sequential item is one that has two or three stages, with the later parts being dependent upon the first. Those students who fail on the first part will automatically be unable to do well on the second or third. An obvious example is giving a dictation and then asking the students to translate the paragraph into English. Those who were not able to write the dictated sentences receive a double penalty. Another example is the test item with a blank in which they are supposed to write the correct form of a verb (given in the first language) in the second language. If they do not know the vocabulary word, it is impossible for them to give the correct form of the verb.

14. Sample fairly the material covered. The teacher should strive on each examination to sample fairly all the objectives and all the various types of activities included in the lesson plans. She may be unable to write specific items testing all the concepts taught, but by randomly sampling those taught in class, she should receive scores that are representative of the students' total learning. This statement also implies two other important concepts in testing: (a) all four language skills should be tested, and (b) items of varying levels of difficulty should be included.

One effective aid for obtaining a random sample is to keep a checklist of all material covered in the view and review in each of the language skills. Using this outline, the teacher should have little difficulty sampling the content in each of the language skills at various levels of difficulty. Attempting to implement the guidelines mentioned in this paragraph, the teacher may tend toward examinations that are too long. Over any given amount of material the possibilities for items are almost unlimited, and the teacher must refrain from attempting to include everything. Testing each selected concept or form once is sufficient. In testing verbs, for example, there is no need to include more than one item testing the ability to use the first-person singular form. In fact, testing all four language skills permits the teacher to test some forms or concepts in one skill and others in another skill, thereby shortening considerably the necessary length of the test.

15. Allow sufficient time to finish. This statement must be qualified in the case of listening and speaking. All students must answer the same listening items given at the same speed. This also applies to speaking tests given in the laboratory, in which all students must respond at approximately the same time. On the written portions of the examination, however, some students will be able to finish much more quickly than others. Since this variety of speeds is common in most classes, and since having to turn in an unfinished test is frustrating to most students, the teacher should take care to allow everyone to finish before collecting the papers. He can accomplish this trick of keeping everyone busy, either by giving the faster students extra-credit questions or by permitting the slower students to omit certain difficult items on the test. The teacher is protecting the students' right to answer all the items, but he cannot permit them to sit and meditate over particular items. Quizzes especially must be completed quickly and collected. Normally, those students in a second-language class who wait for a sudden flash of inspiration continue to remain in the dark. In the case of languages, they either know it or they do not, so little is accomplished by letting the few who are unwilling to accept their fate waste valuable class time.

16. *Make the test easy to grade, if possible.* Of course, making the test easy to grade is not a primary consideration, but the teacher must arrange her time as efficiently as possible. One way of decreasing her work load is to consider beforehand the amount of time necessary to grade the examination. By choosing types of items that can be graded quickly, she can eliminate some unnecessary work. One simple example is to have the students always place their answers in a column to the left of the number of the item rather than filling in a blank or circling the letter of the correct answer in multiple-choice questions. Their answers then become a list that can be graded almost in a single glance. Another technique that greatly speeds up the grading of examinations is to grade one group of items on all the papers before continuing to the next section. By grading in this fashion, the teacher has the correct answers memorized after the first few papers, and her speed increases tremendously. Grading the entire test of each student before proceeding to the next student's paper is much slower. Writing the number of errors in each section in the margin will speed up the tabulation of the total score at the completion of the last section. Too, preparation of an answer key along with the test is a time-saving device.

Of course, grading tests in which students select answers is easier and quicker than grading tests in which students give their own answers in writing or speaking. In this sense, normally it takes less time to grade tests over the receptive skills than over the productive. This relative ease in grading, however, is counterbalanced by the fact that the preparation of good objective tests in which the students select answers take longer to prepare than short-answer and essay-type questions. Since a test covering all four skills must, by definition, include both selecting and giving answers, the teacher needs to gain expertise in preparing and grading both types of items.

17. Go over the test immediately afterwards, if possible. The students' interest is highest during and immediately after a test. The teacher should take advantage of this peak of interest by giving the correct answers as soon as he collects the papers. Some teachers prefer to have the students exchange papers and grade them in class. At any rate, the point is that an examination is also a learning experience, and as such, it is always preferable to review the correct answers with the students. The best time to clarify difficulties and doubts is at the end of the test. The students should never have to wait more than a day, possibly two, to see the results.

18. Help those students with problems to determine specific areas in need of improvement. Whether or not the test is indeed a learning device depends a great deal upon the teacher. He can return the tests with a lengthy harangue about the lethargy and apathy of the younger generation, or he can praise the students for their fine work, when they deserve it. He can scold them for the poor grades, or he can indicate just what their problems seem to be by means of short notations on the tests or in personal interviews. The student in question may need to work with sounds, with vocabulary, or with grammar. The student may need additional practice in listening, speaking, reading, and/or writing. The teacher can provide assistance not only with identifying the problems, but also with suggesting ways and means of improvement. A personal interview may also reveal affective-social problems with which the teacher can help even though they may have little to do with second-language learning per se.

19. Test each concept only once. Testing a single concept more than once not only inflates the true score of those students who know the correct answer; it deflates the true score of those students who do not know the answer. For example, in a group of items testing the students' knowledge of regular verb endings of a single class, one item testing each of the person forms in the singular and the plural covers all the concepts and forms. Additional items not only take additional time and cause extra work but falsify the results as well.

20. Give credit for what a student knows. Although the argument that a response is not correct unless it is entirely correct can be defended strongly, and often is, such a method of grading test papers is not fair to the students. A closer examination of the question often reveals that the students have been asked to make more than one decision in answering the item. It is each decision that should be given credit separately rather than one single grade that is either totally correct or totally incorrect. In working with object pronouns, for example, some students may know the correct form but err in placing them correctly in the sentence or vice versa. In choosing between the indicative and subjunctive, some may choose the right mood of the verb but fail to make it agree with its subject or vice versa. The point is that the teacher should grade from the point of view of what the students do know rather than rejecting all but perfect responses. When testing language skills, the teacher should place primary stress on the ability to communicate. Although students who take rather marked liberties with the grammar of the second language obviously do not deserve as good a grade as those who are able to express themselves with great fluency and with very few errors, they have accomplished the major goal in second-language learning, and they deserve credit for being able to communicate.

21. Distinguish between recall and recognition tests. In taking a *recognition test,* the students select the correct answer from a number of alternatives. The alternatives may range from two in true-false questions to more than two in a multiple-choice test (normally three, four, or five) to several grouped items in a matching exercise. The tendency is to have fewer distractors in listening comprehension items and more in reading items. Since listening and reading are receptive skills, recognition-type questions are most suited to the testing of these two skills.

In taking a *recall test,* the students must produce the cued responses rather than select the appropriate one. A recall test measures the students' ability to apply functional understanding in order to produce language. Recall items, then, must be used to test the productive skills, speaking and writing, since the nature of the skill itself involves production rather than recognition. One commonly used type of recall item is to ask students to write answers to personalized questions such as "What's your name?" The principle of testing only one language skill at a time can be modified in this case, since in the normal language situation the receptive skills quite commonly serve as stimuli to the productive skills.

22. Distinguish between discrete items and global items. Clark (1972) identifies discrete items and global items. A discrete item consists of a short stimulus followed either by an answer to be chosen (a recognition item) or a space for an answer to be given (a recall item). The important characteristic of a *discrete item* is that it tests only one point. An example of a discrete item is a question followed by four possible replies. An example of a *global item* is a longer passage followed by a series of questions testing comprehension of content. The purpose of such an item is to test one of the language skills in a more sustained sequence.

23. At some point in the learning sequence, the students should have to choose between various grammar structures. Tests, as well as exercises, should foster the assimilation of each component of the language system into a large, meaningful whole. To be discouraged is the memorization of fragmented chunks of information that can be placed in indicated slots on tests, but that the students cannot use in any context involving a choice. After the students have studied the past tense, they should be able to complete an exercise in which they use past tense verb forms. However, if they are going to learn to use the language, they should also be able to choose when to use the present or the past and to use both in the same exercise as the context indicates. Students should be able to complete an exercise on a test labeled *direct object pronouns.* They must also be able to reach the point at which they can use both direct and indirect object pronouns in the same exercise if they are ever to achieve any functional ability to employ these forms for purposes of communication. On each test there should be some items in which the students must make choices that indicate functional control of the components of the language system.

24. Be prepared to incorporate new types of items. The best place to find new types of test items is in the teacher's own classroom. If at all possible, the students should be asked to perform only those types of exercises and drills that they have been doing in class. There is no need to resort to the exotic or the esoteric in the preparation of test items. The object is to assess the language *skill* that has been developed in the work being done in class. However, if the teacher feels obliged to "do something different," the bibliography at the end of this chapter contains sources for "new" ideas. She should have as a ready reference the most complete listing of example test items to date, *Modern Language Testing: A Handbook* by Valette. (See Selected References.)

CONCEPTS OF TESTING

The first concept normally mentioned in a discussion of testing is that of *validity.* The test is sound when it tests what it purports to test, i.e., when it tests entirely or in a random sample all the objectives and content of the material being learned.

Another often mentioned concept is *reliability.* The implication of this term is that the test continues to give the same or similar results on successive occasions.

Both validity and reliability are concepts with which the teacher is most likely familiar even though he may not be able to define the words themselves. Certainly, he should examine his own tests to determine the relationship between the content of the examination and the activities pursued in the class.

Standard error of measurement is an important concept to be kept in mind while assigning grades for a particular score on a test. Standard error implies that a certain amount of error is part of each test score. The amount of error varies from test to test. Therefore, a student's true score probably lies between one standard error above and one standard error below the score the student received on the examination. For example, if Mary's score was 85 on a test with a standard error of 3, the odds are rather high, 68 percent, that her true score is somewhere between 82 and 88.[1]

Two other concepts with which the teacher should be familiar are *item difficulty* and *item discrimination*. Item difficulty refers to the percentage of students who answer the item correctly; item discrimination is a measure of which students answer the item correctly. Item discrimination involves comparing the student's answer on the item with her total score on the examination. For the item to have high discrimination, those students who give the correct answer should be those students who receive the higher scores on the test.

Even if the means are not available to him for a complete item analysis by computer, he may want to check the difficulty and discrimination of certain items by a show of hands in class or by a subjective estimate gained while grading the examinations. The teacher should always grade the papers or examine them carefully afterwards in order to improve his testing techniques and in order to determine what the focus of the follow-up discussion should be.

With regard to level of difficulty, only the first few items in each part of the examination should be so easy that most students will get them right. The remaining items should be increasingly difficult. One of the characteristics of a good examination is that the range of scores be sufficiently spread out to guard against chance deviation from one letter grade to another. For example, when the B's on the examination range from 59 to 61 and the standard error of measurement is 3.5, then any given student's grade could go from a C+ to an A- merely by chance. Therefore, the examination should be difficult enough to insure a proper range of scores for the purpose of assigning grades and to challenge the brighter students in the class. At the same time, the test should not be so difficult as to discourage the students. Most good test items are answered correctly by 60 to 85 percent of the students. Certainly, any item in which the correct answer is chosen by fewer than a guessing percentage is not a good item. For example, in a multiple-choice question with four possible answers, any time fewer than 25 percent of the students select the correct answer, something is wrong with the item or with the teaching leading up to the test.

With regard to discrimination, the teacher needs to keep in mind that his better students should be answering the questions correctly. He should reexamine any item answered properly by the less able students, but missed by the more capable. Such an item has obviously failed to discriminate the knowledge level of the students properly.

---

[1]Sixty-eight percent of the scores on a test having a normal distribution fall within one standard deviation above and below the mean scores on the test. *Standard error of measurement* follows the same principle. See Lemke & Wiersma (1976) in the Selected References section of this chapter.

In improving his test preparation, the teacher should begin by reconsidering his objectives and his classroom activities in relation to the test. After this, he can begin to revise the items themselves. Many items, of course, will need to be discarded or completely revised. Others may need to have only one distractor changed to improve the quality of the item. All distractors should make sense if they are to fulfill their function. Writing three distractors that would seem plausible if the students do not completely understand the item requires a great deal of thought and time. A good item is often ruined by the failure to work on the item until the teacher thinks of satisfactory distractors. Writing the stimulus and the answer is not too difficult. The secret to a successful item, however, is equivalent to the success of the distractors. Since writing such items does require much time, the teacher should, in his own self-interest, begin an item file during his first year of teaching and faithfully improve and expand it in succeeding years.

Sample Objective Test Items

The following examples are not intended to provide a classification of item types, but to demonstrate the concepts of item difficulty and item discrimination. The items are designed to test listening comprehension and reading. The items are multiple choice, and the correct answer depends either on an application of knowledge of vocabulary or an understanding of structure. Item difficulty, i.e., the proportion choosing each alternative, is given in the first column to the left of the letter of each choice. Item discrimination, i.e., the alternative correlation with total score, is given in the right column. A good item has a high positive correlation in the left column opposite the correct answer, and high negative correlations in the right column opposite the incorrect answers. These correlations indicate that the students with the higher scores on the test chose the correct answer and vice versa.

1. Good listening comprehension and/or reading items (vocabulary):

J'habite New York. Je n'ai pas envie de prendre le bateau pour aller en France. Cette fois je vais prendre _____.

.188	-.255	a. le train
.079	-.237	b. l'autocar
.109	-.160	c. le métro
.624	.441	*d. l'avion

Señora, ¿quiere usted que sirva la carne ahora?

.020	-.118	a. ¿Cuánto es la ganancia?
.608	.430	*b. No, espere usted un rato.
.137	-.219	c. Sí, hay mucho ganado.
.235	-.279	d. No sirve para nada.

2. Good listening comprehension and/or reading item (grammar):

¿Vinieron ellos a la inauguración?
.641 .370   *a. No, no pudieron aceptar la invitación.
.109 -.260   b. Sí, pude ir.
.250 -.222   c. No, no vinimos en coche.

3. Good reading item (grammar):

—¿Se va a casar con el rubio o con el moreno?
—Eso no lo _____ hasta el domingo próximo.
.083 -.267   a. supimos
.229 -.221   b. saldremos
.458 .503   *c. sabremos
.229 -.200   d. sepamos

All the preceding items are good items from the point of view of item difficulty and item discrimination because an acceptable portion of the students answered the questions correctly. The positive correlations with correct answers and negative correlations with incorrect answers indicate that the better students answered the items correctly. Item number 3 was difficult, but the figures show that its discriminative power was very high, i.e., the best students got the question right. Even the best items can be improved. In the preceding examples some distractors were chosen by a very small percentage of the students. Some distractors should be changed for more realistic choices if the students have not understood the items completely.

4. Poor listening comprehension and/or reading item (vocabulary):

Wo kommen Sie her?
.543 .096   a. Sie kommt aus Clinton in Iowa.
.163 .010   b. Ich komme mit dem Zug.
.209 -.018   *c. Ich komme aus Lafayette.
.085 -.159   d. Sie fahren nach Deutschland.

5. Poor reading item (vocabulary):

Bonn ist _____ der Bundesrepublik Deutschland.
.008 -.211   a. das Gebäude
.938 .131   *b. die Hauptstadt
.008 -.076   c. die Reihe
.047 .031   d. der Salz

6. Poor listening comprehension and/or reading item (grammar):

¿Qué era necesario?
.188 .155   *a. Que dejara el puesto.
.708 -.282   b. Que pague la cuenta.
.104 .221   c. Que lo llamó anoche.

7. Poor reading item (grammar):

Paul rêve de son voyage à Paris. Il _____ pense souvent.
.386 .172   a. en
.123 -.171   b. le
.465 -.023   *c. y
.026 -.099   d. lui

An item is inherently poor because it is either too difficult or too easy or because it fails to discriminate between those students receiving higher scores and those receiving lower scores on the test.[2] The results obtained from any item may be unsatisfactory either because of a flaw or because the students had not been taught to make the correct selection.

In the preceding examples the correlations indicate that these items were not discriminating between better and slower students. In item number 4, for example, the better students were guessing either a or b with a few of the better and a few of the slower choosing c. Too, the correct answer was chosen by fewer than a guessing percentage. The only definite information obtained from the item was that students who chose d did not do well on the test in general and that it was a poor item in particular. Distractors a, b, and c should be rewritten.

For ranking purposes, item 5 was too easy and failed to discriminate. Distractors a, c, and d need to be changed, the first two to more plausible choices and d to an item that will not deceive almost 5 percent of the better students.

Item 6 has an unsatisfactory difficulty correlation, and the discrimination correlations reveal that the better students selected c, a wrong answer, and the slower students chose b, also incorrect. The item would seem to be a good one, but the results reveal that it is not. One can only conclude that this item

---

[2]The reader should recognize that the purpose of criterion-referenced tests is to determine what the students have learned. Therefore, the concepts of item difficulty and item discrimination are much less important than the validity of the test when the teacher is stressing achievement of course content rather than student ranking. However, although often used to obtain rankings, this same type of discrete item can serve a very useful function to test specific aspects of the second language. In other words, good objective test items often used for ranking purposes can also be used as criterion-referenced items.

was not valid for the group of students taking the test. Evidently, they had not learned to distinguish between a cue that would elicit past subjunctive and present subjunctive or between indicative and subjunctive.

In the case of item 7, almost 47 percent of the students answered the question correctly, but almost 39 percent of the better students chose a as the correct answer. Either the context of the stimulus did not make the meaning entirely clear to the students, or they had not learned the difference between *en* and *y* and the contexts in which each is used. Changing distractor a would eliminate much of the problem with the item, but the results seem to indicate that the difference between *en* and *y* should be retaught.

The reader should notice that many of the same items can be used to test either listening comprehension or reading. Of course, those that are too long, too complex, or that have blanks in the middle of the sentence should be rewritten. Too, the reader should realize that item analysis reveals the problem, i.e., what should be changed, but not the solution.

TESTING PROCEDURES

Learning requires feedback. Otherwise, the learners have no means of judging the extent and appropriateness of their learning. Although the second-language learners' feedback should not be limited to the objective testing program, carefully prepared tests can be an important component in clarifying progress to the students and in specifying individual strengths and weaknesses.

Tests can encourage or discourage. Tests can promote cognitive achievement and productive affective-social attitudes, or they can produce negative effects, canceling much of the teacher's gains in choosing suitable objectives and teaching-learning activities for the students. For the most part, student reaction depends upon how well the teacher correlates the content of the tests with class goals and activities. Students who participate in class, learn the material, and practice the skills should know what to expect on a test and they should be able to do well. Tests should support, not surprise. Test format should be consistent and predictable from classroom activities.

One testing procedure that provides feedback in a supportive manner is to give a short, formative, self-graded test over each grammar item during the class period following its coverage in the view class activities. The format is quite simple. The teacher gives the students five or six items. To answer these items the students must demonstrate a knowledge of the structure being studied. Afterwards, the students supply the correct answers, thereby giving all students an opportunity to grade their papers and an opportunity to check their progress up to that point. Answering the questions takes only a few minutes, yet each student receives regular progress reports prior to the graded test.

Testing Competence

Since the second-language learner must understand the language system in order to use the language to communicate, approximately one half of each test should be designed to test comprehension of and ability to produce and manipulate the components of the language system. At the beginning levels, when the students are working with hearing, pronouncing, reading, and writing sounds, the student's knowledge of the sound system should be tested. Also, each test should contain items designed to determine the student's knowledge of the grammar and the vocabulary of the unit. At more advanced levels, items testing the sound system are less important, but grammar and vocabulary should continue to be emphasized.

The teacher should remember in preparing test items that the objective is to test student *understanding* of the language *system*. That is, she should construct the items in such a way that the students cannot answer rotely. Given the limited time available in any class period, items such as *Give the first-language equivalents of the following list of words,* and *Write the first-person singular of each of the following irregular verbs,* should be discarded in favor of such items as *Give the words that will correctly complete each of the following sentences,* and *Write the appropriate forms of the verb* to be *in the following conversation.* Too, all structures taught should be tested. Tests that contain only grammar items do not cover the entire spectrum of the language system. Testing for competence should also cover, as taught, vocabulary and sounds.

Some teachers may test only rote learning of vocabulary and grammar. Others test in context, but they test only grammar with a few vocabulary items for variety. Still others may want to test only performance skills and to ignore entirely items geared toward the validation of the acquisition of competence. As attractive as the latter may appear, following such a procedure would be detrimental to student learning for two important reasons. First, including items on grammar, vocabulary, and sounds encourages students to study and learn the component elements of the language. If they have been asked to learn a list of vocabulary words in the lesson, some of those words should appear on the test. Second, the results of test items over the basic unit material summarize for the students specific concepts and content that should be reviewed and indicate to them how they may strive to improve in future units.

Where does the teacher obtain types of test items? The answer is simple—from the text and from selected classroom activities. (Examples of exercises designed to develop competence are given in each of the skill chapters and in the chapters on general guidelines and lesson planning.) These are exercises in which the students demonstrate the ability to produce and manipulate forms in meaningful contexts. From the point of view of instructional objectives, items testing for competence are based on cognitive-behavioral objectives. If the teacher decides, for some reason, that types of items other than those previously practiced in class should be incorporated into tests, she should purposefully make them a part of the class hour on occasion so that the students will be prepared for such items.

Testing Performance Skills

Performance skills involve the receiving or sending of messages in the second language. Approximately one half of each test should involve testing each student's ability to go from thought to language or vice versa. The student should be aware from the beginning of the course that he will be expected to demonstrate on each test an answer to the question, "What can you do with what you have learned in this unit?" Accomplishment of communicative competence is a must in any second-language class. (This statement is not meant to deny the value of second-language classes taught in the first language, a common practice in some schools at present. However, their value lies in areas other than language study per se.)

As is true when testing for competence, ideas for the format and content of performance skills tests should come directly from the classroom activities. (Examples of performance skills activities are given in each of the skill chapters and in the chapter on lesson planning.) Whatever second-language activities the students have been doing in class they should be expected to do on the test. These activities should be practically the same as those practiced in the "real" language portions of the class hour. The students should be able to talk about material in the text and be able to relate the content to their own lives. For example, the students have just had a unit dealing with the future tense in which they had opportunities to use real language skills dealing with their future career plans. For the test, they should be prepared to listen to and give a summary (in the first language) of a conversation on tape in which a similar topic is discussed; to read similar material; to tell or write about their plans; or to carry on a conversation with someone else about future hopes, dreams, and plans. The objectives being tested in this portion of the test are a combination of cognitive, behavioral, and affective-social. One suggestion for encouraging student input and for focusing the students' attention during the course of the unit is to invite them to assist in the selection of topics to be used in class activities, and subsequently to be a part of the examination over the unit.

For the most part, items testing for competence will be discrete. Tests of performance skills may contain both discrete and global items, but items requiring sustained reception or production of language will, of necessity, be global. Although some teachers shy away from the use of global items because they are more time-consuming to grade and less objective, the qualities inherent in the communication process mandate that such items be included in tests of productive performance skills. At this stage of testing, objectivity, which has been maintained in testing for competence and in other lower-level performance skills, is less important than the necessity of demonstrating to the student that the ability to use the language in a "real" language situation is an important goal. The preceding statement is not meant to imply that the teacher should not strive to maintain as much objectivity as possible in grading speaking tests and essays, but to stress the need for such items, whatever their shortcomings. For example, as a means of maintaining objectivity, many teachers have used oral multiple-choice items to test listening comprehension, yet even native speakers have trouble with such items. Answering an oral multiple-choice question demands extreme concentration and a high ability to abstract. A more practical approach would be to read the students a narrative or a conversation and let them summarize (in the first language) the main points of what they understood. Scoring can be accomplished by counting a set number of points for each piece of information the student mentions, with comprehension being the basic criterion.

One of the problems associated with global items is establishing a fair grading system. One system is to determine the characteristics of the speaking or writing to be assessed. For example, the teacher may decide to grade pronunciation, grammar usage, vocabulary usage, and general fluency in speaking and the latter three in writing. He can then establish criteria such as the following:

(5) expresses himself well with practically no errors
(3) communicates fairly well but with noticeable errors
(1) practically incomprehensible
(0) no response

The resultant score can be converted into any number of points allotted to the item by multiplying.

Another problem with regard to global items is the amount of time required to grade student answers. A practical solution is to divide this portion of the test into two parts: one fourth for a receptive skill and one fourth for a productive skill. The particular skills being tested can be rotated so that the teacher does not have quite so much work to do on any given test. For example, he might give a listening comprehension test and a writing test over one unit. The next unit test would contain a reading and a speaking test. This procedure permits the teacher to test all four language skills periodically without making the work load too burdensome. The ideal, of course, is to test all four language skills on each examination; and if the teacher has the time and energy, he should do so.

In this author's opinion, one way to improve testing is to permit as much individual variation as possible. With regard to sounds and grammar the system is finite, so each student must of necessity learn as much of the system as her ability allows. However, vocabulary is an almost infinite system, and it is a personal system as well. No two people have the same vocabulary or the same preference for words commonly used. It would seem that each student might well be given the prerogative of learning those words, within agreed-upon guidelines, that she feels would be most useful to her. One way to accomplish such a goal and to relieve the students of the burden of attempting to memorize each and every word in the unit is to grant the students the privilege of choosing which vocabulary items they want to answer. The same is true for the four language skills. Each is an infinite system, and we should permit each student the right to express herself in her own unique way. By focusing on the ability to communicate with regard to the topics of the unit rather than on specific grammar and vocabulary to be used to talk about the topic, the teacher recognizes that the conversion of thought to language is a personal, creative process that will be different for each second-language learner.

Testing Speaking

Because speaking tests are seldom given in the language classroom, this facet of testing is being given special consideration in this chapter. The exclusion of speaking tests should not be too severely criticized because the reasons for not including them are practical and valid. Some teachers are not aware of the various techniques for testing speaking. Others feel that a subjective evaluation based on classroom performance is sufficient. For those who do not have language laboratories, systematic procedures are difficult, if not impossible. Tests to accompany most textbooks do not include sections testing the speaking skill. And last, but certainly not least, is the question of time. Many teachers feel they do not have the time to prepare or grade speaking tests.

On the other hand, the teacher cannot expect her students to take seriously any goal that is not tested. Their whole educational background has conditioned them to study for examinations and to consider that the content of these examinations covers the important objectives of the course. Therefore, if the teacher is really serious about having the students concentrate on speaking, she must include some form of testing on speaking ability. Granted such testing does take more time, but good teaching takes time. Written tests take more time to grade than listening or reading tests, but such tests are commonly given.

As was mentioned previously, the most common way of evaluating the students' speaking ability is the teacher's subjective evaluation of the students' work in class. Certainly this approach is practical in that it takes very little time. The disadvantage is that no class grade can be as important psychologically to the students as a test grade. However, if the teacher decides that she does not have the time to do more in testing speaking, she should emphasize to the students that they are being given a grade on their speaking ability and that this grade is an important part of their grade in the course. To assist the students in improving and to demonstrate to the students that this grade is indeed a fact, she should keep notes on the students' progress and point out to them at the end of each grading period what their grades are and what their weaknesses and strengths are. She should tell them, for example, those sounds they pronounce well and those they need to improve. She can even point out specific structures that they use only hesitantly or not at all and suggest work on which they might concentrate to better their oral mark.

A preferable alternative to the class grade as an indication of speaking ability is to give short speaking tests in class. In this type of test the teacher prepares a long list of personalized questions based on the material being tested. She then proceeds down the list, asking questions of students in a random fashion. As they answer, she grades their responses. By asking the question, waiting a few seconds for the students to formulate an answer, and demanding a prompt reply, the teacher has sampled quite well the students' ability to answer personalized questions based on the vocabulary and structural content of the text. The advantages of this approach are that it does stress in a test situation the importance of the ability to speak the language, and it is not especially time-consuming. The disadvantages are that only the ability to answer teacher-chosen questions is tested and that asking all students questions that are equally difficult is impossible.

Another version of the procedure outlined in the preceding paragraph is to ask the students to come to the teacher's desk to answer personalized questions from a prepared list. The teacher may, for example, ask each student five or ten questions. In asking the questions, he must be careful to insist upon definite time limits as the students respond. The good students can answer up to ten questions per minute or more, but slower students need more time. One solution to this problem is to ask each student questions for one minute. The results are then scaled and letter grades assigned.

Another method of testing speaking in the case of more advanced students is to require them to come in for a personal interview. The advantage of this procedure is that it resembles very closely a true language situation. The disadvantage is that some students will most likely be even more nervous during the interview than in the normal test situation. Also, the grade must be assigned on the basis of a global, subjective evaluation. If the teacher decides to test speaking by means of a personal interview, she should prepare the students carefully and provide them with definite topics upon which to focus their study while preparing for the test.

A practical procedure for testing interaction in groups of two or more is to have students make a recording. A topic, chosen from those practiced during the work with the unit in class, is given to the students. They then go to some quiet spot where they use a tape recorder to record their conversation. Their performance is later graded by the teacher. Ideally, someone is present to handle the tape recorder and to prompt the students if they need assistance.

For those teachers whose schools have tape recorders in all the booths in the language laboratory, the fairest, most objective, most complete, and in the long run probably the most efficient approach to testing speaking is to record the students' answers. The advantages to this procedure for testing are many: (1) All students answer the same questions. (2) The teacher can stop the tapes as she grades in order to be completely sure of the grade she is giving. (3) All difficulty levels of the speaking skill from pronunciation to sustained oral response to a single stimulus can be included. Oral pattern drills, for example, which are basic to the audio-lingual technique of skill development and which are seldom tested as they are taught, can be an important part of a test given in the laboratory. Such a test becomes a true test of the skill that the students have been practicing. The disadvantage is that, in the beginning, such a test may take a considerable amount of time. (This author found, for example, that it is possible to give a speaking test containing 125 points in a recorded time of fifteen minutes. The recorded student responses varied from two to three minutes.)

There are two time-consuming blocks to efficient testing in the laboratory that the teacher should plan to eliminate before considering seriously the possibility of giving speaking tests in the laboratory. First, the students must record only their responses, not the stimuli. Second, the individual student tapes should all be transferred to a single tape. The first problem can be solved by recording the examination in the following fashion. After the stimulus, the teacher should allow approximately ten seconds for the students to prepare their responses. She then makes a sound on the tape, a bell perhaps, which indicates to the students that they are to start their tape recorders and give their answers. As soon as she has had time to give the answer twice quickly, she signals the students to stop their tape recorders and get ready for the next question. It is extremely important that the procedure outlined above be carefully followed for two reasons. First, unless all students answer at approximately the same time (the pause before responding facilitates the probability of some synchronization), the slower students merely need to imitate their neighbors' answers. Second, if the students are permitted to turn off their recorders as soon as their answers are completed, the teacher will not have sufficient time to record the grades without stopping the tape recorder. The second problem is easily solved by having a lab assistant collect the tapes and rerecord the students' answers all on one tape. It is doubtful that grading such a tape will require any more time than grading a typical writing test.

Testing Culture

Often students do not realize that the teacher is attempting to teach aspects of the second-language culture. One of the principal reasons for this lack of awareness is that culture is usually not a fundamental component of the class content. The teacher may attend to culture by inserting ideas as they occur to him during the class period and subsequently fail to check student comprehension or recall of these points on the test. If culture is to be an important goal in the second-language class, it must be taught and tested systematically. Currently, the most practical approach to testing culture is to test the facts.

TYPES OF GRADING SYSTEMS

In recent years, due to an expressed dissatisfaction with grades and grading systems by some educators, alternative grading systems have been developed and adopted on an experimental basis.[3] The most common types of grading systems that are currently practiced in the schools are as follows:

1. Traditional letter grades or percentage grades. These are still the most commonly used among all the grading systems.

2. Essay type evaluation and conferences. This is the second most commonly practiced approach, especially in the elementary schools.

3. An advising system. In this approach the students are advised as to their progress. However, grades are given without the student's knowledge and kept on record.

4. The contract system. The student makes an agreement with the teacher that says that if he does a given amount of work he will receive a certain grade. The student has the option of choosing the amount of work and the grade he wants to work for at the beginning of the contract.

5. The mastery approach. Based on predetermined behavioral objectives the students must demonstrate mastery of the material at a teacher-selected level (commonly 80 percent) before he is permitted to move on to new content.

6. Pass/fail. Normally, the student's grade record is kept by the teacher. However, only pass or fail is entered into the student's permanent record. *Credit versus no credit* is another name for this type of approach.

---

[3]Much of the organization and content of this section is based on "Testing as Communication" by Jorstad. See Jorstad (1974) in the Selected References section of this chapter.

7. *Blanket grading.* Under this system all students receive the same grade.

8. *Variable credit.* In individualized classes, some schools have adopted the practice of giving credit for the work that the student does during the course of the semester or year. As soon as the student finishes so much material, he receives credit for that work. He may receive credit for more or less than a year's work depending upon the material covered.

9. *Credit only.* An idea associated with variable credit is to grant credit only. No failures are ever recorded on the student's record. If and when he completes his work successfully, he receives credit for what he has learned.

10. *Retaking examinations.* Another practice closely related to the recording of credit only is that of permitting students to retake examinations if the scores are unsatisfactory. The justification for retesting is that the primary goal is to get the students to learn the material.

Closely allied to the movement away from the more popular traditional grading system (which Jorstad [1974] says has slowed down considerably) has been the obvious grade inflation that has tended to accomplish the goals of those opposing grades without abolishing the grading system as such. Jorstad (1974), for example, quotes a survey conducted by the Minneapolis Public Schools which found that of the letter grades reported in the senior high schools in Minneapolis, 25 percent were A's. In second-language classes almost 50 percent of the grades were A's. A comparison of grades received with scores received on the SAT examinations indicates a lack of consistency somewhere in the students' educational program.

GRADING AND RECORDING GRADES

Evaluation is a continual process beginning with the first day of class and ending when the final grades are given. During this period, both subjective, informal judgments and prepared tests are utilized in order to obtain a complete picture of instruction and student achievement. Both forms of evaluation are equally important, but they are utilized in different ways. Subjective evaluation by the teacher of student performance in the classroom serves primarily as feedback to the teacher, and the students, of how things are going. This immediate feedback enables the teacher to make adjustments that will improve weaknesses in her teaching procedures. Classwork also provides the students with immediate feedback relating to their progress in the class.

For the purposes of assigning a letter grade in the course, more objective types of measurement are generally used. Test results provide black-and-white statistics upon which to base grades. Often students are reluctant to accept grades based on subjective estimates of achievement, but they are able to understand and accept test scores. Test results also impress upon students their strengths and weaknesses in language much more strongly and more clearly than do success or failure during class recitation. In this sense, tests are more for the students, and for the parents, than for the teacher. Nor should the teacher allow herself to be misled by groans of complaint at the mention of examinations. In spite of the fact that most students dislike having to take tests, most in moments of seriousness will admit their value. Certainly, a good grade on a test is a positive reinforcement for a job well done and an incentive for those who scored lower than their capability to work harder next time.

The teacher should always have all students' grades legibly recorded in the grade book. The grades should be arranged in an orderly fashion with the final grade based on a fair and impartial system. Any student or parent should have the right to see these grades and to check to determine whether an error was made in calculation. In fact, the teacher should encourage those students who do not understand their grades to come in *after* school, so that she can show them how the grades were determined.

There are various systems for recording grades. Some teachers record letter grades, others use a ten-point scale, and others use a percentage scale of one hundred points. The specific system chosen depends, of course, on the teacher's preference, but after she has decided, she should always: (1) convert any and all test and quiz scores to that system in order to facilitate adding all the scores at the end of the grading period, and (2) carefully explain the system (and in the case of numbers, how they are converted to letter grades) to the students at the beginning of the year and encourage them to keep track of their grades. No alert student should be surprised by the grade he receives. Although less manipulation of figures is required using letter grades and a ten-point scale, the scale of one hundred points spreads the students' scores out in a broader range and makes it much easier to distinguish between letter grades. At times, the teacher using the other systems may become involved with fractions that may make fine distinctions confusing.

CONCLUSION

Although some teachers and many students have been increasingly critical of tests and testing programs, teaching and learning without some form of continuous and cumulative evaluation of learning seems idealistic, impractical, and inefficient. Learning implies change, but change that is undertaken without careful consideration of the results of prior learning may be more harmful than beneficial. Classroom evaluation, both the spur-of-the-moment, subjective judgments and the more formal, prepared tests, provides the necessary feedback to maximize the effectiveness of classroom instruction and the efficiency of classroom learning. Distasteful as the process and the results may be at times, both to the teacher who has to prepare and to grade the tests and to the students who have to prepare for and take them, they do furnish needed bases for the teacher to improve his teaching and for the students to expand their knowledge of and ability in the subject. Subjective evaluation and prepared classroom tests remain important components in the instructional process. Not only do they provide feedback in learning, but they also help to motivate and, in the case of those students who do well, give a feeling of satisfaction for a job well done.

REVIEW AND APPLICATION

DEFINITIONS

1. contract system of grading, p. 509
2. discrete vs. global items, p. 496
3. domain-referenced test, p. 488
4. item difficulty, p. 498
5. item discrimination, p. 498
6. mastery system, p. 488
7. recall vs. recognition items, p. 496
8. reliability, p. 497
9. standard error, p. 497
10. validity, p. 497
11. variable credit, p. 510

DISCUSSION

1. Discuss the relationship between subjective and objective evaluation.
2. Outline the relationship among objectives, classroom activities, and test items.
3. Discuss the various types of tests and the purposes and uses of each type.
4. What type of test format would best incorporate the general guidelines for testing?
5. Recall and examine with the other members of the class the types of test items that have been included in past second-language tests you have taken.
6. Discuss the problem of recording and giving grades, especially the emotional aspects of grading, both from the students' and teacher's points of view.
7. Is the test really a learning device as used in the typical classroom? Explain why or why not.
8. What is your opinion of grade inflation? Should some changes be made? If so, what?

ACTIVITIES

1. Examine copies of different types of tests and classroom tests prepared by different second-language teachers. Discuss the good and bad points of each type.

2. Prepare an objective, an activity, and a test item for (a) competence, (b) a performance skill, and (c) an aspect of culture.
3. Prepare a test over the week's lesson plan you did in chapter 14.

SELECTED REFERENCES

Birznieks, P., and Birznieks, M. (1966) Written Production Tests for the Audio-Lingual Classroom. *German Quarterly*, 29: 358–64.

Bockman, J. F., and Bockman, V. M. (1973) Contracts versus the Commitment Process. *Foreign Language Annals*, 6: 359–66.

Bornscheuer, J. H. (1973) The Grade Contract and the Language Class. *Foreign Language Annals*, 6: 367–70.

Brière, E. J. (1971) Are We Really Measuring Proficiency with Our Foreign Language Tests? *Foreign Language Annals*, 4: 385–91.

Brooks, N. (1964) *Language and Language Learning* (2nd ed.) New York: Harcourt Brace & World. Pp. 199–225.

Brooks, N. (1967) Making Your Own Tests. In M. R. Donoghue (Ed.), *Foreign Languages and the Schools*. Dubuque, Iowa: William C. Brown. Pp. 285–302.

Bryant, W. H. (1975) On Grading Compositions Objectively. *Canadian Modern Language Review*, 31: 260–63.

Carroll, J. B., and Sapon, S. M. (1958) *Modern Language Aptitude Test*. New York: Psychological Corp.

Chastain, K. (1965) *Testing Program* (and *Key*) *for Spanish for Secondary Schools*. New York: Heath.

Chastain, K. (1969) Prediction of Success in Audio-Lingual and Cognitive Classes. *Language Learning*, 19: 27–39.

Clark, J. L. D. (1972) *Foreign Language Testing: Theory and Practice*. Philadelphia: Center for Curriculum Development.

Davies, A. (Ed.) (1968) *Language Testing Symposium: A Psycholinguistic Approach*. London: Oxford University Press.

Deitz, P. (1961) An Oral Performance Rating Sheet. *French Review*, 35: 54–58.

Educational Technology, vol. 14, June, 1974.

Gordon, W. T. (1974) Object-Oriented Oral Testing. *Canadian Modern Language Review*, 31: 72–74.

Grittner, F. M. (1969) *Teaching Foreign Languages*. New York: Harper & Row. Pp. 341–60.

Harris, D. P. (1969) *Testing English as a Second Language*. New York: McGraw-Hill.

Huebener, T. (1965) *How to Teach Foreign Languages Effectively* (rev. ed.) New York: New York University Press. Pp. 212–25.

Jakobovits, L. A. (1970) Foreign Language Attitude Questionnaire. In J. A. Tursi (Ed.), *Foreign Languages and the "New" Student*. Northeast Conference Reports. Pp. 17–30.

Jarvis, G. A. (1970) Systematic Preparation of the Multiple-Choice Listening Test. *NALLD Journal*, 5: 18–25.

Jorstad, H. L. (1974) Testing as Communication. In G. A. Jarvis (Ed.), *The Challenge of Communication*. Skokie, Ill.: National Textbook. Pp. 223–73.

Kalivoda, T. B. (1970) Oral Testing in Secondary Schools. *Modern Language Journal*, 54: 328–31.

Lemke, E., and Wiersma, W. (1976) *Principles of Psychological Measurement*. Chicago: Rand McNally.

Macintosh, H. G., and Morrison, R. B. (1969) *Objective Testing*. London: University of London Press.

Modern Language Association (1965) *MLA-Cooperative Foreign Language Tests*. Princeton, N.J.: Educational Testing Service.

Pimsleur, P. (1965) *The Pimsleur Language*

Aptitude Battery. New York: Harcourt Brace & World.

Pimsleur, P. (1966) Testing Foreign Language Learning. In A. Valdman (Ed.), *Trends in Language Teaching.* New York: McGraw-Hill. Pp. 175–214.

Pimsleur, P. (1970) New Approaches to Old Problems Through Testing. *Canadian Modern Language Review,* 27: 23–32.

Politzer, R. L. (1970) *Practice-Centered Teacher Training: French (Spanish).* Philadelphia: Center for Curriculum Development.

Rivers, W. M. (1968) *Teaching Foreign-Language Skills.* Chicago: University of Chicago Press. Pp. 286–317.

Stack, E. M. (1960) *The Language Laboratory and Modern Language Teaching.* New York: Oxford University Press. Pp. 128–31.

Stack, E. M. (1966) *The Language Laboratory and Modern Language Teaching.*

(rev. ed.) New York: Oxford University Press. Pp. 184–207.

Upshur, J. A., and Fata, J. (Eds.) (1968) Problems in Foreign Language Testing. *Language Learning,* Special Issue.

Valette, R. M. (1965) Oral Objective Testing in the Classroom. *German Quarterly,* 38: 179–87.

Valette, R. M. (1967a) Improving Multiple-Choice Grammar Tests in German. *German Quarterly,* 40: 87–91.

Valette, R. M. (1967b) Laboratory Quizzes: A Means of Increasing Laboratory Effectiveness. *Foreign Language Annals,* 1: 45–48.

Valette, R. M. (1967c) *Modern Language Testing: A Handbook.* New York: Harcourt Brace & World.

Wright, W. A. (1970) Testing: Examples and Suggestions for Use with L. F. I., Level 1. *Canadian Modern Language Review,* 27: 33–43.

Conclusion to Part Two

How the task of the second-language teacher has changed! In the "good old days" teaching grammar and correcting a few translations were deemed sufficient. Teachers explained, and the students absorbed. The work became harder as the goal changed to one of drilling language habits into the students. Teachers expended huge amounts of energy orchestrating the class in choral, group, and individual drill. Now the ideal has shifted to teaching the "whole" person. Suddenly, the teachers' obligations have multiplied enormously. In response to the exigencies of the times, teachers are being asked to deal with the students' emotional as well as their mental growth.

The teacher's expanding role would be difficult enough if all she had to consider was a greater responsibility for the students' attitudes and feelings. At the same time, however, the more recent theories of learning and language support models that make her tasks of choosing objectives, selecting appropriate teaching-learning activities, and evaluating student achievement even more complex than that of her predecessors in second-language teaching. The second-language teacher now faces the assignment of teaching the whole spectrum of language skills to the whole student.

The overall goal of part 2 of this text has been to deal with these new emphases in second-language teaching. The complexities of the task are tremendous, but so is the potential for improving second-language teaching. As means are sought to accommodate their increased responsibilities, teachers must consider their students' psychomotor, cognitive, and affective-social characteristics. Their conception of the student must encompass the students' psychomotor and mental capabilities, attitudes, and social relationships.

As the teacher prepares objectives and selects teaching-learning activities for the students, he can conceive of learning as being either internally or externally directed. For example, he can view learning as being under his direction in that he controls the stimuli and the reinforcers, or he can think of learning as being under the control of the learner in that learning is internally activated and directed. He can think of the learner as needing to be conditioned and reinforced, or he can think of the learner as needing to be guided and assisted. He can think of learners as being shaped or as shaping their own learning. The indications are that the teacher will encounter both types of learners in his classes. Based on research findings and the need to promote internally directed learners, the approach taken in this text has been to outline cognitive procedures best suited for internally directed learners and to recommend supplementary conditioning drills for those students who require additional habit-formation practice.

The order in which second-language skills are taught seems to vary depending upon the objectives involved and the second-language learner's level of proficiency. In teaching the sound system and sound-symbol association, the teacher proceeds in the following fashion: listening, speaking, reading, and writing. However, in developing competence, i.e., in learning vocabulary and structural patterns, and in initial stages of productive performance, the written skills should realistically precede the other skills. This is due to the fact that they can be processed at slower speeds and therefore can serve as a preliminary step toward the high-speed, mental processing necessary in the oral skills. At intermediate and advanced levels many students would seem to have the requisite base to go from any of the four language skills to any other provided the linguistic and semantic level of the content is not beyond their level of learning. At any level any language skill can reinforce content learned in any of the other skills.

During the entire language-learning sequence the teacher must be constantly concerned with student reaction and attitude. Attitude affects achievement, and achievement in turn affects attitude. In order to promote positive attitudes, the teacher tries to maintain a sensitivity to the class atmosphere and to be responsive to changes occurring from time to time. She wants the students to do well, and she lets them know it. She is ready to support her interest in them with positive actions. She realizes that the students must be willing to do the work to gain an elementary competence in the language and that they must be interested in participating in real language activities in the class. She is especially mindful of the fact that communicative competence involves affective as well as cognitive and behavioral components and that productive skills must be generated internally by the students.

As the class progresses through the year, the teacher's major concern is with "maximizing." First, he needs to maximize student satisfaction and confidence. Second, he needs to maximize the percentage of students who are actively participating at any one time in the class. Third, he needs to maximize the amount of class time that is spent productively in real language activities. And fourth, he needs to maximize student familiarity with the second-language culture.

As teachers seek to maximize positive student attitudes, participation, and achievement, they first attempt to present all new material in a way that is meaningful to the students. From this cognitive base, they assist the students in gaining an internalized competence in the language system and afterwards provide opportunities for receiving and producing meaning-carrying messages in the second language both individually and in social interaction situations. They attend to all components of language and all stages of the second-language learning sequence, and they sequence the material to facilitate student progress. During the entire process, they are watchful for those students having difficulties and are prepared to help them overcome their problems. The procedures for achieving competence and/or for correcting deficiencies depend upon the needs of the particular student.

In order to use the available class time as efficiently as possible, the teacher is ever alert to ways in which to diminish the percentage of the class devoted to the production and manipulation of language forms. Two promising techniques for accomplishing this objective at the moment are to: (1) ask the students to learn to produce and manipulate forms in take-home cognitive writing exercises, and (2) combine the practice of forms and communication in meaningful exercises and activities.

Given the current state of knowledge concerning language learning, delineating all the specific characteristics of language learning is not possible. However, the assumption can be made that two factors are always involved in language learning. First, from the point of view of the learner and his internalized language system, all language learning is meaningful. Second, all real language exchanges involve the exchange of meaning. In this sense, the vital components of any language situation are that they be meaningful and that they convey meaning from one speaker of the language to another.

The greatest need in second-language teaching is to develop additional ways and means of relating the language to the students and of practicing real language skills in real situations within the classroom context. More activities that could occur in the second-language situation with which the students can identify and in which they are interested are needed. The learner must be given many opportunities to "play with" the creative construction of language. He must be put into situations in which language becomes thought and vice versa.

The challenge presently facing second-language educators is to make language learning in the classroom come alive for the students. What is needed is greater insight into and an expanded vision of how this reality and vitality can be best achieved for each student. Following the general sequence and procedures suggested in part 2 of this text is a beginning, but the author's desire is that each teacher will add his personal contribution to improving the science of our art and the art of our science.

APPENDIX 1
THE FIRST DAY OF CLASS

The first day is the most important day in any given class. From this first encounter with a second language and with the teacher, the students form their initial impressions of what the class is going to be like. From the teacher's point of view, the first class, especially for a first-year teacher, may be quite nerve-racking. The new teacher is not only nervous; often she is concerned about a plan to follow on the first day. The more experienced teachers need to reconsider each year what they do on this all-important day. In general, there are several subjects to be included on the first day of class.

1. Greeting. First, the teacher should manage a warm, sincere smile as he welcomes the students to his class. The greeting can be in the second language. Whether they understand exactly is not important. They will get the message that in this class they are going to learn to speak and use the second language.

2. Administrative chores. As quickly as possible, the administrative details, such as the completion of enrollment forms, seating charts, or whatever, should be dispensed with.

3. Getting acquainted. Give the students cards asking them to write such personal information as name, address, phone number, etc. on the front. On the back of the card they can write a short autobiography and a summary of their major interests and activities. (This information can be a most valuable source of information during the course of the semester.) As the teacher checks the names, she is presented with an excellent opportunity for the class to begin to get acquainted. She asks the students to introduce themselves and to tell something about themselves. As soon as they have introduced themselves, she should give them a short summary of her background, so they can begin to feel acquainted with her.

4. Rules and regulations. The rules and regulations to be followed in the class should be outlined to the students. At no time should the students be surprised when disciplined. They should know exactly what is expected. In general, the fewer rules the better. (In setting up his rules, the teacher should stress that these rules are intended to help the class run more smoothly and to help them learn more in the class. The teacher may well reinforce this positive emphasis by dwelling a few minutes on the importance of rules in all aspects of life. Rules help people rather than hinder them. As an example, he can mention such a commonly understood practice as always driving on the right-hand side of the road. Driving on the highways would be quite nerve-racking if all drivers did not accept this rule.) For most classes, four rules seem to be sufficient. (a) In order for the class to proceed, everyone is expected to be ready to begin work when the bell rings. Nor is anyone free to leave until dismissed at the end of the hour. (b) In order to be able to pronounce the new sounds they will be learning and to avoid the "mess" of gum improperly disposed of, gum is prohibited except on days of written tests. The teacher can foster a cooperative spirit in the class by telling the students that no penalties are involved and that he will remind them if they forget. (c) In order to learn the maximum amount possible, each person, including the teacher, should pay attention to whoever is talking. (d) Each student is expected to be courteous at all times, courtesy being defined as having the most fun one possibly can without bothering someone else. An alternative practiced by some teachers is to involve the students in the selection of rules that would be most beneficial to their learning for the semester.

5. Grading system. The students are always justifiably interested in grades, and the teacher should outline on the first day how the grades are determined and how they are converted into the final grade for the six weeks or for the semester. For example, the class will have a test over each chapter. There will be no quizzes. At the end of each grading period, there will be a major examination over the entire grading period. Each six weeks, a class grade will be given. For the grade on the report card, the class grade will count one fourth, the chapter tests will be half, and the examination one fourth. Those grades will be graded on the following scale: A—95–100, B—85–94, C—75–84, and D—65–74. Any similar outline enables them to keep track of their grade for the course. There should be few, if any, surprises when the grade cards are distributed.

6. *Why study a second language?* At the beginning of the course, and thereafter, the teacher should try to interest and motivate the students to learn a language. The first day of class is a good time to give them some reasons for studying a language just in case they do not have any.

7. *How to study a second language.* For those students who have no prior experience studying a second language, the teacher should give some idea of the ways in which they can approach second-language study. The following hints should help students to learn a second language:

a. Attend class regularly and participate in all class activities.

b. Respond to every problem your instructor poses in class, no matter who is called on to answer. You can respond mentally and then check your accuracy when the answer is given. If you do this regularly, you will have hundreds more practice opportunities than if you merely sit and wait your turn.

c. Complete every assignment on time. The programs in many assignments are designed to prepare you specifically for the class session that follows.

d. Experiment to discover how you learn best. You may do the assignment first and use the summary to review and check what you have learned. In reverse, you may study the summary first and use the assignment to find out whether you understand the details.

e. Keep a vocabulary list and study it for two to four minutes every day. . . .

f. Read aloud in Spanish for two or three minutes every day to improve your pronunciation and fluency.

g. From the very beginning of the course, think and talk to yourself in Spanish, using whatever Spanish you have learned. This can be done at any time when you do not need to use your mind for other things, e.g., while brushing your teeth, waiting for a bus, eating alone.[1]

h. Know what the objectives are for each chapter and organize your study and practice around these goals.

i. Be prepared to give an oral or written summary of all the dialogs and/or readings.

j. Be prepared to talk or write about the content of the chapter.

k. Participate in all the class activities, so that you can get feedback as to how you are teaching.

l. Do not get discouraged by errors or the failure to achieve language skills

---

[1] Lamadrid, E. E., et al. (1974) *Communicating in Spanish.* Level One. Boston: Houghton Mifflin. Pp. vii–viii.

immediately. Everyone who learns a language makes mistakes, and skills must be developed over a period of time.

8. Course goals. The teacher should outline for the students in exact terms what he would like for the class (both the teacher and the students) to accomplish in the course. He should describe both language skills and culture as well as specific sounds, vocabulary, and grammar to be covered. Most important of all, he should pledge his commitment to the students to do his best to help each and every one of them to be a successful second-language student. (A pledge he should remember to honor throughout the year!)

9. Acquaint the students with the book. The teacher should spend a few moments discussing her objectives and the book. She can point out the important features of the text, and she should explain to the students how the class is going to proceed through the book. For example, she can tell them approximately how much time she plans to spend on each chapter and what types of homework they will be expected to do.

10. Assign names in the language. An extra element in establishing a second-language atmosphere can be added by giving the students names in the second language. These names become their real names in the classroom.

11. Introduce the first assignment. Toward the end of the hour, the next day's lesson should be previewed and the homework assigned.

12. Give them something to take away. Whether or not the needed expressions occur in the lesson previewed, the students should be able to say something in the second language by the time they leave class. At least, they should be able to say, "Hi, how are you?" and to answer, "I'm fine, thanks. And you?" One possibility to help the students to get acquainted more quickly and to teach them something to say by the end of the first class is to use the activity suggested in the chapter on speaking, in which the students move about the class asking and giving each other their names (see page 348).

APPENDIX 2
SELECTING A BASIC TEXT:
A SUBJECTIVE EVALUATION

How many teachers of Spanish are satisfied with the text adopted for use in their classes? If conversations heard and overheard at meetings of the faithful are a reliable indication, many teachers are critical of the texts that they are presently using. Coupled with this discontent is a perpetual optimism with regard to the promise of new materials. Apparently, most teachers are somewhat like voters, who are said to vote against rather than for. Part of this dissatisfaction is due, of course, to the fact that many teachers find themselves in the situation of having to teach from materials which they have not chosen. But the question arises as to whether they would be any happier after a year or two with materials which they themselves had selected. What criteria would they have used?

The following comments are directed toward the problem of selecting a basic language text. The author is well aware that his ideas do not correspond to many of those reflected in the evaluation lists currently available. The criteria now used by most teachers are aimed toward some objective means of evaluating the text or series of materials. However, with these lists it is quite possible to become so busy examining trees that the forest is lost in a maze of branches, i.e., of minor aspects of the text. In this writer's opinion, a general,

Reprinted, by permission, from *Hispania*, September 1971.

subjective evaluation would be more satisfactory. After all, the acid test of any materials is the compatibility between these materials and the personality and teaching practices of the teacher. Teaching is a subjective interpretation of textual materials to and with the students. The long lists of criteria can be shortened and simplified, thus allowing a more satisfactory personal opinion of the proposed text.

Another reason for abandoning current guidelines for use in textbook selection is that many are obviously biased toward a particular method of language teaching, generally the audio-lingual approach.[1] Such a built-in preference is not justifiable from the point of view of our present state of knowledge about language teaching and language learning. Although Barrutia (1966) and Ney (1968) have defended audio-lingual practices in recent articles, even they have been more moderate in their claims and much more lenient in their receptiveness to a variety of teaching practices within the audio-lingual context than were early proponents of the method. Other writers have been more critical. Wolfe (1967) objects to the artificiality of dialog memorization and pattern drill repetition. Belasco (1969) asserts, "When problems of sentence embedding are considered, the prospect of a dialog-drill saturated grammar becomes utterly impossible." Saporta (1966) seconds the above statement and summarizes the theoretical objection to audio-lingual practices when he states, "All models of learning based exclusively on imitation and reinforcement fail to account for the ability of anyone who has mastered a language to produce and understand novel utterances."

Carroll (1965) has observed that, at the present time, language teachers seem to be divided into two groups with regard to theories of language learning: (1) the audio-lingual habit theory and (2) the cognitive code-learning theory. He continues by stating that neither theory has an appreciable amount of research evidence to support its position. It is his feeling that a synthesis incorporating the most effective practices of each method "will yield a dramatic change in effectiveness."

Each of the two predominant methods of language teaching has its adherents. Neither has solid theoretical support, although recently the trend seems to be more toward placing an emphasis upon the importance of cognition in language learning (Chastain, 1969). Lacking definite theories upon which to base his teaching procedures, the language teacher is forced to rely upon his own assumptions about language, language learning, and the language learner. The following assumptions are those which seem most logical in the mind of this writer and are those upon which he would base his criteria for selecting a text.

---

[1]Although the current trend seems to be to distinguish between *method* and *approach*, the two terms are used interchangeably in this paper.

Assumption 1: A student learns to do what he does. If he devotes most of his time to reading, he learns to read. If he spends the major portion of the hour doing pattern drills, he learns to speak what one investigator has termed *patternese* (Briere, 1968). If he is given the opportunity to express himself in the language, he learns to communicate.

Assumption 2: A student needs to feel successful. He initially comes to class excited about the prospect of being able to express himself in a different tongue. However, after serving a few times as an example to his classmates of the teacher's superior knowledge of Spanish, or after several frustrated attempts to do homework for which he has been inadequately prepared, he begins to find other more agreeable and attainable goals upon which to focus his interest and attention. The teacher's task, or perhaps obligation, is to develop confidence in the student in his ability to learn this strange sounding language.

Assumption 3: A student should be offered a variety of activities. (It is for this reason that students prefer a book with many chapters or lessons. They feel as if they are moving along faster and doing more things.) Most students sit forty to seventy minutes in each class for four or five classes a day listening to some teacher talk. Most teachers could not endure the very things they expect of the students. Teachers are obligated to change the pace in class as often as possible, and no teacher has more possibilities at his disposal than a foreign-language teacher.

Assumption 4: A student must be led through three steps in the acquisition of language. (a) He must understand the concept involved. (b) He must drill the structure in order to develop a certain facility in manipulating its sounds and forms and in order to promote its retention. (c) He must be given an opportunity to utilize previously drilled material to express himself on some topic with which he is acquainted.

Assumption 5: A student approaches language mastery. He does not suddenly acquire it. A great disservice has been done to language teaching by the idea that with three records and a short period of free time, one can learn to speak a foreign language. It is up to the text and the teacher to arrange the material sequentially in such a way that the student gradually approaches the mastery of each section of the text. Nor should the teacher expect too much. At the 1968 Kentucky Foreign Language Conference, Theodore Mueller said that after twenty years in this country he still understands only 60 percent of the dialog in a movie, 40 percent at the theater, and 10 percent of the jokes he hears.[2]

Assumption 6: A student requires practice in all four language skills. This

---

[2]Professor Mueller, a non-native speaker of English, is currently professor of French in the Department of French Language and Literature at the University of Kentucky.

separate attention to each of the four language skills is necessary for several reasons. (a) There is some evidence to indicate that students have a sense modality preference in learning (Pimsleur et al., 1963–64). A given student may feel more comfortable and learn more rapidly by using the book while another may prefer to depend upon oral presentations. (b) Each skill can complement and reinforce concepts learned in the other. (The connotation here refers to concept formation.) (c) Students are, in general, eye-oriented in academic subjects. (d) There is not as much carry-over from one skill to another as one might suppose. (The connotation here refers to skill formation.) (e) All four skills are necessary in the normal process of communicating with our fellow humans.

Assumption 7: A student wants to know about the people of the country. Language in the classroom often becomes so abstract that students have difficulty relating to the subject. The teacher should take advantage of all appropriate situations in which he has an opportunity to relate these funny sounds to real places, people, and events.

Assumption 8: A student is a normal human being, sometimes frightfully so. He does what he has to do in order "to get by." Naturally, he attends class because it is compulsory, but getting him to do homework is another matter. Since teachers realize that he must be exposed to as much language as possible, it is the teacher's responsibility to provide definite homework assignments which are a necessary prerequisite to successful performance in the classroom the next day.

The following criteria for selecting a text all grow out of a consideration of the preceding assumptions. Many minor points will not be mentioned here. The attractiveness of the text, for example, is obviously noticed at first glance. Supplementary teaching aids such as tapes, records, evaluation materials, etc. are not given special mention here because the same basic criteria which apply to the text also apply to the teaching aids.

1. Vocabulary and content of the dialogs and/or reading materials. The crucial point in language teaching, the continually frustrating barrier in the classroom, is the jump from drills to self-expression. The student must be given the opportunity to express his ideas in the foreign tongue. He must be afforded the opportunity to transfer the knowledge learned in class to situations in which he talks about his own life. This chance to talk or write about himself is the most important aspect of language acquisition because it deals with actual communication. Kelly says in the introduction to *Learning French the Modern Way*, the second edition, "No one truly acquires language skills until he uses them to express himself—such self-expression is not only possible from the outset, it is essential" (Evans et al., 1967). Other writers use different terms (Belasco [1968] calls it *liberated* expression. Jarvis [1968] refers to it as *real* language.) to designate this phase of language learning, but all agree that such practice is essential if the student is to acquire active language skills.

Although it is the most important, "real" language is the phase of language teaching most often neglected. To a large extent transfer of structure and vocabulary to practice in meaningful context is the responsibility of the teacher. If he is able to use the vocabulary and situational content of the text to develop conversational situations about the student, his home, his school, his interest, etc., then he will be able to demonstrate to the student the importance of drill as a means toward the goal of language expression and the fun of being able to express oneself in another tongue. If he feels comfortable with the vocabulary, if he feels the student can use this vocabulary to talk about his life, then the teacher and the class can begin to bring language alive as together they go beyond the exercises included in the text. Of course, the more material of this nature provided in the text the better, but the content of any contextual, personalized practice depends upon the vocabulary of the text and its arrangement into meaningful units by the teacher. Gaarder (1967), for instance, is talking about this very problem when he states, ". . . the drills and their follow-up exercises—and usually even the basic dialogs—are in effect so devoid of logical, consistent, situational reality that they do not provide the student with significant life experience in the foreign language—*do not give him anything meaningful to talk about. . . ."*

2. Emphasis placed upon the three steps in language acquisition. In traditional texts, most of the content is devoted to grammatical explanation in order to insure student understanding of structure. Audio-lingual texts are filled mostly with dialogs to memorize and drills with which to practice basic structures to the point of automatic response. Neither type of text has in the past provided sufficient amounts of "real" language practice. Perhaps this is an aspect of language teaching which can be provided adequately only by the teacher himself in his own class, but at least the authors should indicate an awareness of this state of language acquisition. The question which a teacher must consider in evaluating a text is whether the authors develop an under-standing of structure and whether sufficient amounts of understandable drill exercises are provided.

Before drill can be of any great value as far as structure is concerned, the student must be made aware of that structure. This presentation need not involve grammatical explanation, but the student's attention should be fo-cused on the structural relationship to the rest of the sentence, its forms and changes, and its function in the sentence. The presentation may be made in a variety of ways. However, the use of English is not a plague which must be avoided in all cases. Presentation should be made in minimal, accomplishable steps in order to lead the students slowly and with a minimum of errors. It is by focusing on single, understandable aspects of the language that the text can help him bypass the pitfalls of language learning.

Once the students are aware of the structure, they should be given the opportunity to manipulate it. In pattern drills as well as in the presentation of structure, the text must be careful to lead the students with a minimum of error and a maximum of confidence. The sentences should be short and deal with only one aspect of the language at a time. Too many texts rush the students directly into a test situation by combining several elements at once. The drills should proceed from easy to difficult, from teaching drills to test drills in which the students can determine whether or not they have learned the material. All drills should involve some manipulation of structure rather than passive repetition. Along with this point, too many texts have drills which are too long. Six to eight sentences are enough. If more are added, the students tend to lose "consciousness" and are not actually aware of the manipulation which they are performing. Here is an example in Spanish which might be used in teaching direct object pronouns. Rather than have thirty sentences in which the students replace a noun direct object with a direct object pronoun, have drills of six sentences each in this order: (a) replacing a feminine noun with *la*; (b) replacing a masculine noun with *lo*; (c) replacing singular nouns with singular pronouns (a test drill over a and b which were teaching drills); (d) replacing feminine plural nouns with *las*; (e) replacing masculine plural nouns with *los*; (f) replacing plural nouns with plural direct object pronouns (a test drill over d and e which were teaching drills); and (g) a test drill over all of these forms.

3. The four language skills and culture. There is not as much transfer from one language skill to another as one might think. All the skills need to be practiced. Does the text include provisions for the practice of all four language skills? Many texts are not properly balanced to include all aspects of language learning. This is true of both traditional and audio-lingual texts.

Culture is another consideration. No text can be written without points of interest which are contained in the language. However, the text needs to give the students more information concerning the people about which they are studying. Preferably this should be presented in short, simple sections in the language as soon as the students' vocabulary is sufficiently developed.

4. Sequence of developing the language skills. The importance of the proper progression of difficulty in the materials has previously been alluded to in earlier criteria. There is no need to expound further except to re-emphasize the fact that the text and the teacher must begin where the student is and develop his skills over a period of time until the goals of the course have been reached.

5. Possibilities should be included in the text for some type of homework in preparation for the next class meeting. This material should be such that definite tasks can be assigned. The content of the assignment should be such that diligence will be rewarded and rewarding. In other words, the student should be able to complete the assignment successfully without undue frustration, and he should acquire some skill or knowledge which will help him to participate more fully in the planned classroom activities, i.e., to learn the language better.

In summary, language teaching at the present time appears to be in a process of synthesis. Lacking clear-cut research evidence to guide his decisions, the language teacher must rely upon his past teaching experience. Although such a procedure is not very scientific, who can say assuredly that such is not a more valid approach as far as the individual teacher is concerned? The outgrowth of this same type of reasoning is that the teacher follows a simplified set of guidelines in evaluating available texts, a set of guidelines which he answers subjectively based upon his particular teaching techniques and past experience. By selecting a text with a content which can be personalized to the student's interests, the teacher can more readily provide opportunities for real language practice. By selecting a text which provides for all three steps in the acquisition of language and for all four language skills, the teacher can more easily provide a variety of activities in the classroom and at the same time give the students an opportunity to practice all four language skills. By selecting a text in which all three phases of language acquisition are emphasized and in which the building up of all language skills is carefully sequenced to avoid gaps in skill development, the teacher, demonstrating his awareness that language mastery is a slow process occurring over a period of time, can more easily maintain the shaky feeling of confidence with which the students comes to foreign-language class. By selecting a text which includes the people as well as the language, the teacher can more readily help his students to relate to the language. And by selecting a text in which provision is made for daily homework, the teacher can more easily expand the number of student contact hours with the language.

REFERENCES

Barrutia, R. (1966) Some Misconceptions about the Fundamental Skills Method. *Hispania*, 49:440–46.

Belasco, S. (1968) Developing Linguistic Competence. *Modern Language Journal*, 52:213.

Belasco, S. (1969) Toward the Acquisition of Linguistic Competence: From Contrived to Controlled Materials. *Modern Language Journal*, 53:187.

Brière, E. (1968) Testing ESL Among Navajo Children. *Language Learning* (August):16.

Carroll, J. B. (1965) The Contributions of Psychological Theory and Educational Research to the Teaching of Foreign Languages. *Modern Language Journal*, 49:273–81.

Chastain, K. (1969) The Audio-Lingual Habit Theory Versus the Cognitive Code-Learning Theory: Some Theoretical Considerations. *International Review of Applied Linguistics*, 7/2:97–106.

Evans, J.; Baldwin, M.; and Kelly, L. L. (1967) *Learning French the Modern Way.* (2nd ed.) New York: McGraw Hill. P.1.

Gaarder, A. B. (1967) Beyond Grammar and Beyond Drills. *Foreign Language Annals*, 1:110.

Jarvis, G. (1968) A Behavioral Observation System for Classroom Foreign Language Skill Acquisition Activities. *Modern Language Journal*, 52:336.

Ney, J. W. (1968) The Oral Approach: A Re-Appraisal. *Language Learning*, 17: 3–13.

Pimsleur, P.; Sundland, D. M.; and McIntyre, R. D. (1963–64) Under-Achievement in Foreign Language Learning. *International Review of Applied Linguistics*, 1-2: 124–26.

Saporta, S. (1966) Applied Linguistics and Generative Grammar. In Albert Valdman (Ed.), *Trends in Language Teaching.* New York: McGraw-Hill. Pp. 81–92.

Wolfe, D. L. (1967) Some Theoretical Aspects of Language Learning and Language Teaching. *Language Learning*, 17:174–79.

APPENDIX 3
SOURCES OF NEW IDEAS

Once the teacher enters the classroom on her own, the responsibility for improvement rests on her shoulders. Seldom, if ever, and then usually only if she is desperate enough to ask for assistance, does she receive any specific suggestions regarding her teaching such as those she received during the student teaching period. For the first two or three years, everything is new and exciting, and she is so busy that she does not pause often to reflect on what she is doing. Later, she begins to crave new ideas and to feel that she is stuck in the cycle of never-ending imitation similar to that described by Wordsworth when he said, "Man acts as if his whole vocation were merely endless imitation." His problem, that of finding new ideas and of pruning unproductive habits and techniques, is shared by all teachers. The purpose of this appendix is to urge the teacher never to abandon the search for improved techniques and to suggest sources for new ideas.

Above all, the teacher should subject her own teaching to a continuous self-criticism. Self-evaluation is extremely difficult, but it is the only form of criticism that many people are willing to accept. One good procedure for self-appraisal is for the teacher to make a tape recording or a video tape recording of *at least* one class each semester This type of evaluation reveals many aspects of the class that are not evident any other way. Listening to (or viewing) her class gives the teacher an opportunity to take inventory, i.e., to determine exactly what is happening in her class. She should then compare the results of this inventory with the desired outcomes. When what is going on does not correspond with what she wants to happen, she should begin to search for methods and means to institute changes in her procedures and consequently in the students' activities.

The teacher can be more exact and objective in her inventory if she uses a specific observation scale. Since the emphasis in this book has been that the students learn to do what they do, the observation scale that follows deals with student activity in the classroom.[1]

Scale for the Classification
of Student Activities

I. "Real" language
   A. Oral interaction
   B. Listening comprehension
   C. Speaking
   D. Reading comprehension
   E. Writing
   F. English
II. Drill and/or exercises
   A. Listening
   B. Responding
      1. Orally
         a. Chorally
         b. Individually
      2. In writing
   C. Reading aloud
      1. Chorally
      2. Individually
   D. English
III. Presentation of new material
   A. Participating
      1. First language
      2. Second language

---

[1]Those educators who are familiar with interaction analysis as proposed by Flanders, Amidon, et al. may prefer to emphasize the interaction between the teacher and the students in their observations. However, it appears that modifications of the typical interaction analysis are necessary in observing second-language classes. If the reader is interested in the application of interaction analysis, he should consult Grittner, *Teaching Foreign Languages*, pp. 327–40 and/or Jarvis, "A Behavioral Observation System for Foreign Language Skill Acquisition," *Modern Language Journal*, 52 (October 1968), pp. 335–41.

B. Receptive
  1. First language
  2. Second language
IV. Activity not related to language acquisition
  A. Nonrelated topics
  B. Silence or confusion

The teacher takes inventory simply by keeping score of what he hears (or observes) during the class. To record the students' activities, he makes a mark (I) opposite the appropriate description each five, ten, or fifteen seconds. (Since this is a random sample of what is happening, one would suspect that it would make little difference which time interval is used except that, naturally, the fiften-second interval is easier to record and to total.) By using the system of crossing the previous four tallies in marking the fifth (IIII), he can later very quickly determine the totals for each category; for "real" language, drill and/or exercises, presentation of new material, and activity not related to language acquisition; for each of the four language skills; for practice in the receptive and in the productive skills; and for the proportion of time spent in the second language and in the first language. The teacher who is interested in the interaction in the classroom can contrast the entries in which the students were listening with those in which the students were responding either in "real" language or in drill or exercise activities.

One other point needs to be made. Recording a random sample of the students' activities does not provide any objective, quantitative evaluation of the number of responses, i.e., of the pace of the class. The teacher should be aware of this gap and include a subjective evaluation of this factor as he analyzes his class.

The students can also be a potential source of new ideas for the teacher. In the first place, he can learn from them which activities help them to learn best, which are most interesting, and which they would like to see abandoned. As well as helping him to choose what to discard, what to modify, and what to keep, the students often have ideas that can be developed into interesting and productive teaching-learning situations. Student input of this type can be especially helpful in the area of ideas for real language topics.

In addition to taking stock in his own classes, the teacher should also look for new ideas outside his classes. For example, he should have a collection of additional texts at hand and examine them regularly. Quite often another author has included a presentation or an activity that is not in the adopted text and that had not occurred previously to the teacher.

During the school year he should take advantage of any and all opportunities to observe other teachers in action. These visits may be made to classrooms in his own school or in others. Many school systems now have provisions for a day off each semester or each year to visit programs in other schools. Nor should he limit himself to language teachers. Teachers in other fields have ideas that may be applicable to his own. Working with student teachers can be a valuable learning experience for the cooperating teacher as well as for the student teacher, and the teacher should welcome such "fresh" sources of new techniques.

Attending language meetings and reading the language journals can be informative, interesting, and often inspiring. Information gained from language meetings is not limited to that gathered from the speeches. Discussions with other teachers are opportune moments to share ideas and perhaps even resources of one type or another such as tapes, cultural materials, etc. Many journal articles deal with problems related to teaching and to the problems of the profession. The advertisements in the journals provide leads to new books, records, realia, etc.

The most valuable source of new ideas, however, resides within the teacher himself. Limited only by the scope of his own creativity and spurred on by his desire to improve his teaching, the teacher certainly can develop new classroom procedures and techniques on his own. The more insight his experience and knowledge give him into the whole teaching-learning process the more proficient he should become in tapping his own source of new ideas. May his fountain never run dry.

APPENDIX 4
THE LANGUAGE LABORATORY

Although most methods texts include an entire chapter on the language laboratory, the author decided against following this standard pattern for the following reasons:

1. The language laboratory is more appropriately included in a discussion of aids and means to develop language skills than in a discussion of skill development itself.
2. The principles of teaching and skill development are the same for both the lab and the classroom. No basic distinction with regard to principles of teaching need be made.
3. Much of the "know-how" necessary to conduct a class in the lab must be gained through actual demonstrations of and practice with the equipment itself. This is one case, among many, where a book does not suffice.
4. Even one chapter would not be sufficient to include all the needed information on all the hardware and its uses. The reader should consult additional sources dealing directly and specifically with language laboratories.

The conversion of a major portion of the second-language teachers in the United States to the audio-lingual approach was indeed a revolution. However, it was not the only one. At the same time as this rapid change was taking place in methodology, a technological revolution was also sweeping the country. Hundreds of schools purchased tape recorders and installed language laboratories in order to complement the new classroom procedures being advocated. While it was generally conceded that a language laboratory was not necessary for successful audio-lingual teaching, proponents of the method recommended highly that they be incorporated into the school's second-language program. At the same time, task dissatisfaction with language laboratories and their future potential justify a general discussion of the purposes, results, and possibilities of language laboratories and second-language teaching.

Purposes

The use of the tape recorder and the language laboratory in second-language instruction was the logical outgrowth of teaching techniques aimed at conditioning language habits by means of minimal step learning, active response by the students, and immediate reinforcement. Introducing the use of machines to assist in practicing pattern drills was the direct application of Skinnerian principles of learning to the classroom situation. Therefore, lab time was spent in intensive language drill. This drill, in general, took the form of pronunciation practice, mimicry-memorization, or pattern practice.

The tape recorder and the lab were conceived of originally as a means of drilling sounds and structural forms. They were touted as being a tireless drillmaster that performs the tedious chores while leaving the teacher free to concentrate on the creative aspects of teaching. The teacher could now devote her efforts to getting the students to use the language in the classroom. The days of frustrated extraction of answers were over. With the lab the students would be able to respond appropriately and without hesitation to the teacher's questions. The picture was rosy, and the numbers of tape recorders and language laboratories increased rapidly.

Results

The results generally obtained, however, have failed to support the early optimism. Students have been unable to respond automatically; nor have they reacted favorably to overlearning language forms to the point of nonthoughtful responses. Once the novelty of the lab disappears, some students form an intense dislike for the lab sessions. Others are uninspired, uninterested, and inattentive. One of the major problems in many labs is how to control the vandalism. This vandalism is usually not malicious. Apparently, high school-age students just have too much energy to be able to fold their hands discreetly in their laps and concentrate on listening to drills for the entire lab period.

Many second-language teachers themselves have been less than enthusiastic after the first year or two with the lab. They often feel that the students learn more in the classroom, and they react sympathetically to a group of listless students in the lab by not going to the lab as often as desirable. Too, they feel they do not have time for the additional preparation and planning that an efficient lab session requires. Often, the scheduled lab period does not fit into the teacher's daily plans, so it becomes more convenient not to follow the assigned schedule.

As the initial enthusiasm for language labs has waned, comparisons have been made attempting to evaluate their effects on achievement. The results of these studies have been inconclusive and, in the case of the Keating Report and of the Pennsylvania Project, controversial. The following four studies selected for presentation here reflect the major findings.

The Keating report   In 1963, Keating published a report in which the achievement of students who had not practiced in a lab was compared with the achievement of students who had. Three language skills—reading, listening, and speaking—were tested. The results revealed many significant differences, and all favored the no-laboratory group except one. The conclusions drawn were that students with high IQ's were severely disadvantaged by work in the language laboratory. The achievement of students with lower IQ's was relatively unaffected by having studied in a language laboratory.

The Keating study was more a survey of results than a controlled experiment. In this sense, it was more a descriptive study of what was "going on" than what might be true in the ideal situation. The criticism of the *Keating Report* was loud and severe.[1] Most of the objections centered around the lack of controls in comparing the two groups.

The Lorge study   In 1964, Lorge published the results of two successive experiments in New York City. In this study there were five groups: (1) laboratory daily, record-playback equipment; (2) laboratory daily, audio-active equipment; (3) laboratory weekly, record-playback equipment; (4) laboratory weekly, audio-active equipment; and (5) no laboratory. These students were tested in sight reading; oral answers to oral questions; comprehension; and conventional skills. In the overall rating of sight reading, the order of

[1]For additional details see *Modern Language Journal*, 48 (April 1964):189–210.

achievement from highest to lowest was 1, 2, 3, 4, and 5. In answering oral questions, the ranking was 5, 1, 2, 4, and 3. In comprehension at fast speed, the groups ranked 1, 2, 3, 5, 4. At slow speeds, the order was 2, 5, 3, 4, 1. In the total score for conventional skills, the order based on achievement was 1, 5, 2, 4, 3, with 1 and 5 being significantly better than 2, 4, and 3. In addition to achievement, the percentages of students continuing from third to fourth year were compared, and it was found that a much higher percentage of laboratory students continued into fourth year (Lorge, 1964).

The Lorge study has not been subjected to the intense criticism received by the Keating report. The focus was smaller: the first-, second-, and third-year French classes in one school in 1961 and the second-year French classes in two schools in 1962. The controls were more adequate than in the Keating study. In the study the following factors were listed as being related to successful use of the language laboratory: (1) amount of time spent in the lab, (2) types of equipment, (3) kinds of taped materials, and (4) the teacher's ability to handle the lab equipment. The overall conclusion was that groups of students assigned to regular periods of laboratory practice as part of their required French course made greater gains than comparison groups in several areas, and that speaking and listening skills were the new objectives of second-language study. The investigations showed that these skills can be effectively practiced in the laboratory (Lorge, 1964, p. 419). Undoubtedly, the author's conclusions are valid. At the same time, it is interesting to note that in the production of oral language to answer oral questions the no-laboratory group achieved the highest scores.

The Pennsylvania project   In Pennsylvania, Smith (1970) conducted an extensive experiement involving French and German students in many different high schools. Basically, his objective was to compare students taught audio-lingually with students taught by more traditional methods. However, one of the related problems studied was that of the effect of lab practice on achievement. The results indicated that using the lab twice each week had no discernible effect on the students' achievement scores.

The Pennsylvania study, like the Keating investigation, lacked the tight controls possible in a small-scale study. Attempts were made to maximize uniform procedures and to minimize the disparity that tends to creep into a project of such large scope. But complete control in studies involving large numbers of schools, teachers, and students is possible only to a limited degree. This study has generated much critical comment.[2] Most of the

[2]For more detailed discussions of the project's strengths and weaknesses the reader should consult *NALLD Newsletter*, 3 (March 1969); *Modern Language Journal*, 53 (October 1969); *Foreign Language Annals*, 3 (December 1969).

criticism has been directed toward the lack of controls, the manner in which the lab was used, the tests used to evaluate achievement, and the conclusions drawn by the investigators.

Smith's study Another study was that of Smith (1969) of Purdue, who conducted a two-year investigation comparing the effectiveness of electronic classrooms and two types of language laboratories, record-playback and audio-active. In addition, he included a control group that had no classes in the laboratory. Students in French, German, and Spanish were included, and their achievement in listening, reading, and speaking was tested. The overall trend favored the equipment groups over the control group. (It should be noted that this trend on the end-of-term examinations was not consistent. In two instances—listening in French and speaking in Spanish—achievement was significantly higher in the electronic classroom group than in the control. In three cases—speaking in French and reading and speaking in German— significant differences were found between the language lab record-playback group and the control group. In each comparison in which there was a significant difference, the data indicate that the group superior to the control group, whether electronic classroom or language lab, was also significantly better than the other equipment groups as well.) In this study, data concerning attitude and interest were also collected. There was no significant difference in the attitude of the control group and the equipment groups. Student interest in all groups dropped. However, interest dropped less in the control group than in the equipment groups in French. The same results were generally true in German, but they were varied in Spanish.

Discussion of Results and Future Possibilities

The differences of opinion that are associated with the audio-lingual approach also surround the language laboratory. Those teachers who are successful using audio-lingual techniques base much of their work on practice in the lab. Those who do not subscribe to audio-lingual procedures often allow the labs in their schools to remain unused most of the day. Neither subjective evaluation nor research evidence has been able to gather sufficient force to convince the profession to use the lab wholeheartedly or to discard it entirely. Certainly, everyone is aware that the lab is no cure-all. The problems that plagued the second-language teacher prior to the lab still exist, as perplexing today as ever.

The predicted benefits have not materialized, but is the fault that of the lab itself or of the way it is used? Too often the teacher has been hindered in his attempts to utilize the lab facilities to the fullest by administrative procedures and technical failures. Too often the teacher has depended upon the lab equipment to do the job while he relaxes from his labors for a few minutes. Too often he has viewed the tapes as substitute teachers sufficient in and of themselves. Too often he has failed to integrate the lab session into the total sequence of skill development, of going from understanding through drill to application. Too often he has not made his objectives clear to the students. Too often he has not taught the follow-up class activities in such a way that the students can realize that the lab does help them to learn to use the language. Too often he has not included lab work as part of the grade in the course. Too often he has ignored the need for variety of activities in the lab as well as in the classroom. And too often he has not included skills acquired in the lab as a basic and important component on the examinations in the course.

Certainly some of the original justifications outlined in support of the lab are as logical as ever. The lab still allows the students to hear better as they listen to the voices of several native speakers via recorded tapes and to their own voices through the headphones. The lab still provides a place in which all the students can practice simultaneously in relative isolation from the other students. And the lab still makes it possible for the teacher to listen to individual responses and to work with individual students without interrupting the practice of the other students.

In the beginning, perhaps too much was expected of the lab. Overzealous claims may have tended to cause some teachers to overestimate its possibilities and to underestimate their own role in using the lab. The language laboratory as it is used has apparently had relatively little effect on achievement in second-language classes. This unexpected outcome is discouraging, but it should not be considered disastrous. Innovation is needed. An expansion of the past conception of the lab as a "drillmaster" is in order. Can the lab be utilized, for example, in the presentation of new material? Postlethwait of Purdue uses the tape recorder to teach basic concepts in his audio-tutorial approach to teaching introductory biology. Smith of Purdue has adapted the same self-teaching concept to Spanish in the form of "auto-span" tapes prepared to teach basic structures in the elementary Spanish course. What are the potentialities of the lab with regard to application activities? One would think that its potential for listening comprehension practice could be more fully exploited than is true at present. Is it possible to include work in all four language skills in the lab session? Practice in the written skills might relieve some of the boredom associated with the lab. How can one include a variety of activities and still maintain an intensive practice session? What are the possibilities for using the lab as a basic tool in some aspects of diversifying instruction? And at least one more question needs to be asked. Can the lab be adapted to implement cognitive approaches to language teaching? The teacher needs to investigate the lab's potential in the presentation of new material, in application activities, in teaching the written skills, and in the implementation of cognitive approaches to second-language teaching. He must seek new means of providing a variety of activities within the lab period.

REFERENCES

Keating, R. F. (1963) *A Study of the Effectiveness of Language Laboratories.* New York: The Institute of Administrative Research, Teachers College Columbia University.

Lorge, S. W. (1964) Language Laboratory Research Studies in New York City High Schools: A Discussion of the Program and the Findings. *Modern Language Journal,* 48:409–19.

Smith, P. D. (1970) *A Comparison of the Cognitive and Audio-lingual Approaches to Foreign Language Instruction: The Pennsylvania Foreign Language Project.* Philadelphia: The Center for Curriculum Development.

Smith, W. F. (1969) The Language Laboratory and the Electronic Classroom: A Comparison of Their Relative Contribution to Achievement in Three Languages in the Comprehensive High School. Unpublished doctoral dissertation, Purdue University.

APPENDIX 5
PROFESSIONAL ORGANIZATIONS AND
JOURNALS

All teachers, experienced or inexperienced, bear the responsibility for staying abreast of current developments in education and in their academic area. One way of promoting personal professional growth is to participate in professional organizations. Being an active professional gives teachers opportunities to share hopes, concerns, practices, and materials with colleagues and at the same time to support their profession. The professional journals published by many of these organizations serve as a medium for keeping posted on changes being discussed and implemented and for sharing one's own ideas and classroom practices. Following is a description of the major organizations and journals.

Educational Organizations and Journals

American Association of University Professors (AAUP). The AAUP is a national organization (with local chapters) for college and university professors. The organization's primary concerns are with principles of academic freedom, tenure policies, and salaries and economic benefits. In cases of departure from their principles, the violating institutions are censured by the organization. Members are informed of new developments in the *AAUP Bulletin* published at the following address: Publications Office, *AAUP Bulletin*, Suite 500, One Dupont Circle, N. W., Washington, D. C. 20036. The summer issue of the *AAUP Bulletin* contains a detailed study of the economic status of the profession.

American Federation of Teachers (AFT). The AFT is connected with the AFL-CIO. As teachers have become more militant in their demands for higher salaries, increased benefits, and improved working conditions, membership in AFT has risen. Membership in the AFT is highest in metropolitan areas and among younger teachers. The AFT is making attempts to move into college and university teaching. The rivalry between the AFT and the NEA is quite strong. The organizational framework includes national, state, and local groups. The AFT publishes the *American Teacher*, a journal devoted to labor news related to education. The journal is published at 1012 14th Street, N. W., Washington, D. C. 20005.

National Education Association (NEA). The NEA is a national organization to which state and local groups belong. It is the largest organization of educators. The competition with the AFT has caused the organization to adopt a more militant position with regard to many issues in education. There have been suggestions that the AFT and the NEA merge. Two major stumbling blocks have prevented a merger to this point: (1) The AFT's affiliation with the AFL-CIO, and (2) the fact that administrative personnel may not join the AFT. Both organizations are concerned with the problems facing teachers and education. The NEA publishes *Today's Education*, a journal dealing with current problems in the classroom and in education. The address is 1201 16th Street, N. W., Washington, D. C. 20036.

Second-Language Organizations and Journals

Two different types of organizations exist at the national level and in many states. In both instances there is an organization of teachers of all second languages and an organization of teachers of each specific language.

ALL LANGUAGES

American Council on the Teaching of Foreign Languages (ACTFL). ACTFL is the national organization of teachers of all second languages including teachers of the classics and English as a second language. The national ACTFL meeting is held each year at Thanksgiving. ACTFL publishes *Foreign Language Annals,* automatically received by ACTFL members; it also sponsors *The ACTFL Review of Foreign Language Education.* ACTFL also provides various types of insurance at reduced rates. The ACTFL offices are at 62 5th Avenue, New York, New York 10011.

Foreign Language Annals is "dedicated to advancing all phases of the profession of foreign language teaching." The goal is to serve the interests of teachers, administrators, and researchers at all levels of second-language instruction. The editorial policy is to give preference to articles that "describe innovative and successful teaching methods, that report educational research or experimentation, or that are relevant to the concerns and problems of the profession." Since 1968, an annual review of foreign language education has been published. The purpose of this annual review is the "collection, analysis, synthesis, and interpretation of the work of the profession." The latest volume is entitled *Perspective: A New Freedom.*

Many states have a state organization of all language teachers. These groups usually sponsor one or two state meetings per year, and some publish a state language newsletter.

The National Federation of Modern Language Teachers Associations. The National Federation publishes *Modern Language Journal.* As stated on the front cover, this is a journal "devoted primarily to methods, pedagogical research, and to topics of professional interest to all language teachers." The emphasis is on teaching methodology. The business manager is Wallace G. Klein, 13149 Cannes Drive, St. Louis, Missouri 63141.

The Ontario Modern Language Teachers' Association. This association publishes *Canadian Modern Language Review,* which contains articles dealing with teaching of modern languages and book reviews. Their business address is 34 Butternut Street, Toronto, Ontario M4K 1T7.

SPECIFIC LANGUAGES

The following organizations were formed to help promote the study of the particular language or languages involved and to assist teachers in their language area. The major activities of each are the annual national meeting and the publications sponsored by each. However, they also sponsor other services such as group flights to the foreign country at reduced rates, names for pen pals, culture units, placement services, etc. Of course, the national organization also serves as a collective voice representing the professional interests of the members.

American Association of Teachers of French (AATF). The current executive secretary is F. W. Nachtmann, AATF, 57 E. Armory Avenue, Champaign, Illinois 61820. The AATF publishes *French Review,* a journal containing articles on literature, civilization, and teaching. Regular departments are editor comments, pedagogical news, reader replies, and professional and association news as well as a section of book reviews.

American Association of Teachers of German (AATG). For additional information on the AATG journal, *German Quarterly,* write to *German Quarterly,* 339 Walnut Street, Philadelphia, Pennsylvania 19106. The primary emphasis is on literature and literary analysis, although there is an occasional pedagogical article. German pedagogical articles are included in *Die Unterrichtspraxis,* published twice each year by the AATG. This journal contains three sections: (1) Teaching Literature, (2) General Contributions, and (3) More on Culture.

American Association of Teachers of Italian (AATI). The AATI publishes *Italica,* a journal emphasizing literary articles and reviews. The editorial office is located at 601 Casa Italiana, Columbia University, New York, New York 10027.

American Association of Teachers of Slavic and East European Languages (AATSEEL). AATSEEL publishes *The Slavic and East European Journal.* Most of the articles deal with literature, language, and linguistics. A few discuss teaching procedures. Members also receive the *AATSEEL Newsletter.* Subscriptions should be sent to Joe Malik, Jr., Secretary-Treasurer, Department of Russian and Slavic Studies, Modern Languages 340, University of Arizona, Tucson, Arizona 85721.

American Association of Teachers of Spanish and Portuguese (AATSP). The AATSP publication is *Hispania,* a journal devoted to the interests of the teaching of Spanish and Portuguese. There are sections on literature, Shop Talk, FLES, Notes on Usage, Fact and Opinion, F-L Currents, Notes and News, Chapter News, Hispanic World, Books of the Hispanic World, Reviews, Instructional Media. The secretary-treasurer is Richard B. Klein, Holy Cross College, Worcester, Massachusetts 01610.

Teachers of English to Speakers of Other Languages (TESOL). TESOL publishes *The TESOL Quarterly,* a pedagogical journal containing articles dealing with professional needs, materials, methods, testing, psychology and sociology of language learning, curriculum, and research in language learning. TESOL also publishes *TESOL Newsletter,* a newsletter informing members of meetings, in-service training and other professional developments. The address is TESOL, 455 Nevils Building, Georgetown University, Washington, D. C. 20057.

Regional Conferences on Language Teaching

In addition to the meetings sponsored by national organizations, regional meetings are held annually in various parts of the country. These include the Northeast Conference on the Teaching of Foreign Languages, the Southern Conference on Language Teaching, the Central States Conference on the Teaching of Foreign Languages, and the Pacific Northwest Council on Foreign Languages. The proceedings of the first two conferences are published in the

Northeast Conference Reports and *Dimensions* respectively. Reports of three Central States conferences have been published.

Journals of Applied Linguistics

International Review of Applied Linguistics (IRAL). IRAL is published by Julius Groos Verlag of Germany and is available from Oxford University Press, 200 Madison Avenue, New York, New York 10016. The stated aim of this journal is "to provide a common meeting ground for researchers concerned with applied linguistics in its various forms." Most of the articles are written in English with abstracts in French and German. Contributors are from various countries, and the distribution is international in scope.

Language Learning. The emphasis in this journal is upon theoretical discussions and reports of studies dealing with applied linguistics. There are no advertisements. The address is 2001 North University Building, Ann Arbor, Michigan 48104.

State Departments of Education

The departments of education in each state also sponsor a meeting, or meetings, during the year for teachers of second languages. In addition, the office of the state supervisor of foreign languages is an excellent source of information and assistance.

INDEX